Rennyo and the Roots of
Modern Japanese Buddhism

International Institute
for Comprehensive Shinshu Studies
Ōtani University

Rennyo and the Roots of Modern Japanese Buddhism

Edited by
Mark L. Blum and Shin'ya Yasutomi

OXFORD
UNIVERSITY PRESS
2006

OXFORD
UNIVERSITY PRESS

Oxford University Press, Inc., publishes works that further
Oxford University's objective of excellence
in research, scholarship, and education.

Oxford New York

Auckland Cape Town Dar es Salaam Hong Kong Karachi
Kuala Lumpur Madrid Melbourne Mexico City Nairobi
New Delhi Shanghai Taipei Toronto

With offices in

Argentina Austria Brazil Chile Czech Republic France Greece
Guatemala Hungary Italy Japan Poland Portugal Singapore
South Korea Switzerland Thailand Turkey Ukraine Vietnam

Copyright © 2006 by Ōtani University

Published by Oxford University Press, Inc.
198 Madison Avenue, New York, New York 10016
www.oup.com

Oxford is a registered trademark of Oxford University Press

Library of Congress Cataloging-in-Publication Data
Rennyo and the Roots of Modern Japanese Buddhism /
edited by Mark L. Blum and Shin'ya Yasutomi.
    p. cm.
Includes bibliographical references and index.
ISBN-13 978-0-19-513275-5
ISBN 0-19-513275-0
1. Rennyo, 1415–1499.   2. Shin (Sect)—Doctrines.
I. Blum, Mark Laurence.   II. Yasutomi, Shin'ya, 1944–

BQ8749.R467R45 2005
294.3'926—dc22   2004056812
[B]

2 4 6 8 9 7 5 3 1

Printed in the United States of America
on acid-free paper

Foreword

In conjunction with the commemoration in 1998 of the 500th anniversary (by Japanese counting) of the death of Rennyo, a large number of memorial services and other events were held. One of these was a series of panels on Rennyo set up as a special section on June 22 within the 48th annual meeting of the Japanese Association for the Study of Buddhism and Indian Religion (Nihon Indogaku Bukkyōgaku Gakkai) held on the campus of Ōtani University. A great many scholars read informative articles, divided into two groupings: "Rennyo within the History of Religious Thought" and "The Faith of Rennyo and the Modern World." The Shinshū Research Institute at Ōtani University collected many of these and other essays from scholars in Japan and abroad for a volume published in Japanese under the title *Rennyo no sekai* (The World of Rennyo).

The achievements of Rennyo are nothing less than a "restoration of Shinshū." Not only did he pull the essence of Shinshū out from the mud, where it found itself a century and a half after the death of the founder, Shinran, but Rennyo also spoke to a great many people who had lost their direction in life during the troubled age that was the fifteenth century in Japan, and with plain language he extended to them the opportunity to know Shinshū. In the end, Rennyo turned the Shinshū religious organization into an enormous social entity. As a result, during the Muromachi period Shinshū acutely dealt with a host of social issues, political, economic, occupational, feminist, family-centered, and so on, giving birth to a new way of being human.

Ōtani University is an educational and research institution bearing the tradition of the Shinshū organization and is thus founded upon the spirit of this faith. Accordingly it must be said that we are also confronting the issues surrounding a "restoration of Shinshū in today's world." In this climate of the diversification of values within the flood of information that is our society, what message can Shinshū bring to people who have similarly lost their direction in life? Whether it be in societies of advanced capitalism or in societies where people are focused on fighting off starvation, wherever individuals have had their humanity taken away, what prescription can Shinshū offer them? In facing problems such as these, what we learn from Rennyo is that the value of both advantage and disadvantage is without limit.

I would like to express my gratitude for the hard work of Professors Mark L. Blum and Yasutomi Shin'ya for putting together this volume as part of the efforts of the International Buddhist Research Unit of the Shinshū Research Institute at Ōtani University. It is an honor for us that this volume is being published by the renowned Oxford University Press, realizing our wish to make research on Rennyo available to a wider readership.

Kurube Teruo
President, Ōtani University

Acknowledgments

The many events held in Kyoto in conjunction with the celebration of the 500th anniversary of Rennyo's death ranged from special religious services to academic debates to animated feature films. For Shinshū believers affiliated with one of the two Honganji, this was a time of excitement and religious reflection. Everyone, it seemed, flocked to the Kyoto National Museum to see the special Rennyo exhibit jointly sponsored by both religious institutions. This book should be seen properly as part of that collection of events. We wish to thank all the people who have contributed their time and energy to this project. In particular the scholars, students, and staff of the Shinshū Research Institute at Ōtani University, where this and many other Rennyo-related projects were conceived and supported, deserve special recognition for their efforts.

Rennyo is one of only a handful of religious figures without whose story Japanese history simply could not be told, but in the West there has been scant appreciation of his role. It is our sincere hope that this collection of essays will serve to open up greater appreciation and dialogue about his impact.

Contents

Abbreviations

CWS	*The Collected Works of Shinran.*
Cartas que os Padres e Irmãos	*Cartas que os Padres e Irmãos da Companhia de Iesus escreuerão dos Reynos de Iapão & China aos da mesma Companhia da India, & Europa, des do anno de 1549 ate o de 1580.*
Kikigaki	*Rennyō Shōnin go'ichidaiki kikigaki.* References are to edition in SSZ, unless otherwise stated.
Letters	The collection of Rennyo letters known variously as *Ofumi* 御文, *Gobunsho* 御文書, or *Shobunshū* 諸文集. References are either to compete edition in RSI or to traditional five-bundle compilation in SSZ.
Rogers	Minor L. Rogers and Ann T. Rogers, *Rennyo: The Second Founder of Shin Buddhism.*
RSG	*Rennyo Shōnin gyōjitsu.* Inaba Masamaru, ed.
RSI	*Rennyo Shōnin ibun.* Inaba Masamaru, ed.
SSZ	*Shinshū shōgyō zensho.*
SSS	*Shinshū shiryō shūsei.*
T	*Taishō shinshū daizōkyō* 大正新修大蔵経.

Contributors

Authors

Alfred Bloom: Emeritus Professor, Religious Studies, University of Hawaii

Mark L. Blum: Associate Professor, East Asian Studies, State University of New York—Albany

Ruben L. F. Habito: Professor, Theology, Southern Methodist University

Ikeda Yūtai: Emeritus Professor, Shin Buddhist Studies, Doho University, Nagoya

Kaku Takeshi: Associate Professor, Shin Buddhist Studies, Otani University, Kyoto

Katō Chiken: Professor, Religious Studies, Tokyo Polytechnic University, Tokyo

Kinryū Shizuka: Abbot, Enmanji Temple (Shinshū Honganji-ha), Shin Totsugawa, Hokkaidō

Kuroda Toshio (1926–1993): Professor, Japanese History, Osaka University, Otani University

Kusano Kenshi: Professor, Japanese History, Otani University

William R. LaFleur: E. Dale Saunders Professor in Japanese Studies, University of Pennsylvania

Matsumura Naoko: Professor, Sociology, Otani University

Minamoto Ryōen: Emeritus Professor, History of Japanese Thought, Tohoku University, Sendai

Terakawa Shunshō: Emeritus Professor, Shin Buddhist Studies, Otani University

Stanley Weinstein: Emeritus Professor, Buddhist Studies, Yale University

Yasutomi Shin'ya: Professor, Shin Buddhist Studies, Ōtani Daigaku (Otani University), Kyoto

Translators

Mark L. Blum

Maya Hara: Kyoto National Museum

Sara Horton: Assistant Professor, Religious Studies, Macalester College

Thomas Kirchner: International Research Institute for Zen Studies, Hanazono University, Kyoto

William Londo: Assistant Professor, History, Saint Vincent College

Eisho Nasu: Assistant Professor, Rev. Yoshitaka Tamai Professor of Jodo Shin Studies, Institute of Buddhist Studies, Berkeley

Jan van Bragt: Former Director, Nanzan Institute For Religion and Culture, Nagoya

Rennyo and the Roots of
Modern Japanese Buddhism

ABOVE: Rennyo portrait (scroll).

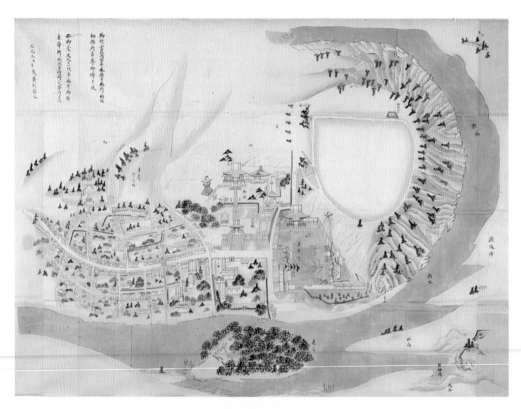

ABOVE: Yoshizaki Inlet map (scroll).

MARK L. BLUM

Introduction

The Study of Rennyo

In the annals of Japanese history, Rennyo (1415–1499) is a figure of enormous influence known primarily for fashioning the Honganji branch of Jōdoshinshū into an institution of growing strength at a time when so many others were weakened by profound political, social, and economic disruption, including ten years of civil war. Rennyo created or was at the forefront of new paradigms of religion, economics, and social structure that not only enabled him and his church to survive violent attacks but led to the accruing of unprecedented power and influence among all classes of society, from peasants to courtiers. As a result Rennyo is seen by some as a savior figure, by others as an ambitious daimyō. The more sympathetic view regards him as the "Second Founder of Jōdoshinshū," who not only saved the sect from destruction by its enemies but also, through his energetic and inspired leadership, united many of its disparate communities under the institutional banner of Honganji, put it on sound financial footing, rightly established it as the dominant branch of the sectarian legacy of Shinshū founder Shinran (1173–1262), and in the end ensured the survival of Shin Buddhism as a whole. The less sympathetic view sees Rennyo as a skilled politician who distorted many of Shinran's philosophical positions in order to create a massive feudal institution of significant wealth, financially fueled by ignorant populations of believers in whose eyes Rennyo had the power to determine their postmortem fate.

Rennyo has thus been of great interest to many Japanese scholars in various fields, most commonly Buddhist studies, religious studies, political science, social and economic history, sociology, art history, and woman's studies, among others. But critical writing on Rennyo outside Japan did not begin until the 1970s, when Michael Solomon and Minor Rogers coincidentally completed dissertations on Rennyo in 1972,[1] and Stanley Weinstein published his groundbreaking "Rennyo and the Shinshū Revival" in 1977.[2] James Dobbins helpfully situated Rennyo in the context of the medieval history of Jōdoshinshū in his *Jōdo Shinshū: Shin Buddhism in Medieval Japan*, but since Rennyo was the subject of just one chapter, the book precluded any detailed presentation of problematic issues.[3] It was not until the publication of *Rennyo* by Minor and Ann Rogers in 1991[4] that we saw a full-length study on this man and his times. That study is an enormously useful guide and contains translations of most of Rennyo's *Letters*, but the concerns in this volume are considerably different from the areas where that work displayed its most critical analyses (countering Marxist interpretations, defending Rennyo's use of *anjin* as equivalent to Shinran's term *shinjin*, for example). In the decade since it was written, there has been a huge outpouring of interest in Japan attendant upon the celebrations commemorating the 500th anniversary of Rennyo's death. Particularly between 1997 and 2000 (by Japanese counting, the anniversary year was 1998), throughout the country there were a great many lectures given, ceremonies held, art exhibited, television programs and films shown, and a significant amount of new scholarship published. Since both branches of Honganji are located in Kyoto, this old capital city was the center of much of this activity, including an unprecedented Rennyo Exhibition at the Kyoto National Museum and a special subconference devoted to Rennyo at the annual meeting of the Association for Indian and Buddhist Studies held at Ōtani University that year. Forty of those papers were published in Japanese in the volume entitled *Rennyo no sekai*, and seven of the writings in this volume are translations or modified versions of those essays. If this number seems large, in fact there is much more: if one includes the modern translations of Rennyo's writings, more than sixty books about Rennyo have been published in Japan since 1997. Considering the general paucity of materials extant from the Muromachi period, this much activity reflects a much broader and more creative use of materials; in essence we have had a veritable renaissance of Rennyo studies. In selecting essays for this volume, the editors have tried to reflect many of these new approaches to communicate the richness of this field.

We cannot presume to know who this man was, but by any reckoning he was remarkable. Only seven years into his tenure as abbot of Honganji, the temple is attacked by warriors again and again until all buildings are burned to the ground. Rennyo barely escapes with his life, and while in exile not only restores Honganji but expands it into a church of national prominence with political power that rivals the greatest religious institutions of his day. It is well known that Shinshū priests have always taken wives openly after their training, but Rennyo married no less than five times, fathering twenty-seven children. While it is naïve to presume that a pristine form of Shinshū had remained unchanged from the time of Shinran until Rennyo assumed the abbotship, there is no question that he wrought many changes within Honganji that eventually affected all branches of the sect. While critics fault Rennyo for expanding the institution at the expense of its spirituality, the significant number of new converts to the Honganji religious paradigm as redefined by Rennyo suggest otherwise. Rennyo did revise and reshape both the religious institution and its religious message, but how much was lost in those revisions and how much was gained is subjective. For though we are somewhat able to grasp the *form* of Shinshū and specifically Honganji culture under its prior leaders—indeed many of their writings are extant—we can never be certain how much the differences we perceive today in rhetoric and inferred organizational structure under Rennyo's tenure reflect meaningful differences in belief, practice, and perception, and how much merely changes in the way things were expressed in the more than 200 years that separate Shinran and Rennyo.

From our point of view today, more than five centuries after his death, Rennyo thus presents two historical faces: one spiritually appealing, magnetic, and humble; the other politically savvy, powerful, and with responsibility for the lives of tens of thousands. Even putting aside any trace of the "great man" notion of history, Rennyo nonetheless occupies a unique position in Japanese history as having transformed a relatively small religious sect in troubled times into a national organization of wealth and power. Many of the essays examine Rennyo's utilization of the symbols of his church's authority, but the fact that those symbols grew significantly in stature under his leadership tells us that Rennyo's presence itself was substantial, suggesting that in Rennyo we find both personal charisma *and* his institutional genius. Given the Weberian dictum that the mark of a truly charismatic leader is administrative incompetence, Rennyo presents a real enigma. How could both these extremes be combined in the same individual? Is our understanding of the man so off the mark that we have the wrong picture entirely? Or does the example of Rennyo essentially disprove Weber's doctrine? How much of Rennyo's success was actually due to his efforts, how much credit should be given to the attractiveness of Shinran's doctrine, and how much is a result of social, political, and economic factors is a problematic underlying all the essays here.

The fact is that before the time of Rennyo, his church, the Honganji, was only one among many branches of Shin Buddhism, itself only one among many so-called new schools of Pure Land Buddhism that were established in the previous two centuries. Moreover, Shinran's institutional legacy itself was rather weak compared with the other new developments in his time; that is, the branches of Shinran's lineage do not appear to have been among the more socially and politically prosperous or prominent among the many that sprang from Hōnen's disciples in the thirteenth century. The fifteenth-century religious landscape of Japan into which Rennyo was born was dominated by major institutions of an earlier age, such as Mount Hiei, Miidera, Kōfukuji, and the like, as well as the presence of the new Gozan orders of the Rinzai school in the capital with its strong bakufu support.

Among the newly established Pure Land schools based on Hōnen's legacy that had only grown in size and influence through the two centuries since Hōnen's death, it was the Chinzei and Seizan branches of the Jōdoshū, and the Jishū founded by Ippen, that appear to have been most influential when Rennyo first came on the scene. Even among the various lines of Shinshū, most scholars see the Takada and Bukkōji branches as overshadowing the Honganji before Rennyo's impact was felt. When the allegedly amoral and anti-authoritarian values manifest in the behavior of Honganji followers in Ōmi Province caused such ire among the leaders of Mount Hiei as to provoke the sending of troops to suppress them (discussed in chapter 7), the leaders of the Takada school were only too quick to write to the abbot of Enryakuji to clarify how their interpretation of Shinran's teaching differed from that found in Honganji-affiliated communities. Indeed, the very weakness in the political presence of Honganji during this crisis early in Rennyo's leadership is illustrated by the fact that Honganji was finally able to negotiate an end to the armed attack against it by reaffirming its status as a branch temple within the Enryakuji institution of Mount Hiei, essentially making a public denial of its own autonomy. But that was during the Ōnin War, when most of the powerful military households were engaged in open conflict, tens of thousands of troops fought on the streets of the capital, and a general lawlessness pervaded the region.[5] It was many years before Rennyo decided it was safe to return to the capital for the reconstruction of Honganji, and the choice of Yamashina outside the urban center and the fortresslike structure that was built there is only one manifestation of his appreciation of the need for self-protection. That need resulted in various alliances with people and institutions of power, most famously with Miidera and the warlords Togashi Masachika and Hosokawa Masamoto. In 1493, six years before Rennyo's death, Masamoto would overthrow the shōgun and run the bakufu through his chosen successor, in essence becoming the most powerful man in the country. And as his power increased, so did his role as protector of Rennyo and Honganji. By this time Rennyo had administrative control over thousands of peasant soldiers, and Honganji eventually reached a position of political and religious prominence that rivaled Enryakuji and Mount Hiei itself. Under his tenure many Shin communities achieved more economic and political independence than they had ever known, and some even instituted democratic systems of government at the local level. Rennyo was courted by daimyō for the size and commitment of his community, and a major part of his legacy was an institution in Honganji that seemed commensurate with that of a feudal domain in many of its functions, prompting some to see Rennyo himself as a daimyō. After Rennyo's death, Honganji only grew stronger, whereupon Nobunaga sought its destruction as he had destroyed Mount Hiei, and yet it was the one domain that he was unable to conquer.

As was already noted, these events are not in dispute; how Honganji got to this point is disputed, however, as is the nature of its religious role in Rennyo's time. For those who see the growth of a religious organization on this scale to be impossible without an attractive and fulfilling spiritual message that both captures the imagination of its adherents and satisfies their religious needs, Rennyo's achievement, whatever it meant politically, is primarily in the area of formulating a coherent religious message. For those who see the growth of any social institution as primarily about power relations and their management, the key to understanding Rennyo lies in his strategies of control over his congregations and the infrastructure he created for his church that continued for many generations after his death. Indeed one of the most satisfying aspects of this project has been the discovery that nearly all the contributors do not regard these as mutually exclusive interpretations, and the reader will gain an appreciation of the unmistakable fact that Rennyo was a successful religious leader *and* successful political leader.

The sixteen essays that follow this introduction are divided into three parts: historical studies that examine Rennyo in the context of the history of Japan, Japanese religion, and Japanese Buddhism; Shinshū studies, which consider Rennyo and his era in terms of issues particular to the sectarian study of Shinshū; and comparative religion contributions that look at the legacy of Rennyo in terms of religious issues common to European traditions. A brief summary of some of the salient points made in the each of the essays follows.

The biographical outline of Rennyo's life written by Yasutomi Shin'ya not only presents what is currently known about the circumstances of his youth, succession to the abbotship of Honganji, geographical movement, and approach to his community, it also opens with the impact that the political instability of Rennyo's time had upon his outlook, an oft-repeated theme in all the essays. Here we see how the watershed moment in Rennyo's career is probably Enryakuji's formal announcement, on the ninth day of the first month in 1465, of its intention to destroy the Ōtani Honganji complex in Kyoto where Rennyo resided and the subsequent attack that came the next day. While that raid only partially destroyed Honganji, another attack in the third month essentially finished the job. Attacks on other Honganji communities followed, and when the bakufu finally persuaded Enryakuji to cease its persecution of what was then called *Ikkō-shū*, this point did not come until the fifth month of that year. These events illustrate the freedom of the Mount Hiei power brokers to move at will at that time, but they also highlight the fact that when Rennyo began his campaign to reconfigure the Honganji community he did so under the stress of exile. Rennyo's thought then, must be seen against this background: he lived his entire life during a period of enormous social instability, even after Honganji was rebuilt in Yamashina on the outskirts of Kyoto, when traditional centers of power like the court and the bakufu enjoyed only limited influence over the nation.

Kuroda Toshio is famous for categorizing the "establishment" Buddhism of the Kamakura period as *kenmitsu taisei*, a term that combines the words for exoteric and esoteric forms of Buddhism to indicate a religious, social, and political worldview common to all major forms of institutionalized Buddhism in the twelfth and thirteenth centuries. While Kuroda has argued that by and large the so-called new schools of Buddhism were generally viewed merely as heretical forms of that paradigm, and thereby did not seriously challenge it, in chapter 3 he recognizes the writings of Shinran as having "aimed at surmounting the shortcomings of *kenmitsu* thought." In looking at Rennyo, Kuroda reminds us that political unrest was not the only socially meaningful characteristic of society in the fifteenth century. Rennyo lived also at a time when the sociopolitical structure of the *shōen* or manorial system in which three centers of power—court, shōgun, and religious institutions—were being replaced by individual daimyō ruling their domains as autonomous units of power. The breakdown in the *kenmitsu* power structure naturally led to a loss of authority of the old, established institutions such as Mount Hiei and the subsequent rise of interest in local cults and newer forms of Buddhism. Kuroda stresses the importance of the fact that Rennyo was speaking to a populace in which an intellectual approach to religion was much more widespread than in previous centuries when a small elite of highly educated charismatic scholar-monks determined the direction of religion. Rennyo's message should therefore be seen in the context of this "transitional" society when many people were seeking more direct control over their environment; the peasant *ikki* leagues and their uprisings are but one example. Similarly, Rennyo reinforces Shinran's assertion that true religion not only deserves a place separate from secular power structures but also fundamentally need not define itself by its relationship with those secular structures.

Next, Stanley Weinstein in chapter 4 provides a useful comparison between Shinran and Rennyo as leaders of Shinshū culture. Weinstein views Shinran as rather pure and unbending in his refusal to sacrifice his religious integrity to the demands of society. By comparison, Rennyo was "the builder" who did what was necessary to create the edifice of Honganji. Weinstein frames our understanding of Rennyo within the evolution of Japanese scholarship in the postwar period, pointing out how Rennyo had garnished an enormous amount of interest among historians, both Marxist and otherwise, because of his apparent promotion of self-empowerment movements among the populace. When Weinstein shows how, unlike Shinran, Rennyo exhibits strong sectarian consciousness and professes a doctrine in which resolute faith leads not only to the Pure Land in the next world but material benefits in this one, it calls to mind similar rhetoric from the Protestant Reformation. It raises the specter of a doctrine of "predestined salvation of the elect" in Rennyo, an association that also emerges from the contributions of Katō Chiken (chapter 15) and William LaFleur (chapter 16).

Matsumura Naoko in chapter 5 then examines Rennyo's take on what Kasahara Kazuo has labeled the Shinshū tradition of *nyonin shōki*, a twist on the phrase *akunin shōki*. *Akunin shōki*, itself a paraphrase of chapter 3 of the *Tannishō*, is Shinshū jargon for a position attributed to Shinran that if good people are accepted into Amida's Pure Land, how much more so does the Buddha welcome the bad (or the evil). Kasahara thus understood Rennyo's overt religious acceptance of women to have followed the precedent of Zonkaku,[6] who inferred that because women are seen as inherently limited as a karmic given, one should infer that it is to women that the Buddha's message is directed most intensely. Matsumura recognizes the importance of this issue for Rennyo, yet finds his view of women decidedly ambivalent. On the one hand Rennyo is clear that his sectarian tradition does not accept any differences between the spiritual potential of men and of women. On the other he repeats the traditional view that women are hindered by the infamous formula known as the "five obstacles and three submissions," and he sent one of his daughters into the house of the shōgun as a concubine, presumably to cement political ties with his church. Citing Kyōgen scripts and other contemporary sources, Matsumura shows how women were becoming increasingly recognized for their contributions in the Muromachi period, yet in areas such as divorce, society's presumption of male superiority for the most part remained unshaken. What is perhaps most fascinating here is the fact that while traveling from community to community Rennyo encouraged women to form gender-specific study groups, or *kō*, for lay and monastic alike; these strike Matsumura as strikingly similar to the self-empowering solidarity groups that began forming in the last quarter of the twentieth century.

The essay by Kinryū Shizuka (chapter 6) utilizes documents written by European Catholic missionaries dating from the latter half of the sixteenth century to bring in new information on Shinshū in the century after Rennyo. Although unavoidably distorted to some degree, this material contains many things we can learn about the immediate post-Rennyo era, not the least being the forms that Shinshū took at the folk level, where many of these descriptions are based. Here we see a considerable amount of *honji-suijaku* and esoteric religious expression in which there is a rich symbolic interplay between Amida and Kannon as wish-granting savior figures and the forms in which they manifest. The phrase *namu-amida-butsu* itself was analyzed for its symbolic content, and Kinryū also shows how many of these ideas are echoed in Edo period *dangibon*, thought to represent popular sermons. Ever aware of the danger of losing souls to incorrect religious teachings, the priest Valignano, for example, declares, "No matter what sins one has committed, [the priests]...chant the name of Amida or Shaka, and so long as one truly believes in the virtue of this act, those sins will be completely cleansed. Therefore, other atonements are completely unnecessary...this is the same as the teaching of Luther." For the missionaries, this *Ikkō-shū* was a religion of peasants. But it was also a religion that inspired great piety and loyalty; their records tell of rural *dōjō* where the members assemble thrice daily for services, and of the decapitation of a *dōjō* leader for "heresy" by a Christian daimyō in Kumamoto.

Kusano Kenshi's contribution in chapter 7 looks at the initial military attack on the Ōtani Honganji that first drove Rennyo from the capital. By examining documents produced by Mount Hiei to justify the raid, Kusano illustrates how the accusations leveled against Shinshū by Enryakuji are clearly linked to Rennyo's activities, accusing the Honganji of practices that slander both buddhas and kami. An interesting part of the criticism is over the name of *mugekō-shū* adopted by many of the Honganji-affiliated groups in the Ōmi area, which is associated with a doctrine wherein an "unhindered" Amida Buddha empowered his believers to feel similarly unrestricted in their activities. Kusano points to Rennyo's destruction of Buddhist icons (also discussed in chapter 9) as one of the most serious of the accusations. He gives examples that show how the frequent admonition in Rennyo's *Letters* against the open disdain displayed to local kami is testimony that that kind of thing was quite prevalent among Honganji followers, for they are criticized for ignoring pollution customs that result in desecrating shrine precincts. As Kusano suggests, this is not only about the ancient religion we now call Shinto but also about disrupting the political hierarchy embedded in village organizations centered around shrines.

In chapter 8 Minamoto Ryōen offers an analysis of how Rennyo's thought paved the way for the phenomenon known as *myōkōnin*, the name given to a number of lay saints in this tradition. Although most people associate myōkōnin with the Edo and Meiji periods, in fact such individuals begin to emerge during Rennyo's leadership, and Minamoto focuses on the example of Akao-no-Dōshū (d. 1516). Minamoto believes that Rennyo's nenbutsu hermeneutic, coupled with his promotion of the doctrine known as *kihō ittai*, "unified body of individual and Dharma," changed the culture surrounding Shinshū such that it led to these remarkably inspired individuals. In particular, Rennyo's shift from Shandao's view of nenbutsu as a call to personal commitment and practice to one in which both virtues are seen to be emanating from the Buddha himself through the believer clarified a point on which Shinran was not consistent. Echoing the mysticism in the *Anjinketsujōshō* (and Kōsai), Rennyo writes of the attained individual who "knows" the Buddha, who has a "dialogue" with the Buddha, and in his later years this is how he described one who has attained the goal of *shinjin* or *anjin*. This dialogic attitude is typical of the mature Rennyo and suggests that he himself could well have served as a prototype for the myōkōnin. Minamoto's essay is thus an important reminder of the fact that Rennyo not only inspired the community-based form of Shinshū that dominated Honganji from the sixteenth through the twentieth century but also created a new path for the intensely spiritual individual who derives inspiration from discipline and personal religious experience rather than from a communal setting.

In chapter 9 Mark Blum looks at Rennyo's use of religious icons as a means of communication. He asks us to consider the production and distribution of hanging scrolls under Rennyo's tenure as commensurate with the composition and distribution of his *Letters* for the purpose of establishing and confirming relationships, dictating norms of belief, and thus delineating Honganji culture as a whole. Although Honganji had a prior tradition of bestowing sacred scrolls to its outlying affiliated communities, dating back to the time of Shinran, Rennyo plunges into this activity in a way unprecedented in its sheer volume and expense. But Rennyo's relationship with visual forms of the sacred was a complex one, and this chapter echoes Professor Kusano's focus on the significance of Rennyo's period of burning Buddhist icons and its direct impact on the justification for the persecution of Honganji during his leadership. The essay uses the example of Shinshū icons in Rennyo's day to draw our attention to the societal impact of religious icons in Japanese history as a whole, for we know that a wide freedom in iconic expression in Shinshū was significantly curbed under Rennyo when ritual use of the ten-character *myōgō* scroll initially favored by Rennyo himself and many Shin leaders before him, including Shinran, had to be proscribed after it was demonstrated to provoke intense, at times violently repugnant reactions by some of the leaders on Mount Hiei.

Chapter 10, the first essay in the Shinshū studies part, is Terakawa Shunshō's look at the Shinshū view of *ōjō* or Birth in the Pure Land, usually abbreviated here as Birth. This key concept is of crucial importance because there has been considerable misunderstanding of the implications of it in Japanese Pure Land thought; it is too often reified to nothing more than postmortem rebirth in a paradise. Terakawa first looks at Shinran's final statements on it, in his seldom-read *Jōdo sangyō ōjō monrui* and better-known *Ichinen tanen mon'i* and *Yuishinshō mon'i*. Key here is the fact that Shinran directly ties the Pure Land goal of *ōjō* to broader religious issues such as the attaining of *nirvāṇa*, the epiphanic experience of *shinjin* (the "believing mind"), and the Tanluan's twofold notion of the believer's merit transfer (*huixiang*, Japanese *ekō*). Terakawa stresses that our understanding of Rennyo's statements on practice, faith, and realization must be seen within the context of Shinran's understanding of *ōjō* as being something realized in *this* lifetime, not after death. The problem lies in the fact that Rennyo frequently uses language that beseeches the Buddha to "help me in the next life." Through his masterful understanding of Shin doctrine, Terakawa weaves an interpretive tour de force that maintains Shinran's more radical position within Rennyo while finding room for his shift in emphasis.

Kaku Takeshi in chapter 11 provides a window into how Rennyo was resurrected by some as an authoritative religious thinker in the Meiji period, when Buddhism faced government persecution and criticism from many quarters as an anachronistic institution anathema to modernization. He notes that no less a figure than Fukuzawa

Yukichi praised Rennyo for his take on the concept of *obō-buppō*, or "imperial law and the Buddhist law," which he read as advocating the modern legal principle separating church and state, an interpretation that led to Rennyo's *Letters* becoming better studied than Shinran's own writings during the Meiji period. When Kiyozawa Manshi emerged as a leading Shinshū intellectual in the 1890s, his insistence on modern, critical sectarian studies caused a rift between conservative and reform movements within the church. Examining the contribution of Soga Ryōjin, a disciple of Kiyozawa, Kaku argues that Soga sought to resolve this conflict by redefining Rennyo and his doctrines. Over the years we see how Soga writes of Rennyo as social reformer on the one hand and religious mystic on the other, and it is fascinating to see how much Soga and Kiyozawa were taken with Rennyo's embrace of both the *Tannishō* and the *kihō ittai* doctrine, the latter also discussed in Professor Minamoto's essay (chapter 8). Kaku clarifies for us how the Ōtani branch (Higashi Honganji) of Shinshū created the underpinnings of its modern doctrinal position on the basis of a *Tannishō*-centered philosophy running from Shinran to Rennyo to Kiyozawa to Soga. In Soga's words, this attitude is characterized by an approach common to these thinkers such that Buddhism is not regarded as a perfected form to be acceded to, but something to be "understood . . . through their own experiences."

In chapter 12 Alfred Bloom considers Rennyo's legacy in the context of the postwar period and his potential for inspiring progressive developments within the Honganji institution. He reminds us that Rennyo regarded the Honganji church itself as the historical manifestation of the working of the Buddha's wisdom and compassion, yet he warns against tendencies toward rigidity and inflexibility that may emerge from an acceptance of this view today. Bloom notes that Rennyo himself transformed the institution significantly, even reformulating church rhetoric to emphasize the afterlife, turning away from Shinran's focus on the experience of awakening. Bloom affirms this movie as a natural and healthy to adapt to one's surroundings in ways that are innovative if they succeed in communicating your message. As an illustration of how Rennyo's considerable communication skills were employed to this end, Bloom notes the important liturgical role in Honganji temples of Shinran's *Wasan* and *Shōshinge*, a legacy of Rennyo's efforts, begun in Yoshizaki, to print and distribute these texts so that Shin communities could each have copies for their own services. We also know that Rennyo promoted the organization of small voluntary associations usually called *kō*, also discussed in chapter 5, whose leaders he kept in his confidence, giving them his imprimatur for self-government in the service of providing a space for religious activities. It was these local groups that he was able to tie together despite geographical separation into the broad, national organization that Honganji became. Rennyo thus promoted a model of local democratic groups that were tied to a mother church that otherwise remained essentially feudal in structure.

Ikeda Yūtai has spent a number of years studying Rennyo's *Letters*, and in chapter 13 he examines the observation that these are directly inspired by and therefore another expression of the philosophy of the *Tannishō*. Such was the conclusion of a commentary on the *Tannishō* by Ryōshō in the eighteenth century and was asserted again by Soga Ryōjin, as is discussed in chapter 11. Ikeda considers the implications of the text-critical findings of Miyazaki Enjun, who discovered that some twenty-five years had elapsed between the writing of individual sentences in the extant text copied by Rennyo, meaning that Rennyo kept this book with him over a long period of time. After discussing Rennyo's famous colophon to the *Tannishō*: "This should not be shown indiscriminately to those who lack karmic good roots," Ikeda provides a valuable analysis of the interpretive "differences" so bemoaned by that work as understood by Rennyo, according to statements in his *Letters*. Ikeda divides Rennyo's notion of heresy into four categories: (1) misunderstanding of nenbutsu practice, (2) secret practices and doctrines within certain local communities (called *hiji bōmon*), (3) public pronouncements of Shinshū doctrine before nonbelievers, and (4) teaching non-Shinshū doctrines, false doctrines, or for money.

In chapter 14, the final chapter in the Shinshū studies part, Yasutomi Shin'ya presents an example of the rich folklore tradition that has grown up around Rennyo and is little known outside Japan, offering a multifaceted interpretation of a folktale associated with Rennyo's four-year residence in Yoshizaki. A kind of *setsuwa* tale, this story has a clear religious message and found its way into the normative pictorial biographies of Rennyo but also enjoyed retelling in nonreligious contexts. A story in which women are the central characters, it concerns the tragedy of death within a family and the resultant acute spiritual needs of the remaining family members, expressed in tension between a mother-in-law and her son's widow. Yasutomi offers three interpretations of the story: as a blueprint for a Nō drama, as a statement about the traditional prejudice against women in Japanese Buddhism, and as a symbolic representation of the regional conflict between the religio-political paradigm of Honganji and that of the indigenous mountain cults in the Hokuriku area such as the one surrounding Mount Haku, or Hakusan, a mountain where ascetic, shugendo practices continue to the present day. The story communicates a number of important aspects for understanding Rennyo: that he was explicit in his doctrine of equality of men and women before the Buddha, and at times even reflected Zonkaku's earlier view, discussed in chapter 5, that Shinran's doctrine implied that women were the precise object of the Buddha's compassion; that he was enamored of Nō drama and incorporated Nō elements into his own preaching style; and that there was always some degree of social and political upheaval brought on by the expansion of Honganji's influence over an ever-widening geographical area under Rennyo's leadership, of which the *ikkō ikki* peasant uprisings are only the most salient example. The last point illustrates the complex relationship between Honganji under Rennyo and the local cults today we put under the rubric Shinto.

Chapter 15 offers a sample of Katō Chiken's extensive work comparing the lives and religious ideas of Rennyo and Martin Luther. Katō is struck not only by the similarities in their religious outlook but by their personalities as well. He notes that both were happy in domestic settings, a fact he sees as indicative of their devotion to deepening the religious consciousness of the common people. Intrigued with Luther's concept of an "invisible church," Katō implies that Honganji under Rennyo probably progressed under a similar principle. At the very least, the examples shown here of the parallel problems faced when leaders like Rennyo and Luther attempt to realize an idealized religious community suggest the need for further inquiry into areas of consonance and dissonance between religious visions and social realities, especially for the history of Buddhism, where, outside of Śrī Lanka, Tibet, and some Chan studies, such inquiry is particularly lacking. In any case, Katō concludes that the many similarities between Luther and Rennyo naturally arise because both expound ideologies that stand on a doctrine of "faith alone," or in modern Shin language, "absolute Other-Power." This notion begs other questions: (1) Since Rennyo never used either expression, how would we understand his response to Katō's analysis? (2) Is there a similar denial of free will in Rennyo's writings to that seen in Luther's anti-Erasmus 1525 polemic *De servo arbitrio*, for there is a glaring tension between Rennyo's affirmation of universal access to the Pure Land and his belief that Birth there is not open to people born without the right karmic endowment from their previous lives? The tension between Luther's own commitment to universalism and his sense of predestination thus suggests there may be a similar presumption of a community of "the elect" lurking in Rennyo.

William LaFleur in chapter 16 considers an often overlooked aspect of Rennyo: his expression of joy. In fact Rennyo frequently uses expressions of elation to express the experience of faith, and we err in omitting this as an essential part of his message of hope. LaFleur sees this as part of a lineage of openness that defined a new religious outlook, beginning with Hōnen and moving through Shinran to Rennyo. It is not only that these forms of Pure Land Buddhism consciously distanced themselves from the secret, "hiddenness" of the older Tendai forms of Japanese Buddhism, but that they also brought a new message of confidence regarding karma to the general population, many of whom feared that their occupations precluded them from salvation. An important aspect of this openness is Rennyo's attitude of treating his followers as "fellow practitioners" rather than as disciples. This combination of humble authority and openness in Rennyo suggests a deep-seated faith in the value of freedom for bringing people to liberation though faith. LaFleur contrasts this attitude with that displayed by the Grand Inquisitor questioning Jesus in Fyodor Dostoyevsky's novel *The Brothers Karamazov*. Set in sixteenth-century Europe, a time close to that of Rennyo, this priest justifies burning heretics at the stake because, as he explains to Jesus, freedom of thought in religious matters is too oppressive for the people who actually yearn for "miracle, mystery, and authority" which the Catholic Church is able to provide. Professor LaFleur argues that Rennyo consciously moves away from all three of these elements of religion because of his focus on experience and openness.

In the final chapter Ruben Habito brings us back to the twenty-first century by considering the impact of Rennyo upon how the Shin sect has conceived its international role today. Given that Shin Buddhism under Honganji has become both large and influential both inside and outside of Japan, he asks its leadership important questions about its future direction. Comparing Honganji thought and structure to that of the Roman Catholic Church, Habito seeks to make Shin leaders more aware of the issues involved in the "translation" and "contextualization" of the religion for an international audience. This point is particularly important for our evaluation of the legacy of Rennyo because, for Habito, Rennyo appears to have changed many of Shinran's core positions regarding the religious world outside of Shinshū. Focusing on the problem of alterity, Habito recognizes the central role that Rennyo had in shaping the Shin attitude toward the non-Shinshū world over the last 500 years, and this thoughtful essay functions as an open call for Shin to move beyond that history in order to clarify once again how Honganji as an institution can provide leadership for its believers to see other institutions of power in society today, such as the emperor and state power in general, especially in light of the complicity of both Higashi and Nishi Honganji during World War II. As an example of how a political statement from a church leader must be understood in its original context so as to limit the scope of its normative value to later generations, Habito points to Paul's letter to Titus, which, though advocating willful submission to political authority, was subject to varying interpretations over time.

Although there is little to suggest that the world in which Rennyo lived, the fifteenth century, should be considered even a premodern stage of Japanese history, the legacy of Rennyo nonetheless deserves recognition for its contribution to many of the institutional and cultural developments that we take for granted today as emblematic of Japanese Buddhist institutions in the modern period. We might consider these changes under the rubric of innovative sectarian integration, defined as a successful reworking of sectarian precedent in ways that redefined the relationship between religious idealism and institutional need. Successful in this context means growth in size and social stature of the organization, an undeniable fact in the case of Honganji, but one not without attendant controversy as well. But while the changes wrought by Rennyo have not pleased everyone, modern schools of Buddhism in Japan have all been influenced to some degree by his creative strategies of communication. I specfically refer to those that successfully infused lay populations throughout the country with a sense of identity to their sect as a national entity. By devoting considerable attention to the standardization of such things as retreats for study and practice, pilgrimage, funerary rituals, fund-raising, norms of behavior, support for women, and the assimilation of local dōjō into the greater church, Rennyo's integration of local, regional, and national forces reflects an institutional vision that formed a prototype for what later became normative in Japanese religion in the premodern and modern periods.

Having left such a deep imprint on Shinshū culture and Japanese history as a whole, Rennyo continues to be the object of historical scrutiny today. His repeated encounters with tragedy—the Ōnin war,[6] persecution and destruction of his church, exile, sectarian infighting—without giving in to despair suggest the strength of his courage and vision but also make him a compelling figure of considerable interest. However one imagines the experience of living at a time of such great insecurity, Rennyo emerges as a charismatic leader who deeply understood the anxieties of his age and fashioned a response that met with overwhelming acceptance. With the tens of books and hundreds of articles on Rennyo published in Japan in the past decade, the editors of this study make no claim of comprehensiveness. We only hope that this collection makes a small contribution to the understanding of this figure and his times, and serves to stimulate further research.

Notes

1 Minor L. Rogers, "Rennyo Shōnin 1415–1499: A Transformation in Shin Buddhist Piety," Ph.D. dissertation, Harvard University, Cambridge, Mass., 1972. Ira Michael Solomon, "Rennyo and the Rise of Honganji in Muromachi Japan," Ph.D. diss., Columbia University, New York, 1972.

2 Stanley Weinstein, "Rennyo and the Shinshū Revival," in *Japan in the Muromachi Age*, ed. John W. Hall and Toyoda Takeshi (Berkeley: University of California Press, 1977), 331–358.

3 James Dobbins, *Jōdo Shinshū: Shin Buddhism in Medieval Japan* (Bloomington: University of Indiana Press, 1989).

4 Minor L. Rogers and Ann T. Rogers, Rennyo: *The Second Founder of Shin Buddhism* (Berkeley, Cal.: Asian Humanities Press, 1991).

5 See Mary Elizabeth Berry, *The Culture of Civil War in Kyoto* (Berkeley: University of California Press, 1994).

6 Lasting nearly a decade, the Ōnin war was a tragic saga that destroyed much of the capital and yet ultimately decided nothing of consequence politically.

PART I

HISTORICAL STUDIES

YASUTOMI SHIN'YA

The Life of Rennyo

A *Struggle for the Transmission of Dharma*

Rennyo, the eighth abbot of the Honganji, played an extremely significant role in the history of the Jōdoshin school. He not only reestablished the stagnant religious organization of Honganji but also revitalized the concept of *shinjin* (faith) for this school of Japanese Buddhism. Therefore, Rennyo has long been known as the restorer (*gosaikō shōnin*) of the tradition and today is called the second founder (*chūkō shōnin*) of what is called Shinshū, or the Jōdoshin school:

> Within the tradition of the Master [Shinran] Shōnin, the essential teaching is the one thought-moment of entrusting [*tanomu ichinen*]. Therefore, from generation to generation, our masters have always referred to entrusting [*tanomu*]. However, people did not clearly understand what to entrust. Our great grand master [*zenzenjū shōnin*] [Rennyo] therefore composed the *Letters* in which he clarified [the meaning of entrusting as] "to discard the sundry practices and single-heartedly entrust [ourselves to] Amida to save us in the afterlife [*goshō tasuketamae*]." Because of this, he is [regarded as] the restorer [of the tradition] [*gosaiko no shōnin*].[1]

In this passage, the essence of Rennyo's restoration of the tradition is stated clearly and concisely. Rennyo used the phrase "entrusting Amida" (*mida o tanomu*) to demonstrate the foundation of the Jōdoshin school faith to the people of his time. Rennyo's life coincides with the middle of the Muromachi period (1392–1573), a time of social upheaval and natural disasters. Treason undercut the previous military ethic of loyalty, exemplified by the assassination of the Shōgun Ashikaga Yoshinori (1394–1441) by his subordinate, Akamatsu Mitsusuke (1373–1441). Frequent famines plagued the populace, and peasant uprisings shook the country like earthquakes. Power struggles among the political elite eventually escalated into the great war that occurred during the Ōnin and Bunmei eras, from 1467 to 1477.

Such discordance marked a turning point in the religious lives of the populace.[2] The almost continuous state of war made people feel extremely anxious about the future. People were in search of a peaceful land and stable home and were hungry for spiritual consolation. Witnessing how quickly worldly happiness could be destroyed in a single fiery battle, they truly experienced impermanence. Under such circumstances, they needed strong convictions to survive. Rather than simply devoting themselves to communal religious practice—such as formulaic praying for the peace of the nation or a good harvest of the five grains—people needed to participate freely and sincerely in individual practices of faith that could sustain them through these catastrophes.

The methods of propagation used by the established Buddhist schools, which emphasized this-worldly benefits (*genze riyaku*) and prayer rituals (*kitō*), did not satisfy people's spiritual demands. Nor did their abstract doctrinal formulas capture the hearts of people. Faced with the collapse of the preexisting social order, people increasingly clamored for spiritual autonomy. In such times, what Rennyo accomplished can truly be called a religious reformation. He broke with the existing Buddhist teachings, which had become tailored to aristocratic tastes and imprinted with other Japanese religious customs, and revived the original spirit of the Buddhist path.

However, Rennyo had to take drastic actions to accomplish his goals. As was mentioned earlier, Rennyo wrote his *Letters* to urge people to cast away other practices, pejoratively labeled "sundry practices" (*zōgyō*), and he taught that one should take refuge in the Buddha Amida single-heartedly for "salvation in the afterlife" (*goshō tasuketamae*). On the basis of this theory of faith, Rennyo would dismantle closed and self-righteous organizations of secretive medieval Shinshū communities, which were essentially constructed on the practice of taking refuge in a teacher (*chishiki kimyō*), and would enable ordinary followers to participate more actively in the broader medieval society. Applying this principle, he also severely criticized the practices of "entrusting through donations" (*semotsu danomi*) and "thieflike faith" (*monotori shinjin*) in which leaders of Shinshū communities treated followers as their own property. He curbed the power of the head priests of these regional communities and disbanded their private organizations.

The line of Rennyo's propagation extended from Katada and Yoshizaki to cities in the western provinces. Replacing the teaching of Jishū, which had been popular during the fourteenth and fifteenth centuries, the teaching of Shinshū was widely received among townspeople, including merchants, artisans, and sailors. The teaching also gained popularity among people who were becoming objects of discrimination, such as entertainers, women, and those engaged in certain trades.[3]

Rennyo's views on such groups, particularly women, are noteworthy. At that time, women's roles in society were grossly undervalued. Despite the fact that they constituted half the population, they labored under the oppressive ideology of the five exclusions and three submissions (*goshō sanshō*).[4] However, Rennyo did not subscribe to the notion that women could not attain buddhahood; perhaps he was influenced by his many close yet tragic relationships with women—he was separated from his mother at an early age, he was preceded in death by four of five wives,[5] and among his numerous children six daughters predeceased him. Especially toward the end of his life, Rennyo stressed that among the ordinary sentient beings whose evil karma is deep and heavy (*zaiaku jinjū no bonbu*), women were precisely the kind of beings (shōki) whom Amida would work to save. He taught that women should not worry simply because they were women; rather, by realizing faith (shinjin), everyone could certainly attain buddhahood at the moment of Birth in the Pure Land through the saving hand of Amida Buddha. Women could thus be saved just as they are.

In these and other issues, Rennyo had to overcome incredible difficulties to succeed in restoring the tradition. This short essay will examine some of his struggles. Although Rennyo's activities in his later life are well known through the ample historical materials, such as the Kūzenki,[6] gathered by his close disciples, there are few reliable materials on his earlier life, a period crucial in the formation of his religious organization.

Birth and Early Years

Rennyo's early years coincide with the growing pains of the developing Jōdoshinshū institution. Over a period of 150 years following the death of Shinran, his gravesite slowly grew into a locus of religious activity for his lineage. Located in the Ōtani foothills of Higashiyama, what began as a mausoleum gradually took on the features of a monastery, with the temple name Honganji first appearing in historical records in a document dated Genkyo 1 (1321). This was shortly after the site of Hōnen's (1133–1212) grave, located in the same vicinity of Higashiyama, came to be recognized under the name Chion'in based on a similar institutional model. Honganji, it should be remembered, was established by Kakunyo (1270–1351), whose wish was to "rectify misunderstandings and reveal the truth" (haja kenshō).

Approximately one hundred years after the establishment of Honganji, in Ōei 22 (1415), Rennyo was born at Honganji, Higashiyama Ōtani, Kyoto. His father, Zonnyo (1396–1457), was twenty years old, and his grandfather, Gyōnyo (1376–1440), was forty. The name of Rennyo's mother is not known, but it is said that she was a servant of his father or grandfather, so her social status must have been very humble.

The circumstances of Honganji at that time would make a significant mark on young Rennyo's life. According to the Honpukuji yuraiki (A Record of Hompukuji's History), "The head temple was deserted without a single visitor in sight. People living there led very lonely lives."[7] In contrast, the same record notes the prosperity of Bukkōji: "Around Ōei 20 (1413), Bukkōji at Shirutani was crowded with people because of [the temple's] use of salvation registers [myōchō] and portrait lineages [ekeizu]."

Although Honganji and Bukkōji were both the Jōdoshin school temples, they fell under the administration of the Tendai school, the former as a branch temple of the Shōren'in and the latter under the authority of Myōhōin, both Tendai temples of some authority.[8] Each therefore used Tendai protocols (igi), but Bukkōji in particular from early in its history made use of salvation registers and portrait lineages in order to appeal to the populace.

When Rennyo was six years old, his birth mother left Honganji. It is generally agreed that she left because Rennyo's father, Zonnyo, had married Nyoen-ni (d.

1460), the daughter of the lord of the Ebina clan, who was a close associate of the Shōgun Ashikaga Yoshimitsu (1358–1408). It is said that Rennyo's mother left the following words to the boy before leaving: "I beg you to restore the tradition of [Shinran] Shōnin during your lifetime."[9] His mother both lamented the derelict state of Honganji and entrusted Rennyo with the revival of Shinshū, so as to focus on the salvation of women and the weak. It is further recorded that Rennyo, inspired by his mother's words, at the age of fifteen pledged to restore the Shinshū tradition, saying, "During my lifetime, I pledge to propagate the tradition of [Shinran] Shōnin everywhere."[10]

Youth and Clerical Training

Rennyo received his ordination to become a Buddhist priest at Shōren'in[11] in Kyoto in the summer of Eikyō 3 (1431), taking the name Kenju as his priestly name (*jitsumyō*) and Rennyo as his Dharma name (*hōmyō*). Honganji was still floundering in financial difficulties, but, although there were often shortages of food and clothing, Rennyo diligently practiced and studied Buddhism. Among Rennyo's teachers, Kyōgaku (1395–1473), [abbot] of Daijōin at Kōfukuji in Nara, is very famous. Kyōgaku was very close to Rennyo's father, because Kyōgaku's mother, Shōrin (d. 1442), grew up within the Honganji complex in Ōtani, Kyoto.[12] Rennyo was later able to obtain land in Yoshizaki in Echizen Province thanks to his connections to Kyōgaku. Rennyo also studied the Jōdoshin school teachings with the help of his father and his uncle Kūkaku (fifteenth century).[13]

In addition to studying Buddhism, in Eikyō 6 (1434), when Rennyo was twenty years old, he took his father's place at Honganji as manuscript copier of Shinshū scriptures. Currently, the manuscripts of Shinshū scriptures in table 2.1 are those he made before his succession to the office of the abbot of Honganji.[14]

Of all the manuscripts he copied, *Tannishō* is considered the most significant. Although the exact date of this manuscript is not known, Furuta Takehiko, a modern historian, suggests that the text was copied when Rennyo was forty-three or forty-four years old and the colophon was written separately when he was approximately sixty-five.[15] Although Rennyo was a priest in the lineage of Honganji, the *Tannishō* was transmitted within the lineage of Yuien (1222–1288), one of Shinran's direct disciples. Although Kakunyo's writings include some direct quotes from the *Tannishō* and, based on an account in volume 3 of the *Bokie kotoba*, we know that Kakunyo and Yuien did indeed know each other, Kakunyo does not mention Yuien or the *Tannishō* in his own writings. Thus, from the standpoint of the Kakunyo-Rennyo line, the *Tannishō* was identified with a competing Shinshū lineage, and prevailing custom rendered it almost unthinkable for a religious leader to give public recognition to a text central to a different lineage by copying it and distributing it among its own followers. Apparently Rennyo did not adhere to such old customs; he adopted the *Tannishō* as a significant scripture revealing the fundamental teachings of the Jōdoshin school. Although Rennyo's tradition also originated in Shinran, his lineage was transmitted through the blood lines of

TABLE 2.1 Shinshū scriptures copied by Rennyo

Year		Age	Text	Author
Eikyō 6	(1434)	20	*Jōdo monruiju shō*	Shinran
Eikyō 8	(1436)	22	*Sanjō wasan*	Shinran
Eikyō 10	(1438)	24	*Jōdo shin'yōshō*	Zonkaku
			Kudenshō	Kakunyo
Eikyō 11	(1439)	25	*Nenbutsu ōjō yōgishō*	Hōnen
			Gose monogatari	Ryūkan
Kakitsu 1	(1441)	27	*Jōdo shin'yōshō*	Zonkaku
Bun'an 3	(1446)	32	*Gutokushō*	Shinran
Bun'an 4	(1447)	33	*Anjinketsujōshō*	*unknown*
			Mattōshō	Shinran
Bun'an 5	(1448)	34	*Gensō ekō kikigaki*	*unknown*
Bun'an 6	(1449)	35	*Sanjō wasan*	Shinran
			Nyonin ōjō kikigaki	Zonkaku
Hōtoku 1	(1449)	35	*Godenshō*	Kakunyo
Hōtoku 2	(1450)	36	*Kyōgyōshinshō*	Shinran
			Godenshō	Kakunyo
Kyōtoku 2	(1453)	39	*Sanjō wasan*	Shinran
Kyōtoku 3	(1454)	40	*Ōjōyōshū* (nobegaki)	Genshin
			Kyōgyōshinshō (nobegaki)	Shinran
Kyōtoku 4	(1455)	41	*Bokie kotoba*	Jūkaku
Kōshō 3	(1457)	43	*Saiyōshō*	Kakunyo
			Jimyōshō	Zonkaku

Kakunyo and Zonkaku, he nevertheless felt free to absorb teachings contained in the scriptures of other lineages of the Pure Land tradition to nurture his own faith and the faith of others.

Another important influence in Rennyo's life was his travels. According to the *Rennyo Shōnin goichigoki*, during his early years Rennyo traveled twice to the eastern provinces with his father, following in the footsteps of the founding master Shinran, first in Bun'an 4 (1447) when he was thirty-three and then in Hōtoku 1 (1449) when he was thirty-five years old.[16] Especially during his first journey, he traveled long distances on foot and his sandals cut into his feet, leaving permanent scars.[17]

His trips to the eastern regions were, however, not simply pilgrimages tracing Shinran's legacy. They were also tours of inspection. Rennyo planned to investigate new areas in which to propagate the teachings, to examine the actual conditions of Shinshū in the eastern regions.

Although in his early days Rennyo was so poor that he reputedly "read the scriptures by the moonlight,"[18] until his succession to the office of chief abbot he lived contentedly in his lowly positions within Honganji. In Kakitsu 1 (1441), at the age of twenty-seven, Rennyo married Nyoryō, daughter of Taira no Sadafusa of the Ise clan. Although Rennyo would eventually marry five women, it was with Nyoryō that he had his first four sons and three daughters.

Birth of an Abbot and Propagator

Rennyo's father died in Chōroku 1 (1457), when Rennyo was forty-three. Zonnyo was survived by two sons, four daughters, and his wife, Nyoen. Nyoen (or Nyoen'ni) hoped that her elder son, Ōgen (also Renshō, 1433–1503) would be appointed an abbot of Honganji. However, Nyojō (1412–1460), a brother of Zonnyo and the head priest of Zuisenji in the town of Inami, strongly supported Rennyo as the candidate. Because of this support Rennyo became the eighth Dharma Master (*hossu*) of Honganji's office as chief abbot.

Rennyo's first act as abbot was to remodel the Honganji offices, removing the upper seating level in the chamber of the Custodian [of the Founder's Shrine] (*rusushiki*) and thereby placing all seats at the same common level. While working as his father's assistant, he had realized that the seating arrangement was divisive, creating a false sense of "upper" and "lower" offices. Rennyo's remodeling was clearly based on Shinran's statement, "I, Shinran, have no disciples" (*Tannishō* 6). In Shinshū, faith (*shinjin*) is considered a virtue transferred from the Tathāgata Amida; therefore all are considered equal. Rennyo not only understood this ideal, he put it into practice in his everyday life. He expressed this understanding in a radical way with the phrase, "I cast away myself."

> I cast away myself, take a seat at the common level [*hiraza*], and sit equally together [*dōza*]. That is because [Shinran] shōnin said, "Within the four oceans, persons of *shinjin* are all brothers and sisters." I too want to live in accordance with these words. By sitting together, I hope we might clarify what is not clear and more easily attain faith [*shin*].[19]

Thus is it recorded in the *Honganji sahō no shidai* (An Outline of the Rituals and Practices of Honganji) that Rennyo ordered all seats be made level because the dissemination of the Buddha Dharma to all people "cannot be done if you behave like a superior person [*jōrō*]."[20] Physically removing the upper seats seems easy enough, but changing a long-held Honganji custom would be impossible without Rennyo's strong resolve to "cast away" himself.

Rennyo continued his active propagation of Shinshū teaching in a variety of regions, particularly Ōmi, Settsu, and Mikawa Provinces. These activities are known from physical evidence such as his handwritten notes on the reverse sides (*uragaki*) of *myōgō* scrolls, portraits, and copies of the pictorial biography (*eden*) of Shinran.[21]

In order to bring Shinran's teaching of nenbutsu salvation to the hearts of people in this politically unstable period, Rennyo first had to root out the unorthodox beliefs deeply held by many. To accomplish this, he studied not only the orthodox teachings of Shinran but also unorthodox traditions. Between the ages of fifteen and forty-three, Rennyo occupied only lowly positions within Honganji, and while this must have been a difficult period for him, it seems to have been also very productive. Later on as chief abbot, his main concern would be how to make the teachings he learned during this period easily understandable to ordinary people.

After becoming chief abbot, Rennyo began his propagation throughout Ōmi Province at the invitation of Ōmi residents, such as Dōsai (1399–1488) of Kanegamori.

He distributed ten-character *myōgō* scrolls written in gold ink on dark blue paper as *honzon* (main objects of worship) to be enshrined at the practice halls of his followers. Rennyo first gave one of these scrolls to Zenka in the Yamada village of Kurita-gun in the additional third month (*uru'u sangatsu*) of Chōroku 2 (1458), one year after becoming abbot.[22]

Until this time, the Jōdoshin school followers had simply used their own individual *honzon*, which included various types of objects. Many people used the six-character *myōgō* scroll (*na-mu-a-mi-da-butsu*) or the nine-character *myōgō* scroll (*na-mu-fu-ka-shi-gi-kō- nyo-rai*) in various scripts and formats. For others, the *kōmyō honzon* (*myōgō* scroll with the rays of light in the background) were often used. Some followers enshrined portraits or wooden statues, or pursued salvation registers and portrait lineages.

Rennyo's choice of the ten-character *myōgō* (*ki-myo-jin-jip-pō-mu-ge-kō-nyo-rai*) was based in his belief that the genuine *honzon* of Shinshū is the *myōgō* scroll. He maintained that "[As the object of worship,] a portrait [*ezō*] is preferable to a wooden statue, and a *myōgō* scroll is preferable to a portrait,"[23] as an expression of orthodoxy, because use of *myōgō* scrolls follows the spirit of the founding master Shinran and is in accordance with Kakunyo's instructions.[24]

At about this time, at the request of Dōsai, Rennyo began writing his *Shōshinge tai'i* (An Outline of the *Shōshinge*),[25] a commentary the *Shōshinge*, a verse section from Shinran's *Kyōgyōshinshō*. During this same period he also began writing the *Letters*, by which he sought to transmit Shinran's teaching to the common people. Although this method of dissemination is unique to Rennyo, the origin of *Letters* is related to the genre of medieval literature called *kanahōgo* commonly used by the founders of new Buddhist groups during the Kamakura period (1192–1333). *Kanahōgo* are collections of "Dharma messages" (*hōgo*), usually written on a single sheet of paper, in which Buddhist teachers concisely explain lofty doctrinal principles in colloquial Japanese; they are written in the mixed *kana* and *kanji* scripts, which are more easily understood by the common people than the Chinese-syntax *kanbun*, which are written for the professional clergy. Shinran wrote quite a few such Dharma messages in letters (*shōsoku*) to his followers in the eastern provinces after he returned to Kyoto. Rennyo himself made a copy of a collection of Shinran's letters, the *Mattōshō* (Lamp for the Latter Age), in the second month of Bun'an 4 (1447).[26] Rennyo's *Letters* were undoubtedly inspired by Shinran's letters.[27]

Rennyo's use of *Letters* was, however, somewhat different from that of Shinran's correspondence with distant followers. Rennyo *Letters* used as a method of teaching in combination with direct oral propagation. As is known from the popularity of a style manual for letter writing, the *teikin ōrai*, written during the Nambokuchō (1336–1392) and early Muromachi periods, many people were learning to read and write at this time. The *Letters* thus became a most fitting media for propagation. Rennyo's restoration of the Jōdoshin school tradition greatly depended on his letter writing. Shinran's letters provided the model, and the master's other writings influenced the content and expression found in Rennyo's *Letters*. Particularly the *Anjinketsujōshō* (On Establishing the Settled Mind) contributed to Rennyo's thought, as well as the critical spirit of the *Tannishō*, the doctrinal significance of which was discovered by Rennyo. Further studies are necessary for an understanding of Rennyo's process of letter writing.[28]

Rennyo himself was well aware of the significance of *Letters* for the Shinshū tradition. For example:

> These *Letters* are the mirror for the Birth of ordinary sentient beings. There are those who think that I attempt to establish a [new] teaching with these letters, but this is a great misunderstanding.[29]

And elsewhere:

> The holy teachings [*shōgyō*] are [often] read in wrong ways and [expressions] are not always fully understandable. As for the *Letters*, however, people do not make any mistakes reading them.[30]

There is little doubt that Rennyo's *Letters* played an irreplaceable role in the spread of Shinran's teachings throughout society during this period of civil war.

Breaking Old Customs and Conflicts with the Established Powers

Rennyo's propagation created large communities of Shin followers around Shiga-gun and Yasu-gun in Ōmi Province. Concurrently, Rennyo carried out bold iconoclastic actions: "[he burned] the objects of worship and other articles not in accordance with the tradition [to heat the water] whenever he took a bath" (*Kikigaki*, 221); he created and distributed the ten-character *myōgō* scroll known as the *mugekō honzon* (object of worship of unhindered light); and he promoted the exclusive practice of nenbutsu and dismissed all others as mere "sundry practices."

In Kanshō 2 (1461) Rennyo officiated the two-hundredth memorial service of the founding master Shinran at Ōtani Honganji established by Kakunyo in the eastern quarter of Kyoto. The middle day of the service was scheduled to be on the twenty-eighth of the eleventh month, which is Shinran's memorial day. The service was a great success, with crowds of people said to have gathered from far and near; the previously declining Honganji was beginning to see signs of its future prosperity.

However, its rising popularity strongly provoked the priests of Enryakuji on Mount Hiei. On the eighth day of the first month in Kanshō 6 (1465) the priests of Mount Hiei assembled at the Western Pagoda to discuss the indictments against Honganji and adopted a resolution to destroy the temple. On the ninth day of the first month — the day after the resolution passed — the priests of Mount Hiei attacked the Ōtani Honganji with approximately 150 armed men. This incident was the first direct confrontation between Honganji and forces from the so-called exoteric-esoteric Buddhist establishment against the followers of Shinshū. Rennyo escaped unharmed and eventually found his way to the Kanegamori community in Ōmi Province, where he took up residence.

However, the forces of the Mount Hiei were not satisfied with the destruction of the Honganji edifice in the capital. Their army moved on to Kanegamori on the twenty-third of the third month and attacked Rennyo's followers defending Kanegamori. The resistance forces (*ikki*) of Rennyo's followers retreated at his order, but the next day the Hiei forces also attacked Akanoi, where a stronghold of Rennyo's followers gathered near Kanegamori.[31] This persecution of Rennyo's followers by Mount Hiei in 1465 is called the Kanshō persecution [of the Dharma] (*Kanshō no hōnan*).

As the result of the Kanshō persecution, not only did Rennyo lose the Ōtani Honganji, the base of his propagation, but his activities in Ōmi Province ended as well. He could only continue by moving from Kyoto to Settsu, then Kawachi Provinces. At this time, the regions surrounding Kyoto were fractured into many small autonomous powers. The Kitabatake clan had established its stronghold in Ise Province and had strong ties to the eastern provinces via Pacific sea routes. In Ōmi Province the Rokkaku clan, a branch of the Sasaki clan, the provincial governors (*shugo*) of the area, had established an autonomous domain at the southern shore of Lake Biwa. In northern Ōmi the Asai clan, subjects of the Kyōgoku clan, which itself belonged to the Sasaki clan, had similarly established its autonomous domain. In the midst of these small domains in the western provinces, governed by the regional powers, Honganji would develop into an independent religious power adapting to local conditions as necessary, eventually with significant political implications.

In the second month of Ōnin 1 (1467) Enryakuji pardoned Honganji and reinstated it as a branch temple within its own institution. Rennyo boldly took the statue of Shinran, originally enshrined at Honganji but removed after Honganji's desruction to Annyōji in Kurita-gun, Ōmi Province, and moved it to Honpukuji in Katada, at the foot of Mount Hiei. In the same year the warlords Hatakeyama Yoshinari (d. 1490) and Hatakeyama Masanaga (1442–1493) began fighting at the forest of Goryō in Kyoto, a battle that eventually developed into the great Ōnin War (*Ōnin no tairan*). Society was thrown into confusion. In Katada, to the east of the capital, the people controlled the thriving fishing and sailing business on Lake Biwa. In this region lived a Shinshū follower named Hōjū (1396–1479), whose family had become affiliated with Honganji during the time of Rennyo's grandfather, Gyōnyo. Rennyo frequently visited the homes of Shinshū believers in the Katada area to propagate the teaching, and Hōjū would support this effort by organizing large groups of Shinshū followers at his practice hall.

During the uprising in Kanegamori at the time of the Kanshō persecution, many in the Katada community had fought for Rennyo and he regarded them as the most trusted of Shinshū followers. Even after the persecution, skirmishes against Shin followers by the Hiei priests continued, despite the Muromachi bakufu's attempts to stop them. In order to avoid further confrontation, Rennyo ordered his followers to halt the uprisings against the forces of Mount Hiei. Hōjū acted as a negotiator between the two sides and played no small role in the peace that was finally achieved between Hiei and Honganji.

During the negotiation at Enryakuji, Hōjū brought a *mugekō honzon* scroll and, hanging it on the pillar in front of the Konponchūdō (the main assembly hall), he explained its origin and the teaching of the Jōdoshin school in a dignified manner. The Hiei priests, however, made no response to his doctrinal presentation, perhaps because they had already been promised the considerable sum of eighty *kanmon* of cash they had requested as compensation. The Tendai priests attending the meeting concluded the following:

> In every country and province, all kinds of people, including the most ignoble, carelessly handle this object of worship. The decision of the three [main] temples [of Enryakuji] should not be disregarded. Therefore, from now on, the use of [this object of worship] should be strictly banned. However, this [particular] object of worship now displayed is permitted.[32]

In Shinshū lore, the object of worship brought by Hōjū is known as the *tozan myōgō*, or "the scroll of the Sacred Name that went up to Mount [Hiei])."

However, on the ninth day of the first month of Ōnin 2 (1468) a group of Katada people attacked a ship chartered by Shōgun Ashikaga Yoshimasa (1436–1490). The authorities ordered Mount Hiei, which oversaw the Katada area, to take disciplinary action against the Katada people, triggering a harsh response. In the incident known as the great suppression of Katada (*Katada ozeme*), the entire township of Katada was burned to ashes during a five-day assault by the forces of Enryakuji. Again escaping danger, in Bunmei 1 (1469) Rennyo moved to the Chikamatsu region of Ōmi, and with the permission of Miidera (Onjōji) he built a temple that he named Kenshōji. There he enshrined the statue of Shinran. Rennyo could now perhaps breathe more easily, since Miidera tended to act as a counterforce against the powers of Enryakuji on Mount Hiei. It was the only temple in Ōmi with which the forces of Mount Hiei could not interfere.

Move to Yoshizaki

Over the next few years the Ōnin Wars intensified and Kyoto found itself the center of the armed confrontations, resulting in the destruction of the greater part of the city. Buddhist temples in and around Kyoto were drawn into the conflict and many people fled the capital, including religious leaders such as the well-known Zen monk Ikkyū Sōjun (1394–1481). Rennyo had no choice but to suspend his plan to return to the original site of Honganji in the Ōtani section of Kyoto.

Looking for a fresh start, in the fourth month of Bunmei 3 (1471) Rennyo decided to move to Yoshizaki in Echizen Province in the Hokuriku region. It is not clear why he selected this particular geographical site, but of the many different theories, the following three are most compelling.[33]

1. Members of the Honganji clan, such as his uncle Nyojō, had already established a foundation in this area and the nenbutsu teaching had already become popular there.
2. Rennyo was personally close to Asakura Takakage (1428–1481), the warlord governing Echizen.
3. Kyōgaku at Kōfukuji in Nara owned estates (*shōen*) in this area, and Rennyo was promised support from him.

In the seventh month of Bunmei 3 (1471) Rennyo obtained a piece of land in Yoshizaki and built a temple on top of the promontory that juts out into Lake

Kitagata. From his letters, we know that his propagation activities soon expanded into communities in the Shin'etsu and Ōshū regions as well, and by the next year pilgrims from all over the country began visiting Yoshizaki. Rennyo's new center at Yoshizaki soon developed into a large-scale religious township.

Institutional Expansion at Yoshizaki

Records suggest that as a popular leader, Rennyo made great efforts to capture people's hearts and paid careful attention to their needs. From his clothing and food to his manner of speaking, he consciously tried to become friendly with people and accept them as equals, and this approach seems to have further strengthened his religious charisma. Rennyo's stay at Yoshizaki lasted only four years, yet activities during that period won him everlasting fame in the history of Jōdoshinshū. It is thus accepted today that a new tradition of Honganji was born at this time. Let us examine four aspects of Rennyo's effort to created this new tradition during his Yoshizaki period.

Distribution of Six-Character Myōgō Scrolls

As was mentioned earlier Rennyo began distributing six character *myōgō* scrolls as the main object of worship (*honzon*). Previously he had used the ten-character *myōgō* scroll, *ki-myo-jin-jip-pō-mu-ge-kō-nyo-rai*, but, because the Mount Hiei forces alleged that Rennyo was establishing a new school called *mugekō*, he changed to the more widely accepted six-character sacred phrase *na-mu-a-mi-da-butsu*. Many of these were written by Rennyo himself, and he produced a massive number of six-character *myōgō* scrolls beginning from this period.[34] As new Shinshū groups formed in "practice halls" or *dōjō* throughout the country, Rennyo's *myōgō* scrolls were often at their center.

Propagation by Letters

Rennyo also wrote many instructional letters (*Letters*) to guide his followers, especially after he moved to Yoshizaki. Living in the midst of war, people sought genuine religious peace of mind, and Rennyo responded to their needs by expounded the simple message that "the afterlife [in the Pure Land] is indeed the blissful result in eternity."[35]

During his stay in Yoshizaki, Rennyo wrote seventy-eight *Letters*, approximately half of the 158 extant dated letters that he produced over his lifetime. Clearly, Rennyo had transformed his method of propagation from his oral preaching in Ōmi Province to dissemination by writing. It is believed that it was primarily through this propagation with *Letters* that Rennyo's religious organization rapidly expanded in the Hokuriku region. In the *Letters* during his early Yoshizaki period, he explained such fundamental Shinshū concepts as the teachings that faith is essential (*shinjin ihon*) and the cause of Birth is accomplished in everyday life (*heizei gōjō*).[36] In the latter part of this period, however, his emphasis shifted to criticizing his followers for their unorthodox understandings and secretive practices (*hiji bōmon*), such as "entrusting through donation" (*semotsu danomi*) and "taking refuge in a teacher" (*chishiki kimyō*), and he admonished them against anti-social activities, which had become increasingly visible as their numbers grew.[37]

Formation of Local Congregational Meetings (*kō, yoriai*)

As the social and religious foundation of Shinshū, local congregational meetings, or *kō*, were central in nurturing followers' faith (*shinjin*). These meetings derive from aristocratic Buddhist services at the great temples and the imperial court from the early Heian period (794–1192), such as the food offering service (*itsukie*), the eight lecture meetings on the *Lotus Sutra* (*hokke hakkō*), and the lecture meeting on the *Saishōkyō* or *Sutra of the Golden Light* (*saishōe*). With the growing popularity of the Pure Land teachings, over time these meetings spread among the common people, providing religious rituals unobtainable elsewhere.

The meetings served a broad variety of functions. They unified people both here and in the afterlife through fervent pledges as in the twenty-five samadhi meetings (*nijūgozanmai kō*) from the time of Genshin (942–1017). They provided funeral rituals, occasions for group pilgrimages to spiritual sites, and a variety of recreational activities. Many later developed into financial cooperatives called *tanomoshikō*, or "trustworthy meetings." Despite their miscellaneous functions, they all developed spontaneously and shared a grass-roots and communitarian character.

Among Japanese religions, the organizational structure of Honganji developed by Rennyo was unique in maximally utilizing the functions and organization of these local congregational meetings. In the Jōdoshin school, the congregational meeting was the social center, providing for both the material and spiritual needs of its members, especially during the medieval and early-modern periods. It is not clear exactly when the Shinshū adopted the congregational meeting system, but it is known that the followers of Katada Honpukuji organized one of the first of such groups. During the Bunmei era (1469–1487) such gatherings, called *yoriai*, developed vigorously in the villages of the Hokuriku region in conjunction with the rapid establishment of semi-autonomous unified villages (*sō*) and were occasions when literate village leaders would read the one of Rennyo's *Letters*.[38]

Following Rennyo's guidelines, the leaders of these gatherings often served as the cultural and social councilors of their communities.

Standardization of Rituals Using the Shōshinge and Wasan

Rennyo also worked to reform the ritual practices of his school so that Shinran's teaching could become a part of the followers' everyday lives. To do this, he paid particular attention to two of Shinran's compositions: the *Shōshinge* section in the chapter on Practice in the *Kyōgyōshinshō*, and three of his *Wasan* (*Jōdo Wasan*, *Kōsō wasan*, and *Shōzōmatsu Wasan*) collections, which are hymns composed in Japanese.

In Bunmei 5 (1473) Rennyo published a woodblock print edition of the Shōshinge and the three collections of Wasan in four volumes and made them the basis of the Honganji ritual chanting service. A note on the Honganji rituals comments on this change:

> After Rennyo Shōnin moved down to Yoshizaki in Echizen Province and adopted the ritual of reciting the six [Wasan] following the nenbutsu, he stopped the ritual of Rokuji raisan. Priests of the assembly hall at Zuisenji also remember that they [began to] practice the recitation of six Wasan at that time.[39]

The Rokuji raisan, which is a ritual recitation of Shandao's Ōjōraisan six times per day, was performed at Honganji prior to Rennyo in line with the liturgical tradition established by Hōnen. Changing this service to the recitation of Shinran's Shōshinge and Wasan, he shifted the focus to the words of Shinran, emphasizing the sectarian independence of Honganji from all other Jōdo or Pure Land schools based in the Hōnen lineage. By having this printed while in Yoshizaki, he at once established a standard liturgy unique to the Honganji organization.

Yoshizaki as a Religious Township and Conflict with Authorities

Rennyo's propagation received overwhelming support from the Hokuriku populace, and the number of visitors to Yoshizaki increased rapidly. Rennyo made note of this development in one of his Letters:

> Everyone knows that followers of our sect—priests and laypeople, men and women—flock to the mountain in pilgrimage, particularly from the seven provinces of Kaga, Etchū, Noto, Echigo, Shinano, Dewa, and Ōshū. This is extraordinary for the last age and appears to signal something.[40]

In Yoshizaki, many houses were built as residences for local priests and followers. These residences, called taya, also provided lodging for pilgrims. The area was gradually developing into a township. The prosperity of Yoshizaki area, however, became a source of conflict with the two preexisting powers in the area: the Buddhist establishment and the warlord government. The former consisted of the powerful religious establishments of Heisenji and Toyowaraji (also Toyoharaji), whose practices were centered in the traditional worship of nearby Mount Hakusan. They grew increasingly concerned about Rennyo's rapidly expanding organization and had essentially the same fears as those that had emanated from Enyakuji on Mount Hiei regarding Rennyo's activites in Ōmi Province. The second power structure to take notice were provincial warlords, especially the Kai clan, which was warring with the Asakura clan to control the Echizen region. The Kai grew increasingly ambitious to obtain control of the prosperous Yoshizaki area.

The sense of crisis intensified during the first month of Bunmei 5 (1473). Sensing imminent danger, Shinshū followers in Yoshizaki began to fortify the town to protect it from invading enemies. Rennyo was not happy to see his followers preparing an uprising, and he began writing Letters concerning his followers' rules of conduct (*okite no ofumi*) during the ninth month of Bunmei 5 (1473), approximately two and half years after he began propagating in Yoshizaki. The main issues in these letters are as follows:

1. Do not belittle the various *kami* shrines and the teachings of other schools (including the folk practices of avoiding things that are impure and inauspicious [*monoimi*]).
2. Never slight the provincial governors (*shugo*) and local land stewards (*jitō*).
3. Firmly hold the faith (*shinjin*) of Other-Power within your own heart deeply and determinedly.

Despite Rennyo's orders, his followers began acting recklessly against these powers. Troubled, Rennyo moved to Chōshōji in Fujishima in Bunmei 5 and began preparations to return to Kyoto. However, the priests and followers in the *taya* residences in Yoshizaki forcefully brought the reluctant Rennyo back to Yoshizaki.

The administrators of the temples in Hakusan and Tateyama had allied themselves either with the provincial governors and local land stewards or with warrior bands (*rōnin*) and were preparing to stop the further expansion of Honganji influence in the area. Worried about the situation, Rennyo urged his followers to restrain themselves to avoid creating friction with the authorites, using the words "laws of the state" (*ōbō*) and "laws (Dharma) of the Buddha" (*buppō*) together—traditional phrasing that implies cooperation with civil authorities—for the first time in a *Letter* issued in 1474.[41] And just as the tension between Rennyo's followers and the local powers in Yoshizaki escalated, Honganji followers in Kaga Province also faced a crisis situation. In Kaga, the followers of the Takada lineage of the Shinshū, who had begun propagating Shinshū even before Rennyo's time and who were no less Dharma descendants of Shinran, felt alarmed by the expansion of Rennyo's religious organization and began suppressing his followers in armed conflicts by allying with the governor, Togashi Kōchiyo (d. 1474).

In order to prevent counter-uprisings by his followers, Rennyo wrote the following restraining order:

> Do not slight the provincial military governors and local land stewards, claiming that you have attained faith; without fail meet your public obligations [*kuji*] in full....Besides this, in particular, take the laws of the state as your outer aspect, store Other-Power faith deep in your hearts, and take [the principles of] humanity and justice [*jingi*] as essential.[42]

Shinshū teaching does not require its followers to observe the usual Buddhist precepts. Therefore Kakunyo, third abbot of Honganji, adopted a system promoting the five virtues (*gojō*) of the mundane world as rules of conduct for the school.[43] Based on this, Rennyo instructed his followers to "take the laws of the state as authoritative" (*ōbō ihon*)[44] and advised them to uphold secular laws and not to confront the secular powers.[45]

Nevertheless, conflicts between Honganji followers and the secular powers grew worse. On the twenty-eighth of the third month, Bunmei 6 (1474), the main hall of the temple in Yoshizaki was completely destroyed by an act of arson. In the seventh month the followers in Kaga Province rose in arms together with Togashi Masachika (1455–1488), an older brother of Togashi Kōchiyo who was competing with Kochiyo for the governership of the province. The allied forces of Masachika and the Honganji followers destroyed the forces of Kōchiyo and the Takada followers. Masachika took the governorship of Kaga, and Honganji followers were allowed to practice freely. This peace arrangement was short-lived, however. In the following year, Bunmei 7 (1475), a confrontation arose between Masachika and the Honganji members. Facing another crisis, Rennyo determined more rules of conduct (*okite*) and publicized them broadly among his followers. However, one of Rennyo's most trusted followers, Rensō (d. 1499), schemed against the master's wishes and incited the hot-blooded followers to revolt.

Yamashina Honganji

After wave after wave of uprisings, the spiritual decline of Yoshizaki led Rennyo to leave Yoshizaki, taking with him his third son, Renkō (1450–1531). He traveled first to Obama in Wakasa Province by boat, and then continued through Tanba and Settsu Provinces, eventually to settle at Deguchi in Kawachi Province. In Deguchi village, Rennyo's follower Kōzen (d. 1520), a priest from Iwami Province, offered Rennyo lodging in his own home. Rennyo did not wait a day to begin new propagational activities, and by the end of Bunmei 8 (1476) he had already built temples in Sakai and Tonda, both in Settsu Province.

It is believed that because of Rennyo's presence, the number of Shinshū followers rapidly increased. However, the new followers did not always understand Shinshū faith, and many retained unorthodox practices. Even in Deguchi, Rennyo had to battle this problem. The many expressions of frustration found in the *Letters* of this period, such as "this is utterly deplorable" (*asamashi asamashi*) or "this is absurd" (*gongo dōdan no shidai*),[46] reflect Rennyo's frustration with this situation. But what kind of unorthodox practices were they?

Here are some references to this problem in Rennyo's *Letters*:

"Thieflike" Faith (monotori shinjin):

... with such views, [these people] go around to visit Shinshū followers, read scriptures to propagate the teaching, and, above all, without permission they falsely call themselves representatives of the head temple [Honganji], using flattering and untrue words to make a living by stealing goods from [the followers].[47]

Teaching Outside the Orthodox Transmission:

[These people] propagate the teaching using strange words and phrases that are not our transmitted doctrine. This should not be permitted.[48]

Secret Teachings (hiji bōmon):

Sometime in Bunmei 7 or 8, Seichin Bizen, a resident of Nodera in Mikawa Province, gave a secret teaching [*hiji bōmon*] to Yasuda Kazunosuke, a son of Jōken of Kōshu in Ise Province. This transmission is secretly conveyed in Yoshizaki.[49]

Rennyo encountered these kinds of unorthodox practices in Deguchi. However, the existence of unorthodox interpretations and practices was, in a sense, proof that Shinshū spirituality was at least still alive. If Rennyo could first cure the diseases and defects in people's spiritual lives, he could then lead them into healthy spiritual development. Hoping for their growth in the right direction, he continued his efforts to establish organizational bases in strategic places.

Rennyo returned to the Kinai region hoping to build a new temple where he could enshrine the statue of Shinran that had been entrusted to Miidera. In other words, he intended to rebuild Honganji. Rennyo had never moved the statue to Yoshizaki, nor had he attempted to move it to his temporary residence at Deguchi or to the new temples in Sakai and Tonda. He strongly believed that the statue of Shinran belonged in Kyoto, and rebuilding the destroyed Ōtani Honganji was to be his final mission.

The great war during the Ōnin and Bunmei reigns ended in 1477, when Rennyo was in Sakai. In the first month of Bunmei 10 (1478) he left Deguchi and headed to Kyoto, where people were at long last in high spirits at the prospect of reconstructing the city after the war. Rennyo was sixty-four years old, and the long-awaited reconstruction project of Honganji was now to begin.

Rennyo chose Yamashina in Yamashiro Province (an area lying east of present-day Kyoto city) as the site for the new Honganji. Many reasons have been offered for his selection of Yamashina. According to one record (*Itokuki*), it was Dōsai of Kanegamori who recommended Yamashina.[50] Modern historians also point out Rennyo's relationship to Daigoji, which governed the village of Nomura. Whatever other circumstances there may have been, Rennyo's vision that Honganji must be in Kyoto was the most significant reason for his selection.

As construction began in Bunmei 10 (1478), Rennyo moved to a hermitage in a village called Nomura in Yamashina. His third wife, Nyoshō, died in the same year. In Bunmei 12 (1480) the construction of the Founder's Hall (Goeidō) was completed. The statue of Shinran was brought from Ōtsu, and the next year the construction of the Amida Hall (Amidadō) was completed. The entire construction project was finished in Bunmei 15 (1483), creating a huge new complex of temple buildings that far exceeded the size of the original Ōtani Honganji.

Yamashina Honganji was built in three sections surrounded by three layers of protecting walls and trenches, with the third section including a "temple-town" (*jinaichō*) with a residential zone accommodating townsfolk. Thus a settlement for a general Shinshū community was finally established. The creation of the religious township allowed residents to enjoy an autonomous lifestyle within the city. Rennyo defined the people's vocations variously as "services for the needs of the Buddha Dharma"[51] and "services for the needs of the Tathāgata and [Shinran] Shōnin,"[52] just as in Europe John Calvin (1506–1564) had introduced the idea of working ethics based in Christianity by defining work as service to God.[53]

The Final Years

The restoration of Honganji, which Rennyo had dreamed about since his days as a lowly scribe, finally came true for him at the age of sixty-nine. Followers came from all over the country to worship at the Yamashina Honganji, now so successful that it seemed an entirely different beast from the formerly destitute Ōtani Honganji. Seeing the growth of Honganji in Yamashina, other Shinshū lineages joined Rennyo's religious organization as their leaders affiliated themselves with Rennyo, one after another. In Bunmei 13 (1481), Kyōgō (1451–1492) of Bukkōji became a disciple of Rennyo and brought many Bukkōji followers with him.[54] In the following years Zenchin (1389–1465) and the lineage of Gōshōji joined, and later in Meiō 2 (1493) so did Shōe (1475–1557) of Kinshokuji.[55] All leaders of other established Shinshū branches, they brought with them an equal or greater number of followers as were in Rennyo's group. In one massive charge, Rennyo's organization expanded nationally.

But with the growth of Yamashina Honganji, the increased numbers of worshippers who visited Honganji brought doctrinal problems, as many clung to unorthodox practices common to their place of origin:

> Meanwhile, in recent years, [some] have confused people to the extreme by spreading distorted teachings [*higa bōmon*] not discussed in our tradition. Others, reprimanded by local land stewards and domain holders (who are themselves entrenched in wrong views), have come to view our tradition's true and real faith [*anjin*] as mistaken.[56]

Bracing up his old bones for fresh exertion, Rennyo remonstrated with these people, a fact that is reflected in a letter of the eleventh month of Bunmei 15 (1483), where he lists three rules of conduct (*okite*) to be followed by all.[57] The fact was, after the construction of Yamashina Honganji, Rennyo's Shinshū organization now faced problems of diplomacy that came with increased interest from the aristocracy and people with powerful political status. In Bunmei 12 (1480), for example, on the fourteenth of the tenth month, Hino Tomiko (1440–1496), the wife of Shōgun Ashikaga Yoshimasa, visited the newly constructed Yamashina Honganji. Rennyo recorded the event in a letter in which he unabashedly displays his joy:

> Recently, Her Eminence [Hino Tomiko] visited us and inspected the Founder's Hall (Goeidō). Such a visitation has never happened before. It does not appear to be insignificant.[58]

Rennyo later even describes Honganji as a prayer-offering site (*chokugansho*) for the prosperity of the imperial family.[59] These records reveal how the association between Honganji and the powers of the bakufu and the imperial family grew closer.

Does this suggest that Rennyo had developed a craving for power? Or was he rather simply attempting to secure peace and prosperity for Honganji and his followers by smoothing relationships with the established powers? Modern historians often note that because of these political maneuvers, Rennyo was allowed to build Yamashina Honganji without interference by Mount Hiei only ten years after the Ōtani Honganji had been destroyed during the Kanshō persecution.

Meanwhile, at about the time the construction of Yamashina Honganji was completed, in Kaga Province the confrontation between bands of Shinshū uprising groups (*ikkō ikki*) and Governor Togashi Masachika had grown critical. In Chōkyō

1 (1487) Shinshū followers once again staged an armed uprising while Masachika was in Ōmi with his army. Masachika hastily returned to his domain but was forced by the Shinshū army to commit suicide in the following year. This incident is remembered as the Chōkyō uprising (*Chōkyō no ikki*), when Kaga become "a country owned by Shinshū followers" (*monto no mochitaru kuni*).

Coincident with the end of the Chōkyō uprising, in Entoku 1 (1489), Rennyo wrote a letter to his fifth son, Jitsunyo (1458–1525), granting him the office of custodian (*rusushiki*), thereby making him the head priest of Honganji. Jitsunyo was not a man of high intellectual caliber like his father, but Rennyo recognized that his personality was honest and trusted that Jitsunyo would protect and maintain the religious organization. In fact, Jitsunyo was to fulfill this mission very successfully. After transferring the responsibilities of temple administration to Jitsunyo, Rennyo retired to Nanden, located within the ground of the Yamashina Honganji, presumably feeling content with his accomplishments.[60]

Yet Rennyo's efforts at propagation did not end with his retirement. He continued to give religious writings to his followers, adding his signature (*kaō*) on the reverse side (*uragaki*). The number of *Letters* sent to his followers in fact increased after his retirement. Including only the letters that are clearly dated, forty-four were written after his retirement in Entoku 1 (1489).

In Meiō 5 (1496) he visited Osaka in Settsu Province. There he had the idea of building a temple as his retirement residence at the strategically important spot between the branches of the Yodo River. The temple, completed in the next year, later became Ishiyama Honganji. One may consider that the temple in Osaka was built in preparation for expansion to the western provinces. However, it is not definite that at the age of eighty-two Rennyo, was still thinking of expanding his religious organization. It seems natural that he was interested in Settsu Province, the gateway to the western regions, and so decided to reside in Osaka, but this area of his life requires further investigation.

Rennyo had never flagged in his efforts to disseminate Shinshū teachings as he moved his base from Kyoto to Ōmi, Hokuriku, Yamashina, and then Osaka, but finally he began to feel ill in the fourth month of Meiō 7 (1498):

> Early in Meiō 7 (1498) he first began to feel ill.... [then] Kōken sōzu [Jitsunyo] sent him an invitation. He went to the capital [Kyoto] on the twentieth of the second month [of Meiō 8 (1499)].[61]

Very old now, he had perhaps originally planned to die in Osaka, but he suddenly decided to return to Yamashina Honganji.[62] By the second month of Meiō 8 (1499) he realized that his days were numbered and left Osaka for Yamashina. There he spent his remaining days talking to his children and disciples and often wandered through the areas surrounded by walls and trenches. He visited the temple on the twenty-seventh day of the second month, and his time there is recorded sentimentally.[63]

On the nineteenth of the third month he was no longer able to eat food; and on the twenty-third his pulse became unstable. Finally, at noon on the twenty-fifth, he accomplished Birth in Pure Land at the age of eighty-five as if quietly falling asleep:

In the middle of the hour of the horse [noon], he lay down, placing his head to the north and facing west. His last breath reciting the nenbutsu stopped as if he had gone to sleep. He was eighty-five years old.[64]

The cremation was held next day; the site eventually became Rennyo's mausoleum in Yamashina. Rennyo was given the posthumous title of Shinshōin 信証院.

Notes

1 *Jitsugo kyūki* 124, *Gyojitsu* p. 100, *Kikigaki* 188, SSZ 3.577.

2 Kuroda Toshio says this turning point is marked by (1) dissolution of estates (*shoen*), (2) the fall of the exoteric-esoteric establishments (*kenmitsu taisei*), and (3) the rise of common people ("*Tenkanki no Shidosha*" The leader in turning age 1 "*Rennyo*" Nanba Betsuin, pp. 131–132, 1986, April).

3 See Amino Yoshihiko 網野善彦, *Zoku Nihon no rekishi o yominaosu* 続日本の歴史をよみなおす (Tokyo: Chikuma Shobō, 1996), 166–171, based on the *Honpuku atogaki*.

4 On this problem, see chapter 5.

5 Rennyo married five times, outliving all but his last wife. Their names are Nyoryō 如了 (d. 1455), Renyū 蓮祐 (d. 1470), Nyoshō 如勝 (1448–1478), Shūnyo 宗如 (d. 1484), and Rennō 蓮能 (1465–1518).

6 The *Kūzenki*, compiled by Rennyo's disciple Kūzen 空善 (d. 1520) sometime in the early sixteenth century, contains a somewhat hagiographic record of Rennyo's activities over an eleven-year period at the end of his life, including his funeral.

7 *Honpukuji yuraiki*, "A Record of Hompukuji's History," *Shusei*, p. 661.

8 Inoue Toshio, "*Honganji*" (Tokyo: Shibundo, 1966) 102, 149.

9 *Rennyo Shonin itokuki*, SSZ 3.870.

10 *Rennyo Shonin itokuki*, SSZ 3.871.

11 The Shōren'in was the same temple where Shinran was ordained.

12 See the first fascicle of Kyōkaku's diary, *Kyōgaku shiyōshō*, at *Zoku gunsho ruijū* (Tokyo: 1971).

13 Miura Shūkō "Honen to Rennyo," in Hayashiya Tatsusaburō and Asao Naohiro, ed., *Shinpen Rekishi to Jinbutsu* (Tokyo: Iwanami Shoten—Iwanami bunko 33-166-2, 1990), 205.

14 *Rennyo shikigoshū*, SSS 2.374–378.

15 Furuta Takehiko, *Shinran shisō* (Tokyo: Fusanbō, 1975), 433–434.

16 *Rennyo Shōnin goichigoki* 152, SSS 2.529.

17 *Kikigaki* 301, SSZ 3.608.

18 Ibid. 145, SSZ 3.567.

19 *Kūzenki* 93, RSG 35–36; *Kikigaki* 40, SSZ 3.543.

20 *Honganji sahō no shidai* 172, RSG, 237.

21 *Rennyo uragakishū*, SSS 2.379–407.

22 Ibid., 379.

23 *Kikigaki* 69, SSZ 3.549.

24 See Kakunyo's *Gaijashō* 2, SSZ 3.66–67.

25 Rennyo's *Shōshinge tai'i* is at SSZ 3.385.

26 *Rennyo shikigoshū*, SSS 2.375

27 See the opening essay by Katada Osamu in SSS 2.9–45.

28 Hosokawa Gyōshin, "Shinshū chūkō no shigan: tokuni Rennyo no Honganji saikō ni tsuite" (The wish to restore Shinshū: On Rennyo's reestablishing of Honganji), *Ōtani gakuhō* 48–3 (January 1969), 6.

29 *Rennyo Shonin ichigoki* 112, SSS 2.453; *Kikigaki*, 177, SSZ 3.573–574; RSG 97.

30 *Mukashi monogatariki* 8, RSG 252; *Kikigaki*, 53, SSZ 3.546, SSS 2.611.

31 From a section of the *Honpukuji yuraiki* entitled "Ōtani goryū hakyaku no koto," at SSS 2.665–669.

32 *Honpukuji yuraiki*, SSS 2.668

33 See Sasaki Yoshio, *Rennyo Shōnin-den no kenkyū* (Kyoto: Chūgai Shuppan, 1926), 66–68; Tanishita Kazumu, "Rennyo Shōnin no Yoshizaki senkyō ni tsuite," *Rekishi Chiri* 62–4 (1933), 313–328; and Minamoto Ryōen, *Rennyo* (Tokyo: Kōdansha, 1993), 178.

34 The following conversation is recorded from this period: "Once when Rennyo said, 'There is no one who has written *myōgō* more than I,' Kyōmonbō replied, 'Very few people have done it even within the three nations [of India, China, and Japan].' Rennyo responded, 'That may be true.' Then Kyōmonbō replied, 'That is most wonderful.'" *Kūzenki* 35, RSG, 13; *Rennyo Shōnin goichigoki* 76, SSS 2.519.

35 *Letter* 1.10, eleventh day, ninth month, Bunmei 5 [1473], Rogers, *Rennyo*, 161, SSZ 3.417.

36 These two doctrines are typical of the religious attitude that typifies Shinshū thought then and now, emphasizing the importance of taking an active role in the creation of one's religious identity. *Shinjin ihon* expresses the doctrine that the attainment of *shinjin* is of paramount importance in the lifetime of any Shinshū believer. *Heizei gōjō* expresses the doctine that one should aim to accomplish the path itself within this lifetime.

37 The term *hiji bōmon* refers to unorthodox belief communities existing within Shinshū. *Semotsu danomi* points to unethical practices by priests who solicited money or other forms of compensation for the performance of rituals, healing, and magic tricks. The phrase *chishiki kimyō* refers to extreme devotion to one's teacher to a point considered unhealthy.

38 Rennyo is quoted as saying, "If priests, elders, and heads [of villages] seriously took refuge in the Buddha Dharma, all other people would also become familiar with the teaching." *Eigenki* 6, RSG 260.

39 *Honganji saho no shidai* 46, RSG, 194.

40 *Letters* 1.7, SSZ 3.411; Rogers, 150.

41 *Letters* 2.10, dated the thirteenth day, fifth month, Bunmei 6 (1474).

42 *Letters* 2.6, dated the seventeenth day, second month, Bunmei 6 [1474], SSZ 3.434; Rogers, 180.

43 *Gaijashō* 3, SSZ 3.67–68. The five are humanity, righteousnous, decorum, wisdom, and faith.

44 *Letters* 3.12 and 13, SSZ 3.472, 473; Rogers, 215.

45 In a recent lecture, Professor Okuwa Hitoshi has offered a new perspective on Rennyo's sense of secular law which differs from the usual view. According to Okuwa, Rennyo's *ōbō* is not that of rulers, but *daihō* (great law) of people which was established as a self-governing rule for their community. See "*Rennyo Shonin no ōbō*" (Higashi Honganji Shuppanbu, 1997), 20–21.

46 The phrase *gongo dōdan no shidai* is particulalry common; for example, see RSI, 274, 290, 310, 313, 320.

47 *Letters* (*Jogai*), third month, Bunmei 9 [1477], RSI, 255

48 *Letters* (*Jogai*), twenty-seventh day, seventh month, Bunmei 8 [1476], RSI, 264.

49 *Letters* (*Jogai*), first month, Bunmei 9 [1477], RSI, 269.

50 SSZ 3.875–6.

51 *Kikigaki* 162, 260, 263, at SSZ 3.570, 597, 599.

52 *Kikigaki* 169, 313, at SSZ 3.579, 612.

53 The early view on the resemblance between Shinshu and Protestantism would be traceable to Max Weber's *Gesammelte Aufsätze zur Religionssoziolog*, 3 vols. (Tübingeu,

Mohr 1920–1921). See Mori Ryūkichi 森龍吉 "Rennyo to Karuvan: keizai rinri o meguru Shinshū to Purotesutantizumu Tono hikakuron ni kanrenshite" (Rennyo and Calvin in Terms of a Comparative View on the Ethics of Economy between Shinshu and Protestantism), *Nihon bukkyō gakkai nenpō* 37 (1972), repr. *Rennyo Taikei* 2 (Hōzōkan, November 1996), 426–538.

54 Kyōgō, also known as Renkyō, was the twelfth abbot of Bukkōji.

55 Both Zenchin and Shōe married into the family, Shōe marrying two of Rennyo's daughters (the first one died) and Zenchin marrying a younger sister of Jitsunyo's wife, Nyoyū.

56 *Letters* 4.5, twenty-first day, eleventh month, Bunmei 14 [1482], Rogers, 226, SSZ 3.482.

57 *Letters* 4.6, SSZ 3.484.

58 RSI, 105–106. Dated twelfth day, eighth month, Bunmei 5 [1473].

59 RSI, 326; dated Bunmei 13 [1481]; *RennyoShonin Itokuki*, SSZ 3.876–7.

60 *Kūzenki* 1, RSG 3. *Kikigaki* 164, SSZ 3.571.

61 *Rennyo Shonin itokuki*, SSZ 3.880–881.

62 "Fall and spring have slipped away, and it is already the middle of early summer in this seventh year of Meiō; I have grown old—I am eighty-four. This particular year, however, I have been seriously beset by illness." *Letters* 4:13, Rogers, 237, SSZ 3.495.

63 "[Rennyo] visited the temple on the twenty-seventh. On the way back, he was so reluctant to part from his followers that he made his cart go backwards so that he was able to see them all [as he left]. *Kūzenki* 127, *Gyojitsu*, 45.

64 *Rennyo Shonin itokuki*, SSZ 3.885.

3

KURODA TOSHIO
TRANSLATED BY THOMAS KIRCHNER

Leaders in an Age of Transition

Rennyo and the Shin Buddhist Institution

Immediately after the Japanese defeat in World War II there was a period when the so-called feudalistic character of Japanese Buddhism was much discussed. At this time there were within the Jōdo Shin sect many loud calls for a "return to Shinran" (although of course this was not the first time such calls had been issued) and much investigation of the historical background of Shin's feudalistic institutional structures and its doctrines promoting submission to political authority. It was concluded by some that it was Rennyo, the eighth *hossu* (head abbot) of Honganji, who had distorted Shinran's teachings and established the feudalistic character of the Shin sectarian organization.

I myself played no role in the discussion (I lacked the requisite doctrinal knowledge and was in no position to participate anyway), but I do remember feeling a bit baffled by arguments of scholars who placed all the blame on Rennyo and situated their own viewpoints on the lofty spiritual level of Shinran. In the first place, I felt, it is only because of Rennyo that the modern Shin Buddhist institution exists at all. Even more to the point, if Shin Buddhism in the immediate postwar era was dangerously out of touch with the times, then surely what was needed above all was Rennyo's capacity as a religious thinker and social activist to see into the subtle workings of the society in which he lived.

My field is Japanese medieval history; I have no deep understanding of Buddhist or Shinshū doctrine and am not versed in the biographical details of Rennyo's life. Nevertheless, as a historian I cannot help noticing the large mark that Rennyo has left on history. In this essay I would therefore like to present my view of Rennyo's position in the overall context of Japanese religious development.

An Era of Social and Historical Change

Those who compare Shinran and Rennyo tend to do so solely on the basis of Shinshū doctrine, but it must be remembered that the two figures were separated by nearly two centuries and that the sociohistorical conditions under which they operated were markedly different. Shinran lived during the Kamakura era (1185–1333), the middle of the Japanese *chūsei* (medieval period), when religious orthodoxy was represented by *kenmitsu bukkyō* (exoteric-esoteric Buddhism),[1] that is, by the traditional sects of what is commonly called "Old Buddhism." Textbooks today stress that during the Kamakura period the "New Buddhist" schools founded by figures such as Hōnen and Shinran came into positions of dominance, but the evidence indicates that at the time these movements were quite marginal and were seen as rather heretical.

The orthodox *kenmitsu* sects, their place in the medieval establishment secured by the official sanction of the governing authorities and their own enormous socioeconomic power, tended to be quite secularized and formalized, but despite such signs of degeneracy they continued to hold much spiritual appeal for the populace. It was within this historical context that Shinran preached a "true Buddhism" (*shinjitsu no bukkyō*) appropriate for the times. Hence the particular character of his writing, sparkling with a taut logic aimed at surmounting the shortcomings of *kenmitsu* thought.

Rennyo was born in 1415. There is much of interest in his early and middle life, but it was during his later life that his truly influential work began. The years between 1471, when he moved his base of operations to Yoshizaki in the province of Echizen (present-day Fukui Prefecture), and 1499, when he died at the age of eighty-five, may be seen as his most productive period. This was the time when the Ōnin War (Ōnin no Ran; 1467–1477) was ushering in the century-long period known as the Sengoku Jidai (Warring States period), during which the governmental and social order presided over by the Muromachi bakufu (1338–1573) was thrown into a state of utter confusion.

However, the historical situation that faced Rennyo was not characterized by disorder alone. In addition to being a time of upheaval and unrest, it was a time of historical and social transition, and in this its particular significance lay. Three particular aspects of this period are of special interest.

The Age of an Awakened Populace

The first of these factors was the gradual breakdown of the old medieval social and political order, whose socioeconomic foundation was the *shōensei* (the landed estate system)[2] and whose sociopolitical structure was the *kenmon taisei* (system of ruling elites, made up of the imperial court and aristocracy [*kuge*], the bakufu and samurai authorities [*buke*], and the principal religious institutions [*jike*]). This old order shifted toward the pattern characteristic of the Warring States period, when individual daimyō warlords ruled over independent domains and, later, toward the centralized bakufu system that governed Japan during the Tokugawa period (1600–1868).

This shift represented a fundamental revolution in the social and political structures of Japan, a revolution far-reaching enough to be described as a change in historical eras. The populace formed leagues known as *ikki* to protect their livelihoods and press their political demands; the warriors attempted to expand the areas under their control through incessant war and conflict; and the *kuge* experienced a rapid decline in their fortunes. This was the reality within which Rennyo had to operate, regardless of what his personal preferences might have been.

However, this situation by itself cannot be said to have necessitated any direct action by a religious figure like Rennyo. A more important factor (the second of the three factors referred to) was the contemporary state of the erstwhile religious orthodoxy, the religious establishment ideologically undergirded by the principles of *kenmitsu* Buddhism. This establishment, which for so long had sustained and regulated the spiritual life of the Japanese, was now in a state of utter collapse[3] because of the general breakdown of the former social and political order. Consequently the newer religious traditions such as Zen, Jōdo, Hokke, and Shinshū could operate openly with no fear of opposition by the older sects. Despite the breakdown of the old *kenmitsu* institutional order, however, there was a widespread persistence of *kenmitsu* viewpoints and practices in syncretized, vulgarized forms, and these profoundly influenced the beliefs of the newer schools. Examples of this influence were the popular cults of the fox spirit (*koshin*), the gods of good fortune (*fukujin*), the gods of disease (*yakubyōgami*), and the gods of recovery (*chiryōgami*), along with such practices as the worship of lewd deities (*inshi*) and the transmission of "secret doctrines and practices" (*hiji bōmon*). Thus the challenge directly facing Rennyo in his capacity as a religious thinker was to confront and overcome these lingering influences and establish a new mode of religious belief. This is the aspect of Rennyo's work that I would like to emphasize; whether or not Rennyo utilized the popular uprisings and domanial strife to spread his religious teachings is at best a secondary consideration.

The third factor to be considered is the broad scale of the historical transition within which Rennyo was operating. It represented a shift from an older, simpler era characterized by devotion, undisguised emotion, and rustic simplicity to a more modern age in which the dominant virtues were diligence, intelligence, and secular sophistication. It is beyond the scope of this essay to discuss exactly why such profound changes occurred in the human emotional and spiritual makeup, but it should be obvious from the historical evidence that between the medieval and modern eras such a transition in behavior and outlook did indeed take place. An age was approaching in which religious attitudes were determined by an awakened populace, not by an educated intellectual elite or the spirit-fearing, superstitious masses.

The moves initiated by Rennyo demonstrate his grasp of the character of this new, transitional age. These moves were not the organic outgrowths of an evolutionary process within Shinshū itself, but were deliberately made by Rennyo in recognition of the new forces that were shaping society: the rural *ikki* leagues (acknowledged in his relocation of the sectarian headquarters in Yoshizaki) and the urban commercial and manufacturing interests (acknowledged in his subsequent residence in Ishiyama in the Osaka region). Rennyo was, in effect, a new type of intellectual leader ideally suited to guide the new type of Japanese commoner.

The new and highly effective form of proselytization developed by Rennyo was the *ofumi*, referred to here in their collected form as the *Letters*. The word *ofumi* literally means "letter," but the *ofumi* were not just ordinary letters; as the much revised, highly polished manuscripts (written in Rennyo's own hand) make evident, they were designed in both form and content to serve the purpose of spreading the Shin teachings. Shinran may have been an eminent teacher and spiritual guide, but Rennyo was a perceptive innovator capable of creating an approach to proselytization that, through such works as the *Ofumi*, *Shōshinge*, and *Wasan*, has sustained the spiritual life of the Shin Buddhist believer to the present day. In many ways his activities resembled those of Luther and Calvin, the leaders of the Protestant Reformation who were his rough contemporaries. Rennyo grasped the relationship between society and religion, not on an abstract level of theories or ideals, but on the practical level of social interaction; this fact is evident in the manner in which he organized the lives of the common people. Shinran may have explored the very foundations of human existence, but his thought lacked the elements necessary to operate on a more practical, societal level.

Rennyo's qualities of foresight in reading the developments of the age in which he lived are also clearly evident in his concept of *buppōryō* (佛法領), or Realm of the Buddha Dharma. Let us now examine this key concept.

The Realm of the Buddha Dharma in the Present Age

At the close of one of his *Letters*, dated the twenty-eighth day of the fourth month of Bunmei (1475), Rennyo writes:

> Our tradition is the Realm of the Buddha Dharma. How absurd it is to ignore the Buddha Dharma even as, through the strength of the Buddha Dharma, we live as we please according the standards of the secular world.[4]

Here Rennyo identifies as the defining characteristic of "our tradition"—that is, the Shin Buddhist organization—the fact that it constitutes the Realm of the Buddha Dharma. As in the *Rennyo Shōnin goichidaiki kikigaki* (hereafter *Kikigaki*), where Rennyo states that "our morning and evening devotions are our duty to the Tathāgata and Shinran Shōnin," Rennyo's words point to his belief that the Honganji tradition represented a domain ruled by the Buddhas and Shinran. His attitude toward this sacred domain is clearly expressed in the following passage, also from the *Kikigaki*:

> While Rennyo was walking in the corridor, he noticed a scrap of paper fallen on the floor. "We mustn't waste the property of the Buddha Dharma Realm," he said, carefully picking up the scrap with his two hands.[5]

The first thing to note here is the implied comparison between the realm of "the Buddha Dharma" and the realm of "the world" (*seken*), that is, the realms of

"Buddha's Law" (*buppō*) and "Imperial Law" (*ōbō*: political power and secular order). This comparison undoubtedly emerged against the historical backdrop of violent territorial disputes that marked late medieval Japan. Nevertheless, there was a qualitative difference between the Realm of Buddha Dharma and the secular realm of Imperial Law. The Realm of Buddha Dharma was strictly the realm of faith, the realm of (in the words of the *Kikigaki*) "entrusting oneself entirely to Namu Amida Butsu." Although Rennyo does not hold the notion that the Pure Land exists in the present world just as it is, such statements as "There are many in society who are hungry and cold; that we can eat as much as we wish and wear as many clothes as we need is due to the benevolence of Shinran" and "We should be worshipful, for retribution will without fail strike those of no faith" underscore his belief that "our tradition" comprises the portion of the world regulated through the Buddha's benevolence and punishment. Thus he states that "the one tradition of Shinran is the Law of Amida Nyorai (Tathāgata)." This tradition is the organization of Honganji believers, those for whom this world is the place in which one lives the life of faith, and this is why it is known as the Realm of Buddha Dharma.

There are scholars today who interpret this "realm" to mean those regions, such as the Kaga domain (present-day Ishikawa and Toyama Prefectures), that came under the political control of the Shin sect as the result of uprisings by Shin followers (*ikkō ikki*) in the late fifteenth and sixteenth centuries, but this use of the word is far different from that intended by Rennyo. For Rennyo, the Realm of Buddha Dharma was nothing more and nothing less than that realm within the everyday world which centered on the Honganji organization and was guided by the Tathāgata and Shinran.

In order to understand exactly what Rennyo meant by this way of thinking, it is important that we realize the conditions under which it emerged. Although it is beyond the scope of this chapter to go into a detailed analysis of the historical circumstances of Rennyo's time, it should be kept in mind that during the period of his proselytization Japan was still under the sway of traditional Buddhist-influenced social concepts dating back many centuries. The forces of *kenmitsu* Buddhism that controlled medieval society had from ancient times held to the view that the proper relationship between the Imperial Law (the government authorities) and the Buddhist Law (the *kenmitsu* temple-shrine power complexes [*jisha seiryoku*] of Nara and Kyoto) was one of mutual aid and dependence, like "the two wings of a bird, the two wheels of a cart." Rennyo, however, took a rather different view, seeing the religious sphere as existing on a different level from that of the secular sphere.

Next we must consider the various ways of thought prevalent in Rennyo's time. One such way, needless to say, was the calculating, profit-seeking outlook of the daimyōs, warriors, and merchants—this was an avaricious secularism that wasted not so much as a side glance at Buddhism and other religious traditions. Buddhism, for its part, contained sects with distinct connections to political forces. The Zen sect, for example, extended its influence under the patronage of governmental leaders and wealthy merchants; and the Hokke sect followers, emphasizing the congruence of politics and religion, saw union with political power as the means to spread the True [Buddhist] Law. For Rennyo, rooted as he was in the teachings of Shinran, such views constituted either a muddying of the faith or a dangerous fanaticism. In my view, Rennyo's concept of the Buddha Dharma Realm emerged from a thoroughly thought-out attempt to define the proper mode of being of a community of Buddhist believers in an age when religion and politics were either in a state of conflict or of syncretism.

A Historical Demand

Rennyo's attitude toward the relation between the Imperial Law and the Buddhist Law is expressed in such statements as "Take the Buddhist Law as your master, and the world as your guest" and "Affix the Imperial Law to your forehead, but deep in your inner heart maintain the Buddhist Law" (both from the *Kikigaki*). From the *Letters* we have "Outwardly stress the Imperial Law, inwardly treasure faith in Other-Power, and take worldly virtue as your foundation"[6] and "Make Imperial Law your foundation, give precedence to virtue, follow the accepted ways of worldly righteousness, and deep in your inner heart store the spiritual peace of our tradition."[7]

Some scholars interpret such words as indicating that Rennyo taught the primacy of Imperial Law (*ōbō ihon* 王法為本), but it is unlikely that this was the case. Since Rennyo preaches that Imperial Law and the social virtues of benevolence and righteousness should prevail *outwardly*, but that *inwardly* faith in Other-Power should stand above all else, it is clear where his true emphasis lies. Two aspects of his teaching may be seen here. First is his belief that the standards of secular life differ from those of the life of faith—his belief, in other words, that politics and religion are separate. For Rennyo, religion was a matter for the inner spirit of the individual, and thus distinct from political and secular pursuits. Second is his stress on the centrality of religion and the foundational nature of faith (*shinjin ihon* 信心為本). Hence his words, "Take the Buddhist Law as your master, and the world as your guest."

Rennyo is not simply preaching a division between politics and religion, nor still less is he recommending a crude deception for the sake of social appearance. Quite the contrary: to live in deep religious faith even as one follows the laws and common-sense ways of the world is to live life as the expression of a profound reflection upon the nature of human existence. The devotion of thought to such matters is, I believe, the most important thing one can do. It is a way of living, both humble and devout, that examines and recognizes not only the glory, beauty, and potential of human life but also its sorrow, ugliness, and limitation. At the same time it manifests the type of courageous attitude that meets its secular responsibilities and does what it can to realize a more ideal form of government and society. Such an attitude, while accepting and submitting to the structures of government and authority, is neither indifferent to society nor directly bound up with the social forms or political processes. What is important is striving toward the ideal with an attitude of courage.

I believe that it was from this standpoint that Rennyo preached the separation of politics and religion and stressed the fundamentality of faith. The concept of the Realm of Buddha Dharma was a prescient and historically significant pointer toward an inner, spiritual life in the upheavals of the late medieval period.

An Uncompromising Attitude toward Corruption

I have always believed that the true life of Shinran's thought emerges from a spiritual tension rooted in distress at faith perverted by falsity and misunderstanding and at society overwhelmed by injustice and confusion. One does not find in the teachings of Shinran any easy formulas for salvation nor guaranteed paths to happiness and prosperity. Shinran, in other words, never preached that one could ignore due reflection on one's own humanity, refuse to address problems that have to be overcome, then gain Birth in the Pure Land through lip-service nenbutsu and formalistic ritual. "The nenbutsu is the single path free of hindrances. Why is this? To practitioners who have realized *shinjin*, the gods in the heavens and birth bow in homage, and Māras and nonbuddhists present no obstruction."[8]

Rennyo's concept of the Realm of Buddha Dharma may be seen to emerge from this same uncompromising attitude toward social and religious corruption and the taut logic and profound self-reflection to which it gave birth.

What the People Sought

Although the expression "Realm of Buddha Dharma" was Rennyo's creation, and although it may be seen to express a central aspect of his thought, it quite seldom appears in his work—to the best of my knowledge there are only four examples (including the two that I cited earlier) in all of his extant writings. There may be some who question whether such a scanty body of samples can justify the importance I have assigned to this term.

I believe, however, that the "Realm of Buddha Dharma" appeared far more often in Rennyo's work, although a thoroughgoing analysis is beyond the scope of this article. This notion, of course, raises the question as to why so few examples remain. To answer this question I must leave the discussion of "Rennyo the man" for the moment and turn to later historical factors, factors that exemplify the complex and severe nature of the historical process.

It is indisputable that because of Rennyo's proselytization, the teachings of "a society of faith headed by the Tathāgata and Shinran" and "a realm in the present world governed by the benevolence and retribution of the Buddha" spread widely throughout the populace of medieval Japan. Leaving aside for the moment the question of whether these teachings can be linked with the notion of the Realm of Buddha Dharma, the fact of their wide acceptance is clearly reflected in their wide dissemination due to the spread of the Shin-sect leagues known as *ikkō ikki*.

The term *ikkō ikki* is generally used today in reference only to the uprisings led by these Shin-sect leagues during the Sengoku era, but at the time it referred to the leagues themselves: *ikkō* (lit., single-minded) is another name for the Jōdoshin sect, and *ikki* originally meant something to the effect of "uniting in an egalitarian community." In contrast to the authoritarian, lord-and-vassal power structure of the domains led by nobles and warriors, the *ikki* organizations were more republican in nature. They were instituted by the common people as a means of survival during the turbulence of the Sengoku era. If these were not "Realms of Buddha Dharma," then what were they? Of course a critical examination of the historical facts relating to the *ikki* reveals all manner of betrayals and contradictions, and it serves no purpose to gloss over such failings. Yet surely the aspiration of the comon people for a "Realm of Buddha Dharma" is clearly reflected in the basic ideal of the *ikki*.

Degeneration and Distortion of the Ideal

Unfortunately, this aspiration was not to be fulfilled through an appropriate development of the concept of the Realm of Buddha Dharma.

First of all, the secular establishment observed the enormous growth in the areas (such as Kaga domain) controlled by the *ikkō ikki*—that is, by the Honganji organization—and concluded that this was simply another "realm" in the ordinary sense. According to the *Kokon dokugo*, published in 1568 by Rennyo's grandson Kensei (1499–1570),[9] already in the Bunmei era (1469–1487) the bakufu, the *kuge* (court representatives), and the main temple/shrine headquarters had petitioned Honganji to have the *Ikkō ikki* forces return the *shōen* landed estates to their original owners, claiming that this was the command of the emperor. Rennyo, though apparently vexed that this was not a matter relating to the Realm of Buddha Dharma, secretly directed the local authorities to do so "as it was the imperial will." (This, incidentally, is the third appearance of the term "Realm of Buddha Dharma" in Rennyo's extant writings.)[10]

Again, according to the *Yamashina gobō no koto narabi ni sono jidai no koto* (1575), compiled by Rennyo's son Jitsugo (1492–1583),[11] Hosokawa Masamoto (1466–1507) requested Honganji in 1506 to issue contingents of believers from the Settsu and Kawachi areas (both in the region of present-day Osaka) to aid him in his siege of Yoda Castle during his campaign against Hatakeyama Yoshihide (d. 1532). Jitsunyō (1458–1525),[12] annoyed by the request and facing the strong opposition of the Settsu and Kawachi congregations, finally fulfilled his obligation to Hosokawa by sending a thousand followers from Kaga. In this way the "Realm of the Buddha Dharma" was inexorably dragged into the political arena.[13]

These factors that transformed and perverted the idea of the Buddha Dharma Realm sent roots into the inner ranks of the Shin Buddhist institution. The *Honpukuji kyūki*, a Sengoku-era record from the Katada area of the Ōmi Domain (present-day Shiga Prefecture), contains the following statement:

> If one donates goods to the Buddha Dharma Realm, then the noble families of the *hossu's* relatives will seek one out and extend words of praise [this is the fourth appearance of the term "Realm of Buddha Dharma"].[14]

Katada Honpukuji had been the center of the Shin Buddhist congregation in the Ōmi region since the time of Rennyo and had contributed greatly to the development of the Shin organization. In time, however, a temple associated with a sibling (*ikkēshū*) of the *hossu* was built nearby and from about 1520 embarked upon a rather vicious campaign of pressuring Honpukuji. This well-known fact, repeatedly documented in the *Kyūki* records, should be kept in mind when one is reading passages like the one just cited:

> It is a serious mistake to believe that the *hossu* is unaware of clergymen and believers throughout the land who fail to make donations. If they are not careful on this point, their salvation is uncertain. If they desire heavenly assistance, they should make donations, no matter how small.[15]

There is little point in going into further detail on this issue—it is plain that the concept of the Buddha Dharma Realm now referred to the domain under the jurisdiction of the Honganji *hossu*, with his authority to render "uncertain the salvation" of those who did not support him. The Buddha Dharma Realm, in other words, had become simply another power structure for the exercise of exploitation and political control.

By the end of the Sengoku era things had moved even further in this direction. Ishiyama Honganji, the Shin Buddhist headquarters on Naniwa Bay in the present-day Osaka area, comprised an elaborate fortresslike complex with magnificent temple buildings and a large "temple town" (*jinai machi*) surrounded by walls and moats. The head abbots—the tenth *hossu* Shōnyo (1516–1554), eleventh *hossu* Kennyo (1543–1592), and twelfth *hossu* Kyōnyo (1558–1614)—possessed a political authority every bit the equal of that of the contemporary Sengoku warlords. Here again, rather than detailing the historical details, I will assess some of the more salient—and tragic—features of the Shin Buddhist institution of this period.

Aside from the questions of whether the *ikkō ikki* were true to their own ideals or were misunderstood by secular society, it is undeniable that by the late medieval period these leagues had gained control of territories as vast as the domains of the feudal daimyō. Claim though one might that the Realm of Buddha Dharma was not the same as a secular domain, the fact remained that it operated as a political power structure and was under the control of a *hossu* who was as involved with ritual duties and political maneuverings as the most powerful daimyō of the time. Indeed, by this time the *hossu* had assumed almost dictatorial powers. They could excommunicate, or even execute, those who opposed their wishes or failed to show the proper degree of respect. "The benevolence and retribution of the Tathāgata and Shinran" mentioned by Rennyo was now "the benevolence and retribution of the *hossu*," while the *ikkeshū* were notorious in their arbitrary exercise of the authority they gained through their family ties with the head abbot.

In this way the ideal of the Buddha Dharma Realm was distorted into something quite different than originally intended. The politicization of the Realm may be seen as one of the factors leading to Oda Nobunaga's campaign against the *ikkō ikki*, in which Ishiyama Honganji was destroyed and the political power of the Shin Buddhist organization broken. In the course of the conflict countless numbers of peasant believers, fighting from a sincere determination to defend their faith, lost their lives. Little was left but the corpses of these believers and a huge group of unlettered nuns, the uncomplaining—and perhaps rather overawed—followers of the *hossu* within the vast power structure of the Honganji organization. It is understandable why, for generations afterwards, Nobunaga was referred to among certain segments of the peasantry as the Great Evildoer and Enemy of Buddhism.

During the Tokugawa period (1600–1868) the introduction of the *danka* system turned the temples into instruments of governmental control.[16] In complying with this system the Shin Buddhist clergy assumed, de facto, the primacy of the Imperial Law. With the coming of the Meiji era the new government instituted policies suppressing Buddhism and promoting State Shinto as the new national religion; here again the Shin Buddhist institution went along, supporting the notion of Japan not as the Realm of Buddha Dharma but as "the Land of the Kami" (*shinkoku nihon*).

Here we must keep in mind that with the coming of the Sengoku era and the concomitant collapse of the *kenmitsu* system, Honganji had become a central part of the Japanese religious establishment, aristocratic in nature and with ties to the imperial family, having been designated a *monzeki* temple in 1559 under Kennyo. The sect thereby lost its critical stance and, with it, the ideological tautness that had once distinguished it. Lost too were the spirit of the founder, Shinran, and Rennyo's ideal of the Buddha Dharma Realm.

Notes

This chapter originally appeared as "Tenkanki no shidōsha" 転換期の指導者, in *Rennyo* 蓮如, ed. Minami Mido Shinbun, Osaka: Nanba Betsuin, 1986, 128–146.

1 *Translator's note*: *Kenmitsu Bukkyō* is a central concept in Kuroda Toshio's Buddhist historical thought. In contrast to the traditional model of Japanese Buddhist historical development, which saw the Buddhism of the Nara period (710–94) as characterized by the so-called Six Schools (Kusha, Jōjitsu, Ritsu, Hossō, Sanron, and Kegon), the Buddhism of the Heian period (794–1185) as characterized by the Tendai and the Shingon sects, and the Buddhism of the Kamakura period (1185–1333) as characterized by the so-called New Buddhism of the Zen sect, Nichiren sect, Jōdo sect, and Jōdoshin sect, Kuroda proposed a view that emphasized what he called *kenmitsu* (exoteric / esoteric) Buddhism.

His basic contention is that during medieval times the new forms of Kamakura Buddhism were fairly peripheral, whereas the old forms tended to dominate religious affairs. Certainly, they were the ones that controlled the most temples, clerics, and material resources, and whose religious outlook was recognized as mainstream. The word *kenmitsu*...refers to the body of beliefs and practices that bound medieval religion together as a coherent and comprehensive worldview. The scope of this worldview went beyond the parameters commonly ascribed to Buddhism, for it included beliefs associated with kami, which today are categorized as Shinto. Under this *kenmitsu* umbrella separate lineages or schools were recognized—the number of Buddhist schools was traditionally set at eight (*hassū*: Tendai, Shingon, and the six Nara schools)—and they each developed their own exoteric teachings (*kengyō*), doctrinal systems that rationalized and undergirded religious practices. But they were all united in their common recognition of the efficacy of esoteric beliefs and practices (*mikkyō*). ("Editor's Introduction: Kuroda Toshio and His Scholarship," by James C. Dobbins, *Japanese Journal of Religious Studies* 23:217–32, [1996] p. 222).

2 *Translator's note*: The *shōen* were large landed estates located away from the urban population centers. They were generally owned by absentee court nobles or religious organizations and managed by proprietors that lived on the premises. First appearing in the eighth century and continuing in gradually changing form until the sixteenth century, they comprised one of the central institutions of medieval Japan.

The mature estate, emerging in the mid-11th century, proved to be an extremely successful way of securing a balance between the demands of the ruling class for income and the demands of the populace for a stable livelihood. Not only did the *shōen* serve as the primary means through which the ruling class tapped the wealth of the countryside, but it also provided the residence, workplace, and the source of sustenance for peasants and estate managers alike....As one of the primary production units in medieval Japanese society, the *shōen* held a central place in the economic and social history of Japan. (*Japan: An Illustrated Encyclopedia* [Tokyo: Kodansha, 1993.] p. 1401.)

3 The present-day Old Buddhist sectarian organizations (see note 1) consist of reorganized forms of their Heian-period counterparts.

4 RSI, 236.

5 SSZ 3.611.

6 RSI, 181.

7 RSI, 256.

8 From *Tannishō* 7, at SSZ 2.777; CWS 665.

9 Abbot of Kōkyōji in the Kaga Domain.

10 SSS 2.720b.

11 Third son of Rennyo and abbot of Gantokuji in the Kaga Domain.

12 Ninth *hossu* of Honganji.

13 *Yamashina gobō no koto narabi ni sono jidai no koto*, entry 72, at SSS 2.555b-556.

14 The name *Honpukuji kyūki* refers to five texts written by the father and son team of Myōshū (n.d.) and Myōsei (1491–1560), who protected Rennyo against the armed aggression of Mount Hiei. The quote here is from a work titled *Honpukuji atogaki* at SSS 2.651b.

15 Ibid.

16 The word *danka* indicates the households affiliated with a particular temple; the term is composed of the two elements *dan* 檀 (from a transliteration of the Sanskrit *dānapati*, lay believers who give donations to the ordained sangha) and *ka* 家 (from the Japanese *ka*, also pronounced *ie*, "family" or "household"). During the Tokugawa period, under the *terauke* 寺請 system, every household in Japan was required to register as the *danka* of a nearby temple, and the temples were in turn required to report to the government regarding the *danka* associated with them. The ostensible purpose of this was to suppress Christianity, but the system was used to control the population as a whole.

4

STANLEY WEINSTEIN

Continuity and Change in the Thought of Rennyo

The two names that most likely come to mind first when one thinks of the great teachers and leaders of the Jōdoshinshu in the premodern period are Shinran and Rennyo. These names are known not only to students of Japanese religion or followers of the Shinshū school but also to most ordinary Japanese, since these names figure prominently in high school textbooks.

Kurata Momozō's biographical novel about Shinran, *Shukke to sono deshi* ("The Monk and His Disciples"), continues to enjoy popularity today, eighty years after it was first published,[1] and despite the prediction of the eminent Marxist historian Hattori Shisō[2] in 1947 that Rennyo would not likely be chosen as the subject of a novel or play, the life of Rennyo, as the popular Japanese writer Itsuki Hiroyuki noted,[3] has in fact been dealt with by a number of novelists including Matsugi Nobuhiko, Niwa Fumio, and more recently, from a woman's perspective, by Minagawa Hiroko.[4] Thus Shinran and Rennyo remain familiar and appealing figures to large numbers of laypeople who do not think of themselves as being particularly religious.

In the traditional Shinshū view, Shinran is regarded as the founder (*kaisan shōnin*) of the Shin denomination, whereas Rennyo is seen as the reviver (*go-saikō shōnin* or *chūkō shōnin*).[5] It was Shinran's profound and unique religious experience in the thirteenth century, specifically his insightful reading of the Pure Land scriptures and his deep, personal understanding of the teaching of *tariki shinjin* (acceptance of the absolute grace of Amida Buddha), that formed the basis of the doctrines and faith that came to be known as the True Teaching of Pure Land (Jōdoshinshū).

Shinran did not discover until relatively late in his spiritual journey what he ultimately concluded was the highest truth of the Pure Land faith, namely, the teaching of *tariki shinjin*. He started his religious career as a novice on Mount Hiei, devoting himself to scriptural study and the chanting of the nenbutsu in the fashion of the Tendai school. In 1201, at the age of twenty-eight, he became a disciple of Hōnen, from whom he learned the *senju nenbutsu* (the exclusive practice of chanting the nenbutsu). When the senju nenbutsu was suppressed and Hōnen's fellowship was banished from Kyoto in 1207, Shinran was laicized and exiled to Echigo, a province facing the Japan Sea. This experience affected him profoundly: from that time on he began to describe himself as *hisō hizoku* (neither a monk nor a layman) and subsequently took a wife and started a family.

When Shinran was pardoned in 1211 along with other members of Hōnen's fellowship, he did not return to Kyoto, the center of Japan's political and cultural life, as did Hōnen, but stayed on in Echigo for another three years with his family, sharing with the local people his understanding of the Pure Land faith. In 1214 Shinran, now forty-one years of age, moved to Hitachi in eastern Japan. Here he devoted himself to teaching the common people about the Pure Land faith while working on the draft of his major doctrinal work, the *Kyōgyōshinshō*. In about 1232 Shinran, by now resolute in his belief in *tariki shinjin*, as his wife, Eshinni, attests,[6] finally moved back to Kyoto, where he spent the remaining years of his life writing on matters of faith and trying to provide guidance to the various groups of *monto* (believers) he had left behind in Echigo and the Kantō region by discussing matters of faith with emissaries of the monto and engaging in correspondence with individual believers.[7]

Shinran was a truly remarkable Buddhist teacher: a man of great humility who always strove for the truth but who was nevertheless plagued by doubts and uncertainty until his last years; an earnest seeker with a deep awareness of his own limitations and sinfulness; someone who would never compromise what he believed to be the true teaching of the Buddhist scripture for the age in which he lived regardless of how the secular or religious authorities might react. For Shinran the message of the Pure Land scriptures and the Pure Land patriarchs came down to the acceptance of the gift of faith from Amida that enables one to attain in this life the state of *shōjōju*, that is, the state in which one is assured of Birth in Pure Land and achieves a profound peace of mind.

In Shinran's view, no mediation by priest or monk, no formal affiliation with a temple, was necessary to attain salvation; Amida's compassion was aptly expressed in the words *sesshu fusha* (Amida embraces all and rejects none). Unlike other Buddhist teachers, Shinran never formally accepted disciples.[8] Those who turned to him, those with whom he shared his faith, he called "friends" (*dōbō*) or "fellow wayfarers" [on the spiritual journey] (*dōgyō*), but never "disciples" (*deshi*), since this term implied a type of hierarchy that was alien to Shinran's view of the path to Pure Land. Later local traditions notwithstanding, Shinran likewise built not a single temple. His followers established "religious associations" (*kō* 講) and came together at *dōjō* (small gathering places) which were presided over by an "elder" (*otona* 乙名).

Although Shinran was successful in establishing numerous small-scale associations during his sojourns in Echigo and Kantō, all evidence shows that after his return to Kyoto he led a simple, unassuming life, so much so that unlike his teacher Hōnen and the founders of the other Kamakura schools, Shinran goes unmentioned in contemporary accounts. Nichiren (1222–1282), an unremitting critic of Pure Land Buddhism who died twenty years after Shinran, rails against Hōnen in many of his writings but does not make a single reference to Shinran.

Similarly, the *Jōdo homon genru shō*,[9] written by Gyōnen (1240–1321), which is the first comprehensive history of Pure Land produced in Japan, does not contain a word about Shinran, even though it devotes an entire chapter to Hōnen and his disciples and was written forty-nine years after Shinran's death.[10]

In many respects Rennyo represents the very antithesis of Shinran. Born a century and a half after the death of Shinran, Rennyo was a tenth-generation blood descendant (counting Shinran as the first generation) of Shinran's through the latter's daughter, Kakushinni. Unlike Shinran, whose life was marked by an intense search for the true meaning of Amida's vows, Rennyo was born into a family that for generations had been raised on the truths that Shinran had experienced only after a lifetime of study and introspection. Shinran arrived at his unique interpretation of *tariki shinjin* toward the end of a life of intense searching and questioning, whereas Rennyo learned this doctrine at his father's knee and then devoted his early years to an extensive study of the major writings and sayings attributed to Shinran. According to the testimony of Rennyo's sixth son, Renjun, Rennyo studied the *Kyōgyōshinshō*, and the *Tannishō*, as well as Zonkaku's (1290–1373) definitive commentary on the *Kyōgyōshinshō*, the *Rokuyōshō*.[11] Shinran was born into a secular household and was ordained into the Tendai order on Mount Hiei as the first step in his search for the truth of Buddhism; Rennyo was born into a family that had been ordained priests, albeit married ones, for generations.

Despite the eminence of Rennyo's lineage owing to its descent from Shinran, Rennyo's family and indeed their temple in Ōtani in Kyoto, the Honganji, had fallen on hard times by the early fifteenth century. The number of monto had grown steadily since Shinran began his proselytization in Echigo Province, and the Kantō region two centuries earlier, but the Honganji was not the principal beneficiary. The monto associations and *dōjō* were loosely organized and many, probably a majority, had become affiliated with Shinshū temples, such as the Senjuji in Shimotsuke and the Bukkōji in Kyoto, that claimed, often dubiously, a lineage that extended back to some of Shinran's better-known semi-clerical followers.

Mastering the teachings of his humble, self-effacing ancestor was not the only thing on the mind of young Rennyo. According to Renjun, Rennyo resolved at the age of fourteen to revive the "Dharma lineage" (*hōryū*) of Shinran, that is, to make the Honganji the sole spiritual focal point of the monto.[12] Whereas Shinran had not established a single temple or taken a single disciple, Rennyo had built a succession of large temples, first at Yoshizaki in Echizen in 1471, then at Yamashina in Kyoto in 1479, and finally at Ishiyama Osaka in 1496. In the same vein, whereas Shinran had spent the last thirty years of his life in relative obscurity occupying himself with writing and teaching, the latter half of Rennyo's life, which coincided in part with the Ōnin War (1467–1477), reflected the turbulence of the times and its impact on Rennyo: the burning of the Ōtani Honganji in 1265, his flight from Kyoto, his involvement during his sojourn in Yoshizaki between 1471 and 1475 in the cataclysmic monto peasant uprisings known as *ikkō-ikki*, his taking up residence in Yamashina in 1478, where he undertook the construction of a new Honganji, and finally his retirement in 1489 at the age of seventy-four. Shinran was unknown to the influential people of his day; Rennyo, with the mass following he commanded as a result of his vigorous evangelism and his honored status as Shinran's lineal descendant, was regarded by the feudal lords (*shugo daimyō*) with a mixture of awe and fear.

As was noted at the beginning of this chapter, Shinran has traditionally been regarded as the founder of the Jōdo Shinshu, and he is retrospectively listed as the first chief abbot (*hossu*) of the Honganji, whereas Rennyo is viewed as the "reviver" (*chūkō shōnin*) of the Shinshū and is counted as the eighth chief abbot of the Honganji. As the historical records make clear, when Rennyo was born, the Honganji had for some time been in a period of decline; the structures were decaying, visits by the monto were infrequent, and resources were scarce. That Rennyo dramatically reversed the fortunes of the Honganji during his long tenure as chief abbot and turned the Honganji into one of the most powerful forces in the late Muromachi period is beyond dispute. He also deserves credit for his relentless and, on the whole successful, struggle against the various distortions of Shinran's teachings—the so-called *ianjin*—that were current in his day. As a result of his lifelong effort to bring the scattered monto groups in Hokuriku, the Kantō, and other regions under the umbrella of the Honganji and to establish the primacy of the Honganji among the groupings, Rennyo occupies a unique position among the chief abbots, and that position is what the appellation *chūkō shōnin* reflects.

While Rennyo's contributions in building the Honganji into a major institutional force have not been questioned, we do not find the same unanimity with regard to Rennyo's relationship to Shinran in matters of doctrine. The traditional view has been that Rennyo is a true successor to Shinran, one who accepted Shinran's teachings without alteration or distortion. It was of course always recognized that Rennyo's style differed from Shinran's: Shinran wrote highly technical doctrinal works in Chinese such as the *Kyōgyōshinshō, Jōdo monruiju shō, Gutokushō*, and *Nyūshutsu nimon geju*[13] to explain and justify his Pure Land faith, whereas Rennyo, apart from his short commentary in Japanese on the *Shōshinge*,[14] wrote no learned treatise on doctrine. Which is not to say that Rennyo did not leave behind a considerable corpus of writing. Quite the contrary, for we have a collection of 211 letters, the so-called *Ofumi* (*Letters*), written in what is usually described as "plain, simple Japanese." These letters, eighty of which are now available in an excellent annotated English translation by the late Professor Minor Rogers,[15] offer penetrating insights into Rennyo's view of Shinshū faith and how that faith should be expressed within the constraints of the then feudal Japanese social order.

In the traditional view of Rennyo and Shinran, then, Shinran was seen as the scholar, the intense, introspective seeker, the man who lived much of his life in obscurity, whereas Rennyo was the activist, the builder of the Honganji as a major institution, the popular proselytizer who made the essence of Shinran's teachings accessible to the broad masses of monto. Although differences of style were recognized, Rennyo was perceived as faithfully following the teachings of Shinran.

In more recent times, however, the question has been raised from a variety of perspectives whether Rennyo, in his desire to establish the primacy of the Honganji and make Shinran's ideas comprehensible to the masses, did not deviate from Shinran's understanding of the Pure Land teachings either deliberately or unwittingly. In the late 1940s the study of Japanese history and religion, freed from the political and societal constraints of the prewar years, began to move in new, hitherto unexplored directions. For a variety of reasons, not the least of which was Rennyo's close involvement with the peasant uprisings of the late fifteenth century, Rennyo became the object of close scholarly scrutiny. As the exhaustive bibliography of Professor Amagishi Jōen published in 1984 shows,[16] fifty-four scholarly books (not to mention sixty-seven popular books) and 450 scholarly articles were published on Rennyo between 1948 and 1984, a period of thirty-six years. One can only speculate on how many books and scholarly articles have appeared since 1984.

A number of historians, perhaps beginning with Professor Hattori Shisō, as well as some scholars from within the Shinshū itself, have asked whether Rennyo in his self-defined mission to bring the scattered monto groups under the authority of the Honganji did not compromise, or at least dilute, some of the basic teachings and attitudes of Shinran for the sake of expediency. Certainly this question needs to be thoughtfully examined. Shinran never saw himself as the founder of a new religious order as did, say, Saichō (767–822) or Kūkai (774–835). As was noted, Shinran had no formal disciples, built no temples, brooked no hierarchy within his fellowship. With Rennyo a starkly different picture emerges. Rennyo had an exceptionally strong sense of Shinshū as an independent school with its own distinctive lineage that was competing with several long-established, officially recognized schools. As Professor Izumoji Osamu reports, Rennyo uses the term *tōryū* ("this tradition/lineage") ninety-nine times in forty-four letters and the synonymous term *ichiryū* eighteen times in fourteen letters.[17] It bears noting that these terms are frequently used with the name or title of Shinran in combinations such as *tōryū Shinran Shōnin* ("Shinran Shōnin of this tradition"), *tōryū Shōnin*, and *tōryū kaisan Shōnin* ("the saintly teacher [Shinran] who is the founder of this tradition"). It comes as no surprise to those familiar with Shinran's rejection of sectarianism that the terms *tōryū* and *ichiryū* were never used by Shinran to refer to his own groups of followers.

For Shinran, salvation was realizable only by reliance upon the eighteenth Vow of Amida. The moment one accepted the gift of faith (*ichinen hokki*), one entered the ranks of the *shōjōju*, "those whose rebirth in Pure Land is assured." True faith (*shinjitsu shinjin*) in Amida's promise of salvation brought immediate benefits in this world (*genze riyaku*), but unlike the teachers of the other schools of Buddhism, who saw these as *material* benefits, such as recovery from illness or acquisition of wealth, Shinran regarded the benefits that accrued in this world as being essentially *spiritual* in nature. Furthermore, as Shinran, paraphrasing a passage in the *Mahāparinirvāṇasūtra* (*Nehangyō*) declares, "one who puts his faith in the Buddha [= Amida for Shinran] should not also put his faith in non-Buddhist divinities."[18]

In some of his letters Rennyo seems to embrace Shinran's view unambiguously: "Put aside all practices [other than what are taught in the eighteenth Vow], and relying solely on Amida Nyorai, dismiss from your mind [all thoughts of] other Buddhas and kami."[19] Four months later Rennyo uses even stronger language when he compares all kami and their ilk (i.e., Buddhist divinities other than Amida) to "useless playthings" in this life, and to emphasize this point Rennyo quotes the Confucian maxim, "The loyal subject does not attend two lords; the chaste wife does not serve two husbands."[20]

But as hostility toward the monto continued to intensify in the early 1470s, partly as a result of their exclusive practices, Rennyo appears to have sought an accommodation with the established order—something that Shinran never did. In a letter written on the seventeenth day of the second month of 1474 [sixth year of Bunmei] Rennyo altered his position, writing that Amida Buddha embodied (or "contained within himself") all kami, Buddhas, and bodhisattvas, so that when one relies (*tanomi*) only on Amida, one is in fact taking refuge in all Buddhas, bodhisattvas, and kami.[21]

By holding that Amida contains within himself all the Buddhas, bodhisattvas, and kami, Rennyo seems to be reverting to the then popular doctrine of *honji suijaku*, namely, that the native kami are none other than Japanese manifestations of Buddhist divinities, particularly as this doctrine was espoused within the Shingon school and depicted in the maṇḍala, with Dainichi Nyorai at the center emanating outward in manifestations of Buddhas, bodhisattvas, and various types of kami. It is axiomatic in Shingon to say that Dainichi Nyorai is the embodiment of all Buddhas, bodhisattvas, and other divinities. Rennyo of course does not make such a bold statement about Amida, but his language appears to represent a departure from Shinran's view of Amida. For Shinran, the moment the believer gave rise to true faith (*shin no ichinen*), one of the ten benefits of that faith to be immediately manifested in this life (*genshō jisshu no yaku*) was that the various kami would protect the believer in his religious endeavors (*myōshu goji*).[22] This view of the role of the kami as protectors of those who recite the nenbutsu is not identical with the view that the kami are contained within Amida and are objects of refuge, which is the position Rennyo takes in his letter of the seventeenth day of the second month in 1474.[23]

In the same remarkable letter Rennyo writes:

> Those who regard the next life as being of supreme importance and with resolute faith seek rebirth in Pure Land—such people will, needless to say, be saved in their next life. And even if these people do not desire anything for this life, their [wish for rebirth in Pure Land] will spontaneously become a prayer [for material benefits] in this life.[24]

Rennyo's choice of language here is extraordinary in his description of the person of resolute faith seeking rebirth in Pure Land. He writes that not only does it go without saying that such a person will be saved in the next life (*goshō no tasukaru koto*), but also that the very wish to reach Pure Land is spontaneously transformed into a *kitō*, a "prayer"; this is a common word that invokes the image of receiving material benefits in this world, a notion firmly rejected by Shinran. As was noted, for Shinran, True Faith in the eighteenth Vow brings its own rewards in this world, the *genze riyaku*, but these are spiritual in content and do not arise from *kitō*, a word that never occurs in any of Shinran's writings.

Whereas Shinran devoted his life to a search for the ultimate truths of Buddhism and felt no need to accommodate the secular authorities, Rennyo, having a different temperament and living under different circumstances, believed in the necessity of compromise to secure the survival and prosperity of the Jōdoshinshū headed by the Honganji lineage. Shinran, basing himself on a deeply personal reading of the three

Pure Land scriptures, the writings attributed to Mahāyāna Indian thinkers such as Nāgārjuna and Vasubandhu, the works of Chinese Pure Land monks, and most immediately the teachings of Genshin (942–1017) and Hōnen, ultimately came to the conclusion that salvation in the age in which he lived could be achieved only through *tariki shinjin*. And it was this idea that he proclaimed tirelessly in his doctrinal writings, the many letters he sent to his scattered followers, known as the *Goshōsoku shū*, and the intimate talks he had with devoted followers preserved in the *Tannishō*.

Professor Bandō Shōjun observed that Rennyo's thought is characterized by a kind of dualism (*nigen heiretsuteki ronpō*) that is absent in Shinran,[25] whose position may be summed up by the phrase *shinjin ihon*, that is, "'faith [in the compassionate vow of Amida Buddha] must be the foundation [of our daily life and everyday activities]." Although Rennyo also affirms the notion of *shinjin ihon*, he tends to think in terms of complementary categories. Thus Rennyo juxtaposes "the law of the ruler' (*ōbō*) to "the law of the Buddha" (*buppō*), a duality that figures prominently in his thinking. In one letter Rennyo urges the monto both "to follow publicly the law of the ruler and to resolutely hold on in one's heart to faith in Amida's salvific power, while making secular moral obligations the foundation [for daily life].[26] In another letter he asserts that the monto should "regard the law of the ruler as the foundation [for daily life], give priority to secular moral obligations, and conform to worldly conventions, while deeply holding to the faith transmitted by our lineage.[27]

Rennyo left little doubt in his letters about what he meant by "giving priority to secular moral obligations and conforming to worldly conventions." In the eleventh month of 1473 he drew up a list of eleven rules incumbent on all monto, which included prohibitions against treating Buddhist and Shinto deities with contempt, criticizing other schools, and engaging in any type of intolerant behavior. Monto were instructed to show respect to *shugo* (military governors) and *jitō* (estate stewards) and to refrain from eating fish and meat, drinking sake, or gambling at religious services.[28] The monto were also cautioned not to try to convert people of other sects or proclaim their own beliefs openly. Rennyo further admonished them to pay their taxes in full[29] and to adhere to the code of secular ethics.[30] It is difficult to imagine Shinran uttering words such as these in light of the outrage he expressed toward the government (Rennyo's "law of the ruler") in the epilogue to his *Kyōgyōshinshō* for its unjust treatment of Hōnen and other devotees of the *senju nenbutsu*. Shinran wrote: "The emperor at the top and the ministers of state beneath him have turned their backs on Buddhism; they have flouted justice, made a show of their anger, and exacted vengeance."[31] It might be noted here that the editors of the standard edition of the Shinshū scriptures, the *Shinshū shōgyō zensho*, which was first published in 1940—a time when ultranationalist ideology was dominant— excised Shinran's criticism of the emperor in the *Kyōgyōshinshō*,[32] presumably in accordance with Rennyo's injunction to "conform to worldly conventions," that is, to avoid conflict with the authorities.

One does not have to look far for other examples of Rennyo's dualistic thinking. Professor Bandō has written on Rennyo's unique view that the assurance of rebirth in Pure Land that we receive in this life as a result of faith (*shōjōju*) and the attaining of nirvāṇa in the next life (*metsudo*) are two distinct benefits.[33] Professor Nadamoto Aiji[34] has discussed the differences between Rennyo and Shinran in their respective interpretations of the *gan jōju mon*[35] and has attempted to reconcile Rennyo's controversial injunction to "beseech Amida for salvation in the next life" (*goshō tasuke tamae to Mida wo tanome*[36] with Shinran's view that salvation is "spontaneously" (*jinen*) assured to all who have accepted Amida.[37] Professor Yamazaki Ryūmyō has focused on the prominence of the concepts of "impermanence" (*mujō*) and "the next life" (*goshō*) in Rennyo's writing and thinking, terms that are never used by Shinran.[38]

Given the complexity of Shinran's doctrinal writing, the subsequent elaboration of Shinshū doctrine by Kakunyo (1270–1351) and Zonkaku, and the very different circumstances in which Rennyo found himself in the fifteenth century when Japan was undergoing unprecedented violent social and political upheavals, it is not surprising that Rennyo chose to adopt new methods of proselytization and new phraseology for disseminating Shinran's teachings. It is a matter of ongoing dispute among scholars whether Rennyo's unique interpretations and choice of language represent attempts on his part to make Shinran's thought more accessible to the masses and to make the essence of Shinran's teachings more palatable to the secular authorities or whether Rennyo's interpretations and language signify a deviation from Shinran's fundamental beliefs.

What is beyond dispute, however, is the truly monumental role Rennyo played in transforming the scattered fellowships of monto into what has become the largest Buddhist denomination in Japan today. It seems safe to say that were it not for the unflagging efforts of Rennyo, Shinran would probably not be the nationally, indeed internationally, known, respected, and beloved figure that he is today. Therefore it is entirely fitting that we commemorate the 500th anniversary of the passing away of Rennyo Shōnin by expressing our gratitude for his remarkable accomplishments.

Notes

1 *Shukke to sono deshi* first appeared in 1917. It was soon translated by Glenn Shaw, and this translation was published in 1922 by Hokuseido.

2 See Hattori Shisō, *Rennyo*, reprinted as vol. 14 in *Hattori Shisō zenshū* (Tokyo: Fukumura Shuppan, 1974), 19–20.

3 Itsuki Hiroyuki, *Rennyo: seizoku guyū no ningen zō*, Iwanami shinsho 343 (Tokyo: Iwanami Shoten, 1994).

4 Matsugi Nobuhiko, *Watashi no Rennyo*, published in 1981 by Chikuma Shobō; Niwa Fumio, an 8-volume novel called *Rennyo*, published in 1982–1983 by Chūō Kōronsha; Minagawa Hiroko, *Ransei tamayura: Rennyo to onna-tachi*, published in 1991 by Yomiuri Shinbunsha.

5 For the term *kaisan shōnin* see Rennyo's *Letters*; see RSI letter nos. 39, 41, 50, and 74, pp. 134, 141, 166, and 225. For an early use of the term *gosaikō shōnin* see *kikigaki* in *Rennyo, Ikkō ikki, Nihon shisō taikei* 17 (Tokyo: Iwanami Shoten, 1972), 145. From the Edo period on *chūkō shōnin*, a word synonymous with *gosaikō shōnin*, was a commonly employed appellation of Rennyo. On the term *chūkō* see the *Kōshinroku* of Genchi 玄智 (1734–1794) fasc. 5, at SZ 64.200–204.

6 *Eshinni shōsoku* (Letters of Eshinni), SSZ 5.101.

7 Shinran's letters to his believers are arranged in several collections: *Mattōshō*, *Shinran Shōnin goshosoku shū*, *Kechimyaku monjū*, and *Zenshō bon goshōsoku shū*, all of which can be found in Nabata Ōjun and Kabutogi Shōkō, eds., *Shinran shū, Nichiren shū*, vol. 82 of *Nihon koten bungaku taikei* (Tokyo: Iwanami Shoten, 1964).

8 Note the often quoted line from the *Tannishō*: "[I] Shinran do not have even a single Jōdo hōmon genrushō, disciple" 親鸞は弟子一人ももたずさふらう. SSZ 2.776.

9 T No. 2687, 84.192–201.

10 See Mark Blum, *The Origins and Development of Pure Land Buddhism: A Study and Translation of Gyōnen's* Jōdo Hōmon Genrushō (New York: Oxford University Press, 2002), esp. pp. 41–45, which discuss possible reasons for Shinran's absence from Gyōnen's text.

11 See *Renjun ki*, in RSG 64.

12 Ibid.

13 All three works to be found in volume 2 of SSZ.

14 *Shōshinge taii* is at SSZ 3.385, RS1 23.

15 Rogers translated the collection of letters known as the *Gojō ofumi* or *Jōnai ofumi*.

16 Included in Kimura Takeo, ed., *Rennyo Shōnin no kyōgaku to rekishi* (Ōsaka: Tōhō Shuppansha, 1984), 366–399 (written horizontally, this actually begins on 399 and progresses toward 366).

17 See Izumoji Osamu, *Ofumi Rennyo, Tōyō bunko*, vol. 345 (Tokyo: Heibonsha, 1978), 372.

18 佛に帰依せん者は終にまたその余の諸天神に帰依せざれ, at *Kyōgyōshinshō*, SSZ 2.175. For the original passage that Shinran has abridged see the *Daihatsu Nehangyō*, fascicle 8, T No. 374, 12.409c.

19 もろもろの雑行をさしきて、一向に弥陀如來をたのみたてまつりて、自余の一切の諸神 ☒ 諸仏にもこころをかけず…, at *Letters* 32, dated "the last ten days" (gejun) of the ninth month of the fifth year of Bunmei [1473], RSI 124.

20 The two quotes are また一切の諸神なんどに今生にをいて 用にもたたぬせせりごと and 忠臣は二君につかえざれ、貞女は二夫にまみえず, in *Letter* 43, dated the thirteenth day of the twelfth month of the fifth day of Bunmei [1473], RSI 152.

21 またあらゆる諸神諸仏菩薩もことごとくこもれるなり。阿弥陀一仏をたのめば、一切の仏菩薩一切の諸神に帰するいはれあり, in Letter 54, RSI 177–178.

22 *Kyōgyoshinshō*, SSZ 2.72.

23 Letter 54, RSI 177.

24 Ibid., 178.

25 Bandō Shōjun, "Shinran to Rennyo," 1988; reprinted in Kakehashi Jitsuen et al., eds., *Rennyo taikei* (Kyoto: Hōzōkan, 1996), vol. 2, p. 140.

26 外には王法をおもてとし、内心には他力の信心をふがくたくわえて、世間の仁義をもって本とすべし. RSI 180.

27 まづ王法をもって本とし、仁義をもって先として、世間通途の義に順じて、当流 安心をば内心にふかくたくはえて. *Letter* 86, dated twenty-seventh day of the first month of the seventh year of Bunmei [1475], RSI 256.

28 Letter 38, dated the seventeenth day of the eleventh month of the fifth year of Bunmei [1473], RSI 177.

29 Letter 54, RSI 179.

30 The preceding four sentences are taken with minor changes Stanley Weinstein, "Rennyo and the Shinshū Revival," in *Japan in the Muromachi Age*, ed. John W. Hall and Toyoda Takeshi (Berkeley: University of California Press, 1977), 355–356.

31 Kaneko Daiei, ed., *Kyōgyōshinshō*, in *Iwanami Bunko* 5813–16 (Tokyo: Iwanami Shoten, 1957), 444; Hoshino Genpō et al., eds., *Kyōgyōshinshō*, in *Shinran*, vol. 11 of *Nihon shisō taikei* (Tokyo: Iwanami Shoten, 1971), 257–258.

32 SSZ 2.201.

33 Bandō, "Shinran to Rennyo," p. 141.

34 Nadamoto Aiji, "Shinran Shōnin to Rennyo Shōnin," in Kimura Takeo, ed., *Rennyo shōnin no kyōgaku to rekishi* (Tokyo: Tōhō Shuppan, 1984), 55–58.

35 Specifically the passage in the *Muryōjukyō* explaining the fulfillment of the Eighteenth Vow. See T No. 360, 12.272b9.

36 See, for example, *Kikigaki* articles 185 and 188, in *Nihon Koten bungaku tai kei* 17.144–145.

37 See, for example, Shinran's *Songō shinzō meimon (kōhon)* SSZ 2.581, lines 1–5.

38 See Yamazaki Ryūmyō, "Shinran to Rennyo no shūkyō jōkyō ni tsuite: jingi-kan wo chūshin to shite," in Futaba Kenkō, ed., *Zoku Kokka to shūkyō: kodai, chūsei hen (Nihon bukkyōshi kenkyū 3)* (Kyoto: Nagata Bunshōdō, 1981), 271–313, and "Rennyo ronkō 蓮如論 考," *Musashino joshi daigaku bukkyō bunka kenkyūsho kiyō* 14 (1996).

5

MATSUMURA NAOKO
TRANSLATED BY MAYA HARA

Rennyo and the Salvation of Women

Rennyo's Statements on Women

Rennyo is known to have actively preached on the salvation of women and their birth into the Pure Land. In looking at Rennyo's eighty extant *Letters* (*Jonai ofumi*), twenty-eight refer to women. According to Minowa Shūhō, four characteristics can be seen in the way Rennyo viewed women.[1]

1. The view that men and women are equal. For example, Rennyo writes: "[In t]he fundamental principle of Master Shinran...no distinction at all is made between male and female, old and young" (1:2).[2] "To receive that faith.... It does not matter if one is good or evil, male or female" (2:7).[3]

2. The view that the five obstacles and three submissions of women and the ten transgressions and five grave offenses of an evil person are synonymous. For example, "People of evil [karma] who have committed the ten transgressions and the five grave offenses and women, burdened with the five obstacles and the three submissions—all of whom have been excluded from the compassionate vows of all the buddhas of the ten directions and the three periods" (2:8).[4] "[W]hen we inquire in detail about the vows of all the buddhas, we hear that they were unable to save women burdened with the five obstacles and evildoers who have committed the five grave offenses" (4:3).[5]

3. The view that women possess the five obstacles and three submissions and cannot be saved in this condition. "[Women are] wretched creatures of deep evil karma, burdened with the five obstacles and the three submissions" (1:10).[6] "Because the bodily existence of women is defined by the five obstacles and the three submissions, they are burdened with deep evil karma exceeding that of men" (5:7).[7] This view is most prevalent in Rennyo's letters.

4. The view that held women in contempt. "We must realize that, unbeknownst to others, all women have deep evil karma; whether of noble or humble birth, they are wretched beings" (5:14),[8] "because of the depth of their evil karma and doubts" (1:10).[9]

The first two types of letters appear to address both men and women, while the latter two seem to be addressed specifically to women. The difference in the various letters is thought to derive from the objective in each letter. Moreover, the fact that so many letters show Rennyo to be extremely conscious of women reflects upon his deep concern for the salvation of women. Regarding the condescending and disparaging language in the latter two examples, this point needs to be discussed as a direct problem related to Rennyo's view of women. However, in order to examine Rennyo's efforts to liberate women, I would first like to interpret his expressions of women in the context of the age in which they lived and to show that women in fact viewed themselves in that way. The later results from such expressions are a different matter. Regarding this point, Rennyo's ideas on the salvation of women, their birth into the Pure Land, and becoming a buddha, he explains that "women can be saved all the more so, because they are the worst human beings with deep and grave defilements." This hermeneutic of what can be classified as *nyonin shōki* (女人正機, the idea that the Buddha's compassion is directed toward women) can be seen as derived from Shinran's theory of *akunin shōki* (悪人正機), wherein the Buddha's message is understood as explicitly for the salvation of the evil. This is the explanation, for example, given by Kasahara Kazuo.[10] On the other hand, there is also the idea that Rennyo interpreted "evil and ordinary beings of the Last Dharma Age and women who possess the five obstacles and three submissons" to represent "all us sentient beings." In this view, he equated women, evil persons, and "us," stressing the idea that both men and women could equally achieve buddhahood. This is the interpretation of Ikeda Yūtai.[11]

Although these views split on the matter, they both reflect the fact that Rennyo lived in an age in which the prejudice and exclusion of women was rooted in the contempt toward them from an earlier time as well as from the beginnings of Buddhism, when achieving buddhahood was based on the idea of "transforming into a man" or "changing from a woman and becoming a man." Living in an age when such views were prevalent and when the existence of women in the buddha lands could not be imagined, Rennyo boldly and clearly taught the idea of women's salvation (birth in the Pure Land and achieving buddhahood) and reached the hearts of many women. Furthermore, this position was connected to the realization of the theme of Rennyo's life work in reviving the teachings of Shinran.

Women in Kyōgen

There have been many discussions regarding the reasons why Rennyo was so dedicated to the salvation of women, more so than other religious figures. One reason was Rennyo's personal experiences such as the separation from his mother in his early childhood, the antagonism toward his stepmother, his having to part with his own children when he was young and poor, and the deaths of four wives and seven daughters.[12] In addition, Rennyo was acutely aware of the powerful role that women played through his contact with people from all walks of life.[13]

Here, I would like to examine the circumstances of women in that period through their portrayal in the comical plays of *kyōgen*, a popular form of theater in the Muromachi period (1392–1573) and of course still performed today. Kyōgen plays, which are mainly set in the agrarian villages in the provinces around Kyoto, "express events and situations rooted in reality and reenact the daily lives of its nameless characters in the colloquial language of the time."[14] Among these are various comical plays in which women are the central character, known as *onna kyōgen* (woman kyōgen), and those that play on the themes of choosing a son-in-law, having him move to the wife's family, or the fighting that went on between the husband and the father-in-law, known as *muko kyōgen* (son-in-law kyōgen). All such works vividly depict the daily lives of commoners and the relationship between families and between husband and wife. Here is an excerpt from a short play entitled *Hōshi ga haha* that offers a candid insight to the conditions of commoners:[15]

HUSBAND (*in a drunken state*): I'm giving you leave. Get out!...How can you not leave when your husband is telling you to do so!

WIFE: What a sad thing you say!...I feel sorry for our son who will be left alone....My parents would be surprised to hear what you said. But I think it best that I return to my parents' home.

(*Later the husband awakens from his drunken stupor to find that his wife is gone.*)

HUSBAND: Have you seen a woman about twenty years in age? The mother of our child works hard for us all year round. In the spring, she gathers fern. In the summer, she plants rice. In the autumn, she harvests the rice. In the winter, she weaves. The clothes she weaves, our trousers, our coats, our summer kimono, who will do the weaving? I miss my dear wife, the mother of our child.

(*In the end, the husband finds his wife and joyously celebrates.*)

HUSBAND: Come here, my sweet wife, come here.

WIFE: Yes, yes, I understand.

(*And the story ends happily.*)

In this story, the wife, given leave by her husband, returns to her parents' home. Here we see that a woman in a patrilocal marriage is relatively weak and submissive to her husband. On the other hand, the words of the husband reveal that the young wife is not only the mother of their child but a vital existence in operating the daily labors of a small-scale farmhouse. Along with childrearing, the wife engages in various farming activities throughout the year, and in the winter she weaves the family's entire wardrobe. Year in, year out, her days are filled with work in order for the family to be self-sufficient. One can see that the survival of a family is dependent on the wife.

In another example of *onna kyōgen* we find a slightly older couple in the play *Oko sako*.[16] Here the story develops around the exchange between Oko and his wife over how to press charges against their neighbor, Sako, whose cow ate their crops:

> OKO: This year, they say, is a bumper crop. My rice field has yielded a beautiful crop and I am so happy.
>
> WIFE: As you say, my lord. Your rice field has yielded well and there is nothing more felicitous than this.
>
> OKO: It is thanks to you, who have worked so hard. Certainly, this is most satisfying.
>
> WIFE: If you say so. It was worth it and I am all the more pleased.... However, you and I have both broken our backs to harvest this crop and that Sako's cow ate our crops. This is most disheartening....
>
> OKO: Could you, my wife, go and put this forth to the lord of our landed estate?
>
> WIFE: How can I go to the lord while you are here? Isn't it for you to go to the lord?
>
> OKO: ...It is no wonder that everyone praises my wife so. I am not good with words...so I am asking you to prepare the case as if you were the arbiter, for you surpass men.

From this dialogue, we find that the relationship between husband and wife seems close to that of lord and servant; the husband and wife use different second-person adjectives to address each other that reflect the disparity of their positions.[17] Moreover, even though they worked together to plant their field, the husband expresses it as "my field" and the wife acknowledges this fact by referring to it as "your field." Nonetheless, though it was considered the man's duty to bring the issue to the arbiter, his recognition of her superior "way with words" leads to the wife training the husband on exactly what to say. In the end, the more the wife's abilities are manifested as she practices the litigation with her husband, the more comical the scene becomes.

Themes about strong-minded women, such as in *Oko sako*, often appear in the *muko kyōgen* plays about son-in-laws, in which various customs of welcoming the son-in-law to the wife's home are depicted. Many of these play upon the tension when the bridegroom first enters his father-in-law's home, and this is where the comedy develops. In this category are also plays that focus on the exchange between young newlyweds. In such plays, the portrayal of the young husband and wife is often that of an uneducated, uncultured husband coupled with an intelligent wife, such as in the scene in *Ryōri mukō* in which a husband is impressed by his wife's ability to read and write when she makes sense of a document on the proper etiquette for son-in-laws.[18] In another example, this one from *Okadayū*, a husband forgets the name of a sweet that he was treated to at his father-in-law's house, so he has his wife memorize the poems in the *Wakan rōeishū* until he is able to recall the name.[19] In these situations, the comic element is from an ignorant husband paired with a wife of superior upbringing and abilities who is praised for these qualities even by the husband.

There are also plays, such as *Mizukake muko*, that depict a husband who is extremely conscious of his status as son-in-law having a water fight with a father-in-law who cultivated the field next to his.[20] The wife comes across her husband and her father fighting and is caught between the two. Nonetheless, eventually she takes the side of her husband and runs off with him hand-in-hand. A similar ending can be seen in *Morai muko*, in which a drunken husband goes to his father-in-law to retrieve his wife. In both plays, there is a strong bond between the couples that surpasses parent–child relations.[21]

There are also kyōgen depicting the importance of a woman's social role. In *Kawarataro* and *Oba ga sake*, for example, it is a woman who makes the rice wine essential for the family's livelihood but who becomes entangled in problems with a husband or nephew who thinks the best way to sell it is through intimidation or extortion.[22]

Through these examples, we can glimpse the actual living situations of the commoners of the time. Moreover, the cooperation between husband and wife in the management of small-scale agrarian families, in addition to family life and the relationship between husband and wife, especially regarding the family's financial well-being, is dependent on the abilities of the wife, who is often portrayed as a loud, boisterous woman who supports every aspect of the family's livelihood.

Kyōgen generally shows us a good-for-nothing husband with a wife who, in such plays as *Ishigami*, *Kamabara*, and *Mikazuki*,[23] laments that "He views the triple-world [the entire universe] as his home but has no regard whatsoever for his household. Day and night, he sleeps where he pleases and has me fix the leaking roof." The husband typically praises his wife, as in *Ishigami*: "Though my woman is especially boisterous, when it comes to taking care of the house, she works hard night and day." This vivid contrast between a good-for-nothing husband and a strong-willed, hardworking wife who places the utmost importance on her family invites laughter. Of course, there is some exaggeration in these stories, but the audience sees realistic examples and, in many cases, even in the fights between husband and wife, a deep bond between the two is emphasized in a way that people can relate to and feel comfortable laughing at.

Another example of the importance of women at this time can be seen in the local festivals, or *matsuri*. Among the relatively advanced, well-established rural communities in the traditional five regions in and around the capital, village cooperative associations were formed at this time to run the local festivals, which were both public events and political occasions. In addition to the "shrine groups," or *miyaza*, composed of men of stature to supervise the festivals, there were also some separate women's groups called *nyōbō za* or *onna za*, in which women gathered on their own with wine to enjoy their own company. There are examples of women having important roles, from providing offerings to the deities all the way up to supervising the running of the festival itself.[24] This was a remnant from ancient times, when women played religious roles in making *sake* and overlooking divine affairs. Moreover, as rice cultivation spread, land came to be used year round and agricultural output increased, and women tended also to other work related to agrarian life. Thus the woman's economic arena expanded and their position was strengthened. Further, with the development of transportation and a merchandise economy, people began to trade, and as an economy based on selling and buying goods developed, women again became involved. In *Shichijūichiban shokunin utaawase*, a collection of poems and pictures of seventy-one artisans showing the various working situations of the Muromachi period, the merchants and salespeople of food items, clothes, and sundries, such as *sake*, rice cakes, rice, beans, fish, tofu, noodles, cotton, sashes, cloth, wrapping paper for kimono, and brooms, are all women.[25] In addition, many documents show that space was rented to women to operate stores and that some women were in charge of fixed marketplaces in town for exchanging goods. Women also were active in weaving, textiles, dyeing, and embroidery, and there were many women artisans.[26]

Nonetheless, these instances were localized. Even if women were active in certain economic sectors, the structure of the society was based on class and a patriarchal system. The power relationship between men and women did not equal change. According to Tabata Yasuko, "In every strata of society in the Muromachi period, the patriarchal structure was reinforced. Moreover, the power to divorce lay in the hands of the husband. Husbands and wives were like lords to servants."[27] Society in general was pervaded with a value system in which males occupied a dominant position. Therefore women with talents, knowledge, learning, wit, or wisdom who exceeded their husbands became the protagonists on stage through laughter. Moreover, a plot like that of *Dondarō*, which depicts a main wife as "a boisterous woman in the southern part of the capital" and a concubine as "a gentle woman in the northern part of the capital," is probably realistic. No matter how much ability a woman had, "even a useless man was a man" (*Oko sako*) and "even an untalented man was a man" (*Okadayū*). In such a period and in such social circumstances, the hardships of women in daily life were abundant.

Buddhism's Ambivalent Legacy for Women

Rennyo's letters emphasize repeatedly that if women realize their karmic evil through the five obstacles and three submissions and if they without a doubt take refuge in Amida Buddha, then they will all be saved. Buddhist thought, which from ancient times had a great influence on the spiritual world of the Japanese in various respects, controlled the daily lives of the common people. The acceptance of the idea of the five obstacles of women is an example of its impact. In *Ryojin hishō* (Secret Selection of Rafter Dust), a collection of popular *imayō* poems from the late Heian period compiled by Emperor Goshirakawa (1127–1192), many poems reflect this idea. "Though women possess the five obstacles and are far from the purity of the Pure Land, just as the lotus blooms in muddy water, even the naga princess became a buddha." "If the naga princess became a buddha, then may I also become so? The clouds of the five obstacles are thick, but the Tathagata's moon ring cannot be concealed."[28] Regardless of how one became a buddha, the idea of the five obstacles in regard to women began to penetrate the people's minds. In Rennyo's letters as well, the emphasis on the five obstacles and three submissions was acknowledgement that this idea was widely held among women. In *Ryōjin hishō* one poem expresses the feelings of the many who lamented having to go against the Buddhist precept of taking life: "Even if we are living in this world of impermanence, we must work as fishermen at sea and as hunters in the mountains to make a living. By doing this, we are distanced from all the buddhas. What are we to do in our lives hereafter?" Because of these issues, Shinran (see *Tannishō*) and later Rennyo suggested the need to clarify the salvation for hunters and fishers (see *Letters* 1:3).

When the ideas on the five obstacles and three submissions of women came together with the spreading idea of defilement and impurity, the female biological features of menstruation and childbirth came to be labeled the "red impurity" and the "white impurity," which only women possessed, thus reinforcing the view that women were defiled and must be excluded from sacred places of purity. The spread of the belief in the *Blood Pool Sutra* (*Ketsubonkyo*)[29] in the fifteenth century, around the time Rennyo's letters were written, took place within such a context. An apocryphal text, the *Blood Pool Sutra* explains that the bleeding that accompanies childbirth defiles the earthly deities.[30] Women defile the waters by using in the mountain streams to wash their clothes that were soiled by childbirth; and when they offer tea brewed with that water, they defile holy people (and by extention, the buddhas and gods as well). Through this sin of defiling the buddhas and gods, women are destined to fall into the "Blood Pool Hell." It is said that this sutra already existed in Japan from around the fourteenth century, and by the early fifteenth century there were records of mountain ascetics of the Tendai lineage who would throw this sutra down onto a place they regarded as the Blood Pool and would hold prayers, in order to save women who fell into the Blood Pool Hell because of the blood defilement of childbirth or who themselves died while giving birth. From that time until the modern period, this idea prevailed in the minds of many. According to Miyata Noboru, even in the early modern period, at the women's Nenbutsu associations (*nenbutsukō*) in the Kantō region they recited such poems as "Being born as a woman, in order to give birth, one has her menstruation, which is impure and defiled. Be careful not to wash this in the rivers" and "Being born as a woman, repeatedly read the *Blood Pool Sutra*. Uphold others and uphold yourself, together wishing to be born in the Pure Land."[31]

As in Rennyo's own life, there were many at that time living in extreme poverty who had to face war, natural disasters, famine, epidemics, and the loss of loved ones. In addition to the [inevitable] separations brought about by these calamities, people also faced separations due to abortion, infanticide, and having to abandon or sell off their children. Like Kyōgen, there are several well-known Nō plays, also loved in the Muromachi period, that depict the heroine as a crazy and frantic mother looking for her lost child. In the opening scene of *Sakuragawa*[32] a slave trader announces himself; this is a story about a child who was bought and then resold. In *Hyakuman*[33] a mother is looking for her child in a crowd. They both sing: "I parted with my husband because he has died, and I parted in life with my child, how my heart lies confused." In other rlays there are songs that portray a child who is abandoned because of his physical handicaps as in *Semimaru*,[34] or because of another's lie about him (*Yoroboshi*).[35] Parting in life and in death, or longing to be with a child, who may be dead or alive, a mother's heart continues to wander in darkness. "Truly, each time, I am born and reborn, I am tied to the path of parent and child. In this short life, the ties to the triple-world, where does it eternally point to?" (*Hyakuman*)

Surrounded over and over by notions of karmic evil such as the five obstacles and three submissions, defilement by menstrual blood and giving birth, dealing with the familial separation or discord with the difficulties of living a life of attachments, which themselves are difficult to sever, women who aspired for liberation were compelled to wish for Birth into the Pure Land in the next life, for the karmic gain from making donations or entry into monastic life; they look with anticipation toward asceticism, shamanism, magic, folk belief, and superstition. It is also thought that belief in the *Blood Pool Sutra* and its pictorial explanations by nuns are manifestations of such tendencies:

> While women's hearts may be true, their inclination to doubt is serious and their tendency to regard many things as impure is even more difficult to cast off. Lay women in particular, absorbed in practical matters and concerns for children and grandchildren, only devote themselves to matters of this life.... They go through their days aimlessly. This is the way most [women] live.... They should put aside their inclination to engage in sundry practices, cast off all thought of courting favor with the kami and other buddhas through expressions of adulation ... and accepting their evil and useless state, adopt an attitude of taking refuge in the Tathāgata [Amida] in the most profound way. (*Letters* 2:1)[36]

The reason that Rennyo, who even in his old age was said to have traveled so often to the various provinces to spread the teachings that "the straw of his shoes was worn out and cut to pieces" (*Kikigaki* 303), wrote this, which was known as the "letter [encouraging] repeated practice" (*osarai no sho*), was perhaps because he grasped the situation of many women as they really were and was able to see into their hearts without any illusions. Understanding that they were tossed about by hardship and feelings of doubt, envy, attachment, anxiety, and sorrow in their daily lives, Rennyo hoped to inspire them to brighten the darkness in their hearts and rediscover their joy and the will to live. At the same time, Rennyo himself saw this as a theme in his own life.

Rennyo and the Creation of Women's Groups

Rennyo was especially concerned with the salvation of housewives, that is, women who lived as lay followers, who supported the daily life of the family, who bore and raised the children, and who, in shouldering various hardships, simply could not enter monastic life. The terms frequently found in Rennyo's letters that refer to female disciples or devotees (*ama-nyūdō, ama-nyōbō*) are said to indicate wives in their thirties and forties.

Rennyo thus explained that the key to that salvation was found in the words of Shinran's poems (*goeika*): "In this world, it is better to put aside thoughts of becoming a nun [to tread the traditional path], just accept whatever horns you end up with as a female cow." Echoing the maxim "Though one's head may be shaven, his heart may not be," Rennyo added "Form is not necessary; the single [simple or pure] mind should be the foundation."[37] In other words, it is precisely the Original

Vow of Amida Buddha that will save someone who has not taken the tonsure and continues with normal life burdened with karmic sin. If one can only believe in the wonderous power of the Vow without doubt, one is sure to be received by the Buddha.

In this way, he explains, "This Other-Power faith—how readily we understand it!" "The Name [of the Buddha]—how readily we practice it!"[38] Therefore "women who have renounced the world while remaining in lay life" (*zaike no ama-nyōbō*)[39] and "unlettered women who have renounced the world" (*ichimon fuchi no ama-nyūdō*),[40] in other words, even uneducated and ignorant housewives who have neither read the sacred texts nor have specialized knowledge, if they seek salvation single-heartedly from Amida Buddha, are saved. They are saved not from some special dispensation but precisely because they do not argue the issue with logic but accept their karmic limitations of their own accord and earnestly trust the Buddha that such women are welcomed. If housewives, who have much influence in the daily lives of ordinary families, can attain *shinjin*, then "even though they are not specialists, the Buddha's power will assist others to hear the rejoicing of such female religious [*ama-nyūdō*] and come to believe."[41] Thus the faiths of others, especially one's children and grandchildren, will be nurtured. Even from this point of view, the salvation of women was considered very important.

Rennyo also wrote, "Just get together, join together, and discuss the Buddha Dharma,"[42] always encouraging four or five people to gather together to discuss the Buddhist teachings. But we can take special note that he highly valued women's salvation through the fact that he organized religious discussion groups known as *kō* ("co-fraternities") that were restricted to women. Called women's group, wives' group, or renunciates' group (*nyoninkō* 女人講, *nyōbōkō* 女房講, *amakō* 尼講), they formed a community where women could speak out and be heard and could affirm their faith. These groups were opened as places to recite Buddhist gathas (songs), listen to Rennyo's letters, and have critical dialogue about their faith, thus deepening their belief. The reaffirmation of their Birth into the Pure Land in the afterlife through the reflection of their own life and forgetting about their daily hardships, human relations, and other worries gave them the will to live their present life. These *kō* thus were places where women had the opportunity to liberate themselves. Women were tied to a stratified social system in which prejudice and discrimination toward them were strong. In these meetings, restricted to women only, they could meet on equal grounds, free to discuss things openly; they could disclose to their friends the circumstances of their lives and their selves—their hardships, worries, anger, dissatisfaction, and also their ideas on faith. On occasion they probably "had time to leisurely spend a day and night with each other."[43] This opportunity can be thought of as the process and actualization of identity, of establishing their subjecthood, where the socially weak could escape their own minority consciousness and seek to take back their original self.

This form is interesting in that it corresponds to current theories on the liberation movement 500 years later; women aimed to change their personal and social situation in the latter half of the twentieth century. In the 1960s and 1970s, women created countless numbers of small groups with the goal of reforming awareness ("consciousness raising") through open discussions on the realities of their lives. For the first time, they were able to live as the subject of their own life, history, and movement and they decided that without this activity there would be no true freedom for women. They rejected the pattern of dependence on organizations and leaders that had been the norm up to that point and demanded that each person be her own subject. These new theories came to be called new or radical feminism, within the so-called second wave of feminism from the late 1960s on. In any case, clearly these women's groups in Rennyo's time (*nyoninkō*) promised salvation in the next life at the same time as they provided a radiant moment in which women could enjoy their present life in happiness and peace. In that sense, they have contributed much to the liberation of women.

However, a problem remains. "Though there are a myriad of things that sadden and trouble us, take heart in the Buddha Dharma that you will be saved in the afterlife, no matter what. If you rejoice, this is the Buddha's benevolence."[44] If this call were established as a belief, one may perhaps personally attain salvation. And the belief that no matter how difficult things may be now, the affirmation that one will surely be saved by the hands of Amida and born in the Pure Land after death gives one the strength to live through the present moment and to accept and endure the realities of life. However, it is one thing to consider this in a world in which human rights, equality, and social justice are a given and conclude that this kind of religious thinking is not conducive to the struggle to realize those ideals, but it is quite another to suggest that for people in the medieval period who had no indication that such changes were even possible the conviction of personal salvation in the next life led to such acceptance of their current situation that they lost the vector of their will to revolution. This distinction is related to the point where the assessment of Rennyo's ideas on the salvation of women in later years diverged. Can it not be said, however, that here a problematic point remains, and that theories on the opposition to oppression and liberation from it that had immense political circumstances such as the peasant movements of *ikko-ikki* cannot completely resolve it? Rennyo's teachings on the salvation of women in regard to their liberation undoubtedly was a definite contribution. However, from a historical perspective, it is seen over time through the present, is it not going too far to say that his method of teaching women's salvation was in danger of stereotyping the image of deeply sinful women with the idea of the five obstacles and three submissions?

Itsuki Hiroyuki characterized Rennyo as the man who possessed both "the sacred and the profane."[45] If we were to go by this description, we could then understand that because Rennyo considered the sacred to mean *shinjin* (faith, and by extension, the revival of Shinran's teachings), the most important theme in his life, he firmly confronted the secular or profane, which to him was reality, and used this scheme effectively. Thus, for the sake of the sacred, Rennyo was not afraid of being covered in the profane. In other words, his lifestyle was the fulfillment of living a dialectic between sacred and profane. Rennyo writes:

> In particular, take the laws of the state as your outer aspect, store Other-Power faith deep in your hearts, and take [the principles of] humanity and justice [*jingi*] as essential.[46]

[O]utwardly, take the laws of the state as fundamental and do not hold any of the kami, buddhas, or bodhisattvas in contempt; do not slander other sects or other teachings. Do not slight the provincial military governors or local land owners, but meet fixed yearly tributes and payments of officials in full. Besides that, take (the principles of) humanity and justice as essential. Inwardly, rely singleheartedly and steadfastly on Amida Tathāgata for (Birth in the Pure Land) in the afterlife.[47]

This emphasis on the laws of the state and the principles of humanity and justice as the basis of faith was an expedient to carry through *shinjin* as the basis of faith. In *Eigen kikigaki*, Rennyo states, "I would first like to teach three people the Dharma. The three are the priest, the village councelor, and the village head, each in their own capacity. If they come to believe in Buddhism, then people everywhere will come to believe the Buddha Dharma, which will no doubt prosper."[48] [By appealing to the village authority,] we can see the rational, shrewd, and directed way in which Rennyo went about accomplishing both the acquisition of faith and the spread of Shinran's teachings.

In regard to Rennyo's use of secular means to achieve the sacred end, I would also like to briefly discuss this as it relates to his relationship with the dominating class. With the exception of his third wife, Nyoshō (1448–1478), Rennyo's wives all came from powerful managerial families, perhaps as a result of the high social position of Honganji at the time. However, in terms of the treatment of his children, who were strategically placed in influential positions for future benefits, the situation was somewhat different. Beginning with arranging for his eldest son, Junnyo (1442–1483), and his ultimate successor, Jitsunyo (1458–1525), to be taken in by the Great Minister of the Left, Hino Katsumitsu, Rennyo established various relationships with aristocratic families such as the Hino for his other sons. He even went as far as to place his fourth daughter, Myōshū (1459–1537), in the household of the Shōgun Yoshimasa as a concubine (*sokushitsu*). In *Ransei tamayura*, Minagawa Hiroko wrote that Myōshū, later known as Sakyō Dayū, was presented as a concubine because Rennyo wanted to create a tie with [the power in] Kyoto and so presented his daughter to the shōgun in return for the latter's assistance to Honganji.[49]

Although the veracity of this story is uncertain, it is a fact that he used his daughter as leverage to draw himself closer to power and surely within the political conditions of the time he ascertained the effect of this plan to create his strategy realistically. Moreover, as a "stronghold of the Buddha Dharma," he stationed his many sons in various temples that served as the focal points in distinct areas, and placed his daughters as wives or concubines of ministers. This too was in line with his strategy. Utilizing the profane—the real—in order to achieve the sacred—the revival of the Buddha's Dharma—was greatly effective in expanding the teaching and establishing his religious organization. However, at the same time, with the later expansion of the organization, we see that worldly principles such as patriarchal authority and a hereditary system of authority came to take root. The realism of this unsurpassed realist and man of ideas was fully directed toward women as well. Starting with an objective recognition of how women actually lived and how they were commonly viewed in society, what Rennyo sought in his doctrine of the salvation of women was not only to confirm their salvation in the afterlife but also, by doing so, to provide a means for women to get beyond their present troubles so that they themselves could obtain the power to live subjectively.

Notes

This chapter originally appeared as "Rennyo to josei no sukui: oboegaki" 蓮如と女性 の救い: 覚え書き, in *Rennyo no sekai* 蓮如の世界, ed. Ōtani Daigaku Shinshū Sōgō Kenkyūjo, Kyoto: Bun'eidō, 1998, 699–714.

1 Minowa Shūhō, "Ofumi ni manabu, Part I" in *Dobo*, 1995, p. 7. The order of the four categories have been rearranged in my essay.

2 SSZ 3.404; Rogers, 144.

3 SSZ 3.433; Rogers, 181.

4 SSZ 3.433; Rogers, 182.

5 SSZ 3.478; Rogers, 221.

6 SSZ 3.416; Rogers, 160.

7 SSZ 3.504; Rogers, 247.

8 SSZ 3.511; Rogers, 253.

9 SSZ 3.416; Rogers, 161.

10 Kasahara Kazuo, *Fumetsu no hito, Rennyo* (Tokyo: Sekai Seiten Kankō Kyōkai, 1993), 164–165. See also his *Nyonin ōjō shisō no keifu* (Tokyo: Yoshikawa Kōbunkan, 1975).

11 Ikeda Yūtai, "Rennyo Shōnin no nyonin jōbutsu setsu no kadai," *Shinran kyōgaku* 60 (1992), 80–91.

12 See Mori Ryūkichi, *Rennyo*, in *Kōdansha gendai shinsho* 550. (Tokyo: Kōdansha, 1979). See also Yamazaki Ryūmyō, "Rennyo ni okeru shinkō kōzō ni tsuite (3)" *Musashino joshi daigaku kiyō* 18.

13 Ibid.

14 From the *kaisetsu* of Koyama Hiroshi, ed., *Kyogenshū* (Tokyo: Iwanami Shoten, *Nihon koten bungaku taikei* 42, 1960), 3.

15 The script of *Hōshi ga haha* can be found in Koyama Hiroshi, ed., *Kyōgenshū*, vol. 42–43 of *Nihon koten bungaku taikei*, and has been translated in Karen Brazell, ed. *Twelve Plays of the Noh and Kyōgen Theaters* (Ithaca, N.Y.: Cornell University, East Asian Papers, no. 50, 1990).

16 A version of *Oko sako* is found at *Kyōgenshū* 2, vol. 43 of *Nihon koten bungaku taikei*.

17 He addresses her with the second-person pronoun *wagoryo* and she calls him *konata*. Both these forms express affection toward someone intimate, yet they also mark a disparity of station, as *wagoryo* is directed to an equal or someone of lower status and *konata* implies an unmistakable degree of politeness or deference.

18 *Ryōri muko*, traditional kyōgen, is in the *Kyōgenki*, ed. Hashimoto Asao in *Shin nihon koten bungaku taikei*, vol. 58.

19 *Okadayū* is published at vol. 4 of *Ōkura toramitsubon kyōgen-shū*, ed. Hashimoto Asao, in *Kotenbunko* (Tokyo: Koten Bunko, 1990–1992). *Wakan rōeishū* is a poetry collection compiled in 1012 by Fujiwara Kintō (d. 1041) containing poems written in both Japanese and Chinese. There are 804 poems, so when the husband gives the wife the task of memorizing them he is not only asking a nearly impossible mental feat for her but one that would stretch on seemingly infinitely in time.

20 A version of *Mizukake muko* can also be found at *Kyōgenshū*, vols. 42–43 of *Nihon koten bungaku taikei*.

21 A version of *Morai muko* can also be found at Kyōgenshū, vols. 42–43 of *Nikon koten bungaku taikei*.

22 A version of *Kawarataro* is published in vol. 3 of *Ōkura toramitsubon kyōgen shū*, ed. Hashimoto Asao, but *Oba ga sake* is in Kyōgenshū, vol. 42–43 of *Nihon koten bungaku taikei*.

23 *Ishigami*, *Kamabara*, and *Mikazuki* can all be found in Koyama Hiroshi, ed., Kyōgenshū, vol. 42–43 of *Nihon koten bungaku taikei*.

24 Sōgō Joseishi Kenkyūkai, ed., *Nihon josei no rekishi: onna no hataraki chūsei* (The History of Japanese Women: Women's Work in the Medieval Period) (Tokyo: Kadokawa Shoten, 1993).

25 There is a reproduction of a 1784 woodblock edition containing both pictures and text of the *Shichijūichiban shokunin utaawase* in *Edo kagaku koten sōsho*, vol. 6, ed. Higuchi Hideo et al. (Tokyo: Kōwa Shuppan, 1977).

26 Wakita Haruko, *Nihon chūsei joseishi no kenkyū* (Tokyo: Daigaku Shuppankai, 1992).

27 Tabata Yasuko, *Nihon chūsei joseishi ron*, (Tokyo: Hanawa Shobo, 1994), 285.

28 Enoki Katsurō, ed., *Ryojin hishō*, in *Shinchō Nihon koten shūsei*, vol. 31 (Tokyo: Shinchosha, 1979), 285.

29 There are various versions of the *Ketsubonkyō*, the full title of which is *Bussetsu daizō shōgyō kechibonkyō*. See *Zoku gunsho ruijū* 28, vol. 2, and the 1910 ed. of the *Dainihon zokuzōkyō* at 1-87-4.

30 Tagami Taishū, "Furoku: seisabetsu o jochōshita *Ketsubonkyō*," an appendix to his *Bukkyō to seisabutsu* (Tokyo: Tokyō Shoseki, 1992).

31 Miyata Noboru, "Josei to minkan shinkō" in *Nihon josei shi 3: Kinsei*, ed. Nihon Joseishi Sōgō Kenkyūkai (Tokyo: Tokyō Daigaku Shuppankai, 1982), 238.

32 *Sakuragawa* can be found in many editions. See Koyama Hiroshi et al., eds, *Yōkyokushū* 2, vol. 59 in *Shinpen Nihon koten bungaku zenshū* (Tokyo: Shōgakkan, 1998).

33 *Hyakuman* can be found in the first volume of *Yōkyokushū*, ed. Yokomichi Mario et al., *Nihon koten bungaku taikei*, vol. 40.

34 The Nō play *Semimaru* is at Koyama Hiroshi et al., eds, *Yōkyokushū* 2, vol. 34 in *Nihon koten bungaku zenshū*. Tokyo: Shōgakkan, 1975.

35 *Yoroboshi* can be found in the first volume of *Yōkyokushū*, ed. Yokomichi Mario et al., *Nihon koten bungaku taikei*, vol. 40.

36 SSZ 3.424. The translation is that of the editors due to errors in Rogers, 171–172.

37 *Kikigaki* 24. SSZ 3.538, where it is entry number 25.

38 *Letters* 2:15. SSZ 3.448; Rogers, 192.

39 *Letters* 5:3. SSZ 3.501; Rogers, 244.

40 *Letters* 5:2. SSZ 3.500; Rogers, 242.

41 *Kikigaki* 96. SSZ 3.556, where it is entry 95.

42 *Kikigaki* 201. SSZ 3.581.

43 Oguri Junko, *Nyonin ōjō* (Kyoto: Jinbun Shoin, 1987), 127.

44 *Kikigaki* 300. SSZ 3.608, where it is entry 298.

45 Itsuki Hiroyuki, *Rennyo: seizoku guyū no ningenzō* (Tokyo: Iwanami Shinsho, 1994).

46 *Letters* 2:6, SSZ 3.434; Rogers, 180.

47 *Letters* 3:13, SSZ 3.473; Rogers, 215–216.

48 *Eigen kikigaki*. Written between 1521 and 1533, this was a record of Eigen 栄玄, priest of Jutokuji in Kaga. At SSS 2.588.

49 Minagawa Hiroko, *Ransei Tamayura* (Tokyo: Kodansha, 1995), 119, 219.

6

KINYRŪ SHIZUKA
TRANSLATED BY WILLIAM LONDO

The *Ikkō-shū* as Portrayed in Jesuit Historical Documents

In the latter half of the fifteenth century, as a result of the determined efforts of Rennyo, abbot of Honganji, the religious organization known as *ikkō-shū* 一向宗 was established and soon came to have such power that its influence was felt throughout society. Research aimed at better understanding the situation at that time has progressed significantly through studies of Honganji in the Sengoku era as well as studies of Rennyo and successive generations of leaders of the organization. However, the nature of proselytization by these organizations in various areas, and the actual situation in these areas, has not yet been ascertained, because the historical documents that record the situation on the front lines simply do not exist in the collections of Honganji and other temples.

Certain Jesuit historical documents are a valuable resource for remedying this lacuna. Francis Xavier first arrived in Kagoshima in 1549, fifty years after the death of Rennyo. From that time on, many missionaries energetically spread Catholic teachings throughout Kyūshū and Shikoku and the Kinai region of Japan. These missionaries made a large number of minutely detailed reports concerning the state of the various Buddhist schools they encountered, including information about their teachings. Records of this sort reach into the first half of the seventeenth century, but because the purpose of this chapter is to illuminate the situation of the *ikkō-shū* during the *Sengoku* era, it will survey only those records covering the century following the death of Rennyo, that is, up to the end of the sixteenth century.

Because the credibility of such documents is affected by the level of comprehension of the missionaries as "hearers" and the level of understanding they conveyed in their reporting as "speakers," these documents may be seen as having secondary or tertiary value at best. Furthermore, the appropriateness of terms used in translation must also be considered, though even among specialists in Japanese history there is virtually no one who is able to read all the documents of the Sengoku era and completely ascertain their meaning. Moreover, given that questions remain about the extent to which Japanese "speakers" of the time concretely grasped the teachings and true circumstances of the religious schools to which they belonged, it is possible to see particularly important Japanese documents from this period as having relatively lesser or greater value.

The Jesuit documents partly tell what the missionaries heard and partly tell how they felt about it. The latter parts unquestionably contain malicious and self-righteous statements, but because the missionaries' main intent was to grasp the actual situations of the various Buddhist sects they encountered, their records of what they heard are not necessarily completely distorted.

Buddhas and Bodhisattvas according to the Jesuits

First let us consider a letter from 1562 found in the *Iesusu kaishi nihon tsūshin* (*Communiqués from Japan by Jesuit Missionaries*).[1] It reads:

> There are two main types of *hotoke* idols (Mida and Shaka), and from these have arisen ten religious sects...one of these hotokes is called Amida 阿弥陀. The first character of the name Amida, *a* 阿, refers to all male saints. The second character, *mi* 弥, refers to all female saints. The third character, *da* 陀, means all will be saved...the name Amida means that every male and female saint will be saved (1). The pagans chant the name of Amida with great enthusiasm, and in May when the barley harvest is finished, they make offerings of barley to those who serve this Buddha and request prayers for the souls of their ancestors. They form into groups and go into the streets chanting "Amida butsu," and dance while parading (2)....As the child of the King of the East, Amida married and had two children (Kannon and Seishi), but after his wife died, he undertook many ascetic practices. Looking to her, he made forty-eight vows in order that the devout would be saved, and in order to atone for girls he canonized his wife as a saint and preached that girls would not be saved unless they made offerings. The two children gathered their mother's bones and kept them as sacred treasures (3). Furthermore, she is revered as the god of medicine as well. The two children are the sun and the moon (4), and it is said that whoever calls their names will be saved. One of these children has many disciples. Three sects stem from this head (Jōdoshū, Shinshū, Jishū); these sects attract many people, and a large majority of Japanese people belong to them.

This quote has the sense of being only a rough outline of how tathāgatas and bodhisattvas figure in Jōdoshū, and it is tempting to disregard it because today we know that members of the *ikkō-shū* probably would not have made such assertions. However, looking at this passage in detail reveals an unexpected reality. The section marked (1) contains the so-called "esoteric reading" (*mikkyōteki jikunshaku*) of the Buddha's name,[2] that is, the belief that each individual sacred character carried a sacred meaning and power, a belief that was generally accepted in the religious world of that time.

With reference to the section of the quote marked (2), in a passage treating the *tendō* nenbutsu custom in the early modern gazetteer called *Shinpen Hitachi kokushi* we read:

> Every year in the third month...men and women gather...chant prayers [*ganmon*], beat drums, ring gongs, chant the nenbutsu....They begin at daybreak and

continue until sundown. Sometimes they chant hymns praising the name of the Buddha [*butsumyō wasan*]....When the barley harvest is finished...when the time to sow rice arrives, it is a nenbutsu performed for the purpose of praying to the deity Tendō for the calming of wind and water.[3]

It seems possible that what is described in section (2) is the custom of the *tendō* nenbutsu. Needless to say, a variety of incantational nenbutsu practices besides the *tendō* nenbutsu were omnipresent in the early part of the Edo era, including the *himachi* nenbutsu and the *higan* nenbutsu. Associated with agricultural rituals, these were used in ceremonial offerings to the spirits of ancestors and prayers for good harvest. Iba Myōrakuji[4] was a powerful temple in the Bukkōji sect until 1739, when it switched its affiliation to the Honganji sect. In its archives is an illuminated altar scroll (*kōmyō honzon*) attributed to Shinran in which the sacred name of the Buddha (*myōgō* 名号) is the central image, but this particular scroll is also called the "agriculture sacred name" or "insect-repelling sacred name" and is known for playing a major role in efforts to promote agriculture in villages during the Edo era.[5]

As for section (4), there are at least three works written by Zonkaku (1290–1373), the eldest son of Kakunyo (1270–1351) of Honganji that relate similar ideas. According to his *Shojin hongai shū*, the Buddha Yakushi (Bhaiṣajyaguruvaiḍūrya-prabha) rules over the Jōruri world to the east, while the Bodhisattva Kannon (Avalokiteśvara) is revealed to be the heavenly son of the sun (Nittenshi) and Seishi (Mahāsthāmaprāpta) is in fact the heavenly son of the moon (Gattenshi). Likewise, the *Kenmyōshō* states, "The light of the sun is a manifestation of Kannon; the light of the moon is the authority of Seishi."[6] A belief system combining Amida and Yakushi in the form of a married couple is quite interesting indeed.[7]

With respect to section (3), which contains the striking phrase "sacred treasure," in the *Hōonki* of Zonkaku we read:

> In the *Shinjikan kyō* we find that...Kannon manifests the profound virtue of a great teacher and is crowned [*hōkan*] with Amida. Seishi shows his deep gratitude to [his] mother and father, and in the midst of winter, [he] inters the bones of his mother and father.[8]

Also, in Zonkaku's *Kenmyōshō* we read:

> Kannon illuminates the forms of all sentient beings in the five realms with the light from within himself, and saves them from their agony. Numerous beams of light radiate from the heavenly crown on the head of Seishi, producing many varieties of merit.

Zonkaku wrote the first of these works while he was living in Bingo (present-day Hiroshima Prefecture), and the second he wrote at the request of Meikō (1164–1227), who was representative of the Araki branch of Shinshū in Bingo.[9]

The word crown (*hōkan*) also appears often in *dangibon*, texts used for teaching that often include notions drawn from popular religion. In the *Shinshū shidō shō* by Zonkaku (essentially a copy of the contents of his *Hōonki*) and in the *Bumo kyōyōshō* we find, "Out of filial piety the Bodhisattva Seishi places the bones of his parents in an urn and wears it as a jewel in his crown." In the *Shichō onjuji* we also read, "Kannon wears the his master Amida Buddha in his crown." The *Jigō shōnin shinshi mondō* as well says, "Shōtoku Taishi...is the incarnation of Kannon Bodhisattva....And Kannon, the original essence (*honji*) [of Shōtoku], honors his own teacher by wearing Amida as a jewel in his crown.[10]

Writings such as the preceding suggest that the contents of the 1562 Jesuit letters are not mere fiction, but that the Jesuits did put effort into listening to the claims of the *ikkō-shū*. What the missionaries encountered was the northern *ikkō-shū*, but exactly what kind of *ikkō-shū* was it? That is to say, we should recognize existence of both the *ikkō-shū* of Bukkōji with Zonkaku as its doctrinal leader, and the *ikkō-shū* branch founded by Ryōgen (1295–1336), whose teacher was Meikō.[11] If we take this to be the case, we can say that the influence of the Meikō and Bukkōji branches of Shinshū encompassed a wide variety of buddhas and bodhisattvas based on Amida Nyorai, and that these groups, which carried on the functions of encouragement of agriculture, Yakushi (i.e., healing), and the interment of remains (*nōkotsu*), played a primary role in the daily life of the time. After the early part of the *sengoku* era, the Kōshōji lineage stemming from Bukkōji quickly spread over all of western Japan. But rather than spreading into areas where it had not been before, it seems this lineage inherited the doctrines of the Bukkōji and Meikō groups in a kind of "re-expansion."

Nenbutsu and the Buddha Name

Esoteric explications of the six characters of *na-mu-a-mi-da-butsu*, similar to those found in section (1) of the passage cited earlier, can be found in other *dangibon* as well. For example, in the *Shin ketsumyakushō* it is explained as follows:

> What is called the *hōben hosshin* [of Amida][12] is born from the two characters *a* + *un* 阿吽 [Skt. *a-hūṃ*]. If one holds Yang (*yō* 陽) for one thought-moment [*ichinen*] and one breath, and *a* 阿 for one breath, the character *mi* 弥 will come into existence as a result of this single-thought [contemplation]. By offering what is called "mind" 心, the *dharmatā* is realized. By contemplating Yin (*in* 陰), the character *da* 陀 will come into existence in the place where *un* is received....*Nan* 南 is the father, *mu* 无 is the mother. Therefore, the father is the Buddha name (*myōgō*), the mother is radiance [*kōmyō* 光明].[13]

Furthermore, in *Nihon kyōkai shi*,[14] the Jōdo shū six-character *myōgō* (i.e., *namu Amida Butsu*) is explained as follows: "the word *namu* 南無 includes the *a* for inhalation and *u* for exhalation."

This being the case, exactly how was the Shandao (613–681) explication of the phrase *namu-amida-butsu*, which occupied the mainstream position in the Jōdo sect, understood by the missionaries? The following interpretation appears in a communiqué from Hakata, Kyūshū, dated the ninth month of 1576: "'Amida' is the proper name of the idol; *Butsu* means 'redeemer,' and *namu* means 'please save us.' Because of this, when the three parts of the prayer are combined, it means 'Redeemer Amida, please save us.'"[15] However, it is not clear whether this explanation came from Rennyo's *Letters* or from Jōdo school sermons.

In any case, we know that the esoteric and Shandao explications of *namu-amida-butsu* intermingled and spread together at the end of the Sengoku era. It is difficult, however, to distinguish who opted for which interpretation. Rather, it seems more likely that Jōdo-shū and *ikkō-shū* adherents used these old and new interpretations together. If we press this argument further for the case of the *ikkō-shū*, it is impossible to verify any real spread of the so-called "Shinran branch" interpretation of *namu-amida-butsu*, perhaps because of its difficulty or abstractness. Moreover, it is important to note that the phrase "*tasuketamae*" (help me) in the *Letters* was not read as such; rather, it was read as "*sukuitamae*" (save me) after the fashion of the so-called "*Letter* to the ignorant of the Latter Age."[16] Given that salvation is perceived as a result of one's own efforts in an esoteric interpretation, it would be quite surprising if they had made an effort to avoid this kind of minor oversight.

There is an important reason why the missionaries paid attention to the equivalence between the *myōgō* and the nenbutsu. A 1573 communiqué notes that chanting the nenbutsu was the only way of "saving the soul," and that chanting it yielded salvation no matter what sins had been committed.[17] In the *Nihon Junsatsuki* of Valignano as well, we see "No matter what sins one has committed, [the priests]...chant the name of Amida or Shaka, and so long as one truly believes in the virtue of this act, those sins will be completely cleansed. Therefore, other atonments are completely unnecessary," and so the conclusion that "this is the same as the teaching of Luther" should all the more be regarded as dangerous.[18] Furthermore, concerning the voicing of the nenbutsu, the Jōdoshū nenbutsu is done in a loud voice, whereas the nenbutsu of the *ikkō-shu* is to be done quietly, "chanting in an inaudible voice."[19]

Ikkō-shū on the Front Lines

A letter dated the fifth day of the ninth month of Eiroku 9 (1566) allows us to comprehend what sort of everyday religious observances occurred in regional branch temples and *dōjō*:

> At the monastery, every morning at between three and four A.M. a bell is rung and all the members of this sect, regardless of the rain, snow, or cold and despite the very early hour, immediately get up, wait for the gate to the hall to be opened, and enter. Every day there is a sermon. The great majority of the members of this sect go to the monastery three times a day and offer prayers for long periods of time. All of the priests of the *ikkō-shū* are married.[20]

Thrice-daily practice, daily sermons, and long periods of prayer suggest a condition of very dedicated religious activity. It is unclear whether the "long hours of prayer" centers on the chanting of the nenbutsu or refers to the *shōshinge wasan* liturgy implemented by Rennyo in which Shinran's *Shōshin nenbutsu-ge* and *wasan* are recited. However, there were also Sakai merchants who "read the scriptures of Shaka every day in the same way the priests do,"[21] and if we suppose the "scriptures of Shaka" to be the *shōshinge wasan*, there is a good possibility that it was the *shōshinge wasan* that was recited at this monastery.

References to *ikkō-shū* adherents called *kojimoto, kuimoto,* or *koshimoto* appear frequently in Jesuit communiqués. The communiqués say they are "preachers," "supporters of the sect," "persons who marry as laypeople and are granted [marriage] licenses by the head of their sect," "persons who live off the offerings of ordinary citizens...part of which they support themselves with, and part of which they send off to the head temple in Sakai." They undoubtedly refer to the people running the *ikkō-shū dōjō* in general area of western Japan.[22] When the Christian documents report a heresy imbued in simple farmers and sharecroppers in the seaside village of Sumoto in Amakusa, Kumamoto,[23] it was probably the result of the head priest of this kind of *dōjō* as well. It should be added, however, that the Kirishitan ruler of Sumoto "dealt with this priest by decapitating him, displaying his head atop a stake stuck in the ground, and hanging the false scriptures (sutras, possibly a *shōban ofumi,* in the form of a scroll) around the neck of his corpse."

In the eyes of the missionaries, the *ikkō-shū* was a "sect of farmers."[24] Toyotomi Hideyoshi (1537–1598) also seemed to hold the perception that the membership of the *ikkō-shū* was "limited to peasants and those of humble birth."[25] There certainly were a few members of the *ikkō-shū* who were of samurai rank,[26] but the overwhelming majority were people of no rank. In examining Jesuit documents, one sees that the missionaries were most concerned with the conversion of "nobles" such as the proprietors of *shōen.* If they could convert the proprietors, the missionaries could expect that the vassals (*kashin*) and cultivators (*ryōmin*) of the proprietors would convert en masse. Of all the Buddhist sects, this approach most resembles the kind of proselytization promoted by the Nichiren-shū. It does not seen to have been practiced by the *ikkō-shū* at this time, however.

Among the correspondence with Honganji from the end of the medieval era and the beginning of the early modern era we find mention of "wife (*kaka*), girl (*hime*), mother, wife (*ofukuro*), daughter, lady-in-waiting (*otsubone*), widow," and so forth, listed individually.[27] The process of implementing Hideyoshi's cadastral survey program that was vigorously carried out throughout the nation at this time tended to displace women for "being of no use."[28] In one communiqué, Toyotomi Hideyoshi says, "The Buddhist priests are tied to men and tied to women, that is, they have close friendships with the parishioners of their temple (*danka*)," and because of this, the communiqué records that Hideyoshi "didn't much care for" the *ikkō-shū.*[29]

It is said that when a close confidant of the *sengoku daimyō* Ōtomo Sōrin (1530–1587) fell gravely ill, his aunt visited him. The Christian documents record that "At the end she said to him, 'Before long I will see you again in the paradise of Amida.'"[30] This woman, who was from Bungo (most of Oita prefecture), gave the *kue issho* 具会一処 sermon (concerning the gathering of the saved in the Pure Land) from the *Amida sutra* to demonstrate that salvation occurred at that place. Today there may be a variety of perspectives concerning whether or not this kind of thing is only "foolishness," but when one compares it with reported examples of the embarrassing activities practiced by the "new religions" in Japan, such as healing illness with "holy water" or reducing a fever by drinking water containing the dust of a picture of Christ,[31] the activities within a *vihāra* of 400 years ago do not seem that outmoded at all.

Absolutist Perceptions of the Honganji Suzerains

The Honganji suzerain who appears in Jesuit communiqués was the twenty-third abbot Kennyo (1543–1592). Records concerning how *ikkō-shū* followers viewed the head of the school at that time can be found in various places. For example, it was noted that the followers were as grateful to Kennyo "as they were grateful to Amida. The reason for this is that the followers believed that he and his successors were incarnations of Amida." Elsewhere it is said that Kennyo "was regarded as an oracle-giving holy priest, and it was believed that Amida himself lived within him."[32] Futhermore, "The farmers even consider the head priest of Honganji as a *deus* known as the living Amida."[33] In their view, Kennyo = incarnation of Amida = living Buddha.

Oddly enough, the *ikkō-shū*, referred to as "the Osaka sect *ikkō-shū*,"[34] is never called the sect of Shinran or the sect of Rennyo.[35] An awareness that the founder of the school and the one who revived it should be treated as important had not yet become widespread in the *ikkō-shū*; ultimately it was only the central object of worship (*honzon*) Amida Nyorai and whoever was the Honganji leader at the time whose existence was absolute.

The people of the time most commonly used the custom of prostration to show their respect. In one report it is noted that "When they saw him (Kennyo), whether of high rank or low, everyone without exception put their faces to the ground and prostrated themselves, and many tears flowed."[36] Not surprisingly, after his defeat in the Ishiyama war, Kennyo likewise could not help but "prostrate himself at the feet of" Toyotomi Hideyoshi as Hideyoshi looked down upon him from his high seat.[37] However, despite Hideyoshi's high position, his mother's response was different:

> When the door to his (Kennyo's) room was opened, everyone prostrated themselves, touching their heads to the floor and worshipping him, venerating him very much as if he were Amida himself. The mother of the *kanpaku* (Hideyoshi) also conducted herself the same way.

The prostration of the shōgun's mother was probably "done in the same manner as the great majority of Japanese farmers,"[38] and she had probably learned from their example. As a matter of fact, Hideyoshi's mother was not a *ikkō-shū* adherent; her funeral was conducted at the Daitokuji, a Rinzai Zen temple.

For eleven years the *ikkō-shū* organization led by Kennyo directed all its energy toward battling the authority of Oda Nobunaga (1534–1582). Among the various regional *sengoku daimyō* were those who looked favorably on the *ikkō-shū* and those who viewed it with caution. The wife of Ōtomo Sōrin had the impression that "a king [of the Togashi clan] had been exiled, and the province he had ruled (Kaga), was now a territory controlled by *ikkō-shū* priests."[39] Indeed, this statement was made in 1587, ten years before Hideyoshi's proscription of Christianity (from fear of similar territorial authority).

In his final years, Oda Nobunaga built Sōkenji Temple in Azuchi 安土 (in Gamō, Shiga prefecture) and made a broad appeal for worshippers. According to one view, the central image there is said to be of Nobunaga himself. The this-worldly benefits of visits to this temple are enumerated in the following:

When one comes to this place (Sōkenji) to worship, one's body is likewise enriched owing to the virtue of visiting this temple....People who have no heirs in the way of sons or daughters are at once blessed with offspring and good fortune, and they achieve great peace and prosperity....They live long lives of 80 years, and their illnesses are cured instantly.[40]

This sort of promise of immediate benefit reflects such a common and vulgar religious outlook that it seems almost too far from the image we have of Nobunaga as a pioneer carving out a new era. When one thinks of how being defeated by this kind of person must have affected the religious outlook of Japan for some time afterward, one cannot help but be deeply moved.

Conclusion

This essay has investigated what Jesuit communiqués from Japan have to say about the *ikkō-shū* of the time and its adherents. I have tried to present a glimpse of the "real image of *ikkō-shū* life" that is almost completely unobtainable from the archives of Honganji. Roughly another half-century of Jesuit documents remain. In addition, there are quite a few other records in existence, composed by the Dutch traders in Nagasaki and the embassies from Korea, which treat the world of Buddhism in the early modern (*kinsei*) era. Studying them is a task that is directly related to the one I have undertaken here, and my sense is that another look at the descriptions given here indicates that the *ikkō-shū* of the Sengoku era, in its very close coexistence with the Jōdoshū, looked to the people of that time as if it were in fact part of Jōdoshū. I will particularly bear this point in mind if I have an opportunity to read these reports and communiqués again.

Likewise, *dangibon* were not simply ways of playing with Buddhist sermons. It is quite possible they might best be regarded as guides used for proselytizing on the front lines, created under competing pressures from other religions, and motivated to show how to make the leap into the world of esotericism. If we tentatively accept this to be the case, then traces of the vigorous religious efforts of the *ikkō-shū* may be recoverable from them. At the very least, I believe that too much emphasis has been put on critiquing particular *dangibon* by seeing to what extent they diverge from the sermons of Shinran or Rennyo, and this had led to a lack of appreciation of their historiographic value.

Finally, I am concerned about the fact that these various kinds of documents have been handled in different ways and appear in a variety of different historical document collections. Naturally new translations are better than earlier ones, and I have therefore not taken into account which page of the earlier translation the later translation comes from. When I have used other studies, common sense dictates that I give references to these earlier scholars' works. In cases where I have used compilations of documents, the reason I have decided it was acceptable not to give recognition to the work of earlier scholars is that I was unable to ascertain to whom credit belonged.

Notes

This chapter originally appeared as "Iezusukai shiryō no ikkō-shū" イエズス会史料の一向宗, in *Rennyo no sekai* 蓮如の世界, ed. Ōtani Daigaku Shinshū Sōgō Kenkyūjo, Kyoto: Bun'eidō, 1998, 445–458.

1 Murakami Naojirō, trans., and Yanagiya Takeo, ed., *Iezusu kaishi Nihon tsūshin-jō*, in the series *Shin ikoku sōsho* [New Series on Documents from Foreign Countries] (Tokyo: Yūmatsudo, 1969), vol. 1, 297–298; hereafter *Nihon tsūshin*. Original text appears in *Cartas que os Padres e Irmãos da Companhia de Iesus escreuerão dos Reynos de Iapão & China* (Tenri, Japan: Tenri Central Library, 1972 [facsimile]), 99; hereafter *Cartas Que os Padres e Irmãos*. This section covers the years 1549 to 1587. Brackets appearing in documents quoted herein contain annotations by me.

2 Mitsui Shūjō, "Renshi kyōgaku no rekishiteki igi ni tsuite," *Shūgakuin Ronshū* 60 (August 1988), 32. The belief that characters themselves have sacred power is the flip side of the view that *zenchishiki* (those who help one on the Buddhist path) and tathāgatas (Nyorai) are equivalent.

3 *Shinpen Hitachi kokushi*, originally compiled in two volumes by Nakayama Nobuna (1787–1836) and Kurita Hiroshi (1835–1899) and published by Kanō Yozaemon in Mito in 1899. See reprint by Miyazaki Hōonkai and Hitachi shobō (1969), 630.

4 Iba Myōrakuji is located in Kanzaki–gun, Nōtogawa–chō, Shiga Prefecture.

5 This scroll is formally called the *Den Shinran hitsu kōmyō honzon*. See Nishiguchi Junko, "Ekeizu ni miru 'ie' no saishi, *Gekkan hyakka* 288 (October 1986), 18–29.

6 SSS 1.707 and 756. See also Matsumoto Takanobu, *Chūsei ni okeru honjibutsu no kenkyū* [Research into *honjibutsu* in the Medieval Era] (Tokyo: Kumi Koshoin, 1996). (I was directed to this by Yamada Masanori.)

7 Itō Shinichi et al., eds., "Sagara shi hōdo [Rules of the Sagara Clan]," in *Chūsei hōsei shiryō shū* [Compilation of Historical Documents on Medieval Law] vol. 3 (Tokyo: Iwanami Shoten, 1965), 33. See also the Luis Fróis (Froes) monograph, *Tratado em que se contem muito susinta e abreviadamente algumas contradições e deferenças de custumes entre a gente de Europa e esta provincia de Japão* (1585); hereafter *Tratado*. This is translated into Japanese as *Nichiō bunka hikaku*, Okada Akio ed. and trans., published together with *Nihon Ōkokuki* by Avila Giron, Sakuma Tadashi et al., trans. and ed., in *Daikōkai jidai sōsho* (Tokyo: Iwanami Shoten, 1965), vol. 11, p. 550. The yamabushi traversed mountains and fields collecting medicinal herbs and such, and it is believed they played a role in Yakushi becoming equated with medicine and healing, since the characters 薬師 were used not only to represent the Buddha Yakushi but also as a word for doctor, also pronounced *yakushi*, from which we have *yakuzaishi* 薬剤師, pharmacist.

8 SSS 1.801.

9 SSS 1.811 and 955. See also Kinryū Shizuka, *Rennyo* (Tokyo: Yoshikawa Kōbunkan, 1997), 25.

10 *Shinshū shiryō shūsei* 5.357, 618, 177, and 1109. Also preserved at Katada Honpukuji, in addition to the mid-Muromachi original of the *Bumo kyōyō shō*, are an early Muromachi copy of Zonkaku's *Ketchishō*, a mid-Muromachi copy of his *Shoshin hongai shū*, and a copy of Ryōkai's *Tariki shinjin kikigaki*. See *Kosha kohan Shinshū shōgyō genzon mokuroku*, ed. Honpa Honganjiha Shūgakuin (Kyoto: Kōkyō Shoin, 1937), 235–236, entries 838, 839, 840, 855. 857. Also included are documents relating to the Araki branch and Bukkōji.

11 The Meikō subgroup of the *ikkō-shū* belonged to the Araki branch in the Kantō region. After the Nambokuchō era, it developed in the Chūgoku (Bingo) region as well.

12 *Editors' note:* This is a Shinshū term for what would otherwise be the *nirmāṇakāya* form of the Buddha, that is the manifest form seen in history. Literally, *hōben hosshin* represents *upaya-dharmakāya*, that is, an active form of the otherwise nonmanifesting

dharmakāya, who appears in order to carry out the Buddha's vows of compassion for sentient beings. In Shinshū usage, the *hōben hosshin* is what is designated as the form we perceive with our normal sense operations. Usually this refers to images, but here the audience is told they have the power to invoke the Buddha by a focused production of sound, akin to the use of mantras in meditation.

13 SSS 5.327. Kinryū Shizuka, *Rennyo*, 25–26. See also Kinryū Shizuka, "Ikkō-shū no shūha no seiritsu," in *Kōza Rennyo* [Lectures on Rennyo] vol. 4, ed. Jōdo Shinshū Kyōgaku Kenkyūsho (Tokyo: Heibonsha, 1997), 219–220.

14 Ema Tsutomu et al., trans. and ed., *Nihon kyōkai shi* vol. 2, vol. 10 of *Daikōkai jidai sōsho* (Tokyo: Iwanami Shoten 1970), 472. Original text in João Rodriguez Tçuzzu, *História da Igreja do Japão* (Lisbon: Biblio do Palácio da Ajuda, repr. 1953). On page 473 of the *Nihon kyōkai shi* we read, "Life itself is breathing in and out," taken from Saichō's *Chū-Muryōgikyō* (T No. 2193, 56.203), where there is an explanatory note about the Sanskrit belief known as *a-un* based on inhalation and exhalation. See writings by Rodriques that appear in *Nihon kyōkai shi* 2. Also the *Buppō no shidai ryaku nukigaki* (written ca. 1605; in Ebisawa Arimichi, H. Cieslik, et al., eds., *Kirishitan sho, Haiyasho*, at *Nihon shisō taikei* 25.111) offers an explanation of this with reference to divination, noting that "in divination, the south is the direction taken toward fire." In SSS 8.229, Hosokawa Gyōshin links the Three Truths with the three characters of the name Amida.

15 *Nihon tsushin* vol. 2, at *Shin ikoku sōsho* 2.322; *Cartas Que os Padres e Irmãos*, 370. Also *Nihon kyōkaishi* vol. 2, 472 introduces the interpretation "Amida Buddha, please save us" for the six characters.

16 *Letters* 5:1, known as the *matsudai muchi no ofumi*. *Rennyo Shōnin ibun*, 470–471, letter no. 172.

17 Jesuit Historical Document Archive, city of Rome; trans. in *Dai Nihon shiryō* series 10, vol. 19, 142.

18 Matsuda Kiichi, Sakuma Tadashi, et al., trans. and ed., *Nihon Junsatsuki* (Tokyo: Heibonsha Tōyō Bunko, 1973), 31. Original text appears in Alejandro Valignano, *Sumario de las cosas de Japón, Adiciones del sumario de Japón* (1592), ed. José Luis Alvarez-Taladriz, vol. 1, *Monumenta Nipponica Monographs* No. 9 (Tokyo: Sophia University, 1954). A passage nearly the same as this quote from the *Nihon Junsatsuki* also appears in a communiqué from Shiki 志岐, Nagasaki (present-day Kumamoto Prefecture) dated 1571, ninth month, fourth day. See *Nihon tsūshin* 2.272. The "Yasokai shi shokanshū" in *Nagasaki kenshi: shiryōhen* 3.51 is also the same.

19 Letter from Joãn Rodriguez Giran dated twelfth day, first month, 1613, in Matsuda Kiichi et al., eds., *Jūroku–shichi seiki iezusukai nihon hōkokushū*, II-1 (first volume in second group), published in 15 volumes (Kyoto: Dōbōsha, 1987), 298 (hereafter *Nihon hōkokushū*). This collection of communiqués was compiled after *Nihon tsūshin*. Concrete details concerning the chanted nenbutsu of Jōdoshū also appear in Luis Frois, *Nihon shi* [History of Japan] vol. 3, Matsuda Kiichi and Kawasaki Momota, trans. (Tokyo: Chūō Kōron sha, 1980): 251. Original text appears in Luis Frois, *Historia de Japam*, 5 vols. (Lisbon: Biblioteca National, 1976).

20 *Nihon tsūshin* 1, 369.

21 Frois, *Nihonshi* 3, 263; *Historia de Japam* vol. 2, 36. On p. 218 it also says, "[In] Osaka…in the magnificent houses of certain wealthy pagans…as many as sixteen lanterns are hung and an altar to Amida is present."

22 "Rōma-shi Iezusu kai monjokan monjo," in *Dai Nihon shiryō*, series 10, vol. 19, pp. 142, 164; *Nihon tsūshin* 2.322. See also Kodama Shiki, *Kinsei shūkyō no tenkai katei* (The Development Process of Medieval Shinshū) (Tokyo: Yoshikawa Kōbunkan, 1976), 140–147.

23 "Annual Report of 1590," in *Nihon hōkokushū* I-1, 175–176. Original text in *Copia di due lettre annue scritte dal Giapone del* 1589 &1590. (Milan: Pacifico Pontio Impressore della Corte Archiepiscopale, 1593), 90–91.

24 *Nihon kyōkaishi* 2.220; *Historia Igreja do Jāpao*, 110–111.

25 Frois, *Nihonshi* 1.327; *Historia de Japam* 4.405.

26 "Annual Report of 1596," in *Nihon hōkokushū* I-1, 258.

27 See the letter labeled *konshi uketorijō* in the archive of Chōanji in Kusatsu, document bearing the seal of someone named Lower Official (*gekan*) Shōjō, unknown year, twelfth day of the eighth month, and twenty-eighth day of the second month. See also the *kanjinchō* (money-raising ledger) dated the fourth day of the eleventh month, Keichō 16 (1611), in Tokyo Daigaku Henshansho, ed., *Dai Nihon shiryō* series 12 vol. 9 (Tokyo: Tokyo University), 198–205. Furthermore, though the typical image of the women of this time is that they were oppressed by the custom of *goshō sanshō*, or "five preclusions" (i.e., women would not become Brahmā, Benten, Indra, Māra, a Cakravartin king, or a buddha) and "three familial obligations" (first to father, then to husband, then to son), in *Nichiō bunka hikaku*, by Ruisu Furoisu, 526, we read, "In Europe, possessions are jointly held by a couple. In Japan, each person owns his or her own share. Sometimes the wife will loan money to the husband at a high rate of interest," and "In accordance with their foul character, it is typical for the husband to divorce the wife. In Japan, a wife often divorces her husband." On p. 527 as well, the custom of "Japanese women having the freedom to go wherever they like without informing their husbands" is also mentioned. These statements stand in sharp contrast to received wisdom concerning *goshō sanshō*. I believe this kind of information should be taken into account when considering women in the *Sengoku* era.

28 Asao Naohiro, "Jūroku seiki kōhan no Nihon," in Asao Naohiro et al., eds. *Iwanami kōza Nihon tsūshi*, vol. 11 (Tokyo: Iwanami Shoten, 1993), 38.

29 "Annual Report of 1596," Supplement, in *Nihon hōkokushū* I-2.313. In Kanda Chisato, "Ikkō-shū to Kirishitan," *Tōyō daigaku bungakubu kiyō* 22 (50-*shū shigakka hen*), 17. An interesting observation is made that "it is thought that the customary relationships between parents and children, husbands and wives, and lords and vassals...meant that the faith was jointly held by everyone in those relationships, and that everyone bound together by those relationships received salvation and awakening at the same time."

30 "Annual Report of 1589," *Nihon hōkokushū*, I-1, 130; *lettre annue*, 452.

31 *Nihon tsūshin* 1.50–55. Also Ōita-shi Shi Hensan Iinkai, ed., *Ōita-shi shi* (Oita: Oita Shi) 2.313. See also Kinryū Shizuka, *Rennyo*, 94.

32 Frois, *Nihonshi* 3.217, and 5.261; *Historia de Japam* 2.6 and 5.105.

33 *Nihon kyōkaishi* 1.220.

34 Frois, *Nihonshi* 4.114; *Historia de Japam* 2.249.

35 This was pointed out to me by Takeda Takemaro.

36 *Nihon hōkokushū* III-5.277. Letter from Joãn Francisco dated 1580, ninth month, first day.

37 Frois, *Nihonshi* 1.174; *Historia de Japam* 4.186.

38 Frois, *Nihonshi* 1.274; *Historia de Japam* 4.33.

39 *Nihon tsūshin* 2.353.

40 Frois, *Nihon shi* vol. 5.134; *Historia de Japam*, 3.332.

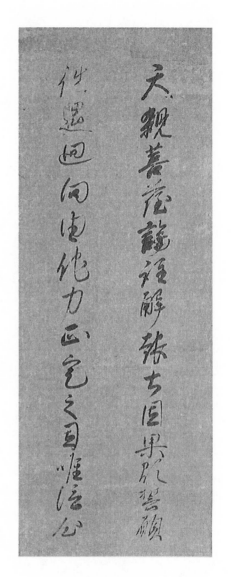

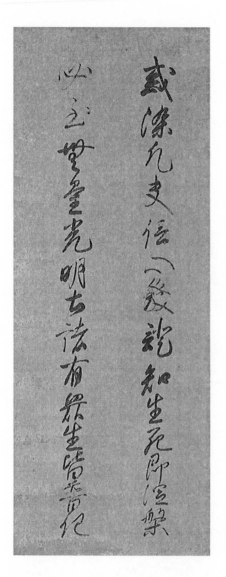

ABOVE LEFT: Shōshinge panel one (scroll).
ABOVE RIGHT: Shōshinge panel two (scroll).

右斯三帖和讃幷正信偈

四帖一部者末代写興際

枚木開之者也而已

文明五年 癸巳 三月 日

FAR LEFT: Six character Myōgō (scroll).
NEAR LEFT: Sanjō Wasan postscript (scroll).
RIGHT: Ten character Myōgō (scroll).

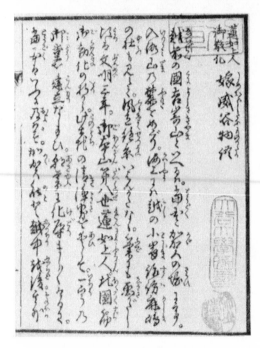

ABOVE: Tale of the
Flesh-Adhering Mask—picture

LEFT: Tale of the
Flesh-Adhering Mask—text

7

KUSANO KENSHI
TRANSLATED BY EISHO NASU

The Kanshō Persecution

An Examination of Mount Hiei's
Destruction of Ōtani Honganji

In the first year of Chōroku (1457), Rennyo was appointed the eighth abbot of Honganji, succeeding Zonnyo (1396–1457), who passed away in the same year. It is well known that Rennyo, eager to revitalize Jōdoshinshū, had begun proselytizing activities, especially in the southern part of Ōmi Province, immediately after his succession to the abbot's office. However, it is also well known that his activities temporarily came to a standstill with the destruction of the Ōtani Honganji, known as the Kanshō Persecution (*Kanshō no hōnan*), led by the Tendai militia-priests of Mount Hiei (*Hieizan shuto*) in the sixth year of Kanshō, or 1468.

The cause of the Kanshō Persecution, however, has yet to be fully explained. What reason did the priests on Mount Hiei have for carrying out the destruction of the Ōtani Honganji? Past studies of the incident have generally attributed the cause to such popular notions as feelings of resentment toward the sudden expansion of Honganji's influence among the priests on Mount Hiei,[1] or the Tendai organization's greed for more tribute (*reikin*) from Honganji.[2] Although some studies depict the incident as a religious confrontation, many simply explain that the cause of the incident was that Honganji had promoted the heterodoxy (*jagi*) known as *mugekō-shū*, the "teaching of unhindered-light."[3] Although these may have been part of the reason, I believe that the causes lay in wider issues related to the social and political changes wrought by the ideologies inherent in Rennyo's movement.

Although the power of Mount Hiei dominated religious society in medieval Japan, and Honganji was merely a branch temple (*matsuji*) of Enryakuji on Mount Hiei, in order for the priests on Mount Hiei to employ armed forces within the capital city of Kyoto, the seat of the imperial court and the head office of the Muromachi bakufu, they needed a "just cause" (*taigi*) both to avoid public criticism and to secure the consent of the imperial and bakufu powers. That the Hiei priests worked to create a rationale for their attack is indicated by the facts that prior to the destruction of Ōtani Honganji, the priests sent a letter of indictment and that they had a closed meeting (*heirō*) at the Gion shrine a day before the incident took place.

Thus the Hiei attack did not occur spontaneously but was a premeditated action carried out with meticulous preparation.

Through an examination of the logic of the Hiei priests' accusations that led to the Kanshō Persecution, I hope to clarify both the reasons for the persecution and some aspects of the internal situation of Rennyo's religious organization.

Mount Hiei's Allegations: The Contents of the *Eizan Chōjō*

Prior to the attack on the Ōtani Honganji, the Mount Hiei authorities sent a letter known as the *Eizan chōjō* (Letter of Indictment from Mount Hiei), notifying the administrators of Honganji of Hiei's charges.[4] However, the contents of the letter have never been examined thoroughly, perhaps because it is generally assumed to have been written from the monologic perspective of the attackers. Thus I will begin by presenting the letter and identifying the issues in it. It is addressed to Honganji:

> In Kanshō 6, on the eighth day of the first month, the assembly of the continuous sutra chanting priests [sanctioned by] the emperor's decree (*chokugan fudankyōshū*) held a meeting at the Saitōin regarding the charges against Higashiyama Honganji. According to the case [against the temple],…the temple has been unlawfully promoting single-hearted and exclusive practice (*ikkō senju*) and following the wrong view of slandering the three treasures (*sanbō hihō no hekiken*). In accordance with traditional rules and principles, as a matter of course [the registration of such a temple] should be suspended and revoked. In addition to [this allegation, the temple] uses the name of *mugekō* (unhindered light) to establish an [independent school] of teaching (*shū*) and has been spreading the teaching among ignorant men and women and demonstrating the teaching to the lowly young and old. [As a result], in village after village people throng together and burn buddha statues and sutra scrolls and show disdain for the gentle lights of the kami (*shinmei no wakō*). Their acts following the wicked path (*jaro*) are unbearable to see. Their wicked deeds of evil are intolerable to hear. They are the enemy of the Buddha (*butteki* 仏敵). They are the enemy of kami (*shinteki* 神敵). For the sake of the true Dharma and for the sake of our country, they should not go unpunished. [The license of the temple] should have been revoked already, when we had a closed meeting last year. However, we temporarily suspended [our decision], since [the temple] submitted a petition containing words of intervention from the abbot (*monzeki*) [of Shōren'in]. To this day, however, the incidents of [misbehavior of the temple's followers] have never stopped and are further multiplying. We cannot tolerate their repeated violations any longer. Hereby, the assembly [of the continuous sutra chanting priests] have unanimously passed a resolution to dispatch temple servants (*kunin*) [of Mount Hiei] and shrine servants (*inujinin*) [of Gion shrine] to demolish completely the buildings of the temple and shrine [at the Ōtani Honganji].
>
> The above is addressed to Honganji.

The allegations begin with the statement that Honganji was unlawfully promoting the teaching of single-minded and exclusive practice (*ikkō senju*) and following the wrong view of slandering the three treasures (*sanbō hihō no hekiken*). This part of the letter is based in abstract ideology and is difficult to use as a resource for the examination of the charges.

The case is presented in the section following the sentence that begins "In addition to...." The charges state that Honganji is indicted because of (1) having established a school called *mugekō*, and (2) spreading this teaching among ignorant men and women, and the lowly young and old. (3) As a result of the propagation of the teaching, those people described in the second accusation thronged together and began burning buddha statues and sutra scrolls, and (4) they became contemptuous of local deities. Therefore, the priests on Mount Hiei passed a resolution to destroy the Ōtani Honganji in order to (a) protect the true Dharma and (b) protect the country.

The first and second accusations are thought to be aimed directly at Rennyo's proselytizing activities. As many scholars have pointed out, the first charge—establishing a school called *mugekō*—was based on Rennyo's use of the ten-character *myōgō* scrolls which were given to his followers during this period as *honzon*, or objects of worship. On the scroll, the ten-character name of Amida, *ki-myō-jin-jip-pō-mu-ge-kō-nyo-rai* 歸命盡十方无碍光如来 is written in large script using gold ink (*kindei*), and the scroll is therefore called the *mugekō honzon*. The accusers claimed that Rennyo's teaching was thus a new school (*shū*) called *mugekō-shū*.[5] At the time the name *mugekō-shū* was broadly used to identify Rennyo's religious organization, and it is not difficult to imagine that the name was used because it conveyed a special meaning broadly understood in society at large.

The second charge against Honganji—spreading the teaching among ignorant men and women and the lowly young and old—is also connected to Rennyo's activities. The main areas of Rennyo's proselytizing efforts were village communities in southern Ōmi Province. According to a recent study, all members of a community, from village leaders to ordinary peasants, were known to accept Rennyo's teaching.[6] The Hiei priests' reference to "ignorant men and women" and "the lowly young and old" would thus have included all members of these communities, both leaders and peasants. Although this language reveals the priests' sense of superiority over village residents as nothing but ignorant and ignoble people, it should also be noted that their use of such expressions might be taken as evidence that they have moved beyond a simple view of the uneducated populace, since they make an effort to despise even "the lowly young and old."

The first and second charges are accusations against Rennyo himself, but they also present the *Eizan chōjō's* fundamental allegations against Honganji. I will examine these issues in detail in the next section.

The third and fourth charges are accusations regarding the actions of people in Ōmi Province who received Rennyo's teaching. The accusation in the third charge—that people thronged together to burn buddha statues and sutra scrolls—agrees with other records that document the attack by Hiei priests the Kanshō Persecution. For example, according to the *Tōji kakochō* (Records of Past Events at Tōji), the reason for the attack against the people of Kanegamori, one of the strongholds of Rennyo's religious organization in Ōmi Province, was that they "threw statues of Amida Buddha into the river and burned paintings and wooden statues of buddhas."[7] It also said that Rennyo himself often "burned objects of worship and other articles that were against his tradition every time he took a bath," that is, in order to heat the bath water.[8] Burning objects of worship and other articles that contravene Shinshū teachings was a part of Rennyo's method of proselytization. We can imagine that Rennyo's actions would have made such a strong impression upon the people of Ōmi Province who accepted his teaching that some villagers would have scrutinized their local Buddhist statues and scriptures to determine whether they accorded with the teaching of Shinshū and then burned those articles judged as inappropriate. From this indirect historical evidence, it is reasonable to conclude that the third charge, that people thronged together to burn Buddhist statues and sutra scrolls, was based in fact.

The fourth charge—contemptuous behavior toward local deities among Rennyo's followers—is documented by Rennyo himself in his *Letters* issued after Bunmei 5 (1473) when he was proselytizing at Yoshizaki in Echizen Province after the destruction of Honganji. In order to avoid conflicts with other religious powers in the region, Rennyo chastised those followers who scorned local deities or the buddhas and bodhisattvas worshipped by other traditions. In his letters he says, for example, "Do not slight various kami, buddhas, and bodhisattvas,"[9] and "One should not neglect various kami and various bodhisattvas."[10] It is well known that during Rennyo's Yoshizaki period there were people within Rennyo's religious organization who did belittle the various kami, buddhas, and bodhisattvas.

In the *Eizan chōjō*, such offenses are referred to simply as "showing disdain for the gentle lights of the kami" (*shinmei no wakō wo keibetsu su*) with no mention of any specific activities. However, this charge, together with the third charge, condemns offenses of people who followed Rennyo's teaching, and describing those offenses simply as "showing disdain for the gentle lights of the kami" would have been sufficiently understood by the people at that time. According to my assessment, the phrase "showing disdain for the gentle lights of the kami" itself is strongly related to the scornful comments in the priests' second charge against the people in Ōmi Province, despising them as "ignorant men and women" and "the lowly young and old," as I will soon discuss in greater detail.

In this section I have examined the allegations against Honganji made by the priests on Mount Hiei in the *Eizan chōjō*. The priests elaborated their charges of the alleged criminal offenses committed by Rennyo himself (allegations 1 and 2) and by the people who followed his teaching (allegations 3 and 4). However, since the activities described in (3) and (4) were understood by the Hiei priests as having derived from Rennyo's proselytizing activities described in (1) and (2), the core condemnations are contained in allegations (1) and (2).

The Crime of Establishing an Independent Sect

As was already mentioned, Rennyo used a scroll on which was written in large characters *ki-myō-jin-jip-pō-mu-ge-kō-nyo-rai* as the object of worship to propagate his teaching in Ōmi Province, and his religious organization was therefore popularly called *mugekō-shū* (the "school of unhindered light"). This expression is found in the writings of Kyōgaku (1395–1473)[11] of the Daijōin of Kōfukuji in Nara, who was related to Rennyo through marriage and acted favorably toward him, and even by

Jinson (d. 1508),[12] Kyōgaku's successor, who also maintained friendly relations with Honganji. Other records from a slightly later period also show that the name was used by warriors and priests in Noto,[13] Echigo,[14] and Kai[15] Provinces. Thus the name *mugekō-shū* seems to have been commonly used to identify Rennyo's religious organization beyond the borders of both social classes and geographical areas.

It is also noteworthy that Rennyo's religious organization was also labeled *mugekō-shū* by the followers of the Takada branch of Shinshū, which, like Rennyo's group, claims Shinran (1173–1262) as its founder. In a letter issued on the fifth day of the seventh month in Kanshō 6 (1465), Shinne (1434–1512), the tenth abbot of Senjuji of Takada-ha, uses the term to distinguish Rennyo's followers from the Takada followers:

> The [priests] of Mount [Hiei], having confused us with the followers of the *mugekō* [teaching], held a meeting of the assembly of priests of the three pagodas [on the mountain] and determined to dispatch their temple servants to persecute our followers. They dispatched more than fifty temple servants of Mount [Hiei] (*sanmon kunin*) led by a temple officer (*gyōji*) of Sanuki Province to Echizen and Kaga Provinces. Responding to this incident, more than ten representatives of our followers of these two provinces traveled to the capital city and submitted a petition to the temple on Mount [Hiei] asking them not to confuse us with followers of the heretical *mugekō*, because we are different from them, since our tradition has received the transmission of [Dharma] lineage through a different founder. Therefore we should not be confused with them and we do not deserve to be persecuted by the temple [on Mount Hiei]. Upon receiving [this petition], the [assembly of priests of the] three pagodas held another meeting and agreed, in accordance with accepted regulations (*kenpō*), that the followers of the Takada Senjuji should not be persecuted. They issued a document of confirmation to this ignorant priest. They also sent letters of confirmation to our branch temples in all provinces. This genuinely fulfilled my wish.[16]

This letter indicates that immediately after the Kanshō Persecution the followers of the Takada branch of Shinshū were seen as a faction of Rennyo's religious organization and became targets of Hiei's attacks. In order to avoid the persecution, members of the Takada *monto* appealed to Mount Hiei that they were different from Rennyo's religious organization—that is, "followers of the heretical (*jarui*) *mugekō* teaching"—because, they maintained, they had received "the transmission of Dharma lineage through a different founder (*besso sōjō*)." This petition was apparently approved by the priests on Mount Hiei, and Shinne expresses his satisfaction because Hiei issued letters of confirmation to him and the branch temples in all provinces.

By emphasizing "the transmission of Dharma lineage through a different founder," Shinne was maintaining that the Takada followers belonged to the lineage of Hōnen (1133–1212), not Shinran, as is seen in a document called *Senjuji Echizen no kuni matsuji monto chū mōshijō an* (Letter from Senjuji drafted to address to the followers of the affiliated temples in Echizen province), which states, "our tradition belongs to the lineage founded by Hōnen Shōnin."[17] Responding to the Takada followers' petition, Mount Hiei issued a letter of confirmation (*andojō* 安堵状) entitled *Enryakuji Saitōin shūgijō an* (Letter drafted to announce a resolution passed by the priests of Saitōin at Enryakuji):

Regarding Senjuji of Ōuchi no shō in Shimotsuke Province, since they are the head temple of the practice halls (*dōjō*) of the single-minded exclusive practice of the nenbutsu (*ikkō senju nenbutsu*), and since from long ago until this day they have never betrayed the rules of conduct set by their founder when they spread their Dharma lineage, they should [properly be called] the followers of single-minded practice (*ikkō-shū*). Upon hearing their petition, [it has been determined that] in accordance with the just law they should not be confused with the ignorant people who call themselves *mugekō* and should not be persecuted. Thus it is ordered in this folded paper (*origami*).[18]

It should be noted that in this document Senjuji and its followers are identified not as *mugekō-shū* but as *ikkō-shū*.

In this letter, the name *ikkō-shū* does not carry with it the sense of enmity seen during the Kamakura period, when it was used to indicate the practitioners of single-hearted exclusive practice (*ikkō senju*), such as members of Hōnen's religious organization. Instead, the name *mugekō-shū* has become the new symbol of heretical teachings, perhaps because they belonged to the lineage of Shinran.[19] Therefore, it is necessary to examine the origin of the name *mugekō-shū* and what kind of impression it gave to people in the society at that time.

The etymological origin of *mugekō-shū* can be traced to the term *mugekō butsu* (Buddha of unhindered light), an epithet of Amida Buddha found in the *Larger Sukhāvatīvyūha-sūtra* (*Dai Muryōjukyō*). In the sutra, Amida Buddha's virtues are likened to the twelve kinds of light, and *mugekō butsu* is the third name of the "Buddha of the twelve lights" (*jūnikō butsu*).[20] It is also based on a passage in the *Jōdoron* (*Jingtu lun*, "Discourse on the Pure Land"), attributed to Vasubandhu, that states, "O, World-Honored One, I single-mindedly take refuge in the Tathāgata of unhindered light (*mugekō nyorai*) throughout the ten directions and aspire to be born in the land of bliss."[21]

Japanese Pure Land masters in the Kamakura period commonly used the epithet. For example, Hōnen said, "The light of that buddha (*mugekō butsu*) shines through all the mountains both large and small surrounding Mount Sumeru and embraces sentient beings in this realm without hindrance."[22] Ippen (1239–1289) is also recorded as saying "The mind awakening faith in the Original Vow of Amida who embraces both good and evil equally, this is the virtue of the Buddha of unhindered light (*mugekō butsu*)."[23] In these passages, the name *mugekō butsu* is used to express the idea that nothing hinders Amida Tathāgata's salvation, because his light of salvation reaches all human beings whether good or evil. Shinran, too, the subject of our scrutiny, demonstrated a similar understanding of this name, saying, the "Buddha of unhindered light is spoken of thus in order to indicate that this buddha seeks to save all beings, unhindered by their being wretched and evil."[24]

Rennyo, however, introduced a unique interpretation of this name in his *Shōshinge taii*, said to have been given to Dōsai (1399–1488) of Kanegamori in Ōmi Province. In the text, Rennyo says, "The name Buddha of unhindered light expresses the unhindered aspect of the auspicious light of Amida Buddha because no person or doctrine can stop it."[25] He understands the name *mugekō butsu* to represent the particular aspect of Amida in which the Tathāgata's salvific light cannot be hindered by what he terms *ninpō* 人法. Ninpō has many possible meanings and therein lies the problem. As a Buddhist term translating *sattva* and *dharma*, ninpō can mean person and doctrine or teaching, sentient beings and the material substance of which sentient beings are made, or by extension the categories of sentient and insentient. As an ordinary Japanese word, however, the ninpō refers to "human (*nin*) law (*hō*), or a way [of behaving] that [all] human beings must maintain."[26] People thus might interpret this passage to mean that the salvific light of *mugekō butsu* could not be hindered by any "human law," including not only moral and ethical rules of conduct but also the laws of government. Therefore, it is possible that this interpretation could be turned into criticism against all sorts of regulations that constrained people at that time. In fact, this passage of the *Shōshinge tai'i* is based on a passage found in Shinran's main work, *Kyōgyōshinshō*. The passage there is taken from *wuliangshoujing lianyi shuwenzan* by Kyŏnghung (ca. 681) which reads, "[He is called] *Mugekō butsu*: because there is no ninpō that obstructs him."[27]

In addition is a comment by a Rinzai monk, Keijo Shūrin (1440–1518), a Gozan literary figure. In his *Kanrin koroshū*, Shūrin makes the following comment about the *ikkō-ikki* Shinshū uprising that took place in Kaga Province during the Bunmei era (1469–1486):

> A confused man [started a teaching] called *ikkō-shū*. He attracted the populace (*hyakushō*) with pipes and drums, and people gathered [around him] like swarming ants or a flock of crows. Denouncing the [teachings of] other schools, he converted them to [the *ikkō-shū*] faction. Moreover, these people even killed guard officers and stole collected taxes and tributes. Their forces were unstoppable. Long ago [in China] during the Mongolian Yuan dynasty, there was an ordinary citizen who [started a group] called the Lotus Society and spread the teaching of *mugekō*. He called himself a spiritual leader, extensively engaging in demonic activities. The so-called *ikkō-shū* [must be] an offshoot of this teaching of *mugekō*.[28]

In this passage Shūrin compares the forces of the *ikkō-ikki* to the followers of the Teaching of the White Lotus (*bailianjiao*) in China, which led to the destruction of the Yuan dynasty (1271–1368). The latter part of this passage is especially noteworthy. Shūrin explains that long ago during the Yuan dynasty there was a peasant who used the name of the White Lotus Society, a nenbutsu association established by Huiyuan (334–416) of Mount Lu, and spread the teaching of *mugekō*. He says that this man called himself a spiritual leader and extensively practiced demonic affairs. Shūrin then attacks Rennyo's religious organization by claiming that Rennyo's *ikkō-shū* is an "offshoot" (*ryūa*), or of the same lineage, of the teaching of *mugekō* of the Teaching of the White Lotus. Maintaining that the followers of the Teaching of the White Lotus, led by Zhu Yuanzhang (1328–1398), who overthrew the Yuan dynasty, also spread the teaching of *mugekō*, he criticizes Rennyo's religious organization because it is also known by the term *mugekō-shū*, suggesting an association with rebellion.

These records indicate that behind the first charge in the *Eizan chōjō* lay suspicion toward the potentially subversive nature of Rennyo's movement. The teaching of *mugekō butsu*, understood as emphasizing that Amida Tathāgata's salvation is unhinderable by any "human law" (*ninpō*), might lead people to neglect the existing order of society and in the end result in the destruction of the nation itself. It is this fear that perhaps led the priests of Mount Hiei to the assertion that Ōtani Honganji must be destroyed to protect the country. I believe that this allegation was based on the widely accepted public view of *mugekō butsu* as a subversive group, so that the priests on Mount Hiei did not have to explain the reasons for their accusations in detail.

The content of the charge of "establishing a school called 'Unhindered Light'" was thus raised to appeal to the negative public impression of the *mugekō butsu* movement and provided a strong foundation for justifying Mount Hiei's persecution of Rennyo' religious organization. In the next section I will examine the meaning of the second charge against Honganji: spreading the teaching among ignorant men and women and the lowly young and old.

The Crime of Spreading the Teaching among Ignorant Men and Women, the Lowly Young and Old

I believe that the content of the accusation of "spreading the teaching among ignorant men and women and the lowly young and old" is connected to the criticism of "showing disdain for the gentle lights of the kami" (*keibetsu shinmei wakō*). Therefore, I will first examine the concrete meaning of "disdain for the gentle lights of the kami" and the kind of actions that were subject to that criticism.

Examples of the scandalous behavior of Rennyo's followers are recorded in the *Tadatomiōki*, covering the years 1496 to 1505, the diary of Shirakawa Tadatomi, the head officer of kami affairs (*jingi haku*) within the imperial court. Although the date of the record, Meiō 5 (1496), is thirty years later than Kanshō 6 (1465), Rennyo was still alive at that time:

> The ninth month of Meiō 5 (1496). [The society of] the lesser nobility (*jige*) is filled with [the followers of] the *ikkō-shū* in recent years. I am gravely concerned about [its popularity]. I do not mean that I despise the recitation of the nenbutsu. However, those people are so devoted to the temple that they do not [even] observe the thirty-day period of avoiding [the shrine] because of the impure pollution of death (*fujō shie*). They dare to trespass into the shrine households [with polluted bodies], infecting many others with their pollution. This kind of thing is beyond words. The evil of pollution (*eaku*) is the evil of demonic spirits (*kijin*). These people should be removed [from noble society].[29]

Tadatomi accuses the followers of the *ikkō-shū*, that is, members of Rennyo's religious organization, of not even observing the thirty-day period of avoiding shrine precincts when tainted by death pollution. They dare to walk in and out the kami shrines with polluted bodies and spread their pollution to many others. He reveals his unconcealed hatred for them by saying that, since the kami hate pollution, those followers of the *ikkō-shū* should be expelled.

Shirakawa Tadatomi was the second son of Masakaneō (n.d.), who had been the head officer of kami affairs three successors before Tadatomi. Although he belonged to a sublineage of the Shirakawa family, which had inherited the title of head officer of kami affairs in the imperial court, Tadatomi had been hastily appointed to the position because Sukeujiō (n.d.), Masakaneō's grandson and a direct descendant of the main-lineage (*chokkei*) of the Shirakawa family, had abruptly resigned in Entoku 2 (1490) from the position at the age of thirty-nine because of illness. However, the cause of Sukeujiō's illness was also a source of concern about pollution brought to shrines by *ikkō-shū* followers. Konoe Masaie (1444–1505) in his diary, *Gohōkōinki*, comments upon it in a record of the fourth day of the seventh month of Entoku 4 (1492):

> I heard that the head officer (*haku*) [of kami affairs] third rank [Sukeujiō] has been displaying [signs of] madness since the fourth month, and now he is not capable of comporting himself in public any longer. I heard that he has a three-year-old son whose mother is a daughter of [the head priest of the] *ikkō-shū*. Such is the result when an officer serving the kami becomes personally mixed up with the polluted and impure (*oe fujō*).[30]

In fact, the woman who married into the household of this Sukeujiō was Rennyo's seventh daughter, Yūshinni (1463–1490).[31]

As was recorded in the *Gohōkōinki*, Sukeujiō had to resign from his position because of his "displaying signs of madness" and becoming incapable of "comporting himself in public." Masaie offers the explanation that it is because "an officer serving the kami becomes personally mixed up with the polluted and impure." Masaie believes that the cause of the display of madness was that, although Sukeujiō served the kami as the head officer of kami affairs (*jingi haku*), he had married a polluted and impure daughter of the head priest of the *ikkō-shū* of Honganji.

Shirakawa Tadatomi's unusually strong feeling of hatred toward the *ikkō-shū* followers, as I have explained, is difficult to understand unless, like Masaie, Tadatomi himself believed that Sukeujiō's retirement was due to illness lay in this explanation.

These documents demonstrate that the followers of the Honganji *ikkō-shū* were generally considered by aristocratic society to be "impure with the evil of pollution." One of the most significant reasons for this view was that the followers of Honganji were not afraid of and did not protect against the pollution of death and dared to come into shrines to kami in a polluted state. Such outrageous behavior was incomprehensible to the aristocratic families. But how did these Honganji *ikkō-shū* followers acquire such attitudes toward the deities and their shrines?

In order to understand this behavior, we must first examine Rennyo's comments on local deities. In his *Letters*, for example, Rennyo taught his followers to take refuge absolutely and solely in Amida, saying that one must "take refuge in Amida wholeheartedly" (*tada hitosujini mida ni kisu*)[32] in order to accomplish Birth in the Pure Land; he strongly urged his followers "not to entrust their minds to any other buddhas, bodhisattvas, and kami" (*yo no butsu bosatsu shoshin nimo kokoro wo kakezu shite*),[33] and "to cast away altogether any intention to obey other kami and buddhas" (*shoshin shobutsu ni tuishō mōsu kokoro wo minamina sute*).[34] Rennyo's remarks inevitably produced contemptuous attitudes toward local deities and the buddhas and bodhisattvas of other schools, which are also mentioned by Rennyo during his Yoshizaki period. In order to avoid conflicts with other schools and lineages, Rennyo began reprimanding his followers for their attitudes toward other buddhas and kami with the logic that, since "within the one buddha, Amida, all other kami and buddhas are embraced" (*mida ichibutsu no uchi niwa, issai no shoshin shobutsu mo komoreru*),[35] "one should not neglect other kami and bodhisattvas" (*shoshin shobutsu omo orosoka ni subekarazu*).[36] However, those who had already accepted Rennyo's earlier teaching were not easily swayed by this new line of reasoning.

In Ōmi Province, since Rennyo had adamantly taught his followers to take refuge solely in *mugekō nyorai*, they undoubtedly lost any feeling of veneration for other kami, buddhas, and bodhisattvas, and their contemptuous behavior especially toward the kami became conspicuous.

The clash of local custom and institutional ideology can be seen on other fronts as well. Another of Rennyo's *Letters*, issued toward the end of the ninth month of Bunmei 5 (1473), is instructive as a window to the behavior of Shinshū followers in their private meetings:

> For years, the followers at Chōshōji have been seriously at variance with the Buddha-Dharma. My reason for saying this, first of all, has to do with the leader of the assembly (*zashū*). He thinks that to occupy the place of honor and drink before everyone else and to court the admiration of those seated around him, as well as that of others, is really the most important aspect of the Buddha-Dharma. This is certainly of no use for birth in the land of utmost bliss; it appears to be just for worldly reputation.[37]

In this letter Rennyo criticizes the manner in which his followers hold their meetings (*yoriai*) at Chōshōji. A person identified as the "leader of the assembly" who occupies the seat of the "place of honor" and drinks before everyone else does is criticized for thinking that the most important thing in the Buddha-Dharma is to court the admiration of others; but this is certainly of no use for his "birth in the land of utmost bliss." Rennyo's criticism is in keeping with his refusal to designate a particular "leader of the assembly" as based in his ideal of the equality of group members. His egalitarian ideal, at least for now, must be given proper recognition.[38]

This letter has generally been taken as evidence of the gradual emergence of hierarchical order within village meetings as demonstrated by distinctions of higher and lower seats and the order of usage of the sake cup.[39] According to my assessment, however, this should instead be understood as an indication that the meetings were held according to existing customs rather than in the manner intended by Rennyo when he began to promote meetings in village communities for honoring the Buddha's Dharma and realizing *shinjin*, the entrusting mind of faith. In fact, the preexisting model of the community meeting was that of the *miyaza*, or shrine meeting:

Takamaki Minoru, in his book *Miyaza to sonraku no shiteki kenkyū*, gives a general overview of how shrine meetings were held:

> In addition to regional differences in the time of establishment and distribution of *miyaza*, there are also great regional differences in the structure of these meetings. Generally they can be divided into the Kinai region and its surrounding areas, and into western and eastern Japan. First, looking at the Kinai region and its surrounding

areas, there are differences in the forms of *miyaza* depending on the structure of *sōson* (unified villages) during the medieval period and structure of villages during the early modern (*kinsei*) period. In areas where the social class of community leaders of *sōshō* (unified *shōen*) or *sōson* was comprised of authorities such as local strongmen, local samurai, supervisors of village communities, and minor supervisors in residence, *miyaza* were under the leadership of the *otona* (elders) of these authorities, and during worship services the leadership class always occupied the higher seats and the ordinary people occupied the lower seats. In other *sōson* lacking a leadership class, however, the ordinary people who were the leaders of the meeting moved into higher seats according to rules of seniority, with [the most senior members] becoming *otona* leaders.[40]

The Chōshōji meetings criticized by Rennyo in his letter seem to have been held in a style very close to the *miyaza* described by Takamaki.

If this is the case, Rennyo's egalitarian manner of holding meetings as places to realize entrusting minds would have conflicted with the existing *miyaza*-style social order governing village communities. Such confrontations with the existing order must have occurred repeatedly in villages influenced by Rennyo's teaching, and, combined with the followers' tendency to neglect local deities, must have threatened the *miyaza*-style social order in some villages. The derogatory attitudes and behavior of the *ikkō-shū* followers toward shrines, as strongly denounced in the *Tadatomiōki*, thus arose in conjunction with new ideas about village social order.

It is highly possible that these trends were witnessed in Ōmi Province during the Kanshō era, leading the priests of Mount Hiei to charge Rennyo's followers with "showing disdain for the gentle lights of the kami" and reinforcing aristocratic impressions of the *ikkō-shū* followers of Honganji as people of "impure pollution." Allegations concerning these followers' behavior were in this way connected to the accusations against the actions of "ignorant men and women," who did not even know the meaning of death pollution, and the acts of "the lowly young and old," who spread pollution in front of shrines.

Conclusion

I have examined the charges against Honganji in the *Eizan chōjō*, focusing on the two charges of (1) "having established a school called *mugekō*" and (2) "spreading the teaching among ignorant men and women and the lowly young and old." On one hand, these charges were deliberately exaggerated with the intention of destroying Honganji and Rennyo's religious organization, but on the other hand, they were based on actual conditions existing within the organization. In that sense, it is not too far off to think that the *Eizan chōjō* is a document that justifies Hiei's desire to destroy Honganji by raising issues of concern to the powers of both the imperial court (*kuge* authority) and the Muromachi bakufu (*bushi* authority).

The charge of "having established a school called *mugekō*" was raised in order to give the impression that Rennyo's religious organization ignored the norms of society and country and, therefore, if left unchecked might bring about the destruction of the country itself. This accusation was further amplified by a Zen monk who criticized an *ikkō-ikki* movement in Kaga Province during the Bunmei era. After that, the name *mugekō-shū* become broadly used in Hokuriku and eastern

Japan to identify the religious organization of Honganji. The charge of "spreading the teaching among ignorant men and women and the lowly young and old" seems to have been connected to the accusation of "showing disdain for the gentle lights of the kami." These charges point to the social customs of pollution avoidance, especially among the aristocratic class, and they reflect the attributes of the powerful shrines and temples standing at the top of the *miyaza*-style social order of village communities. These justifications, which portray the realities of Rennyo's propagational activities and the behavior of the *ikkō-shū* followers, allowed the priests of Mount Hiei to carry out their premeditated attack on Ōtani Honganji without resistance from the secular authorities.

Subsequently, Rennyo and his followers acquired a vast estate in the Yamashina area in Kyoto in Bunmei 12 (1480). There they built a new head temple, the Yamashina Honganji, including a town within the temple grounds (*jinaimachi*). Although Yamashina was not located within the inner capital, it stood at an important crossroad adjacent to the eastern border of Kyoto and was strategically important for the military powers. Once Honganji reestablished its head temple in this location, the priests of Mount Hiei demonstrated almost no concern for the temple. Had the character of Hiei changed only fifteen years after the Kanshō Persecution of 1465? Or had the situation surrounding Honganji changed? These very important questions are related to this topic, and I hope to address them in a future work.

Notes

This chapter originally appeared as "'Kanshō no hōnan' ni tsuite" 「寛正の法難」につ いて, in *Rennyo no sekai* 蓮如の世界, ed. Ōtani Daigaku Shinshū Sōgō Kenkyūjo, Kyoto: Bun'eidō, 1998, 537–553.

1 For example, see Inoue Toshio, *Ikkō ikki no kenkyū* (Tokyo: Yoshikawa Kōbunkan, 1968).

2 See Kasahara Kazuo, *Ikkō ikki no kenkyū* (Tokyo: Yamakawa Shuppansha, 1962).

3 For example, see Honganji Shiryō Kenkyūjo, ed., *Honganjishi*, vol. 1 (Kyoto: Jōdo Shinshū Honganji-ha, 1961), 310–312.

4 *Eizan chōjō* is contained in the *Kanegamori nikki batsu*, at SSS 2.701, where it is called *Eizan yori furaruru kenshō*.

5 See *Honganjishi*, vol. 1. See also Kanda Chisato, *Ikkō ikki to Shinshū shinkō* (Tokyo: Yoshikawa Kōbunkan, 1991); Kinryū Shizuka, *Rennyo* (Tokyo: Yoshikawa Kōbunkan, 1997). Another noteworthy work is an article by Hayashima Yūki, "Honganji Rennyo no myōgō honzon to sengoku shakai: jūji myōgō wo sozai to shite," *Kyoto-shi rekishi shiryōkan kenkyū kiyō* 10 (1992 [published by Kyōto Rekishi Shiryōkan]). In this article Hayashima examines artistic and visual meanings of the *mugekō honzon* and points out its social functions. This article is also reprinted in *Rennyo taikei*, vol. 4, ed. Kakehashi Jitsuen, Nabata Takashi, and Minegishi Sumio (Kyoto: Hōzōkan, 1996), 285–325.

6 Kojima Michihiro, "Heichi jōkan ato to jiin, sonraku: Ōmi no jirei kara," in *Chūsei jōkaku kenkyū ronshū*, ed. Murata Shūzō (Tokyo: Shinjinbutsu Ōraisha, 1990), 397.

7 Kanda, *Ikkō ikki to shinshū shinkō*, 207.

8 *Rennyo Shōnin ichigoki* 158, in Katada Osamu, ed., SSS 2.459.

9 Shobunshū 40, SSS 2.169.

10 Shobunshū 61, SSS 2.187.

11 As recorded on the twelfth day of the first month in Kanshō 6 (1465) in *Kyōgaku shiyōshō*, in Shinshū Ōtaniha Kyōgaku Kenkyūsho, ed. *Rennyo Shōnin gyōjitsu* (Kyoto:

Shinshū Ōtaniha Shumusho Shuppan, 1994), 38. (Though the title is the same, this is not RSG.)

12 As recorded on the first day of the eleventh month in Bunmei 6 (1474) in *Daijōin jisha zōjiki*, ibid., 87.

13 From a letter entitled, "Oki Munetomo, Miyake Toshinaga rensho shojō" printed in *Wajima shi Kōtokuji monjo*, 1974. Kigoshi Yūkei introduced this document to me.

14 *Niigata kenshi shiryōhen* 3, *chūsei* 1 (Niigata: Niigataken, 1982).

15 *Kai no kuni Myōhōji ki*, in Hanawa Hokiichi, ed. *Zoku gunshoruijū*, 30–1 (Tokyo: Zoku gunshoruijū kanseikai, 1902, 1925, etc.), 282.

16 From letter number 3 in the collection, "Shinne shojō," at SSS 4.72–73.

17 *Senjuji Echizen no kuni matsuji monto chū mōshijō an*, SSS 4.163.

18 *Enryakuji Saitōin shūgijō an*, in the "Seujuji Moujo (字)" collection at SSS 4.164.

19 For example, see Makino Shinnosuke, ed., *Shinsei Shōnin ōjōdenki*, in *Shinsei Shōnin godenki shū* (Tokyo: Sanshūsha, 1931).

20 *Muryōjukyō*, in SSZ 1.16.

21 *Jingtu lun*, in SSZ 1.269.

22 From the "Hōnen shōnin seppō, kōmyō kudoku" section of the *Saihōshinanshō* in SSZ 4.72.

23 *Ippen shōnin goroku*, in *Nihon shisō taikei*, vol. 10, *Hōnen, Ippen* (Tokyo: Iwanami Shoten, 1971), 300.

24 *Shinran Shōnin goshōsokushū* 9, at SSZ 2.711. Translation from CWS 1.571. (vol. 1.)

25 *Shōshinge tai'i* (Saihōji bon), SSS 2.123.

26 *Nihon kokugo daijiten* (Tokyo: Shōgakkan, 1974).

27 *Nihon shisō taikei* 11.184. The *Muryōjukyō jutsumonsan* passage by Kyeong-heung is at Translation from CWS 1.201. T No.1748, 37.155c3.

28 *Kanrin koroshū*, in Kamimura Kankō, ed., *Gozan bungaku zenshū*, vol. 4 (Tokyo: Gozanbungaku Zenshū Kankōkai, 1936).

29 *Tadatomiōki*, a record from the ninth month of the fifth year of the Meiō era, cited in Tsuji Zennosuke, *Nihon Bukkyōshi* (Tokyo: Iwanami Shoten, 1951), 6.137 (Chūsei hen 5).

30 Record of the fourth day of the seventh month, Entoku 4 (1492). *Gohōkōin-ki* published in 4 vols. facsimile ed. as vols. 22–25 in *Yōmei sōsho* (Kyoto: Shibunkaku, 1990).

31 *Hino ichiryū keizu*, at RSG 275, and SSS 7.527. See also *Hogo no uragaki* 反古裏書 by Kensei, in SSS 2.740.

32 Shobunshū 29, in SSS 2.162.

33 Shobunshū 29, in SSS 2.162.

34 Shobunshū 44, in SSS 2.172.

35 Shobunshū 53, in SSS 2.182.

36 Shobunshū 62, in SSS 2.188.

37 Shobunshū 33, in SSS, 2.165. Translation from Rogers, 163.

38 I tentatively say "at least for now" because there are as yet many questions about group membership that must be resolved: for example, did membership include all strata of people in village communities, did they necessitate the separation of men and women, and so on.

39 See Kasahara Kazuo, *Ikkō ikki no kenkyū*.

40 Takamaki Minoru, *Miyaza to sonraku no shiteki kenkyū* (Tokyo: Yoshikawa Kōbunkan, 1986), 56.

8

MINAMOTO RYŌEN
TRANSLATED BY MARK L. BLUM

Late Rennyo and the
Myōkōnin Akao no Dōshū

I have addressed the problems associated with the formation of *myōkōnin*[1] in the early period of Rennyo's life by considering the example of Kanegamori no Dōsai (1399–1488). During this period Rennyo followed Shinran in adopting the standpont that viewed faith (*shinjin*) as the true cause for Birth. Within Rennyo, however, new ideas were beginning to emerge.[2] In the *Mattōshō*, Shinran distinguished "one thought-moment nenbutsu of faith" (*shin no ichinen*) and "one thought-moment nenbutsu of practice" (*gyō no ichinen*) as fundamentally different yet inseparable, asserting that neither can exist without the other. By contrast, Rennyo began to think it prudent to focus on faith as the core of doctrine, and came to see the importance of affirming the phrase "faith in the merit transfer of the Other Power" (*tariki ekō no shin*). This is summed up in the dictum "*shinjin* is the true cause, *nenbutsu* is the expression of gratitude." It is on this philosophical basis that the deeply religious Kanegamori no Dōsai formed his relationship with Rennyo.

Now in the latter period of Rennyo's life, while he continues to assert this same doctrine of "*shinjin* is the true cause, *nenbutsu* is the expression of gratitude," he also offers a new formulation of the six characters that constitute the nenbutsu, as well as a new interpretation of the notion of *kihō ittai* 機法一体, or "unified body of the subject of faith and Dharma." This new combination, moreover, appears to have strengthened the proselytizing power of his teachings enormously, showing significant impact.

Interpreting the Nenbutsu

Rennyo's construction of a rationale for the six characters in the nenbutsu transformed the relationship between man and tathāgata into a personal relationship, bringing about a dialogue between them. The combination of this new interpretation of the six characters of the nenbutsu together with the doctrine of the unified body of individual and Dharma also led to a more dynamic relationship between these two elements. On the level of the meaning of the six characters, it led to a *myōkōnin*-like formation as seen in the figure of Akao no Dōshū (d. 1516). A similar *myōkōnin*-like formation resulting from the union of the "six-character formula" and the "unified body of individual and Dharma" emerged more than 400 years later in the modern *myōkōnin* Asahara Saiichi (1850–1932). I have written on Saiichi elsewhere.[3] Here I will only look at the figure of Akao no Dōshū.

The first attempt to explain the Pure Land teachings by way of interpreting the six characters of the nenbutsu (*na-mu a-mi-da butsu*) was made by Shandao (613–681). In the Xuanyifen (Japanese: Gengibun) chapter of his *Guanjing shu*, Shandao conceived of this notion, writing:

> To say the word *namu* [expresses] the taking of refuge; it also means [the practice] of committing oneself to Birth by merit transfer. To say *Amida-butsu* is precisely that [act of] practice. It is with this meaning that one will attain Birth without fail.[4]

Shandao interpreted the six characters in *na-mu a-mi-da butsu* (Chinese: *nan-wu a-mi-tuo fo*) to include three meanings—"taking refuge," "desiring Birth and transferring merit toward realizing that goal," and "praxis"—and that is why Shandao's and later interpretations of the nenbutsu phrase are referred to by the rubric known as the "six-character interpretation." The first word, *namu*, comes from the Sanskrit *namas* but was interpreted in China as an expression of entrusting in the mind of the Buddha, expressed by the set phrase "to take refuge" (from the three refuges). Since faith in the mind-set of the tathāgata is reflective of an attitude of desiring to be reborn in the Pure Land, the word *namu* also includes the meaning of merit transfer as a commitment in one's aspiration to achieving or enabling Birth. And as the Name of Amida Buddha has been designated as "the practice for Birth," the holy name *amida-butsu* itself is endowed with the meaning of praxis. Thus the formula *namu amida butsu* includes the elements of commitment *and* practice, both necessary for Birth, making it possible to proclaim that those who invoke the Name will be reborn in the Pure Land without fail.

The chart shown here is an illustration of Shandao's interpretation (however, the markings connecting Amida Buddha and merit transfer as a commitment to enable Birth reflect interpretations not in Shandao; this will be discussed later).

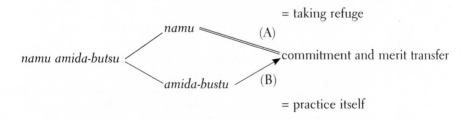

With this in mind, let us consider Rennyo's hermeneutic of the six characters that make up the nenbutsu. His ideas can be divided into two. One adds a new interpretation to the fundamental position reflected in the interpretation of Shandao in the Xuanyifen chapter of his *Guanjing shu*. The other diverges from Shandao in asserting that the commitment and merit-transfer aspect are workings of Amida Buddha. Let me first examine the former position.

From one of Rennyo's letters we have the following statement:

> 1. Grasping the *shinjin* of the Other Power is nothing other than this. We say that confirmation of *shinjin* comes when one fully grasps what the six characters [of the nenbutsu] *na-mu a-mi-da-butsu* actually mean. When we consider the embodiment of *shinjin* itself, it is as defined in the [*Larger*] *Sūtra* as "the joy of *shinjin* upon hearing the holy name."[5] It is also as Shandao glossed thus: "To say the word *namu* [expresses] the taking of refuge, and also means [the practice] of committing oneself to Birth by merit transfer. To say *Amida-butsu* is precisely that [act of] practice." *Namu* means to abandon all other forms of practice and to humbly request Amida Buddha singlemindedly, without doubt. The four characters of *a-mi-da-butsu* means Amida Buddha with extraordinary ease saves sentient beings who single–mindedly take refuge in him. To realize the embodiment of *namu amida butsu* in this way means to grasp *shinjin*. In other words, this what we refer to as the practitioner of nenbutsu who has deeply realized the *shinjin* of *tariki*.[6]

Next is a letter by Rennyo that explains the act of merit transfer as a commitment to enable Birth as a function of *namu* and taking refuge:

> 2. When the Tathāgata Amida was still in training as a bodhisasttva for the purpose of establishing the means by which ordinary persons could be born in his land, he understood that such persons found it difficult to accomplish their own transfer of merit for Birth because it depended entirely on their own efforts (*jiriki*). To aid these ordinary persons he therefore labored long and hard, ultimately accomplishing the turning over of his own merit so he could bestow merit transfer to us. So when we take refuge by means of the single thought-moment [concentrated] in the word *namu*, this very merit transfer is thereupon bestowed upon us. Since it is not a merit transfer achieved on the side of ordinary beings, this merit transference of the Tathāgata is called the *non–merit transfer* from the practicioner's side.[7]

In this discussion, merit transfer as a commitment to enable Birth is an activity of Amida. This aspect cannot be seen in Shandao. In the chart, outlining Shandao's concept of the relationship between Amida Buddha and merit transfer as a commitment to enable Birth, I added the line with the arrow (→) to indicate consideration of Rennyo's position. This position, moreover, also indicates his thoughts on *tariki* merit transference.

Although there is some difference between the positions expressed in (1) and (2), I want to point out the main difference from the standpoint of Shandao. Shandao divided the six characters of the invocation of the name into three parts: "taking refuge," "merit transfer as a commitment to enable Birth," and "practice." Rennyo, on the other hand, divided the invocation into only two parts: *namu* and *amida-butsu*. This position is most clear in quotation (1), where Rennyo takes Shandao's two elements of "taking refuge" and "merit transfer as a commitment to enable Birth" and collapses them as referring to the same thing. He then rereads "taking refuge" as *namu*, and "practice" as *amida-butsu*, resulting in a conclusion that sees the two meanings of *namu* and *amida-butsu* as the body or essence (体) of *namu amida-butsu*. In other words, *namu* means "humble request to Amida

Buddha made single-mindedly, without doubt, and after abandoning all other forms of practice," and *amida-butsu* means salvation itself, "the principle by which [Amida Buddha], with extraordinary ease, saves sentient beings who single-mindedly take refuge in him." And realizing this "principle" is what is meant by *shinjin*. The possessor of this *shinjin* is "the practictioner of nenbutsu who has deeply realized the *shinjin* of *tariki*."

Like the thinkers of the Chinzei and Seizan branches of Jōdo-shū, Rennyo did not accept Shandao's interpretation verbatim. First of all, he followed Shinran's interpretation of the six character invocation, which took the position that "The phrase 'merit transfer as a commitment to Birth' refers to the mental freedom of the Tathāgata who, in having established his Vows, transfers to sentient beings the practice [by which they attain Birth]."[8] On the fundamental issue of Other-Power merit transfer, they take exactly the same position, but in Shinran we see two types of interpretation: one is of a piece with Shandao's view of "merit transfer as a commitment to enable Birth" as stated in the *Songō shinzō meimon* mention of the "commitment to Birth of the practicioner,"[9] and the other reflects his statement in the chapter on practice in the *Kyōgyōshinshō* previously quoted, "Tathāgata's merit transfer as a commitment to enable Birth." This situation was neglected, leading to a state of perplexity for later preachers of the faith. No one had reached the structural conclusion of Rennyo's interpretation of the six-character invocation, which combined both positions by idenifying "merit transfer as a commitment to enable Birth" with *namu* and *amida-butsu*. It is my opinion that Rennyo owes a great deal in this understanding to the intellectual impact of the philosophy of "unified body of individual and Dharma" found in the *Anjinketsujōshō*.

Rennyo's Nenbutsu and *Myōkōnin*

Next I will take up the question of how the formation of the *myōkōnin* tradition in the Shinshū religious organization is related to Rennyo's move which took the threefold interpretation of the six-character invocation of the Name and changed it into a twofold interpretation based on *namu* and *amida-butsu*. The best approach to this problem is to see how Rennyo's interpretation of the six-character nenbutsu evolved over time in the record of his thoughts, words, and activities collected in the *Rennyo Shōnin go-ichidaiki kikigaki*, abbreviated here as *Kikigaki*. Let us first look at three of Rennyo's comments on Shandao's statement, "*Namu* indicates taking refuge; this means a commitment to enable Birth through transfering merit":

1. [Rennyo said] "*Namu* means taking refuge [*kimyō*]; 'Taking refuge' means to ask Amida for help in one thought-moment. Also, merit transfer as a commitment to Birth is [the process by which] great merit and great virtue are suddenly given [by the Buddha] to the being who aks for assistance. The embodiment of this is none other than *namu amida-butsu*.[10]

2. *Shinjin* is, at the time of the one thought-moment when one implores Amida for help, the sudden state of salvific assistance bestowed [by the Buddha]; we call this *namu amida-butsu*.[11]

3. *Namu* is taking refuge, and this state of mind is that of asking [the Buddha] for help. And in the state of mind of taking refuge, one feels that mind [of the Buddha] transferring merit [to oneself for] the commitment to Birth.[12]

In the glosslike explanation in (1), we are only given a general, somewhat abstract description. In (2) the angle has changed, and instead a particular formula of faith is expounded which, in extolling *namu amida-butsu* as the form of help that suddenly manifests when one asks for that help in one-thought moment, expresses a union between the subject of that faith taking refuge in the Buddha and the salvation itself. In (3) he has deepened his penetration within the mind of the believer to offer the explanation that there is a sympathetic response between the mind of the subject of this faith which has completely asked the Buddha for help and the mind of the subject for salvation. The "doctrine" relevant to this notion of salvation inevitably brings forth the problem of *anjin* within the living experience of the believer's faith.[13]

The world of faith manifest in statement (3) is, I believe, the doctrinal standpoint that opened up the possibility for the path of the *myōkōnin*. In the realm of (3), the Tathāgata and the believer begin a dialogue. At the end of his life, while reciting the invocation of *namu amida-butsu*, Rennyo maintained a dialogue with the Tathāgata. He distanced himself from the use of abstract language which referred to the Tathāgata as a *sambhogakāya buddha*, preferring references to a "living buddha" as in "the individual who single-mindedly and humbly requests help is one who is well aware of the tathāgata."[14] The individual who "knows" the Tathāgata in this way is the self who "feels the mind of merit transference as a commitment to Birth."

In terms of religious philosophy, Rennyo's position remained unchanged from his original standpoint of "*shinjin* as the orthodox cause [for Birth], invocation as requital for the Buddha's benevolence." But in the way he relished *shinjin*, there is a depth to Rennyo's writings at this time not seen in the *Letters* written during his younger years. As a believer, Rennyo began to look more and more like a *myōkōnin* in his later years, focusing on this continual dialogue with "Tathāgata." The pious followers of Rennyo now began to walk the same path that Rennyo walked, developing their own dialogues with the Tathāgata. From this collective experience, the religious nature of Jōdoshinshū deepens considerably.

The widespread acceptance of the notion of a dialogue between Tathāgata and believer came about as a result of the doctrinal establishment of Rennyo's interpretation of the nenbutsu, particularly in regard to the unification of *namu* and *amida-butsu* that he asserted. That is, it was a result of the establishment of an "I–thou" relationship (here one is reminded of the fact that Rennyo's disciple Kanamori no Dōsai called the Buddha by the pronoun "you" [*anata*]). And among the believers under Rennyo's influence, some referred to the Buddha as an intimate, calling him *nyorai-sama, nyorai-san*, and in some cases even as a parent with the form *oya-sama*, all of these forms using the Japanese titles of courtesy *san* or *sama* normally applied to known people.[15] For these people, this unending dialogue with the Buddha led them to a dialogue with themselves; in other words, we are seeing the expression of a remarkably frank internal dialogue in a form that Rennyo, the leader of their religion, never clearly indicates. I am not in a position to know how much this expression of dialogue with the Buddha and dialogue with the self enriched the religious world of Jōdo Shinshū, but the fact that so many were attracted to the *myōkōnin* from both within and without the Shinshū organization appears to have been the result of the directness of this expression as well as the depth and purity of its religiousness. The most brilliant example of such a person is Akao no Dōshū.

Akao no Dōshū

Among all the known examples of *myōkōnin*, there is no one about whom we have so many anecdotes as Akao no Dōshū. Despite questions about the veracity of the stories, they all nevertheless betray a certain consistency, allowing us to gain a fairly good picture of what type of person this man was. Anyone trying to create an image of him would be drawn to these statements. But without being drawn into the anecdotal literature, let me first introduce two passages in the *Kikigaki* where Dōshū is mentioned simply as a believer:

> Dōshū said, "I may continually hear the same words, but I still have the same sense of gratitude I felt the first time [I heard them]."[16]

> "When one thinks that they cannot do what their spiritual advisor has suggested, it is truly deplorable. But howsoever one has been instructed, if these words come [from their spiritual advisor] then one should be resolved to the fact that they will indeed get it done. After all, in that we become buddhas in this very body as ordinary persons, is there really anything that we should think we cannot do? For that reason, if [I] said 'Dōshū, dig Lake [Biwa] of Ōmi[17] by yourself,' he would respond by saying, 'As you wish.' Is there really anything that, if so asked, one cannot do?"[18]

The first statement does not make sense in the context of normal worldly experience. On the level of usual human intellectual knowledge, repeatedly hearing something we already know creates stress. But in the realm of spirituality, the truth uncovered by Śākyamuni 2,400 or 2,500 years ago still makes sense today. These words of Śākyamuni have been repeated over and over as they pass from one generation to another. Those who are always able to hear these timeless truths as if they were fresh, new ideas are truly religious people. But for nearly all of us this is impossible. Dōshū, however, was someone who was able to do this. The fact that he has been considered one of the *myōkōnin* can be understood from this fact.

The second quotation can lead to a completely opposite result depending on who is giving the orders. Herein lies the danger of religion. The recipient must have the ability to judge intuitively the validity of the words in the commands he receives and the truthfulness of the person giving those commands. Because people like Dōshū and Shinran (in the *Tannishō*) undergo a fundamental rejection of self such that they are convinced they have no ability to avert falling into hell anyway, I think they were able to see the true nature of their teachers and understand the truth in their words. But when religious followers have not gone through this denial of self, the situation is dangerous.

With the following comments by Rennyo about Dōshū, I would now like to consider the contents of the document entitled *Akao no Dōshū kokoroe nijūichi kajō* (Twenty-one Rules Resolved by Akao Dōshū).[19] This statement of self-discipline was put together by Akao no Dōshū himself on the twenty-fourth day of the twelfth month of 1501, two years and nine months after Rennyo's death. Before I read this *Dōshū kokoroe nijūichi kajō*, I had the impression that Dōshū was a person of integrity and intense self-reflection. In particular I had assumed he fit into the category of "ascetic monk," somehow different from the other so-called *myōkōnin* such as Shōmatsu 庄松 (1800–1872) or Asahara Saiichi, mentioned earlier. But when I read this text I realized how completely mistaken I had been. While it is true that Dōshū did have a personality of integrity and self-reflection, and that this marks him as different from the *myōkōnin* of the late Edo period, such issues are relevant only to the way in which *myōkōnin* are seen by society and have nothing to do with the essence of what makes someone a *myōkōnin*. On the issue of "ascetic monk," however, while he did live an intentionally austere life, it was not motivated by the usual objective of such people, which it to gain enlightenment by means of the most difficult forms of religious practice. Dōshū put himself through austerities after his attainment of faith so that he would not forget his sense of gratitude toward the Buddha, who accomplished the forty-eight vows that created Amida's Pure Land. This motivation is fundamentally different from the self-imposed way of living based in what can only be called a *jiriki* approach to austere practice.

The *Akao no Dōshū kokoroe nijūichi kajō* is not a systematically organized work. At the end of the first year of Bunki (1501) Dōshū decided to write down a number of things he had long been contemplating, particularly after the death of Rennyo. A series of short statements meant to serve as a kind of guideline to further discipline himself, these are clearly issues that gushed forth from within him, and it reads like a beautiful song. The main topics, as was pointed out by Iwami Mamoru,[20] are the following:

1. [Considering] the important matter ahead in the next life [where we have a chance to reach buddhahood], as long as one is alive one cannot loosen one's discipline.

2. To let anything outside the Buddha's Dharma be of serious concern to oneself is completely unacceptable; in other words, if this happens it must be overturned.

3. One should not back off from [contemplating the doctrines of Buddhism]; if one finds one has relaxed in this, that state of mind must be yanked out.

The rest is little more than variations on these themes. As a whole, the twenty-one points made here are reponses to what was taught to him by Rennyo, whom he traveled over many mountains to see in Yamashina, a report of how Dōshū intends, in his own way, to maintain those principles. For example, I think we can read statement one, as well as variations on this theme in statements twelve, seventeen, and twenty, as Dōshū's reponse to the following comment by Rennyo, which is recorded in both the *Kikigaki* and *Jitsugo kyūki*: "If even one individual is determined to gain faith, abandon yourself in your effort [to assist him]; such abandonment of the self is not an abandonment at all."²¹ In order to help even one believer attain a true faith, Rennyo was not reluctant to give up his own life. Dōshū's response was suitably stern, as in this passage from statement twelve:

> Even if one were to starve to death or freeze to death in this life, if such events were to lead to resolving the major issue of the next life, then one could nevertheless be satisfied knowing that what one has been seeking from immeasurable kalpas in the past has finally been realized. You must discipline yourself utterly, to immediately give rise to astonishing surprises.

There are also a number of anecdotes that show him putting his life on the line in pursuit of religious truth.

On the issue of *shinjin*, there are too many examples to give them all. His comments in sections seventeen, "One should immediately correct the mistaken understandings of fellow seekers," and nineteen, "No matter how many times it occurs, one must follow the advice of others," are both included in the *Jitsugo kyūki* as well, and they appear to express direct acceptance of Rennyo's dictum recorded in the *Kikigaki*:

> Rennyo Shōnin said, "Speak up, say what is on your mind." He would say that those who refuse to speak make him shudder, adding "Whether you have faith or don't have faith, just say what you are thinking. If you state what is on your mind, others can understand what you are thinking, and you can be corrected by someone else. Just say what is on your mind.²²

In section six Dōshū makes the statement, "Knowing that things here are mysteriously illuminated, even if no one here knows about it, bad things must be reversed." This is obviously a reflection of Rennyo's comment, "People are ashamed of what their friends or colleagues might see, but do not fear the thoughts of buddhas. It is only what the buddhas and bodhisattvas mysteriously see that we should fear."²³ Considering the fact that the *Akao no Dōshū kokoroe nijūichi kajō* was written before both the *Jitsugo kyūki* and *Kikigaki* were compiled, these correlations confirm the latter texts to be considerably faithful representations of Rennyo's sayings. In addition, from the section that closes the *Akao no Dōshū kokoroe nijūichi kajō*, we have the following:

> Repeatedly I call to you, my mind, not to violate the rules and principles [of the path], internally to maintain the confidence and gratitude of the one thought-moment [of *shinjin*], and externally to take the deepest care [with others].

It has been pointed out by Satō Taira that this excerpt mirrors the content of letter 4:2 in Rennyo's *Letters*.²⁴

This is not to say that everything in this document by Dōshū is under the influence of Rennyo. And even sections that do show the influence of Rennyo often also contain strong elements of Dōshū's personal orientation. A good example of the former can be seen in article eight of the *Akao no Dōshū kokoroe nijūichi kajō*, where Dōshū states:

> To expect to be esteemed in the world because you have faith in the Dharma is utterly contemptible. If such thoughts do arise in you, you would do well to redirect

your thoughts instead toward the fact that faith in the Buddha's Dharma is there
to settle the issue of Birth, the most important thing in life.

Statements like these transcend the teachings of Rennyo; these are born from the
individual experience of Dōshū and his motivation to discipline himself.

The individuality of Dōshū can be seen even further in the following statements.
Based on the assumptions of the difficulties surrounding the path to faith in *tariki
shinjin*, Rennyo made statements such as "Do not accept your state of mind as is,
but discipline your mind." Similarly, Dōshū said in article twenty-one, "Be severe
with yourself, strive to the limits of your pain." For Rennyo, saying "Be severe with
your thoughts" was quite enough, but Dōshū changed this to "Be severe with
yourself." Here we see how Dōshū seemed to be uncomfortable without something
more concrete, and the language of "Strive to the limits of your pain" (*tashinamikiru*)
is similarly missing from Rennyo's vocabularly. In contrast to the literary expression
illustrative of Rennyo's well-rounded, broad personality, Dōshū exhibits nothing of
the scale of Rennyo but he does share a certain thoroughness. There are three
places in the *Akao no Dōshū kokoroe nijūichi kajō* where Dōshū used an expression
not seen in Rennyo, "that state of mind must be yanked out" (*shinjū wo hikiyaburu*):
sections three, ten, and thirteen. We see this thoroughness in his willing destruction
of his present state of mind in statements in which Dōshū is not bothered by the
prospect of baring his own mind and exposing it to others. This eccentricity of
Dōshū is in fact the source of his integrity.

However, if a person's integrity is limited to this sort of thing, then even if he
is thorough in his sense of morality, we still see no hint of religiosity. Within the
Akao no Dōshū kokoroe nijūichi kajō, statements ten, twelve, and twenty-one contain
elements not seen in the others. I was particularly moved by these sections, and I
concur with Iwami's readings of ten and twenty-one. Here is section ten in full:

> Whenever I think, "My thoughts are that dreadful," I feel miserable, sad, and in
> pain. Until now I have always sought forgiveness, but nevertheless whenever I feel
> that my mind is in such a state, I keenly feel my worthlessness, my sadness, and
> everythings seems so wretched. It is precisely because in my former life I also had
> a mind that was useless that my present condition is as it is today. But when I think
> of that, my feelings of wretchedness have no limit. If I should see you at the end
> of all this,[25] I will still feel miserable. Yet somehow I seem to be one who has
> received the unknowing protection of the Buddha. I earnestly seek forgiveness for
> all that I have felt guilty about up until the present day, and will proceed with full
> acceptance of what [the Buddha] has said.

The biggest problem with this passage is that we do not know to whom it was
directed. Iwami thinks it is directed to You [the Tathāgata], whereas Satō feels it is
directed to Rennyo. Satō's reasoning is based on the fact that the this section ten is
associated with Dōshū's writing on the eve of a memorial to Rennyo two years and
nine months after his death, and thus should be read as a narrative directed at a
Rennyo who had returned to the Pure Land. This view also gives consideration to
the fact that Dōshū considered Rennyo to have been an incarnation of Amida
Buddha.[26] I thought this to be a cogent argument. On the other hand, considering
that Dōshū was so faithful a disciple of Rennyo, I think that he followed Rennyo's

teachings and indeed Rennyo's own practice of speaking directly to the Buddha. If one considers the intimacy of the thoughts expressed in the statements in this document, then the theory that he was speaking to Rennyo is plausible, but when we consider the fact that the doctrines that Dōshū encountered from Rennyo during the latter's later years were centered upon his interpretation of the six-character nenbutsu and the theory of the unity of Dharma and practicioner, and that Rennyo at this time continually told his followers that he was nothing more than a spiritual advisor to them (*zenchishiki*), we should probably see Dōshū as an accomplished disciple of Rennyo. Therefore I think it is more natural to favor the theory that he was directing his statements to the Tathāgata.

In order not to forget the effort made by the Tathāgata to accomplish his vows, Dōshū's ability to empathize resulted in his sleeping on top of firewood representing the forty-eight vows of the Buddha. Thus it is not at all strange to consider the intimacy displayed by his thoughts to be directed to the Buddha. Having said that, however, I also feel it is important to take into account the fact that he considered Rennyo himself to have been an incarnation of the Tathāgata. It seems quite possible that Dōshū did not even realize himself that his appeal to the Buddha and feelings of emotional attachment to Rennyo had become fused together in this text. But I nevertheless believe that basically they are written as an appeal to the Buddha. From this position I think we can conclude that, for example, article ten is not directed specifically to Rennyo, but that all twenty-one articles of the *Akao no Dōshū kokoroe nijūichi kajō* are expressions of Dōshū's response to Rennyo and his teachngs.

Any further analysis of this problem seems moot. Let me end this discussion by saying that I concur with the opinion of Iwami:

> I see Dōshū as a strong personality, solemnly engaged in self-examination. This sentiment undergirds the all twenty-one articles in this document. But there is another important characteristic of his personality that also comes through in two of the articles, particularly article ten. This passage repeatedly expresses a deep pathos where even his rigorous self-examination has disintegrated. This expresses not strength but a bottomless weakness. Is *shinjin* something so weak?... Is *shinjin* characteristic of someone who throws himself down before the Buddha, the unlimited weakness of someone prostrate before the Buddha?[27]

There is one more article among the twenty-one that calls for such a reading. This is the final assertion, number twenty-one. Although it is somewhat long, I quote it in full:

> How miserable is this mind of mine. If I am to attain resolution of the one great matter of the next life, I must not be concerned with issues of how many of something [I have] but be prepared mentally to go the end of anywhere in order to follow whatever you say. I am in a state of mind wherein I would go even to China or India in search of the Dharma. Such is the resolution in my heart, and I will follow your words without guilt, enduring anything [たしなみ候わん] in pursuit of the truth of the Dharma. And yet I know that this is not an easy thing to do. I have said this to you over and over again, mind of mine: remember that this life happens only once, and it is not a very long life at that! Even if one were to starve to death or freeze to death, do not look back. Do not relax your concern

for the critical issue of the next life. Do not diverge from what I have said repeatedly: you must discipline yourself in striving as if your life depended on it. Repeatedly I call to you, mind of mine, not to violate the rules and principles [of the path], internally to maintain the confidence and gratitude of the one thought-moment [of *shinjin*], and externally to take the deepest care [with others].

After his dialogue with the Tathāgata in article ten, Dōshū concludes in his final remarks in article twenty-one by dialoguing with himself. This dialogue is an outgrowth of his dialogue with the Buddha and can be seen as a natural development. The very fact that this type of dialogue was written down has enormous signficance in the history of religious thought. In the fact that he dared to do this lies his contribution to the noncontrived spirituality of the *myōkōnin*, and we should consider him to be the person who triggered this whole approach.

But for Dōshū himself, these dialogues with his own mind are replete with an intensity of his beseeching himself for something more. We see a sense of self engaged in a life that has put his very life on the line in the pursuit of truth, a self that attempts to lead a life of faith as repayment for the pain and suffering undergone by the Tathāgata over eons of disciplined practice. Thus he calls out to his own mind: do not slacken your resolve regarding the singular issue of the next life, be strict with yourself and strive to the limit of your pain. He further entreats his mind to maintain rules and principles, as well as a sense of confidence and gratitude in his faith of one thought-moment. Article twenty-one ultimately ends with a call to execute care in one's behavior toward others, echoing similar statements in Rennyo's *Letters*.

There is a tension in this document that we do not see in the material related to the *myōkōnin* of the Edo period and afterward. It brims with a vigor that refuses to allow even a moment of laziness. We can probably attribute this energy to Dōshū's personality, the period in which he lived, and the fact that, according to what has been transmitted about him, he was the son of a former minister of the politically unsuccessful southern court, and hence his family had removed itself from society. Also relevant may be the fact that he lived in rather severe conditions in the mountains, where people must live according to how they actually feel.

In addition to the two articles cited earlier, there is another passage that includes something I had never imagined associated with Dōshū. This is the discussion of self-discipline required for the religious life as seen from the point of view of "surprise" described in statement twelve. This section provides an important clue as to how this severe life of faith was made possible by a novel and flexible religious sensitivity:

If the kind of surprises that rattle your senses do not to occur within the mind, you should think, "Oh, how dreadful. What a waste. In this life, even if one were to starve to death or freeze to death, if such events were to lead to resolving the major issue of the next life, then one could nevertheless be satisfied knowing that what one has been seeking from immeasurable kalpas in the past has finally been realized." You must disciple yourself utterly, in order to immediately give rise to astonishing surprises. But if even then there are no surprises, then you will know that this means that this self may have received some form of punishment [from the Buddha]." The mind should then be ripped apart, for then when you meet a fellow seeker and ritually praise the Buddha, you will be intensely surprised.

In this rather short passage, the word "surprise" occurs no less than four times. Even for someone who has attained faith, aside from the specific time when that first occurs, that sort of experience becomes part of a daily routine and the joy gradually lessens, the faith continuing more by force of habit. What he is saying is that when someone suddenly realizes that he has lost the feelings of intense "surprise" and joy at learning that even someone like one's own self is saved, he should think, "Ah, how dreadful. What a waste. In this life, solving the major issue of the next life and being able to attain Birth, even if I were to starve or freeze to death, is precisely what I have been seeking over immeasurable kalpas, and it has finally been satisfied." Then he should discipline himself and surprises will occur. But if even then no surprises come, then what does what one do? In that case, Dōshū says that one should consider the fact "that this means that this self may have received some form of punishment from the Buddha." The mind should then be "ripped apart," and upon meeting fellow seekers if you ritually praise the Buddha, you will be intensely surprised.

Aristotle said that surprise was the fountainhead of philosophy, and intellectual surprise is precisely that. But surprise is not limited to intellectual pursuits. The real world in which we live contains a variety of forms of hidden surprises. While it is true that to some degree intellectual progress brings with it a corresponding disappearance of surprise in our lives, the other side of this phenomenon is that by forgetting our experience of surprise we also forget about the meaning of being human itself. Our minds become drained of fresh emotions. The "surprise" mentioned in Dōshū's statements here represents the latter case.

Rennyo said:

> When you hear something, you should always feel the rarity of it, as if you are hearing it for the first time—this is the way someone of faith is supposed to be.... No matter how many times you hear of this one thing, it should always sound as rare as if it is the first time.[28]

When Dōshū speaks of something being *arigataki*, "rare and deserving of gratitude," this sentiment corresponds to Rennyo's use of the word *mezurashiki*, "rarity" here. When Dōshū is praised by Rennyo as having said, "Whenever I hear just these same words, I feel the same gratitude [*arigataki*] as the first time I heard them,"[29] it is because he has taken care not to lose that thought-moment of surprise that comes from "this self who is destined to fall being saved." But on top of this, Dōshū also realized that his existence was that of someone who was not surprised at what he should have been surprised at. Thus whenever he noticed himself not being surprised by what should have surprised him, he would utter the word "dreadful" (*asamashi*).

Notes

This chapter originally appeared as "Kōki Rennyo to myōkōnin Akao no Dōshū" 後期蓮如と妙好人赤尾の道宗, in *Rennyo no sekai* 蓮如の世界, ed. Ōtani Daigaku Shinshū Sōgō Kenkyūjo, Kyoto: Bun'eidō, 1998, 291–307.

1 The term *myōkōnin* 妙好人, "wondrous person," was coined to designate certain saintlike laymen in the Shin tradition from the Muromachi period onward who gained recognition for their humility, faith, and charisma.

2 See Minamoto Ryōen, *Rennyo*, in *Jōdoshū no shisō* 12 (Tokyo: Kodānsha, 1993), 266–267. On Shinran's thoughts on this matter, see SSZ 2.261, 263, and 268.

3 Minamoto Ryōen, "Myōkōnin Asahara Saiichi to Rennyo—hitsotsu no shiron," in Jōdo Shinshū Kyōgaku Kenkyūjo, ed. *Rennyo Shōnin kenkyū* (Kyoto: Nagata Bunshōdō, 1998).

4 T 37.250a28.

5 T 12.272b9.

6 *Letters* 5:11; SSZ 3.508.

7 *Letters* 3:8; SSZ 3.463.

8 *Kyōgyōshinshō*, SSZ 2.22.

9 SSZ 2.567.

10 *Kikigaki* 6, SSZ 3.532.

11 *Kikigaki* 7, SSZ 3.533.

12 *Kikigaki* 8, SSZ 3.533.

13 Regarding this problem, see Minamoto, *Rennyo*, 354.

14 *Kikigaki* 83, SSZ 3.552.

15 In spoken Japanese, *anata* is a polite second-person pronoun; the word *nyorai* is the Japanese word for *Tathāgata*, one of the epithets of all buddhas and often a preferred form in the Shin tradition.

16 *Kikigaki* 131, SSZ 3.564.

17 Rennyo is referring to Biwako, the largest lake in Japan.

18 *Kikigaki* 192, SSZ 3.578.

19 *Akao Dōshū kokoroe nijūichi kajō* is at SSS 2.712–713.

20 Iwami Mamoru, *Akao no Dōshū* (Kyoto: Nagata Bunshōdō, 1956), 109.

21 *Kikigaki* 114, SSZ 3. 560.

22 *Kikigaki* 86, SSZ 3. 553.

23 *Kikigaki* 133, SSZ 3. 564.

24 See note 12 on p. 373 of Mizukami Tsutomu and Satō Taira, eds. *Myōkōnin*, in *Daijō butten—Chūgoku Nihon hen*, vol. 28 (Tokyo: Chūō Koronsha, 1987).

25 This may be a reference to his deathbed, or it may indicate his state after reaching the Pure Land.

26 Minakami and Satō, *Myōkōnin*, 373.

27 Iwami, *Akao no Dōshū*, 128–129.

28 *Kikigaki* 130, SSZ 3.564; *Jitsugo kyūki* 64, RSG, 86.

29 *Kikigaki* 131, SSZ 3.564; *Jitsugo kyūki* 65, RSG, 86.

9

MARK L. BLUM

Rennyo Shōnin, Manipulator of Icons

The Iconic and Aniconic in Buddhism

There can be no question that the role of icons in the history of Buddhism suggests a pantheistic system. At least this would be the view of Roy Rappaport, who, in *Ritual and Religion in the Making of Humanity*, understands this to be the case when religious images have different roles for different people within a given culture. This means, of course, that religious images in Buddhist cultures may take on an array of context-specific meanings, but also that ancient symbols with well-established pedigrees of meaning may, at some point, find those pedigrees torn up and thrown out. In Rennyo we find just such an example of pedigree burning. Rennyo is known for many accomplishments in his successful drive to reshape the landscape of the Jōdoshin school of Japanese Buddhism into one wholly dominated by his Honganji line, but one of the least appreciated is his effective use of the visual symbols of his lineage. This essay is an exploration of how Rennyo understood and exploited the iconic power of images for his community and sought to redefine their sacrality. I hope to show that this process is best seen not as a secondary by-product of Rennyo's religious outlook but as something representative of his specific line of thought. In short, Buddhist art for Rennyo was deployed not only as a means to express his personal concept of orthodoxy but also to expand Honganji's religious, social, and political control under his leadership.

Japanese Buddhist images from this period invite a variety of interpretations, cultural matrices that invoke defining metaphors for the religious community and its politics, economics, freedom, security, and history. When considering the relationship of religious art to the people who construct and maintain its meaning, anthropologists have long spoken of the transition from "image" to "symbol." This is said to take place when a visual form dissociates from the specific context that gave birth to it, a process that allows it to function over a broad range of contexts among disparate communities.[1] In Buddhism images typically become symbols rather quickly, for they are readily shared across schools, sects, and nationalities. And yet in its striving during to create an identity separate from the other competing movements in Pure Land Buddhism, Shin walked away from this norm to develop new forms of ritually empowered art that stood out as unique. The result was a plurality of sacred artistic expression and an opening for Rennyo to express his sense of orthodoxy through his personal iconic vocabularly.

Pure Land Buddhism has a long tradition of iconography that is both pictorial and sculptural, as seen in the common images of the Buddha Amitābha in nearly all schools of Buddhism throughout the Mahāyāna world. Indeed visualization meditation is thought to have been at the heart of Huiyuan's (334–416) Amitābha practice, traditionally designated as the beginning of the "tradition" in China.[2] Precisely what the "re-presentation" of the standing Buddha, at times surrounded by bodhisattvas, is supposed to mean is not entirely clear, however. Neither is the believer's relationship to that icon nor how that relationship is established, recreated, or confirmed when he faces it. At the very least we can say it is fundamental to the process of defining the religious consciousness of a community not only by providing an established, accessible referent to the sacred, but also by demonstrating the relationship between the believer and the sacred. When we consider some of the unusual developments in the religious symbols of Jōdoshinshū during the fourteenth and fifteenth centuries, it is clear that these manifold expressions reflect both a diversity and an evolution in religious consciousness within Shinshū cultures of the time. Rennyo's reaction to this situation was to push for standardization in iconography, even while his own conception of sacred art became more diversified as he grew older. That notwithstanding, the success of his endeavors with icons played no small role in his expansion of the perception of the Honganji as a kind of symbolic mother asserting its authority to clarify the distinct religious identity of Shin Buddhism, particularly as opposed to other forms of Pure Land belief and practice.[3]

Differing perceptions of religious symbols or icons indicate differing presumptions of functionality as well, and the resultant disparity often creates a tension not easily resolved. We expect the presence of some degree of this tension because icons by their very nature are not mere signs, they are *representative* signs. In the case of medieval Japan, there is much evidence suggesting that certain icons entailed strong community identification, which in turn gave these icons exalted status. Well-known examples are the Amida Triad at Zenkōji in Nagano and the Shaka Triad of Seiryōji in Kyoto, both of which were copied many times and installed at other religious institutions throughout the country. The grandest example of this phenomenon, of course, is the Great Buddha (daibutsu) Tōdaiji, a colossus large enough and politically imposing enough to enjoy, at least traditionally, the entire nation as its community. An example of a single image with similar authority is the Kannon at Kiyomizudera in Kyoto, which acquired unique power and prestige among hundreds of other Kannon images throughout the country.

As communities identified with their images, so images came to represent communities. This was true for individual images such as the Kannon at Kiyomizudera as well as entire categories or rubrics of images, such as "statues of Maitreya." How the politically powerful dealt with images was thus a fundamental manifestation of their religious and political outlook. At times this could become destructive, for threatening an image of representative stature directly threatened its supporting community. There are three ways in which Rennyo's career was intimately linked to this gestalt:

1. Rennyo's role as representative of a received iconic tradition of Shin Buddhist that was both imagistically rich and iconoclastic.
2. The persecution of Rennyo and burning of the Honganji complex for the alleged crime of destroying Buddhist icons.
3. Rennyo's wielding of icons within Shin for the purpose of defining its iconic orthodoxy.

Rennyo was not the first leader to understand and exploit the power of sacred art to authenticate Honganji as the true inheritor of the legacy of the founder Shinran (1173–1262); for that honor we can look to Kakunyo's commissioning of the biography scrolls of Shinran. We even know that Zonnyo, Rennyo's father, had hanging scrolls made with sacred images similar to those created by Rennyo. But the intensity and personal effort poured into the production and distribution of *honzon* scrolls by Rennyo was unprecedented, and it manifests his confidence in this method of communication as making a significant contribution to his efforts to expand Honganji's influence.

Since Buddhist images enshrined on an altar rarely occur singularly, in Japan focus came to be placed on the central image, called *honzon* 本尊. Thus while there may be many iconic forms imbued with religious significance in a place of religious ritual, it is only the *honzon* that is regarded as the *representative* image or icon of that community or institution. For example, despite the popularity of images of the bodhisattva Kannon (Avalokiteśvara) in Japan, as evidenced in the cult surrounding the Kiyomizudera image, as an assistant devoted to Amida in the cosmology of the many Pure Land sūtras, Kannon frequently appears on altars with Amida Buddha but usually together with the Buddha's other assistant, called either Daiseishi or Seishi (Mahāsthāmaprāpta), in a parallel position flanking Amida and thus indicative of secondary status. The *honzon* in this environment is clearly Amida Buddha and the iconic display known as an Amida Triad (*Amida sanzon*). By contrast, at Kiyomizudera and a great many other temples, Kannon is the *honzon*, the central object of devotion and ritual in that space.

Another important distinction is in the medium used to express the icon. One can carve a sculpture of the devotional object, paint a picture of it, or write its name or a ritually uttered phrase that invokes his presence; any of these may be used as a ritual object and can serve as *honzon*. At times individuals or schools within the Buddhist tradition could take strong positions on what form an image should take, such as that taken by the Tang Pure Land patriarch Shandao (613–681), who said that Amida must be depicted standing rather than seated. Two-dimensional art also played in a important role in the spread of meditative and ritual practices on Pure Land themes when they were too complex to represent in three dimensions. This tendency is particularly strong in connection with the sutra known as the *Guanjing*.[4] In general, however, the presumption was that given a choice of how to depict a buddha or bodhisattva, tradition favored concreteness: sculpture was regarded as ideal, painted pictures were next, and written names were considered the least desirable. This ordering can be understood by reference to the legends attached to famous images, such as the Udayana statue of Śākyamuni carved in his presence, that presume a level of resemblance in a carved statue that is unattainable in a painting. But while painted images are suggestive of mental pictures of actual three-dimensional forms, textual representations are devoid of visual cues altogether. It is also probably no coincidence that the cost of material, time, and skill required to produce each form parallels its perceived religious value.

The Iconic Legacy of Shinshū

Rennyo survived the attacks from Mount Hiei in 1465 by escaping first to Ōmi and then as the attacks followed him, to Yoshizaki in Echizen Province. Part of the lore accompanying these events describes how he safely protected the Honganji image of Shinran during his escape from Kyoto, restored it, and ensured that it was temporarily enshrined in various locales before arriving "home" in the rebuilt Honganji in Yamashina in 1480.[5] The heroic qualities of this story reflect not only the celebrity of Rennyo but the transcendent power of the Honganji church itself as symbolized in its icon's ability to survive adversity. The full narrative, beginning with Rennyo's escaping the burning temple with the statue on his back and ending with its reenshrinement fifteen years later in a rebuilt Founder's Hall that was bigger and more beautiful than any previous structure, is akin to myths of righteous kingdoms once vanquished that rise again with intrepid leadership, with Rennyo playing the role of gallant knight. Since Honganji began as a shrine to Shinran, episodes like this one only reinforced the Shinran cult within it, and today the halls enshrining Shinran are far larger than those enshrining Amitābha in both Nishi and Higashi branches of the Honganji.[6]

This gallant story is one of many that testifies to the crucial iconic role of Shinran's image for Honganji,[7] and it naturally leads us to inquire of Shinran's own ideas about representation and its power. Let us briefly review what we know of the iconic legacy Shinran gave to his community, how it was understood, and how that understanding evolved into the fifteenth century, two hundred years after his death.

The faithful in Japan built upon the iconic legacy of Amitābha-centered Buddhism in East Asia from the very inception of Buddhism's introduction to the country in the fifth and sixth centuries. There is considerable production of Amida statues and scholarly treatises on the doctrines associated with the Amidist faith throughout the Heian period in the dominant Tendai and Shingon schools through the efforts of Ennin, Ryōgen, Genshin, Kakuban, and many others. Best known are the Tendai practices of *kanbutsu* and *nenbutsu* samādhi, as well as the deathbed rituals described by Genshin in his *Ōjōyōshū*. All of these require images and involve concentrated visualization. In Genshin's rather encyclopedic *Ōjōyōshū*, the Buddha is always beautiful and exhibits a definite otherworldly transcendence. A good example is the Amida statue at the Byōdōin in Uji.

Like Genshin, Hōnen's doctrine emphasized the descent of the Buddha to man, depicted in *raikō* (or *raigō*) paintings where the Buddha comes down from Sukhāvatī to greet someone facing death. But Hōnen embraced what was called the mud of this world in a way Genshin did not—at the time in his life when Genshin retreated to Yokawa, Hōnen came down to live in the capital. In extolling the unique power of the spoken nenbutsu as opposed to Genshin's stress on visualization nenbutsu, Hōnen delineated an approach to praxis that could, at least in principle, be performed entirely without an image. But in fact we know that under Hōnen's leadership monastic settings for nenbutsu practice remained the norm and nenbutsu recitation practice in group settings have presumably almost always been done before a statue. In his extant writings, however, Hōnen is not consistent on this point. Granted that many of the writings attributed to Hōnen have now fallen into question, the relatively well-accepted *Gyakushu seppō* itself indicates not only that the locale for nenbutsu practice should have a standing image of Amida on an altar and that the *raikō* ritual similarly require a standing statue, but also that other forms of representation are acceptable, such as what we might call the "universal light" form. He is explicit that painted or drawn Buddhas can have just as much transformative power as carved images, even in the *raikō* ritual.[8]

In fact, the iconic issue that most concerned Kamakura period Pure Land thinkers was whether the image of the Buddha should be standing or sitting, not whether it should be carved or painted.[9] Insofar as Hōnen quotes a line from Shandao insisting on the authoritative value of standing Buddhist sculpture, Shandao's phrase for this, *licuo jixing* (立撮即行), *rissatsu sokugyō* in Japanese pronunciation, soon emerged in the Jōdo school as defining its own orthodox position.[10] However strong Hōnen's reverence for Shandao, however, his personal valorization of the transformative power of spoken nenbutsu without samādhi attainment not only signified a break somewhat from the Tendai tradition, it also inevitably created a legacy that shifted ritual focus from visual images of the Buddha to linguistic representations of the Buddha. This resulted in a kind of iconic divide among the various sectarian lines that descend from Hōnen, with what we regard today as the Jōdoshū taking a conservative stance that rhetorically cleaves to the Shandao *licuo jixing* position, and Shinran and Ippen generally favoring linguistic forms.[11]

Shinran and *Honzon*

The fact that Hōnen mentions nonstandard forms of representation is important for understanding Shinran, because while Shinran is known for jettisoning the *raikō* ritual, his later use of linguistic forms of *honzon* would not have been possible without Hōnen's recognition of the sacrality of drawn images as *honzon* commensurate with sculpture. Hōnen thus forms an important link both doctrinally and iconographically between the older Heian Pure Land culture so elegantly expressed by Genshin and the *raikō* artists, and the newer forms of religious expression in Shinran, Kōsai, Ippen, and others.

Shinran himself never clarified his position on the form that a *honzon* should take, but he produced textual scrolls and an essay on scroll inscriptions, both of which led to Rennyo's initial preference for linguistic scrolls as his choice of representation. Around the time when the so-called furor over his son Zenran's behavior resulted in the latter's banishment,[12] that is, when he had passed the age of eighty, Shinran began to draw sacred phrases on silk scrolls. As a rule these were given to his disciples who, it is presumed, used them as *honzon*. The practice probably had humble beginnings—Shinran's responding to his students' yearning to take something of him home with them as a keepsake after a visit—since Shinran left no written record of his motivation. Shinran wrote one of the *myōgō* or ritually intoned phrases directed to the Buddha, and to this the image of a lotus dais was usually drawn in by someone else, and the full form also contained quotations from the *Larger Sukhāvatīvyūha Sutra* and Vasubandhu's *Pure Land Treatise* (*Jingtu lun*) written out on strips of paper that were glued above and below Shinran's calligraphy.

After Shinran died, these scrolls became highly prized, and seven are extant today. The parallel with Nichiren's Lotus Sutra mandala known as *gohonzon* seems obvious—both use language as sacred object—but there are important differences. Nichiren initially insisted this form of *honzon* was the only form of orthodoxy he recognized, a proclamation that required uniformity among all communities under his guidance; he thus created a great many scrolls and over 100 are extant. By contrast, Shinran left no such instructions, he drew very few scrolls, and we cannot even be sure that he intended his scrolls to be used as *honzon* at all. Nichiren's form is moreover overtly Tantric in conception, with an array of names of kami and bodhisattvas surrounding the sacred name of the Lotus Sutra; it is a complex, pluralistic form labeled a mandala by Nichiren himself, implying layers of meaning that may be hidden to the uninitiated. Shinran's focus, on the other hand, is the ultimate in simplicity: one phrase, nothing more, though sutra quotations were later added. The precedent for Nichiren's form is painted mandalas that evolved out of the need to include a plurality of sacred objects in one space and are thus symbols of a pantheon of sacred images. The basis of Shinran's conception is rather a single, unified vision of the infinite and reflects Hōnen's exclusive nenbutsu, which itself expresses a kind of polemic against the Tantric culture of Tendai, so evident in Nichiren's creation.

For the Shinshū tradition, Shinran's scrolls are said to embody a new conception of sacred imagery conceived and executed as language. But there are problems with this depiction. For one, the use of *bīja* characters as representations of the sacred, typically identified as a Tantric form of expression, has a long history prior to Shinran; in addition, the outline of the lotus dais that identified the sacred phrase as metaphorically indicative of the expected picture of a buddha is also a typical motif for *bīja* representations. It remains unclear what Shinran's *myōgō* scrolls were intended to express. Did he want them to have iconic value as a new form of metaphoric sign-image? Or were they merely symbols, and if so, of what? Were they meant to re-present a *verbal picture* of a statue of Buddha (itself a symbol), or the concept of *dharmakāya*, or the actual Buddha, or the individual's faith, the promise of Birth in the Pure Land, or the link between believer and Buddha, or the ritual experience of reciting the *myōgō*?

Unlike Nichiren, moreover, Shinran used three different sacred phrases in his scrolls, something that suggests he did not conceive of them as a new orthodoxy.[13]

After Shinran's death these textual scrolls become increasingly viewed as a symbol for Shinshū itself. This view is due partly to the fact that scrolls served as *honzon* for many Shinshū communities, often hung in little more than rural *dōjō*, where believers gathered in farmhouses and where sculptured buddhas would be prohibitively expensive. The ritual use of Shinran's text scrolls thus served to confirm this medium as legitimate *honzon* within Shin culture. Rennyo picks up on this tradition and expands it.[14]

But among the scrolls used as *honzon* in Shinshū *dōjō*, painted images of Amida were just as common as textual *myōgō*, and the fact that one of Shinran's extant scrolls is quite stylized and clearly made by a professional artist confirms his sensitivity to the iconic yearnings of his followers. In any case, when a *dōjō* grew into something larger and more substantial, that is, when they sought the appellation *jiin*, which conferred a certain legal legitimacy as monastery, the community generally sought to upgrade their *honzon* to a standing statue of the Buddha. Until the time of Rennyo, there was no explicit resistance to this sort of change, though it might not have pleased Kakunyo, as will be discussed. Even today we have no small amount of evidence that Shinran himself also displayed reverence for images.[15] In fact, of the seven extant *myōgō honzon* scrolls created by Shinran (including one for which he only wrote the inscriptions but had an artist create the calligraphy), five are at held today at Senjuji and a sixth is at Myōgenji, another Takada-branch temple, even though Senjuji has always used an Amida Triad statue as *honzon*, also said to have been given as a gift by Shinran. Shinran lived at a time when portraiture of patriarchs was regarded as worthy of being placed on the altars of monasteries, and this form of representation also became common in Shinshū temples, including representations of Shōtoku Taishi, a famous example of which is also at Senjuji. This interchangeability suggests that idealized images, portraits, and language were commonly revered as objects of religious ritual. There is nothing to suggest that Shinran regarded the *myōgō* scroll as normative.[16]

The cult to Shinran that was created after his death is also part of this paradigm. We know that when the gravesite of Shinran was turned into a shrine large enough to hold ceremonies, the image on the altar, that is, the *honzon*, was not Amida but a sculpture of Shinran himself. We also have evidence that images of Hōnen were similarly revered ritually as *honzon*. The final chapter in the Hōnen biography *Hōnen Shōnin gyōjō ezu*, for example, states that Kūamidabutsu was so taken with Hōnen that he regarded him as a living buddha. He asked the artist Fujiwara Nobuzane to paint a portrait of Hōnen, which he then placed on an altar and revered as *honzon* throughout his life.[17] We should also remember that the epilogue to Shinran's *Kyōgyōshinshō* explains that after Shinran asked Hōnen for permission to copy his *Senchakushū* and received it with a personalized Hōnen inscription added, he then asked Hōnen for permission to borrow and copy a portrait of Hōnen himself, a request that Hōnen not only granted but used as an occasion to add a much longer inscription summarizing the prooftext of the eighteenth vow and its enactment through nenbutsu. Now while we do not know what Shinran did with this image of Hōnen, the *Kechimyaku monjū*, a collection of Shinran letters, probably compiled in the generation after Shinran's death, refers to the Hōnen image with the personally written inscription as a *honzon*,[18] reflecting the identical combination of image and inscription described in the portraits of patriarchs discussed in Shinran's *Songō shinzō meimon*.

Nevertheless a rhetoric developed within Honganji that describes the liturgical *myōgō* scrolls as the orthodox form of *honzon*. In Shinshū today, particularly the Honganji branch, the official doctrinal position affirms that the proper *honzon* should be a scroll depicting one of the sacred *myōgō* that expresses entrusting oneself to Amida Buddha.[19] What I am suggesting here is that in querying how and why modern interpreters of the Honganji tradition came to the conclusion that Shinran *preferred* a textual icon rather than a pictorial one, we cannot overlook the role Rennyo played in this process of legitimation. Although it may be difficult to determine why Shinran began his dissemination of linguistic *honzon* only after reaching the age of eighty, this fact may indicate a certain development in his thought on what *honzon* for his communities signify and therefore what they should look like. In fact there is a similar pattern of change in how Rennyo approached *honzon*, since he, unlike Shinran, was explicit in the value he saw in using a certain conception of *honzon* to express his notion of ritual orthodoxy. Also unlike Shinran, Rennyo was aggressive in using the medium of *honzon* and associated notions of orthodoxy to expand his personal influence under the aegis of Honganji among disparate Shinshū communities.

Honzon Forms between Shinran and Rennyo

After Shinran's death, his lineage expanded in both membership and iconic forms. The best-known Shinshū writers from this period are Kakunyo (1270–1351), Shinran's great grandson, and Kakunyo's son Zonkaku. Kakunyo played an important role in establishing his family lineage at the center of the branch called Honganji, and in defining what that branch stood for.

Chapter 2 of Kakunyo *Gaijashō* (1337) contains a section on *honzon*. Here Kakunyo asserts unequivocally that Shinran did not rely on the standard *honzon* among Pure Land devotees in his time, namely a wooden statue of Amida as described in the eighth contemplation of the *Guanwuliangshou jing* (*Kangyō*), but instead preferred the ten-character ritual phrase of devotion to the Buddha of Infinite Light (*ki-myō jin-jip-pō mu-ge-kō nyo-rai*).[20] The essay also gives tacit recognition, however, to the fact that "it is commonplace to enshrine paintings of the blessed images of the founder and patriarchs in the transmission of the teachings over the three nations."[21] For a document that is overwhelmingly dogmatic—the title means *Reforming Heretical Doctrines*—the tone here is saliently accepting of other forms of *honzon*. In other words, although Kakunyo's intention was aimed at establishing the ten-character *myōgō* as the orthodox *honzon* for the Honganji community, he also acknowledged the use of portraits and statues as *honzon*.

The next significant marker of Honganji views on *honzon* is found in the writings of Zonkaku (1290–1373), the eldest and brightest son of Kakunyo. Although disallowed by his father to succeed him, he was arguably the most brilliant Shinshū thinker in the two centuries separating Shinran and Rennyo, and his writings had a major influence on Rennyo's thought.

Zonkaku's *Zonkaku sode nikki*[22] reveals a situation quite different from the picture painted in Kakunyo's *Gaijashō*, where the ten-character *myōgō* is designated as normative.[22] Zonkaku describes statues of Amida Buddha, statues of both Amida Buddha and Śākyamuni Buddha, various sacred *myōgō* formula, paintings, statues, and paintings of ancient patriarchs, and even portraits of leading disciples of Hōnen and Shinran as *honzon*. Confronted with this plethora of iconic forms, Zonkaku's rhetorical legacy for Rennyo is *not* to define what the orthodoxy should be. Unlike Kakunyo, who, though not entirely exclusive in his attitude, moved toward narrowing Shinshū conceptions of *honzon*, Zonkaku sought instead to open it up.

Further evidence of Zonkaku's different approach to *honzon* can be found in his argument favoring a nine-character *myōgō* phrase, *na-mu fu-ka-shi-gi-kō nyo-rai*. In another essay, the *Benjutsu myōtaishō*, he goes into some detail about this and in fact, of the more than fifty entries in the *Sode nikki*, the vast majority of linguistic *honzon* have this nine-character phrase. This fact is noteworthy because among the six extant *myōgō honzon* written in Shinran's hand, none has the nine-character but most are written using the ten-character phrase.

Zonkaku also refers to the use of portrait lineage charts as *honzon* in this work. Whereas Kakunyo mentions the display of patriarchs, in Zonkaku we see the development of scrolls displaying portraits of abbots of one's own temple. Reflecting this trend, there is a new form of *honzon* in his era that combines text, iconic image, and lineage portraits of both patriarchs prior to Shinran and local abbots. Replete with light rays painted with gold dust, these scrolls were called "illuminated honzon" (*kōmyō honzon*). A complicated art form, full discussion of which will be deferred to another venue, the illuminated *honzon* also reflect the inclusive side of Shin culture. The fully developed form contains something akin to a *myōgō* triad, with three different forms of the ritualized Name standing on lotus flowers, a standing Amida and Śākyamuni between them, with bodhisattvas and patriarchs of India and China on the left side, Hōnen, Shinran, and the abbots of a particular temple on the right side, and Shōtoku Taishi on the bottom. The effect of the illuminated *honzon* is striking but it is also very busy, and we may infer from this form a wide range of sacred objects revered by Shinshū communities in the fourteenth and early fifteenth centuries.

Rennyo's Violence against Icons and Its Repercussions

Born only forty years after the death of Zonkaku, Rennyo came into power as the leader of Honganji in a much more insecure age. The Ōnin Wars devastated the capital and debilitated the political establishment so badly that Rennyo lived the last twenty-five years of his life under great pressure to form political alliances primarily to protect his community. This was the time when peasant uprisings against local authorities were frequently associated with Shinshū and thus known as *ikkō-ikki*, and it is also the time when Shinshū, particularly the Honganji branch under Rennyo's leadership, expanded dramatically.

Before we look at Rennyo's creation and dissemination of *honzon* and what his efforts meant to his doctrinal and political identities, let us turn to one rather curious aspect of Rennyo's relationship with icons: he often burned them and, according to his enemies, threw some into the Kamo River. The fact that Rennyo destroyed Buddhist statues is confirmed by its mention in documents written from opposing political perspectives. Assessing *why* he engaged in this type of behavior or discerning what it meant to his community is more difficult.

The sources for these actions of Rennyo all seem basically to agree that some of the leaders of Mount Hiei could not abide Rennyo's acts of "throwing Amida Buddha [statues] in the river and burning wooden and painted images of Buddha."[23] A large center of Shinshū activity at that time, the Honpukuji in Ōmi, has a record from this period called *Honpukuji atogaki* which mentions that when people saw their Buddhist statues and paintings fall into disrepair with age, they would bring them to Rennyo. He put them in a box and when they were literally falling apart he would use them to feed the fire that heated the bath for the temple. He called the resultant bath "hot water of merit."[24] A significantly different impetus for icon destruction can be found in a statement by Rennyo's tenth son, Jitsugo, in his *Jitsugo kyūki* (also known as *Rennyo Shōnin ichigoki*). Jitsugo was born very late in Rennyo's life and he was just eight when his father died. In this case he tells his readers that he learned this information from Jitsunyo, his elder brother by thirty-four years and the son who succeeded Rennyo to the head of Honganji. As Jitsugo explains:

> During the time of the leader before last [Rennyo], any *honzon* that seriously contravened [the principles of] our tradition or worse was brought in to be burned whenever a bath was being prepared.[25]

These and other references to Rennyo's practice of destroying images of buddhas can thus be separated into two categories: disposing of old, decrepit icons, and the willful destruction of icons for ideological reasons. The usual interpretation of the latter course of action is that these were images of Amida that originally came from other sects of Buddhism such as Tendai or Shingon and were being used by Shinshū congregations; Rennyo objected to this practice in order to enforce his demand that the iconicity of Amida Buddha for Shin must be within strict guidelines. This view is often hailed as supporting the orthodox sectarian Shinshū position today that defines the sect's *honzon* as the linguistic *myōgō honzon*.[26]

Rennyo grew up with hanging portraits of Zennyo (1333–1359) and Shakunyo (1350–1393), the fourth and fifth leaders of Honganji, that depicted them wearing traditional yellow robes and surplices (*kesa*). It is also recorded that Rennyo decided these images were to be burned because everyone should follow the example of Shinran and wear only robes that were light black in color.[27] Realizing the delegitimating implication in doing this, at the last moment he changed his mind and the portraits were not destroyed. Nevertheless he had his followers mark these portraits as "bad examples" (*waroshi*) of what Shinshū clergy should look like. Jitsugo of course sees Rennyo as a courageous reformer, and his apologetic view of this behavior has led to the traditional Honganji view that such actions only served to strengthen the church.

Chiba Jōryū is of the opinion that Rennyo began burning *honzon* soon after he took over the helm of Honganji; that is, in 1457 at the age of forty-three.[28] He sees this act as one example of the extreme self-confidence, some might say overweaning pride, that Rennyo held in his personal understanding of who Shinran was and what he had taught. There is certainly no example before him of any Shinshū leader burning "incorrect" icons relating to the Honganji view of Buddhism. Later we will look at what Rennyo's view of a "correct" icon needed to be, but it is interesting that in Jitsugo's and all other accounts of Rennyo's icon burning, no one took the daunting step of broaching the subject of what a "correct" icon was or should look like. This fact is probably due to a number of factors, such as plurality of *honzon* that persisted among Shin communities during Rennyo's tenure and even after it, but it also suggests how much easier it was to indicate what was heretical than what was orthodox in Honganji culture. Rennyo's violence toward icons suggests that his efforts to define the orthodoxy of Honganji, and by implication Shinshū as a whole, were not limited to the pronouncements in his letters on practice, attainment, deportment, relations with secular authorities, and so forth, but were also directed to the form and use of icons. Today we presume that Rennyo must have identified this or that icon as representative of this or that belief, but search as we may, nowhere does he leave that sort of statement.

But Rennyo could not burn buddhas for very long without bringing attention to himself. As Honganji's influence spread in Ōmi, the areas surrounding Lake Biwa, the leaders on Mount Hiei apparently felt encroachment upon their sphere of influence and religious worldview,[29] and finally a decision was made to attack the Honganji institution by destroying its monastic complex and desecrating the grave of Shinran. The description of their rationale found in the *Kanegamori nikki batsu* and repeated later in the *Sōrinshū* by Ekū is explicit about the public affront of Rennyo's destruction of Buddhist icons and scriptures.[30] According to the *Tōji shikkō nikki*, the Honganji complex based at the grave of Shinran in Ōtani in Higashiyama was attacked in order to punish Rennyo first for throwing statues of Amida in the river, but burning pictures and sculptures of unspecified buddhas are also mentioned.[31]

In this politically charged environment when alliances could mean life or death, there are three documents that also illustrate just how tense leaders in the monastic community outside of Honganji became in response to what befell Rennyo and Honganji. In addition to the *Kanegamori nikki batsu* and *Tōji shikkō nikki*, a third and more detailed contemporary reference that confirms Rennyo's destruction of Buddhist icons is a statement attempting to define the traditions and belief system of the Takada branch of Shin Buddhism called *Kenshōryū gishō* written by Shinne (1434–1512), the tenth abbot of Senjuji, the central administrative temple for the Takada line.[32] Senjuji is known for its Amida Triad and statue of Prince Shōtoku. Although relations with Rennyo were initially friendly, strong rivalry quickly developed when Takada-associated individuals began joining Honganji affiliates. A number of Rennyo's activities were criticized in the *Kenshōryū gishō*. He was accused of advocating a doctrine that considers religious paintings and sculptures to be only *hōben*, that is having utilitarian rather than inherent value. This charge illustrates the faith within the Takada culture in a sacred presence rather than mere likeness or representation in icons, and tells us that Rennyo was adamant about rejecting that viewpoint.

Other sins of Rennyo alleged by Shinne include regarding nenbutsu practice as *jiriki*, removing images of Shōtoku Taishi from altars, and throwing away paintings and sculptures of the Buddha, tantamount in Shinne's eyes to "committing one of the five grave sins." Interestingly, Shinne compares Rennyo's intolerance to that of Nichiren.[33] Such critiques of Rennyo from rival Shinshū leaders must be seen against the background of possible raids from Mount Hiei upon their own structures, and reflect their need to publicly make plain that they do not stand with Rennyo. There is some degree of consensus, therefore, in the statement from Mount Hiei that its attacks on Rennyo and his complex are justified "because such behavior is the enemy of the buddhas, the enemy of the gods; [thus] for the sake of the true law and for the sake of the nation, this cannot go unpunished."[34] The operative principle here is that by destroying Buddhist icons, Rennyo damaged the religion, and by damaging the religion, Rennyo damaged the *nation*. Rhetoric that regards an attack on Buddhism as an attack on the nation is not new; there is precedent for this sentiment from at least the Kamakura period in secular writings such as the diary of Kujō Kanezane, in religious documents such as in the *Kōfukuji sōjō* of Jōkei and *Risshō ankokuron* of Nichiren, and in historical fiction such as the *Heike monogatari* and *Azuma kagami*.[35]

But the statements in these documents regarding threats to Buddhist institutions as assaults on society appear largely as by-products of warfare and thus differ from Rennyo's "violations" which are motivated by aspirations to ideological purity. Rennyo was motivated solely by a felt need to reform his own school; he expressed his concerns about "contravening" icons' presenting a wrong view of Shinshū. Though there is nothing to suggest that Rennyo spoke out in any general way against Buddhist imagery, the visceral response to him suggests that fear of Honganji's encroachment by Mount Hiei, Senjuji, and others stemmed from a fear his behavior might impact their own communities. Their responses also illustrate the power of icons within Japanese culture in general. No one has suggested that Rennyo destroyed Buddhist imagery naïvely or without understanding the implications of such behavior, and indeed such a hypothesis would be difficult to consider seriously. His actions might appear to have initially caused him more than a slight setback, yet considering how his manipulation of religious icons aided the expansion of his power, a more plausible explanation of his thinking should stem rather from his appreciation of the gravity of what he did. That is, while he may not have anticipated the degree of violence that his actions would bring, he was well aware of the strong identification between iconography and sectarian affiliation among Shinshū believers and this was precisely why, as head of the Honganji church, he felt he could not allow "mistaken" views of these symbols of the faith to continue. Indeed, the reaction of Shinne and the Tendai monks on Mount Hiei taught him just how much power there was in icons.

Rennyo's Dissemination of *Honzon* Scrolls in the Expansion of Honganji

Aoki Kaoru has called Jōdoshinshū a *kakejiku kyōdan*, a "religious institution of hanging scrolls," because of the widespread use of this form of icon as its *honzon*, or central image.[36] Although this tradition in prototype form dates back to the time of Shinran himself and, as has been mentioned, there were many forms of *kakejiku* used prior to Rennyo, it is largely through the efforts of Rennyo that these scrolls began to be standardized and regarded as the orthodox or representative *honzon* for Shin Buddhism as a whole. Following the basic form initiated by his father, Zonnyo, Rennyo was the first leader to see the value of this activity for creating common ritual forms within Shin communities, and he put considerable effort into expanding and standardizing this medium for any Shin community that showed interest. Since he makes only indirect references to his creation and distribution of *honzon* scrolls, we need to examine the traces of his activities in this area to ascertain what he hoped to achieve by this endeavor, how his scrolls were received, and how this activity was linked to his iconoclastic activities discussed previously. We will consider the first two questions forthwith and deal with the third after a brief overview of the content and construction of the scrolls themselves.

Consideration of the first questions must begin with the fact that Rennyo clearly saw a need for greater communication between Honganji and the many Shinshū communities with whom it maintained some sort of relationship. It is to this end that Rennyo wrote his so-called pastoral *Letters*, looked at in some detail in chapter 13 of this volume, but discussed to some extent in all the essays. Rennyo's *Letters* were often generated in response to queries that came to him over points of doctrine, ritual, or practice, and they show him taking an unusually active role in the affairs of many dōjō outside Honganji, probably more so than any previous Honganji leader.

Rennyo's distribution of *honzon* scrolls is of a piece with his official letter-writing, and many of the themes seen in the *Letters* also appear in the scrolls. The most central themes common to the two media of self-expression are the "rectification of heresy" and the assumed authority of the leader of Honganji to speak for Shinran's legacy as his descendant and thereby to declare what such rectification should be.

We know that by the end of Rennyo's life the size and prestige of Honganji had grown exponentially, and it is generally accepted that his concern for individual communities proved effective in creating feelings of allegiance from within the dōjō toward the Honganji. Although it may seem that as icons the "message" that was conveyed through these scrolls was never explicit; in fact just as the *Letters* provided a vehicle for dispensing his rulings to create uniformity in doctrine and practice, Rennyo's distribution of *honzon* scrolls also sent clear statements about Honganji's views on orthodoxy. In addition, because these served as *honzon* and had Rennyo's name personally written on the back, they probably enhanced the prestige of Rennyo even more than did his *Letters*. I say this because while the members of a community might have a letter from Rennyo read to them when they received it and its content might affect the community's leadership in some way, we would not expect the community as a whole to be repeatedly reminded of the letter's message. Rennyo's scrolls, however, are presumed to have been hung as *honzon*; thus every time an individual or group gathered before the altar, their ritual practice was performed immediately before a visual reminder of Rennyo, at times even before an image of Rennyo himself. Sharing something of the image *and* symbol mentioned here earlier, each scroll was revered by each community as unique to that community.

Yet in terms of content, they were all within a narrow iconic range, and in sharing common elements Rennyo's scrolls affirmed the connection between himself and the Honganji he represented, the dōjō, the communities that dōjō represented, the founder Shinran, and the unassailable religious authority of the Buddha. Insofar as the nature of this connection or relationship was hierarchical, at least from Rennyo's point of view, the creation, sending, and acceptance of a *honzon* scroll allowed him to assert a degree of administrative authority over a dōjō and its community, thus serving his ideological goals as well. In other words, through the distribution of scrolls Rennyo affirmed the authority he needed for his letters to have real force as rulings.

While it is difficult to speak with confidence about the role that the distribution of these scrolls played in Rennyo's overall success, a few points are warranted. First, to a significant degree Rennyo managed to establish a publicly accepted norm for defining the orthodoxy of religious icons for all branches of Shin, not only those directly under Honganji's jurisdiction. At a time when there was significant variety in iconic expression among Shinshū groups, this distribution contributed a certain uniformity at least to the form of the ritual practice that defined what made a community Shinshū as opposed to other groups dedicated to the Buddha Amida. The most salient example of this phenomenon is his rejection of the illuminated *honzon* form. Extremely popular throughout many Shin communities in the fourteenth and fifteenth centuries, it was especially common in dōjō and temples affiliated with Bukkōji and Senjuji. Although Rennyo had no authority in these other branches, the impact of his opposition to this form upon all Shin congregations is a measure of his ability to affect the Shinshū culture as a whole. We see this in the fact that while illuminated *honzon* continued to be created in the late fifteenth and early sixteenth century, they were in decreasing numbers, and by the end of the sixteenth century the form had disappeared entirely. Rennyo's denigration of the illuminated *honzon*, which display both Amida and Śākyamuni standing perfectly parallel, almost as mirror images of each other, is seen in the following comment:

> To be "with one mind, in one direction" means [to be focused] in regard to Amida Buddha, and not to line up two buddhas. That fact that we relate to only one master thus reflects the same principle. Just as it says in a non-Buddhist work, "A loyal minister does not serve two rulers; a chaste wife does not have two husbands."[37]

Statements like this show Rennyo's decision to align himself with what we may call the Kakunyo-hermeneutic within the Shin tradition. That is, as a leader of a major branch of Shinshū in the second half of the fifteenth century, Rennyo encountered examples of both the "narrow construction" interpretive stance of Kakunyo and the "liberal construction" viewpoint of Zonkaku regarding doctrines, icons, rituals, and the like within Shin communities. He borrowed from both thinkers, but in general we should categorize Rennyo as a narrow constructionist, and nowhere is this stance more evident than in his attitude toward religious icons.

Rennyo's view of sacred art thus forms an integral part of his religious gestalt, but even in limiting our concern to art production, we can discern a means for Rennyo to assert the preeminent status of Honganji vis-à-vis the other branches of Shinshū. This can be seen in the content of those scrolls created whereby Rennyo's claim to authority is evident in expressions of Dharma lineage *and* family lineage. I am referring to the many extant scrolls which depict Shinran and Rennyo facing each other, where it is implied that that Shinran is speaking directly to Rennyo. Sometimes one of the sacred *myōgō* phrases such as the nenbutsu is drawn between them, asserting the authority of the linguistic *honzon* at the heart of the transmission.

A third important dimension of the Rennyo scrolls is that they were personalized in a way that inspired strong ties between Rennyo and the leaders of these communities. Inscriptions on the back of each scroll included Rennyo's personal signature and also conferred a kind of baptismal or "Dharma" name upon the receiver. This naming bolstered the status of the local leader within his community and confirmed his position within the lineage descending from Shinran, both of which naturally created a sense of obligation (*on*) to Rennyo.

Four basic ritual objects were promoted and distributed by Rennyo as *honzon*: *myōgō*, images of Amida Buddha, images of the founders Shinran or Hōnen, and images of Rennyo himself. Some of the Rennyo images appear with Shinran, and there are also a few portraits of disciples, the seven patriarchs of Shinshū, and Shōtoku Taishi. Rennyo also had copies made of a Shinran biography scroll (*eden*) from the Kōei era (1342–1345). In all cases the media are painted scrolls, and all were produced with inscriptions on the reverse side usually bearing Rennyo's name.

Since many different iconic forms were used, one wonders if there was a sequence to them or if different forms were produced for different ritual purposes. We can answer the latter question in the affirmative, since the same temple could receive as many as five or six different scrolls from Rennyo over the years and there is nothing to suggest one replaced another. Unfortunately the inscriptions do not mention particular rituals or services, so we cannot know for certain what events, if any, prompted the painting and sending of a particularly themed scroll.

Regarding which type of icons were produced when, Aoki has put together a chart that shows that although certain forms are more clustered in certain time periods, with one exception these clusters do not suggest ideological movement on Rennyo's part.[38] The exception is the switch from the ten-character to the six-character *myōgō*, which will be discussed later. Typically a temple or dōjō first receives a ten-character *myōgō* from Rennyo, then later a portrait of Shinran or Shinran together with one or two people in the lineage, and still later a biographical picture scroll of Shinran. However, at least two congregations received these images in reverse order, which suggests they were created in response to requests for specific ritual purposes.

Rennyo's production of the ten-character *myōgō honzon* can be dated as early as 1458, one year after his succession to the leadership of Honganji, and production regularly continues until the Kanshō Persecution of 1465. The form on the front of the scroll is based on Shinran's artistic conception repeated by Kakunyo and others, distinguished by a lotus dais drawn beneath the sacred phrase, borrowed from Tantric forms.[39] In general, Rennyo's *myōgō honzon* can be divided into an elaborated gold form and a plain black form. The elaborate form was the first manner in which he began to express himself; it is seen in the early years of his sacred scrolls, from

1458 through some minor variations until production ceased abruptly in 1465. This conception had moved from the Shinran prototype into a form much brighter and bigger in conception. Unlike the Shinran-generated scrolls, which are done in plain ink on white silk or paper, Rennyo's forms strongly suggest that from the beginning he was working with an *edokoro*, or an office of commissioned professional artists. He often used paper or silk that had been dyed or painted indigo, and his characters are square and thus abstracted. In other words, spontaneity was sacrificed for iconicity. A similar move can be seen in the illuminated *honzon*. This is a crafted form of writing; first outlines are drawn and then they are filled in, in a type of writing called *utsuoji* (also *utsuhoji* and *utsuwoji*), deriving from the similar technique of *kago moji*. Again reminiscent of the illuminated *honzon*, these outlines are filled in with gold paint and then gold light rays are painted around them extending to the edge of the scroll. The number of light rays is typically forty-eight in Rennyo's form, a number not seen earlier in *myōgō* painting but the significance is obvious, mirroring the forty-eight vows of compassion made by Amitābha while still a bodhisattva. Indeed we see the same number of light rays in scrolls of the Buddha coming from Rennyo.

The Kanshō Persecution changed all this, however, for Rennyo essentially abandoned this form after this incident. One criticism of Rennyo cited in the Mount Hiei justification for its attack mentions his dissemination of and therefore identification with the ten-character *myōgō*. Indeed most of the ten-character scrolls had been given to groups in the Ōmi region surrounding Lake Biwa, an area Hiei regarded as within its sphere of influence. Many of the Ōmi congregations were somewhat overzealous and were accused of burning Buddhist statues and scriptures they did not care for, of denigrating Shinto kami, and other offenses. Identifying strongly with Shinran's legacy, including his esteem of the ten-character *myōgō*, many took its *mugekō* phrase, meaning "unimpeded light," as the appropriate name for their own movement. Mount Hiei saw implications of hubris, antinomianism, and political independence in the name "unimpeded" and felt compelled to take action.[40] To reduce tensions, Rennyo and other Shin leaders thereupon dissociated themselves from the ten-character *myōgō* and it largely fell out of use thereafter.

After the destruction of the Honganji temple and his eventual move to Hokuriku, Rennyo not only abandoned the ten-character *myōgō* but put more energy into producing portraits as well. He had produced a few of these forms earlier but they were clearly of secondary concern compared with the ten-character *myōgō* scrolls. In this new phase of his career, Rennyo also devoted considerable energy to writing pastoral *Letters*, and the frequent reference to the authority of portraits and the six-character *myōgō* in them confirms their centrality to his mission.

While his portraits of Amida after the Kanshō Persecution retained the previous form of gold light rays on a dark background, in the six-character *myōgō*, *na-mu a-mi-da butsu*, he revertsed to a style much closer to the Shinran prototype, black ink without the embellishments of colored paper or light rays. After some time, Rennyo also produced nine-character and even ten-character *myōgō* again, but they remained in a simple, calligraphic style close to that used by Shinran, with the lotus dais added as the only adornment. There is one extant Amida scroll created by

Rennyo's father, and this image is also done with rays of light. Thus it appears that Rennyo was not creating entirely new forms of icons but was modifying existing structures. Compared with his father's work, Rennyo's buddhas occupy a much larger percentage of the space inside the frame of the painting. The number of light rays in Zonnyo's work is eighteen, probably intended to suggest the eighteenth Vow of Dharmākara. Rennyo's portraits of Amida always contain forty-eight rays of light, which depict either the entirety of Dharmākara's vows or, as Miyazaki Enjun speculates, a multiple of four times twelve, based on Shinran's notion of the twelve forms of light emanating from a buddha, which later developed into the twelve buddhas of light who are depicted as twelve small buddhas around ten-character *myōgō* and standing Amidas from this time. In any case, though flat and iconic, Rennyo's portraits of Amida are nonetheless dynamic and often visually stunning.[41]

Even more interesting, however, is Rennyo's production and distribution of scrolls that depict patriarchs, also frequently used as *honzon*. The subject matter varied but generally included paintings of Hōnen, Shinran, founders of a local temple, or Rennyo himself. In the early period Rennyo also produced what are called *renza-zō*, or images of two or three patriarchs, most commonly Shinran and himself. The variety in content reflects a freedom of expression that probably was more of a reaction to the variety of requests coming from the congregation than any felt need in Rennyo to express diversity. One, for example, contains portraits of Shōtoku Taishi, Shinran, and Zonnyo, certainly not what we would expect to see enshrined on a Shinshū altar today.

Most Rennyo portraits of Shinran are from the Bunmei period, 1469 to 1487, that is, after the destruction of Honganji, but there is one that dates to 1464.[42] The image of Shinran seen in this 1464 image and his later ones as well are clearly modeled on the famous Anjō portrait painted when Shinran was eighty-three years old and now held at Nishi Honganji. But Rennyo altered the Anjō image layout in one critical way: he changed the fabric edging on the platform (*raiban*) from the originally depicted *kōrai beri* pattern to an *ungen beri* pattern. The *ungen beri* pattern indicates a thick tatami mat with an imperial-type brocade around its edge—typically this was used only in paintings of emperors, but it also appears in portraits of monks of the highest rank. Portraits of "common" shōgun typically do not have the *ungen beri* pattern; it does appear with Ashikaga Yoshimitsu and Hideyoshi (but not with Nobunaga), for example. With this move, Rennyo signals not only Shinran's historical status commensurate with the highest monastic figures in Japanese history, but also the fact that his aristocratic lineage (and thereby Rennyo's own) is not to be forgotten. This 1464 image is the earliest extant example of a Shinran portrait with the added *ungen beri* motif, which thereafter became the normative pattern for all later Shinran portraits.[43]

There are nineteen extant dual portraits of Shinran and Rennyo attributed to Rennyo, most from the Bunmei period. According to Igawa Yoshiharu, stylistically they fall into two patterns: a *renza* form, in which Shinran is merely lined up above Rennyo, and a *taiza* form, where they are more at angles to each other. All dual portraits done before the Kanshō Persecution of 1465 are the former type, depicting the order of succession somewhat impersonally. After 1465 both forms were produced, but the *taiza* form, which suggests a dialogue is taking place, seems to be increasingly preferred. After 1470 Rennyo decided to separate the two images, and the single scroll with both portraits was replaced by two separate scrolls. Aoki speculates that these were hung in such a way as to face the *honzon* to remind the congregation of the historical lineage present, but he offers no theory to explain these changes in Rennyo's approach. I would suggest that what we are seeing is Rennyo's growing need to express the transmission process in a more corporeal manner because it served his goal of raising the profile of Honganji. That is, conscious of competing lineage claims in the Takada and Bukkōji branches as Dharma heirs of Shinran, Rennyo strove to exploit his unique legitimacy as both Dharma and blood heir to the founder. The *renza* form reflects the idiom of the illuminated *honzon* and, it might be added, other precedents of using portraiture to substantiate lineage that was imported from China in the Southern Song. Within the Zen school and at Sennyūji, individual portraits were hung side by side to suggest their historical link. In the *taiza* form a conversation between master and disciple is added, bringing the *process* of transference into the foreground. Here we see a new intimacy as Rennyo spiritually "hears" Shinran's message. Separating the *taiza* images by the insertion of a *honzon* only adds the Buddha to that conversation.

The many portraits of Rennyo himself are also noteworthy for their clarity and quantity. According to the *Yamashina gobō no koto narabi ni sono jidai no koto*,[44] Rennyo first allowed his portrait to be made at the age of thirty-three, and in his sixties he ordered the production of a great many. For the first rendition a Kanō artist named Shōshin (1430–1530) was hired. Aoki has pointed out that the dates of this story are impossible because Shōshin would have been only fifteen years old at the time, and Rennyo does not become the leader of Honganji until ten years later, at age forty-three. Speculating a scribal error of ten years renders it plausible, however, for it gives us the year when Rennyo was installed as Honganji abbot, and Shōshin was then twenty-five.[45] This entry confirms that Rennyo invested in continuing the Honganji *edokoro* tradition, dating from the Kamakura period, of hiring professional artists for portraits, and in his case also adding the production of *myōgō* or iconotext *honzon*.

As mentioned earlier, Rennyo usually wrote an inscription on the backing paper of the scrolls he disseminated.[46] Typically he recorded what was depicted on the front, when it was produced, and for whom it was intended. This detailed approach was extremely unusual if not unprecedented and played an integral role in how the production of these scrolls served his administration.[47] Rennyo's disciplined regularity in both *controlling* the content and form of these *honzon* scrolls and *describing* precisely how they were to be understood by means of these inscriptions produced a new medium for expressing his view of iconic orthodoxy and thus Shin orthodoxy as a whole. At the same time they added a personal touch that was also new. His views appear innovative at times but always display consciousness of traditional Shin artistic customs. Rennyo's early stylized ten-character *myōgō honzon*, for example, follow the precedent of Kakunyo in using both an unnatural square style of calligraphy and an open lotus dais motif. But unlike Kakunyo, Rennyo added to the back his signature and the name of the person to whom the scroll is going, and drops the earlier convention of adding strips of paper above and beneath the *myōgō* on which are written quotations from scripture, something Kakunyo inherited from Shinran's example. Rennyo thus removes anything beyond the central image on the face of the scroll, and has the effect of directing the viewer's interest to his personal inscription, albeit written on the back side.

Rennyo was not the first to add such inscriptions, but he developed a formula that is fairly regular and that shows respect to the recipient. There are extant similar inscriptions written by Rennyo's father—both give a date and personal signature (*kaō*)—but otherwise Zonnyo's follow no fixed pattern in order or content. Rennyo's always follow the same pattern, betraying a certain deliberateness in his task. Rennyo's inscriptions always begin on the right somewhere in the middle of the paper with the phrase "Shaku Rennyo of Ōtani Honganji" followed by his signature. Then slightly higher on the page the next line contains the date. The third line gives the name of the type of image drawn on the front and is always written much higher and in much larger characters, sometimes three to four times larger. Then lower and returning to the same small size characters, the next two lines usually give the location of the community center or temple where this is to be installed and its name followed by the word *honzon*. Finally, one more line set lower and usually ending at the horizontal level of Rennyo's signature, contains the Dharma name of the person who has requested the scroll, usually the congregation's leader.

There has been great interest in interpreting the texts of these inscriptions by Rennyo and subsequent leaders of Honganji in the sixteenth century, particularly since Kitanishi Hiromu pointed out their importance to the creation of a more advanced infrastructure within branches of Shinshū, especially Honganji.[48] Those discussions are too complex to summarize here, but a few points are worth repeating.

First, as noted there are prior examples of *honzon* scrolls with inscriptions of similar content, both by Zonnyo and among other branches of Shinshū. But in Rennyo's scrolls, although his name is the first thing one sees, it is positioned at the same height as that of the name of the "requesting party" (*ganshu*), the person receiving the scroll. This suggestion of spiritual equality not only mitigates their unequal political relationship but does so in sharp contrast to scrolls produced by later leaders of Honganji; over the next 200 to 300 years the name of the *monshu* (Honganji abbot) gradually moves higher relative to the *ganshu* to emphasize their status disparity.

Rennyo's inscriptions also create a precedent in consistently rendering the recipient's name in the form of a Dharma name; previously, if the recipient's name was given at all, it could be either the Dharma name or the secular name. Since there are very few surviving letters from this period confirming induction into a lineage via appointment of a Dharma name to the individual, it appears that Rennyo was using the gift of these *honzon* scrolls as his means to do just that. Hayashima Yūki points out that in beginning each inscription with the words "Shaku Rennyo of Ōtani Honganji"[49] followed by his signature, Rennyo adds a personal confirmation that this scroll is officially sanctioned by himself as representative of Śākyamuni Buddha, Shinran, the Honganji lineage and thereby Amitābha Buddha, and implicitly all the Pure Land patriarchs who came before him, and thus is to be revered as a bona fide sacred *honzon*.[50] Aoki has pointed out that in this self-identifying phrase Rennyo also sought to implant within Shinshū culture an identification between Shinran, the Ōtani locale, and the Honganji church. It had become common practice to associate Hōnen with the name Kurodani, a place where he had practiced; it was not unusual, for example, to refer to Hōnen as "Kurodani Shōnin." Clearly Rennyo wanted to create a similar association between Shinran and Ōtani. Unlike Kurodani, however, Ōtani loomed large for Rennyo not as a place where Shinran lived, but as the memorial gravesite of Shinran, where the Honganji church began.

The public acceptance of the Shinran–Ōtani–Honganji gestalt that Rennyo sought was thus for the goal of establishing his own lineage as the most authoritative among all branches of Shin. Clearly Rennyo saw this link as necessary to imbue these scroll *honzon*, whether pictorial or linguistic, with full religious power. From another point of view, someone had to sponsor the artist to create the scroll, and someone had to certify that the merit accrued for this action was going to the person who instigated the endeavor—the requesting and ultimate receiving party—and not the artist. This line in Rennyo's inscription thus confirms that the role of Honganji is that of guarantor of the relationship between donor/requesting party and the ultimate authority figures of Rennyo, Shinran (for portraits), or the Buddha (for sacred phrases).[51]

Although we cannot know how these *honzon* scrolls were viewed by the groups who received and often requested them, there is little doubt that this medium proved extremely effective in strengthening the bonds between local groups and the central authoritative church of Honganji. After Rennyo established the practice of using the scroll to confer lineage status, subsequent generations of Honganji leaders expanded the inscription medium to establish someone's function or status within their community or Honganji as a whole. The social ranking of priests within the Honganji organization was not well established until after Jitsunyo, the successor to Rennyo; it was also sometime in the sixteenth century that requesting groups were first expected to pay honorariums to the monshu for the privilege of receiving the bona fide *honzon* scroll. According to Hayashima, under Rennyo's financial system, funds were collected primarily during the yearly Hōonkō celebration of the anniversary of Shinran's death. While he finds evidence to suggest funds went to the Honganji for scrolls with Shinran's image on them, this did not happen for *myōgō* scrolls. But while the deepest gratitude and sense of affiliation may have been to Shinran, the founder, all forms of Rennyo's *honzon* represented a concrete promise of a post-mortem Birth in the Pure Land for Shinshū believers.[52]

Conclusion

Each Buddhist community in Japan has had a *honzon* or central icon installed on the altars of its dōjō, temples, and monasteries as a matter of course since the beginning of Buddhism's arrival. As a public face for these communities, the *honzon* came to represent them, and as much as the strict doctrines of the religion may insist that these are empty signs, the numerous stories of the miraculous associated with these images combined with incidents of political conflict that arose in connection with them testify to their enduring power and authority.

Testimony to Honganji's valuation of sacred art is the fact that it was probably the first of the so-called new schools of Kamakura Buddhism to establish an *edokoro*, or administrative office to handle its artistic needs. When Rennyo rose to the leadership of Honganji, he inherited a tradition of its chief abbot, or monshu, producing scrolls in response to requests from Shinshū communities. But this practice was not done systematically, it remained rather small in scale, and therefore prior to Rennyo the creation and distribution of sacred art does not appear to be of central importance to the culture of Honganji and Shin in general.

Rennyo's insight was to recognize the potential that creating and distributing religious icons held for expanding Honganji's influence. He understood how art worked as a powerful medium of communication between the Honganji and it supporting community centers. Sending a *honzon* scroll contributed to the vitality of the receiving dōjō or temple and strengthened the relationship between that group and the Honganji leadership. From the moment his succession was confirmed, Rennyo devoted energy to the production of scrolls to be given to this and that Shin community. No doubt this activity led to other communities hearing about it and asking for their own. As the requests came in, Rennyo responded, signing the back of each one and duly noting the location of the requesting group and its leader, recording the year, month, and day, and describing precisely what was depicted there, all confirming his personal approval of what the icon was, its form, and to whom it was given. Affixed to the back of a scroll when it was mounted, these inscriptions also contained the Dharma name of the person making the request, evidence that one's admission into the official Shinshū lineage had been recognized by Honganji. By first sending a community a scroll depicting Shinran, or himself "communicating" with Shinran, and then a second scroll with a *myōgō* or sacred phrase favored by Shinran, Rennyo thus was able to clarify his special authority as family descendant and Dharma descendant of Shinran, an assertion that played a key role in the expansion of Honganji under his leaderhsip.

Although known for his many activities devoted to standardizing beliefs and practices within Honganji and Shin as a whole, when it came to his production and distribution of sacred scrolls, there is ample evidence of a freedom to embrace different forms of the sacred, including even Shinto.[53] But Rennyo did not begin this way. For the first decade of his tenure he produced primarily portraits of Shinran and the ten-character *myōgō* as *honzon* scrolls for distribution. Considering the popularity of the illuminated *honzon* at that time, it is plausible to infer a motivation here to produce a new norm for Shinshū iconography that explicitly rejected that complex form while maintaining some of it elements. After the Kanshō Persecution and destruction of Shinran's grave, Rennyo's exile from Kyoto led to a change of heart and a more flexible approach to what artistic forms could represent Honganji. The ten-character *myōgō* was, in general, replaced by the six-character phrase, but his production of scrolls continued apace. In addition to the political heat that accompanied the ten-character *myōgō*, Rennyo may have discovered that despite his view that this was Shinran's own preference, the six-character *myōgō* was received more enthusiastically, since *namu amida butsu* was the one ritually invoked phrase that *everyone* knew and that had roots in popular religious consciousness far deeper than the ten-character *myōgō*, or *kimyō jinjippō mugekō nyorai*.

In the end, Rennyo realized that as long as his signature was on the back, regardless of content his scrolls would have the enduring significance of being both personalized gifts to the head of the receiving congregation and "permanent" symbols of that individual group's status as full members of the wider congregation known under the rubric of Honganji. This meant Rennyo was free to create a range of iconic forms that could all work as *honzon*, including portraits that authenticated the lineage of a temple or dōjō by including Shinran, himself, and the founder or current head monk of that temple. It is also the reason that, as small congregations grew larger and more prosperous, they could put aside their scroll for a statue of Amida without appreciably changing the religious content of the icon that held their congregation together. Even then the *honzon* scrolls were never abandoned, only redefined as something brought out and hung for specific rituals.

To receive a *honzon* scroll signed by Rennyo gave many a sense of belonging to Shinran himself, since Rennyo was able to claim a bloodline to the founder that none of the leaders of the other Shinshū factions could. And lest we think that the physical scroll itself was the location of the power of that bond, it is worth recalling a quote from Rennyo, found the *Jitsugo kyūki*:

> *Honzon* should be hung [on the altar] until they fall apart; the sacred teachings should be read until [the books] fall apart.

Notes

1 James Fernandez, "The Mission of Metaphor in Expressive Culture," *Current Anthropology* 15:2 (1974), 120, based in some form on Sapir (1934) and Morris (1955).

2 The discovery by Tsukamoto Zenryū of a sudden shift from the construction of Maitreya statues to those of Amitābha in the Longmen caves of China has long since served as convincing evidence of the pervasiveness of sudden spread of belief in Amitābha in the sixth century. See Tsukamoto Zenryū, *Shina bukkyōshi kenkyū: hokugi-hen* (Tokyo: Kōbundō, 1942), 355–609.

3 There were many forms of Pure Land belief and practice active in Japan in Rennyo's time that Honganji competed with. In addition to other large factions or branches of his own Shinshū lineage, most notably the Takada and Bukkōji, the Chinzei and Seizan branches of the Jōdoshū and the Jishū founded by Ippen were also widespread in their influence both inside and outside the capital.

4 *Guanwuliangshou jing*, T No. 365, 12. This work appears some time in the sixth century in China and inspired a great many commentaries and new practices among Sui and early Tang Buddhist thinkers. See Kenneth Tanaka, *The Dawn of Chinese Pure Land Buddhism: Ching-ying Hui-yüan's Commentary on the Visualization Sutra* (Albany, N.Y.: SUNY Press, 1990), and Mark L. Blum, *The Origins and Development of Pure Land Buddhism: A Study and Translation of Gyōnen's Jōdo Hōmon Genrusho* (New York: Oxford University Press, 2002), 149ff.

5 Initially it was housed at Honpukuji in Ōmi, and then, when Honpukuji came under attack by Mount Hiei, it was entrusted to Miidera, near Ōtsu, a rival faction of Tendai and a far more secure location.

6 Nishi Honganji is formally known as Jōdoshinshū Honganji-ha, and Higashi Honganji as Jōdoshinshū Ōtani-ha. It is tempting to consider this story not as enhancing the Shinran cult within Honganji but as a product of it, but both processes have been at work.

7 On this theme, see James Dobbins, "Portraits of Shinran in Medieval Pure Land Buddhism," in *Living Images: Japanese Buddhist Icons inHistorical Studies Context*, ed. Robert Sharf and Elizabeth Sharf (Stanford, Cal.: Stanford University Press, 2001), 19–48.

8 *Gyakushu seppō*, 234.7.

9 This discussion in the *Gyakushu seppō*, is in Ishii Kyōdō, ed. *Shōwa shinshū Hōnen Shōnen zenshū*. Kyoto: Heirakuji Shoten, 1955, 234.

10 See T No. 1753, 37.265c17–266a6. Shandao insisted that a seated Buddha did not have the same power to save one from delusion.

11 That is, once the doctrine of standing sculpture is given a doctrinal name in *rissatsu sokugyō*, this is repeated again and again in later Jōdoshū writings, notably by the dominant Chinzei and Seizan branches, as the normative orthodox position, but that does not tell us what each temple and *dōjō* actually used on their altars. Today Jōdoshū temples all apparently have standing statues of Amida Buddha.

12 The long-established story of Shinran's break with his son and expected Dharma heir Zenran based on Shinran's extant letters is now in dispute. See Mori Shōji, "Shokan ni miru Shinran to Jishinbō Zenran," *Tōyōgaku ronsō* 28 (2003), 27–83. See also Hiramatsu Reizō, "Zenran gizetsujō no shingi ni tsuite," *Ryūkoku daigaku ronshū* 432 (1988), 19–30.

13 Five of the extant seven have the ten-character *myōgō* pronounced in Japanese *ki-myō jin-jip-pō mu-ge-kō nyo-rai* (taking refuge in the Tathāgata of the Unimpeded Light of the Ten Directions), a phrase taken from a verse in Vasubandhu's *Jingtulun*.

14 There is no evidence that Shinran or his immediate disciples built monasteries (*jiin*) in the traditional sense, instead preferring more intimate and far less formal community meeting centers (*dōjō*). Often created in rural areas where people had few resources, these centers were usually housed in what were little more than modified family dwellings; they are sometimes referred to as "thatched halls" (*sōdō*). See Mikogami Eryū, "Shinshū kyōdan no honzon" in *Bukkyō kyōdan no kenkyū*, ed. Yoshimura Shuki (Kyoto: Hyakka-en, 1968), 450. See also Dobbins, "Portraits of Shinran," 66, and Akamatsu Toshihide and Kasahara Kazuo, *Shinshūshi gaisetsu* (Kyoto: Heirakuji Shoten, 1963), 76.

15 For example, when Shinran traveled to Hokuriku he stayed for some time at Kinshokuji in Ōmi and prostrated himself before the Amida sculpture there, said to have been made in the image of the Amida at Zenkōji. Kinshokuji later became the center of the Kibe branch of Shinshū, but there is no record of its abandoning its sculpture for a scroll. When he stayed in the Kantō area, he spent most of his time among either the Inada community, which used a statue of Shōtoku Taishi for their honzon or the Takada group who venerated an Amida Triad carved in wood. Buddhist images often have origin legends, and the story of the Amida Triad sculpture installed at the Takada main temple, Senjuji (then a *dōjō* called Nyoraidō), centers on this *honzon* being personally donated to the community by Shinran himself, who brought it from Zenkōji as a copy of the famous icons there. We know that Shinran did make a pilgrimage to Zenkōji, an important center of faith in Amida Buddha in his time, and that replications of the original Zenkōji Amida Triad as seen in these two examples, despite its being designated as a secret image (*hibutsu*), were numerous and highly prized in the Kamakura period. On Zenkōji, see Donald McCallum, *Zenkōji and Its Icon* (Princeton, N.J.: Princeton University Press, 1994).

16 See Chiba Jōryū, ed., *Shinshū jūhō shuei*, vol. 1: *myōgō honzon* (Kyoto: Dōbōsha, 1988) 185, and Mikogami, "*Shinshū kyōdan no honzon*," 449.

17 Coates and Ishizuka, *Hōnen the Buddhist Saint* (Kyoto: Chinon'in, 1925), 781; Ikawa Jōkyō, ed., *Hōnen Shōnin-den zenshū* (Osaka: Hōnen Shōnin-den zenshū Kankōkai, 1961), 315.

18 SSZ 2.723. Cited in Miyazaki Enjun, *Shinshūshi no kenkyū (jō)* (Kyoto: Nagata Bunshodō, 1987), 384–385.

19 All modern Shinshū dictionaries state the anachronistic nature of this view and have entries on these phrases, called *songō* or *myōgō*, whereas they do not have entries for *songyō* or *shinzō*, the words used in medieval texts to indicate painted images or sculpture as well as portraits of both historical and ahistorical figures.

20 SSZ 3.66–67. This section is read very differently in the *Complete Works of Shinran*, quoted in translation on p. 142 of volume 2. The difference in reading stems partly from how the adverb *anagachi* is understood here; they take it as "purposely" and I take it as "not necessarily," and presumably because of sectarian influence *agame-mashimashiki* is translated there as "adopted for the altars" instead of simply "revered," essentially grandfathering the passage into something that ties Shinran more concretely to what Kakunyo finds normative. This passage is often quoted to explain why Shinran preferred expressions of the Name rather than images.

21 SSZ 3.66.

22 *Zonkaku sode nikki*, at SSS 1.892.

23 The earliest source of this information is the entry for the sixth year of Kanshō (1465), *Tōji shikkō nikki* 3.23. For a discussion of these materials, see Kanda Chisato, *Ikkō ikki to Shinshū shinkō* (Tokyo: Yoshikawa Kōbunkan, 1991), 206ff.

24 *Honpukuji atogaki*, in SSS 2.660a.

25 *Jitsugo kyūki (Rennyo Shōnin ichigoki)* 158, in SSS 2.459a. The same line is also found in *Rennyo Shōnin gojōjō* 47, SSS 2.479.

26 See Daiki Naohiko, "Butsuzō no shōshitsu," *Rekishigaku kenkyū* 675 (September 1995), 1–17.

27 Presumably the yellow robes signified rank and black robes expressed the absence of it.

28 Chiba Jōryū, "Rennyo no ikonokurasumu," *Nihon Bukkyōshi no Kenkyūkai*, ed. Chiba Jōryū Hakase koki kinen: *Nihon no shakai to bukkyō* (Kyoto: Nagata Bunshodō, 1990), 11.

29 See chapter 7 in this volume.

30 The *Kanegamori nikki batsu*, at SSS 2.701b. *Sōrinshū*, ch. 8, at *Shinshū taikei*, 17.289.

31 On the *Tōji shikkō nikki*, see Daiki, "Butsuzō no shōshitsu," and Kanda, *Ikkō ikki*.

32 The *Kenshōryū gishō* is at T No. 2673, 83.841.

33 *Kenshōryū gishō*, 844c. The five are patricide, matricide, killing an Arhat, injuring a buddha, or causing disharmony within the Saṃgha. Any of these crimes bring rebirth in hell and in some circles prevent the person from liberation.

34 *Kanegamori nikki batsu*, 701b.

35 *Yamashiro Daigoji sōjishu mōshijōan* contains an account of the burning of the main hall at Daigoji in 1296 by a group of brigands, or *akutō*, that is described as an angry assault on the Nation (*kokka*) and on the Saṃgha (*jimon*), at *Kamakura ibun* No. 19091. *Heike monogatari* comments in chapter 2, regarding the burning of Zenkōji in 1179, that the loss of the Buddha icon there reflects the breakdown in both the Buddhist and the Imperial law. A similar lament is found in the *Azuma kagami* in reference to the burning of Tōdaiji in 1184. Kanezane's diary refers to an entry for the sixteenth day of the eleventh month of 1185 in his *Gyokuyō*. For these and other examples, see Daiki, "Butsuzō no shōshitsu."

36 Aoki Kaoru. "Honzon, eizō ron," *Kōza Rennyo* 2 (Tokyo: Heibonsha 1997), 13.

37 *Letters* 2:9; SSZ 3.438. This quote is from the *Siqi*.

38 Aoki, "Honzon," 26.

39 The use of Sanskrit or Tibetan letters as *bīja* symbols drawn atop a lotus dais is quite common in a Tantric context, and in East Asia in particular the Sanskrit vowel *a* written in Siddham is often seen. But there is also a precedent of placing Chinese characters on lotus seats; see the Heian-period Lotus Sutra written with each character drawn on a lotus from the Shōsōin now held at the Nara National Museum.

40 These accusations are mentioned in a document called *Eizan yori furaruru kenshō* (called *Eizan chōjō* in chapter 7), which is contained within the *Kanegamori nikki batsu* at SSS 2.701. See Inoue Toshio, *Ikkō ikki no kenkyū* (Tokyo: Yoshikawa Kōbunkan, 1968), 308–316, and also Kanda, *Ikkō ikki*, 206–214.

41 See also the *Kōmyō kenmitsu shō*, text no. 31 in SSS 5.

42 This is held at Akanoi Fukushōji in Moriyama, Shiga Prefecture.

43 Aoki, "Honzon," 36–39. Aoki also points out that in the early portraits Shinran's robe covers most of the platform edging, making the pattern depicted somewhat hard to see, but as Rennyo get older the robe recedes and this becomes more and more prominent. By the time of Jitsunyo, there is no obstruction of the edge.

44 *Yamashina gobō no koto narabi ni sono jidai no koto* entry 68, at SSS 2.555. This document, by Jitsugo (1492–1584), dates to 1575 but is based on earlier materials describing many daily affairs of Honganji during the Yamashina era.

45 The *Honpukuji yūraiki* states that their image of Rennyo was the first he ever allowed to be made, and they have a dual portrait of Rennyo and Shinran with an inscription dated 1461, two years after Rennyo assumes the leadership. See *Shinshū shiryo shūsei* 2.665. Aoki discusses these ponts on pp. 40–41 of "Honzon."

46 These are typically referred to as *uragaki* in Japanese. The exceptions were the scrolls produced under Rennyo that were not intended to remain in one locale. As movable *honzon*, they would be hung in different *dōjō* as needed, giving them a temporary quality; therefore they were constructed with paper rather than silk, and they have no named recipient or congregation.

47 Hayashima Yūki. "Honganji Rennyo no myōgō honzon to sengoku shakai: jūji myōgō wo sozai to shite," *Kyōto-shi rekishi shiryōkan kiyō* (1992), 222, states that to his knowledge there are no earlier examples of this type of inscription accompanying religious scrolls.

48 See Kitanishi Hiromu, *Ikkō ikki no kenkyū* (Tokyo: Shunjosha, 1981), 774. Kinryū Shizuka and Kanda Chisato have also looked at the information and how it is positioned on the back of the scroll and drawn quite different inferences about the hierarchical relationship between the person who requests and receives the scroll and the head of the school who supplies it. Kinryū Shizuka's argument is at "Sengokuki Honganji kyōdan no uragaki-kō," *Nenpō chūsei-shi kenkyū* 13 (1988), 1–20. For Kanda Chisato, see his *Ikkō ikki to Shinshū shinkō* 196–205. These debates concern largely the feudal nature of this relationship, but this is a matter of course, given the nature of society at that time. Rennyo is undeniably in a position of power in this relationship as head of his church, and the granting of a request for a *honzon* brings with it an inevitable confirmation of his authority and thereby an affirmation of that power relationship.

49 The prefix *shaku* (釋) is an abbreviation of *Shakamuni* and marks an individual as having received the monastic precepts and thus joined the lineage of Śākyamuni.

50 Hayashima, "Honganji," 224.

51 Kanda, *Ikkō ikki*, 204–205.

52 Hayashima, "Hanganji," 233–237.

53 Shigaraki Takamaro refers to a recent discovery of a Rennyo inscription on what appears to be a scroll with the liturgical name of the kami of the Tenman shrine, or Tenman

Daijizaiten. This Daijizaiten is derived from the Sanskrit Maheśvara, but it was widely understood even in Rennyo's time as merely a *honji-suijaku* overlay added to the kami Tenjin or Tenman, who is the deification of Sugawara no Michizane. See Shigaraki, "The Problem of the True and the False in Contemporary Shin Buddhist Studies: True Shin Buddhism and False Shin Buddhism," *Pacific World* 3:3 (2001), 46.

PART II

SHINSHŪ STUDIES

10

TERAKAWA SHUNSHŌ
TRANSLATED BY MARK L. BLUM

Shinran and Rennyo

Comparing Their Views of Birth in the Pure Land

If you ask people to suggest an example of the formation of a powerful tradition over generations in Japanese Pure Land Buddhism many might point to the lineage formed by the Hōnen–Shinran link and then add Rennyo. If one then added what sacred writings would represent this line, we would perceive a continuity of thought in the traditional line that runs through the *Senchakushū* of Hōnen (1133–1212),[1] the *Yuishinshō* of Seikaku (1167–1235),[2] the *Tannishō* of Yuien (d. 1289),[3] and the *Letters* of Rennyo (1415–1499). This tradition is based on an understanding of the Buddhist path as a "path to Birth via nenbutsu," an understanding that is certainly recognized by anyone today.

Of course, if you ask how we should understand the concept of *ōjō* itself, translated here as "Birth," then you are standing squarely within the concerns of this tradition. As someone connected with the tradition of Shinran, I would first like to inquire as to how Shinran comprehended *ōjō*.

At the present time, understanding of *ōjō* can go in a variety of directions and one cannot avoid some sense of confusion. But during Shinran's time understanding was also quite varied, and it is a mistake to assume that there was unanimity of belief on this matter. It was within just such a context that Shinran examined his own view of *ōjō* at the end of his life and left an essay expressing his personal understanding of it. That composition is called *Jōdo sangyō ōjō monrui*.[4] In the terse sentences of this monograph Shinran explores a wide variety of views regarding the meaning of *ōjō*, ultimately labeling his own view the "Birth based in the *Larger Sūtra*." Since the opinion expressed here is consistent with the views described in his main work, the *Kyōgyōshinshō*, I believe we can rely on this work to ascertain Shinran's understanding of Birth in the Pure Land.

In his *Jōdo sangyō ōjō monrui*, Shinran organized the various views of *ōjō* into three categories, the names of which he takes from the three core sutras of the Pure Land school:

1. *Ōjō* as described in the *Larger [Sukhāvatīvyūha] Sūtra*: Birth that is hard to conceive of.

2. *Ōjō* as described in the *Contemplation Sūtra*: Birth beneath two trees in the forest.
3. *Ōjō* as described in the *Smaller [Sukhāvatīvyūha] Sūtra*: Birth that is hard to imagine.

Of these three, Shinran is most positive about *ōjō* as defined by the *Larger Sūtra* compared with *ōjō* in the *Contemplation Sūtra* or *Kangyō* and *ōjō* in the *Smaller Sūtra* or *Amidakyō*. His label, the "Birth that is hard to conceive of," is reminiscent of the language he uses to describe the *hongan*, or Original Vow itself, a "covenant inconceivable." In other words, we can make the assumption that Shinran's description of this issue as being something hard to conceive of is precisely so because it is based on the "covenant inconceivable." Furthermore, since Shinran also describes this as "the core teaching of the *Larger Sūtra*," we can also take this to represent the fact that his understanding of Birth is based on what is preached in the *Larger Sūtra*. As a result, we should take this phrase to represent Shinran's personal understanding of *ōjō*.

The Two Forms of Merit Transfer

Shinran writes:

> From the two forms of merit-transfer in relation to the Tathāgata, the person who has attained "faith" [*shingyō*] without fail resides in the stage of being among the group of assured.[5] For that reason, we use the term *tariki*....This is the core teaching of the *Larger Sukhāvatīvyūha Sūtra*. This is also called Birth that is hard to conceive of.[6]

These words come from his concluding remarks on the *Larger Sūtra*. Here without doubt we see two aspects of Shinran unique understanding of *ōjō* according to the *Larger Sūtra*. First is his understanding that *ōjō* according to the *Larger Sūtra* or "Birth that is hard to conceive of" means Birth that is realized through the two kinds of merit transfer of the Tathāgata. Second is that the concrete expression of *ōjō* according to the *Larger Sūtra* lies in the fact that one resides in the position of being among "the assured."

On the first point, Shinran is saying that Birth in the Pure Land is realized by means of the two forms of merit transfer toward the Tathāgata, especially that of the gratitude expressed in transferring merit in the aspect of *going to* the Pure Land (*ōsō ekō*). On the meaning of merit transference in this aspect of going, Jinrei (1749–1817), a Shinshū scholar from the early modern period, explained it this way:

> It refers to the time from when one attains the understanding of "faith" (*shinjin*) in this Sahā world, are then born in the Pure Land, and continues up to realizing the enlightenment of nirvāṇa. Transferring merit on our return from the Pure Land means to return to this defiled world. Returning to this defiled world from the Pure Land, one works for the salvation of all sentient beings.[7]

The modern scholar Hoshino Genpō wrote in his *Kōkai Kyōgyōshinshō*:

The aspect of going denotes the form of one's going to the Pure Land. Since our going to the Pure Land is something that is given completely by the Buddha, it is referred to as the merit transference in the aspect of going. The aspect of returning denotes the form of one who has returned to this world to save sentient beings after having achieved Birth in the Pure Land. This activity, the returning aspect, is also bestowed to us from the Buddha, and so it is called the merit transference in the aspect of returning.[8]

These two opinions reflect the common understanding of the two aspects of merit transference, and in particular the aspect of going to the Pure Land. But although it is clear from these explanations what these two kinds of merit transfer are, especially the aspect directed at going to the Pure Land, such understanding is all too often missing from modern treatments. Witness, for example, the following explanations in two highly respected modern dictionaries:

Bukkyō jiten

This refers to the event of being born in another world when one's life in this world is over, and in Pure Land thought came to refer to leaving behind this defiled land and going off to a so-called "pure land."...But even if we say that the idea of Birth has its origins in the notion of being reborn in heaven, there is a major difference between the two notions. The concept of being reborn in heaven does not transcend the limits of transmigration, whereas achieving Birth in the Pure Land means leaving behind the wheel of rebirth and reaching the realm of buddhas....In Jōdoshinshū, two forms of Birth are discussed: spontaneous birth in a land of [the Buddha in] a true reward [body], and womb birth in a land of [the Buddha in] an expedient [body]. Also, when Birth in the Pure Land is determined in this world, it is called "immediate Birth" [*sokutoku ōjō* 即得往生]; when one is born in the Pure Land, this is called "Birth that is hard to conceive of" [*nanshigi ōjō*].[9]

Bukkyōgaku jiten

Leaving this world at the end of one's life to be born in the other world....In Jōdo Shinshū, there are two types of Birth explained, immediate Birth [*soku ōjō*] and expedient Birth [*ben ōjō*]. Or, there may be three forms of Birth posited, where "immediate birth" is called Birth that is difficult to conceive of [*tariki* nenbutsu, Birth of the eighteenth Vow], "expedient Birth" is called Birth that is difficult to imagine [*jiriki* nenbutsu, Birth of the twentieth Vow], and "Birth beneath two trees in the forest" [Birth by a variety of practices of the nineteenth Vow]. In Shinshū, it may also be stated that when it is confirmed through the attainment of *shinjin* that Birth is possible, this is called "immediate attainment of Birth" [*sokutoku ōjō*]. This is also Birth without losing the body [confirmation of Birth during one's lifetime, i.e., with a defiled body] and is contrasted with Birth with losing the body [Birth that occurs when the physical body dies].[10]

Leaving aside the issue of how appropriate these explanations are, despite all the detail about Birth in Shinshū with or without losing the body, or Birth in a womb or spontaneously, the three types of Birth, and so on, it is noteworthy that there is no mention of the relationship between Birth and the transfer of merit toward this goal.

The second point I would like to make concerns the issue of joining the "group of the assured" while in this life, and on this point the dictionary explanations do seem to reflect the generally held views. However, the understanding of Birth expressed when Shinran spoke of Birth according to the *Larger Sūtra* was of a concept of joining the assured not seen in these discussions; namely, the confirmation of being on the path to nirvāṇa. Moreover, Shinran called this the "core teaching of the *Larger Sūtra*, the Birth that is difficult to conceive of." Therefore, in order to understand what Shinran really had to say about Birth, we must approach this not with our preconceptions but with an open mind to appreciate the discourse that he actually used to express himself.

Shinran's View of Birth and Merit Transfer

The special characteristics of Birth that Shinran expressed when he used the phrase "Birth according to the *Larger Sūtra*" concerns the realization of this by means of the two forms of merit transfer. Shinran's basic position can be seen in his view of the other two forms of Birth that he does not see as having presumed the two forms of merit transfer. That is, Birth according to the *Contemplation Sūtra* refers to yearning for the Pure Land after transferring the merit one personally has accumulated in all one's good karmic action; and Birth according to the *Amida Sūtra* is Birth that one asks for only by means of the power inherent in transferring merit accrued from personally [evoking] the Buddha's holy name, because one cannot accept the inconceivable wisdom of the Buddha. These other forms of Birth are the means by which one embraces the hope of reaching that world when facing one's final moments; they are notions of Birth that spring from the expectation of confirmation that one hopes will come from the encouragement of nenbutsu practice. By contrast, what Shinran called Birth according to the *Larger Sūtra* is the Birth that is naturally realized by means of the two types of Tathāgata merit transfer. This interpretation implies, to put it more concretely, something more along the lines of a doctrine whereby someone who engages in nenbutsu by believing in the Original Vow resides naturally and spontaneously in the "group of the assured" in this world and then, upon his next birth, treads the path to the final goal of unsurpassed nirvāṇa.

But what precisely is this twofold Tathāgata merit transference that realizes Birth according to the *Larger Sūtra*? To understand Shinran's fundamental understanding of this, we should first note this *Wasan*:

> Abandoning the *duḥkha* of the beginningless spin of *saṃsāra*
> In expectation of the unsurpassed nirvāṇa,
> The debt [*ondoku*] toward the two forms of Tathāgata merit transference
> Is truly difficult to repay.[11]

As this verse shows, for Shinran the merit transfer directed at the objective of going to the Pure Land and the merit transfer directed at the objective of returning from the Pure Land are both expressions of *ondoku* (恩德), the feeling of indebtedness from having received the blessing of the merit transferred from the Buddha. This is the first point to keep in mind regarding Shinran's understanding of these two forms of merit transference. The second is that the person who is able to realize this indebtedness arising from these two forms of merit transference will have his life transformed from being locked into transmigration to being definitively at the stage of the group of the assured. Enacting the transfer of merit directed at reaching the Pure Land does not simply reflect a notion of Birth in the Pure Land, it also implies residing among the group of assured that is standing on the great path to final, complete nirvāṇa. Let us look at how Shinran expressed this.

Shinran expresses a most positive attitude toward merit transference for the goal of Birth in his *Kyōgyōshinshō*, but the most condensed presentation can be found in the section on "Birth according to the *Larger Sūtra*" in his *Jōdo sangyō ōjō monrui*. This is the backbone of Shinran's thought on this matter. Here are the main points of his argument:

1. There is *true practice* (*shinjitsu gyōgō*) in the merit transference of the Tathāgata for the goal of Birth. In other words, it is a manifestation of the compassionate vows inherent in the invocation of the names of all the buddhas. The compassionate vow [at the base of] invoking the name is as stated in the *Larger Sūtra* (text of the Vow is then quoted here.) The text of the accomplishment of the compassionate vows [of the Buddha] regarding entrusting in invoking the name is as the sūtra says (text of the confirmation of the Vow is quoted here).

2. In addition there is a *true faith* (*shinjitsu shinjin*). This is what is manifest in the compassionate vows [guaranteeing] Birth via nenbutsu. These vows of compassion that one entrusts oneself to are stated thus in the *Larger Sūtra* (the eighteenth Vow is quoted here).

3. In addition there is a *true realization* (*shinjitsu shōka*). That is what is manifest in the compassionate vows of inevitably reaching the final annihilation (*metsudo*) [of defilements that is nirvāṇa]. The *Larger Sūtra* states the following compassionate vow [as an expression] of [the Buddha's] realization. (Quote from the sūtra of a vow that promises everyone in his realm is assured of reaching *metsudo*.) The sūtra [confirms] this attainment of final annihilation, the realization of nirvāṇa, in the text that narrates the accomplishment of this vow (another quote from the second fascicle).

4. The person who has attained this true invocation and this true entrusting has been promised to be enabled to reside at the rank of the group of the rightly assured. Residing among the group of rightly assured has also been described as reaching the [stage of] equivalent [to a buddha's] enlightenment. It is also preached that this equivalent enlightenment stage is the same as that of Maitreya Bodhisattva, who has only one lifetime remaining before buddhahood. That is why the *Larger Sūtra* says "the next one is like Maitreya."[12]

From these passages we see how individual is Shinran's understanding of merit transference directed toward Birth. Shinran states that "regarding the merit transference of the Tathāgata directed toward Birth, there is true practice, true faith, and true realization. What he means is that the activity of this meritorious debt or merit transference toward Birth is manifest in the lives of sentient beings. The concrete form of this true practice is the action of "recitation of the name of the Tathāgata of Unhindered Light," characterized in the fascicle on practice (in the *Kyōgyōshinshō*) as "the great practice." On his notion of the true *shinjin*, Shinran likewise in the fascicle on faith (in the *Kyōgyōshinshō*) identifies this as the self-realization of faith as confessed by Vasubandhu in the beginning of the section entitled *Gathas seeking Birth* (in the *Jingtu lun*) in the phrase, "With a singularity of mind I take refuge in the Tathāgata of Unhindered Light in the Ten Directions." This is none other than the so-called practice and faith of the selected Original Vow, which is precisely the ground where Jōdoshinshū makes its presence known.

In addition, Shinran enthusiastically speaks of the central issue of the attainment of true realization. We can find this discussion in the fascicle on attainment (in the *Kyōgyōshinshō*):

> Ordinary beings replete with spiritual defilements [reside in a] a mass of budding [anxieties which spring from] the sinful defilements of saṃsāra. But if they obtain the mind and practice of the merit transference directed at Birth, immediately they become counted among the Mahāyāna group of those assured. And because they reside among the group of assured, they will reach nirvāṇa without fail.[13]

As an excellent scholar-monk of the Buddhist tradition, Shinran was well aware that true realization meant "the ultimate attainment of unsurpassed nirvāṇa." But at the same time he also accepted positively the fact that for the individual residing in the community of assured whose steps are taken toward the inevitable attainment of nirvāṇa, this true attainment occurs in one's present condition. This is a point that needs to be stressed.

Merit Transference and Religious Attainment in This Life

Thus Shinran takes the activity of "leaving behind sentient beings and crossing this ocean of transmigration"[14] (going to the Pure Land) as an indebted blessing in the form of merit transfer for the goal of Birth that is realized within the lives of sentient beings by means of true practice, true *shinjin*, and true attainment. These three doctrines are each seen as having their roots in vows, that is, the vow of all the buddhas invoking the name, the vow of Birth by nenbutsu, and the vow of attaining nirvāṇa without fail. From this point of view, Shinran's sense of merit transfer for the goal of Birth is, by means of these three Original Vows which he refers to alternately as "the selected Original Vows of Amida Buddha of merit transfer for the goal of Birth," or as "the Tathāgata's benevolence manifesting within sentient beings to which we are indebted." Shinran's understanding of the third Vow, Expressing confirmation of the attainment of nirvāṇa without fail, is especially important. On this he says:

> The person who has attained this true invocation and this true entrusting have been promised to be enabled to reside at the rank of the group of the rightly assured. Residing among the group of rightly assured has also been described as reaching the [stage] equivalent [to a buddha's] enlightenment.[15]

He thus understands the vow's intention to have been accomplished as the individual's *inevitability* of reaching nirvāṇa, and he describes this as the state of someone in his present situation billowing with true attainment. Shinran's own comprehension of Birth in every instance stands upon this understanding of the merit transfer directed toward the goal of Birth. To clarify this further, let us look at a more advanced statement on this point in his *Ichinen tanen mon'i*:

> The vow of attaining nirvāṇa without fail expounded in the *Larger Sūtra* pledges "If in becoming a buddha, the people and devas in my world do not reside in the community of the rightly assured who reach nirvāṇa without fail, may I not attain buddhahood." The accomplishment of this vow is explained by Śākyamuni as "The sentient beings born in that world all reside in the community of the rightly assured. Why? Because in that world all forms of the [other two] groups of the communities of the misguided and indeterminate are not present."...In this way what Dharmākara Bodhisattva vowed was explained by Śākyamuni for us living with the five stains to be "The sentient beings born in that world will all reside in the community of the rightly assured. Why? Because in that world all forms of the [other two] groups of the communities of the misguided and indeterminate are not present." In the statements by these two honored ones, the description of Birth as confirming the stage of the community of the assured is itself a statement on residing in a stage of nonbacksliding. Because this stage being confirmed means one is in a body that will reach nirvāṇa without fail, this is described as reaching the level of equivalence, or reaching *avaivartika* [the state of nonbacksliding]. It is also known as immediately entering [the status of the] inevitably determinate.[16]

He calls this the "practice and faith of the selected Original Vow" and also "the mind and practice of merit transfer for the goal of Birth." (*ōsō ekō no shingyō*). These terms express the realization of his faith as someone who has joined the community of the assured in this body, in this life. Shinran identifies this state with the state of one who stands in the inevitability of reaching nirvāṇa as implied in the accomplishment of the vow. I have already cited this passage from the chapter on Realization (in the *Kyōgyōshinshō*), which narrates this in a way that suggests activity rather than passivity for the individual life, but I want to match it with an important passage in his *Yuishinshō mon'i*:

> It is the same for ordinary people bound by restrictions, people like meat sellers on the bottom of society [and so forth]. If they can entrust themselves to the inconceivable Original Vow of the Buddha of Unhindered Light, the holy name of enormous wisdom, then they will reach the highest nirvāṇa even while they are filled with karmic afflictions.[17]

If we follow Shinran's argument, then the *ondoku* of the merit transfer for the goal of Birth which expresses Tanluan's "leaving behind sentient beings and crossing this ocean of transmigration" lies most fundamentally with "the selected Original Vow of the merit transfer of the Tathāgata Amida directed toward [those aiming at] Birth." Shinran understood the true reality of this achievement by means of knowing the vow of all the buddhas reciting the Name, the vow of Birth by nenbutsu, and the vow of the inevitability of nirvāṇa. All this is realized within the lifetime of the individual in a very concrete way by means of him or her personally knowing the reality of this achievement, by means of experiencing *shinjin* and the realizing this truth within in their own lives. Thus does the reality of this achievement of the Buddha manifest to sentient beings via their sense of gratitude and indebtedness toward the merit transference that makes their going to the Pure Land a reality. When we think of how we know this, that is, through the process to the realization that I myself reside among the assured who is on the path to the ultimate aim of unsurpassed nirvāṇa, we see how this is something active (rather than passive).

Thus we see how much effort Shinran put into narrating his view of realizing the merit transfer for the goal of Birth. At the risk of sounding redundant, if we follow Shinran's view on this, it is not as simple a matter as it seems. It is all the more obvious that this notion of ōjō is not something that is realized after physical death in the sense of a "future Birth in the Pure Land." Every time Shinran writes of merit transfer directed to the goal of Birth, he always expresses himself in this way. Nevertheless, it seems that we have been saddled with a fixed understanding of Shinran that views his notion of the two forms of merit transfer regarding Birth (ōsō ekō and gensō ekō) as simply a round trip to the Pure Land. I cannot help but look upon this idea in the same way that the Tannishō laments the way that people become "enlightened to their own opinions," missing the uniqueness of what Shinran had to say by a thousand miles.

Pure Land Birth Pointing to Nirvāṇa

As has been mentioned, Shinran refers to this path to self-awareness realized by means of the ondoku of the merit transfer for the goal of Birth as "the core issue of the Larger Sūtra, the Birth that is difficult to conceive of." What he also calls "Birth according to the Larger Sūtra" reflects his understanding of how someone is able to live on this path of self-awareness as a human residing in the community of the assured in his present life, a concrete expression of the real attainment that comes from the gratitude and indebtedness (ondoku) arising from experiencing both forms of merit transfer from the Tathāgata. For another expression of Shinran's understanding of Birth, I return to his Ichinen tanen mon'i:

> Because one attains the true shinjin, one is therefore embraced by the mind of the Buddha of Unhindered Light and never abandoned....In other words, regardless of the passage of time, when it is determined that the individual is at the stage of the community of the assured, it can be said that he or she attains ōjō.[18]

This passage appears to make Shinran's position quite clear, but let me pursue the matter further in the interests of arguing that my own understanding is the correct one.

Shinran has said in these passages that his understanding of what the Larger Sūtra means by "immediate Birth" (sokutoku ōjō) is the determination that by means of attaining shinjin one naturally and immediately attains the stage of the community of the assured. As was seen in the quotation from the Bukkyō jiten, that dictionary's characterization of the Shinshū position as "when Birth is determined in this world, it is called 'immediate Birth'" seems subjective, even inaccurate. Shinran's own realization of immediate Birth is based on the Larger Sūtra's statement that this refers to the individual "residing in the community of the assured, destined to reach nirvāṇa."

To break through the standard understanding and truly see Shinran's unique understanding of the meaning of Birth, one should begin with the suggestion in his statement in the *Ichinen tanen mon'i* that one should "carefully, carefully consider" the statement in the *Larger Sūtra* that confirms the accomplishment of Amida's vows.

Moreover, the understanding of Birth he displays when he labels "Birth according to the *Larger Sūtra*" as a "Birth difficult to conceive of" in his *Jōdo sangyō ōjō monrui* is one viewed from his perspective on the two forms of merit transference. That is, the manifestation of merit transfer for the goal of reaching Birth is felt as a blessing bestowed from the Buddha's true virtue to one self-awakened from obtaining true practice and faith. At that point, one's life is turned away from saṃsāra toward a life that relies on this true merit, that is, a life that manifests the individual's position within the community of the assured. Such a life is naturally characterized by deep feelings of gratitude.

In his *Jōdo sangyō ōjō monrui* Shinran makes the following summary:

> Birth according to the *Larger Sūtra* [is possible through] the Original Vow selected by the Tathāgata, an inconceivable ocean of a Vow, and this is called *tariki* [Other-Power]. This means that by means of the Vow which is the cause of Birth through nenbutsu [*nenbutsu ōjō*], the individual will inevitably reach the goal of the Vow *which is* [enabling that person to realize] nirvāṇa. Residing among the group of assured in this life, he or she knows he or she will reach the true Pure Land of the Buddha in a reward-body. This means that because of the true cause which is the merit transfer from Tathāgata Amida for the goal of Birth, one is *enlightened to the highest nirvāṇa*. This is precisely the core teaching of the *Larger Sūtra*. For this reason, this is called Birth according to the *Larger Sūtra*. [italics added]

Shinran is calling this Birth according to the *Larger Sūtra* because it is a doctrine that is apropos of the core teaching of that sutra. As a final statement of Shinran's own position on all this, here is another quote from the chapter on Realization in the *Kyōgyōshinshō*:

> Thus do we deeply understand the true words of the great sages. The realization of the Great Nirvāṇa is by means of merit transfer from the power of the Vows [of the Buddha]. The benefits that come from the merit transfer used for returning from the Pure Land [*gensō ekō*] is the manifestation of true thoughts for the sake of others.[19]

Rennyo and Shinran

In the history of Japanese Pure Land thought, Shinran's understanding and conception of *ōjō* (Birth) can be considered the highest point in the various formulations of this doctrine. Just how difficult it has been to maintain this understanding over time is a crucial topic for the history of Buddhism, and seeing how the *Bukkyō jiten* from Iwanami Shoten came up with something different is just one of many such examples.

Rennyo appears approximately 200 years after the death of Shinran, making the reconstruction of Shinshū as founded by Shinran his mission in life. Rennyo is quoted to have said, "In this generation I am definitely going to resurrect the Buddha's Dharma." As the leader of this tradition of the Pure Land teachings, Rennyo naturally inherited the Shinshū understanding of Birth and proceeded to add his own characteristics to this position.

One phrase that Rennyo often added to his narration of Birth is "help me in the next life." This takes different forms in different contexts, but whether it be his *Letters*, or in the *Kikigaki*, there is a definite repetition of the idea of *ōjō* as a "future Birth in the Pure Land." In his own, idiosyncratic way, Rennyo nevertheless does display a faithful response to the calling of Shinran's legacy of Birth in the positive sense of joining in the present life the community of the assured, or being on the path to nirvāṇa. We can see this concept in his use of the term *heizei gōjō* (平生業成), "the attainment of practice under normal conditions."[20] Here are two examples of how he uses it:

1. The position of someone who has attained *shinjin* is described in the [*Larger*] *Sūtra* as "immediately attaining Birth; dwelling in a nonbacksliding [state]." In [Tanluan's] Commentary this is also called "with the arising of a single-thought nenbutsu [*ichinen*], one enters the community of the rightly assured." This reflects the discourse of [Birth] without the experience of being greeted at one's death by the Buddha and his attendants [*raigō*] and signifies the attainment of practice under normal conditions [*heizei gōjō*].[21]

2. In general, in our school we speak of this as "with the arising of a single-thought nenbutsu, one enters the community of the rightly assured." After one realizes that it is because of the manifestation of previously sewn good karmic activity that one is afforded the opportunity in the course of ordinary life to hear about the principle in the Original Vow of Amida Buddha that saves us, one then understands the origins of the Original Vow, meaning it is not one's own power [*waga chikara*] but by means of the *tariki* of the Buddha wisdom that has been bestowed upon us that we come to understand. In other words, this is the meaning of the attainment of practice under normal conditions. Thus "the attainment of practice under normal conditions" refers to the condition whereby the individual has truly heard this principle and is in a stage where he or she feels that Birth is determined, fixed, which is also called "with the arising of a single-thought nenbutsu, one enters the community of the rightly assured," or "the attainment of practice under normal conditions," or "immediately attaining Birth; dwelling in a nonbacksliding [state]."[22]

This phrase, "the attainment of practice under normal conditions," is something that Rennyo is thought to have taken from Kakunyo's writings and is probably an expression of the standpoint where the matter of *ōjō* is completed or accomplished. Shinran would term this the identity of one residing in his current state in the community of the assured as a result of attaining *shinjin*. As such this is definitely a statement of understanding that the path to Birth has been attained, and thus from these two letters we know that Rennyo sought to express a position that was in line with this tradition. We can see the same sentiment in the following well-known letter by Rennyo:

> The gist of what we teach in this tradition of [Shinran] Shōnin is based in *shinjin*. For that reason, we abandon the other miscellaneous forms of practice, and since we single-mindedly take refuge in Amida Buddha, our Birth is confirmed by dint of the power in the inconceivable vows [of that buddha]. This position is interpreted as meaning "with the arising of a single-thought nenbutsu, one enters the community of the rightly assured," and the recitation nenbutsu that follows must reflect an attitude of performing nenbutsu to exhaust the debt owed to the tathāgata who has determined my Birth for me.[23]

Rennyo endeavored to resurrect the self-realization implicit in Shinran's faith, and yet Rennyo could never meet Shinran face to face. Instead he had to study Shinran through understanding displayed in the works of Kakunyo and Zonkaku and then succeed to a Shinshū thus conceived. In addition to his assuming the leadership of Honganji, Rennyo's position was complicated by the fact that Japan was immersed in terrible military conflict during most of his life, which corresponds to the latter Muromachi period. And those who tried to stand with him in the awareness he inherited from Shinran as "fellow practicioners" were people living in a chaotic world. Such severe conditions, it seems to me, brought forth to him the question of the salvation of ordinary people in a defiled world in the Latter Age and moved him toward a role of leading the people closer to the salvation embodied in the enlightenment attained by Hōnen.

"To attain *shinjin* is to comprehend the eighteenth Vow. To comprehend the eighteenth Vow is to comprehend the form of *namu amida butsu*." In this understanding of the Sacred Name (*myōgō*), Rennyo for some reason bypasses Shinran to rely on the traditional interpretation of Shandao and Hōnen regarding the six characters that make up the nenbutsu. Shandao clarified the meaning of the Sacred Name within this phrase by saying that "with this meaning one attains Birth without fail." Shinran glosses this statement to the effect that " 'to attain Birth without fail' is an expression denoting the fact that one obtains a position of nonbacksliding," which unmistakably refers to his understanding of residing in the community of the assured in one's present life (*genshō shōjōju*).

By contrast, Rennyo's hermeneutic looks somewhat different, expressed in phrases such as "please save me in the next life" (*goshō tasuke tamae*) and "the next life is the single most important issue [in this one]" (*goshō no ichi-daiji*). These are expressions of Rennyo's own thoughts on the subject of Birth, but should we not also consider them as the resignation of a Rennyo accepting the urgent supplications of the people in an age of upheaval? And in response to those needs, Rennyo asserted the following:

> For those whose *shinjin* of one thought-moment is confirmed [*ichinen no shinjin sadamaran tomogara*], each one will attain Birth in the Pure Land—ten out of ten, one hundred out of one hundred. There is nothing further to worry about.[24]

When Rennyo asserts that "each and every person will be born in the Pure Land of a [buddha in] reward body [*saṃbhogakāya*]; there is absolutely nothing to doubt about this," he shows us how inspired he was by Shandao's conviction in the latter's reading of the "inevitability of attaining Birth." But one more point I would like to draw attention to is the fact that the attainment of this conviction is an event that unmistakenly occurs in this life. It cannot be denied that Rennyo's statement that "one will attain Birth" expresses a certain softening of the tension expressed in the understanding found in Shinran's similar statements. Not only that, but when "one will attain Birth" is asserted, the time when the realization of the Birth occurs is implied to be during one's final moments or at the moment of death itself. When this is finally realized, Rennyo maintains Shinran's position by saying the accomplishment of the matter of Birth happens during one's normal lifetime, and that attainment of conviction in the confirmation of Birth occurs during the present life, when one produces the single-thought [of *shinjin*]. Thus does the basic understanding of Rennyo on the issue of Birth attempt to express agreement with what he inherited from Shinran.

Notes

This chapter originally appeared as "Shinran to Rennyo: ōjō rikai wo megutte" 親鸞と蓮如: 往生理解をめぐって, in *Indogaku Bukkyōgaku Kenkyū* 91 (46–1), 1997, 1–11.

1 T No. 2608, 83.1; SSZ 1.929. Usually pronounced *Senjakushū* in the Shinshū tradition.

2 T No. 2675, 83.910. Seikaku was another disciple of Hōnen, elder to Shinran, who also exerted a deep influence on Shinran's thinking. Shinran wrote a commentary to Seikaku's *Yuishinshō* that is called *Yuishinshō mon'i*, with two extant recensions at SSZ 2.621 and 639.

3 T No. 2661, 83.728; SSZ 2.773.

4 *Jōdo sangyō ōjō monrui*. There are two recensions of this text, at SSZ 2.543 and 551.

5 *Translator's note*: This is a statement of inevitability regarding one's future religious attainment, translating the Sanskrit *niyata-samyaktva*. In a Pure Land context, it can either refer to reaching the Pure Land or have the more general meaning of attaining enlightenment. Terakawa's argument hinges on reading a final enlightenment meaning in Shinran's usage, based on statements such the one quoted from the fascicle on attainment in the *Kyōgyōshinshō* where Shinran states that "they reside among the group of assured they will reach nirvāṇa without fail."

6 SSZ2.554.

7 Jinrei, *Kyōgyōshinshō kōgi shūsei*, 9 vols., orig. ed. in *Bukkyō taikei* (Tokyo: Bukkyō Taikei Kanseikai, 1918; rep. Kyoto: Hōzōkan, 1975), 1.244.

8 Hoshino Genpō, *Kōkai Kyōgyōshinshō*, rev. ed., 6 vols. (Kyoto: Hōzōkan, 1994), 1.40.

9 Nakamura Hajime et al, eds., *Bukkyō jiten* (Tokyo: Iwanami Shoten, 1989), 86.

10 Taya Raishun, Ocho Enichi, and Funahashi Issai, eds., *Bukkyōgaku jiten: shinpan* (Kyoto: Hōzōkan, 1995), 44.

11 *Shōzōmatsu wasan* 49 (48), SSZ 2.521.

12 *Jōdo sangyō ōjō monrui*, expanded version, SSZ 2.551.

13 SSZ 2.103.

14 A quote from Tanluan's *Jingtu lunzhu* (*Jōdo ronchū*), his commentary on the *Jingtu lun*, at T No. 1819, 40.836b.

15 *Jōdo sangyō ōjō monrui*, SSZ2.552.

16 *Ichinen tanen mon'i*, at T No. 2657, 83.694c; SSZ 2.606.

17 *Yuishinshō mon'i*, at T No. 2658, 83.701c–702a; SSZ 2.628.

18 SSZ 2.605.

19 *Translator's note*: *Kyōgyōshinshō*, at T No. 2646, 83.620c; SSZ 2.118. Terakawa stops short here of explaining Shinran's view of this second type of merit transfer but directs the reader to his treatment of this issue in his book *Shinran no shin no dainamikkusu* (Chiba: Sōkōsha, 1993).

20 *Heizei gojō* is a Shinshū term which denotes the attainment of the path before death, created to differentiate the Shinshū position from that of Jōdoshū sects. The latter takes a contrasting position called *rinjū gojō*, whose goal is said to be attained at the moment of death.

21 *Letters* 1:2; SSZ 3.404; RSI, 69.

22 *Letters* 1:4; SSZ 3.406; RSI, 88.

23 *Letters* 5:10; SSZ 3.507; RSI, 60.

24 *Letters* 5:4; SSZ 3.502; RSI, 439.

11

KAKU TAKESHI
TRANSLATED BY MAYA HARA

Rennyo's Position in Modern Shin Buddhist Studies

Soga Ryōjin's Reinterpretation

R ennyo's impact on the religious ideas and institutional organization of Shin Buddhism was not limited to the turbulent medieval period in which he lived, but continued on through the modern period. This chapter will focus on how Rennyo was viewed within the Higashi Honganji Ōtani denomination of Jodoshinshū in the modern period through one of its most eminent twentieth-century thinkers, Soga Ryōjin (1875–1971).[1] Formerly, the religious organization of Higashi Honganji controlled a feudal, conservative image of Rennyo as reflected in *shūgaku* (宗学), or traditional sectarian studies,[2] of the Ōtani denomination, which Soga and other Shin reformers such as Kiyozawa Manshi (1863–1903)[3] challenged. Therefore they were, for a time, defrocked. Soga, who came from a family belonging to the Ōtani branch, struggled against the opposition and oppression from his religious organization, which regarded Rennyo as its absolute ecclesiastical authority. By challenging and redefining Rennyo's position and significance in the modern period, Soga came to define and shape the course of Modern Shin Buddhist Studies in the Ōtani branch.

Rennyo's Position in Modern Shinshū Studies

In the latter part of the Edo period (1604–1867) both Higashi and Nishi Honganji established ecclesiastical hierarchies that placed the descendants of Shinran at the pinnacle of their religious institutions, which by then were based on the Tokugawa government's religious policies that required systematic delineation of head and branch temples.[4] Each sect also created an official and authoritative *shūgaku* in accordance with the government's educational advancement programs. These programs represented the religious organization and served as a vehicle to carry out the social and educational reforms of the chief abbots of the respective denominations.[5] Shin *shūgaku* originally referred to the general study of religious doctrine. For the Ōtani denomination,[6] traditional sectarian studies, that is, the apologetic and doctrinal study of Shin Buddhism, was the means to secure and strengthen the organizational hierarchy of the sect. The *Letters of the Restorer Saint*, Rennyo, as a canonical source of authority, were made absolute and served as the standard measure of orthodoxy or heresy in the sect. Both the religious organization and the *shūgaku* it sponsored emphasized the importance of adherence to the *Letters* and ensured the position of the leaders of Honganji as "the good teachers [*zenchishiki*], [the only true] successors in the transmission [of teaching]."[7]

However, with the Meiji Restoration, Japan's feudal age came to an end, opening the way for the modern period. For Honganji, which had come under the aegis of the religious policies of the Tokugawa government, this was a time of crisis. The Ōtani organization was confronted in the early Meiji period by the government's promotion of Shinto as the state religion and by official anti-Buddhist activities (*haibutsu kishaku*), as well as by the spread of Christianity due to new national policies that allowed its proselytization throughout the country. The sect attempted to redefine its sociopolitical role by showing complete support to the emperor system and by establishing educational associations, such as the Dharma Preservation Society to counter advances being made by Christianity in Japan.[8]

In an effort to show loyalty to the emperor system, Rennyo's words were utilized to represent a doctrine as the basis for contemporary Shin discourse within Higashi Honganji on the relationship between state law and Buddhist law (*ōbō buppō*) through the concept of the two truths of "worldly truth and absolute truth" (*shinzoku nitai*). For example, in 1875 the twentieth head priest of the Ōtani branch, Gonnyo, and in 1904 the twenty-third head priest Shōnyo, each wrote declarations to their adherents expressing the need to respond to the demands of the national emperor system by submitting to secular order. They expounded a doctrine promising Birth in the Pure Land in the afterlife if one expressed gratitude, loyalty, and filial piety to the emperor in this present life and took a position of commitment regarding the proper teaching of truth.[9]

The influential Meiji-period educator Fukuzawa Yukichi (1835–1901), who advocated the separation of state and religion, also asserted the value of the concept of the two truths because it limited the inner problems of faith and gave importance to secular authority. Fukuzawa thus praised Rennyo's *Letters* as being the most appropriate "religion" for the modern imperial nation-state.[10] In his *Letters*, Rennyo wrote:

> [T]ake the laws of the state as your outer aspect, store Other-Power faith deep in your hearts, and take [the principles of] humanity and justice (*jingi*) as essential. Bear in mind that these are the rules of conduct that have been established within our tradition.[11]

Such statements by Rennyo, which encouraged unquestioning obedience to the laws of the secular state, were attractive as an apologetic for Honganji's political situation, with Rennyo's words being utilized to justify the religious insitution's stance toward the polity of the modern Japanese nation-state. Sectarian studies of the Ōtani denomination thus came to support the institution's official position of accommodation with government policy and, as a result, any tendency to neglect or criticize Rennyo was suppressed. Sectarian scholars placed such great importance on the research of Rennyo's *Letters* in the early Meiji period that, for some, *shūgaku* came to mean the study of the *Letters*.[12]

However, in the midst of the political and social changes taking place in Japan, structural reform within the Ōtani denomination also came to the foreground. Soga reminisced in his later years:

> The traditional way the teachings have been transmitted [in our time] within the religious organization and its schools has ignored dealing directly with Shinran. Instead, [everyone] followed the Tokugawa-period style of examining Shinran through Rennyo.[13]

By the mid-Meiji period, young aspiring intellectuals within the sect began challenging the conservative advocates of *shūgaku* and urged progressive religious teaching. In 1895, three years before the 400th Memorial Service of Rennyo, a group surrounding Kiyozawa Manshi, a charismatic teacher who inspired Soga and whose ideas later became central to the development of Modern Shin Studies, submitted a proposal to reform the temple administration in charge of doctrinal studies. In 1896 Kiyozawa's group began publishing the journal *Kyōkai Jigen* (Timely Words for a Religious World), in which they again urged institutional change. Fearing conflict from within, the conservative authorities of the sect attempted to crush outright the reform movement centered around Kiyozawa, and in 1897, they condemned Kiyozawa and his supporters to expulsion according to sectarian ordinances. In the same year, advocates of traditional *shūgaku* formed an association called the Kanrenkai, which proclaimed an old slogan, "cherish the head temple and protect the Buddha Dharma" (*aizan gohō*). It also worked to oppose all ideas on Modern Shin Studies that began with Kiyozawa. In *Kyōkai Jigen*, Kiyozawa criticized the formation of the association saying:

> The Kanrenkai attempts to determine doctrinal orthodoxy and heresy on the basis of the misconception that confuses Shinran's teachings with that of sectarian studies, which is based on the research of later scholars. Ultimately, it is no more than a form of partisanship whose assertions, if realized, will leave the sect in a lamentable state.[14]

In the midst of this heated dispute between reformers and conservatives, Rennyo's 400th Memorial was welcomed in 1898.

Soga Ryōjin's Position in Modern Shin Studies

While Soga was a student at Shinshū University, founded by Higashi Honganji, he witnessed the oppression of the reform movement by the faction that advocated sectarian studies. In 1896 he signed a written declaration by some Shinshū University students against *shūgaku*, showing that he sympathized with Kiyozawa's movement from an early age. Moreover, in a special issue of the journal *Mujinto* (Inexhaustible Light) commemorating Rennyo's memorial, Soga contributed a short article entitled "The Highest Truth of Rennyo's Teachings," in which he criticized *shūgaku* as being too erudite and obscure and not being true to Rennyo's original intentions.[15] He remarked that *shūgaku* distanced itself from Rennyo's teachings, whose purpose was simplicity and immediacy. Soga first praised Rennyo by saying:

> As a revivalist of Buddhism, a propagator of loyalty to the emperor and reformer of social morality, [Rennyo] defined the historical basis of a national religion, and always preached morality to reform social principles. These are what make him great.[16]

This was the general view that many inside and outside of the sect held of Rennyo in that period.

However, Soga went on to elucidate that beyond this common view of Rennyo, there was a higher truth (*shintai*) which Rennyo sought. Regarding the various opinions on secular truth (*zokutai*), Soga explained his own view of this highest truth, referring to it as the "Master's religious doctrine" (*shōnin no shūgi*), a concept set against secular *and* sectarian ideas. Soga argued that the impact of Rennyo's teaching lay in his clear and simple language:

> All the fundamental teachings of the Master [Rennyo] can be found in his approximately eighty letters. The plain and lucid letters were the sole enterprise of our "Restorer Saint." When someone asked peasants and rustics about the pacified mind (*anjin*) in Shinshū, they always answered in one sentence: "We simply entrust ourselves to Amida to save us in the afterlife."[17]

Further, Soga asserted that "Rennyo was a great social reformer, who was thought to be subversive and disruptive in his day and age, not a conservative authoritarian leader."[18] In view of the circumstances Soga faced, the so-called "conservative authorities" that he referred to were the advocates of *shūgaku*, and the "great social reformer" meant the modern-day reformers of the teachings of the Ōtani denomination as represented by Kiyozawa. Soga also asserted that Rennyo based true religious understanding on whether or not one had faith. He showed how decidedly different this concept was from the approach taken by the proponents of *shūgaku*, who reacted to the reform movement led by Kiyozawa by attempting to defrock its members. By presenting his views on Rennyo's teaching in this way, Soga tacitly unfolded his critique against the views held by those running the organization's sectarian studies. However, at this point his most radical criticism was not yet fully developed. Although he sympathized with the religious studies movement centered around Kiyozawa, Soga did not yet touch upon the definitive core of Kiyozawa's idea of Buddhist learning, which was a quest for the understanding of the relationship between the Tatāgatha and the self. Realizing this teaching was to become the fundamental turning point in Soga's radical interpretation of Rennyo's doctrine.

For Soga, Rennyo's teaching was embodied in the concept of what is known in Shin Buddhism as *kihō ittai*, or "the unity of the individual's faith and the Buddha Dharma," and in Kiyozawa's idea of the "correspondence between the finite and infinite" (*yūgen to mugen no taiō*). This critical view came to life only when Soga fully stood on Kiyozawa's doctrinal understanding, eventually leading to his full confrontation with sectarian studies.

The Transformation of Soga's Interpretation of Rennyo

After Kiyozawa's death, Shinshū University, founded by Kiyozawa in Sugamo, Tokyo, was moved to Kyoto by the authorities in charge of sectarian studies. Soga began challenging the views of Rennyo espoused in *shūgaku* by focusing on Rennyo's interpretation of *kihō ittai*, the unity of faith and the Dharma. Soga reminisced that in his youth he was deeply moved by Rennyo's teaching of the unity of the faith of sentient beings and the Dharma: "In my youth, I was drawn to the *Anjinketsujōshō*,[19] in which the concept of the unity of faith and the Dharma appears, in the same way [as I was drawn to] *Tannishō*."[20] In Rennyo's letter entitled "The Oneness of the Person [to Be Saved] and the Dharma [that Saves]," there is a passage, "What is the meaning of *Namu-amida-butsu*? Furthermore, how are we to entrust ourselves to Amida and attain Birth in the fulfilled land?"[21]

Underlying the six characters of the Buddha's name (*rokuji myōgō*), which is believed to contain the workings that allow all sentient beings to be born into Amida's Pure Land, is the unity of faith and the Dharma. Rennyo laid out the immediate relationship between sentient beings and Amida and taught that one should "cast away the sundry practices,"[22] thus clarifying the true meaning of the pacified mind (*anjin*) in Shinshū. Although Rennyo highly valued the concept of the unity of faith and the Dharma, this idea was not unique to him. It was introduced early on in the Seizan branch of the Pure Land sect (such as in *Anjinsho* by Shōkū (1177–1247) and was also incorporated by Kakunyo (1270–1351) and Zonkaku (1290–1373) in the laying of the foundations of Shinshū teaching.[23] Rather than simply uncritically accepting Rennyo's understanding of the *Anjinketsujōshō* and other past interpretations, Soga sought the practical meaning of "responsiveness" (*kan'ō* 感応) as expressed by the idea of unity. "Responsiveness" was originally a Tendai concept, in which *kan* (feeling) represents the awareness of the Tathāgata by sentient beings and *ō* (response) is the Tathāgata's response itself. For Soga, "responsiveness" was a spiritual awakening that surpassed intellectual comprehension. He explains that through the central theme of *shōmyō nenbutsu* (reciting the Buddha's Name) in *Tannishō*, Rennyo clarified the actual practice of the unity of faith and the Dharma, and through the "two aspects of deep belief" (*nishu jinshin*),[24] especially the understanding of the deep belief of faith, he clarified the distinction between the role of the faithful individual and the Dharma.[25] Soga asserted in a lecture for Rennyo's Memorial:

> To clarify the role of the faithful individual and the Dharma was one of the greatest achievements of Master Rennyo. In other sects, the unity of faith and the Dharma was considered a nonduality between sentient beings and the Buddha (*shōbutsu funi*), but [this position] confuses it with the thought of the Tendai school at that time. Regarding this and the directing virtue of the Other-Power (*tariki ekō*), Rennyo thoroughly clarified the issue through his division of the capacity of sentient beings to accept the Buddha's teaching from the capacity of the Buddha to save us. For this reason, for the 450th Anniversary, our most important task is to create a study that elucidates these capacities.[26]

In this way, Soga saw that Rennyo's life work was expressed in the self-realization of faith in the directing virtue of Other-Power through the capacities of sentient beings and the Buddha. Until then, Rennyo had been misinterpreted because this point had not been fully understood. The major difference between the conservative advocates of *shūgaku* and the reformers in understanding Rennyo could be seen through this single point, and by illuminating this, Soga reshaped the understanding of Rennyo in the modern period.

The deepening of Soga's understanding of the unity of faith and the Dharma can be seen in two phases. The first phase is through an existential appreciation inspired by Kiyozawa; the second, through the religious quest of the bodhisattva Dharmākara, who became Amida Buddha. The definitive means by which Soga received Kiyozawa's understanding is through the idea that the Tathāgata's salvation does not exist apart from our belief and that our salvation lies in the awakening to our finitude.[27] Soga explains:

> This faith (of Kiyozawa) in regards to the Tathāgata's salvific power is called the unity of subjective faith and objective Tathāgata. This faith is also called the unity of the Buddha mind (which arises in ourselves as faith, the active faith that provides grace) and the ordinary mind (the evil, sinful self that is saved by this faith, a passive faith that is accepted and received), in terms of the self existing in eternal darkness.[28]

In other words, Kiyozawa's idea of the correspondence between the finite and infinite is a subjective, modern expression of Rennyo's theory of the unity of faith and the Dharma. Thus Soga's task was then to clarify this one point in Rennyo's teaching of the unity of faith and the Dharma as a doctrinal theme. Soga began to develop this idea of the "unity of faith and the Dharma" through his interpretation of what he called "the Tathāgata and myself":[29]

> I am not limited to calling the Tathāgata "Thou"; I directly call the Tathāgata "myself." Those who believe in "self power" (*jiriki*) proudly boast, "I am Tathāgata!" Those of other Pure Land sects vainly lament this life, saying, "The Tathāgata is the Tathāgata." We are surprised by the wonderous meaning of "the Tathāgata is me." At the same time, we are aware that "ultimately, I am me and not the Tathāgata."[30]

Soga argued that the relationship between "the Tathāgata and myself" is often confused. Some are immersed in concepts of "own-nature (*svabhāva*) and Mind Only (*vijñapti-mātratā*)" (as in self power-based teachings) and some are lost in the self power of meditative and nonmeditative practices (as in other Pure Land sects). Thus the relationship between the Tathāgata and oneself begins with the quest for Dharmākara through the intuition that "the Tathāgata in becoming me means the birth of Dharmākara."[31] Here, the meaning of "the unity of faith and the Dharma" is "the six characters of the Buddha's name in this unity, which is already manifested without exception in the single fact of Dharmākara's birth."[32] With the discovery of Dharmākara, Soga is able to present the existential theme of "the Tathāgata in becoming me, saves me." In this way, through Kiyozawa's realization of the limitation of the capacity of sentient beings in his idea of "the correspondence between the infinite and the finite," Soga is able to find meaning in Rennyo's teaching of "the unity of faith and the Dharma" and further develops this in the relationship between the Tathāgata and himself through the existence of Bodhisattva Dharmākara.

For Soga, if the question of Dharmākara was not clarified, the message of Shin Buddhism would be reduced to prayers to Amida for salvation, which was the orthodoxy of the Edo period. Soga worked against this interpretation of Amida as an anthropomorphic savior and Dharmakara as his ancient predecessor.[33] What then was the essence of the self-realization of the relationship between the Tathāgata and myself, which is the unity of faith and the Dharma? Soga's unique understanding is none other than deep entrusting. Deep entrusting is the "deep mind" concretely explained by the Chinese Pure Land master Shandao (613–681), who indicated that the two aspects of the deepen trusting and the Dharma are actually one, and that self-realization via faith means realizing that one is saved by Amida.[34] Shandao wrote in his *Guanjing shu* (*Commentary on the Contemplation Sutra*): "Deep mind refers to the deeply entrusting mind. There are two aspects. One is to believe deeply and decidedly that you are a foolish being of karmic evil caught in birth-and-death [*saṃ sāra*], ever sinking and ever wandering in transmigration from innumerable kalpas in the past, with never a condition that would lead to emancipation. The second is to believe deeply and decidely that Amida Buddha's forty-eight Vows embrace sentient beings and that allowing yourself to be carried by the power of the Vow without any doubt or apprehension, you will attain birth."[35]

In other words, Soga confirmed the reality of "the unity of faith and the Dharma" by means of the realization of one's finitude, expressed in the doctrine of the deep entrusting of the self (*ki no jinshin*). When the sadness of the human condition based upon this realization of the deep suffering that accompanies being born into human life is lost, the vitality of deep entrusting is lost. Soga explained this to be the case because this realization is itself the fundamental opportunity of a religion symbolized in the Name of Amida.

Brought to Life by the *Tannishō*

Soga asserted that "Master Rennyo was inspired by *Tannishō* and through it he was able to find his inner motive to achieve the revival of Shinshu."[36] The oldest extant copy of *Tannishō* was transcribed by Rennyo, and regardless of his seemingly contradictory attitude toward it, if his personal copy had not survived, this text might not have been transmitted to later generations.[37] Although some credit Rennyo for the discovery of *Tannishō*, for Soga it was through *Tannishō* that Rennyo as the revivalist of Shinshū was born. Soga understood Rennyo's Shinshū renewal through the spirit of *Tannishō*, and in modern Japan it was Kiyozawa who rediscovered and reintroduced *Tannishō* to Soga and the wider Shin community.

In 1930 Soga, then a professor at Ōtani University in Kyoto, a reestablishment of the former Shinshū University, was again accused by the highest *shūgaku* authorities of serious differences with the doctrines of the sect. In response to accusations of heresy (*ianjin*) levied against him, Soga submitted his resignation and left the university. Although this act meant he was driven out of the sect, eleven years later while in the midst of World War II, and five years before the 450th Memorial of Rennyo in 1946, Soga was asked to return to Ōtani. At the age of sixty-seven, he returned, this time as a *kōshi* lecturer, the highest academic position in the Ōtani denomination. In the following year he lectured for a month on *Tannishō* for the scholars of the sect in the Ōtani denomination's *ango* lecture series.[38] Ironically, the *ango* was organized by the Takakura Gakuryō, a sanctuary of the same *shūgaku* tradition that had banned Kiyozawa, closed down Shinshū University, deprived Kaneko Daiei (1881–1976) of his clerical title, and labeled Soga a heretic. The year before Soga returned to the university, he made a scathing remark against the *shūgaku* and its interpretation of "the unity of person and the Dharma" as "that complicated dogmatic, metaphysical *shūgaku* of long ago."[39] In these words we can see that Soga's choice of *Tannishō* as the main *ango* text was no mere coincidence. Although there was no direct reference to Kiyozawa, Soga had in mind Kiyozawa's efforts in bringing to light the importance of this document.[40] This thinking is revealed in Soga's writings, which explain that in his youth Soga tried to spread the teaching of *Tannishō* among his colleagues because his teacher Kiyozawa "sought the spirit of Master Rennyo's revival of Shinshū, and at the same time began to prepare for the quickly approaching 650th anniversary of the founding of the sect."[41] In the modern period the *Tannishō* became the prime textual vehicle for bringing Shinran's thoughts beyond the sectarian context (*shūmon*) and played an important role in introducing these thoughts to the general public (the understanding of Shinran by most people today is based on *Tannishō*). Following Kiyozawa's lead, then, Soga tried to discern the meaning of the Shinshū revival under Rennyo through the *Tannishō*. Here Soga realized the "profound historical meaning [of *Tannishō*]" through his lectures and found reason to affirm that "the spirit of Rennyo's Shinshū revival lies in the spirit of lament in *Tannishō*."[42]

The revolutionary idea behind many of Soga's lectures can thus be found in the idea that the spirit of lament in *Tannishō* is based essentially on the "receptiveness and responsiveness" between sentient beings and the Tathāgata. In other words, the circumstances described in *Tannishō* "are no different from the faith (*shinjin* 信心) transmitted by our first teacher [Shinran]." Prior to Soga, this deep entrusting was understood to mean the feeling of powerlessness and despair among sentient beings, premised in the profound trust in the teachings. For Soga, *shinjin* was the essence of *Tannishō*. Thus he asserted that it was through *Tannishō* that Rennyo, the revivalist of Shinshū, came to life.

The Second Revival of Shinshū in 1949 Coinciding with Rennyo's 450th Memorial

The defeat of Japan in World War II in 1945 meant the collapse of the modern Japanese emperor system, which controlled its populace through its State Shinto ideology. This collapse became a major turning point for the administrative operations of many religious organizations in Japan. In the midst of the confusion of defeat, both Higashi and Nishi Honganji began planning celebrations of Rennyo's 450th Memorial of 1949,[43] for which many publications were produced. Especially significant were the publications of *Rennyo* by Hattori Shisō,[44] who took a Marxist materialistic interpretation of history, and *Rennyo Shōnin kenkyū*, edited by Ryukoku University,[45] which held a positivistic historical view. Both proposed new and critical interpretations of Rennyo, which countered the views of the established *shūgaku* approach. For his part, Soga did not adopt these new views and remained silent. In preparation for the celebration of Rennyo's 450th Memorial, Soga gave a public talk in 1948 based on the theme "The Nature of Receptiveness and Responsiveness."[46] Especially noteworthy in this lecture was that Soga openly discussed Kiyozawa's Shinshū revival, something he was unable to do during the *ango* lecture series, which was controlled by conservative sectarian scholars.

Later, in *Daini no Shinshū saikō* ("The Second Revival of Shinshu") Soga wrote:

> In reality, we think of Master Rennyo's endeavors to revive Shinshū generally as having ended with the establishment of the Meiji Restoration, which brought about the downfall of the Tokugawa government.[47]

Soga explained that in associating Kiyozawa with the modern revival of Shinshu, however:

> This second revival was different from Rennyo's revival. For Rennyo, it was limited only to Japan, and generally within the Shinshū following. However, the extent of this second revival is global. Instead of consolidating Shinshu, the objective is to unify Buddhism. ... Lately I have come to realize that the culmination of this great undertaking of the second revival is *Waga shinnen* (My Faith) by Kiyozawa-sensei.[48] I have felt this with the opportunity I had recently to visit the United States.[49]

His reason for indicating Kiyozawa's *Waga Shinnen* as signifying the second Shinshū revival was that "[Kiyozawa] did not start with the Tathāgata; instead, he began with faith (*shinnen*), and taught that the Tathāgata and faith are one." The distinction in Kiyozawa's teaching was that he did not try to analyze a religious doctrine upon the premise that it was complete; rather he understood religious experience as the meaning of truth. In contrast to the traditional stance of *shūgaku*, Soga saw Kiyozawa's ideas as crucial to the foundation of a "Modern Shin Studies" and came to emphasize the traditions of Shinran, Rennyo, and Kiyozawa, who "understood Buddhism through their own experiences."[50] Soga showed that Rennyo was significant in clarifying the relation between the Tathāgata and oneself in a certain time, thus subjectively situating Rennyo within this notion of the tradition of Shinshū rather than through a continued transmission and explanation of his teaching.

Conclusion

For Soga, Rennyo symbolized Shinshū itself. Although Soga opposed the doctrine of the religious organization that viewed Rennyo as the absolute authority, he deeply sympathized with the members of the organization who respected Rennyo. Soga neither ignored nor denied Rennyo and his importance. Although he openly confronted the image of Rennyo that was created and maintained by the legacy of *shūgaku*, which defined him as reviver of the institution on the basis of the *Letters*, he continued to revere the Rennyo who sought to revive faith (*shinjin*) through *Tannishō*. For this reason, he could not be protective of an image of Rennyo upheld by the apologetic sectarian scholars whose doctrine was uncritically premised on Rennyo's faith, nor could he be a mere observer like the nonsectarian scholars who systematically ignored the importance of Rennyo's faith.

Soga's radical stance against the Ōtani sectarian scholars was not only based on religious grounds but also had a historical and epistemological basis that was developed over time in response to the organizational suppression of Kiyozawa and his followers (including Soga himself). Through confrontation with the religious institution, Soga was able to reevaluate Rennyo's importance both doctrinally and historically. By interpreting Rennyo's teaching as the expression of faith rather than as a systematic presentation of doctrine, Soga criticized the absolutist image of Rennyo that was upheld by the authoritarian aspect of his sect and clarified the practical meaning of Rennyo's personal faith.

Notes

1 Soga Ryōjin was born the third son of Ryodo and Tatsu Tomioka in 1875, in Entokuji Temple in Ajikata Village, Nishikanbara District, Niigata Prefecture. In 1890 Soga entered Shinshū Daiichi Chūgakuryō (a Higashi Honganji Shinshū middle school); five years later he attended the Shinshū seminary, Shinshū Daigakuryō. The following year Soga entered Jo'onji Temple in Niigata Village, Minami-kanbara District, Niigata Prefecture. He married Kei, the eldest daughter of Enan Soga, and took her family's name. In 1902 he began teaching Buddhist logic at the newly opened Shinshū University in Tokyo. During his teaching years he published five articles, such as "Meiji 34 ni kansha su" (In Gratitude to 1901), in which he was largely critical of Kiyozawa Manshi's spiritual movement, *Seishinshugi*. However, Soga later came to agree with Kiyozawa's ideas, and in 1903 he joined Kiyozawa's group, and moved to the dormitory Kōkōdō with several of Kiyozawa's students, though by this time Kiyozawa returned to his temple in Ōhara and did not reside with them, due to his illness.

In 1904 Soga became a professor at Shinshū University and lectured on Yogacāra thought. When Shinshū University moved from Tokyo to Kyoto in 1911, Soga resigned and returned to Niigata. For the next six years he absorbed himself in Shin Buddhist Studies and began building his own doctrinal understanding. In 1916 he became a professor at Tōyō University and the editor of *Seishinkai* (The Spiritual World), a publication of Kiyozawa's group. He resigned from Tōyō University in 1924 and the following year his wife passed away. In the same year, he became a professor at Ōtani University and, with Kaneko Daiei, worked to establish the foundation for a new phase in Shin doctrinal studies.

In 1930 Soga authored *Nyorai hyōgen no hanchū to shite no sanshinkan* (The View of Three Minds as the Category of the Tathāgata's Manifestation), for which he was publicly criticized by the academic committee (*jitōryō*) of Higashi Honganji for going against conventional sectarian scholars. For this equivalent of a public declaration of heresy, he resigned from Ōtani University. In 1941, during World War II, he was promoted to the highest academic position of Shin doctrinal studies in the Ōtani Denomination (*Ōtaniha kōshi*) and again became a professor at Ōtani University, where he became professor emeritus in 1951. In 1959 he became the head of the academic committee of Higashi Honganji, and in 1961, at the age of eighty-six, he became the president of Ōtani University, during which time he worked as lecturer and administrator for the modern education of the student body. Soga retired from Ōtani University in 1967, and he passed away in 1971.

2 Hirose Nan'yu defined *shūgaku* as understood in Higashi Honganji as "doctrinal studies in which the object of study is the infallible understanding of a doctrine as established by its founder, who is endowed with the spiritual authority of a particular religious group," in *Shinshūgakushi kō* (Kyoto: Hōzōkan, 1980), 9. Nishi Honganji similarly has had a formal doctrinal studies which is called *Shinshūgaku* or Shinshū Studies. See Rogers, 10.

3 Kiyozawa Manshi was born as Tokugawa Mannosuke, the eldest son of Tokugawa Naganori, a low-ranking samurai of Owari Province (present-day Aichi Prefecture). He was ordained as a priest of the Ōtani denomination at the age of fifteen and had a deep impact on Shin Buddhism's response to the modern world.

4 Various regulations were implemented in the "premodern" Tokugawa period to protect Buddhism, such as the organized systems of head and branch temple hierarchies (*honmatsusei*) and affiliation registration at temples (*shūmon aratame*). See Notto R. Thelle, *Buddhism and Christianity in Japan: From Conflict to Dialogue, 1854–1899* (Honolulu: University of Hawaii Press, 1987); James Edward Ketelaar, *Of Heretics and Martyrs in Japan: Buddhism and Its Persecution* (Princeton, N.J.: Princeton University Press, 1990).

5 Akamatsu Toshihide and Kasahara Kazuo, *Shinshūshi gaisetsu* (Kyoto: Heirakuji Shoten, 1963), 390–399.

6 The Nishi Honganji sect faced similar issues in the modern period. For the purposes of this essay, however, I focus only on the problems that existed within the Higashi Honganji sect.

7 *Gaikemon*, printed under the title *Ryōgemon* at SSZ 3:529; see also Rogers, 280. According to Kogatsu-in Jinrei (1749–1817), who was the most prominent scholar of the Ōtani denomination during the Edo period, from the time of Jitsunyo (1458–1525), Rennyo's fifth son, successive chief abbots of Honganji taught Rennyo's *Letters* to their followers (*Shinshū taikei*, 32.218). Regarding the concepts of orthodoxy and heresy in Jodo Shinshū and in the *Letters*, see James C. Dobbins, *Jodo Shinshu: Shin Buddhism in Medieval Japan* (Bloomington: Indiana University Press, 1989), 7–10 and chap. 9. See also Rogers regarding the authoritarian nature of the *Letters*.

8 Higashi Honganji created the Dharma Preservation Association, Gohōjō, in 1868 as an adjunct school of the Takakura Gakuryō, its main school. The association was intended to foster commitment to the anti-Christian campaign of the Ōtani denomination, said to "defend Buddhism and refute the false doctrine (*bohō boja*)." Classes such as classical Japanese, Confucianism, astronomy, and Christianity were taught. However, in time the society helped to educate students who became reformers within the Ōtani branch and who, through their new education, strongly criticized the policies of their own religious organization and school for being outdated and controlling. Nishi Honganji similarly responded to outside pressures at this time by creating the Gakurin, which offered a parallel curriculum.

9 Regarding this idea, Honganji leader Shōnyo (1516–1554) espoused, "In this life, be good citizens of the emperor; in the after world, become a pure person in the Pure Land" (SSS 6.718).

10 Fukuzawa is famous for saying that religion is like tea. See *Fukuzawa Yukichi zenshū* (Tokyo: Iwanami Shoten, 1969–1971) 16.91–93, where he implies that the difference between religions is so insignificant as to be like the choice between types of tea. But in fact Fukuzawa frequently wrote positively about religion and specifically about Rennyo on more than one occasion, having been raised himself in a family affiliated with Honganji. For his views on the importance of religion in general, see Fukuzawa Yukichi, "Shūkyō no hitsuyō naru o ronzu" (The Necessity of Religion) in *Fukuzawa Yukichi zenshū*, 19.585–587, written in 1876; for Fukuzawa's views on Rennyo, see "Shūshi senpu no hōben" 10.52–58, where he criticizes Christianity's intolerance of other religions and praises Rennyo's ability to separate internal

faith from social obligations. See also Shigematsu Akihisa, "Fukuzawa Yukichi to Bukkyō" in Shigematsu Akihisa, ed., *Shinran, Shinshū shisōshi kenkyū* (Kyoto: Hōzōkan, 1990). See also Fujiwara Masanobu, "Kindai Shinshū to Fukuzawa Yukichi" in Kōkakai, ed. *Kōkakai shūkyō kenkyū ronshū: Shinran to Ningen*, vol. 2 (Kyoto: Nagata Bunshōdō, 1983).

11 Rogers, 180.

12 Yasui Kōdo, "Ōtaniha gakujishi," in *Zoku Shinshū taikei*, 1976 ed., 20.138.

13 Soga Ryōjin, "Shinshū Saikō no Shihyo," in *Soga Ryōjin kōgishū* (Tokyo: Yayoi Shobō, 1977–1990), 10.130.

14 "Kanrenkai wo ronzu," in *Kiyozawa Manshi zenshū* (Kyoto: Hōzōkan, 1953), 4.316–317.

15 Soga, "Rennyo Shōnin no shintai," *Soga Ryōjin senshū* (Tokyo: Yayoi Shobō, 1970–1972), 1.240.

16 Ibid.

17 Ibid., p. 241.

18 Ibid., p. 242.

19 *Anjinketsujōshō* 安心決定鈔, 2 vols., T 89.921, is a Japanese Pure Land treatise of unknown authorship. Some attribute this work to a priest of the Seizan branch, while others have suggested Kakunyo. Nishi Honganji considers this work part of Shinshū canon, whereas Higashi Honganji does not recognize it as such. This treatise explains the nonduality of Birth into the Pure Land by sentient beings and the enlightenment of the Buddha, and it asserts that the "unity of faith and the Dharma" (*kihō ittai*) and the nenbutsu itself are one and the same.

20 *Soga Ryōjin kōgishū*, 1.179. The *Tannishō* 歎異抄 was compiled by a direct follower of Shinran (probably Yuien) after Shinran's death. It became the most important text for Shin Buddhism in modern-Japan through Kiyozawa's influence. (See CWS, vol. 1.661–682.)

21 Rennyo was eighty-three years old when he wrote this letter in 1497. See Rogers, 235.

22 Ibid., p. 294.

23 For differences in the doctrinal understanding of the "unity of faith and the Dharma," see section 2 in Inaki Sen'e, *Rennyo kyōgaku no kenkyu 1: gyōshinron* (Kyoto: Hōzōkan, 1993). In the *Letters*, Rennyo mentions the concept of "the unity of faith and the Dharma" in a total of seven letters, all of which were written in his later years (one at the age of sixty-one and six at the age of seventy-six). The basis for his interest in this concept perhaps lies in his response to the popularity of the teachings of the Chinzei branch of the Pure Land, which espoused that good karma was secured through repeated reciting of the nenbutsu, whereas Rennyo emphasized the absoluteness of faith in the nenbutsu.

24 Shandao interpreted the term "deep mind," *jinshin* (深心), the second of the "three minds" described in the *Contemplation Sūtra* (*Guanjing*), as the mind of deep entrusting. He explained that this deep faith has two aspects (*nishu jinshin*). The first is the awareness of faith (*ki*), whereby the finite and limited self steeped in mental affliction is the object of Amida's vow; the second is the awareness of the Dharma (*hō*), which is the working of Amida's forty-eight vows (which function solely for the sake of such beings). See T No. 1743, 37.271a27, CWS, 1.85.

25 *Soga Ryōjin senshū*, 6.21.

26 Ibid., 11.102.

27 In his memoir, Soga wrote: "What is the main point of Kiyozawa's teaching? He never gave us an answer, he only provided us with the first step in that direction. First of all, his studies were essential. His quest was for the Great Path [*daidō*] never becoming apologetic or assuming. . . . Second, his studies were practical. Third, his studies were liberating and gave

importance to each person's individuality." "Meiji Yonjuyonen Noto" (Notes from Meiji 44 [1911]), reproduced in Soga Ryōjin, *Shūkyō no shikatsu mondai* (Tokyo: Yayoi Shobo, 1973), 120.

28 *Soga Ryōjin senshū*, volume 4, p.334.

29 In 1911, the year of Shinran's 650th Memorial, Shinshū University, which was established in Tokyo by Kiyozawa in 1901, was moved to Kyoto. This move was due to the strife between modern religious studies based in Tokyo and the Takakura Gakuryo, the authority of *shūgaku* based in Kyoto. Soga, who was serving as professor at the university, called the closing of the school "the death of our mother school" and left the university to return to his home in Niigata to lead a life of solitude and contemplation. At this point Soga actively confronted the doctrinal subject of "the unity of faith and the Dharma." However, this theme not only was connected wtih Kiyozawa's religious theme of the "correspondence between the finite and the infinite," a theme that Soga inherited, but it was also one that *shūgaku* took up to bring about the downfall of the "mother school."

30 *Soga Ryōjin senshū*, 4.340.

31 Ibid., 2.408.

32 Ibid., 2.373.

33 Ibid., 2:370–375, 2:408–421.

34 Shandao's twofold explication of religious faith had a major impact on Japanese Pure Land Buddhism after it was featured in Hōnen's writings, and his terminology quickly became doctrinal jargon in the Kamakura period and thereafter. See n. 24.

35 CWS 1.85.

36 *Soga Ryōjin senshū*, 6.20.

37 Rennyo's note affixed to Tannishō states, "This sacred writing is an important scripture in our tradition. It should not be indiscriminately shown to any who lack past karmic good" (CWS, 682).

38 The term *ango* (安居) comes from the Indian word *varsa*, referring to traditional Buddhist rainy-season retreat, which consisted of arduous practice in a set place over a certain period of time. In the Ōtani denomination, *ango* refers to a special lecture series held over a period of several weeks. The record of Soga's *ango* was compiled in a book entitled *Tannisho chōki*, published by Higashi Honganji in 1970, and in vol. 6 of the *Soga Ryōjin senshū*.

39 *Soga Ryōjin senshū*, 11.84. Soga's remark was made in a lecture in honor of Kaneko Daiei's sixteenth birthday in 1941.

40 See *Kan'o no dōri: Rennyo kyōgaku no chūshin mondai* (Kyoto: Chōjiya, 1952); also contained in *Soga Ryōjin senshū*, 11.136–140.

41 In "Rennyo kyōgaku no konpon mondai," in *Soga Ryōjin kōgishū*, 1.194–195, he wrote that "[Rennyo] disseminated the *Tannishō* and clearly and concisely taught Master Shinran's spirit."

42 Ibid.

43 Nishi Honganji held their services April 10–17, 1948, whereas Higashi Honganji conducted them a year later on April 18–25, 1949.

44 Hattori Shisō, *Rennyo* (Tokyo: Shinchi Shobō, 1948).

45 Ryūkoku Daigaku, ed., *Rennyo Shōnin kenkyū* (Kyoto: Chūshū Daishi Yonhyakugojūkai Onkihōyō Jimushō, 1948). Other important works appearing in conjunction with the memorial included Miyazaki Enjun and Mikogami Eryū, *Rennyo Shōnin no shōgai to shisō* (Kyoto: Nagata Bunshōdō, 1948); Iwami Mamoru, *Rennyo Shonin* (Kyoto: Shōsei'en, 1949); and Inaba Shūken, *Rennyo Shonin no kyōgaku* (Kyoto: Ōtani Shuppansha, 1949).

46 "Kan'ō no dori." Later published as *Kan'ō no dōri: Rennyo kyōgaku no chūshin mondai*.

47 "Daini no Shinshū saikō" was given in 1956. See *Soga Ryōjin kōgishū*, 10.44 and 130–131.

48 *The Nature of My Faith*, translated by Mark L. Blum, in *Modern Shin Anthology* (Kyoto: Ōtani University, 1999).

49 "Daini no Shinshū saikō," *Soga Ryōjin kōgishū*, 10.46.

50 Ibid., p. 138.

12

ALFRED BLOOM

Rennyo and the Renaissance of Contemporary Shin Buddhism

Rennyo's Place in the History of
Shin Buddhism

Elsewhere I have summarized important aspects of Rennyo's life which were the basis for his successful effort to revitalize the Honganji and create a major, powerful religious movement in medieval Japan. I have suggested that he offers clues for the renaissance of contemporary Shin Buddhism. Honganji in Japan has called his commemoration a time for innovation, which expresses the spirit of Rennyo. The slogan for the Hawaii Honganji mission, for example, is "Live together, work together, in the spirit of Rennyo." This chapter will look more directly into what we can learn from the spirit of Rennyo and his innovative propagational activities. Both Shinran and Rennyo responded to issues of their own time and circumstance. Differences in their personalities and historical situation show that, while there is a basic unity in their thought, Rennyo adjusted Shinran's fundamental insights to make them more accessible and understandable to the ordinary person of his day. Shinran unintentionally created a more individually oriented movement. His teaching reflects his inward, introspective and subjective, as well as more scholarly or philosophical character. Shinran spoke pointedly of his religious experience and his personal weaknesses or limitations. He clearly rejected the idea that he was a teacher or had disciples, though they honored him. Rennyo, on the other hand, inherited the movement that Shinran inspired. It had already become institutionalized through the efforts of previous abbots of Honganji and other branches of Shinran's lineage. Rennyo was concerned with the fortunes of the community in his time and for the future. His personality was more outgoing. He told little about his own religious change or development. He consciously accepted the role of teacher or leader of an emerging movement. He had to deal with the problems of religious power and authority that accompanied his status. Further, his position as a teacher must be considered in the light of his enormous influence, for which there is little comparison among other medieval teachers.

Perspective on Shinran's Teaching

The foundation of Rennyo's work is Shinran's teaching. Suffice it to say that Shinran emphasized absolute Other-Power in all aspects of religious faith and activity. No matter how evil a person may be, he or she is never beyond the embrace of Amida. Shinran had a vision of Amida Buddha's all-encompassing compassion and wisdom in which every feature of religious life is grounded in Amida Buddha's Vows. Also the assurance we have of final enlightenment liberates us from the many religious fears and superstition common to Japanese society. Shinran's teaching involves a transformation of the self-striving mind to the mind of reliance on and trust in the Vow. Shinran calls it the "turning of the mind" (*eshin*) or the one moment of entrusting (*shinjin-ichinen*). All efforts subsequent to that moment are responses of gratitude and commitment, supremely expressed in reciting *namu-amida-butsu*. The sense of oneness with Amida Buddha, experienced through trust in Shinran's thought, never overwhelms the awareness of our evils. Rather, it prevents presumption or taking Amida's embrace for granted. While conducive to a deep humility, Shinran's faith gives rise to a strong religious commitment and self-concept as a person who has been embraced by Amida Buddha, never to be abandoned.

The Fundamental Character of Rennyo's Teaching

Rennyo shared Shinran's vision of Amida's all-encompassing compassion and wisdom, but he believed that it manifested itself in the world through the Honganji tradition. Being born within an already existing institutional system, Rennyo assumed that it faithfully transmitted the truth of Amida's Vow as interpreted by Shinran. Also he tried to simplify the more complex teaching of Shinran, holding to the principle that in teaching, you select a hundred from a thousand things that might be given, and from a hundred you choose ten. Finally from the ten you select one. As a consequence of his approach to teaching and propagation, there were differences from Shinran in emphases. Rennyo's experiences of the deaths of his wives and several children, as well as the violence of the age, made him keenly aware of the impermanence, unpredictability, and violence in life. In view of the brevity of life and the depth of our evil, the afterlife was of the greatest importance for Rennyo (*gosho-no-ichidaiji*), in contrast to Shinran's stress on the reception of faith and assurance of rebirth in this life. Rennyo drew a clear distinction between this world and the next. The human realm is a place of uncertainty. The land of utmost bliss is one of eternity and should be the object of our aspiration and the decisive settling of mind.

The principle of karma is also strongly upheld and emphasized by Rennyo as the basis for encountering the teaching. The teaching is not to be discussed with anyone whose past good karmic conditions have not matured. Rennyo used the idea to restrain disciples inclined to boast about their faith and ridicule others. The process of deliverance is outlined by Rennyo in five conditions which must be present in order for a person to attain truly settled faith. First is the unfolding of good karma from the past. Second is the meeting with a good teacher. Third is receiving Amida's light; fourth is attaining faith, and fifth is saying the name of the Buddha. We can view these five elements as a simultaneous moment in which we have the good fortune to encounter a teacher who opens for us the truth concerning our spiritual condition and the truth of the teaching.

In that moment we attain trust in the Vow, reject sundry practices, and recite *namu-amida-butsu* in gratitude. It is altogether the one moment of entrusting and attainment of truly settled faith. According to Rennyo, faith is fundamental and is the source of nenbutsu. Faith "is granted by Amida Tathāgata...this is not faith generated by the practicer,...it is Amida Tathāgata's Other-Power faith. The term *shinjin* is taken by Rennyo to be Amida's Other-Power true mind which displaces the believer's mind of self-striving. An alternative term for faith is *anjin* or *yasuki kokoro*, which for Rennyo has essentially the same meaning as *shinjin*, but with emphasis on the aspect of the peace or tranquility that attends reception of faith. As a result, the recitation of the name is for gratitude only, because it flows out from the trusting mind. It is important to note that external appearance or people's outward condition, status, or role in life have no relevance in attaining trust.

Further, on attaining the settled mind, one carries on a normal life, whether it is as a hunter, fisherman, or tradesman. After faith or settled mind is established, nothing is taboo, though keeping "firmly to ourselves the teaching transmitted in our tradition and not giving any outward sign of it; those who do this are said to be people of discretion." Settled faith means also to honor the laws of the state and fulfill public obligations. The relation of Buddhism and the state or society is a key issue in Rennyo's thought, but it must be viewed in the light of his historical situation. Essentially he promoted the western idea of "rendering unto Caesar what is Caesar's and unto God [Buddha] what is God's [Buddha's]."[1] Rennyo interprets the terms *namu* and *amida butsu* in the nenbutsu to emphasize the oneness of the mind of the person of settled faith and the Buddha. It is the action of the Tathāgata that creates the oneness of the Buddha mind and ordinary mind, guaranteeing the ultimate enlightenment of the person of faith. The *namu-amida-butsu* is the verbal, symbolic expression of the reality of that oneness when it is recited in trust and gratitude.

With respect to religious life, the hallmark of Rennyo's teaching is his emphasis that the nenbutsu is only for gratitude, arising spontaneously from the settled mind of faith. He rails against the perfunctory, mechanical, conformist recitation of the name without understanding its essential meaning. In order to encourage his followers to be respectful of other religions, Rennyo exalts Amida Buddha as the Original teacher and Original Buddha of all buddhas and gods. That is, he is the superior and supreme expression of Buddhahood, which includes all other gods and Buddhas within himself. They appear as *upāya* or compassionate means to lead people to the Buddha-Dharma. Shinran's and Rennyo's approach to faith are similar in being subjective and requiring a definite turn of the mind in trust in Amida's Vows. It is expressed in grateful recitation of the nenbutsu. There is a common emphasis in both teachers on the absolute Other-Power foundation of deliverance. They understand that Amida is a power within the heart and mind of the person, bringing about a spiritual transformation, as well as being enshrined as the essence of the nenbutsu itself. Rennyo's term *anjin* or *yasuki kokoro* or settled mind, however, appears within an institutional setting of community and obligatory observances, as well as a variety of rules or guidelines which he instituted to deal with problems in his movement. An important feature of expressing one's settled faith is grateful recitation of nenbutsu while keeping one's eye on the goal of rebirth in the Pure Land. The communal character of faith is expressed through obeying the regulations which Rennyo set down as a means of avoiding conflicts and obstacles to the teaching in the general community.

Rennyo's Mission of Propagation and Education

What ultimately gives Rennyo's life significance is his work of propagation and education which enabled Honganji to become the principal leader of Shin Buddhism. Through his expositions of the teaching he made Shinran's teaching comprehensible to the masses. Without his consistent efforts, it is clear that Shinran's highly personal and subtle teaching would have remained obscure to the ordinary person, though Shinran himself became the object of veneration. The abbots prior to Rennyo engaged in propagation activities, yet Honganji remained a small segment of the Shin movement. Traditionally there have been ten branches, of which the Honganji was one. In the controversy centering on Rennyo's acceptance as abbot, his uncle, Nyojō, argued on his behalf that Rennyo had lifelong dedication, and he participated intimately in Zonnyo's work of copying texts for followers, as well as occasionally representing his father in relations with disciples. When Rennyo became abbot, it was clearly the combination of his personality, his abilities and activities, the times, and the character of his teaching that brought about the momentous change in the fortunes of the Honganji. He was the right man in the right place at the right time. Rennyo's activities included copying texts, undertaking teaching tours, writing objects of worship in the form of name scrolls, granting Dharma names, establishing temples, and writing letters, as well as frequent interviews and meetings with individual disciples. These endeavors were all aimed at securing the relationship of Rennyo and the Honganji with the followers on a deeply personal level. While not all these undertakings were original with him, he made the most skillful and greatest use of the various methods. He also was perceptive in seeing how social dynamics worked in Japanese society when he developed the system of *kō* or small, voluntary associations and described how propagation should proceed.[2] We might say that Rennyo's propagation and education depended on personal relations, communication-publication through copying texts or writing letters, and the like, and social insight.

Copying Texts

In order to instruct followers in an age before printing, it was necessary to copy texts meticulously. Copying was a form of publication in a pretechnological age. The various texts that were copied demonstrate how serious Shinran and his successors were in responding to their followers' desire for understanding the Dharma. In Shin Buddhism the work of copying texts began as early as Shinran, who reproduced various Pure Land works requested by his disciples. Together with composing his own original writings, Shinran copied a variety of Pure Land texts which he thought were useful for understanding his teaching. Zennyo, the fourth abbot of Honganji, is noted for annotating a pictorial biography of Shinran and making a seventeen-volume copy of the *Kyōgyōshinshō* in Japanese translation. He also copied the words of Zonkaku (*Zonkaku hōgo*).[3] There is a record of some fourteen texts copied by Gyōnyo, the sixth abbot; Zonnyo, the seventh abbot; and Kūkaku, a brother of Zonnyo. Zonnyo also initiated the copying of Shinran's hymns (*wasan*), and separated out the *Shōshinge* from the *Kyōgyōshinshō*. He focused attention on that passage because it presented the basic principles of Shin Buddhism in a condensed form. Rennyo later wrote a synopsis of that text known as *Shōshinge taii*.[4] He also published the *Shōshinge* and the *Wasan* collections in block print at Yoshizaki in 1473. The block printing of texts made for wider distribution of texts and broadened the use of the *Shōshinge* and *Wasan*[5] in services in temples or at home. Even before he became abbot, Rennyo made copies of texts for disciples, who often received them when they came to study in Kyoto. At times he substituted for his father in making and signing these texts. We are told that there now exist some forty texts copied by Rennyo. The meticulous work of copying texts undoubtedly contributed to Rennyo's study and absorption of the teaching which underlay his thought in his letters, his major mode of communication.

Teaching Tours

From the time of Kakunyo, abbots made tours around regions where Shinshu congregations were located. Rennyo toured to spread and strengthen the teaching. Before he became abbot, he went to the Kanto region, following the example of other abbots who visited the sacred sites of Shinran's life at least once in their lifetime. Rennyo, however, traveled three times to Kanto. Immediately after becoming abbot, he focused on Ōmi, an area roughly corresponding to Shiga prefecture located east of the capital, where there were many Shin followers. He also went to Mikawa and Settsu, as well as the northern provinces known as Hokuriku. Rennyo's success in drawing adherents through these activities even-tually caught the attention of the forces of Mount Hiei, who attacked Honganji in 1466. It was probably no accident that Rennyo selected Yoshizaki in the Hokuriku area for his base, since the Honganji had had a long association with the region because of the travels of the various former abbots. By 1471, when Rennyo moved to Yoshizaki, there were as many as 119 temples known in the Echizen, Kaga, and Etchū regions. With his arrival in Yoshizaki, the number of temples expanded significantly as members and temples of other sects turned to Rennyo. James Dobbins indicates: "Rennyo's presence in Yoshizaki created a mysterious and powerful chemistry that sparked an unprecedented religious awakening in the region."[6] There were forty-nine additional temples in Inami county in Echizen alone, five times the number that had been there over the previous two centuries. Twenty of these forty-nine temples had previously been affiliated with the Tendai order. Similar developments took place in other regions near Kyoto, in Ōmi, Tōkai, Chūgoku, and Kansai.

Objects of Worship

Shinran's original object of worship was the name *Jin-jip-pō mu-ge-kō nyorai*, which means the Tathāgata of Universal Unhindered Light. He granted Name (*myōgō*) scrolls to leading disciples for their dōjō. In addition to the Name, pictorial representations of Amida were also made. This practice was later followed by Kakunyo, Zonkaku, and succeeding abbots. Zonnyo's diary indicates that he made various types of scrolls at the request of his disciples. Rennyo gave out so many Name scrolls that he was said to have written the Name more times than any other person in history. Some extant scrolls were written with gold paint, a sign of the growing prosperity and influence of Honganji. Ten are listed from 1460 to 1465. The Ōsaka-gobō or Ishiyama temple, where Rennyo finally retired, was financed almost entirely through writing of Name scrolls.

Dharma Names and Temple Names

Another way in which relations with disciples was strengthened was the bestowal of Dharma names. These names began to be conferred when followers came to the Honganji to study. Rennyo followed the precedent set by Zonnyo, and there are numerous extant examples of Dharma names written in his own hand. Temple names indicated the status of a community as a temple based on its affiliation with the Honganji. They marked the transformation of a dōjō to a temple and permitted the members to enshrine an image of Amida rather than a name scroll.

Letter Writing

Perhaps the most striking aspect of Rennyo's activities in education and propagation was his letter writing. However, there were also precedents in Shin Buddhism for this mode of communication. Shinran himself wrote numerous letters dealing with doctrinal questions, disputes among his followers, and persecution. Although it is recorded that Shinran wrote ninety letters, there are presently forty-three existing. Rennyo's letters number over 200, eighty-five of which were selected out by Rennyo's grandson Ennyo (1491–1521) at the direction of Ennyo's father, Jitsunyo, the ninth abbot. These have become virtually sacred text for Shin Buddhists. Most famous among them is the *Hakkotsu no gobunshō*, or Letter on White Ashes,[7] which is used extensively in funeral services. Among these only eleven are originals; the remainder are copies made by others. Rennyo did not write complex doctrinal analyses such as we find in the *Kyōgyōshinshō*, and so modern scholars underestimate him as a scholar or thinker. Nevertheless, the letters were his chosen method for communicating the insights of Shin Buddhism in comprehensible, clear language that the members of the temples could appreciate. Undoubtedly they contributed to his popularity, because such letters as the White Ashes touched the hearts of people with the reality of impermanence and the importance of faith and gratitude in spiritual life.

Rennyo made gratitude a central feature of Shin Buddhism. A general accounting of his letters indicates that in the collection of eighty-five letters, forty-nine conclude with specific exhortations to gratitude, while in others it is implied. He concluded his letters by urging his followers to recite the nenbutsu with gratitude. This became the distinctive approach of Shin Buddhism toward practice and religious reflection.

Rennyo demonstrated his sensitivity to women, who played a great role in his life, by referring to women in fifty-eight letters of the 212 considered authentic. Contrasting Shin Buddhism with other Buddhist traditions, Rennyo stressed that the salvation of women was a primary concern for Amida Buddha. This belief is significant because the religious status of women in traditional Buddhism was lower than that of men. Though Rennyo declared the spiritual equality of women, he did not make clear their social equality. This subject remains a task for our contemporary *saṅgha*. In almost all his letters Rennyo emphasized the human condition, Other-Power faith, recitation of the nenbutsu, and the importance of the afterlife. He set forth rules for social behavior in response to the anti-social attitudes of some followers who used the Shin experience of spiritual liberation to ridicule and denounce other religions and even oppose secular authority. Addressing contemporary issues confronting the community, Rennyo's letters defined the content of faith.

Method of Propagation

The great expansion of Shin Buddhism under the leadership of Rennyo resulted not only from the resonance of his ideas and personality with the people of the time, but also from his understanding how society worked. As Dobbins points out, in the spread of Shin Buddhism, Rennyo benefited from the formation of independent, self-governing villages that attended the end of the manorial economic system. Rennyo's method of propagation consisted of approaching the three most prominent people in any village: the priest, the elder, and the village headman. He maintained that "If these three will lay the basis for Buddhism in their respective places, then all the people below them will conform to the teachings and Buddhism will flourish."[8] This strategy is known as the top-down principle, accepting the hierarchical structure of a village, and has been followed by all religions since ancient times. It presupposes a highly communal and kinship society in which leaders are recognized by all members as having status by virtue of their wisdom and qualities of leadership. Many of these leaders were formerly heads of large farm families in the earlier, declining *myōshu*-estate system. It was a natural extension of the family structure. In our more individualistic age, this strategy would have little effect, but what is important here is Rennyo's sensitivity to the changing nature of the society in which he lived and his shrewdness in recognizing its usefulness.

Concurrent with Rennyo's strategy of reaching the leadership of the society, he also developed the *kō* (講), a voluntary religious association for the nurture and development of personal faith. *Kō* is an ancient Buddhist concept meaning discourse, preaching, or lecture. In time it took on the meaning of a meeting for some religious purpose such as studying a text or undertaking a particular practice. Shin Buddhism today has such things as Nenbutsukō and Hōonkō services. In our modern thinking, a *kō* would be like a cell, a subgrouping of a larger body; We might call it a discussion group or informal fellowship.[9] Though the *kō* might coincide with the village, it was really the social-religious foundation of Shin Buddhism. In time religious and political aspects overlapped, as is evident in the peasant *ikko-ikki* uprisings. One important characteristic is that the *kō* could transcend its local character through its connection with the broad movement of Shin Buddhism. This connectedness was the basis for the enormous power that Shin Buddhism came to hold in medieval society, leading to its struggle with Oda Nobunaga and its division under the Tokugawa. Members would open their homes for meetings, and as these grew into a regular occurrence the home would be called *dōjō*. The size of the *kō* varied from as few as six people to perhaps thousands. They were supported by members' donations. The local *kō* were affiliated with the Honganji through the various levels of subtemple relations. In terms of governance, Rennyo had to combine his democratic spirit with the need for more centralized control necessitated by the social and religious problems that arose within the *kō*. These were the major reasons for locating his sons and daughters in major temples in order to maintain the loyalty of the members under their control.

We can gain some idea of the activities in the *kō* from Rennyo's letters indicating that the members meet monthly (the twentieth-eighth of the month, which was Shinran's death day) in order to discuss their faith. Annual Hōonkō services to express gratitude for the teaching and to commemorate Shinran's death have been typically held for seven days and were greatly stressed by Rennyo. However in his letters he noted that the faith was not always discussed at the meetings as it should be. He criticized the members for turning the meetings into social occasions, forgetting their true purpose. He urged deep discussion and questioning in order to arrive at settled faith. Rennyo was very critical of the clergy who oversaw the fellowships. We can see that the meetings of the *kō* in dōjō and temples provided an opportunity for members to interact and discuss their faith in a more personal way.

The dissemination of the *Shoshinge* and *Wasan* suggests that part of the meeting was devoted to the devotional chanting of these texts, and members and clergy then discussed the teaching. Rennyo also wrote numerous letters marking the anniversary of Shinran's death in which he commented on the meaning of the teaching, and he instructed that these letters were to be read at the appropriate services, in this case Hōonkō. The meetings were clearly also social occasions, though Rennyo desired that the religious purpose be constantly maintained. For him the spirituality of the movement was uppermost. In his overall perspective he recognized that the prosperity of the movement lies not in the prestige of great numbers, but in whether people have faith, and the flourishing of the right sole practice comes about through the will of the disciples who follow.

Rennyo's Personal Style

Rennyo's personal style can be summarized as more open and democratic than what was often seen at this time. The first letter in the authorized collection emphasizes the camaraderie of Shin Buddhism, noting Shinran's declaration that he had not one disciple. Rennyo wore plain gray robes, insisted that even highly ranked clergy within his organization do the same, and removed the preaching platform. He sat on the same level as his followers. It is said he sat knee to knee. He admonished his associates not to keep followers waiting and to serve them food and sake. He did not put on airs, so when he visited followers who had little to offer him, he warmly ate the millet gruel which they ate and spent the night discussing religion with them. He advocated that Nō plays be performed to put people at ease and to teach the Buddha-Dharma anew when followers have lost interest.

But though Rennyo could be solicitous for the welfare of his followers, he was also critical. He castigated the priests who sought more spiritual and financial power over rank-and-file members. He also censured the members for lacking proper religious motivation for their participation or for their lack of engagement with, discussion of, and understanding of the doctrine.

Conclusion

We can see there are many dimensions to Rennyo's activities and style that successfully brought Shin Buddhism to a peak level of support in the medieval period. The determination with which all Honganji abbots have labored offers suggestions for how we might strengthen Shin Buddhism in today's age of turbulence and transition, but it is with Rennyo that we particularly notice comradeship, communication, critique, commitment or deep religious motivation, and understanding as keys to the future strength of Jōdoshinshū.

Notes

1 For example, in a letter written from Yoshizaki dated the thirteenth day of the fifth month, 1474, Rennyo asserts, "You must be careful never to carelessly say 'I am someone who reveres the Dharma and has attained *shinjin*' before the authorities in your province, such as the military governors [*shugo*] or warrior land stewards [*jitō*]. Do not fail to perform your public duties." RSI, 192; SSZ 3.441.

2 See pp. 170–171.

3 The *Zonkaku hōgo* is at SSZ 3.353.

4 The *Shōshinge taii* was written in 1460 in response to a request from Kanamori Dōsai; it is at SSZ 3.385.

5 *Wasan* are liturgical hymns written by Shinran in Japanese, in contrast with his doctrinal theses, which are all written in Chinese.

6 James C. Dobbins, *Jōde Shinshū: Shin Buddhism in Medieval Japan* (Bloomington: Indiana University Press, 1989), p. 137.

7 RSI, 182; SSZ 3.513

8 Dobbins, *Jōde Shinshū*, p. 139.

9 *Kō* were the smallest social unit that supported—emotionally, politically, and financially—both local dōjō and the national *honzan* of Honganji.

13

IKEDA YŪTAI
TRANSLATED BY SARAH HORTON

The Characteristic Structure of Rennyo's *Letters*

The Spirit of "Lamenting Deviations"

Rennyo's composition of numerous letters is said to have greatly fascilitated the restoration of Shinshū which occurred under him.[1] This chapter reconsiders the nature of these letters through an examination of their structure.

The words of Rennyo's mother, as related in the *Rennyo Shōnin itokuki*,[2] suggest an early influence which contributed to his desire to restore Shinshū:

> Ōei 27 [1420]. The master [Rennyo] was six years old. On the twenty-eighth day of the twelfth month, the mother spoke to her six-year-old child, revealing what was in her heart: "It is my wish that during this child's lifetime, he will restore the tradition of the master [Shinran]." With that, she departed for an unknown destination.[3]

The *Itokuki* also declares:

> From the age of fifteen, the master [Rennyo] first began to earnestly aspire to restore Shinshū. It grieved him to think how the school had languished in previous generations. He constantly prayed that somehow he would be able to reveal the teachings of the master [Shinran] in all places, far and near. In the end, he did restore [Shinran's teachings].[4]

Thus Rennyo made his mother's wish his own goal. The origin of his desire to restore Shinshū must be sought, as previous scholars have pointed out, in his relationship to the *Tannishō*.

The first to note the relationship between Rennyo's *Letters* and the *Tannishō*, and to suggest the doctrinal lineage they share, was Ryōshō of Myōon'in (1788–1842) in his work *Tannishō monki*.[5] Soga Ryōjin (1875–1971) went a step further by declaring in the *Tannishō chōki* that the spirit of restoration is none other than the spirit of "lamenting deviations."[6] Although the following paragraph has been widely read, I will quote it again here:

It goes without saying that the *Tannishō* "laments that which deviates from the true faith transmitted by the Master [Shinran]." The true faith thus transmitted is the two types of deep belief (*nishu jinshin*), found throughout the *Tannishō*, which have been handed down from the time of Master Zendō (Shandao). It is these two types of deep faith that overturn the two states of mind, meditative and nonmeditative (*jōsan nishin*), elucidating the metaphor of the two rivers [of greed and anger] and shedding light on the faith of the Boundless Vow [Amida's Eighteenth Vow]. This was, I believe, the way of Master Zendō's own enlightenment. The spirit and feeling of "lamenting that which deviates from the true faith transmitted" is, I strongly believe, the spirit behind the restoration of Jōdo Shinshū. Perhaps because of this, Rennyo indicated that "This is an important scripture in our lineage. It should not be shown indiscriminately to those who lack [sufficient] karmic good [roots]" (*mu shukuzen ki*). I firmly believe that the spirit behind Rennyo's restoration of Shinshū was none other than the spirit of "lamenting deviations."[7]

Our oldest extant manuscript of the *Tannishō*, copied by Rennyo himself, provides clues to the relationship between Rennyo and this text. In November 1969 Hōzōkan published a photographic reproduction of the manuscript, with a commentary by Miyazaki Enjun.[8] Although he did not record the date of his copying of the text, on the basis of past handwriting it had been thought that Rennyo copied it when he was about sixty-five or sixty-six. Miyazaki explains, however, that reexamination of the manuscript using microphotographs and other technology indicates that Rennyo was around forty years old when he copied the sentence, "The exiled persons were the above eight," which is found in the appendix. He was sixty-five or sixty-six, however, when he copied the next sentence, "The persons executed were as follows," and also when he added the colophon.

In addition, the cover of this manuscript bears the title "*Tannishō*, one copy" and to the lower right of this is the note "belonging to Rennyo." The fact that Rennyo copied the text over a period of many years as well as the existence of this note on the cover suggest that this was his personal copy, something he used throughout his life.

Rennyo copied a wide range of Shinshū scriptures, beginning even before he took over the leadership of Honganji from his father. Although their contents vary, here is a list of seven extant Rennyo manuscripts that have *Tannishō*-like colophons and where they are held:

1. The *Kudenshō*, two fascicles.[9] The first fascicle is in the archives of Fukudadera, Shiga City. The second fascicle is in the archives of Nishi Honganji, Kyoto. The text is dated Eikyō 10 (1439), copied when Rennyo was twenty-three years old.

2. The *Rokuyōshō*,[10] ten fascicles. In the archives of Kōshōji, Kyoto. Dated Chōroku 2 (1458), copied when Rennyo was forty-four years old.

3. The *Kyōgyōshinshō* (in *nobegaki*), seventeen fascicles.[11] In the archives of Nishi Honganji. Dated Kanshō 2 (1461), copied when Rennyo was forty-seven years old.

4. The *Kudenshō*, three fascicles. In the archives of Jōshōbō, Osaka. Dated Bunshō 2 (1467), copied when Rennyo was fifty-three years old.

5. The *Kyōgyōshinshō taii*,[12] one fascicle. In the archives of Shinshūji, Sakai City. Dated Entoku 1 (1489), copied when Rennyo was seventy-five years old.
6. The *Hōnen Shōnin okotoba*, one fascicle.[13] In the archives of Kōtokuji, Kashiwabara City. Dated Meiō 5 (1496), when Rennyo was eighty-two years old.
7. The *Tannishō*, two fascicles. In the archives of Nishi Honganji, probably copied when Rennyo was forty years old.[14]

Despite their similarity, however, none of colophons to these other works contains a harsh statement similar to this one in the colophon of the *Tannishō*: "This should not be shown indiscriminately to those who lack karmic good roots." It is possible that Rennyo intended not to ban or proscribe this work, but rather simply to record that it should be treated with great care, as an "important sacred text of our lineage." These points all indicate that Rennyo had the *Tannishō* at his side from the time of his difficult youth, that is before he became leader of Honganji, to his maturity when he fulfilled his desire to restore Shinshū.

These connections between Rennyo and the *Tannishō* should be explored in light of Rennyo's *Letters*. Elsewhere I have discussed this issue with reference to the first letter, which contains the fundamental positions found in all the letters. I would now like to go a step further, however, and examine the language and ideas contained in Rennyo's *Letters*.

Rectifying Heresy (gaija 改邪)

Starting from his view of "lamenting deviations" as seen in his esteem of the *Tannishō*, how did the restoration of Shinshū advance under Rennyo? In the past, when analyzing Rennyo's Letters, Shinshū scholars always established the category "Purpose of the Letters," saying, for example, "They are to help foolish people achieve true faith" and "They do away with various kinds of aberrant doctrine, taking refuge in that which is true."[15]

Such evaluations stop at simply noting that the *Letters* were written to correct mistaken views. Indeed, the *Letters* speak eloquently to this point. I would like to focus, however, on the implications of this point. Is it possible to say that Rennyo took over from Kakunyo, advancing the restoration of Shinshū by rectifying heresies? This is the question that I want to explore.

First, let us look at the aberrant doctrines discussed in the *Letters*. Professor Sumida Chiken summarizes the situation as follows:

> As has been said in the past, we can count four or six different types [of aberrant doctrine], but I find three: the teaching in the Seizan sect that Birth in the Pure Land has been assured from the time Amida achieved Buddhahood ten kalpas ago (*jikkō anjin*); the teaching in the Chinzei sect that Pure Land Birth cannot be achieved without practicing the spoken nenbutsu (*kushō zunori*), and secret teachings which misrepresent such things as the wisdom of the path of the sages. Teachings such as revering one's teacher as the Buddha (*chishiki danomi*), the

practice of giving gifts to Buddhist monastics as a meritorious act for the achievement of Buddhahood (*semotsu danomi*), and the teaching that those who have
achieved faith are, in this life, already one with Amida (*ichiyaku hōmon*), fall under
these three categories; I find none outside these three.[16]

The letters themselves provide examples of heresy which can be classified into the
following four groups:

1. "Marked differences from our tradition's basic view of *anjin*" (*Letter*
   3:8): There are two: belief that the "pacified mind" (*anjin*) was determined for us when Dharmākara attained buddhahood as Amitābha ten
   kalpas ago (*jikkō anjin*, as in *Letters* 1:13, 2:11, 3:8) and belief that
   recitation of the sacred Name without any understanding of faith is
   sufficient (*mushin shōmyō*, as in *Letters* 1:1, 1:15, 3:2, 3:3, 3:4, 3:5,
   5:11).
2. Anything based in the "secret teachings which are widespread in
   Echizen Province…that are deplorable, and not to be considered
   Buddhist" (*Letters* 2:14). This would include such things as doctrine of
   "the one benefit" wherein the attainment of *shinjin* is taken to mean
   one has attained buddhahood (*ichiyaku hōmon*, as in *Letter* 1:4), the
   practice of worshipping a spiritual guide as an incarnation of the
   Buddha (*chishiki danomi* as in *Letter* 2:11), a variety of nonstandard
   Shinshū interpretations known as "secret doctrines" (*hiji bōmon*, as in
   Letters 2:14), or the secret teaching that ritual worship is unnecessary
   (*fuhai hiji*, as in *Letter* 3:3).
3. The practice of "proclaiming our doctrine before [members of] other
   schools and sects" (as in *Letter* 1:9). This [problem] can be seen in such
   statements as "some see our school as polluted and loathsome " or
   "something taboo" (*mono imi*, as in *Letter* 1.9), or in [admonitions
   against] "acting so that one appears to later generations as a good person
   or follower of the Buddhist teachings" (as in *Letter* 2:2) and "going out
   of one's way to bring attention to the fact that one is a follower of our
   tradition" (as in *Letter* 2:13).
4. The practice of "speaking of teachings that have not been transmitted
   [within our lineage] and misleading others" (as in *Letter* 3:10). This
   includes such unacceptable activities as asking for donations (*semotsu
   danomi*, as in *Letter* 1:11), "relying on their own abilities, some people
   are interpreting texts that have not been properly transmitted and
   [expound] unknown, heretical doctrines" (as in *Letter* 3:11), "[spreading]
   unknown teachings that are not part of our lineage" (as in *Letter* 3:13),
   "turning one's ears to hear twisted [notions] and then opening one's
   mouth to spread it as slander" (as in *Letter* 4:1), spreading our teachings
   among those "about whom it is not known if the person possesses good
   karmic roots" (as in *Letter* 4:5), and participating in services "for one's
   reputation or to be in step with everyone else" (as in *Letter* 4:8).

The discussion of heresies in the *Letters* shares much with Kakunyo's ideas
about destroying aberrant doctrine. Although approximately one hundred years

passed between the time of Kakunyo (1270–1351) and Rennyo (1415–1499), statements from Kakunyo's *Gaijashō* can be placed in the above four categories.

There are statements in the *Gaijashō*, for example, that pertain to the first category. Article one of the *Gaijashō* declares:

> [Extolling] the creation of name registers is based on one's personal view of things and corrupts the lineage of our founder.[17]

And in article two:

> It is likewise wrong to assert a personal interpretation in the use of what are called portrait lineages.[18]

The precursor to the problem raised in the third category is found in Article three of the *Gaijashō*:

> You should not promote yourself in the form of a renunciant or delight in appearing different. Do not wear the skirtless robe (*monashi goromo*) or use a black clerical surplice (*kesa*).[19]

And precedents for the second category above can be seen in the declaration in Article eighteen of the *Gaijashō*:

> Among those who are known as adherents of the Venerable of Honganji (Shinran), there are some who so revere their spiritual guide (*chishiki*) that they liken [this person] to the Tathāgata Amida and regard his or her physical dwelling as a true Pure Land of the Buddha's body of glory [generated] by his unique vows. This is [so absurd as to be] beyond all comment.[20]

Finally, the following statement from the twenty-first article of the *Kudenshō*, also by Kakunyo, can be placed in the first category: "Asserting that one nenbutsu (*ichinen*) does not suffice, we must strive to practice many nenbutsu (*tanen*)."[21]

Although there were of course differences between the circumstances surrounding Kakunyo and Rennyo, their attitudes regarding aberrant doctrine were fundamentally the same. The situation in which Kakunyo found himself is addressed in Zonkaku's (1290–1373) *Haja kenshō shō*. According to this work, there are no words to describe the degree of slander and violence prevalent at that time among the Tendai monks of the path to self-perfection based on Mount Hiei, yamabushi, female shamans, and *yin-yang* masters:

> These monks seem in form to embody the Buddhist teachings and practices, but at heart they are no different from people who renounce the Buddhist doctrine of causation. Hence, they devastate the chapels of nenbutsu followers in place after place, and in each case with every occasion they deceive the adherents of the Pure Land path. They call the paintings and sculptures of Amida heretical images, and they trample them under foot. They declare the sacred writings of Shinshū doctrine to be heretical teachings, and they spit on them and destroy them. In addition they seize and deprive us of dozens of texts, including the three major Pure Land sutras as well as the expositions of the five patriarchs....
>
> Overall their power resounds throughout a thousand world systems, nearly outstripping the *asura*'s legions.[22]

This passage shows that in the time of Kakunyo, there was a crisis situation wherein teaching of the exclusive nenbutsu was in danger of being destroyed not only at the individual level but throughout all of society.

When critically reexamining correspondences between the heresies at the time of Kankunyo and of Rennyo, it becomes necessary to establish not only the relationship between Rennyo and the *Tannishō* but also the relationship between Rennyo and Kakunyo, especially with regard to the *Gaijashō*. Although both the *Tannishō* and the *Gaijashō* address problems with religious institutions, the *Tannishō* remains within the simple framework of a group of fellow believers and monks. The author states that he wrote it so that "there may be no differences in faith among the practitioners in a single room."[23] In contrast, the *Gaijashō* is written from the perspective of an established orthodox institution which, by Kakunyo's time, was based on a clear hereditary line spanning three generations, as the following colophon shows:

> The above text is essential for [the understanding of] the import of the oral transmission handed down from the founder of Honganji, Master Shinran, and Master Ōami Nyoshin, which contains the key to the attainment of Birth in the Land of Recompense (*hōdo*). In past days and years, by humbly receiving the hereditary lineage spanning the three generations of Kurodani (Hōnen), Honganji (Shinran), and Ōami (Nyoshin), the carefully maintained doctrines of the two Buddhas (Amida and Śākyamuni) have served as our eyes and our feet.[24]

Inevitably, then, there are differences between the two texts in their criticisms of aberrant doctrine. The *Tannishō* focuses on examining and rectifying one's own faith, a faith achieved primarily through direct contact with Shinran and his teachings. This emphasis is apparent in the passage "[let there] be no differences in faith among fellow practitioners in a single room," which shows a critical attitude toward one's own faith.

The *Gaijashō*, on the other hand, assumes that an orthodox institution has already been established and attempts to destroy any heresy that is opposed to this orthodoxy. In the same colophon, Kakunyo adds, "I record this in order to destroy heresy and light the lantern of truth."

Kakunyo, through his emphasis on the hereditary line spanning three generations, sought to hold together the institution after Shinran's death. Sensing the danger facing Honganji, he felt he had a historical mission to fulfill. It was inescapable that the institution thus established was unified under the authority of orthodoxy.

It was Rennyo who found himself in the middle of this Honganji institution which had been established by Kakunyo. In the face of this reality, how was he to grapple with his decision to "reveal the teachings of the Master (Shinran) in all places, far and near, during my lifetime"? This problem must have preoccupied Rennyo during the long years before he assumed the leadership of Honganji. Therefore, he read through Kakunyo's *Kudenshō* and *Gaijashō*, and then he turned to the *Tannishō*, all of which had in common "the true faith transmitted from the Master (Shinran)." Rennyo took as his own the spirit of "lamenting deviations" which was the foundation of this true faith. His actions thus conformed to the rectification of heresy which he had inherited from Kakunyo, as can be seen in the correction of abberant doctrine discussed in the *Letters*. It was this that propelled the restoration of Shinshū.

It is undeniable that Rennyo addressed the correction of these aberrant doctrines in his *Letters* from the standpoint of a powerful institution. The *Eigenki* asserts:

> When Rennyo was at his temple in Yamashina, it is not that he thought ill of people.... He said, "There are, however, two of whom I think ill: one who causes unhappiness to his parents, and one who speaks aberrant doctrine. Of these two, I think ill." The news that was received in Kyoto [was that] samurai who spoke ill of Honganji and who confused [other teachings] with the teachings of the founder were extreme enemies of the Dharma.[25]

In addition, article 243 of the *Kikigaki* relates:

> Rennyo heard that in the northern provinces, a certain person was spreading mistaken teachings, saying that they were the teachings of our tradition. Rennyo called Jōyū of the northern provinces to him and said, with great anger, "It is abominable and despicable to attribute [other teachings] to the founder [Shinran]." He gnashed his teeth, saying, "Even I mangle them, I still will not be satisfied."[26]

Such harsh attitudes must be viewed as building on the steps Kakunyo took to rectify heresy, to "destroy heresy and light the lantern of truth."

Conclusion

"Lamenting deviations" and rectifying heresies are, in many ways, contradictory. In the past, this point has impeded studies of Rennyo. In fact, Rennyo worked to create a spirit of unity among fellow believers on the one hand, but on the other, he also formed a power structure with the centralization of power in the Honganji institution, placing his own male descendants (*ikke shū*) at major temples:

> In every generation, good spiritual teachers (*zenchishiki*) have succeeded the founder [Shinran]. Master Rennyo secluded himself in the hall at Osaka, and when Master Jitsunyo went to visit him there, Rennyo said, "[Our] relationship as parent and child is, for both of us, [like] a visit from the founder [Shinran]." His goblet remained on its stand for some time.[27]

These two emphases appear to be opposites. Although this situation essentially places the two sides at variance with each other, Rennyo maintained the contradiction in his own character, which was based on the principle of the centrality of faith, enabling him to lead Honganji through the power of his personality. In this way, Rennyo, more than anyone else, placed himself in the middle of the contradiction while seeking to transmit the patriarchs' tradition of true faith. The contradiction is all the more apparent in the correction of abberant doctrine addressed in the *Letters*, but for precisely this reason Rennyo always returned to his chosen focus on the spirit of "lamenting deviations" and of fellowship (*dōbō*). This was Rennyo's fundamental position.

The composition of the *Gaijashō* shows that the steps taken by Kakunyo to rectify heresy did not stop at simply an emphasis on the orthodoxy of his own position. From among his many writings, Kakunyo's *Gaijashō*, *Shūjishō*, and *Kudenshō* are traditionally referred to as "The Three Works of Kakunyo." Among these three, the *Gaijashō* and the *Kudenshō* may be classified in the same category, because they were composed only six years apart (the *Kudenshō* was written in 1321, the *Gaijashō* in 1327) and both were written at the request of disciples, including Jōsen (1295–1377).

The *Haja kenshō shō*, written in 1324 by Kakunyo's son Zonkaku, tells of societal problems at that time that placed the Honganji institution in danger. Such situations no doubt helped to prompt the writing of the *Gaijashō*. The reasons the *Gaijashō* was written provide further evidence that Kakunyo's activities were driven by his conviction that he had a great historical mission regarding Honganji. Rennyo also felt he had this mission, but in his case the basis of this conviction was the spirit of "lamenting deviations." To the extent that the correction of aberrant doctrine developed in this way, Rennyo surpassed a simple schematic understanding of orthodoxy and heresy. In grasping this concept, we see Rennyo's real intention.

I therefore propose the following metaphor: in Rennyo's *Letters*, which unify the contradiction between "lamenting deviations" and rectifying heresies, the spirit of "lamenting deviations" forms the warp, the spirit of rectifying heresy the woof, of the fabric of the *Letters*. In recent years the act of rectifying heresy has been criticized as merely emphasizing the orthodoxy of one's own position. Actually, however, I believe this is so because the nature of actions taken to rectify aberrant doctrine which occurred when the Honganji became a fixed institution, after Rennyo's death and particularly in modern times, ultimately came to conceal the true mission of the rectification of heresy.

That the *Letters* unify the contradiction between "lamenting deviations" and rectifying heresies tells us that by constantly returning in his practice to his understanding of "fellow practitioners," Rennyo became an outstanding leader of Shinshū. At the same time, it signifies that the restoration of Shinshū which occurred by means of this epistolary communication was nothing other than the revitalization of the original meaning of Shinshū: true faith (*shinjin*).

Notes

This chapter originally appeared as "Ofumi no seikaku kōzō" 御文の性格的構造 in Ikeda Yūtai 池田勇諦, *Ofumi kangeroku* 御文勧化録. Kyoto: Shinshū Ōtaniha Shūmusho, 1998, 29–43.

1 The phrase "lamenting deviations" or *tanni* (歎異) is an allusion to the *Tannishō*, compiled by Yuien (d. 1288). The first half of the *Tannishō* records statements of Shinran, and the second half is largely focused on pointing out improper patterns of belief and practice. Rennyo was the first Shinshū leader to hold up the *Tannishō* as a legitimate transmission of Shinran's ideas on a number of important topics, and his handwritten copy is currently the oldest extant text.

2 *Rennyo Shōnin itokuki*, SSZ 3.869.

3 SSZ 3:870

4 SSZ 3:871.

5 *Tannishō monki* is in *Zoku Shinshū taikei* (Tokyo: Shinshū tenseki kankōkai, 1940), *bekkan*; repr. as *Zoku Shinshū taikei* (Tokyo: Yoshikawa Kōbunkan, 1976), vol. 21. This volume was also published separately by Hōzōkan, 1972.

6 Soga Ryōjin, *Tannishō chōki* (Kyoto: Chōjiya, 1947). Rev. ed. appears in Soga Ryōjin and Soga Ryōjin Senshū Kankōkai, ed., *Soga Ryōjin senshū* (Tokyo: Yayoi Shobō, 1970), vol. 6.

7 *Sōga Ryōjin senshū*, 6.19.

8 Miyazaki Enjun, ed., *Tannishō* (*Rennyo Shōnin shosha*), (Kyoto: Hōzōkan, 1969).

9 A biography of Shinran by Kakunyo, dated 1331 and originally in three fascicles.

10 Completed by Zonkaku in 1360, the *Rokuyōshō* in ten fascicles is the first exegetical commentary on Shinran's *Kyōgyōshinshō*; at SSZ 2. 205. This work was often printed together with the *Kyōgyōshinshō* in the Edo period so the two works could be read simultaneously.

11 The *Kyōgyōshinshō* is the magnum opus of Shinran, containing the most detailed exposition of his thought. Originally in *kanbun* in six fascicles, this *nobegaki* version is extended in length by essentially being rewritten into *wabun*, or Japanese syntax.

12 An essay on the main points in Shinran's *Kyōgyōshinshō* by Zonkaku, dated 1328. It is a work in one fascicle; compare it with Zonkaku's *Rokuyōshō*, written over thirty years later and in far greater detail.

13 It's unclear what is contained in this work because it has a nonstandard title, but probably this is another name for a group of documents known today by the rubric *Hōnen Shōnin gohōgo*. These were collections of various utterances of Hōnen from different contexts compiled at the end of his life and shortly thereafter. There are two in the *Shōwa shinshū Hōnen Shōnin zenshū*, one dated 1201 at p. 1117, another dated 1211 at p. 1131, both also in one fascicle.

14 See RSG 183–190.

15 Quote from Sumida Chiken in Dōhō Daigaku Bukkyō Gakkai, ed., *Rennyo Shōnin no kenkyū* (Nagoya: Bunkōdō Shoten, 1971), 83.

16 Sumida Chiken, *Igishi no kenkyū* (Kyoto: Chōjiya, repr. 1960), 381.

17 SSZ 3.66. The term "name register" or *myōchō* (名帳) refers to a variety of documents that recorded the names of individuals who professed their faith in Shinran's doctrine, a practice started by Ryōgen of the Bukkōji branch of Shinshū. Kakunyo's statement here is a strong polemic against its implied promise of thereby guaranteeing Birth in the Pure Land to the individual. In fact we know that Shinran similarly recorded the names of his disciples.

18 SSZ 3.66. Portrait lineages, or *ekeizu*, were another common way of documenting lineage in the Bukkōji branch. These recorded the abbots of temples and typically included portraits of each person in the lineage.

19 SSZ 3.64.

20 SSZ 3.84.

21 SSZ 3.33.

22 SSZ 3.158–159. Translation based on James Dobbins, *Jōdo Shinshū: Shin Buddhism in Medieval Japan*, (Bloomington, Indiana: Indiana University Press, 1989), 92.

23 SSZ 2.793.

24 SSZ 3.89.

25 RSG 262. This text is also known as the *Eigen kikigaki*, which is how the title is given at SSS 2.588.

26 This is entry 241 in the recension at SSZ 3.593, but it is entry 243 in the *Shinshū kana shōgyō* edition.

27 From the *Eigenki* at RSG 264.

14

YASUTOMI SHIN'YA
TRANSLATED BY MARK L. BLUM

The Tale of the Flesh-Adhering Mask

When Rennyo left the Ōmi area in the third year of Bunmei (1471), he began his proselytizing activities in Yoshizaki, located in a mountainous region in present-day Fukui prefecture. He continued there until the seventh year of Bunmei, and his considerable success during this four-year period is well known. Concerning the impact of his presence, we have the following comment overheard in a conversation between two aristocratic-looking women:

> A lodging has recently been built on the summit of Yoshizaki—there are no words to express how interesting a place it is. There are believers who make the pilgrimage to the mountain from seven different regions—Kaga, Etchū, Noto, Echigo, Shinano, Dewa and even Ōshū! Both men and women come, and everybody knows about the crowds. No one holds back in talking about this.[1]

In the vicinity of Rennyo's residence were built *taya* or lodging rooms for over 200 priests of influence.[2] One can imagine what a bustling scene that remote spot must have become. It is well known that there was an enormous increase in the number of believers who came to follow Rennyo during that period, and it is worth looking at the special efforts Rennyo made to treat women and men equally.

In the Muromachi period the power of women was slowly increasing, but in places such as Yoshizaki in the Hokuriku area[3] north of the capital women still remained restricted by an older culture. It was to these women that Rennyo devoted considerable time communicating his message. Much of this interaction can be seen in the *Letters* (*ofumi*) written to the wives of the priests living in the *taya* in Yoshizaki. This is one example of an extant letter from this period:

> Well now, I want to say to you wives who are living here together with the priests in the *taya* lodgings on this mountain in Yoshizaki that you should understand that this fact itself is the result of karma from your previous lives that is not insignificant. But the meaning of this will be clear to you only when you confirm your *shinjin* [faith] regarding that matter of singular importance, namely the afterlife. So for anyone intending to become a wife [and join this community], it is imperative that you commit yourself to achieving *shinjin*.[4]

Rennyo would frequently gather these wives for Dharma discussion meetings. It is believed he was motivated partially by the death of his own wives and daughters and partially by his having seen the desire for independence among the women he met in that community.

Rennyo's proselytizing efforts in Yoshizaki consisted of informal Dharma discussions, the writing of the *Letters*, the painting and distribution of sacred scrolls with the nenbutsu written as the sacred object, and the printing and dissemination of certain texts written by Shinran such as the *Shōshinge* and three *Wasan*, followed by efforts at encouraging the recitation of these texts by lay followers. In addition, as the organization expanded in the Hokuriku region, he also brought in performers of Nō and popular songs (*utai* 謡) that were popular in the capital, Kyoto. Previously scholars have paid little attention to the role that art played in Rennyo's religious activities, but Kagotani Machiko has done pioneering research in this area.[5] According to the record of Rennyo's tenure at the Yamashina Honganji, in the thirteenth year of Bunmei (1481) he brought in *sarugaku* performers during a service as "Dharma entertainment."[6] Rennyo himself was well versed in Nō theater. He included in his nenbutsu preaching, for example, play titles such as *Seiganji* (Temple of the Vow),[7] taken from the Nō stage, and when he found people sleeping or talking during his lectures, he would say to them, "Time for you to sing!" and make them sing the most dynamic part of a song.[8]

We may glimpse an example of Rennyo's style of preaching in the story passed down in the Yoshizaki town of Kanazuchō in Fukui prefecture called *Yome-odoshi no oni no men* (The Devil Mask of Daughter-in-Law Intimidation), as seen in the illustration in the photo gallery.[9] The story is about an old woman who resents her young daughter-in-law's cherished desire to go to Yoshizaki every night to hear Rennyo. In order to stop her from going to hear the Dharma, the mother-in-law puts on a mask with the face of a devil and pops out along the road to scare her. But then the old woman finds that the mask has stuck to her face and she cannot remove it. Furthermore, after repeated encouragement from her daughter-in-law, she begins to recite the nenbutsu and then suddenly the mask falls off her face onto her lap.

There are two extant masks from this period regarded as treasured art objects and held today at temples in the Yoshizaki area (Nishi Honganji affiliate Yoshizakiji, and Higashi Honganji affiliate Gankyōji). We don't know precisely when this story was born, but we do know that in Rennyo's time it was considered a highly artistic form of Nō theater and was also performed in a Kyōgen adaptation, being performed or sung at artistic intervals between various ritualized activities that were the heart of Shinshū services. In light of its frequent appearance within the context of religious ceremonies, we may thus consider *Yome-odoshi no oni no men* to be but one title among a genre of what we may call "Shinshū educational Nō."[10]

Contents of the Legend

In addition to a devil mask, the temple Gankyōji in Yoshizaki holds a 1611 xylograph print of one version of this story in a text called *Shinshō yome-odoshi nikutsukimen engi*, or *The Genuine Tale of the Flesh-Adhering Mask of Daughter-in-Law Intimidation*.[11] Here is a translation of it in full:

> We shall begin by looking at the origins of this mask. It can be traced back to the time during the Bunmei reign era (1469–1487) when Rennyo Shōnin was residing on this mountain. There was a farmer named Yosoji from a nearby village called Jūraku. This man descended from Yoshida Gen-no-shin, a retainer to Hiyama Jibu'uemon, lord of Hiyama Castle. When the castle fell and Hiyama was routed, Gen-no-shin ended up in Jūraku, where he took up farming. Yosoji was the head of that household at the time of this incident, and he had a wife called Kiyo and two sons. Yosoji and his family, however, were struck by an illness that eventually took the life of Yosoji and both children.
>
> Truly overwhelmed at her loss, Kiyo felt the pain of separation over and over again. Having no choice but to accept the reality of such things as simply the way of the world regardless of what she herself may have wanted, [the widow] nevertheless yearned to do something for the enlightenment of the departed. Admittedly she also hoped to journey herself in the future to the Pure Land, where there is no suffering and where she could once again experience joy with others. Fortunately, just at that time Rennyo Shōnin was residing in Yoshizaki and holding Dharma meetings, which gathered both the high- and low-born. Deciding she wanted to hear what he had to say, Kiyo made the pilgrimage to Yoshizaki on the occasion of the anniversary of her husband's death. Upon meeting face to face with Rennyo, she witnessed all the joy she was hoping to find. Under his encouragement, Kiyo soon experienced that moment of faithful entrusting called *shinjin*, in the end becoming a believer of incomparable strength [and a frequent visitor to Yoshizaki].
>
> However the mother-in-law in her home was a misguided person plagued by an unusual degree of resentment and greed. In her own grief she was reminded daily of losing her son and being separated forever from her grandchildren; she had no interest whatsoever in the future [and no sympathy with Kiyo's faith]. The mother-in-law quickly became resentful of her daughter-in-law's trips to Yoshizaki and tried to convince her not to go. But try as she may, Kiyo was a woman whose faith was second to none and no words were able to dissuade her. The mother-in-law then responded by abusing and punishing Kiyo and keeping her busy with farming chores all day. But the daughter-in-law reacted to this treatment by simply going to Yoshizaki at night.
>
> One day the old woman got the idea that she could halt the daughter-in-law's trips to Yoshizaki by appearing in the form of a [hungry] devil in a small valley en route to Kiyo and threatening the younger woman if she proceeded further. She took out a mask that had been secretly held by her family since the time of her ancestors, matted down her own gray hair, and put on the mask. She then put on a white, unlined garment and hid herself in an area of dense brush in the small valley pass in question and waited. Before she knew it, her daughter-in-law Kiyo came hurriedly down the road reciting the nenbutsu on her way to Yoshizaki. As the wind in the pines created an unearthly sound, the mother-in-law in her devil disguise suddenly leapt out of the brush before her daughter-in-law and did her best to scare her. Kiyo was truly frightened; the hair on her skin stood up. But then, taking the situation as a sign of the kind of thing she had heard about [in Yoshizaki], she calmed her heart and, unperturbed, in a quiet voice sang the following song:
>
>> If you are going to eat [me], eat. If you are going to drink [my blood], drink.
>> But faith in the diamondlike Other-Power will never be consumed.

Then, reciting *namu amida butsu, namu amida butsu,* she walked by the devil and continued on to Yoshizaki.

The old woman returned home before her daughter-in-law and when she tried to take off the mask, sadly she found it affixed to her face. When she tried harder to pull it off, it was excruciating—as if she were pulling off her own skin. She became frantic, worried not only about the mask but about what she would say when her daughter-in-law returned home. There seemed to be nothing she could do. As the mother-in-law brooded over this dilemma, she began to feel she could not go on living. Her hands and feet became numb; she was no longer able to move. Thus did time pass when suddenly the door opened as Kiyo returned from Yoshizaki. Entering the house, she saw the devil that had confronted her in the valley. Shocked, she wondered what was going, on but before she could speak her mother-in-law let out a great scream, "Aahh, I am so ashamed," and began to cry inconsolably. When Kiyo approached and asked what had happened, the mother-in-law dropped all pretense and confessed that it was she who had taken on the form of the devil in the valley, explaining her motivation, and doing it in a way that hid nothing of how she had felt at that time. The daughter-in-law, now speaking through sobs of her own, related that she had heard Rennyo say that regardless of how good or bad someone was, anyone who [sincerely] asked Amida [for help] and recited the nenbutsu would become a buddha. She thus urged the mother-in-law to begin chanting the nenbutsu immediately. Struck by these compassionate words of encouragement mixed with tears from her daughter-in-law that came to rest on top of her own deep sense of shame, for the first time in her life the mother-in-law said *namu amida butsu.* As amazing as it may sound, after only one recitation the mask suddenly fell off and her hands and feet returned to normal. Truly as if she had awoken from a dream, the old woman was now of a mind of self-reflection, and it occurred to her that she herself must find a way to make it to Yoshizaki to hear the teaching. So together with her daughter-in-law she made the pilgrimage and received instruction [from Rennyo], and thereafter both embraced a faith second to none.

The mask was given to Rennyo, and he left instructions that it be shown to others in the future. It was then bestowed upon Yūnen, the founder of this temple [Gankyōji]. This is in fact what is famously known today as the "flesh-adhering mask." The route through the mountains that brought Kiyo to Yoshizaki has come to be known as the "Valley of Daughter-in-Law Intimidation," and the mask itself has been kept here at this temple ever since. The overturning of a past vehicle can become a lesson for a future vehicle, can it not? The point is to take these words to heart, overturn your daily negativity, and, according to the Buddha's teaching, become someone who recites nenbutsu.

Thus goes the famous legend of the *Flesh-Adhering Mask of Daughter-in-Law Intimidation.* There are, of course, many stories of daughter-in-law intimidation throughout the country, but this particular tale from Yoshizaki is one of the oldest and its contents are rather unusual. According to the colophon, this version was first carved in woodblocks and printed in the sixteenth year of Keichō (1611), based on a text written in the first year of Keichō (1596). It was released again in revised editions during the Teikyō (1684–1688) and Bunka (1804–1818) eras, but the basic contents remained unchanged. Probably what we are seeing is an orally narrated story that was transferred to print medium so it could be distributed to the pilgrims who made the journey to Yoshizaki in the early seventeenth century. The characters in the story are Rennyo, Hiyama Jibu'uemon, lord of Hiyama Castle, his retainer Yoshida Gen-no-shin, Gen-no Shin's descendant Yosoji, Kiyo, and Yosoji's mother.

Two elements of the plot that have received attention are the small valley on the way to Yoshizaki where the devil-mask was used to scare the daughter-in-law, and the repentant change of heart of the mother-in-law and subsequent nenbutsu recitation that function as the solution to the problem of the mask attaching itself to her face. There are other versions of this legend that have come down to us. One is contained in a biography of Rennyo compiled from the middle to the end of the Edo period called *Rennyo Shōnin seizui denki*.[12] In this version the husband's name is Ninomata Yosoji, with Yosoji written differently,[13] the intimidation event with the devil mask occurs when the wife is not going to but returning from Yoshizaki, and it is the mother-in-law's change of heart that occurs when she herself hears Rennyo's sermon that is given as the reason the mask drops off.

Nearly all the picture-scroll biographies (*eden*) of Rennyo include a panel depicting daughter-in-law intimidation. This is true even in the earliest picture-scroll biography, the *Rennyo Shōnin sanpuku eden*, dated the ninth year of Tenshō (1581).[14] The tradition of expressing this theme continues in the numerous pictorial biographies known as *Rennyo Shōnin eden* created in the Edo period, and we thus know that the story often figured in something called *etoki*, local preaching events that made use of paintings.[15] Since the story later appears beyond the particular context of the Rennyo biography, its transmission and dissemination via the *etoki* conducted by Shinshū monks during the *hōonkō* and other services must have had an impact on society as a whole. Its spread was further aided by its eventual adoption in theatrical forms such as Kabuki and Bunraku.

The Tale Evolves

It is unclear whether the creation of this *Tale of Daughter-in-Law Intimidation* can be connected to Rennyo himself, but at the very least the doctrinal contents do derive from ideas that Rennyo disseminated. The subsequent development of the tale reflects efforts to make it easy to understand, but it is interesting how the structure of the story calls to mind the traditional four-step process of constructing Chinese poetry, known in Japan as *ki shō ten ketsu* (起承転結), meaning (1) introduction, (2) elucidation of the theme, (3) transition to another viewpoint, and (4) summation. This method was also quite influential in narrative development in classical Japanese literature, and it seems apparent that this was the basic plot structure adopted for the various versions of this *Tale of Daughter-in-Law Intimidation*, as I will explain.

The first stage is to introduce the setting. Here we are told that a mother-in-law and daughter-in-law are living together after the death of the son/husband and children/grandchildren. The widow/daughter-in-law, somewhat obsessed with her husband's death, rushes off after work night after night to Yoshizaki to hear Rennyo's lectures. The mother-in-law cannot stomach this behavior and, in an attempt to stop her, dons the devil mask and appears before the daughter-in-law en route to her destination to scare her into abandoning her quest. Both women, the widow Kiyo who has lost both her husband and her children and the grandmother who lost her son and grandchildren, are described as ill-fated and unhappy. While the young widow takes refuge in Rennyo's teaching on the nenbutsu, attains *shinjin*, and is described as living peacefully, the mother-in-law by contrast is jealous and spiteful, which is her motivation for dressing up as a devil so as to chastise the widow/daughter-in-law.

The second stage takes place at the scene of the devil jumping out to scare the widow, a kind of confrontation between mother-in-law and daughter-in-law. The young widow Kiyo feels her hair stand on end at the sight of the devil but then recalls something she had been hearing for sometime, calms herself, and then responds to what is before her with these words:

> If you are going to eat [me], eat. If you are going to drink [my blood], drink.
> But faith in the diamondlike Other-Power will never be consumed.

Kiyo then recites the nenbutsu and proceeds on to Yoshizaki, apparently unruffled by her experience. As she was set upon by her mother-in-law in the form of a she-devil, this episode illustrates how she entrusts her fearful thoughts to the thoughts of Amida; by putting her palms together and uttering "faith in the Other-Power will never be consumed" and "*namu amida butsu*," she is able to endure the intimidation of the devil. This reaction is meant to portray the image of the young widow as someone who has attained the diamondlike confidence of *shinjin* based on the teachings of Rennyo and the power of that confidence to overcome such difficulties. Rennyo's understanding may be seen in *Letters* 4:13, which elucidate the concept of attaining the path in everyday life at the moment of a single thought-practice of nenbutsu.

In the third stage we find the old woman's face stuck to the mask (Japanese masks cover only the front of the face). We see her anxiety mount as she attempts to remove the mask before the daughter-in-law comes home, but the more she pulls the more it seems like she is peeling off her own skin. Finding herself in a corner with no way out, the mother-in-law contemplates suicide, loses all feeling in her hands and feet, and finds herself frozen, unable to move. The widow Kiyo, in the meantime, is returning from Yoshizaki, emboldened by having listened to Rennyo lecture yet another time. When she opens the door to her home, she is stunned to find the old woman in front of her wearing the devil's mask.

She then addresses the panic-stricken mother-in-law by saying, "In the sayings of Rennyo I have heard that no matter who makes the request to Amida, if that person recites the nenbutsu it will lead to attaining buddhahood. So hurry up and start your nenbutsu practice!" In a letter to the wives of the local *taya* monks dated the eleventh day of the ninth month of Bunmei 11 (1479), Rennyo wrote:

> Having been abandoned by even the tathāgatas of the ten directions and the buddhas in the past, present, and future, women will be saved, to our great joy, by Amida Tathāgata alone, and thus he has already put forth his forty-eight vows [for just such purpose].[16]

We may surmise that it is just this teaching of Rennyo regarding the rebirth of women in Amida's Pure Land that the young daughter-in-law communicated to her mother-in-law. This third section is thus the heart of the story of the flesh-adhering mask and the climax of the story.

The fourth and final stage is a denouement where the older woman becomes remorseful for her earlier attitude and in the end accepts the recommendation of the younger woman to begin nenbutsu recitation. Upon her doing so, the mask suddenly pops off and lands in her lap. She journeys to Yoshizaki with her daughter-in-law, donates the mask, and opens herself up to the teachings of Rennyo. Thus does the tale end.

Although the story as we have it here has been somewhat romanticized, the theme in stage four of the mask falling off and older woman's personal movement toward being restored spiritually as a result of accepting the daughter-in-law's urging to practice nenbutsu is easily misunderstood as illustrating a doctrine in which the nenbutsu has the power to eliminate bad karma and bring happiness. But if we remember that she begins to chant the nenbutsu only after reflecting on her own behavior as expressed in her declaration of shame, it should be clear that this teaching does not diverge from the basic premise of Jōdoshinshū.

Leaving aside the pedagogical use of this story already described, I would also like to offer a few other ways of thinking about it. There are many ways to find meaning here; in particular, the motifs of the mask and the desire to punish the young daughter-in-law who has awakened to faith suggest different intrepretive contexts. The three approaches that seem most plausible are as follows: the story can be viewed as a form of theater, it can be read as a statement about women and family issues, or it can be interpreted from an ethnic, anthropological point of view.

Viewed as Theater

Supported by rich and powerful families during the time of Rennyo, various guilds formed what we think of today as Nō theater, such as the Kanze (観世), Konbaru (今春), Kongō (金剛), and Hōshō (宝生). These flourished in Kyoto and Nara, the most famous being led by the actor and playwright Zeami, and many plays in their repertoire dealt directly with issues related to Buddhist notions of faith. One such common motif of Nō drama utilized a female *shite* or main character who awakens to the teachings of a buddha and is thereby released from a vengeful spirit or ghost.

In the *Jitsugoki* and *Kūzenki* biographical records of Rennyo are references to the fact that Rennyo himself was a great fan of Nō and Kyōgen performances. In his sermons he made practical use of the content of the Nō play *Seiganji* and the Kyōgen play *Torisashi*, and his own style of teaching was transformed by these plays as he increasingly found they helped him bring people into his worldview. When Rennyo was actively expanding the Honganji network into the northern regions of Honshū, he included materials from the songs and Nō theatrical performances popular in the capital as well as Kyōgen humor from around the country. Indeed, the resurgence of Honganji power in the Muromachi period owes a great deal to Rennyo's skillful employment of theatrical techniques.

Kagotani Machiko's interesting thesis is that there was a kind of "Shinshū educational Nō" based on the rise of Nō as a dramatic form at this time and on Rennyo's personal interest in both Nō and Kyōgen. In her view, this story of daughter-in-law intimidation would have been performed on a Nō stage. In this form of theater actors wear masks, and since the mask is supposed to represent the actor's mind faithfully, there are established mask types that the audience recognizes. Kagotani sees the devil mask used here as corresponding to the more common *hannya* mask, one that typically expresses a deep-seated grudge or resentment, and speculates that the daughter-in-law probably would have been wearing a gentle mask such as *ko-omote* or *waka-onna*, both expressing refinement and a woman's kindness or sympathy. The two-horned *hannya* mask is the emotional opposite, employed when a female character feels enmity, resentment, or jealousy. The horns bare the truth of a loathesome mind-set of self-attachment or self-righteousness. This mask has a frightening look that somehow cools the mind of the viewer. These two types of masks symbolize the two emotional extremes for female *shite*.

The mother-in-law depicted in the *Shinshō yome-odoshi nikutsukimen engi* reminds one of the standard female devils who appear on the Nō stage. Female devils in Nō are typically considered human incarnations of a woman's mind in a state of jealousy. Their jealously is often shrouded in lonely desolation deriving from a sense of victimization at the hands of another. In the case of the mother-in-law of Yoshizaki, we similarly find someone seized by resentment directed at, in this case, someone of the same sex — her daughter-in-law. Note how her transformation by means of putting on the devil mask occurs at the precise moment when her actions correspond most closely with her irrepressible feelings of jealousy. In other words, the devil mask has the same theatrical effect as the *hannya* mask.

Looking at Women and Family Issues

What are the effect of these deaths upon the widow and grandmother and their relationship with each other? The widow's efforts to journey to Yoshizaki to hear Rennyo's sermons on the Dharma after the death of her husband and children reflect, in her own words, an inescapable acceptance of the truth. Thus we read:

> Having no choice but to accept the reality of such things as simply the way of the world regardless of what she herself may have wanted, [the widow] nevertheless yearned to do something for the enlightenment of the departed. Admittedly she also hoped herself to journey to the Pure Land in the future where there is no suffering and where she could once again experience joy with others.

This attitude leads Kiyo to rush over to Yoshizaki after her chores on the farm, which as we have noted leads her to finding inner peace.

This analysis begs the question of what Rennyo may have said that helped her, and on this point it is important to reassert the fact that in that social context women were typically viewed as limited both ethically and spiritually simply because of their gender. This prejudice is embodied in the Buddhist doctrine of "five limitations and three submissions."[17] Rennyo statements relevant to this context express a rather complex attitude which, on the one hand, does recognize the prevailing view of a woman's spiritual and ethical limitations and yet, on the other, also asserts a Honganji doctrine that rejects such prejudice in terms of the stated goal of Birth for women based on the Original Vows of Amitābha Buddha. For example, the former position can be seen in the following letter:

> The very fact that someone is born in a female body means that the depth of that person's inherent sin surpasses that of a man, as expressed in [the notion of] the five limitations and three subjugations.[18]

The latter position has been noted earlier in the quoted letter from Bunmei 11.

Rennyo's position on the Birth of women had more than philosophical significance. It is, in fact, believed by many that the Honganji organization expanded as remarkably as it did during Rennyo's tenure precisely because in his proselytizing he expounded a teaching that unambiguously asserted the Birth of women in the Pure Land, despite their traditional estrangement within medieval society.

As was mentioned earlier, the status of women in the Muromachi period when Rennyo lived had improved somewhat,[19] but in the mountains of Hokuriku, where Yoshizaki was located, Rennyo found women held back by the bonds of an older and, to him, anachronistic value system. Thus he was motivated to direct much of his attention to women.

Women nevertheless often faced severe restrictions in society and the home. Generally speaking women were subject to the absurdities of being regarded merely as wives to their husbands and mothers to their children. It was also considered both human nature and an ethical duty to follow an assumed absolute obligation to submit to people of higher social status. Young women generally became wives and went to live in the home of their father-in-law and mother-in-law. At that point it would have been exceedingly difficult for them to go out into the world to do as they pleased without the agreement of their husband's parents. Thus in a typical family of this period we would not expect to see, as we do in this Intimidation story, a daughter-in-law allowed to travel on her own to a meeting place in Yoshizaki to hear Rennyo speak. Within the same-sex relationship of mother-in-law and daughter-in-law, jealousy toward the happiness of one by the other was a common problem, so it is not surprising to see the mother-in-law unforgiving of her daughter-in-law's joy at having found faith. When the mother-in-law dons the "mask that had been secretly held by her family since the time of her ancestors," in essence she is holding up a shield against the daughter-in-law, asserting her own status and protecting her authority as head of the household.

Folkloric Interpretation

Early in this story is the sentence, "Fortunately, just at that time Rennyo Shōnin was residing in Yoshizaki and holding Dharma meetings, which gathered both the high- and low-born." From Yoshizaki, Rennyo organized significant numbers of

Shinshū believers in the entire Hokuriku area to lead to the creation of the Honganji institution as we know it today. At this time he focused his dissemination activities on the domains of Echizen, Kaga, Noto, and Etchū. The wide-ranging energy of so many people organized as well as their potential military power posed a threat to the powers that be: both the *shugo daimyō* who aspired to take control of the region and the preexisting religious organizations in the area took notice. The historian Inoue Toshio has pointed out, for example, that if one maps out the region where Rennyo was actively proselytizing at this time, it corresponds exactly to the area where the cult devoted to the mountain Hakusan was prevalent.[20]

The peak referred to as Mount Haku or Hakusan (白山; White Mountain) is the source of the waters that form both the Kuzuryū River (九頭竜川) in Echizen and the Tedori River (手取川) in Kaga. Hakusan is thus the major source of irrigation for the entire farming area of Hokuriku and is also known as "The Great Mountain Beyond." At that time it was an object of faith for many people in the area who considered it, as the source of their livelihood, sacred. The region surrounding Hakusan has, since ancient times, served as a rich ground for many religious forms, including fusions of Shintō and Buddhist deities, Tantra, and various expressions of pantheism. Rennyo himself was well aware of this heritage and is thought to be commenting on it in various places in his writing. For example:

> Take refuge on your own in the Buddha; take refuge in the Dharma, and take refuge in the Saṅgha. Do not follow other paths, do not worship the heavens, do not ritually enshrine gods and spirits, do not look for auspicious days.[21]

But in addition to asserting a position that "purifies" the mountain faith paradigm prevalent among the rural communities in that area, Rennyo also wanted to assert the importance of committing oneself to *one* buddha. He was essentially asking the local people to free themselves from this older Hakusan-centered faith and instead to take refuge in the one buddha called Amida, thereby changing their status to adherents of Honganji.

Rennyo's message is that there is no need to worship all the various kami and buddhas—even give up your local events and magical ceremonies—for such things are of no value for attaining Birth. However simple and limited this statement may be, it nevertheless often brought out rough behavior among local converts. Indeed, their behavior is an early example of turning half-understood doctrines into an ideology, with all the political implications of that word.

There are examples in his *Letters* of Rennyo admonishing nenbutsu practitioners against slandering the cultures surrounding not only Hakusan, but also Tateyama (立山), and the temples at Heisen (平泉) and Toyohara (豊原). When the old woman takes out a "mask that had been secretly held by her family since the time of her ancestors" in order to punish the relatively young, nenbutsu-practicing daughter-in-law, we may be seeing a symbolic expression of anger in a local, native god whose traditional religious support has been threatened by a newly arrived, competing model of religious authority. One may also see this event as the voice of established Tendai and Shugendō centers in places like Heisen and Toyohara criticizing the Shinshū nenbutsu community. Inoue Toshio, for his part, viewed *The Genuine Tale of the Flesh-Adhering Mask of Daughter-in-Law Intimidation* as a vestige of the conflicted relationship between Rennyo and Hakusan.[22] That is, he saw in it the faith of the local ethnic population voicing opposition to a faith based in the Amida-nenbutsu paradigm. There have been many studies of the relationship between Rennyo and local populations of Hokuriku, and this folk tale is certainly worthy of consideration within that subfield.

Conclusion

This tale of daughter-in-law intimidation is also a tale of the salvation of two women. Both suffered painful losses of loved ones within their immediate family and faced difficult futures. The daughter-in-law was fortunate enough to hear Rennyo's talks directly and was able to gain faith. The mother-in-law had to go through a further painful process of turning herself into a devil out of jealousy, but in the end, through the remonstrations of the object of that jealousy, she too managed to gain faith. In other words, this is also a drama about the salvation of women through faith in nenbutsu, a theme explicit in Rennyo's own writing.

The most commonly read of Rennyo's *Letters* are traditionally bundled into five collections. Among these five, the following letters mention the salvation of women:

> *Letters*   1:7,
>
> 2:1, 2:8, 2:10
>
> 3:7
>
> 4:3, 4:10
>
> 5:3, 5:6, 5:7, 5:8, 5:14, 5:15, 5:17, 5:19, 5:20

Clearly this theme appears quite often and is especially concentrated in the fifth collection, implying that the number of women in his congregation steadily grew to where it became quite substantial.

Within Rennyo's unusually strong concern for the religious education of women many see a deep-seated longing for his mother. A victim of class discrimination on top of gender discrimination, she was unable to secure the permission of the family to be the public, official wife of his father, Zonnyo, and ended up leaving Honganji while Rennyo was still a child. In addition, Rennyo's sympathy must have been stirred by thoughts of the other women in his family he had lost. During the time of his residency in Hokuriku (1471–1475) and even before, illness took the lives of his first wife, Nyoryōni (如了尼), who died in 1455, his second wife, Renyū (連祐), who died in 1470, his first daughter, Nyokei (如慶), who died in 1471, and his daughters Ryōnin (了忍) and Kengyoku (見玉), both of whom died within eight days of each other in 1472. Even after leaving Hokuriku, Rennyo then lost his third wife, Nyoshōni (如勝尼) in 1478, his fourth wife, Shū'nyoni (宗如尼; year of death unknown), and two more daughters (Yūshin 祐心 in 1490 and Nyokū 如空 in 1492). These personal losses of so many women—four wives and five daughters—must have led him not only to encourage women to seek salvation through nenbutsu, but to conclude that women and men must be seen as [spiritually] equal.

Rennyo's view stands in part upon the foundation of Shinran's doctrine of *akunin shōki*, which affirms that Amida Buddha's religious message is above all directed to the unfortunate, to those who have done bad or evil acts. In addition, it is highly likely he was influenced by the ideas of Zonkaku, whose treatise *Nyonin ōjō kikigaki* (Notes on the Birth of Women in the Pure Land) we know he copied in 1446 at the age of thirty-two, before he took up residency in Yoshizaki. Zonkaku strongly argues for *nyonin shōki*, an interpretation of the *akunin shōki* doctrine that regards women as the true object of the Buddha's religious message.

Among all the deaths of women in his family, it was the passing away at age twenty-five of his daughter Kengyoku (also known as Kengyokuni) not long after the family had settled into their new mountain home in Hokuriku that seems to have affected him the most. Her grave is still standing in Yoshizaki. Kengyokuni made the journey to Yoshizaki just at the time when her father's religious activities were beginning there in earnest. A year after her arrival, after a long illness of 100 days, she succumbed. Rennyo's sadness can be seen in a letter he wrote just after her funeral.[23]

The *Daughter-in-Law Intimidation* tale of response to deaths in a family is thus set in Yoshizaki at a time when Rennyo himself had lost a number of close female family members. Many issues associated with the story have not been treated here, such as the various versions of the story as *setsuwa* and authenticity questions that surround the masks currently displayed that are purported to be the actual object. The fact that the story has skillfully woven into it the doctrine of the Birth for women is; however, the most important message here. For the story ultimately stands out as a model of how women restricted by the beliefs and customs of that region find liberation in Rennyo's teachings, and as such it narrates a process of how one turns toward faith in the nenbutsu and attains *shinjin* as well as how that experience itself contributes to a woman's independence. Many generations of Shinshū believers have been moved by it, and thus the tale continues to be told, even to the present day. We thus expect that the tale of *Daughter-in-Law Intimidation* will continue to be passed down to future generations and merit future interpretations as well.

Notes

1 *Letters* 1:7; RSI 105.

2 RSI 104. Called *taya*, the written form of this term in Rennyo's letter is 多屋, but the word is derived from 他屋.

3 Hokuriku (北陸) or "north country" refers basically to a wide, generally mountainous area of Honshū along the Japan seacoast area that was north of the capital of Kyoto. Today it is occupied by the four provinces of Fukui, Toyama, Ishikawa, and Niigata. In this chapter the old provincial or domain names will be used, since these are the forms that appear in the texts of the period. In general, the five premodern domain names that comprised this region are Echizen (Fukui), Etchū (Toyama), Noto (northern Ishikawa), Kaga (southern Ishikawa), and Echigo (Niigata).

4 *Letters* 1:10; RSI 111.

5 Kagotani Machiko, "Rennyo to *Yome-odosi no ohanashi*," *Shinshū kenkyū* 26 (1982), 128–136; "Rennyo to Nōgaku" in Shinshū Rengō Gakkai, ed., *Rennyo taikei*, vol. 1 (Kyoto: Hōzōkan, 1996), 288–316.

6 *Jitsugoki* 30, RSG 156–157; *Kūzenki*, RSG 39–40.

7 Seiganji 誓願寺.

8 *Jitsugoki* 9, RSG 144.

9 See woodblock print of scene from this story at the top of the last page in the photo gallery.

10 Shinshū kyōka nō 真宗教化能.

11 Wada Sōkyū, ed., *Yome-odoshi nikutsuki no men ryaku engi: Rennyo Shōnin go-kyūseki* (Sakai: Gankyōji, 1943). Based on the woodblock entitled *Shinshō yome-odoshi nikutsukimen engi* and dated the sixteenth year of Keichō (1611).

12 Held at Eiganji in Hekinan city in Aichi prefecture.

13 In the Gankyōji text, Yosoji is written 与三次, but in the version in the *Seizui denki* it is written 与惣治.

14 See Gamaike Seishi, "Rennyo Shōnin eden no keifu," in Rennyo Shōnin Eden Chōsa Kenkyūhan, ed., *Rennyo Shōnin eden no kenkyū* (Kyoto: Higashi Honganji, 1994), 122–152.

15 See Asakura Kiyū, *Yoshizaki gobō no rekishi* (Tokyo: Kokusho Kankōkai, 1995), 90. The location of the many versions of this story within the Rennyo picture-scroll biographies are as follows. As all have the same title: *Rennyo Shōnin eden*. Each will be distinguished here by the temple that holds it, with its location given in parenthesis.

   1. Saigenji 西厳寺 (Ōmachi, Nagano)—fourth panel
   2. Shōrakuji 勝楽寺 (Susaka, Nagano)—second panel
   3. Saionji 西恩寺 (Ichimiya, Aichi)—third panel
   4. Hongakubō 本覚坊 (Jōetsu, Niigata)—thirteenth panel
   5. Yoshizawaji 芳沢寺 (Ikō, Shiga)—second panel
   6. Kōshōji 光照寺 (Kyoto pref.)—second panel
   7. Honpōji 本法寺 (Bunkyō-ku, Tokyo)—third panel
   8. Jōkenji 浄賢寺 (Nishio, Aichi)—second panel
   9. Shinnenji 真念寺 (Ōmi-hachiman, Shiga)—second panel
  10. Myōrakuji 明楽寺 (Ikō, Shiga)—third panel
  11. Saikōji 西光寺 (Anakuri, Hyōgo)—third panel
  12. Eiganji 栄願寺 (Hekinan, Aichi)—fourth panel

16 *Letters* 1:10; RSI 112.

17 Five limitations and three submissions *goshō-sanshō* (五障三従), an old tradition in East Asian Buddhism. The five limitations are said to be five attainments which women cannot achieve as women: to become Brahma, Śākra, Mārā, a Cakravartin, or a buddha. The three subjugations are three people whose authority a woman must submit to at varying times in her life: her father, her husband, and her son.

18 *Letters* 5:7; RSI 474.

19 It has been frequently pointed out that Hino Tomiko served in the government. Ichijō Kanera responded to her involvement by praising the idea of women governing the nation. This fact shows how far women had advanced since the Kamakura period, when men were completely dominant. Outside of the upper levels of society as well, women at this time were not limited to devoting themselves to aiding their husbands and sons, but were accepted if they chose a professional path such as craftsperson or running a store.

20 See the chapter by Inoue Toshio called "Hakusan shinkō to Ikkōshū" (Belief in Mount Hakusan and the *ikkō-shū*) in his *Ikkō ikki no kenkyū* (Tokyo: Yoshikawa Kōbunkan, 1968), 265–277.

21 *Letters* 1:9; RSI 110. Here Rennyo is quoting the *Pratyutpanna buddhasaμmukhāvasthita samādhi sūtra*, in Chinese translation as *Banzhou sanmei jing*, T No. 418, 13.901b.

22 Inoue, "Hakusan," 273.

23 This *Letter* is not one chosen for the five bundles that form the standard collection but is found at RSI 82.

PART III

COMPARATIVE RELIGION

15

KATŌ CHIKEN
TRANSLATED BY JAN VAN BRAGT

Rennyo and Luther

*Similarities in Their Faith and
Community Building*

Opening Question

What kind of religious community or congregation can one expect to see develop
in the type of religion for which observances and rites are not important and faith
alone is everything? This chapter investigates this question in connection with
Rennyo, the eighth abbot of the Honganji branch of Jōdōshinshū, who followed
Shinran's conviction that it is only faith (*shinjin*) that matters, and with Martin
Luther (1483–1546), who came to his "salvation by faith only" (*sola fide*) declaration
in a frontal confrontation with the Roman Catholic Church. Of course it must be
understood that the historical and religious backgrounds of these two personalities
differ greatly.

Going to and Coming from the Pure Land

As is generally known, Shinran declared:

> Our going and returning, directed to us by Amida, come about through Other-
> Power; the truly decisive cause is *shinjin*.[1]

"Going" is usually interpreted as: sentient beings going to be born in the Pure Land,
and "returning" as sentient beings, once born in the Pure Land and having become
a buddha there, now returning to this world to work for the benefit of others.
Shinran taught that both of these moments of salvation depend on the power of
the Original Vow. For the sake of my argument, I will interpret these two movements
as two aspects of the same reality. "Going" is then the aspect of firmly believing
that, by Amida's Original Vow, one's salvation is already settled and one's Birth in
the Pure Land already a certainty; and "returning" is then the aspect of being filled
with the joy of one's salvation and therefore wanting to tell others about the Original
Vow and rejoicing in being saved together with others. I think that being able to

carry both these aspects in one's heart at the same time is characteristic of the type of religion that declares absolute Other-Power or "faith-only" to be everything. I further believe that this trait is an important element in regard to community building, since in this case it is also believed that the propagation of the faith and the building of the community themselves depend on Other-Power. The question then becomes how community building on the basis of Other-Power faith is possible.

Luther, who also stressed faith very strongly, formulated these two aspects as follows:

> By faith he is caught up beyond himself into God ["going"]. By love he descends beneath himself into his neighbor ["returning"].[2]

The service of others and the building of the community must find their origin in the joy of having obtained faith. Therein lies, I think, one of the specific traits of community building found in a faith-centered type of religion.

Once Shinran was convinced that his own Birth in the Pure Land was settled by the grace of the Original Vow of Amida Buddha, he put all his efforts into the practice of the path of "returning" and devoted himself to the propagation of the faith with the wish, "May there be peace in the world, and may the Buddha's teaching spread!"[3] We find his idea of the human predicament in sayings like "we who are bound by all our various afflictions (*kleśa*),"[4] and "Such peddlers, hunters, and others [who are called 'lowly' or 'sinners'] are none other than we, who are like stones and tiles and pebbles."[5] I think that it is precisely in the way of feeling this "we" that we discover the basis of the view of community held by people who live by faith. It is true that Shinran did not directly aim at the building of a religious congregation, but I sense in his "we" not the religious organization visible to the worldly eye, but the [purely religious] "invisible community."

Moving from Invisible to Visible Community

When one goes on to form a visible religious congregation out of this invisible community, the self of the person who tries to give shape to this congregation must be the object of honest scrutiny. Shinran confessed that he was "lacking even small love and small compassion. I cannot hope to benefit sentient beings."[6] In the case of Other-Power faith, such a penetrating self-reflection must be the presupposition of all community building, since here the true subject of the community building is not the sentient being, who cannot benefit others anyway, but the Buddha himself. All a human being can do is humbly "to be allowed to help" in the realization of the Will of the Buddha. It is thus a question, not of realizing one's own will, but of endeavoring, earnestly and self-forgettingly, in the realization of the Buddha's community. And I think that Rennyo was the one who tried to put this into practice, with rejection of his own self.

In this essay, I shall thus, first of all reflect on the characteristics of Rennyo's faith (Rennyo himself used the word *shinjin*, but I shall use the word "faith," while incorporating into it the meaning of *shinjin*); and subsequently consider the nature of Luther's faith. Next, I shall investigate the relationship between faith and community building, successively in Rennyo and Luther. Finally, I shall endeavor to clarify the similarity in faith and community building between these two protagonists.

Rennyo's Faith

Some scholars are of the opinion that, while Shinran was actually convinced of "faith of nonretrogression in the present life," Rennyo proclaimed the supreme importance of the afterlife, and that Rennyo thus distorted Shinran's doctrine. Was that really the case? I want to keep that question in mind while investigating the characteristics of Shinran's faith.

Shinran wrote: "As I reflect, I find that our attainment of faith [*shingyō*] arises from the heart and mind with which Amida Tathāgata selected the Vow."[7] He thus held that even faith is brought about by the Vow-mind of the Amida Buddha. For him, *shinjin* was "the straightforward mind directed to us through the selected Vow,"[8] in other words, the single-minded heart bestowed on us through the Vow that Amida selected to save all sentient beings — something that had already been prepared on the Buddha's side for the benefit of sentient beings. He called it, therefore, "the *shinjin* given by Amida."[9] Thus, Birth in the Pure Land is settled right from the moment that one is able to believe that one has received the gift of faith from the Tathāgata.

Why, then, did Rennyo put such a strong stress on the afterlife? He wrote, for example:

> Hence there can be no doubt at all that those who abandon the sundry practices and, with the [awakening of] the one thought-moment, deeply entrust themselves to Amida Tathāgata; to save them in [regard to] the afterlife will all be born in Amida's fulfilled land.[10]

> ...there is deliverance for all those who simply rely deeply, single-heartedly, and steadfastly on Amida Buddha and entrust themselves to [the Buddha] to save them in the afterlife.[11]

> ...when they then feel the thankfulness and joy of being saved in [regard to] the afterlife, they should simply repeat *namu-amida-butsu, namu-amida-butsu.*[12]

However, the same Rennyo also wrote:

> When people who remain in the lay state entrust themselves wholeheartedly to Amida Tathāgata's merciful Vow, while abandoning all attachment to the sundry practices and various observances, and find in their hearts the one-thought of imploring [Amida] single-mindedly and without doubt, Amida Tathāgata immediately sends forth the rays of his light and embraces them. Such is namely the Buddha's heart, which only wants to save. This is also what is meant by the expression "Amida bestowing faith."[13]

Help [salvation] thus comes from the Buddha's side, and even faith is seen as given by the Buddha, Why then, if birth in the Pure Land is settled at the moment of faith and salvation thus realized, would Rennyo have put such strong stress on the afterlife? Would he diverge from Shinran's idea of faith on this point?

Indeed, we can recognize therein an idiosyncratic trait of Rennyo's presentation of faith and also the unique qualities he displayed in the building up of the Honganji community. His point of view, namely, was always "the persons who remain in the lay state," or again, "lay men and women, lacking wisdom in the last age,"[14] "unlettered men and women."[15] Whether or not true faith resided in these people's breast was the overriding concern of Rennyo, the great propagator of the faith.

With his reasoned approach, Rennyo sufficiently grasped the significance of Shinran's "state of nonretrogression in the present life," but he felt that for lay people this was not so readily understandable. And even when they came to grasp it at a certain moment, it was difficult for them to keep this understanding alive. As for Rennyo himself, even if he dwelt in the same state of faith as Shinran, his heart was always where the people were. While understanding the state of faith reached by Shinran, he knew how difficult it is to keep on believing in this way. Proof of this feeling is found in the fact that Rennyo avoided showing the *Tannishō* to the people. He feared that they would misunderstand it.

Also in the case of Shinran himself, even if he had received the gift of such faith from the Tathāgata, things were not so simple. Yuienbō, the compiler of the *Tannishō*, once asked him, "Although I say the nenbutsu, the feeling of dancing with joy is faint within me, and I have no thought of wanting to go to the Pure Land quickly. How should it be [for a person of nenbutsu]?" According to Yuienbō, Shinran's answer was, "I too have had this question, and the same thought occurs to you, Yuienbō!" On that occasion, Shinran made the following honest confession:

> It is hard for us to abandon this old home of pain. Where we have been transmigrating for innumerable kalpas down to the present, and we feel no longing for the Pure Land of peace, where we have yet to be born. Truly, how powerful our afflictions are! But though we feel reluctant to part from this world, at the moment our karmic bonds to this Saha world run out and helplessly we die, we shall go to that Land.[16]

Here Shinran is clearly confessing the difficulty of believing that one is at the present moment already saved by the Tathāgata. This was the case even for Shinran himself, and Rennyo knew how much more difficult it was for his lay people. Would it not be for this reason that Rennyo, in considering faith, took the moment of death as one of his viewpoints, the moment when a person's links with the Saha world have run out?

Of course, there is no doubt that Shinran was thoroughly aware of his salvation at that time, since he also commented on the same occasion:

> What suppresses the heart that should rejoice and keeps one from rejoicing is the activity of our afflictions. Nevertheless, the Buddha, knowing this beforehand, called us "foolish beings possessed of afflictions"; thus, becoming aware that the Compassionate Vow of Other-Power is indeed for the sake of ourselves, who are such beings, we feel all the more confident.[17]

Consequently, Rennyo must have thought that for the ordinary people of his time the idea of birth on the threshold of the afterlife at the moment when links to the Saha world have run out was what was most needed to transmit Shinran's meaning truthfully and without endangering it. Moreover, Rennyo's time was one of wars and upheavals, wherein death was constantly before one's eyes. I submit that this situation also contributed to Rennyo's putting the afterlife into the foreground.

However, what we must pay special attention to at this point is that Rennyo, for all his stress on the afterlife, never taught that salvation was limited to the afterlife. He recommended, indeed, single-mindedly to ask Amida "to save you in [regard to] the afterlife," but he did not say that one should despair of the present world or this life. He scolded the faithful and urged them on, saying, "In the Buddhist Dharma there can be no thought of tomorrow. Hurry up! Hurry up! when it comes to the Buddha Dharma."[18] Birth may occur in the afterlife, but the attainment of faith should not be postponed. Rennyo spurred the people on to do it today, at this very moment. He bade them to hurry up: "With regard to the Buddha Dharma, one should do already today the things of tomorrow."[19] While speaking of the afterlife, he pressed the people for a decision at the present moment.

With his eye on their mood and capacities, Rennyo urged the lay people to come to a decision. "The most important matter of the afterlife" (*goshō no ichidaiji*) and the most important matter of this life are not apart from one another. While speaking of "the most important matter of the afterlife," he was, in fact, speaking of the most important matter in this life. In his endeavor to bring people to have faith in Amida, Rennyo was especially attentive to the heart and mood of the common people. As a result, we can find peculiar—very human and, as it were, "fleshy"—traits in his presentation of our relationship with Amida Tathāgata. Thus he told people the following:

> [In a dream] Amida caught hold of his [Yuirenbō's] sleeve and held on to it firmly, not letting go even when he tried to get away. Thereby we should understand that] "embracing" [*sesshu*] means catching and holding on to one who may want to escape.[20]

Rennyo's faith was principally at one with Shinran's faith, but it somehow gives the impression of being "rawer," more down-to-earth. Shinran's faith of nonretrogression in the present life was pure but difficult to uphold. It might be said that Rennyo rethought it in the direction of birth in the afterlife and remodeled it into a faith whereby one feels safe in self-surrender. Could we not speak here of the difference between a faith born from a strenuous religious quest and a faith reshaped after the feelings of ordinary people?

Luther's Faith

When reflecting on the characteristics of Luther's faith, two sentences found right at the beginning of his *The Freedom of a Christian* provide us with an important indication of his perspective:

> A Christian is a perfectly free lord of all, subject to none. A Christian is a perfectly dutiful servant of all, subject to all.[21]

Luther found the inspiration for these sentences in St. Paul's letters, Romans 13:8 and I Corinthians 9:19, respectively, but he quotes them together and puts them in a sequence that reveals the nature of Luther's faith.

In order to find out why Luther puts these two sentences together, let us first investigate the characteristics of his conversion. It was his attention to the suffering of Jesus that brought Luther to conversion. He became deeply aware that, for the sake of us sinful humans, the sinless Jesus became man and, as a human being, died on a cross: "In order that we may be saved, Christ lowered himself into the middle of our bodily life full of suffering and deigned to take our sins upon himself."[22]

The one who was originally suffering from sin, living in the flesh, and being tested by the feeling of being rejected by God was Luther himself, but Luther felt that Christ had already taken that suffering upon himself. He further became aware of the Will of the Father who made Christ suffer this way for the sake of us humans. Through this feeling that the pain of his own sins had already been suffered on God's side, Luther's idea of God changed drastically. And in this experience, Luther's faith became something utterly different from what it had been before his conversion: he had become aware that even the act of believing is something received from Christ by the Will of God:

> Without a doubt, faith does not come from your works or by your merits. It comes only from Jesus Christ who promised and bestowed it gratuitously.[23]

There is clearly a similarity here with the faith of Rennyo, who said, "It is the Tathāgata who graciously bestows faith." Luther further said, "Faith is the activity of God working within us."[24] But here I want to consider how Luther came to the state of mind wherein he could write:

> We conclude, therefore, that a Christian lives not in himself, but in Christ and in his neighbor. He lives in Christ through faith, in his neighbor through love. By faith he is caught up beyond himself into God. By love he descends beneath himself into his neighbor. Yet he always remains in God and in his love, as Christ says in John 1 [: 51], "Truly, truly I say to you, you will see heaven opened, and the angels of God ascending and descending upon the Son of man."[25]

We should pay special attention to the expressions "ascending [into God]" and "descending beneath himself." It can be considered that these point to something akin to the aspects of going and returning that Shinran pointed out. Once in possession of such a faith, Luther was able to be a free lord, beyond all the shackles of secular reality and, at the same time, to gladly become the servant or slave of all people. Shinran expressed this same state of mind, whereby one finds one's joy in becoming the servant of all, in the following words:

> ...first attaining Buddhahood quickly through saying the nenbutsu and, with the mind of great love and great compassion, freely benefiting sentient beings as one wishes.[26]

It is also along the same line as Rennyo's going all the way in "treasuring his flock of faithful."[27] And I think that this trait is precisely characteristic of the "faith only" type of faith.

Faith and Religious Community in Rennyo

Exactly like Shinran, Rennyo considered his faith as given by Amida Buddha. How then did Rennyo transmit this faith to other people, and how did he go about building his religious congregation?

Rennyo first of all endeavored to radically change his self-consciousness. Until his time there reigned among the patriarchs of the Honganji branch of Shinshū a strong consciousness of continuing the bloodline of Shinran, and thus a marked sense of belonging to an elite or nobility. A problematic issue with the Honganji family was that they tried to extend their teaching authority on the basis of that bloodline. Rennyo tried to rid himself of that sense of nobility and to lower himself to the level of the ordinary faithful.

In the *Kūzenki*, Rennyo's attitude is characterized in the following way:

> I am held up by the faithful and nurtured by them. Did not Shinran say, "I do not have a single disciple; I only have people that walk the way with me"?[28]

Shinran's idea that he did not have a single disciple is based on the "logic of faith," for there can be no question of a master–disciple relationship when faith is given by Amida himself and this faith is the same in himself and others. Rennyo followed this logic even in his daily life. Therein lay the first step in his practice of "returning."

After having changed his own self-awareness, Rennyo also endeavored to change the consciousness of the people. In the purity of his religious quest, Shinran had left the question of accepting the faith to the autonomous decision of the people: "Beyond this, whether you take up and accept the nenbutsu or whether you abandon it is for each of you to determine."[29] But Rennyo had seen more than his share of hardships due to the dire poverty of Honganji temple and his exposure to the ridicule of a stepmother after the early departure of his mother. He thereby learned about the secrets of the human heart and put himself on the side of the common people. And, on the strength of his understanding of the feelings of the common people, he endeavored to change their consciousness.

Rennyo is quoted as saying that "When people walking the same path gather together, they talk things out with each other. And people who express what is on their minds become aware of their feelings and, moreover, they are healed by the others,"[30] or "These people talk straight from the heart. When it is cold, they say that it is cold; when it is hot they call it hot."[31] Therefore, he strongly recommended "One should seek the company of fellow wayfarers and good teachers of the Way."[32] And he racked his brains like a mother who tries to keep her child on the right path by all sorts of means: "On occasion, Rennyo even served sake to people and gave them other things as well. They welcomed these with gratitude and he saw it as a good occasion to get close to people and speak about the Buddha Dharma."[33] Could not one say that, whereas Shinran was a fatherly person, Rennyo had a good deal of a mother about him? As a seeker of the Way, Shinran had paid most attention to the aspect of "going." Rennyo, on the other hand, in trying to change the consciousness of the people and using each occasion to benefit others, found his mission in the practice of "returning."

Rennyo found that one of the causes of Honganji's decline was the fact that Honganji abbots, who had originally been the guardians of Shinran's tomb, had come to imitate the solemn and authoritarian ways of Tendai abbots. He therefore burned all the paraphernalia of these practices to heat up his bath, including gorgeous robes and vestments, leaving behind only what pertained to the holy doctrine of the sect. He also did away with the heightened platform which his predecessors used as a throne to greet visitors. It is recorded that "At the time, Rennyo removed the heightened platform and made it into an ordinary seat on the same level as the seats of the faithful."[34] He must have done that because, in his view, "to put aside my social status and to sit together with you all"[35] corresponded to Shinran's true intent and constituted a practice of "returning."

Negatively, Rennyo burned the books that had no bearing on Jodōshinshū and, positively, he organized the readings of the religious services so that through them everybody would come into contact with Shinran's mind, with Amida Buddha's mind. With that as his aim, he made the nenbutsu and Shinran's Japanese hymns into a set and added to these the letters he himself had written. Moreover, Rennyo traveled indefatigably to spread the faith. The grooves etched into his feet by straw sandals became symbols of his fervent propagation activity: "The traces, where the straw cords had deeply bitten into his feet, were often pointed to and were shown to all the brethren even at the moment of his death."[36]

He was also active with his hands, continually writing the Name of Amida. He kept on writing, "even when his body was ravaged by old age, his hands trembled, and his sight had become dim."[37] His was a whole-hearted practice of "returning" that "only desired others to gain faith."[38] He wanted to "throw away his very body for the sake of the faithful."[39]

The same "returning" consciousness also transpired in his letters. Shinran's prose is impeccable and virile; in Rennyo's prose one finds repetitions, passages that are long-winded, and texts in which he tried to make himself understood with disregard of the grammar: "As to my letters, their prose is strange and the grammar is bad, but my only concern in writing them was: 'Oh, if only I could lead even a single soul to faith!'"[40] This attitude gradually deepened and developed into a spirit of "cherishing the faithful." In welcoming faithful who came to the Honganji temple from outlying districts, for example, he went so far as to take care of their meals. The record tells us about a meal that he served to people that came from afar: "It was so salty that there are no words for it."[41]

Acts of "returning" must reach the inner depths of the hearts of people, and Rennyo strove with everything he possessed to realize that ideal. It was out of these thoughts and acts of "returning" that the religious congregation was born. Through this practice, the "desolate"[42] Honganji started to shape gradually into a community with faith as its bond.

Faith and Community in Luther

Luther wrote:

> Yet he [the Christian] remains in this mortal life on earth. In this life he must control his own body and have dealings with men. Here the work begins; here a man cannot enjoy leisure.[43]

If so, what is to be done?

> Although the Christian is thus free from all works, he ought in his liberty to empty himself, take upon himself the form of a servant, and to deal in every way with his neighbor as he sees that God through Christ has dealt and still deals with him.[44]

It is here that the practice or implementation of "returning" begins.

Luther made the following statement: "The pope is not the vicar of Christ glorified but of Christ crucified. Now the Romanists make the pope a vicar of the glorified Christ in heaven."[45] In my understanding, Luther is criticizing here the Roman Catholic Church for traditionally neglecting the aspect of "returning" in the life of faith. He is pointing out that this Church does not show a sufficient awareness of the figure and the love of the Christ who, although entitled to an exalted position, freely appeared as an ordinary human being and moreover died on a cross:

> Christ needs a vicar in the form of a servant, the form in which he went about on earth, working, preaching, suffering, and dying.[46]
>
> Compare them with each other—Christ and the pope. Christ washed his disciples' feet and dried them but the disciples never washed his feet (John 13:4–16). The pope, as though he were higher than Christ, turns that about and allows his feet to be kissed as a great favor.[47]

For Luther, who believed that faith is something given by God, the distinctions in social status, high and low, nobleman and commoner, had ceased to exist. In God's eye, high or low status does not enter the picture when it comes to people who have received the faith. By the fact that all participate in the same salvation, class distinctions fall away completely. At the same time, all people gifted with faith have the vocation of serving God and being in the service of their fellow human beings. All have become priests. In the view of Luther, who believed in salvation by faith alone, a spiritual and internal community of equal believers is the origin and basis of the Church.

According to Catholicism, Christ himself established a visible Church to continue administering the saving deeds of the God who became a visible human being. This Church is then a community of believers that is endowed with a system of religious leaders instituted by Christ himself: pope, bishops, and priests. Over against this, Luther saw the true Church as a community of believers, linked by faith and invisible to the human eye. He did not recognize therein any ecclesiastical authority that could impose itself on the faithful from the outside.

However, also in the case of the Church it is true that what lives inwardly shows itself outwardly. A spiritual communion of believers also takes on the form of an actual congregation. In other words, there is no need for a visible Church founded by Christ, as Catholicism envisages things, but a visible Church as the community of the people gifted with faith may, of course, take shape. Thus, while Catholicism and Luther both recognized the existence of the Church, their respective ideas on its inner nature diverged greatly.

Anyway, it is clear that Luther conceived of the religious community or Church on the level of "from faith thus flow forth love and joy in the Lord, and from love a joyful, willing, and free mind that serves one's neighbor willingly."[48] For him, the reality of the Church is based on a spirit of service, whereby people, full of gratitude for their salvation, try to turn their neighbor toward God as well; it is based on a "returning" practice that endeavors to lower the self and to make it the servant of all.

After his conversion, Luther worked at changing himself: he started to seek the company of his neighbor and was often found talking and laughing with people. He now declared that "God had created human beings for companionship," considered solitariness a sin, and rejected solitude. In his family home he gathered people and chatted with them, adopted orphans and cared for them, took in sick people, and protected people who were oppressed. The Luther who had left the monastery made the family home take its place as a gathering spot for people and a center of education. To clerics who felt a need for the other sex he recommended marriage. And once he himself was married and children were born, he had no qualms about washing the diapers and hanging them up to dry. Rennyo, incidentally, is also said to have helped with the diapers.

In short, both Luther and Rennyo had placed themselves among the common people and had put their eye, not on the high ground of pope and clergy, but on the "naked human being" with its afflictions and shackles to flesh and self-love. Precisely there they found the aspect of "going," whereby the eye is taken upward into the love of God and, at the same time, the aspect of "returning," which makes the eye continually shift to the flesh of human beings.

For people who could neither read nor write, Luther authored a short, simple *Little Catechism* that people could learn by heart after having it read to them—the same thing Rennyo did through his letters. Luther looked at the community of the faithful not with the eyes of the pope but with the eyes of the crucified Jesus. To borrow R. Bainton's words, for Luther:

> The true Church was a Church of people that are continually forgiven; a Church known only to God; a Church appearing here and there on earth; a small and persecuted flock, ordinarily hidden from view; in a word, a Church in diaspora, bound together only by the bond of the Spirit.[49]

Conclusion

Human beings are forever shackled to the flesh, however, and Luther came to be betrayed by the flesh of the very farmers that he tried to protect. He was equally betrayed by the nobility to whose flesh he had to submit in order to protect the farmers. The invisible Church may be formed inside the souls of people but, when it comes to forming the visible Church, one must throw oneself into the storm of the mundane power struggle and its calculation of gain and loss.

Rennyo too made compromises for the sake of his faithful, but Luther's case was worse: for the sake of the farmers who betrayed him he had to compromise with the power of the nobility. It was a painful ordeal for Luther: whichever way he turned, his name was bound to suffer. The Honganji congregation, built up by Rennyo, would eventually be trampled upon and twisted out of shape by the power of the Tokugawa feudal regime, but at least in Rennyo's own lifetime it was able, albeit in the face of many difficulties, to form unique social structures, such as the "temple villages" (jinaichô). Luther, on the other hand, was obliged to leave the path of Church building to the prince electors (Kurfuersten). This was a tragedy due to the conditions of the age. Still, even when involved such a tragedy, his attitude of building the Church somehow out of the joy of a practice of "returning" is a phenomenon worthy of our attention, particularly with regard to the question of the inner relationship between faith and religious community.

In this perspective, it is worth stressing that, in the type of religion that sees "faith only" as the central point, the subject of the propagation of the faith and of the building of the religious community is none other than Amida Buddha or God. These activities therefore have a different meaning from that in religions in which both "the seeking of enlightenment above" and the "benefiting of sentient beings below" are thought of as having the priests as their subjects.

Luther said that "Christ needs a vicar in the form of a servant, the form in which he went about on earth, working, preaching, suffering, and dying," and, in accordance with this belief, he made himself the servant of all. Rennyo threw away his social position for the sake of the faithful and in his letters described the attitude of Shinran as "only doing his best to be a vicar [ondaikan] of the Tathāgata"[50]

In this attitude found in both Luther and Shinran we find, I think, the kind of link between faith and community building that is proper to religions of "absolute Other-Power" and "Faith alone."

Notes

1 From the Kyōgyōshinshō, at SSZ 2.45. English translation in CWS I.72.

2 Martin Luther, "The Freedom of a Christian" (Von der Freiheit eines Christenmenschen), in Three Treatises, trans. and ed. Martin Jacobs, A. T. W. Steinhäuser, and W. A. Lambert, 2nd rev. ed. (Philadelphia: Fortress Press, 1970), 309.

3 Shinran Shōnin goshōsoku shū, at SSZ 2.697; CWS 1.560.

4 Yuishinshō mon'i, at SSZ 2.646; CWS 1.459.

5 SSZ 2.647.

6 Shōzōmatsu wasan, at SSZ 2.527; CWS 1.422.

7 Kyōgyōshinshō, at SSZ 2.47; CWS 1. 77.

8 SSZ 2.48; CWS 1.79.

9 Tannishō No. 6, SSZ 2.776; CWS 1.664.

10 Letters 5:2. RSI 472; SSZ 3.500–501. Translation from Rogers, 243–244.

11 Letters 5:3. RSI 473; SSZ 3.501; Rogers, 244.

12 Ibid.

13 This Rennyo letter is not found in the standard collection but is at RSI 47; SSS 2.138.

14 *Letters* 5:1. RSI 470; SSZ 3.500; Rogers, 242.

15 *Letters* 5:2. RSI 471; SSZ 3.500; Rogers, 242.

16 *Tannishō* 9. SSZ 2.777; CWS 665.

17 *Tannishō* 9. Translation modified from CWS 665.

18 *Kikigaki* 102. SSZ 3.557.

19 *Kikigaki* 103; SSZ 2.557.

20 *Kikigaki* 205; SSZ 2.582–583. Translation from Rogers, 189, n. 35.

21 *Von der Freyheyt eynisz Christen menschen*, at Martin Luther, D. *Martin Luther's Werke; kritische Gesamtausgabe*, Weimarer Ausgabe (ed.) (Graz: Akademische Druck-u. Verlagsanstalt, 1964–1966), 7.21. For English translation, see Jacobs et al., "The Freedom of a Christian," 277.

22 *Tessaradicas consolatoria pro laborantibus et oneratis*. at D. *Martin Luther's Werke; kritische Gesamtausgabe*, 6.104f.

23 *Von den guten Werken*. Ibid. 216.

24 *Vorrede auf die Epistel S. Pauli an die Römer*. Ibid. 7.10.

25 *Von der Freyheyt eynisz Christen menschen*, 7.38. "The Freedom of a Christian," 309.

26 *Tannishō* 4. SSZ 2.775; CWS 1.663.

27 *Honganji sahō no shidai* 121. At Ōtani Chōjun, ed., *Rennyo Shōnin zenshū* (Tokyo: Kawade Shobō Shinsha, 1989), 245. SSS 2.579.

28 *Kūzenki* 94. RSG 36.

29 *Tannishō* 2; CWS 1.662.

30 *Jitsugo kyūki* 19; RSG 75.

31 *Jitsugo kyūki* 139; RSG 105.

32 *Kikigaki* 150; SSZ 3.568.

33 *Jitsugo kyūki* 148; RSG 108.

34 *Honganji sahō no shidai* 43. *Rennyo Shōnin zenshū* 220; SSS 2.568.

35 *Kikigaki* 40; SSZ 3.543.

36 *Jitsugoki* 14; RSG 148.

37 *Kikigaki* 229; SSZ 3.589.

38 Ibid.

39 Ibid.

40 *Rennyo shōnin go-ichigoki* 100; SSS 2.523.

41 *Honganji sahō no shidai* 96. *Rennyo Shōnin zenshū* 237; SSS 2.576.

42 *Jitsugoki* 8; RSG 144.

43 "The Freedom of a Christian," 294.

44 Ibid., pp. 303–304.

45 "*An den christlichen Adel deutscher Nation*," in *Three treatises*, p. 27.

46 Ibid., p. 54.

47 Ibid., p. 56.

48 Jacobs et al., "The Freedom of a Christian," 304.

49 Roland H. Bainton, *Here I Stand: A Life of Martin Luther* (New York: Abingdon-Cokesbury Press, 1950), 310.

50 *Letters* 1:1. RSI 55; SSZ 3.402; Rogers, 142.

16

WILLIAM R. LAFLEUR

Dancing into Freedom

Rennyo and Religion

For many of us involved in the study of the religions of Japan, Rennyo has until now been more of a reputation than a reality. Although we have had access to important essays by scholars such as Stanley Weinstein and translations done by the late Minor Rogers, Rennyo has remained for many of us a figure, however towering within history, still wrapped in a mist. Therefore, the opportunity for many of us to try to penetrate that mist is welcome indeed. I am not at all a scholar versed in the materials pertinent to understanding Rennyo and his times, but I am appreciative of the opportunity to try to see what I can see of Rennyo. Since my interests are in literature as much as in religion, I will briefly explore an aspect of how these two come together in a portion of Rennyo's writing.

If there is one thing that has impressed me in reading Rennyo's *Letters,* it is the sense of religious *joy* expressed there. It is a joy of the mind and heart but, if I read the letters correctly, it goes into bodily expression as well. I have been especially attracted to the first letter of the first fascicle (I-1), where Rennyo takes a poem from the *Senjūshō*[1] and transforms its secular meaning into one fully in agreement with his own absolute confidence of rebirth in the Pure Land. The original poem, perhaps written by a courtier many centuries earlier, is quoted by Rennyo as follows:[2]

うれしさを	ureshisa wo
むかしはそでに	mukashi wa sode ni
つつみけり	tsutsumikeri
こよひは身にも	koyohi wa mi ni mo
あまりぬるかな	amarinuru kana

My own attempt at a translation of this poem results in the following:

The joy long bound
up within me and the sleeves
of my kimono, is a joy

that tonight flows through
every part of my body.

We cannot be certain about the circumstances of the composition of this poem, but what I find fascinating is that Rennyo quotes it and then quickly goes on to relate it to his own strong belief in the Pure Land. He concludes this section by saying:

Because of this we are so overjoyed that we feel like
dancing—hence the joy is "more than I can contain."

I suspect that one of the reasons I am so drawn to this is that it shows how the classical Japanese poem, the *waka* of thirty-one syllables, can be marvelously versatile. It can be flexible and reusable by being moved into new contexts and significations. Here a courtly poem by an unknown poet has been transformed by a powerful religious thinker into one of deep spiritual significance. Rennyo takes what originally had been an an expression of emotional pleasure, perhaps even one with an erotic dimension, and turns it into an expression of religious exhilaration. If the original poet was making a point about his joy becoming one that filled his physical body, Rennyo says it is the reality of the Pure Land that exhilarates him bodily—so much so that he *wants to dance*!

There is an explanation for why I find this so interesting. I have spent much time during the past few years studying that part of early medieval Japanese Buddhism that is expressed in the idea of the *rokudō*, the six paths or locations wherein beings can be reborn because of karma. Although I am not among those who think that whatever is medieval will necessarily be "dark" whereas what is modern will be "light" and happy, the descriptions of the *rokudō* in medieval Japan are not exactly what one would call "joyful." The overwhelming focus is on pain and suffering that beings will encounter if they violate the moral code of Buddhism. We find lots of sermons, *setsuwa*, and *emaki* describing transmigration through the painful paths—hell, hungry ghosts, animals, *asura*, human kind, and heavenly beings—but the glimpses of religious joy are very few and far between.

That is why reading Rennyo has been so refreshing for me. Although there is religious depth in Rennyo, there is also a lightness of spirit. In reading his *Letters*, I feel like I myself have in some sense been allowed to emerge from the *rokudō*, or at least from the study of it. This feeling is probably not unconnected to the fact that even in the medieval period the Pure Land was conceived of as a location that transcended the six paths of the *rokudō*.

I wish here, however, to pursue another point, and it involves looking more closely at the poem cited by Rennyo. Its central image is important. A person, probably a courtier, says that in the past his joy [*ureshisa*] had been contained or even kept hidden within himself. He writes of its having been "bound up within his kimono sleeves" (*sode ni tsutsumikeri*). But all that has changed—dramatically. During the "present evening" (*koyohi wa*) that joy, formerly bottled up, has literally "overflowed" (*amarinuru*) in and through the "body" (*mi ni mo*) of the poet. It has, we assume, taken on visible, noticeable, outward form. His whole body felt it. Rennyo's interpretation, correct I think, is that the poet is hinting that it makes him feel like dancing—a characteristic way in which *bodily* experienced joy is given expression.

I would lay emphasis on the contrast here. It is between what, on one hand, had been contained, even constrained or hidden, but now, on the other hand, has been given freedom to find uninhibited, outward, visible, even bodily expression. The poet's language makes a contrast between something wrapped up in the sleeves of a kimono and something that can be hidden no longer, something that is now "overflowingly" overt.

The linkage between the deepest reason for joy (*ureshisa*) and this new movement away from "hiddenness" and toward "openness" in religious things is, I think, the core of what happens in the "new" Buddhism seen in the development from Hōnen to Shinran and from Shinran to Rennyo. Although latent and covert in the "older" forms of Japanese Buddhism, this joy had always mixed with and was constrained by a powerful element of *fear*, especially an anxiety about accumulating so much bad karma that a miserable rebirth lay in the future. And, since I have been reading texts (including *setsuwa*) and looking carefully at *emaki* which express *rokudō shisō*, I have the impression that the fear element had often been much stronger in the earlier Buddhism than was its complement, the element of joy. In fact, such anxieties had loomed so large in the prior religious experience of many ordinary people—probably especially those whose livelihood made the taking of animal life unavoidable—that when they came to Shinran and Rennyo, they had some trouble believing the good news they were now hearing about a Buddhism that was fear-free. It was for most people literally too good to be believable.

There is also, I think, a deep and logical link between this *emphasis*—not entirely a new element but at least a new emphasis in Japanese Buddhism—on what is *open and unhidden*, on the one hand, and, on the other, the willingness of Shinran and Rennyo to treat others not as disciples but as companions. In book one of the *Kikigaki* Rennyo asserts, "I put aside my social status and sit with you all"[3] Once religion is no longer a matter of the manipulation of miracles and mysteries by so-called "experts," the need to distinguish sharply between those experts and the ordinary person is dissolved.

This is the beauty of what we find in the letter of Bunmei 3.7.15 (1471) cited earlier, the one in which concealed joy is referred to as having now found outward expression. In that letter Rennyo takes note of the fact that Shinran preferred to refer to those around him *not* as "disciples" (*deshi*) but as "companions and fellow practitioners" (*dōbō dōgyō*).

There are many things that the tradition of Shinran and Rennyo can contribute to the developed understanding and practice of Buddhism in Europe and America, but if one of special importance can be singled out, it would be the important connection between (1) religious experience shaped by joy rather than fear, (2) the emphasis on openness rather than on secret practices and traditions, and (3) a community in which persons are regarded as "fellow practitioners" rather than one divided between those in authority (the experts) and those expected to listen and obey—between *sensei* (teacher) and *deshi* (disciple).

One of the most severe problems faced by Buddhist groups in the West has been that of some Buddhist teachers, both Asian and Western, taking advantage of their revered positions and bringing harm to ordinary practitioners. Although what is sometimes called "the *guru syndrome*" is not, I think, a necessary part of traditional Buddhism, many in the West who practice Buddhism seem eager to treat their teachers not as "fellow practitioners" but as all-wise and all-powerful teachers. Unfortunately, some in positions of authority have at times encouraged that attitude.

Not just Japan but the entire world of religion has something to learn from what happened when the "guru syndrome" went into its most extreme form, namely, what took place within Aum Shinri-kyō. That terrible event is something from which we should all learn.

But the problem is not just one of power-hungry, egotistical persons usurping authority by and for themselves. It is also a problem of many people far too easily and readily *abandoning their own responsibility* to be careful and making themselves prey to manipulation, ready to ascribe all authority in religious matters to another person who assumes a position of "authority."

I was in Japan during the late spring and summer of 1995, when the details about the Aum Shinrikyō cult were being made clear to the media and the public. I found myself thinking about what Fyodor Dostoyevsky (1821–1881) in his novel *The Brothers Karamazov* had written about the dangers lurking in the human psyche in matters of religion.[4] This comes out especially in Ivan's narrative about the Grand Inquisitor. Ivan's story within the novel is fiction intended to reveal a profound fact about humankind and religion. It is set in sixteenth-century Europe—less than a century after the death of Rennyo in Japan and roughly contemporaneous with the suppression of *ikkō ikki*. In Europe people were being killed, often burned at the stake (the infamous *auto de fe*), for having what others considered to be unorthodox religious views. In those centuries authorities within the Catholic Church often authorized the killing of "heretics" but so too did certain groups associated with the Protestant Reformation. It was a terrible time in Europe.

In Dostoyevsky's fiction Jesus returns to this world and is severely disappointed at what he sees happening within his Church. It does not please him to see simple Christians adding pieces of firewood to the fires that burn heretics. But when he becomes critical of such things, he himself is put in prison by the cardinal who serves as the grand inquisitor. This interrogator puts the following question to Jesus: "Why did you come back here to meddle in our affairs?" He goes on to explain to Jesus that the freedom which the savior had brought to human kind had turned out to be too difficult for them to comprehend and use. He reproaches Jesus with these words:

> There is nothing more alluring to man than freedom of conscience, but there is nothing more tormenting either.

He continues:

> We have corrected your great work and have based it on *miracle, mystery, and authority*. And men rejoiced that they were once more led like sheep and that the terrible gift which had brought them so much suffering had at last been lifted from their hearts."[5]

In the end Jesus, whose cause has been completely undermined, is led away.

Dostoyevsky's point, most commentators agree, is that responsibility in these things is not only usurped but also often simply *handed over* by people who are afraid of freedom. While the issue is articulated in his story as a situation within the Catholic Church, Dostoyevsky's insight is one into a problem faced by *all* religions and religious organizations. The Protestant Church in Europe and America has not been able to avoid it, and I have the impression that even Japan's Pure Land and True Pure Land schools of Buddhism did not always escape it either. What Dostoyevsky forces us to see is the dark side of the psychology of religion but also the roots of political totalitarianism in modern societies. Freedom, including freedom in religious matters, is a fine-sounding word. But far too often people given that freedom find it too difficult to use and then sell it cheaply to get other things that they want—nice, cozy mental security most of all. It is then that they can be "brainwashed" or led about like mindless sheep who follow, without question, what they are being told or commanded to do. It is then that they willingly add firewood to the bonfire of a heretic, dress up like "military monks" (*sōhei*) to attack a rival temple, carry on a religious crusade or war, murder doctors or nurses who work in abortion clinics, or open cans of sarin in a Tokyo subway to hasten the end of the world. Our so-called "modernity," we must realize, has not meant that we have shaken off these dangers.

Our capacity to be easily captured by "miracle, mystery, and authority" is, according to Dostoyevsky, what gives us the most trouble. "Miracle, mystery, and authority" form the triad of things of which we need to be cautious. That is why I have suggested here that there is so much to be gained by paying close attention to Rennyo's *Letters*. In them we find an eminently valuable model, one for today as well as the past. For in Rennyo's writing, so-called "miracle" is unimportant; what matters is not a demonstration of supernatural powers but rather the joy available to those who realize the underlying structure of reality. For Rennyo "mystery," and especially "mystification," have no importance in religion. Rennyo asks that we take what was formerly hidden—comparable to things wrapped in the sleeves of a kimono—and make these things "overflowingly" clear and obvious in our world for all to see. And, third, he sees that real authority does not lie in those who are eager to be seen and treated like "authority figures." Rennyo would give up his own special seat and join, like Shinran, in the regard for others as "companions" and "fellow practitioners." These things are connected. There is in them an internal logic of insight and practice and we do well to keep that in mind. They may be needed today as much as ever before.

Notes

1 Nishio Kōichi, ed., *Senjūshō* (Tokyo: Iwanami Bunko, 1970), 242. The *Senjūshō* is a *setsuwa* collection dating to the early thirteenth century whose compilation is traditionally attributed to Saigyō (1118–1190). On Saigyō, see William R. LaFleur, *Awesome Nightfall: The Life, Times, and Poetry of Saigyo* (Somerville, Mass.: Wisdom Publications, 2003).

2 SSZ 3.402. This letter appears in *Rennyo Shōnin ibun,* 56, but in that edition the poem and its commentary are missing.

3 *Kikigaki* 40. SSZ 3.543.

4 Feodor Dostoyevsky, *The Brothers Karamazov,* trans. Constance Garnett (New York: Grosset & Dunlap [1900?], repr. New York: Dutton, 1927 et al.).

5 Ibid., 301.

17

RUBEN L. F. HABITO

Primal Vow and Its Contextualization

Rennyo's Legacy, and Some Tasks for Our Times

A t a symposium at Harvard University Ōtani Kōshin, current leader of the Nishi-Honganji branch of Jōdoshinshū (Shinshū), described a vital task of the followers of Pure Land Buddhism, in his Opening Address, entitled "Shin Buddhism and Christianity: Textual and Contextual Translation":

> Pure Land Buddhism traditionally emphasizes the way of life in each era. That is to say, the teaching of Amida Buddha's Primal Vow must be translated into the emerging context of each new age....Even in Japan at present, the concrete expressions of Buddhist truth, such as the Primal Vow, Pure Land, and *shinjin*, need to be translated and adapted to the contemporary context.[1]

With this statement, Ōtani gave an apt description of the challenge faced not only by Pure Land Buddhists, but also by every religious community in our day, that is, the representation of their core religious teachings within the emerging context of each epoch.

This chapter considers three points in regard to the translation and contextualization of the Buddhist teaching of Amida's Primal or Original Vow (*hongan*) for our times. These are questions that pertain to (1) the relationship of the community of believers to the wider human community, specifically to adherents of other religious traditions, (2) the relationship of the same community to political authority, that is, the state, and (3) the understanding of the religious message on ultimate destiny as it throws light on human behavior in this worldly life.

Rather than being a historical study highlighting specific elements in the life and thought of Rennyo, this chapter takes Rennyo's legacy as a starting point for reflecting on current and future tasks of the adherents of the Honganji communities both in Japan and in the larger global scene, focusing on these three questions.

Rennyo's Legacy

Born more than two centuries after Shinran, Rennyo is looked up to as a religious genius who made Shinran's teachings accessible to the common people, who brought together the followers of Jōdoshinshū under a powerful religious organization that became a bastion of stability during a turbulent period of Japan's history. His pastoral *Letters*, later enshrined as part of the Holy scriptures of Shinshū followers (*Shinshū seiten*)[2] together with Shinran's writings, are characterized by directness and simplicity of style that translated the core of Pure Land teaching in terms that ordinary people of his day could identify with.

One scholar describes Rennyo's achievement as "manifesting Amida's vow, the transcendent, with the transmission of the teaching ensured by the strenghtening and development of the Honganji as an institution."[3] Rennyo's tireless efforts to combat misleading teachings, including mingling with common folk as well as preaching and writing, led to the consolidation of the Honganji community as a powerful religious institution that gave ordinary men and women a sense of belonging in this world and assured them of Birth in the Pure Land in the hereafter. In other words, he made Amida's Primal Vow (the transcendent dimension) manifest in the mundane lives of people of his day (the historical dimension) through the mediation of the religious institution of Honganji.[4]

In this light a question arises: How did Rennyo address the issue of how to relate to people with different religious beliefs and also to relate to political authority?

Passages from his *Letters* offer us a glimpse. For example, *Letters* 2:3 delineates the following three items.

> *Item: Do not slander other teachings and other sects.
> *Item: Do not belittle the various kami and buddhas and the bodhisattvas.
> *Item: Receive faith [*shinjin*] and attain Birth in the fulfilled land.
> Those who do not observe the points in the above three items and take them as fundamental, storing them deep in their hearts, are to be forbidden access to this mountain (community).[5]

The letter goes on to explain that buddhas and bodhisattvas "appear provisionally as kami to save sentient beings in whatever way possible" and that "even if we do not worship the kami in particular, since all are encompassed when we rely solely on one Buddha, Amida, we give credence [to them] even though we do not rely on them in particular."[6]

A statement in *Letters* 3:10 follows up on the same theme:

> *Item: Do not make light of shrines.
> *Item: Do not make light of the buddhas, bodhisattvas, or temples [enshrining deities].
> *Item: Do not slander other sects or other teachings.
> *Item: Do not slight the provincial military governors or local land stewards.
> *Item: The interpretation of the Buddha's Dharma in this province [Echizen] is wrong; therefore turn to the right teaching.
> *Item: Other-Power faith as established in our tradition must be decisively settled deep within our own minds.[7]

Again an explanation is offered: "When we take refuge in the compassionate Vow of the one Buddha Amida, the thought of similarly entrusting ourselves [to the kami] is contained in that... simply realize that when we take refuge in Amida Tathāgata single-heartedly and steadfastly, all the other buddhas' wisdom and virtue come to be encompassed within the one body, Amida [and so become ours].[8]

On the item regarding provincial military governors and local land stewards, the letter enjoins Pure Land followers to "deal carefully with fixed yearly tributes and payments to officials and, besides that, to take [the principles of] humanity and justice as fundamental."[9]

Rennyo was writing to his followers in a context of religious and political turmoil, and his injunctions to them to avoid slandering the kami and other buddhas and bodhisattvas were meant to spare them from needless and conflict with adherents of other religious beliefs. His injunctions to be subservient to political authority indicate his own stance vis-à-vis the *ikkō ikki* uprisings of Shinshū followers against political authority current in his day, and were likewise meant to protect his followers from needless persecution and harassment.[10]

It is to be noted that in giving these injunctions, Rennyo made no attempt to invoke Shinran's authority, such as by quoting a text or saying from the Master. In fact, he was departing from Shinran's own position in two important matters: the attitude of followers regarding the veneration of the kami, and that toward political rulers.[11] He was simply making pronouncements from his authoritative position as leader of the Honganji community, with the provision that those who did not follow his injunctions were to be forbidden access to the community, in other words, were to be excommunicated.

Rennyo's central concern was to ensure that Shinshū followers would be able to live free from needless conflict with followers of other religious teachings as well as with political authorities, and could thereby devote themselves to their mundane tasks empowered by faith (*shinjin*) in Amida's Primal vow, in anticipation of "that most important matter of Birth in the Pure Land in the hereafter" (*goshō no ichidaiji*). Rennyo thus translated Pure Land teachings derived from Shinran into terms that addressed people's needs during a time of social and political turmoil, broadening the popular base and consolidating the Honganji community into a highly organized and hierarchical structure in the process.

Needless to say, from a historical perspective, the implications of his practical decisions for the future development of the Honganji institution are controversial, especially in light of the stance taken by leaders and members of the Honganji communities during Japan's expansionist and militaristic eras. The official Honganji policy came to be enshrined in the Testament left by Kōnyo (1798–1871), twentieth head priest of Nishi Honganji, which defined the relationship of Honganji members to the state in terms of subservience and guardianship.[12]

In our own day, the direct recipients of Rennyo's legacy, that is, followers of the Honganji tradition (inclusive of both the Eastern and Western branches), are faced with a task not unlike Rennyo's: to bring the message of Amida's Original Vow into the context of our age. In this light, the three questions cited call for renewed consideration and constructive reflection. First, how are Honganji followers to relate to the wider community and to members of other religious traditions? Second, how are they to relate to political authority? Third, how are they to understand Rennyo's emphasis on the "important matter of (Birth in the Pure land in) the afterlife" in a way that throws light on their worldly tasks? These are indeed major issues that any religious community seeking to maintain its viability cannot evade; they are questions that leaders and adherents, especially scholars and theologians (*kyōgakusha*) of the Shinshū tradition, are called upon to address.

What follows are reflective considerations of these issues, from a critical yet sympathetic outsider's standpoint, offering elements from the history of the Roman Catholic tradition as reference points.

Three Questions: Comparative Perspectives

There is textual evidence to the effect that Shinran, grounded in his central message of the absolute primacy of an entrusting faith in Amida's vow, took a critical stance regarding the veneration of kami and also regarding political authority. Two centuries later, Rennyo, facing a different context, while also maintaining the absolute primacy of entrusting faith in Amida's vow and being concerned with the well-being and the consolidation of the Honganji followers, is seen as taking a more compromising stance regarding veneration of the kami and toward political authority. The differences in their standpoints on these two key questions cannot and need not be whitewashed; they need to be understood and analyzed in light of the complex sociopolitical issues of their respective times.

Shinran's writings as well as records of his sayings to his disciples (such as the *Tannishō*) indicate that he placed emphasis not so much on looking forward to Birth in the Pure Land in the afterlife, but on living a life in the here and now filled with gratitude for Amida' s boundless compassion, expressed in the recitation of Amida's name (nenbutsu). The devotee who lives in this way is already assured of Birth in the Pure Land and need not be anxious about this matter, being then freed to turn to worldly tasks with assurance and peace of mind. Rennyo, on the other hand, living in an age of uncertainty and turmoil, repeatedly advised Pure Land followers to focus on the most important matter of all, Birth in the Pure Land in the afterlife, dissuading them from needless involvement in the political and social conflicts that marked their times.

What appears, then, is that there is a marked ambivalence, or even tension, within Shinshū tradition, regarding possible responses to the three questions: (1) how to relate to the wider community of nonadherents, (2) how to relate to political authority, and (3) how to understand the message of Birth in the Pure Land in relation to life on this earth. In other words, Shinran and Rennyo appear to be on different sides on these three issues. Giving due regard to this tension and appreciating the complexity of the issues involved would be essential for Shinshū followers in working toward a viable response to these three questions that avoids simplistic approaches, such as taking a few passages from Shinran's or Rennyo's writings as "proof texts" of one's preconceived position on the matter.

In other words, in addition to the appreciation of the religious significance of entrusting faith in Amida's Primal Vow, careful historical investigation, as well as an understanding of current sociopolitical and other factors, would be prerequisites for a viable position in response to the three questions. The hermeneutical endeavors toward arriving at such a viable position would be involved in the contextualization of the core message of the tradition.

In this connection, aspects of the history of the Roman Catholic Church, which began as a small community of believers united in the conviction of having received a message of eternal salvation in their encounter with Jesus Christ, and which has come to be a powerful hierarchical and highly structured world religious institution, come to the fore as points of comparison. Again without going into detail, I will simply indicate some elements that may provide reference for reflection on the three issues at hand, not so much to extol this religious tradition as a model, but precisely to be able to learn from its failures as well as its successes on these three counts.

On the Question of Other Religions

For centuries, the official stance of the Roman Catholic Church vis-à-vis members of other religious traditions was ensconced in the formula *extra ecclesiam nulla salus* (no salvation outside the church).[13] This standpoint has been the basis of exclusivistic and triumphalistic attitudes on the part of members of this Church. However, even since the second century, theologians such as Justin Martyr (ca. 100–165 C.E.) and Clement of Alexandria (ca. 150) have been noted for taking a more inclusive stance that recognized the workings of God's grace beyond the historical confines of the institutional Church.[14]

In recent decades the Second Vatican Council (1962–1965), as an authoritative source of Church teaching, gave guidelines for the Roman Catholic community on basic questions regarding the Church's identity and mission, and it issued official documents that took this more inclusive stance. These documents recognized the distinctive values and truths taught in other religions, yet in a way that did not compromise the Church's traditional position on the absolute nature of God's message of salvation in Jesus Christ.[15] Guided and inspired by the open stance taken by the Second Vatican Council, more and more Catholics have continued to reflect on the question of how to relate to members of other religious traditions in an atmosphere of dialogue and, shedding the triumphalistic and exclusivistic attitudes of past epochs, are able come to this kind of dialogue with humility, open to learning from and cooperating with members of other traditions on matters of religious import.[16]

As Catholics (and Christians of other denominations as well) meet with and relate in positive ways to members of other religious traditions, they find themselves confronted with a basic dilemma: that of being truly open to dialogue with and learning from others while also being faithful to the core message of their own tradition, which affirms that there is an absolute and definitive, universal message of salvation given in and through Jesus Christ that one is called to share with all people. The dilemma has become the basis for differing positions within the Roman Catholic (and wider Christian) community, depending on which side of the dilemma one places weight on. Thus we find varieties of exclusivism, inclusivism, and pluralism, or a combination of these, among possible Christian positions vis-à-vis other religious traditions.[17]

On Relating to Political Authority

The early Church began as a small community of believers who were subjected to persecution by political authorities due to their refusal to worship the gods recognized and prescribed by the Roman Empire. Strengthened by the pronouncement of their Founder that "my kingdom is not of this world" (John 18:36), they regarded God's reign as superior to all political authority on earth and thus were able to keep themselves at a critical distance from political power.

However, with the conversion of Constantine in the fourth century, and the subsequent promulgation of Christianity as the official religion of the Roman Empire, the lines of demarcation between religious and political authority came to be blurred. The position of the bishop of Rome, the seat of the successor of Peter, leader of the apostles, was earlier regarded as *primus inter pares* (first among equals) in the college of bishops, and later evolved into the institution of the papacy, which from the medieval age of Europe onward took on absolute authority as God's representative on earth. A look at the different ways the papacy and hierarchical officials of the Roman Catholic church played roles in the political history of Europe, and vice versa, at the ways political rulers exercised power and influence in religious and Church matters, will show the complexity of the issue of the relationship of the religious community to political authority.

In recent decades the issue of the religious community's relation to political authority has been raised in a fresh way by liberation theologians from Latin America and Asia, as well as by those who disagree with them. Different thinkers present a wide spectrum of positions on the question of relating to particular governments, including outright opposition to the point of armed stuggle, critical collaboration, and co-option through participation or through noninvolvement.

What can be said in sum, therefore, is that there is a complexity of issues in the various positions taken vis-à-vis political authority in the history of the Roman Catholic Church, and that there is no simple formula for presenting "the official Catholic position." Disagreements among Catholics on how to relate to political authority stem from the different stances that can be taken based on differences in the way God's reign is understood as relating to this earthly domain. These differences have manifested themselves in the very history of the Catholic Church itself, with Catholics taking positions on opposite sides of the spectrum vis-à-vis social and political issues.

The Matter of the Afterlife

A key aspect of the Christian message lies in Jesus' proclamation of the coming of the Reign of God (Mark 1:15, etc.). Again, this Reign of God has been understood in various ways: some have seen it as the proclamation of the establishment of political authority with divine sanction through the coming of God's Anointed One, and others have taken it as a message that pertains entirely to the afterlife. Different

New Testament passages can be used to lend support to both kinds of interpretation. The history of the Christian community offers a colorful spectrum on the ways believers have understood the message of the coming of the Reign of God and its implications for their earthly life.

Given these differences, however, it would not be entirely unfair to say that a prevalent mode of understanding throughout Christian history has been of an otherworldly bent. In the New Testament, we read of Paul reprimanding followers of Jesus who have set aside their worldly tasks and simply sit in waiting for the "coming of the Lord." This is one extreme response to the message of the coming of God's Reign, but there have been other forms through Christian history characterized by a denigration of life in this world in the expectation of a glorious heavenly destiny after death. In other words, the emphasis in many Christian writings has tended to be on preparing for entry into the afterlife, rather than on how to live in and address tasks of this world in the light of the Reign of God.

This emphasis has led to attitudes of apathy and indifference toward events in the social and political scene on the part of many Christian followers, or else to a dualistic utilitarianism which regards actions in the earthly realm merely as "means" for meriting heavenly reward.

Thus the basic Christian injunction to "seek ye first the Reign of God" (Matthew 6:33) has led to a variety of responses ranging from an utter otherworldly attitude of denigrating this present life in imminent expectation of the next, to attempts at establishing this reign on this earth through sociopolitical engagement.

On the positive side, however, the belief in the coming of the Reign of God has served to relativize the importance of worldly projects and put a check on the absolutization of earthly goals, whether personal, economic, political, or otherwise. In other words, the religious message of the primacy and ultimacy of God's Reign above everything else has given Christian believers a "critical principle" to examine their actions and goals in the worldly sphere, enabling them to distance themselves from and to criticize political and other forms of worldly authority that would claim their absolute allegiance.

Contextualization of the Core Message: Summary Reflections

In our age, marked by a globalization that heightens our awareness of the religious diversity of our human family, religious communities in different parts of the world can no longer afford to live their religious lives in isolation from or with hostility toward members of other traditions. The question of how to relate to the Other becomes a matter of extreme importance for the continuing viability of any given religious community, not to mention the peace of the entire world. In the words of Jacob Neusner, scholar of the Jewish tradition, "the single most important problem facing religion for the next hundred years, as for the last, is...how to think through difference, how to account within one's own faith and framework for the outsider."[18]

For the adherents of the Shinshū tradition, grounded in the core message of the all-embracing compassion of Amida Buddha embodied in the Original Vow, the task can be described as translating this core message in a way that does not ignore or exclude, but rather embraces "the outsider." This task needs to be carried out, however, in a way that does not simply subsume or assimilate the other without respect for the latter's religious integrity and identity.[19] At this point, there is yet no clear-cut formula for resolving the inherent dilemma and the consequent tensions in this task, and the only way apparent is to continue engaging the Other in encounter and dialogue, to forge new dimensions of mutual understanding and possibly of mutual transformation.[20]

In short, the translation and contextualization of the core message of Pure Land Buddhism in our age calls for this engagement in creative encounters and dialogue with members of other religious traditions, which may open new horizons in understanding the implications of this core message for the wider human community.

One delicate issue that is an ongoing task for Shinshū followers in Japan is how to view the Shinto kami, and also the related question of how to relate to the imperial (*tennō*) system with which Shinto has been historically associated. This issue presents complexities that non-Japanese may find difficult to appreciate: its backgrounds are in the religiopolitical establishment with the emperor at the apex that prevailed over much of Japanese history.[21]

This issue directly connects with the second question, that of relating to political authority. Rennyo's attitude toward political rulers, ensconced in his injunction not to "slight the provincial military governors or local land stewards" and to "deal carefully with fixed yearly tributes and payments to officials,"[22] has been used to foster an attitude of subservience to political authority and has been taken by later leaders of the Honganji (notably Kōnyo and others) to espouse an official policy of defending the state (*chingo-kokka*) and the imperial system in its expansionistic and aggressive wartime endeavors.

A reexamination of the intent of this passage, in the light of the whole context in which Rennyo lived and guided the Honganji community, that is, in the midst of turmoil and conflict and impending political persecution from authorities, would help clarify the extent of its applicability to later ages.

From a comparative perspective, for example, Paul the Apostle writes to Titus to remind the Christian followers that "it is their duty to be obedient to the officials and representatives of the government" (Titus 3:1). This passage has been taken literally by Christians leaders to encourage subservience and to quell resistance even to repressive government authority. It is the same Paul, however, who, under persecution from Roman authorities, writes: "who can separate us from the love of Christ? No troubles, worries, no persecution, no deprivation of food or clothing, no threats or attacks" (Romans 8:35). For Paul, then, there was something much more powerful and compelling than the political authority of the Roman Empire, and that was the Reign of God, to which he had given his whole life and devotion, and so he had a firm basis of faith in this power of God's Reign that enabled him to withstand and overcome suffering and persecution.

Paul had, in other words, a secure foundation that enabled him to see worldly events and realities in critical light. This whole context of Paul's life as dedicated to the establishment of the Reign of God offers a check for a one-sided interpretation of his injunction to be obedient to political authority.

The third point I have raised, the religious message of Birth in the Pure Land, that is, Rennyo's emphasis on what he calls "the important matter of the afterlife," can be seen in this regard as a critical principle that would throw light on how Shinshū followers are called to relate to political authority. Further clarification of this question is indeed a crucial task of the Honganji community, especially in light of its spotted history over the last century vis-à-vis the Japanese religiopolitical establishment centered on the imperial system. This task involves ensuring that the core religious message centered on Amida's Original Vow and Birth in the Pure Land is properly conveyed and given due, and is not made subservient to, used for, or co-opted by political power struggles or systems.

We have taken a brief glimpse at the history of the Roman Catholic tradition merely as one reference point, to throw some light on issues related to the task of the contextualization of a religious message in differing historical ages. This tradition has not been presented as an ideal one by any means, nor as an exemplar to be followed, but simply as a case of a religious community that has had its share of successes and failures in its own history.

The Honganji communities of the Eastern and Western branches, looking back at their roots in Shinran and Rennyo and other leaders of the tradition, have their own history with its own successes and failures to offer as a case study in pursuing the task of the contextualization of their religious message.

Notes

1 Ōtani Kōshin, "Opening Address," in *Amerika no shūkyō wo tazunete / Shin Buddhism Meets American Religions*, ed. Hābādo daigaku shinpojiumu to Beikoku tōbu kenshū ryokōkan, 1986, quoted in Rogers, 40.

2 The name *Shinshū seiten* at this point is a generic title used for what are essentially the canonized texts of each branch of Jōdoshinshū. *Shinshū seiten* thus refers to various compilations of writings held sacred to the tradition of the Honganji branches of Shinshū that have been published under this title since at least 1904. Both Ōtani (East) and Honpa (West) branches of Honganji have their own texts, but Rennyo's *Letters* have always been included.

3 Rogers, 16.

4 Rogers, 20.

5 SSZ 3.428; translation from Rogers, 175–176.

6 SSZ 3.429; Rogers, 176.

7 SSZ 3.466; Rogers, 209.

8 SSZ 3.467; Rogers, 210–211.

9 SSZ 3.467; Rogers, 211.

10 For studies on *ikko ikki*, see Kasahara Kazuo, *Ikko ikki no kenkyū* (Tokyo: Yamakawa Shuppansha, 1962), Inoue Toshio, *Ikko ikki no kenkyū* (Tokyo: Yoshikawa Kōbunkan, 1968), and Kitanishi Hiromu, *Ikko ikki no kenkyū* (Tokyo: Shunjūsha, 1981).

11 The chapter on Transformed Buddha-bodies and Lands (*keshindo no maki*) of the *Kyōgyōshinshō* gives accounts of Shinran's views on kami manifestations, and also contains a famous passage criticizing the imperial rulers and their retinue for "turning their backs on the Dharma," which is frequently cited to indicate Shinran's attitude toward political authority.

12 *Kōnyo Shōnin goikun goshōshoku*, at SSZ 5.771–777. See Rogers, 316–339, for an account of the problems and issues relating to Nishi Honganji's role in the political arena.

13 This position was officially promulgated in the Council of Florence, 1442. See Don Pittman et al., *Ministry and Theology in Global Perspective* (Grand Rapids, Mich.: Wm. Eerdmans, 1996), 44.

14 See Pittman et al., *Ministry and Theology*, 42–63, for developments in Christian perspectives on the question of nonbelievers.

15 See especially the Second Vatican Council's document *Nostra Aetate*, or "Declaration on the Relationship of the Church to Non-Christian Religions," Walter M. Abbott, S.J., general editor, *The Documents of Vatican II* (New York: Guild Press, 1966), 656–674.

16 See Paul Knitter, *No Other Name? A Critical Survey of Christian Attitudes Toward the World Religions* (New York: Orbis, 1985).

17 See Knitter, *No Other Name?* and Pittman, et al., Ministry and Theology, 55–61, for descriptions of the spectrum of Christian positions.

18 Jacob Neusner, "Shalom: Complementarity," in Pittman et al., *Ministry and Theology*, 465–466.

19 The problem noted with Karl Rahner's proposed theological viewpoint, that is, of regarding members of other traditions who live according to their conscience as "anonymous Christians," it is precisely this subsumption of "outsiders" in a way that obliterates their own identity as Other. See Rahner's excerpted article in Pittman et al., *Ministry and Theology*, 87–93.

20 For an account of the possibilities of mutual transformation of members and religious traditions in and through the dialogical process, see John J. Cobb, Jr., *Beyond Dialogue: Toward a Mutual Transformation of Christianity and Buddhism* (Philadelphia: Fortress Press, 1982).

21 For a detailed analysis of the religio-political establishment of State Shinto in Japanese history, see Kuroda Toshio, *Chūsei Nihon no kokka to shūkyō* (Tokyo: Iwanami Shoten, 1975), and Kuroda, *Chūsei Nihon no shakai to shūkyō* (Tokyo: Iwanami Shoten, 1990).

22 *Ofumi* III-10, at SSZ 3.439; Rogers, 209, 211.

A Chronology of Rennyo's Life

Date	Era Year	Age	Event
1415	Ōei 22.	1	2.25. Born in Higashiyama, Kyoto, the eldest child of Zonnyo (age 20).[1]
1420	Ōei 27	6	3. Mother asks for his portrait to be painted (*Kanoko no goei*). 12.28. Mother leaves Honganji.
1422	Ōei 29	8	Stepmother, Nyoen, gives birth to stepsister, Nyojū.
1429	Eikyō 1	15	Announces his determination to restore Honganji.
1431	Eikyō 3	17	Ordained at Shōre'in during summer, receiving Dharma name of Rennyo.
1433	Eikyō 5	19	Stepbrother, Ōgen born, later given Dharma name Renshō.
1434	Eikyō 6	20	5.12. Copies *Jōdomonrui jushō*, written by Shinran.
1436	Eikyō 8	22	3.28. Zonnyo (age 41) succeeds Gyōnyo (age 61) and becomes seventh abbot of Honganji. Mid 8. Copies *Sanjō wasan*, written by Shinran.
1438	Eikyō 10	24	8.15. Copies *Jōdo shin'yōshō*, compiled by Zonkaku, postscript added by Zonnyo. 12.13. Copies *Kudenshō*, written by Kakunyo, and gives to Sōshun, a priest in Ōmi.
1439	Eikyō 11	25	7.29. Copies *Gose monogatari*, attributed to Ryūkan. Last days of 7. Copies *Tariki shinjin kikigaki*, probably written by Ryokai (了海) of Bukkōji.
1440	Eikyō 12	26	10.14. Death of Gyōnyo (age 65).
1441	Kakitsu 1	27	9.7. Copies *Jōdo shin'yōshō*.
1442	Kakitsu 2	28	Birth of first child and son, Junnyo, to Rennyo's first wife, Nyoryō. Rennyo's uncle, Nyojō, builds Honsenji at Futamata in Kaga province.

1446	Bunnan 3	32	Mid 1. Copies *Gutokushō*, compiled by Shinran. Birth of eldest daughter, Nyokei, and second son, Renjō.
1447	Bunnan 4	33	End of 1. Copies *Anjinketsujōshō* (unknown authorship) for Sōshun. 2. Copies *Rokuyōshō* and Zonkaku and *Mattōshō*, a collection of Shinran's letters to his disciples. 5. Travels to the eastern provinces with Zonnyo.
1448	Bunnan 5	34	10.19. Copies *Gensō ekō kikigaki*, probably written by Ryōkai. Birth of second daughter, Kengyoku.
1449	Hōtoku 1	35	5.6. Copies fourth chapter of *Kyōgyōshinshō*. 5.28. Copies *Sanjō wasan* and gives to Shōjō, a priest in Kaga. 6.3. Copies *Anjin ketsujōshō*. Mid 7. Copies *Nyonin ōjō kikigaki*, written by Zonkaku. 10.14. Copies *Godenshō*, biography of Shinran written by Kakunyo, and given to Shinkō, a priest in Kaga. Travels to Hokuriku with Zonnyo.
1450	Hōtoku 2	36	8.11. Copies *Kyōgyōshinshō* at the request of Shōjō. Birth of third son, Renkō.
1451	Hōtoku 3	37	8.16. Copy of *Kyōgyōshinshō* completed with Zonnyo's postscript, given to Shōjō.
1453	Kyōtoku 2	39	11.22. Copies *Sanjō wasan* and gives to the followers in Ōmi.
1454	Kyōtoku 3	40	4.17. Copies *Ōjōyōshū*, by Genshin, and given to Jōshō, a priest in Ōmi. 7.8. Copies *Kyōgyōshinshō*, copied and given to Myōchin in Echizen.
1455	Kōshō 1	41	7.19. Copies *Boki kotoba* (pictorial biography of Kakunyo), written by Jūkaku. Birth of fourth son, Rensei. 11.23. Death of first wife, Nyoryō.
1456	Kōshō 2	42	2.2. Receives gift of a fan from Kyōgaku (経覚), son of Chancellor Kujō Tsunenori and former *monzeki* of Daijōin at Kōfukuji.
1457	Chōroku 1	43	2.20. Copies *Saiyōhō*, written by Kakunyo. 3.4. Copies *Jimyōbō* by Zonkaku. 5.12. Receives gift of *chimaki* rice-dumpling from Kyōgaku. 6.18. Death of father, Zonnyo (age 62). 12.3. Kyōgaku visits Honganji to express his condolences. 12.4. Rennyo returns favor and visits Kyōgaku. Rennyo becomes eighth abbot of Honganji.
1458	Chōroku 2	44	2.4. Copies *Kyōgyōshinshō* and gives to Kyōshun in Kyoto. 7. Monks of Kōfukuji cause trouble for the followers of Shinshū. 8.10. Birth of fifth son, Jitsunyo, to second wife, Ren'yū.
1459	Chōroku 3	45	1.13. Receives gift from Kyōgaku. 1.14. Presents a fan to Kyōgaku in return. Birth of fourth daughter, Myōshū.

1460	Kanshō 1	46	1.26. Death of uncle, Nyojō (age 49).

2.24. Presents hanging scroll of the ten-character Sacred Name (*jūji myōgō*) to Hōju at Katada, Ōmi Province.
3.23. Visits Kyōgaku in Nara.
6. Composes *Shōshinge taii* at the request of Dōsai of Kanegamori, Ōmi Province.
10.4. Death of stepmother, Nyoen.
Birth of fifth daughter, Myōi.

1461	Kanshō 2	47	1.6. Grants another ten-character Sacred Name scroll to Hōjū

and the followers in Katada.
3. Writes the first of his *Letters* (*fude hajime no Ofumi*).
7. Copy made of *Kyōgyōshinshō* in *nobegaki* (Japanese) style and given to Jōhshō in Ōmi Province.
10. Has Anjō portrait of Shinran's (*Anjō goei* or *Anjō miei*) restored.
12.23. Has a dual portrait of Shinran and himself (*Nison renzazō*) painted for Hōjū and the followers in Katada.
Gives a ten-character Sacred Name scroll to Nyokō of Jōgūji, Mikawa Province.

1462	Kanshō 3	48	1.6. Receives gift of mirror from Kyōkaku.

4.3. Visits Kyōgaku and brings him medicine as a present.
Birth of sixth daughter, Nyokū.

1463	Kanshō 4	49	2.11. Sees a firelight performance of a Nō drama (*takigi nō*) in

Nara.
6.7. Jinson (尋尊), son of Chancellor Ichijō Kaneyoshi of the Daijōin in Kōfukuji, visits Honganji and presents 300 sheets of high-quality paper to Rennyo.
6.8 Rennyo visits Jinson and presents a horse and sword in return.
Birth of seventh daughter, Yūshin.

1464	Kanshō 5	50	Continues good relationship with Kyōgaku.

Birth of sixth son, Renjun.
Leads the twenty-fifth memorial service of his grandfather, Gyōnyo.

1465	Kanshō 6	51	1.9. Anti-Honganji monks at Enryakuji formally state their

intention to destroy it.
1.10. Honganji partially destroyed by Enryakuji. Rennyo escapes to Ōmi Province with Shinran's image.
3.21. Honganji demolished again by Enryakuji warrior-monks.
4.24. Enryakuji warrior-monks attack Jōdoshinshū followers in Akanoi, Ōmi Province.
5.10. Bakufu orders Enryakuji to stop their attacks on Jōdoshinshū (*Ikkōshū*) followers.
9.14. Rennyo visits Jinson.
12.9. Rennyo visits Kyōgaku.

1466	Bunshō 1	52	Birth of eighth daughter, Ryōnin.

7.8. Copies *Kyōgyōshinshō* in *nobegaki* style.

8.5. Sends letter to Kyōgaku.
11.21. Annual Hōonkō services held in Kanegamori, Ōmi Province.

1467	Ōnin 1	53	2. Shinran's image moved from Annyōji to Honpukuji in Katada, Ōmi Province.

2.16 Copies *Kudenshō* for Hōen of Kyūhōji in Kawachi Province.
3. Enryakuji leadership issues decree stopping the attacks against Honganji, and Honganji agrees to become subtemple of the Tendai temple Shōren'in.
5. Ōnin War breaks out.
Birth of ninth daughter, Ryōnyo.
11.21. Annual Hōonkō services held at Honpukuji in Katada.

1468	Ōnin 2	54	1.9. Enryakuji plots to attack the Shinshū followers in Katada.

3.12. Orders moving of Shinran's image from Honpukuji to Dōkaku's congregation in Ōtsu, Ōmi Province.
3.28. Signs decree authorizing Jitsunyo as his successor.
3.29. Enryakuji warrior-monks attack Shinshū congregation in Katada and many escape to Okinoshima, a small island in Lake Biwa.
From fifth to tenth month, Rennyo travels to the eastern provinces, following Shinran's footsteps.
Mid 10. Copies *Hōon-kōshiki*, written by Kakunyo.
Mid 10. Travels south to Mount Kōya and Yoshino on the Kii Peninsula.
Gives scroll depicting six-character Sacred Name (*rokuji myōgō*) to congregations in Mikawa Province.
Birth of seventh son, Rengo.

1469	Bunmei 1	55	Spring. Builds priests' dwellings (*bō*) in the southern detached quarters of Miidera, Ōtsu, and names it Kenshōji. Shinran's image enshrined there.

Birth of tenth daughter, Yūshin.

1470	Bunmei 2	56	11.9. Shinshū followers of Katada return home from forced retreat to Okinoshima.

12.5. Second wife, Renyū, dies.

1471	Bunmei 3	57	Early 4. Leaves Ōtsu and returns to Kyoto.

Mid 5. Moves from Kyoto to Yoshizaki, Echizen Province.
7.15. Writes *Letter (Ofumi)* 1:1.
7.18. *Letter* 1:2.
7.27. Builds priests' dwellings in Yoshizaki.
12.18. *Letter* 1:3.

1472	Bunmei 4	58	1. Prohibits public gatherings at Yoshizaki in order to avoid conflicts with other temples in Hokuriku area.

Death of second daughter, Kengyoku.
9.10. Writes letter to Kyōgaku.

1473	Bunmei 5	59	2.8. *Letter* 1:5.

3. First printing of *Shōshinge* and *Sanjō wasan*.
4.25. *Letter* 1:6.

8. Kyōkaku passes away at age 79.

8.12. *Letter* 1:7.

9. Prohibits movements of followers entering and leaving the dwellings of priests in Yoshizaki and later moves to Fujishima.

9. *Letters* 1:8–9.

9.11. *Letter* 1:10.

Mid 9. *Letter* 1:11.

End of 9. *Letters* 1:12–14.

9.22. *Letter* 1:15.

10.3. Returns to Yoshizaki.

11. Issues eleven-article Rule (*okite*) for Shinshū *monto* with admonishments for unacceptable behavior.

12.8. *Letter* 2:1.

12.12. *Letter* 2:2.

1474	Bunmei 6	60	1.11. *Letter* 2:3.

2.15. *Letter* 2:4.

2.16. *Letter* 2:5.

2.17. *Letter* 2:6.

3.3. *Letter* 2:7.

Mid 3. *Letter* 2:8.

3.17. *Letter* 2:9.

3.28. Fire destroys Yoshizaki.

5.13. *Letter* 2:10.

5.20. *Letter* 2:11.

6.12. *Letter* 2:12.

7.3. *Letter* 2:13.

7.5. *Letter* 2:14.

7.9. *Letter* 2:15.

7.14. *Letter* 3:1.

7.26. Honganji followers in Kaga Province enter into alliance with Governor Togashi Masachika to fight against his brother, Yukichiyo, who has allied with Senjuji, a rival Shinshū branch.

8.5. *Letter* 3:2.

8.6. *Letter* 3:3.

8.18. *Letter* 3:4.

9.6. *Letter* 3:5.

10.20. *Letter* 3:6.

11.1. Masachika-Honganji alliance defeats Yukishiyo; Ikkō uprising in Kaga Province involved.

11.13. Jinson writes letter to Rennyo.

11.25. *Letter* 5:2.

Ordination of fifth son, Jitsunyo, this year.

1475	Bunmei 7	61	2:23. *Letter* 3:7.

2:25. *Letter* 3:8.

End of 3. Followers in Kaga province in conflict with Togashi Masachika.

5.7. Issues ten-article Rule in order to restrain followers' actions.

5.28. *Letter* 3:9.
6.11. Jinson writes letter to Rennyo concerning an estate in Kaga Province.
7.15. *Letter* 3:10.
7.16. Visits Futamata in Kaga Province and Zuisenji in Ecchū Province.
8.21. Leaves Yoshizaki, passes through Wakasa, Tanba, and Settsu Provinces and arrives in Deguchi, Kawachi Province.
11.21. *Letter* 3:11.

1476	Bunmei 8	62	1.27. *Letter* 3:12. 7.18. *Letter* 3:13.
1477	Bunmei 9	63	1.8. *Letter* 4:1. 9.17. *Letter* 4:2, signed with *ingō* name "Shinshōin" (信證院) instead of Rennyo for the first time. 9.27. *Letter* 4:3. 10. 27. Copies *Kyōgyōshinshō.* Early 11. Writes *Gozokushō.* 12.2. *Letter* 4:4. Mid 12. Copies *Jōdo kenmonshū*, written by Zonkaku. Birth of eleventh daughter, Myōshō, to third wife, Nyoshō.
1478	Bunmei 10	64	1.29. Leaves Kawachi Province for Yamashina, Yamashiro Province, after deciding it will be the site of a rebuilt Honganji. Begins construction of priests' dwellings in Yamashina. 8.18. Death of third wife, Nyoshō.
1479	Bunmei 11	65	Construction of Honganji continues in Yamashina. 12.30. Ordination of sixth son, Renjun.
1480	Bunmei 12	66	1. Builds a small hall at Yamashina Honganji. 2.3. Begins construction of Founder's Hall at Yamashina. 2.17. Exchanges letters with Jinson concerning an estate in Kaga Province. 3.28. The ridge-beam of Founder's Hall raised. 3.29. Receives a gift (incense burner) from the imperial court for the construction of Yamashina Honganji. 8.28. Shinran's painted portrait installed in what is Founder's Hall and temporary Amida Hall. 10.14. Hino Tomiko, wife of Shōgun Ashikaga Yoshimasa, visits Yamashina Honganji. 10.15. Repairs Anjō portrait of Shinran's again, and has two copies made. 11.18. Moves statue of Shinran, saved from destruction of Ōtain Honganji, from Chikamatsu, Ōtsu, to Yamashina Honganji.
1481	Bunmei 13	67	2.4. Begins construction of Amida Hall at Yamashina Honganji. 2.28. The ridge beam of Amida Hall raised. 6.8. Main image (*honzon*) of Amida Hall installed in a temporary altar. 6.11. Presides over memorial service for twenty-fifth

anniversary of the death of his father, Zonnyo.

6. Kyōgō, fourteenth head priest of Bukkōji, changes allegiances to Honganji.

12.4. The shogunate returns *Boki ekotoba* to Honganji.

1482	Bunmei 14	68	Construction of Honganji continues in Yamashina. 6.15. The altar of Amida Hall completed and main image installed there. 11.21. *Letter* 4:5. A hanging scroll of Amida Buddha, designated on back as *hōben-hosshin sonzō* (reverent icon of *upāya-dharmakāya* [Buddha]), is presented to Keishū, a priest in Mikawa Province. Birth of twelfth daughter, Renshū, to fourth wife, Shūnyo.
1483	Bunmei 15	69	5.29. Death of first son, Junnyo. 8. Construction of Honganji completed in Yamashina. 11. *Letter* 4:6.
1484	Bunmei 16	70	11.21. *Letter* 4:7 (includes a Six-article Rule). Birth of eighth son, Rengei.
1485	Bunmei 17	71	4.4. Restores a ten-character Sacred Name scroll handwritten by Kakunyo. 7.28. Restores the *Kyōshakuyōmon*, handwritten by Kakunyo. 11.23. *Letter* 4:8 (includes Eight-article Rule). Grants a hanging scroll of Amida Buddha to Muryōjuji in Mikawa Province. Gives scroll of his own portrait to Shōrenji in Mikawa Province.
1486	Bunmei 18	72	1. Admonishes followers against appropriating estates owned by shrines and temples. Gves hanging scroll of Amida Buddha to Shōgen, a priest in Mikawa Province. Has a copy made of *Shinran shōnin eden*, pictorial biography of Shinran originally commissioned by Kakunyo and given to Nyokei, a nun of Jōgūji in Mikawa Province. Grants his own portrait to Jōkaku, a priest in Mikawa Province. Fourth wife, Shūnyo, dies.
1487	Chōkyō 1	73	Ikkō uprising in Kaga Province intensifies. Birth of thirteenth daughter, Myōyū, to fifth wife, Ren'nō.
1488	Chōkyō 2	74	5.26. Ikkō uprising in Kaga province lays siege to Togashi Masachika. 6.9. Takao Castle falls and Togashi Masachika commits suicide. A dual portrait is painted of Shinran and Zonnyo for the congregation in Kanegamori, Ōmi Province.
1489	Entoku 1	75	4.28. Donation to Honganji from the imperial court. 8.28. Enacts actual transfer of Honganji abbotship to Jitsunyo, fifth son, and retires to southern hall of Yamashina Honganji. 10. 28. Copies *Kyōgyōshinshō* in *nobegaki* style.

11. 25. Recites *Hōon kōshiki*.
Grants hanging scroll of Amida Buddha to Ekun and Jōkin, both priests in Mikawa Province.
Copies *Kyōgyōshinshō* in *nobegaki* style and gives it to Jōgūji in Mikawa Province.

1490	Entoku 2	76	10.28. Writes a second letter of transfer of institutional authority (*yuzurijō*) for Jitsunyo. Death of seventh daughter, Yūshin. Birth of ninth son, Jikken, to fifth wife, Ren'nō.
1491	Entoku 3	77	Gives his own portrait to Ekun in Mikawa Province. Gives his own portrait to Keijun of Jōmyōji in Mikawa Province.
1492	Meiō 1	78	6. *Letter* 4:9. 7.13. Restores portrait of Zonnyo. Birth of tenth son, Jitsugo, to fifth wife, Ren'nō. Death of sixth daughter Nyokū.
1493	Meiō 2	79	Shōe, chief priest of Kinshokuji, changes allegiance to Honganji.
1494	Meiō 3	80	Birth of eleventh son, Jitsujun, to fifth wife, Ren'nō.
1495	Meiō 4	81	Spring. Builds Gangyōji in Yamato Province. 3. Shinsei (真盛) dies, founder of Shinsei branch of Tendai that centered on monastic form of Pure Land faith and competed with Rennyo in many areas where Honganji had expanded. 6.2. Copies *Kudenshō*, biography of Shinran written by Kakunyo. Fall. Restores Honzenji (Hōkōji) in Yamato Province.
1496	Meiō 5	82	1.11. Copies *Hōnen Shōnin onkotoba*, compilation of Hōnen's writings. 9.24. Designates site in Ishiyama, Settsu Province (Osaka) for construction of new temple for himself. 9.29. Breaks ground for priests' dwellings, in Ishiyama. 10.18. Begins construction of Ishiyama temple, later called Ishiyama Honganji after Yamashina Honganji is destroyed in 1532. 11. Recites *Godenshō* during Hōonkō services at Yamashina Honganji. Birth of twelfth son, Jikkō, to fifth wife, Ren'nō.
1497	Meiō 6	83	2.16. *Letter* 5:8. Early 4. Becomes seriously infirm and is under care of a doctor. 5.25. *Letter* 4:11. End of 11. Construction of living quarters at Ishiyama completed; conducts annual Hōonkō services there. Writes *Letters* 4:10, 5:5, and 5:6. Birth of fourteenth daughter, Myōshū, to fifth wife, Ren'nō.
1498	Meiō 7	84	2.25. *Letter* 4:12.

3. *Letter* 5:14.

Early 4. Taken ill and is examined by doctors.

4.11. *Letter* 4:13.

4. *Letter* 4:14.

5.7. Visits Yamashina Honganji to pay final respects to Shinran's image enshrined in Founder's Hall.

5.25. Makes another trip to Founder's Hall in Yamashina despite illness.

Summer. Writes *Summer Letters* (*Ge no Ofumi*).

11.19. *Letter* 5:9.

11.21. *Letter* 4:15.

Birth of thirteenth son, Jitsujū, to fifth wife, Ren'nō.

1499   Meiō 8   85   2.16. Sends Kūzen to Yamashina Honganji to prepare for his funeral.

2.18. Leaves Osaka once again for Yamashina Honganji.

2.20. Arrives in Yamashina.

2.21. Visits Founder's Hall.

2.25. Takes a walk along the embankment surrounding Founder's Hall.

2.27. Visits Founder's Hall again and bids farewell to followers.

3.1. Talks with Jitsunyo and his other sons.

3.9. Gives parting instructions to sons Jitsunyo, Renkō, Rensei, Renjun, and Rengo.

3.20. Pardons Shimotsuma Rensō.

3.25. Dies at noon.

Note

1 Subject in Event is always Rennyo, unless otherwise named. Numbers initiating lines in Event column indicate month and day. Information based on Ōtani University, ed., *Shinshū nenpyō* (Kyoto: Hōzōkan, 1973), and Minor L. Rogers and Ann T. Rogers, *Rennyo: The Second Founder of Shin Buddhism* (Berkeley, Cal.: Asian Humanities Press, 1992), 373–379.

Glossary

aizan gohō 愛山護法

Akamatsu Mitsusuke 赤松満祐

Akanoi Fukushōji 赤野井 福正寺

Akao-no-Dōshū 赤尾の道宗

akunin shōki 悪人正機

akutō 悪党

amakō 尼講

ama-nyōbō 尼女房

ama-nyūdō 尼入道

Amida 阿彌陀、阿弥陀

anagachi あながち

andojō 安堵状

ango 安居

anjin 安心

Anjō 安城

Annyōji 安養寺

Araki 荒木

Asahara Saiichi 浅原才一

Asai 浅井

Asakura Takakage 朝倉孝景

asamashi あさまし (浅ましい)

Ashikaga Yoshimasa 足利義政

Ashikaga Yoshinori 足利義教

Azuchi 安土

bailianjiao 百蓮教 (J. byakurenkyō)

bakufu 幕府

Bandō Shōjun 板東性純

ben ōjo 便往生

besso sōjō 別祖相承

Bingo 備後

Biwa 琵琶

bohō boja 防法防邪

Bokieshi 慕帰絵詞

Bukkōji 佛光寺

Bun'an 文安

Bungo 豊後

Bunka 文化

Bunmei 文明

buppō 佛法

buppōryō 佛法領

butsumyō wasan 仏名和讃

butteki 仏敵

Chikamatsu 近松

chingo-kokka 鎮護国家

Chinzei 鎮西

Chion'in 知恩院

chiryōgami 治療神

chishiki → see zenchishiki

chishiki danomi 知識だのみ

chishiki kimyō 知識帰命

Chōanji 長安寺

chokugan fudankyō-shū 勅願不断経典衆

chokugansho 勅願所

Chōkyō 長享

Chōroku 長禄

Chōshōji 超勝寺

Chūgoku 中国

chūkō shōnin 中興上人

daidō 大道

Daigoji 醍醐寺

Daijōin 大乗院

daimyō 大名

Dainichi Nyorai 大日如来

dangibon 談義本

danka 檀家 = lay parishoners of a temple

Deguchi 出口

Den Shinran hitsu kōmyō honzon 伝親鸞筆光明本尊

deshi 弟子

Dewa 出羽

dōbō 同朋 (*also* dōhō)

dōgyō 同行

dōjō 道場

Dōkaku 道覚

Dōsai 道西

Dōshū → *see* Akao-no-Dōshū

dōza 同座

eaku 穢悪

Echigo 越後

Echizen 越前

eden 絵伝

edokoro 絵所 • 画所

Eiganji 栄願寺

Eikyō 永享

Eiroku 永禄

ekeizu 絵系図

ekō 廻向 (回向)

ekō hotsugan 回向発願

emaki 絵巻

Ennyo 円如

Enryakuji 延暦寺

Entoku 延徳

Eshinni 恵信尼

Etchū 越中

etoki 絵解き

Fujishima 藤島

fujō shie 不浄死穢

fukujin 福神

Fukuzawa Yukichi 福沢諭吉

Futamata 二俣

gaija 改邪

gan jōju mon 願成就文

Gankyōji 願慶寺

ganmon 願文

ganshu 願主

Gattenshi 月天子

gejun 下旬

gekan 下官

Genchi 玄智

Genshin 源信

genshō jisshu no yaku 現世十種の益

genshō shōjōju 現生正定聚

gensō ekō 還相廻向

genze riyaku 現世利益

Gion 祇園

Goeidō 御影堂

goeika 御詠歌

Gohōjō 御法場

gojō 五常

gongo dōdan no shidai 言語道断の次第

Goryō 御陵

gosaikō shōnin 後再興聖人

Goshirakawa 後白河

goshō 後生

Gōshōji 毫摂寺

goshō no ichidaiji 後生の一大事

goshō no tasukaru koto 後生のたすかる事

goshō sanshō 五障三従

goshō tasuketamae 後生タスケタマエ

Gozan 五山

gyōji 行事

Gyōnen 凝然

Gyōnyo 巧如

haibutsu kishaku 廃仏毀釈

haja kenshō 破邪顕正

Haja kenshōshō 破邪顕正鈔

Hakkotsu no gobunshō 白骨の御文章

haku 伯

Hakusan 白山

hasshū 八宗

Hatakeyama Masanaga 畠山政長

Hatakeyama Yoshinari 畠山義就

heirō 閉籠

Heisenji 平泉寺

heizei gōjō 平生業成

hibutsu 祕佛

Hiei 比叡

Hieizan shuto 比叡山衆徒

higa bōmon 僻法門

Higashi Honganji 東本願寺

hiji bōmon 祕事法門

Hino Katsumitsu 日野勝光

Hino Tomiko 日野富子

hiraza 平座

hisō hizoku 非僧非俗

Hiyama 日山

Hiyama Jibu'uemon 日山治部右衛門

hō 法

hōben 方便

hōben hosshin 方便法身

hōben hosshin songō 方便法身尊号

hōdo 報土

Hōen 法円

Hōjū 法住

hōkan 宝冠

hokke hakkō 法華八講

Hokuriku 北陸

hōmyō 法名

Hōnen 法然

Hongakubō 本覚坊

Honganji 本願寺

honji suijaku 本地垂迹

honmatsusei 本末制

Honpōji 本法寺

Honpukuji 本福寺

Honsenji 本泉寺

Honzenji 本善寺

honzon 本尊

hōon-kō 報恩講

hōryū 法流

Hoshino Genpō 星野元豊

hōshō 宝章

Hosokawa Masamoto 細川政元

hossu 法主

Hōtoku 宝徳

Huiyuan 慧遠 (J. Eon)

hyakushō 百姓

ianjin 異安心

Iba Myōrakuji 伊庭妙楽寺

Ichijō Kanera 一条兼良

ichinen 一念

ichinen hokki 一念発起

ichinen no shinjin sadamaran tomogara 一念信心さだまらん輩

ichiryū 一流

ichiyaku hōmon 一益法門

ikkeshū 一家衆

ikki 一揆

ikkō ikki 一向一揆

ikkō senju 一向専修

ikkō-shū 一向宗

Ikkyū Sōjun 一休宗純

imayō 今様

Inada 稲田

Inami 井波

inshi 淫祀

inujinin 犬神人

Ippen 一遍

Ishiyama 石山

itsukie 斉会

Iwami 石見

jagi 邪義

jaro 邪路

jarui 邪類

jige 地下

jiin 寺院

jike 寺家

jikkō anjin 十劫安心

jimon 寺門

jinaichō *or* jinai machi 寺内町

jinen 自然

jingi 仁義

jingi 神祇

jingi haku 神祇伯

Jinrei 深励

jinshin 深心

Jinson 尋尊

jiriki 自力

Jishū 時宗

jitō 地頭

jitōryō 侍董寮

Jitsugo 実悟

Jitsujū 実従

Jitsujun 実順

Jitsunyo 実如

Jōdoshū 浄土宗

Jōgūji 上宮寺

Jōken 浄賢

Jōkenji 浄賢寺

jōrō 上臈

Jōruri 浄瑠璃

jōsan nishin 定散二心

Jōsen 乗専

Jōshō 浄性

Jūkaku 従覚

jūnikō butsu 十二光仏

Junnyo 順如

Jūraku 十楽

Kaga 加賀

Kai 甲斐

kaisan shōnin 開山聖人

Kakitsu 嘉吉

Kakunyo 覚如

Kakushinni 覚信尼

kana 假名

kanahōgo 仮名法語

Kanamori-no-Dōsai 金森の道西

kanbun 漢文

Kanegamori 金森

Kaneko Daiei 金子大榮

kanji 漢字

kanjinchō 勧進帳

kanmon 貫文

Kannon 觀音

kan'ō 感応

Kanrenkai 貫練会

Kanshō 寛正

Kanshō no hōnan 寛正の法難

Kantō 関東

Kanzaki–gun 神崎郡

kaō 華押

kashin 家臣

Katada 堅田

Katada Osamu 堅田修

Katada ozeme 堅田御責め

Kawachi 河内

keibetsu 輕蔑

Keichō 慶長

Keijo Shūrin 景徐周鱗

kengyō 顯教

Kenju 兼寿

kenmitsu 顕密

kenmitsu taisei 顕密体制

Kennyo 顕如

kenpō 憲法

Kensei 顕誓

Kenshōji 顕証寺

keshindo no maki 化身土巻

ki 機

Kibe 木辺 (*also* 木部)

kihō ittai 機法一体

kijin 鬼神

kimyō 帰命 (帰命)

ki-myō-jin-jip-pō-mu-ge-kō-nyo-rai 帰命盡
十方无导光如來 (歸命盡十方無礙光如來)

Kinai 畿内

kindei 金泥

ki no jinshin 機深信

kinsei 近世

Kinshokuji 錦織寺

kitō 祈祷

Kiyo 清

Kiyozawa Manshi 清沢満之

kō 講

Kōfukuji 興福寺

Kōken sōzu 光兼僧都

kokka 国家

kōmyō honzon 光明本尊

kondei 金泥

Konoe Masaie 近衛政家

Konponchūdō 根本中堂

konshi uketorijō 墾志請取状

Kōnyo 廣如

kōrai beri 高麗縁

kōshi 講師

koshin 狐神

Kōshō 康正

Kōshōji 光照寺 (Yamashina)

Kōshōji 興正寺 (Kyoto city)

Koshu 香取

Kōzen 光善

kue issho 具会一処

kuge 公家

kuji 公事

Kūkai 空海

Kūkaku 空覚

Kusatsu 草津

kushō zunori 口称づのり

Kyeong-heung 憬興

Kyōgaku 經覺 (*also* Kyōkaku)

kyōgakusha 教学者

kyōgen 狂言

Kyōgō 経豪

Kyōgoku 京極

Kyōkai Jigen 教界時言

Kyōnyo 教如

Kyōshun 教俊

Kyōtoku 享徳

matsudai muchi no ofumi 末代无智の御
文

matsuji 末寺

Mattōshō 末灯鈔

Meikō 明光

Meiō 明応

metsudo 滅度

Miidera 三井寺

Mikawa 三川

mikkyō 密教

mikkyōteki jikunshaku 密教的字訓釈

miyaza 宮座

monoimi 物忌

monotori 物取り

monshu 門主・門首

monto 門徒

monzeki 門跡

Moriyama 森山

mugekō butsu 無礙光佛 (无导光佛)

mugekō honzon 無礙光本尊

mugekō nyorai 無礙光如來

mugekō-shū 無礙光宗

Mujinto 無尽灯

mujō 無常

muko kyōgen 聟狂言

Muromachi 室町

mu shukuzen ki 無宿善機

myōchō 名帳

myōgō 名號 (名号)

Myōhōin 妙法院

Myōi 妙意

myōkōnin 妙好人

Myōon'in 妙音院

Myōrakuji 明楽寺

Myōshō 妙勝

myōshu 名主

Myōshū 妙宗

myōshu goji 冥衆護持

Myōyū 妙祐

na-mu a-mi-da butsu 南無阿彌陀佛 (南無阿弥陀仏)

na-mu fu-ka-shi-gi-kō nyo-rai 南無不可思議如來

Nanden 南殿

nanshigi ōjō 難思議往生

Nehangyō 涅槃經

nenbutsu 念佛

nenbutsukō 念佛講

Nichiren 日蓮

nigen heiretsuteki ronpō 二元並列的論法

Nihon Ōkokuki 日本王国記

nijūgozanmai kō 二十五三昧講

ninpō 人法

Nishi Honganji 西本願寺

nishu jinshin 二種深信

Nittenshi 日天子

Nō 能

nobegaki 述べ書き

Nodera 野寺

nōkotsu 納骨

Noto 能登

Nōtogawa–chō 能登川町

nyōbōkō 女房講

nyōbōza 女房座

Nyoen 如円

Nyoen'ni 如円尼

Nyojō 如乗

Nyokō 如光

nyoninkō 女人講

nyonin shōki 女人正機

Nyoraidō 如來堂

Nyoryō 如了

Nyoshin 如信

Nyoshō 如勝

Ōami 大網

Obama 小浜

ōbō 王法

ōbō buppō 王法佛法 (*also* ōhō buppō)

ōbō ihon 王法為本

Oda Nobunaga 織田信長

oe fujō 汚穢不浄

ofumi 御文

Ōgen 応玄

ōjō 往生

Oka dayū 岡太夫

Okinoshima 沖島

okite no ofumi おきて(掟)の御文

Ōmi 近江

ondaikan 御代官

ondoku 恩徳

Ōnin 応仁

Ōnin no ran 応仁の乱

Onjōji 園城寺

onna kyōgen 女狂言

onna za 女座

origami 折紙

Ōsaka-gobō 大坂御坊

osarai no sho 御さらいの章

Ōshū 奥州

ōsō ekō 往相廻向

ōsō ekō no shingyō 往相廻向の心行

Ōtani 大谷

Ōtani-ha 大谷派

Ōtomo Sōrin 大友宗麟

otona 乙名

Ōtsu 大津

Ōuchi no shō 大内庄

oya-sama 親様

raiban 禮盤

raigō 來迎 (*also* raikō)

raikō → *see raigō*

reikin 礼金

Rengo 蓮悟

Renjō 蓮乗

Renjun 連淳

Renkō 蓮綱

Renkyō 蓮教

Rennō 蓮能

Rennyo 蓮如

Rennyo shikigo shū 蓮如識語集

Rennyo Shōnin eden 蓮如上人絵伝

Rennyo uragaki shū 蓮如裏書集

Rensei 蓮誓

Renshō 連照

Renshū 蓮周

Rensō 蓮崇

Renyū 蓮祐

renza 蓮座

rinjū gōjō 臨終業成

rissatsu sokugyō 立撮即行

Rokkaku 六角

rokudō 六道

rokuji myōgō 六字名号

rokuji raisan 六時禮讚

rōnin 浪人

rusushiki 留守職

Ryōgen 了源

Ryōkai 了海

ryōmin 領民

Ryōnin 了忍

Ryōnyo 了如

Ryōshō 了祥

ryūa 流亜

Saichō 最澄

Saigenji 西厳寺

Saihōshinanshō 西方指南抄

Saikōji 西光寺

Saionji 西恩寺

saishōe 最勝会

Sakai 堺

Sakyō Tayū 左京大夫

sanbō hihō no hekiken 三宝誹謗ノ僻見

sanmon kunin 山門公人

Sanuki 讃岐

sarugaku 猿樂

Sasaki 佐々木

Seichin Bizen 誓珍備前

Seiganji 誓願寺

Seikaku 聖傷

Seishi 勢至

Seishinkai 精神界

Seizan 西山

seken 世間

semotsu danomi 施物頼み

sengoku 戦国

sengoku daimyō 戦国大名

Senjuji 専修寺

senju nenbutsu 専修念仏

sensei 先生

senshō 先蹤

sesshu 接収

sesshu fusha 摂取不捨

setsuwa 説話

Settsu 摂津

Shandao 善導

Shigaraki Takamaro 信楽峻麿

Shimotsuke 下野

shin 信

Shinano 信濃

Shinbutsu 真仏

Shinetsu 信越

shingyō 信楽

shinjin 信心

shinjin ihon 信心為本

shinjitsu gyōgō 真実行業

shinjitsu shinjin 真実信心

shinjitsu shōka 真実証果

shinmei no wakō 神明和光

Shinne 真慧

Shinnenji 真念寺

Shinne shojō 真慧書状

shin no ichinen 信の一念

Shinran 親鸞

Shinran Shōnin goshōsokushū 親鸞聖人御消息集

Shinsei 真盛

Shinshō-in 信証院

Shinshū 真宗

Shinshū seiten 真宗聖典

Shinshū shōgyō zensho = 真宗聖教全書

shintai 真諦

shinteki 神敵

shinzō 真像

shinzoku nitai 真俗二諦

Shirakawa Masakaneō 白川雅兼王

Shirakawa Sukeujiō 白川資氏王

Shirakawa Tadatomi 白川忠富

Shirutani 汁谷

shisō 思想

shōban ofumi 証判御文

shōbutsu funi 生仏不二

Shōe 勝恵

shōen 荘園

shōgyō 聖教

Shōjō 性乗

shōjōju 正定聚

shōki 正機

Shōkū 証空

shōmyō nenbutsu 称名念仏

shōnin no shūgi 上人の宗義

Shōnyo 証如

Shōrakuji 勝楽寺

Shōren'in 青蓮院

Shōrin 正林

Shōshinge tai'i 正信偈大意

Shōsōin 正倉院

shōsoku 消息

Shōtoku 聖徳

Shōzōmatsu wasan 正像末和讃

shū 宗

shūgaku 宗学

shugo 守護

shugo daimyō 守護大名

Shūjishō 執持鈔

shūmon aratame 宗門改め

Shūnyo 宗如

sō 惣

sōdō 草堂

Soga Ryōjin 曽我量深

sōhei 僧兵

Sōkenji 総見寺

soku ōjō 即往生

sokushitsu 側室

sokutoku ōjō 即得往生

songō 尊号

songyō 尊形

sōshō 惣荘

Sōshun 琮俊

sōson 惣村 (*also* sō no mura)

Sugamo 巣鴨

Sugawara no Michizane 菅原道真

Sukeujiō 資氏王

Sumoto 栖本

taigi 大義

taiza 対座

Takada (–ha) 高田 (派)

Takakura Gakuryō 高倉学寮

Takeda Takemaro 武田竹麿

tanen 多念

tanni 歎異

Tannishō 歎異抄

tanomoshi-kō 頼母子講

tariki 他力

Tateyama 立山

taya 多屋

teikin ōrai 庭訓往来

Teikyō 貞享

Tendai 天台

Tendō 天道

tendō nenbutsu 天道念仏

Tenjin 天神

Tenman Daijizaiten 天満大自在天

tennō 天皇

Togashi Kōchiyo 富樫幸千代

Togashi Masachika 富樫政親

Tōkai 東海

Tokugawa 徳川

tomogara 輩

Tonda 富田

tōryū 当流

Toyowaraji 豊原寺 (*also* Toyoharaji)

tōzan myōgō 登山名号

ungen beri 繧繝縁

uragaki 裏書

uru'u sangatsu 閏三月

wabun 和文

Wada Sōkyū 和田蒼穹

waga chikara 我が力

Waga shinnen 我が信念

waka 和歌

Wakasa 若狭

Wasan 和讃

Xuanyifen 玄義分

Yakushi 薬師

Yamashina 山科

Yamashiro 山城

Yasuda Kazunosuke 安田主計助

Yodo 淀

Yome-odoshi no oni no men 嫁おどしの鬼の面

yoriai 寄合

Yoshida Gen-no-shin 吉田源之進

Yoshimasa 義政

Yoshizaki 吉崎

Yoshizakiji 吉崎寺

Yoshizawaji 芳沢寺

Yosoji 与三次 (*also* 与惣治)

yūgen to mugen no taiō 有限と無限の対応

Yuien (Yuienbō) 唯円 (唯円坊)

Yūnen 祐念

Yūshin (Yūshinni) 祐心 (祐心尼)

zashū 座衆

Zenchin 善鎮

zenchishiki 善知識 (*also* zenjishiki, chishiki)

Zendō → *see* Shandao

Zenka 善可

Zenkōji 善光寺

Zennyo 善如

Zenran 善鸞

Zhu Yuanzhang 朱元璋 (J. Shu Genshō)

zōgyō 雑行

zokutai 俗諦

Zonkaku 存覚

Zonnyo 存如

Zuisenji 瑞泉寺

Bibliography

Primary Sources

CANONS AND COLLECTIONS

Bukkyō taikei	佛教大系. 38 vols. Tokyo: Bukkyō Taikei Kanseikai, 1918; repr. Kyoto: Hōzōkan, 1975.
Cartas que os Padres e Irmãos	*Cartas que os Padres e Irmãos da Companhia de Iesus escreuerão dos Reynos de Iapão & China aos da mesma Companhia da India, & Europa, des do anno de 1549 ate o de 1580.* 2 vols. Facsimile repr. of the 1598 ed. Tenri: Tenri Central Library, 1972. Facsimile also at Maia, Portugal: Castoliva, 1997.
Chūsei hōsei shiryō shū	中世法制史料集. 5 vols. Tokyo: Iwanami Shoten, 1965–1978.
CWS	*Complete Works of Shinran.* Trans. Dennis Hirota et al. Kyoto: Jōdo Shinshū Hongwanjiha, 1997.
Daikōkai jidai sōsho	大航海時代叢書. Ikuta Shigeru 生田滋, Aida Yū 会田由, et al., eds. 26 vols. Tokyo: Iwanami Shoten, 1965.
Dai Nihon shiryō	大日本史料, 482 vols. Tokyo Daigaku Shiryō Hensansho, ed. Tokyo: Tokyo Daigaku Shuppankai, 1906; repr. 1968.
Historia de Japam	Frois, Luis (d. 1597), 5 vols. Lisbon: Biblioteca National, repr. 1981.
Kamakura ibun	鎌倉遺文. 50 vols. Takeuchi Rizō 竹内理三, ed. Tokyo: Tokyodō Shuppan, 1971–1997.
Koten bunko	古典文庫. 670 vols. Tokyo: Koten bunko, 1949–2002.
Nihon hōkokushū	*Jūroku–shichi seiki Iezusukai Nihon hōkokushū* 十六・十七世紀イエズス会日本報告集. 15 vols. Matsuda Kiichi 松田毅一, trans. and ed. Kyoto: Dōbōsha, Series I (5 vols.) 1987, series II (3 vols.) 1990, series III (7 vols.) 1992.
Nihon koten bungaku taikei	日本古典文学大系. 77 vols. Takagi Ichinosuke 高木市之助 et al., eds. Tokyo: Iwanami Shoten, 1957–1968.
Nihon koten bungaku zenshū	日本古典文学全集. 51 vols. Tokyo: Shogakkan, 1970–1976.

Nihonshi	日本史. Translation of Frois, Luis *Historia de Japam*, trans. Matsuda Kiichi and Kawasaki Momota 川崎桃太. 12 vols. Tokyo: Chuō Kōronsha, 1977–1980.
Nihon shisō taikei	日本思想大系. 66 vols. Takagi Ichinosuke 高木市之助 et al., supervising eds. Tokyo: Iwanami Shoten, 1971–1982.
RSG	*Rennyo Shōnin gyōjitsu* 蓮如上人行實. Inaba Masamaru 稲葉昌丸, ed. Kyoto: Otani Daigaku Shuppanbu, 1928; repr. by Hōzōkan, 1948, 1983.
RSI	*Rennyo Shōnin ibun* 蓮如上人遺文. Inaba Masamaru, ed. Kyoto: Hōzōkan, 1937; repr. 1948, 1983, 1990.
Rennyo Shōnin zenshū	*Rennyo Shōnin zenshū: gengyō hen* 蓮如上人全集：言行篇. Ōtani Chōjun, ed. Tokyo: Kawade Shobō Shinsha, 1989.
Shin ikoku sōsho	新異国叢書. 29 vols. Tokyo: Yūshōdō, 1968–2003.
Shin Nihon koten bungaku taikei	新日本古典文学大系. Rev. ed. of *Nihon koten bungaku taikei*. Tokyo: Iwanami Shoten, 1989–2003.
Shinpen Nihon koten bungaku zenshū	新編日本古典文学全集. Rev. ed. of *Nihon koten bungaku zenshū*. Tokyo: Shogakkan, 1994–2002.
Shinshū sōsho	真宗叢書. 13 vols. Shinshū Sōsho Henshūjo 真宗叢書編輯所, ed. Kyoto: Maeda Koreyama Ryōwajō Koki Kinenkai, 1927–1930; repr. in Kyoto by Rinsen Shoten, 1978.
Shinshū taikei	真宗大系. 37 vols. Shinshū Tenseki Kankōkai 真宗典籍刊行会, ed. 1917–1925; repr. Tokyo: Kokusho Kankōkai, 1974.
Shinshū zensho	真宗全書. 74 vols. Tsumaki Chokuryō 妻木直良, ed. Kyoto: Zōkyō Shoin, 1913–1916; repr. Tokyo: Kokusho Kankōkai, 1974–1977.
Shintei zōho Kokushi taikei	新訂増補国史大系. 62 vols. Kuroita Katsumi 黒板勝美, ed. Kokushi Taikei Henshūkai, ed. Tokyo: Yoshikawa Kōbunkan, 1951–1981.
Shōwa shinshū Hōnen Shōnin zenshū	昭和新修法然上人全集. Kyoto: Heirakuji Shoten, 1955.
SSS	*Shinshū shiryō shūsei* 真宗史料集成. 13 vols. Ishida Mitsuyuki 石田充之 and Chiba Jōryū 千葉乗隆, supervising eds. Kyoto: Dōbōsha, 1974–1983.
SSZ	*Shinshū shōgyō zensho* 真宗聖教全書. 5 vols. Shinshū Shōgyō Zensho Hensansho 真宗聖教全書編纂所, ed. Kyoto: Ōyagi Kōbundō, 1969–1970.
Yōmei sōshō	陽明叢書. 57 vols. Yōmei Bunko 陽明文庫, ed. Kyoto: Shibunkaku, 1975–1996.
Zoku gunsho ruiju	続群書類従. Orig. ed. by Hanawa Hokinoichi 塙保己一 et al. 71 vols., 1911–1928. Rev. 3rd ed. in 74 vols., Tokyo: Zoku Gunsho Ruiju Kanseikai, 1959.
Zoku shinshū taikei	続真宗大系. 20 vols. Shinshū Tenseki Kankōkai, ed. Tokyo: Shinshū Tenseki Kankōkai, 1938–1941; repr. in different configuration by Kokusho Kankōkai, 1976.
Zoku shiryō taisei	続史料大成. 22 vols. Takeuchi Rizō 竹内理三, ed. Rev. and expanded edition, Kyoto: Rinsen Shoten, 1976.
Zoku zōkyō	Full title: *Shinsan Dainihon zokuzōkyō* 新纂大日本続藏經. 90 vols. Kamamura Kōshō 河村孝照, ed. Tokyo: Kokusho Kankōkai, 1975–1989. repr. of *Manji zokuzōkyō* 卍大日本續藏經, Kyoto: Zōkyō Shoin, 1912.

INDIVIDUAL TEXTS

Akao no Dōshū kokoroe nijūichi kajō 赤尾道宗心得二十一箇条 by Dōshū 道宗. Gyōtokuji 行徳寺 ed., *Akao no Dōshū kokoroe nijūichi kajō* 赤尾道宗心得二十一箇条, published by Gyōtokuji, 1977; SSS 2.712–713; .

Amidakyō: See next entry.

Amituo jing 阿彌陀經, full title: *Foshuo amituo jing* 佛説阿彌陀經 *Bussetsu amidakyō*. T No. 365, 12.340.

Anjinketsujōshō 安心決定鈔. Author unknown. T No. 2679, 83.921; SSZ 3.615.

Anjinsho 安心抄 by Shōkū 證空. *Jōdoshū Seizanryū hitsuyōzō* 浄土宗西山流必要藏, vol. 3.

Azuma kagami 吾妻鏡, author(s) unknown. *Shintei zōho Kokushi taikei*, vols. 32–33.

Banzhou sanmei jing (*Pratyutpanna buddhasaṃmukhāvasthita samādhi sūtra*) 般舟三昧經 *Hanju sammaikyō*. T No. 417, 13.897 and No. 418, 13.902.

Benjutsu myōtai shō 辨述名體抄 by Zonkaku 存覺. SSZ 5.235.

Bokie kotoba 慕歸繪詞, biography of Kakunyo 覺如 written by Jūkaku 從覺. SSZ 3.769.

Bumo kyōyōshō 父母教養鈔, attributed to Zonkaku. SSS 5.617.

Buppō no shidai ryaku nukigaki 仏法之次第略抜書, author unknown, *Kirishitan sho, Haiyasho* キリシタン書 • 排耶書, ed. Ebisawa Arimichi 海老沢有道, H. Cieslik, et al., eds. Nihon shisō taikei, vol. 25. Tokyo: Iwanami shoten, 1970.

Bussetsu daizō shōgyō kechibonkyō 佛説大藏正教血盆経: See *Dacheng zhengjiao xuepen jing*.

Chū Muryōgikyō 註無量義経 by Saichō. T No. 2193, 56.203.

Contemplation Sūtra: See *Guanwuliangshou jing*

Dacheng bensheng xindiguan jing 大乘本生心地観経. T No. 159, 3.291.

Dacheng zhengjiao xuepen jing 大藏正教血盆経, full title *Foshuo dacheng zhengjiao xuepen jing* 佛説大藏正教血盆経. *Zoku zōkyo* 1–87–4.

Daijōin jisha zōjiki 大乘院寺社雑事記 by Jinson 尋尊, 12 vols. Tsuji Zennosuke 辻善之助 ed., Tokyo: Chōshobō, 1931–1937; repr. Tokyo: Kadokawa Shoten, 1964. Also in *Zoku Shiryō taisei*, vols. 26–37.

Dai Muryōjukyō: See *Wuliangshou jing*

Eigenki 榮玄記: See next entry.

Eigen kikigaki 榮玄聞書 by Eigen 榮玄. Also known as *Eigenki* 榮玄記. SSS 2.588; RSG 257.

Eizan chōjō 叡山牒状: Popular name for next entry.

Eizan yori furaruru kenshō 叡山ヨリ触ラルル憲章, in *Kanegamori nikki batsu* 金森日記抜. SSS 2.701.

Enryakuji Saitōin shīgijōan 延暦寺西塔院衆議状案 by Keijun 慶純. SSS 4.164.

Gaijashō 改邪鈔 by Kakunyo. SSZ 3.64.

Gaikemon 改悔文, attributed to Rennyo, under the title *Ryōgemon* 領解文. SSZ 3.529.

Gensō ekō kikigaki 還相廻向聞書, attributed to Ryōkai 了海. *Bukkōji shōbushū* 佛光寺小部集, Bukkyōshi Gakkai, ed. No. 4 in the series *Bogo sōsho* 戊午叢書. Kyoto: Bukkyōshi Gakkai, 1923.

Gobunshō 御文章, compilation of Rennyo's *ofumi* (*Letters*). SSZ 3.402.

Godenshō 御傳鈔 by Kakunyo. SSZ 3.639.

Gohōkōinki 後法興院記, diary of Konoe Masaie 近衞政家 (1444–1505). Facsimile in *Yōmei soshō*, nos. 22–25, Kiroku monjo hen, vol. 8.

Goichidai kikigaki: See *Rennyo Shōnin goichidaiki kikigaki*.

Gojō ofumi 五帖御文: See *Gubunshō*.

Gose monogatari 後世物語, attributed to Ryūkan 隆寛. SSZ 2.757; *Shinshū taikei* vol. 31.

Goshōsoku shū: See *Shinran Shōnin goshōsoku shū.*

Gozokushō 御俗姓, also called *Gozokushō ofumi* 御俗姓御文. By Rennyo. SSZ 3.519.

Guanjing: See *Guanwuliangshou jing.*

Guanjing shu 觀經疏 *Kangyōsho*, full title: *Guanwuliangshou fojing shu* 觀無量壽佛經疏 *Kanmuryōju bukkyōsho*, by Shandao 善導 (Zendō). T No. 1753, 17.245.

Guanwuliangshou jing 觀無量壽經, *Guanjing* 觀經; full title: *Foshuo guanwuliangshou fojing* 佛說觀無量壽佛經. T No. 365, 12.340.

Gutokushō 愚禿鈔 by Shinran 親鸞. SSZ 2.455.

Gyakushu seppō 逆修説法, by Hōnen 法然, in Ishida Kyōdō 石田教道, ed., *Shōwa shinshū Hōnen Shōnin zenshū*, 232.

Gyokuyō 玉葉, diary of Kujō Kanezane 九条兼實. Tokyo: Kokusho Kankōkai, 1906; repr. 1969.

Haja kenshō shō 破邪顕正鈔 by Zonkaku. SSZ 3.155.

Heike Monogatari 平家物語. Takagi Ichinosuke 高木市の助, ed., *Nihon koten bungaku taikei*, vols. 32–33; Kajihara Masaaki 梶原正昭 and Yamashita Hiroaki 山下宏明, eds., *Shin Nihon koten bungaku taikei*, vols. 44–45.

Hino ichiryū keizu 日野一流系図 by Jitsugo 実悟. RSG 275; SSS 7.527.

História da Igreja do Japão by Tçuzzu, João Rodrigues (1561–1634). Lisbon: Biblio do Palácio da Ajuda, 1953; and in 2 vols, Macau: Noticias de Macau, 1954–1955.

Historia de Japam by Luis Frois (1532–1597), 5 vols. Lisbon: Biblioteca National; repr. 1981.

Hogo no uragaki 反古裏書 by Kensei 顕誓. SSS 2.740; *Zoku Shinshū taikei*, vol. 15.

Hōnen Shōnin gohōgo 法然上人御法語 by Hōnen. Two texts with slightly different content in *Shōwa shinshū Hōnen Shōnin zenshū*, 1117 and 1131.

Hōnen Shōnin onkotoba 法然上人御詞. Compilation of Hōnen's writings copied by Rennyo. Unpublished manuscript held at Kōtokuji 光徳寺, Osaka prefecture.

Honganji sahō no shidai 本願寺作法之次第. RSG 175; SSS 2.559.

Honpukuji atogaki 本福寺跡書 by Myōsei 明誓. SSS 2.629.

Honpukuji yuraiki 本福寺由来記 by Myōshū 明宗. SSS 2.661

Hōonki 報恩記 by Zonkaku. SSS 1.801; SSZ 3.256.

Hōon kōshiki 報恩講式 by Kakunyo, at SSZ 3.655.

Hōshi ga haha 法師が母, anonymous Kyōgen play. In *Kyōgenshū ge* 狂言集 下, Koyama Hiroshi 小山弘志, ed., *Nihon koten bungaku taikei*, vol. 43.

Hyakuman 百萬 by Zeami. In *Yōkyokushū jō* 謡曲集 上, Yokomichi Mario 横道満理雄 and Omote Akira 表章, eds., *Nihon koten bungaku taikei*, vol. 40,

Ichinen tanen mon'i 一念多念文意 by Shinran. T No. 2657, 83.694; SSZ 2.604.

Iezusu kaishi nihon tsūshin イエズス会士日本通信, Murakami Naojirō 村上直次郎, trans. and Yanagiya Takeo 柳谷武夫, ed. *Shin ikoku sōsho*, vols. 1–2.

Ippen shōnin goroku 一遍上人語録, author(s) unknown. In *Hōnen, Ippen* 法然 • 一遍, Ōhashi Toshio 大橋俊夫, ed., *Nihon shisō taikei*, vol. 10.

Ishikami 石神, anonymous Kyōgen play. *Kyōgenshū vol. 2* 狂言集 下, Koyama Hiroshi 小山弘志, ed., *Nihon koten bungaku taikei*, vol. 43.

Itokuki 遺徳記: See *Rennyo Shonin itokuki.*

Jigō shōnin shinshi mondō 慈巧聖人神子問答. SSS 5.200.

Jimyōshō 持名鈔 by Zonkaku. SSZ 3.91.

Jingtu lun 浄土論 *Jōdoron*; full title: *Wuliangshoujing youpotishe [yuanshengji]* 無量壽經優 婆提舍 [願生偈] *Muryōjukyō upadaisha [ganshō-ge]*. By Vasubandhu. T No. 1524, 26.230.

Jingtu lunzhu 浄土論註 *Jōdo ronchū*; full title: *Wuliangshoujing youpotishe yuanshengji zhu.* By Tanluan. T No. 1819, 40.826.

Jinguangming zuishengwang jing 金光明最勝王經. T No. 665, 16.403.

Jitsugoki 實悟記 by Jitsugo 實悟. RSG 139.

Jitsugo kyūki 實悟舊記 (実悟旧記) by Jitsugo. Also known as *Rennyo Shonin ichigoki* 蓮如上人一期記. SSS 2.444; RSG 69.

Jōdo kenmonshū 浄土見聞集 by Zonkaku. SSZ 3.375.

Jōdo monruiju shō 淨土門類聚鈔 by Shinran. SSZ 2.443.

Jōdo sangyō ōjō monrui 浄土三経往生文類 by Shinran. SSZ 2.543 and 551.

Jōdo shin'yōshō 浄土新要鈔 by Zonkaku. SSZ 3.119.

Jōdoron: See *Jingtu lun*

Jōdowasan 浄土和讃 by Shinran. SSZ 2.485.

Jōnai ofumi 帖内御文, also *Gobunshō* 御文章, by Rennyo. SSZ 3.402.

Kai no kuni Myōhōji ki 甲斐国妙法寺記, temple history. *Zoku gunsho ruiju*, 30–1.

Kamabara 鎌腹, anonymous Kyōgen play. In *Kyōgenshū ge* 狂言集 下, Koyama Hiroshi 小山弘志, ed., *Nihon koten bungaku taikei*, vol. 43.

Kanegamori nikki batsu 金森日記抜. SSS 2.701.

Kangyō: See *Guanwuliangshou jing*.

Kanrenkai wo ronzu 貫練会を論ず by Kiyozawa Manshi 清沢滿之. In *Kiyozawa Manshi zenshū* 清沢滿之全集. Kyoto, Hōzōkan, 1953, 4.316.

Kanrin koroshū 翰林葫盧集 by Keijo Shūrin 景徐周麟. Kamimura Kankō 上村観光, ed., *Gozan bungaku zenshū* 五山文學全集, Tokyo: Gozanbungaku Zenshī Kankōkai, 1936, vol. 4.

Kawarataro 河原太郎, anonymous Kyōgen play. In *Ōkura toramitsubon Kyōgen shū* 大蔵虎光本狂言集, ed. Hashimoto Asao 橋本朝生, *Koten bunko* 古典文庫, No. 540.

Kechimyaku monjū 血脈文集, letters of Shinran. SSZ 2.717; *Nihon koten bungaku taikei* vol. 82.

Kenmyōshō 顕名鈔 by Zonkaku. SSZ 1.325.

Kenshōryū gishō 顯正流義鈔 by Shinne 眞慧. T No. 2673, 83.841.

Ketchishō 決智鈔 by Zonkaku. SSZ 3.188.

Ketsubonkyo 血盆經: See *Dacheng zhengjiao xuepen jing*.

Kikigaki: See *Rennyo Shōnin go'ichidaiki kikigaki*.

Kōmyō kenmitsu–shō 光明顕密抄, extant text by Ezan 恵山. SSS 5.129.

Kōnyo Shōnin goikun goshōshoku 廣如上人御遺訓御消息, selected letters by Kōnyo 廣如. SSZ 5.771.

Kōsō wasan 高僧和讃 by Shinran. SSZ 2.501.

Kudenshō 口傳鈔 by Kakunyo. SSZ 3.1.

Kulturgegensatze Europa–Japan (1585): Tratado em que se contem muito susintae abreviadamente algumas contradicoes e diferencas de custumes antre a gente de Europa e esta provincia de Japao by Luis Frois (d. 1597), with introduction and annotation by Josef Franz Schutte. No. 15 in the series Monumenta Nipponica monographs. Tokyo: Sophia University, 1955.

Kūzenki 空善記, also called *Kūzen nikki* 空善日記, based on a diary of Kūzen 空善, known as the *Kūzen kikigaki* 空善聞書. RSG 1.

Kyōgyōshinshō 教行信證 by Shinran 親鸞; full title: *Ken jōdo shinjitsu kyōgyōshō monrui* 顯淨土眞實教行證文類. T No. 2646, 83.589, SSZ 2.1.

Kyōgyōshinshō taii 教行信証大意 by either Zonkaku or Kakunyo. *Kokubun tōhō bukkyō sōsho* 國文東方佛教叢書, vol. 1, ed. Washio Junkei 鷲尾順敬. Tokyo: Tōhō Shoin, 1925–1926.

Kyōgyōshinshō kōgi shūsei 教行信証講義集成, by Jinrei 深励, in 9 fascicles, in *Bukkyō taikei*, vol. 25.

Kyōgaku shiyōshō 經覺私要鈔 by Kyōgaku 經覺. *Zoku gunsho ruiju*, vols. 1–6.

Larger [Sukhāvatīvyūha] Sūtra: See *Wuliangshou jing*

Mattōshō 末燈鈔, letters of Shinran. SSZ 2.656; *Nihon koten bungaku taikei* vol. 82.

Mikazuki 箕被, traditional Kyōgen play. In *Kyōgenshū ge* 狂言集 下, Koyama Hiroshi, ed., *Nihon koten bungaku taikei*, vol. 43.

Mizukake muko 水掛聟, traditional Kyōgen play. In *Kyōgenshū jō* 狂言集 上, Koyama Hiroshi, ed., *Nihon koten bungaku taikei*, vol. 42.

Morai muko 貰聟, traditional Kyōgen play. In *Kyōgenshū* 狂言集, Kitakawa Tadahiko 北川忠彦 and Yasuda Akira 安田章, eds. *Nihon koten bungaku zenshū*, vol. 60.

Mukashi monogatariki 昔物語記, author unknown. RSG 249.

Muryōjukyō: See *Wuliangshou jing*.

Muryōjukyō jutsumonsan: See *Wuliangshoujing lianyi shuwenzan*.

Nenbutsu ōjō yōgishō 念佛往生要義抄 by Hōnen. *Shōwa shinshū Hōnen Shōnin zenshū*, 681.

Nichiō bunka hikaku 日欧文化比較, trans. and ed. Okada Akio 岡田章雄. Translation of *Tratado em que se contem muito susinta e abreviadamente algumas contradições e deferenças de custumes entre a gente de Europa e esta provincia de Japão* by Luis Fróis. In *Daikōkai jidai sōsho*, vol. 11.

Nostra Aetate by the Second Vatican Council. In Walter M. Abbott, S.J., ed., *The Documents of Vatican II*. New York: Guild Press, 1966, 656.

Nyonin ōjō kikigaki 女人往生聞書 by Zonkaku. SSZ 3.109.

Nyūshutsu nimon geju 入出二門偈頌 by Shinran. SSZ 2.480.

Oba ga sake 伯母が酒, traditional Kyōgen play. In *Kyōgenshū 2* 狂言集 下, Koyama Hiroshi, ed., *Nihon koten bungaku taikei* vol. 43.

Ōjōraisan 往生禮讃: See *Wangsheng lizanji*

Ōjōyōshū 往生要集 by Genshin 源信. T. No. 2684, 84.33.

Okadayū 岡太夫, traditional Kyōgen play. In *Ōkura toramitsubon Kyōgen shū* 大蔵虎光本狂言, vol. 4, ed. Hashimoto Asao 橋本朝生. Tokyo: *Koten bunko*, No. 540.

Oko sako 右近佐近, traditional Kyōgen play. In *Kyōgenshū 2* 狂言集 下, ed. Koyama Hiroshi, *Nihon bungaku taikei*, vol. 43.

Renjun ki 蓮淳記 by Renjun. RSG, 64.

Rennyo Shōnin go'ichidaiki kikigaki 蓮如上人御一代記聞書, compiled by Kūzen and Rengo. SSZ 3.531; *Nihon shisō taikei* 17.111;

Rennyo Shōnin go'ichigoki 蓮如上人御一期記, compiled by Jitsugo. SSS 2.459.

Rennyo Shōnin ōse no jōjō (gojōjō) 蓮如上人御条条, compiled by Jitsugo. SSS 2.470.

Rennyo Shōnin ichigoki 蓮如上人一語記: See *Jitsugo kyūki*

Rennyo Shōnin itokuki 蓮如上人遺徳記, recorded by Jitsugo, compiled by Rengo. SSZ 3.869.

Rennyo Shōnin seizui denki 蓮如上人西瑞伝記. Held at Eiganji 栄願寺 in Hekinan 碧南 city in Aichi Prefecture, unpublished.

Rennyo uragakishū 蓮如裏書集, editorial name given to collection of Rennyo inscriptions. SSS 2.379.

Rokuyōshō 六要鈔 by Zonkaku. SSZ 2.205.

Ryōgemon: See *Gaikemon*

Ryōjin hisho 梁塵秘抄, compilation attributed to Emperor Goshirakawa 後白河. In *Shincho Nihon koten shūsei* 31 新潮日本古典集成：第 31 回, ed. Enoki Katsurō 榎克朗, Tokyo: Shinchosha, 1979.

Ryōri muko 料理聟, traditional Kyōgen play. In the 1700 ed. of *Kyōgenki* 狂言記, reproduced and ed. Hashimoto Asao 橋本朝生 and Doi Yōichi 土井洋一, *Shin nihon koten bungaku taikei*, vol. 58.

Saishōkyō 最勝経: See *Jinguangming zuishengwang jing*

Saiyōshō 最要鈔 by Kakunyo. SSZ 3.50.

Sakuragawa 桜川, traditional Nō play, Kanze–ryū version in *Kanzeryū, koe no hyakubanshū*, vol. 50, ed. Maruoka Akira 丸岡明. Tokyo: Chikuma Shobō, 1969.

Sanjō wasan 三帖和讃 by Shinran, encompasses *Jōdo wasan* 浄土和讃, *Kōsō wasan*, and *Shōzōmatsu wasan* 正像末和讃. SSZ 2.485, 501, 516.

Semimaru 蝉丸, traditional Nō play. Koyama Hiroshi et al., eds, *Yōkyokushū* 2, vol. 34 in *Nihon koten bungaku zenshū*. As modified by Chikamatsu Monzaemon, Kanze–ryū version in *Kanzeryū, koe no hyakubanshū*, vol. 28, ed. Maruoka Akira 丸岡明. Tokyo: Chikuma Shobō, 1968.

Senchakushū 選択集, full title: *Senchaku hongan nenbutsu shū* 選択本願念佛集. T No. 2608, 83.1; SSZ 1.929.

Senjuji Echizen no kuni matsuji monto chū mōshijō an 専修寺越前国末寺門徒中申状案. SSS 4.163.

Senjūshō 撰集抄, compilation attributed to Saigyō. *Iwanami Bunko*, No. 6746–6749, 黄 (30)–024–1, 黄–139), ed. Nishio Kōichi 西尾光一. Tokyo: Iwanami Shoten, 1970.

Shichijūichiban shokunin utaawase 七十一番職人歌合, author unknown, orginally from Muromachi period. *Edo kagaku koten sōsho* 江戸科学古典叢書, vol. 6, ed. Aoki Kunio 青木国夫 et al. Tokyo: Kōwa Shuppan, 1977; *Shichijūichiban shokunin utaawase*, *Shinsen kyōkashū* 新撰狂歌集, *Kokon ikyokushū* 古今夷曲, ed. Iwasaki Kae 岩崎佳枝 et al., *Shin Nihon koten bungaku taikei*, vol. 61.

Shichō onjuji 師長恩重事. SSS 5.177.

Shiji 史記 (*Shiki*) by Sima Qian 司馬遷. Beijing: Zhonghua shuju 中華書局, 1959. Published as *The Grand Scribe's Records* by Ssu–ma Chien; ed., William H. Nienhauser. Bloomington : Indiana University Press, 1994.

Shinjikan kyō: See *Dacheng bensheng xindiguan jing*.

Shinketsumyaku–shō 心血脈抄, author unknown. SSS 5.327; Shinshū taikei, vol. 36; *Zoku shinshū taikei* 19.

Shinpen Hitachi kokushi 新編常陸国誌, gazeteer of Hitachi province. Nakayama Nobuna 中山信名 (1787–1836) and Kurita Hiroshi 栗田寛 (1835–1899), eds., in 2 vols. Mito: Kanō Yozaemon 加納與右衞門, 1899; Repr. Mito: Hitachi Shobō, 1969.

Shinran shōnin eden 親鸞聖人絵伝, generic name for various pictorial biographies of Shinran. See *Shinran Shōnin ezō, Shinran Shōnin mokuzō, Shinran Shōnin eden* 親鸞聖人絵像、親鸞聖人木像、親鸞聖人絵伝, ed. by Hiramatsu Reizō 平松令三 and Mitsumori Masashi 光森正士. *Shinshū jūhō shūei* 真宗重宝聚英, vol.4. Kyoto: Dōbōsha, 1988.

Shinran Shōnin goshōsoku shū 親鸞聖人御消息集, collection of Shinran's letters. Extant in two recensions, SSZ 2.695 and 2.714; *Nihon koten bungaku taikei* vol. 82.

Shinsei Shōnin ōjōdenki 真盛上人往生伝記. *Shinsei Shōnin godenki shī* 真盛上人御伝記集, Makino Shinnosuke 牧野新之助, ed. Tokyo: Sanshūsha, 1931.

Shinshō yome–odoshi nikutsukimen engi 真正嫁威肉附縁起, traditional folktale. *Yome–odoshi nikutsuki no men ryaku engi: Rennyo Shōnin go–kyūseki* 嫁威肉附之面略縁起: 蓮如上人御舊跡, Wada Sōkyū 和田蒼穹, ed. Sakai 坂井: Ganyōji 願慶寺, 1943.

Shinshū shidō shō 真宗至道抄 by Zonkaku. SSS 5.355.

Shobunshū 諸文集, collection of Rennyo's letters. SSS 2.138.

Shojin hongai shū 諸神本壊集 by Zonkaku. SSS 1.707.

Shōshinge 正信偈, full title: *Shōshin nenbutsu–ge* 正信念仏偈, name applied to verse section at the end of the second fascicle of Shinran's *Kyōgyōshinshō*.

Shōshinge tai'i 正信偈大意 by Rennyo. SSS 2.122 and 130.

Shōshinge wasan 正信偈和讃: See *Shōshinge*.

Shōzōmatsu wasan 正像末和讃 by Shinran. SSZ 2.516.

Shūjishō 執持鈔 by Kakunyo. T No. 2662, 83.735; SSZ 3.37.

Sode nikki: See *Zonkaku sode nikki.*

Songō shinzō meimon 尊号真像銘文 by Shinran. SSZ 2.551.

Sumario de las cosas de Japón, Adiciones del sumario de Japón. José Luis Alvarez-Taladriz. In *Monumenta Nipponica Monogaphs* No. 9. Tokyo: Sophia University (1954).

Tadatomiōki 忠富王記 by Shirakawa Tadatomio 白川忠富王. *Zoku shiryō taisei,* vol. 21.

Tannishō 歎異抄 by Yuien 唯円. T No. 2661, 83.728; SSZ 2.773.

Tannishō chōki 歎異抄長記 by Soga Ryōjin 曾我量深. Kyoto: Chōjiya, 1947. Rev. 4th ed. by Kyoto: Higashi Honganji Shuppanbu, 1970; Soga Ryōjin and Soga Ryōjin Senshū Kankōkai, eds. *Soga Ryōjin senshū* 曾我量深選集 (Kyoto: Yayoi Shobō, 1970), vol. 6.

Tannishō monki 歎異抄聞記 by Ryōshō of Myōon'in 妙音院了祥. Inaba Shūken 稲葉秀賢 ed., Kyoto: Hōzōkan, 1972. Also in 1939–1941 ed. of *Zoku Shinshū taikei, bekkan;* 1976 ed. of *Zoku Shinshū taikei,* vol. 21.

Tariki shinjin kikigaki 他力信心聞書, attributed to Ryōkai 了海 of Bukkōji. *Shinshū taikei* vol. 36.

Tessaradecas consolatoria pro laborantibus et oneratis. Martin Luther, *D. Martin Luther's Werke; kritische Gesamtausgabe,* Weimarer Ausgabe edition. Graz: Akademische Druck– u. Verlagsanstalt (1964–1966), 6:104–134.

Tōji kakochō 東寺過去帳, full title: *Tōji kōmyōkō kakochō* 東寺光明講過去帳, author unknown. In *Zoku gunsho ruiju, zatsubu* 雑部.

Tōji shikkō nikki 東寺執行日記, author unknown. Unpublished.

Tratado em que se contem muito susinta e abreviadamente algumas contradições e deferenças de custumes entre a gente de Europa e esta provincia de Japão. Luis Fróis. Repr. as *Tratado das contradições e diferenças de costumes entra a Europa e o Japão,* ed. de Rui Manuel Loureiro, Macau: Instituto Português do Oriente, 2001.

Von den guten Werken. Martin Luther, *D. Martin Luther's Werke; kritische Gesamtausgabe,* Weimarer Ausgabe (1964–1966), 6:202.

Von der Freyheyt eynisz Christen menschen. Martin Luther, *D. Martin Luther's Werke; kritische Gesamtausgabe,* Weimarer Ausgabe (edition). Graz: Akademische Druck–u. Verlagsanstalt (1964–1966), 7.21.

Vorrede auf die Epistel S. Pauli an die Rōmer. Martin Luther, *D. Martin Luther's Werke; kritische Gesamtausgabe,* Weimarer Ausgabe (edition). Graz: Akademische Druck–u. Verlagsanstalt (1964–1966), 7.10.

Wajima shi Kōtokuji monjo 輪島市興徳寺文書. In *Kōko, Kobunken shiryō* 考古・古文献資料, ed. Wajima-shi shi Hensan Senmon Iinkai 輪島市史編纂専門委員会編, *Wajima shishi* 輪島市史, vol. 3, 1974.

Wakan rōeishū 和漢朗詠集, compiled by Fujiwara Kintō 藤原公任. *Wakan roeishū Ryōjin hishō* Kawakuchi Hisao 川口久雄 and Shida Nobuyoshi 志田延義, eds., *Nihon koten bungaku taikei,* vol. 73.

Wangsheng lizanji 往生礼讃偈 *Ōjō raisan-ge* by Shandao 善導. T No. 1980, 47.438.

Wuliangshou jing 無量壽經, actual title: *Foshuo wuliangshou jing* 佛説無量壽經 *Bussetsu muryōjukyō.* T No. 360, 12.265.

Wuliangshoujing lianyi shuwenzan 無量壽經述文讃 *Muryōjukyō jutsumonsan* by Kyŏnghung. T No.1748, 37.131.

Yamashiro Daigoji sōjishu mōshijōan 山城醍醐寺惣寺衆申状案. *Kamakura ibun,* No. 19091.

Yamashina gobō no koto narabi ni sono jidai no koto 山科御坊事並其時代事 by Jitsugo. RGB 175; SSS 2.541.

Yasokai shi shokanshū 耶蘇会士書簡集. In *Nagasaki kenshi shiryō hen* 長崎県史史料編, vol. 3, Nagasaki-ken 長崎県, ed.

Yoroboshi 弱法師, traditional Nō play. In *Yōkyokushū jō* 謡曲集 上, Yokomichi Mario and Omote Akira, eds. *Nihon koten bungaku taikei,* vol. 40.

Yuishinshō 唯信鈔 by Seikaku 成覚. T No. 2675, 83.91.
Yuishinshō mon'i 唯信鈔文意 by Shinran. T No. 2658, 83.699; SSZ 2.621.
Zenshō bon goshōsoku shū 善性本御消息集 by Shinran. SSZ 2.714.
Zonkaku hōgo 存覺法語 by Zonkaku. SSZ 3.353.
Zonkaku sode nikki 存覺袖日記 by Zonkaku. SSS 1.892.

Secondary Sources: Books

Abe Norio 阿部法夫. *Rennyo shinkō no kenkyū* 蓮如信仰の研究: 越前を 中心として. Osaka: Seibundō, 2003.

Abbott, Walter M., general editor. *The Documents of Vatican II*. New York: Guild Press, 1966.

Akamatsu Toshihide 赤松俊秀 and Kasahara Kazuo 笠原一男. *Shinshūshi gaisetsu*, Kyoto: Heirakuji Shoten, 1963.

Akegarasu Haya. *Rennyo Shōnin–ron* 蓮如上人論. *Akegarasu Haya zenshū* 暁烏敏全集, vol. 13. Ishikawa: Kōsōsha, 1958.

Akegarasu Haya 暁烏敏 and Shikano Hisatsune 鹿野久恒. *Rennyo Shōnin* 蓮如上人. Ishikawa: Bukkyō Bunka Kyōkai, 1948.

Amino Yoshihiko 網野善彦. *Rennyo Shōnin ni manabu: Shinshū kyōdan keisei no shakaiteki kiban* 蓮如上人に学ぶ: 真宗教団形成の社会的基盤. Kyoto: Shinshū Ōtaniha Shūmusho Kikakushitsu, 1993.

——. *Zoku Nihon no rekishi o yominaosu* 続●日本の歴史をよみなおす. Tokyo: Chikuma Shobō, 1996.

Aoki Kaoru 青木馨. *Rennyo Shōnin monogatari* 蓮如上人ものがたり. Kyoto: Higashihonganji Shuppanbu, 1995.

Asaeda Zenshō 朝枝善照. *Myōkōninden kenkyū* 妙好人伝研究. Kyoto: Nagata Bunshōdō, 1987.

Asahi Shinbunsha 朝日新聞社, ed. *Shinran to Rennyo* 親鸞と蓮如. Tokyo: Asahi Shinbunsha, 1992.

Asai Jyōkai 浅井成海監修. *Rennyo no tegami: ofumi / gobunshō gendai goyaku* 蓮如の手紙: お文●御文章現代語訳. Tokyo: Kokusho Kankōkai, 1997.

Asakura Kiyū 朝倉喜祐. *Rennyo: Hokurikuji wo iku* 蓮如: 北陸路を行く. Tokyo: Kokusho Kankōkai, 1995.

——. *Yoshizaki gobō no rekishi* 吉崎御坊の歴史. Tokyo: Kokusho Kankōkai, 1995.

Asano Kenshin 浅野研真. *Rennyo Shōnin no keizai shisō* 蓮如上人の経済思想. In *Bukkyō hōsei keizai kenkyūsho monogaphī* 佛教法政経済 研究所モノグラフィー, vol. 1. Tokyo: Bukkyō Hōsei Keizai Kenkyūsho, 1933.

Asao Naohiro 朝尾直弘 et al., eds. *Iwanami kōza Nihon tsūshi* 岩波講座日本通史, 26 vols. Tokyo: Iwanami Shoten, 1993.

Bainton, Roland H. *Here I Stand: A Life of Martin Luther*. New York: Abingdon–Cokesbury Press, 1950.

Bandō Shōjun 坂東性純, ed. *Daijō Butten—Chūgoku/ Nihonhen*, vol. 29: *Kana hōgo* 大乗仏典 中国●日本篇29: 仮名法語. Tokyo: Chūō Kōronsha, 1991.

Berry, Mary Elizabeth. *The Culture of Civil War in Kyoto*. Berkeley, Cal.: University of California Press, 1994.

Blum, Mark. *The Origins and Development of Pure Land Buddhism: A Study and Translation of Gyōnen's Jōdo Hōmon Genrushō*. New York: Oxford University Press, 2002.

Chiba Jōryū 千葉乗隆. *Rennyo Shōnin monogatari* 蓮如上人ものがたり. Kyoto: Honganji Shuppansha, 1998.

——, ed. *Dangibon* 談議本. *Shinshū shiryō shūsei*, vol. 5. Kyoto: Dōbōsha 1979.

Chiba Jōryū 千葉乗隆. ed. *Honganji Kyōdan no tenkai* 本願寺教団の展開. Kyoto: Nagata Bunshōdō, 1995.

———, ed. *Nihon no shakai to shinshū* 日本の社会と真宗. Kyoto: Shibunkaku Shuppan, 1999.

——— et al., eds. *Rennyo Shōnin ezō, Rennyo Shōnin eden, Shinshū shoha rekidai ezō, Kaiki mokuzō,* 蓮如上人絵像、蓮如上人絵伝、真宗諸派歴代絵像、開基木像. *Shinshū jūhō shūei* 真宗重宝聚英, vol. 9. Shinkō no Zōkeiteki Hyōgen Kenkyū Iinkai. Kyoto: Dōbōsha, 1988.

Chiba Jōryū, Katada Osamu 堅田修, and Miyazaki Enjun, eds. *Rennyo Shōnin ofumi* 蓮如上人御文. Kyoto: Dōbōsha, 1982.

Chigen (Chōshōin 長生院) 智現 (d. 1835). *Rennyo Shōnin Goichidai kikigaki hitsushi* 蓮如上人御一代聞書筆誌. *Shinshū zensho*, vol. 44, 1914.

Coates, Harper, and Ishizuka Ryugaku. *Hōnen, the Buddhist Saint.* Kyoto: Chion'in, 1925.

Cobb, John J., Jr. *Beyond Dialogue: Toward a Mutual Transformation of Christianity and Buddhism.* Philadelphia: Fortress Press, 1982.

Cooper, Michael, trans. and ed. *This Island of Japon: Joao Rodrigues' Account of 16th Century Japan.* New York: Kodansha International, 1973; repr. London: Hakluyt Society, 2001.

Dobbins, James. *Jōdo Shinshū: Shin Buddhism in Medieval Japan.* Bloomington: University of Indiana Press, 1989.

Dōhō Daigaku Bukkyō Bunka Kenkyūsho 同朋大学仏教文化研究所, ed. *Rennyo myōgō no kenkyū* 蓮如名号の研究. Kyoto: Hōzōkan, 1998.

———, ed. *Jitsunyo han, Gojō ofumi no kenkyū: eiinhen* 実如判、五帖御文の研究: 影印篇. Kyoto: Hōzōkan, 1999.

———, ed. *Rennyo hōben hosshin sonzō no kenkyū* 蓮如方便法身尊像の研究. Kyoto: Hōzōkan, 2003.

Dōhō Daigaku Bukkyō Gakkai 同朋大学仏教学会 ed. *Dōhō bukkyō: Rennyo shōnin kenkyū gō* 同朋仏教: 蓮如上人研究号. Nagoya: Dōhō Daigaku Bukkyō Gakkai, 1971.

———, ed. *Rennyo Shōnin no kenkyū* 蓮如上人の研究. Nagoya: Bunkōdō Shoten, 1971.

———, ed. *Ronshū Rennyo: sono shisō to bunka* 論集蓮如: その思想と文化. Nagoya: Dōhō Daigaku Bukkyō Gakkai & Bunkōdō Shoten, 1988.

Dōnryū (Daigyōin 大行院) 曇龍 (1769–1841). *Ryōgemon ryakuge* 領解文略解. *Shinshū sōsho*, vol. 10.

Dōon (Joshinin 浄信院) 道隠 (1741–1813). *Ofumi myōtōshō* 御文明灯鈔, in 15 fascicles. *Shinshū sōsho*, vol. 10.

Dōon. *Ofumi myōtōshō tsūkan* 御文明灯鈔通関, in 2 fascicles. *Shinshū sōsho*, vol. 10.

Dostoyevsky, Feodor. *The Brothers Karamazov.* Constance Garnett, trans. New York: Grosset & Dunlap, 1900; repr. New York: Dutton, 1927.

Ebisawa Arimichi 海老沢有道, H. Cieslik, et al., eds. *Kirishitan sho, Haiyasho* キリシタン書 • 排耶書. *Nihon shisō taikei* 日本思想大系, vol. 25. Tokyo: Iwanami Shoten, 1970.

Ema Tsutomu 江馬務 et al. trans. and ed., *Nihon kyōkai shi* 日本教会史 2 vols. *Daikōkai jidai sōsho* 大航海時代叢書, IX and X. Tokyo: Iwanami Shoten 1970).

Endō Genyū 遠藤玄雄 (1804–1881). *Ryōgemon kōgi* 領解文講義. *Shinshū sōsho*, vol. 10.

Endō Hajime 遠藤一. *Sengokuki Shinshū no rekishizō* 戦国期真宗の歴史像. Kyoto: Nagata Bunshōdō, 1992.

Enen (Kōgonin 香嚴院) 惠然 (1693–1764). *Shinju hongangi* 信受本願義. *Shinshū taikei*, vol. 35.

Enoki Katsurō 榎克朗, ed. *Ryojin hisho* 梁塵秘抄. *Shincho Nihon koten shūsei* 新潮日本古典集成, vol. 31. Tokyo: Shinchosha, 1979.

Fudeuchi Yukiko 筆内幸子. *Shintei – Rennyo Shōnin to sono gonin no tsumatachi* 新訂: 蓮如上人とその五人の妻たち. Ishikawa: Hokkoku Shinbunsha, 1985, rev. ed. 1994.

Fugen Kōju 普賢晃寿. *Chūsei Shinshū kyōgaku no tenkai* 中世真宗教学の展開. Kyoto: Nagata Bunshōdō, 1994.

Fuji Shūsui 藤秀すい. *Gikkyokushū: Ajasseō / Dai Rennyo* 戯曲集: 阿闍世王 • 大蓮如. *Fuji Shūsui senshū* 藤秀すい選集, vol. 7. 1948; repr. Kyoto: Hōzōkan, 1982, 1997.

Fujisawa Ryōshō 藤澤量正. *Rennyo Shōnin Goichidaiki kikigaki kōwa* 蓮如上人御一代記聞書講話. *Seiten kōza* 聖典講座, vol. 3. Kyoto: Nagata Bunshōdō, 1979.

——. *Rennyo Shōnin Goichidaiki kikigaki.* 蓮如上人御一代記聞書. Kyoto: Honganji Shuppansha, 1998.

Fujishima Tatsurō 藤島達朗. *Rennyo Shōnin Goichidaiki kikigaki josetsu* 蓮如上人御一代記聞書序説. Kyoto: Higashi Honganji Shuppanbu, 1976.

Fujiwara Kyōen 藤原教円. *Rennyo Shōnin Goichidaiki kikigaki nyūmon* 蓮如上人御一代記聞書入門. Kyoto: Hyakkaen, 1970.

Fujiwara Tokuyu 藤原徳悠. *Rennyo Shōnin Ofumi no keigo hyōgen* 蓮如上人「御文」の敬語表現. Osaka: Izumi Shoin, 2001.

Fukuma Kōcho 福間光超, Sakurai Yoshirō 桜井好朗, et al., eds. *Ikkyū / Rennyo* 一休 蓮如. *Nihon meisō ronshū* 日本名僧論集, vol. 10. Tokyo: Yoshikawa Kōbunkan, 1983.

Fukuma Kōchō Sensei Kanreki Kinenkai 福間光超先生還暦記念会編, ed. *Shinshūshi ronsō* 真宗史論叢. Kyoto: Nagata Bunshōdō, 1993.

Fukushima Sōyū 福嶋崇雄, Fujitani Shindō 藤谷信道, Kumano Kōyō 熊野恒陽, Yamaori Tetsuo 山折哲雄, and Sasaki Eishō 佐々木英彰. *Bukkōji itansetsu no shinsō* 佛光寺異端説の真相. Kyoto: Hakubasha, 1999.

Fukuzawa Yukichi 福沢諭吉 with Keiō Gijuku 慶應義塾, ed. *Fukuzawa Yukichi zenshū* 福沢諭吉全集. 22 vols. Tokyo: Iwanami Shoten, 1969–1971.

Funahashi Haruo 舩橋晴雄. *Nihon keizai no furusato o aruku: Rennyo kara Ryōma e* 日本経済の故郷を歩く: 蓮如から竜馬へ. Tokyo: Chūō Kōronsha, 2000.

Furuta Takehiko 古田武彦. *Shinran shisō* 親鸞思想. Tokyo: Fusanbō, 1975.

Gitō (Saishinin 最親院) 義陶 (1740–1821). *Ge no ofumi shotsū kōgi* 夏御文初通講義. *Shinshū taikei*, vol. 35.

Hābādo Daigaku Shinpojiumu to Beikoku Tōbu Kenshū Ryokōdan アメリカの宗教を訪ねて: ハーバード大学シンポジウムと米国東部研修旅行, *Amerika no shūkyō wo tazunete* アメリカの宗教を訪ねて: *Shin Buddhism Meets American Religions*. Kyoto: Amerika no Shūkyō wo Tazunete Henshūkei, 1986.

Hachiya Yoshikiyo 蜂屋賢喜代. *Rennyo Shōnin Goichidaiki Kikigaki kōwa* 蓮如上人御一代記聞書講話. Kyoto: Hōzōkan, 1936, repr. 1989.

Haguri Gyōdō 羽栗行道. *Rennyo Shōnin no menmoku: Goichidaiki kikigaki no kaisetsu* 蓮如上人の面目—御一代記聞書の解説. Kyoto: Shinkō to Seikatsusha, 1954.

Hall, John W., and Toyoda Takeshi, eds. *Japan in the Muromachi Age.* Berkeley: University of California Press, 1977.

Harada Mitsuko 原田満子. *Rennyo: ranse o ikiru chie* 蓮如—乱世を生きる智慧. Tokyo: Mokujisha, 1997.

Hashimoto Asao 橋本朝生, ed. *Ōkura toramitsubon kyōgen shū* 大蔵虎光本狂言集, 4 vols., *Koten bunko* 古典文庫, nos 527, 535, 540, and 546. Tokyo: Koten Bunko, 1990–1992.

Hattori Shisō 服部之總. *Rennyo* 蓮如. Tokyo: Shinji Shobō, 1948; repr. as vol. 14 in *Hattori Shisō Zenshū* 服部之總全集. Tokyo: Fukumura Shuppan, 1974.

Hayakawa Kenshi 早川顯之, ed. *Rennyo e no gokai* 蓮如への誤解. Kyoto: Nagata Bunshōdō, 1995.

Hayashi Tomoyasu 林智康. *Rennyo kyōgaku no kenkyū* 蓮如教学の研究. Kyoto: Nagata Bunshōdō, 1998.

Hayashima Kyōshō 早島鏡正, ed. *Rennyo no subete* 蓮如のすべて. Tokyo: Shinjinbutsu Ōraisha, 1995.

Hayashima Kyōshō 早島鏡正, *Rennyo: sono oshie to ikikata* 蓮如：その教えと生き方. Tokyo: NHK Shuppan, 1997.

Higuchi Hideo 樋口秀夫 et al., eds. *Shichijūichiban shokunin utaawase, Shokunin zukushie, Saiga shokunin burui* 七十一番職人歌合、職人尽絵、彩画職人 部類. *Edo kagaku koten sōsho* 江戸科学古典叢書, vol. 6. Tokyo: Kōwa Shuppan, 1977.

Hirai Kiyotaka 平井清隆. *Shōsetsu: Rennyo to sono haha* 小説：蓮如とその母. Kyoto: Nagata Bunshōdō, 1983.

——. *Shōsetsu: nenbutsu ōkoku* 小説 念仏王国. Kyoto: Hōzōkan, 1991.

——. *Rennyo Shōnin no haha to sono miuchi* 蓮如上人の母とその身内. Kyoto: Nagata Bunshōdō, 1996.

Hiramatsu Reizō 平松令三 and Mitsumori Masashi 光森正士, eds. *Shinran Shōnin ezō, Shinran Shōnin mokuzō, Shinran Shōnin eden* 親鸞聖人絵像、親鸞聖人木像、親鸞聖人絵伝. *Shinshū jūhō shūei* 真宗重宝聚英, vol. 4. Shinkō no Zōkeiteki Hyōgen Kenkyū Iinkai. Kyoto: Dōbōsha, 1988.

Hirano Tomeo 平野止夫. *Rennyo: ten no maki / chi no maki* 蓮如：天の巻 ⊠ 地の巻. Kyoto: Hyakkaen, 1948.

Hirose Nan'yu 広瀬南雄. *Shinshūgakushi kō* 真宗学史稿. Kyoto: Hōzōkan, 1980.

Hirose Takashi 廣瀬杲, Ōkuwa Hitoshi 大桑斉, and Tamamitsu Junshō 玉光順正. *Jidai no owari to hajime ni: Rennyo Shōnin gohyakkai goenki wo tōshite* 時代の終わりとはじまりに：蓮如上人五百回御遠忌をとおして. Kyoto: Shinshū Ōtaniha Shūmusho Kikakushitsu, 1999.

Hōjū (Kaigein 開華院) 法住 (d. 1874). *Gaikemon kōgi* 改悔文講義. *Zoku Shinshū taikei*, vol. 9.

Hōkai (Igyōin 易行院) 法海. *Ofumi gengi* 御文玄義. 1811 colophon. *Shinshū taikei*, vol. 32.

Hōkei (Gojōin 五乘院) 寶景 (1746–1828). *Ge no ofumi dainitsū daisantsū daiyontsū kōgi* 夏御文第二通第三通第四通講義. *Shinshū taikei*, vol. 35.

Hokkoku Shinbunsha 北国新聞社, ed. *Shinshū no fūkei: Hokuriku ikki kara Ishiyama gassen e* 真宗の風景—北陸一揆から石山合戦へ. Kyoto: Dōbōsha, 1990.

Hokkoku Shinbunsha Henshūbu 北国新聞社編集部, ed. *Rennyo san—ima wo ayumu* 蓮如さん：今を歩む. Ishikawa: Hokkoku Shinbunsha, 1996.

Honganji Shiryō Kenkyūjo 本願寺史料研究所, ed., *Honganjishi* 本願寺史, in 4 vols. Kyoto: Jōdo Shinshū Honganji–ha, 1961–1984.

——, ed. *Zuroku: Rennyo Shōnin yohō* 図録：蓮如上人 余芳. Kyoto: Honganji Shuppansha, 1998.

Honganji Shiryō Kenkyūjo and Kyōdō Tsūshinsha 共同通信社編集, eds. *Rennyo Shōnin gohyakkaiki kinen Rennyo Shōnin ten* 蓮如上人五百回忌記念：蓮如上人展. Tokyo: Kyōdōtsūshinsha, 1997.

Honpa Honganji Shūgakuin 本派本願寺宗学院, ed. *Kosha kohan Shinshū shōgyō genzon mokuroku* 古写古版真宗聖教現存目録. Kyoto: Kōkyō Shoin, 1937.

Hōrei (of Kaiōin 皆往院) 鳳嶺. *Gaikemon kōgi* 改悔文講義, in 3 fascicles. 1796 Colophon. *Zoku Shinshū taikei*, vol. 9.

Hori Hiroyoshi 堀浩良. *Shōsetsu Rennyo: seinen jidai* 小説蓮如：青年時代. Kyoto: Nagata Bunshōdō, 1972.

Hōsen (Kōsetsuin 廣説院) 法宣 (1803–1867). *Gaikemon zuimonki* 改悔文随聞記. *Zoku Shinshū taikei*, vol. 9.

Hōshi Soun 蓬茨祖運. *Rennyo Shōnin: ofumi ni manabu* 蓮如上人：御文に学ぶ. Nagoya: (Shinshū Ōtaniha) Nagoya Kyōmusho, 1979.

Hoshino Genpō 星野元豊, *Kōkai Kyōgyōshinshō* 講解教行信証. Kyoto: Hōzōkan, 1977–1983; rev. ed. 1994.

—— et al., eds. *Kyōgyōshinshō* 教行信証, in *Shinran* 親鸞. *Nihon shisō taikei*, vol. 11. Tokyo: Iwanami Shoten, 1971.

Hosokawa Gyōshin 細川行信. *Ōtani sobyōshi* 大谷祖廟史. Kyoto: Higashi Honganji Shuppanbu, 1963.

——. *Shinran shisō no bunken kaisetsu* 親鸞思想の文献解説. *Kōza Shinran no shisō* 講座 親鸞の思想, No. 9. Tokyo: Kyōiku Shinchōsha, 1979.

——, ed. *Kodera Junrei Gaido: Shinran/ Rennyo* 古寺巡礼ガイド 親鸞 • 蓮如. Kyoto: Hōzōkan, 1983.

Hosokawa Gyōshin and Kawamura Takeo 川村赳夫. *Rennyo no michi—hōseki* 蓮如のみち (芳跡). Kyoto: Higashi Honganji Shuppanbu, 1996.

Hosokawa Gyōshin, Murakami Munehiro 村上宗博, Adachi Yukiko 足立幸子. *Gendai no Seiten: Rennyo gojō ofumi* 現代の聖典：蓮如五帖御文. Kyoto: Hōzōkan, 1993.

——. *Gendai no seiten: Rennyo Shōnin Goichidai kikigaki* 現代の聖典：蓮如上人御一代 聞書. Kyoto: Hōzōkan, 1996.

Hosokawa Iwao 細川厳. *Rennyo Shōnin Goichidaiki kikigaki sangyō*. 蓮如上人 御一代記聞 書讃仰. Kyoto: Higashi Honganji Shuppanbu, 1989.

Ikawa Jōkyō 井川定慶. *Hōnen Shōnin den zenshū* 法然上人傳全集. Osaka: Hōnen Shōnin-den Zenshū Kankōkai, 1961; rev. and expanded ed. 1967.

Ikeda Yūtai 池田勇諦. *Gaikemon kōsatsu: Shinshū kyōkagaku no kadai* 改悔文考察： 真宗 教化学の課題. Kyoto: Shinshū Ōtaniha Shūmusho Shuppanbu, 1986.

——. *Ofumi Kankeroku* 御文勧化録. Kyoto: Shinshū Ōtaniha Shūmusho Shuppanbu, 1998.

——. *Shinjin no saikō: Rennyo Ofumi no hongi* 信心の再興：蓮如 「御文」の本義. Kunitachi (Tokyo): Jushinsha, 2002.

——, et al. *Ofumi no bun'i* 御文の分位. *Rennyo Shōnin ni manabu* 蓮如上人に学ぶ, vol. 4. Kyoto: Shinshū Ōtaniha Shūmusho Shuppanbu, 1998.

Imada Hōyū 今田法雄. *Rennyo Shōnin: saikō to dendō no shōgai* 蓮如上人： 再興と伝道 の生涯. Kyoto: Nagata Bunshōdō, 1996.

Imai Masaharu 今井雅晴. *Shinran to Rennyo no sekai* 親鸞と蓮如の世界. Tsuchiura (Ibaraki): Tsukuba Shorin, 2000.

Inaba Enjō 稲葉円成. *Ofumi kōyo* 御文綱要. Kyoto: Ōtaniha Angō Jimusho (Higashi Honganji Shuppanbu), 1947.

Inaba Masamaru 稲葉昌丸, ed. *Rennyo Shōnin gyōjitsu* 蓮如上人行実. Kyoto: Ōtani Daigaku Shuppanbu, 1928; repr. Kyoto: Hōzōkan, 1948, 1983.

——, ed. *Rennyo Shōnin ibun* 蓮如上人遺文. Kyoto: Hōzōkan, 1937; repr. 1948, 1983, 1990.

——, ed. *Shohan taikō gojō ofumi teihon* 諸版対校五帖御文定本. Self–published, 1933, repr. Kyoto: Hōzōkan, 1995.

Inaba Shūken 稲葉秀賢. *Rennyo Shōnin no kyōgaku* 蓮如上人の教学. Kyoto: Ōtani Shuppansha, 1949; repr. Kyoto: Bun'eidō, 1972.

Inagi Masami 稲城正己. *Kataru Rennyo to Katareta Rennyo: sengokuki Shinshū no shinkō sekai*. Kyoto: Jinbun Shoin, 2001.

Inaki Sen'e 稲城選恵. *Gobunshō gaiyō: Rennyo kyōgaku no chūshin mondai* 御文章 概 要—蓮如教学の中心問題. Kyoto: Hyakkaen, 1983, repr. 1990.

——. *Rennyo Shōnin no shōgai to sono oshie* 蓮如上人の生涯とその教え. Kyoto: Tankyūsha, 1992.

——. *Rennyo kyōgaku no kenkyū 1: gyōshinron* 蓮如教学の研究 1: 行信論. Kyoto: Hōzōkan, 1993.

——. *Rennyo kyōgaku no kenkyū 2: shukuzenron* 蓮如教学の研究 2 宿善論. Kyoto: Hōzōkan, 1994.

Inaki Sen'e 稲城選恵. *Rennyo kyōgaku no kenkyū* 3: *igiron* 蓮如教学の研究 3: 異義論. Kyoto: Hōzōkan, 1996.

——. *Shinshū yōgo jiten: Rennyo–hen* 真宗用語辞典: 蓮如篇. Kyoto: Hōzōkan, 1998.

Inaki Sen'e and Fukagawa Rinyū 深川倫雄監修. *Rennyo Shōnin ni manabu: go–shōsoku wo itadaite* 蓮如上人に学ぶ―ご消息をいただいて. Kyoto: Nishi Honganji (Fukyōdan Rengō), 1994.

Inoue Keiichi 井上啓一. *Gobunshō no ajiwai* 御文章の味わい. Kyoto: Hyakkaen, 1984.

Inoue Toshio 井上鋭夫. *Honganji* 本願寺. Tokyo: Shibundō, 1962; repr. 1966. *Nihon rekishi shinsho* 日本歴史新書, nos. 51–100.

——. *Ikkō ikki no kenkyū* 一向一揆の研究. Tokyo: Yoshikawa Kōbunkan, 1968.

Inoue Zen'emon 井上善右衛門. *Rennyo Shōnin Goichidaiki Kikigaki ni manabu* 蓮如上人御一代記聞書に学ぶ. Kyoto: Nagata Bunshōdō, 1982; rev. ed. 1994.

Institute of Jodo Shinshu Studies and Hongwanji International Center, eds. *The Rennyo Reader*. Kyoto: Jodo Shinshu Hongwanji–ha, 1998.

Ishida Kyōdō 石田教道, ed. *Shōwa shinshū Hōnen Shōnin zenshū* 昭和新修 法然上人全集. Kyoto: Heirakuji Shoten, 1955.

Ishida Manabu 石田学. Getsumei *Rennyo hyōden* 『月明』蓮如評伝. Kyoto: Nagata Bunshōdō, 1997.

Ishida Mitsuyuki Hakase Koki Kinen Ronbunshū Kankōkai 石田充之博士古稀記念論文集刊行会, ed. *Jōdokyō no kenkyū: Ishida Mitsuyuki hakase koki kinen ronbun* 土教の研究: 石田充之博士古稀 記念論文. Kyoto: Nagata Bunshōdō, 1982.

Ishida Mitsuyuki 石田充之. *Rennyo* 蓮如. Kyoto: Jironsha, 1949; rev. ed. Kyoto: Nagata Bunshōdō, 1993.

Ishii Kyōdō 石井教道. *Shōwa shinshū Hōnen Shōnin zenshū*. Kyoto: Heirakuji Shoten, 1955.

Ishikawa Shundai 石川舜台. *Rennyo Shōnin to hokkoku* 蓮如上人と北国. Kyoto: Gohōkan, 1917; repr. Kyoto: Nishimura Gohōkan, 1935.

Itsuki Hiroyuki 五木寛之. *Rennyo: seizoku guyū no ningenzō* 蓮如: 聖俗具有の人間像. No. 343 in the new red series of *Iwanami shinsho* 岩波新書 Tokyo: Iwanami Shoten, 1994.

——. *Rennyo monogatari* 蓮如物語. Tokyo: Kadokawa Shoten, 1995.

——. *Rennyo: ware fukaki fuchiyori* 蓮如―われ深き淵より. Tokyo: Chūō Kōronsha, 1995.

Iwakura Masaji 岩倉政治. *Myōkōnin Akao no Dōshū* 妙好人赤尾の道宗. Kyoto: Hōzōkan, 1986.

Iwami Mamoru 岩見護. *Rennyo Shōnin no go'ōjō* 蓮如上人の御往生. Kyoto: Ōtani Shuppansha, 1949.

——. *Akao no Dōshū* 赤尾の道宗. Kyoto: Nagata Bunshōdō, 1956; Hōzōkan, 1986.

——. *Rennyo Shōnin* 蓮如上人. Kyoto: Shōsei'en, 1949; repr. Kyoto: Bun'eidō, 1996.

Izumoji Osamu 出雲路修, ed. *Ofumi: Rennyo* 御ふみ: 蓮如. *Tōyō bunko* 東洋文庫 No. 345. Tokyo: Heibonsha, 1978; repr. 1995.

Izumoji Osamu, Kuroda Toshio 黒田俊雄, Kashiwabara Yūsen 柏原祐泉, Amino Yoshihiko 網野善彦, Takashi Akita 高史明他. *Rennyo Shōnin no ayunda michi: Rennyo Shōnin ni manabu* 1 蓮如上人の歩んだ道―蓮如上人に学ぶ 1. Kyoto: Shinshū Ōtaniha Shūmusho Shuppanbu, 1998.

Jacobs, Martin, A. T. W. Steinhäuser, and W. A. Lambert, ed. and trans. *Three Treatises* by Martin Luther, 2nd rev. ed. Philadelphia: Fortress Press, 1970.

Jinrei (Kōgatsuin 光月院) 深勵 (1749–1817). *Gaikemon kikigaki* 改悔文聞書. *Zoku Shinshū taikei*, vol. 9.

——. *Ge no ofumi kōgi* 夏御文講議. Kyoto: Nishimura Kūgedō 西村空華堂, undated but probably Meiji period.

Jinrei (Kōgatsuin 光月院) 深勵 (1749–1817). *Ofumi kōgi* 御文講義, in 8 fascicles. *Shinshū zensho*, vol. 49.

——. *Rennyo Shōnin Goichidaiki kikigaki kōgi* 蓮如上人御一代記聞書講義, in 3 fascicles. *Shinshū taikei*, vol. 29–30.

Jōdo Shinshū Kyōgaku Kenkyūjo 浄土真宗教学研究所, ed. *Rennyo Shōnin: sono oshie to shōgai ni manabu* 蓮如上人‐その教えと生涯に学ぶ. Kyoto: Honganji Shuppansha 1995.

——, ed. *Rennyo Shōnin kenkyū: kyōgihen I & II* 蓮如上人研究：教義篇 I・II. Kyoto: Nagata Bunshōdō, 1998.

——, ed. *Jōdo Shinshū seiten—Rennyo Shōnin Goichidaiki kikigaki: gendaigoban* 浄土真宗聖典‐蓮如上人御一代記聞書：現代語版. Kyoto: Honganji Shuppansha, 1999.

Jōdo Shinshū Kyōgaku Kenkyūjo and Honganji Shiryō Kenkyūjo 本願寺史料研究所, eds. *Kōza Rennyo* 講座蓮如, in 6 vols. Tokyo: Heibonsha, 1996.

Joseishi Sōgō Kenkyūkai 女性史総合研究会, ed. *Nihon joseishi 3: kinsei* 日本女性史 3：近世. Tokyo: Tokyo Daigaku Shuppankai, 1982.

Jungei (of Shinjuin 信珠院) 順藝 (1785–1847). *Ofumi kenkyō* 御文研鏡. *Shinshū taikei*, vol. 32.

Kagai Senmyō 利井鮮妙. *Ge no ofumi kōwa* 夏御文講話. *Shinshū sōsho*, vol. 10.

Kagotani Machiko 籠谷真智子. *Shinshū bunkashi no kenkyū: Honganji no geinō ronkō* 真宗文化史の研究：本願寺の芸能論考. Kyoto Joshi Daigaku Kenkyū Sōkan 京都女子大学研究叢刊, vol. 23. Kyoto: Kyoto Joshi Daigaku, 1995.

Kakehashi Jitsuen 梯實圓 et al., eds. *Rennyo taikei* 蓮如大系, in 5 vols. Kyoto: Hōzōkan, 1996.

Kamata Sōun 鎌田宗雲. *Rennyo Shōnin to "Gobunshō"* 蓮如上人と『御文章』. Kyoto: Hyakkaen, 1995.

——. *Rennyo Shōnin: shōgai to sono oshie* 蓮如上人—生涯とその教え. Kyoto: Tankyūsha, 1996.

——. *Gobunshō kaisetsu* 御文章解説. Kyoto: Nagata Bunshōdō, 1997.

——. *Rennyo Shōnin ni manabu* 蓮如上人に学ぶ. Kyoto: Tankyūsha, 1997.

Kamimura Kankō 上村観光, ed., *Gozan bungaku zenshū* 五山文學全集, in 5 vols. Tokyo: Gozanbungaku Zenshū Kankōkai, 1936; repr. Kyoto: Shibunkaku, 1973.

Kanda Chisato 神田千里. *Ikkō ikki to Shinshū shinkō* 一向一揆と真宗信仰. Tokyo: Yoshikawa Kōbunkan, 1991.

——. *Ikkō ikki to sengoku jidai* 一向一揆と戦国時代. Tokyo: Yoshikawa Kōbunkan, 1998.

Kaneko Daiei 金子大栄 ed. *Kyōgyōshinshō* 教行信証. *Iwanami Bunko* 岩波文庫, nos. 5813–5816. Tokyo: Iwanami Shoten, 1957.

Kanō Minzoku no Kai 加能民族の会, ed. *Rennyo san: monto ga kataru Rennyo denshō shūsei* 蓮如さん：門徒が語る蓮如伝承集成. Kanazawa: Hashimoto Kakubundō Kikakubu Shuppanshitsu, 1988.

Kasahara Kazuo 笠原一男. *Ikkō ikki no kenkyū* 一向一揆の研究. Tokyo: Yamakawa Shuppansha, 1962.

——. *Rennyo* 蓮如. Jinbutsu Sōsho 人物叢書, vol. 109. Tokyo: Yoshikawa Kōbunkan, 1963, repr. 1986.

——. *Nyonin ōjō shisō no keifu* 女人往生思想の系譜. Tokyo: Yoshikawa Kōbunkan, 1975.

——. *Shinran to Rennyo: sono kōdo to shisō* 親鸞と蓮如：その行動と思想. Tokyo: Ronhyōsha, 1978.

——. *Shinshū kyōdan tenkaishi* 真宗教団開展史. 1942; repr. Tokyo: Pitaka, 1978.

——. *Ranse wo ikiru: Rennyo no shōgai* 乱世を生きる：蓮如の生涯. Tokyo: Kyōikusha, 1981.

——, ed. *Rennyo bunshū* 蓮如文集. *Iwanami Bunko*, vol. 33–322–1, 1985. Tokyo: Iwanami Shoten.

——. *Fumetsu no hito: Rennyo* 不滅の人：蓮如. Tokyo: Sekai Seiten Kankō Kyōkai, 1993.

Kasahara Kazuo 笠原一男. *Rennyo* 蓮如. *Gakujutsu bunko* 学術文庫, no. 1224. Tokyo: Kodansha, 1996.

Kasahara Kazuo and Inoue Toshio, eds. *Rennyo / Ikkō ikki* 蓮如 • 一向一揆. *Nihon shisō taikei*, vol. 17. Tokyo: Iwanami Shoten 1972.

Kashiwabara Yūsen 柏原祐泉. *Rennyo Shōnin no montei tachi* 蓮如上人の門弟たち. Video cassette. Kyoto: Ōtani Daigaku, 1998.

Kashiwabara Yūsen, Kuroda Toshio 黒田俊雄, and Hiramatsu Reizō 平松令三, eds. *Kyōdan no Tenkai* 教団の展開. *Shinran taikei: Rekishi hen* 歴史篇, vol. 6. Kyoto: Hōzōkan, 1989.

——, eds. *Rennyo no shōgai* 蓮如の生涯. *Shinran taikei: Rekishi hen*, vol. 7, Kyoto: Hōzōkan, 1989.

——, eds. *Sengokuki no Shinshū* 戦国期の真宗. *Shinran taikei: Rekishi hen*, vol. 8. Kyoto: Hōzōkan, 1989.

Katada Osamu 堅田修, ed. *Rennyo to sono kyōdan* 真宗史料集成2−蓮如とその教団. *Shinshū shiryō shūsei*, vol. 2. Kyoto: Dōbōsha, 1977.

Katō Chiken 加藤智見. *Rennyo to Rutā (Luther): shūkyō kyōdan no genten* 蓮如とルター: 宗教教団の原点. Kyoto: Hōzōkan, 1993.

——. *Rennyo nyūmon* 蓮如入門. Tokyo: Daihōrin Kaku, 1996.

——. *Tariki shinkō no honshitsu: Shinran / Rennyo / Manshi* 他力信仰の本質−親鸞 • 蓮如 • 満之. Tokyo: Kokusho Kankōkai, 1997.

Katō Kyōjun 加藤教順. *Rennyo Shōnin kikigaki dokuhon*. 蓮如上人聞書読本. Kyoto: Hyakkaen, 1971.

Kawade Shobō Shinsha Henshūbu 河出書房新社編集部編, ed. *Zusetsu Rennyo: ikkō namu amida butsu no sekai* 図説蓮如: 一向南無阿弥陀仏の世界. Tokyo: Kawade Shobō Shinsha, 1997.

Kawamoto Gishō 川本義昭, ed. *Zoku Rennyo e no gokai* 続蓮如への誤解. Kyoto: Nagata Bunshōdō, 1997.

Kenzō (Kyōōin 教王院) 賢藏 (d. 1824). *Gaikemon kōgi* 改悔文講義, in 4 fascicles. *Zoku Shinshū taikei*, vol. 9, 1936.

——. *Ge no ofumi shotsū kōgi* 夏御文初通講義. *Shinshū taikei*, vol. 35, 1919.

Ketelaar, James E. *Of Heretics and Martyrs in Japan: Buddhism and Its Persecution*. Princeton, N.J.: Princeton University Press, 1990.

Kikumura Norihiko 菊村紀彦. *Rennyo: sono hito to kōdō* 蓮如−その人と行動. Tokyo: Yūzankaku Shuppan, 1975.

——. *Rennyo: Ranse ni ikita oruganaizā* 蓮如−乱世に生きた オルガナイザー. Tokyo: Suzuki Shuppan, 1988.

Kimura Takeo 木村武夫. ed. *Rennyo Shōninron: mō hitotsu no Ōsaka sengokuki* 蓮如上人論−もう一つの大阪戦国記. Kyoto: PHP Kenkyūsho, 1983.

——, ed. *Rennyo Shōnin no kyōgaku to rekishi* 蓮如上人の教学と歴史. Ōsaka: Tōhō Shuppansha, 1984.

Kinryū Shizuka 金龍静他. *Rennyo* 蓮如. *Rekishi bunka library* 歴史文化ライブラリー, no. 21. Tokyo: Yoshikawa Kōbunkan, 1997.

——, et al. *Rennyo Shōnin to honganji kyōdan* 蓮如と本願寺 教団. Rennyo taikei 蓮如大系, vols. 3-4. Kyoto: Hōzōkan, 1996.

——, et al. *Rennyo Shōnin no mezashita chihei* 蓮如上人の目指した地平. *Rennyo Shōnin ni manabu* 蓮如上人に学ぶ. vol. 2. Kyoto: Shinshū Ōtaniha Shūmusho Shuppanbu, 1996.

Kitanishi Hiromu 北西弘. *Ikkō ikki no kenkyū* 一向一揆の研究. Tokyo: Shunjūsha, 1981.

——. *Rennyo–hitsu rokuji myōgō* 蓮如筆六字名号. Kyoto: Dōbōsha, 1981.

——. *Rennyo, gendai to kyōdan* 蓮如 • 現代と教団. Kanazawa: Hokkoku Shuppansha, 1985.

Kitanishi Hiromu 北西弘. *Rennyo Shōnin hisseki no kenkyū* 蓮如上人筆跡の研究. Tokyo: Shunjūsha, 1999.

——, ed. *Rennyo Shōnin to honganji* 蓮如上人と本願寺. Ishikawa: Hokuriku Chūnichi Shinbusha, 1965.

——, ed. *Shinshū shiryō shūsei* 3: *Ikkō ikki*, 真宗史料集成 3: 一向一揆. Kyoto: Dōbōsha, 1979.

Kitanishi Hiromu Sensei Kanreki Kinenkai 北西弘先生還暦記念会, ed. *Chūsei bukkyō to Shinshū* 中世仏教と真宗. Tokyo: Yoshikawa Kōbunkan, 1985.

Kiyozawa Manshi 清沢滿之, with Nishimura Kengyō 西村見暁 and Akegarasu Haya 曉烏敏. *Kiyozawa Manshi zenshū* 清沢滿之全集. Kyoto: Hōzōkan, 1953.

Knitter, Paul, *No Other Name? A Critical Survey of Christian Attitudes toward the World Religions.* New York: Orbis, 1985.

Kobayashi Hiroaki 小林弘明, ed. *Tetsujin Rennyo: konton no jidai o kakushin shita inobeitā* 鉄人蓮如: 混沌の時代を革新したイノベーター. Tokyo: Sekai Bunkasha, 1998.

Kodama Shiki 児玉識. *Kinsei shūkyō no tenkai katei* 近世宗教の展開課程. Tokyo: Yoshikawa Kōbunkan, 1976.

Kōkakai 光華会, ed. *Kōkakai shūkyō kenkyū ronshū: Shinran to ningen* 2 光華会 宗教研究論集: 親鸞と人間 第 2 巻. Kyoto: Nagata Bunshōdō, 1983.

Komori Tatsukuni 小森龍邦. *Rennyo-ron: toikakeru jinken e no shiten* 蓮如論—問いかける人権への視点. Tokyo: Akashi Shoten, 1998.

Kōrenji Bukkyō Kenkyūkai 光蓮寺仏教研究会, ed. *Renshi kyōgaku kenkyū* 蓮師教学研究, vols. 2–6. Kyoto: Tankyūsha, 1991–1999.

——, ed. *Rennyo e no gokai no gokai* 蓮如への誤解の誤解. Kyoto: Tankyūsha, 1996.

Koyama Hiroshi 小山弘志, ed. *Kyōgenshū* 狂言集. *Nihon koten bungaku taikei*, vols. 42–43. Tokyo: Iwanami Shoten, 1960–1961.

—— et al., eds. *Yōkyokushū ge* 謡曲集 下. *Nihon koten bungaku zenshū*, vol. 34. Tokyo: Shōgakkan, 1975.

Koyama Hōjō 小山法城. *Gobunshō yōgi* 御文章要義. 2 vols. Kyoto: Hyakkaen, 1981.

Kōzon (Jitsumyōin 實明院) 功存 (1720–1796). *Jumyō enzetsuki* 寿命演説記. *Shinshū zensho*, vol. 62.

Kubota Shōei 久保田正衛. *Rennyo* 蓮如. 6 vols. Ōsaka: Shingensha, 1955–1958.

Kūe (Saihōji 西方寺) 空慧 (1661–1746). *Jōdo Shinshū gaikeben* 浄土真宗改悔弁. *Zoku Shinshū taikei*, vol. 9.

Kurata Hyakuzō 倉田百三. *Shukke to sono deshi* 出家とその弟子. Tokyo: Iwanami Shoten, 1917.

Kurihara Gyōshin 栗原行信. *Rennyo no kyūseki to shōgai* 蓮如の旧跡と生涯. Kyoto: Nagata Bunshōdō, 1971.

Kuroda Toshio 黒田俊雄. *Chūsei Nihon no kokka to shūkyo* 中世日本の国家と宗教. Tokyo: Iwanami Shoten, 1975.

——. *Chūsei Nihon no shakai to shūkyō* 中世日本の社会と宗教. Tokyo: Iwanami Shoten, 1990.

——. *Shinkoku shisō to senju nenbutsu* 神国思想と専修念仏. *Kuroda Toshio Chosakushū* 黒田俊雄著作集, vol. 4. Kyoto: Hōzōkan, 1995.

—— et al. *Rennyo ni manabu: Shinshū kyōdan no keisei* 蓮如上人に学ぶ: 真宗教団の形成. Kyoto: Shinshū Ōtaniha Shūmusho Kikakushitsu, 1993.

Kusaka Murin 日下無倫. *Shinshūshi no kenkyū* 真宗史の研究. Kyoto: Rinsen Shoten, 1931.

Kusunose Masaru 楠瀬勝, ed. *Nihon no zenkindai to Hokuriku shakai* 日本の 前近代と 北陸社会. Kyoto: Shibunkaku Shuppan, 1989.

Kyōto Kokuritsu Hakubutsukan 京都国立博物館. *Rennyo to Honganji: sono rekishi to bijutsu* 蓮如と本願寺: その歴史と美術. Catalogue from the exhibit *Rennyo Shōnin gohyakkaiki kinen tōzai gōdō tokubetsu tenrankai* 蓮如上人 500回忌記念東西合同特別展覧会. Tokyo: Mainichi Shinbunsha, 1998.

Kyōdō Tsūshinsha 共同通信社. *Rennyo Shōnin: Rennyo Shōnin Gokyaku Kaiki Kinen* 蓮如上人展: 蓮如上人五客回忌記念. Catalogue from exhibition shown at the Fukui Prefectural Museum, etc. Tokyo: Kyōdō Tsūshinsha, 1997.

LaFleur, William R. *Awesome Nightfall: The Life, Times, and Poetry of Saigyo*. Somerville, MA: Wisdom Publications, 2003.

Luther, Martin. *D. Martin Luther's Werke; kritische Gesamtausgabe*, Weimarer Ausgabe. Graz: Akademische Druck–u. Verlagsanstalt, 1964–1966.

Mainichi Shinbunsha Ōsaka Honsha Henshūkyoku Gakugeibu 毎日新聞大阪 本社編集局 学芸部, ed. *Shinbun kisha ga kaita: Rennyo wo aruku* 新聞 記者が書いた: 蓮如を歩く. Ōsaka: Mainichi Shinbun Ōsaka Honsha, 1998.

Makino Shinnosuke 牧野信之助. *Buke jidai shakai no kenkyū* 武家時代社会の研究. Tokyo: Tōkō Shoin, 1928; new ed., 1943.

——, ed. *Shinsei Shōnin godenki shū* 真盛上人 御伝記集, Tokyo: Sanshūsha, 1931.

Matsubara Taidō 松原泰道. *Rennyo* 蓮如. Tokyo: Tōyō Keizai Shinpōsha, 1998.

Matsuda Kiichi 松田毅一, Sakuma Tadashi 佐久間正, et al., trans. *Nihon Junsatsuki* 日本巡察記. Trans. of *Sumario de las cosas de Japon* by Alejandro Valignano. Tokyo: Chōgensha, 1965; repr. Heibonsha: Tōyō Bunko, 1973.

Matsuda Kiichi and Kawasaki Momota 川崎桃太 trans. *Nihon shi—Furoisu [cho]* 日本史・フロイス [著]. Trans. of *Historia de Japam* by Luis Frois, 12 vols. Tokyo: Chūō Kōronsha, 1977–1980.

Matsugi Nobuhiko 真継伸彦. *Same* 鮫. Tokyo: Kawade Shobō Shinsha, 1980.

——. *Ranse wo ikiru Rennyo no shōgai* 乱世を生きる蓮如の生涯. Tokyo: Chikuma Shobō, 1981.

——. *Watashi no Rennyo* 私の蓮如. Tokyo: Chikumashōbo, 1981.

Matsumoto Takanobu 松本隆信. *Chūsei ni okeru honjibutsu no kenkyū* 中世に おける本地物の研究. Tokyo: Kumi Koshoin, 1996.

McCallum, Donald. *Zenkōji and Its Icon: A Study in Medieval Japanese Religious Art*. Princeton, N.J.: Princeton University Press, 1994.

McMullin, Neil. *Buddhism and the State in Sixteenth–Century Japan*. Princeton N.J.: Princeton University Press, 1984.

Minagawa Hiroko 皆川博子. *Ransei tamayura: Rennyo to onnatachi* 乱世玉響: 蓮如と女たち. Tokyo: Yomiuri Shinbunsha, 1991; repr. *Kōdansha bunko*, 1995.

Minakami Tsutomu 水上勉 and Satō Taira 佐藤平, eds. *Myōkōnin* 妙好人. *Daijō butten: Chūgoku / Nihon hen* 大乗仏典: 中国・日本篇, vol. 28. Tokyo: Chūō Kōronsha, 1987.

Minami Mido Shinbun 南御堂新聞, ed. *Rennyo* 蓮如. Osaka: Shinshū Ōtaniha Nanba Betsuin, 1986.

Minamoto Ryōen 源了圓. *Rennyo* 蓮如. *Jōdo Bukkyō no shisō* 浄土仏教の思想, vol. 12. Tokyo: Kōdansha, 1993.

Mishina Shōei 三品彰英. *Rennyo Shōnin–den josetsu* 蓮如上人伝序説. Kyoto: Nagata Bunshōdō, 1948.

Mitsui Shūjō 満井秀城. *Rennyo kyōgaku no shisōshi* 蓮如教学の思想史. Kyoto: Hōzōkan, 1996.

Miyazaki Enjun. *Hōken shakai ni okeru Shinshū kyōdan no tenkai* 封建社会に おける新宗教団の展開. Tokyo: Sankibō Busshorin, 1957.

——, ed. *Tannishō (Rennyo Shōnin shosha)* 歎異抄 (蓮如上人書写). Kyoto: Hōzōkan, 1969.

——. *Shinshū no rekishi to bunka* 真宗の歴史と文化. Tokyo: Kyōiku Shinchōsha, 1974.

Miyazaki Enjun. *Shinshūshi no kenkyū jō* 真宗史の研究 上. *Miyazaki Enjun Chosakushū* 宮崎圓遵著作集, vol. 4. Kyoto: Nagata Bunshōdō (or Shibunkaku), 1987.

——. *Shinshūshi no kenkyū ge* 真宗史の研究 下. *Miyazaki Enjun Chosakushū*, vol. 5. Kyoto: Nagata Bunshōdō (or Shibunkaku), 1987.

——. *Shinshū shoshigaku no kenkyū* 真宗書誌学の研究. *Miyazaki Enjun Chosakushū*, vol. 6. Kyoto: Nagata Bunshōdō (or Shibunkaku), 1988.

Miyazaki Enjun 宮崎圓遵 and Mikogami Eryū 神子上恵龍. *Rennyo Shōnin no shōgai to shisō* 蓮如上人の生涯と思想. Kyoto: Nagata Bunshōdō, 1948.

Momose Meiji 百瀬明治. *Daijitsugyōka Rennyo* 大実業家蓮如. Tokyo: Shōdensha, 1988.

——. *Shōsetsu Rennyo* 小説蓮如. Tokyo (Kyoto): PHP Kenkyūsho, 1998.

——. *Rennyo: senryaku no shūkyōka* 蓮如: 戦略の宗教家. Tokyo: Gakken, 2002.

Mori Ryūkichi 森龍吉. *Honganji* 本願寺. Tokyo: Sanichi shobō, 1959.

——. *Rennyo* 蓮如. *Kōdansha gendai shinsho* 講談社現代新書, no. 550 (or 401–600). Tokyo: Kōdansha, 1979.

Morris, Charles We. *Signs, Language, and Behavior*. New York: G. Braziller, 1955.

Murakami Naojirō 村上直次郎, trans. and Yanagiya Takeo 柳谷武夫, ed. *Iezusu kaishi Nihon tsūshin* イエズス会士日本通信, in 2 vols. (上下). *Shin ikoku sōsho*, vols. 1–2. Tokyo: Yūshōdo, 1969.

Murakami Sokusui 村上速水, Ōhara Shōjitsu 大原性実, and Tanaka Hisao 田中久夫. *Shinran shisō no shūyaku to tenkai* 親鸞思想と集約と展開. *Kōza Shinran no shisō* 講座親鸞の思想, vol. 8. Tokyo: Kyōiku Shinchōsha, 1978.

Muramatsu Mohei 松村茂平. *Rennyo no homura* 蓮如の炎. Tokyo: Sōbunsha, 1983.

Murata Shūzō 村田修三. *Chūsei jōkaku kenkyū ronshū* 中世城郭研究論集. Tokyo: Shinjinbutsu Ōraisha, 1990.

——. *Shinshiten chūsei jōkaku kenkyū ronshū* 新視点中世城郭研究論集. Tokyo: Shinjinbutsu Ōraisha, 2002.

Nabata Ōjun 名畑應順 and Kabutogi Shōkō 兜木正享, eds. *Shinran shū, Nichiren shū* 親鸞集、日蓮集. *Nihon koten bungaku taikei*, vol. 82. Tokyo: Iwanami Shoten, 1964.

Nabata Takashi 名畑崇. *Honganji no rekishi* 本願寺の歴史. Kyoto: Hōzōkan, 1987.

Naganuma Kenkai 長沼賢海. *Nihon shūkyōshi no kenkyū* 日本宗教史の研究. Tokyo: Kyōiku Kenkyūkai, 1928.

Nakamura Hajime 中村元 et al., eds. *Bukkyō jiten* 仏教辞典. Tokyo: Iwanami Shoten, 1989.

Nakayama Nobuna 中山信名 and Kurita Hiroshi 栗田寛, eds. *Shinpen Hitachi kokushi* 新編常陸国誌. Mito: Kanō Yūzaemon, 1899–1901; repr. Nakaminato: Miyazaki Hōonkai and Mito: Hitachi Shobō, 1969.

Nagasaki Kenshi Hensan Iinkai 長崎県史編纂委員会編, ed. *Nagasaki kenshi* 長崎県史. 8 vols. Tokyo: Yoshikawa Kōbunkan, 1976.

Nihon Bukkyōshi no Kenkyūkai 日本仏教史研究会, ed. *Nihon no shakai to bukkyō: Chiba Jōryū Hakase koki kinen* 日本の社会と仏教: 千葉乗隆博士古希記念.

Niigata Ken 新潟県, ed. *Niigata kenshi* 新潟県史. 37 vols., 24 of which are *shiryōhen* 資料編. Niigata: Niigata Prefecture, 1980–1990.

Ninomiya Takao 二宮隆雄 *Rennyo: shinkō de jidai wo ugokashita otoko* 蓮如: 信仰で時代を動かした男. Tokyo (Kyoto): PHP Kenkyūsho, 1998.

Nishida Shinin 西田真因. *Rennyo Shōnin shiki* 蓮如上人私記. Kyoto: Higashi Honganji Shuppanbu, 1998.

Nishiyama Kunihiko 西山邦彦. *Rennyo Shōnin gojō ofumi kokoroe* 蓮如上人 五帖お文こころえ. Ishikawa: Yokono Shoten, 1993.

——. *Rennyo Shōnin jōgai ofumi himotoki—kaitei-ban*. 蓮如上人 帖外御文ひもとき (改訂版). 1994; rev. ed., Kyoto: Hōzōkan, 1996.

Nishiyama Satoshi 西山郷史. *Rennyo to shinshū gyōji: Noto no shūkyō minzoku* 蓮如と真宗行事：能登の宗教民俗. Tokyo: Mokujisha, 1998.

Nitō Chikō 内藤知康. *Gobushō wo kiku* 御文章を聞く. Kyoto: Honganji Shuppansha, 1998.

Niwa Fumio 丹羽文雄. *Rennyo* 蓮如. 8 vols. Tokyo: Chūō Kōronsha, 1982.

——, et al. *Rennyo ni deau* 蓮如に出会う. Tokyo: Ōbunsha, 1986.

Nobutsuka Tomomichi 延塚知道. *Daihi no hito: Rennyo—Ōtani daigaku kaihō'seminā shiriizu* 1 大悲の人：蓮如［大谷大学開放セミナー シリーズ 1. Kyoto: Ōtani Daigaku, 1998.

Nobutsuka Tomomichi, Miharu Chishō 三明智彰, Andō Fumio 安藤文雄, Fujitake Myōshin 藤嶽明信, Kaku Takeshi 加来雄之, and Ichiraku Makoto 一楽真. *Rennyo Shōnin: Shinran Shōnin no oshie ni ikita hito* 蓮如上人—親鸞聖人の教えに生きた人. Kyoto: Higashi Honganji Shuppanbu, 1996.

Nyosei (of Emyōin 惠明院) 如晴 (1652–1722). *Gaikemon kashō* 改悔文科鈔. *Shinshū taikei*, vol. 35.

Oguri Junko 小栗純子. *Nyonin ōjō* 女人往生. Kyoto: Jinbun Shoin, 1987.

Ōhara Shōjitsu 大原性実. *Rennyo Shōnin kenkyū* 蓮如上人研究. Kyoto: Hyakkaen, 1948.

——. *Rennyo Shōnin to sono shūkyō* 蓮如上人とその宗教. Tokyo: Meiji Shoin, 1949.

——. *Rennyo goroku ni kiku* 蓮如語録に聞く. Tokyo: Kyōiku Shinchōsha, 1964; repr. 1981.

Ōita Shishi Hensan Iinkai 大分市史編纂委員会, ed. *Ōita Shishi (chū)* 大分市史 （中）. Oita: Oita-shi, 1987.

Okada Akio 岡田章雄, trans. and ed., et al. *Ruis Furoisu, Nichiō bunka hikaku* ルイス・フロイス日欧文化比較. *Daikōkai jidai sōsho*, vol. 11. Tokyo: Iwanami Shoten, 1965.

Okamura Yoshiji 岡村喜史. *Rennyo: kinai, tōkai wo iku* 蓮如：畿内・東海を行く. Tokyo: Kokusho Kankōkai, 1995.

Okazaki Bijutsu Hakubutsukan 岡崎市美術博物館編 ed. *Heisei jūnendo tokubetsu kikakuten– higashi no kokoro, nishi no kokoro: "Rennyo / Rutā / Minshū"* 平成 10 年度特別企画展　東の心・西の心「蓮如・ルター・民衆」(English title: Rennyo & Martin Luther). Aichi: Okazakishi Bijutsu Hakubutsukan, 1998.

Okazaki Kyōku Rennyo Shōnin 500 Kaiki Goenki Iinkai Rennyo Shōnin kenkyū Iinkai 岡崎教区蓮如上人五〇〇回忌御遠忌委員会蓮如上人研究委員会. *Rennyo: anakashiko no sekai* 蓮如：あなかしこの世界. Aichi: Shinshū Ōtaniha Okazaki Kyōmusho, 1998.

Ōkuwa Hitoshi et al. 大桑斉他. *Rennyo Shōnin no ōbō* 蓮如上人の王法. Vol. 3 in the series *Rennyo Shōnin ni manabu* 蓮如上人に学ぶ. Kyoto: Shinshū Ōtaniha Shūmusho Shuppanbu, 1997.

Ōmine Akira 大峯顯. *Rennyo no radikarizumu* 蓮如のラディカリズム. Kyoto: Hōzōkan, 1998.

Oniki Yōshū 鬼木沃洲. *Gojō hōshō kōyō* 五帖宝章綱要, in 2 fascicles. Shinshū sōsho, vol. 10.

Osada Tsuneo 長田恒雄. *Hi no hito: Rennyo* 火のひと・蓮如. Tokyo: Hōbunkan, 1964.

——. *Rennyo Shōnin: "Goichidai Kikigaki" to sono ikikata* 蓮如上人—『御一代聞書』とその生き方. Tokyo: Tokuma Shoten, 1972.

Ōsaka Shiritsu Hakubutsukan 大阪市立博物館, ed. *Tokubetsuten—Ōsaka no machi to Honganji* 特別展：大阪の町と本願寺. Ōsaka: Mainichi Shinbunsha Ōsaka Honsha, 1996.

Ōsuga Shūdō 大須賀秀道. *Goichidaiki kikigaki kōyō* 御一代記聞書講要. Kyoto: Ōtaniha Ango Jimusho (Higashi Honganji Shuppanbu), 1949.

——. *Saikō no shōnin* 再興の上人. Kyoto: Ōtani Shuppansha, 1949.

Ōtani Chōjun 大谷暢順. *Rennyo "ofumi" dokuhon* 蓮如［御文］読本. Tokyo: Kawade Shobō Shinsha, 1991; repr. Kōdansha gakujutsu bunko 講談社学術文庫, no. 1476, Tokyo: Kōdansha, 2001.

——, ed. *Rennyo Shōnin zenshū: gengyōhen* 蓮如上人全集: 言行編. Tokyo: Kawade Shobō Shinsha, 1989.

——, ed. *Rennyo Shōnin zenshū* 蓮如上人全集. 4 vols. Tokyo: Chūō Kōronsha, 1998.

Ōtani Chōjun and Nonaka Ekei 野中恵契, eds. *Teihon gojō ofumi* 定本五帖御文. Tokyo: Kawade Shobō Shinsha, 1995.

Ōtani Daigaku 大谷大学, ed. *Shinshū Nenpyō* 真宗年表. Kyoto: Hōzōkan, 1973, repr. 1993.

——, ed. *Rennyo Shōnin ten: Shinshū Ōtaniha (higashi Honganji) shūhō kōkai: Ōtani daigaku hakubutsukan–gaku katei kaisetsu 10–shūnen kinen* 蓮如上人展: 真宗大谷派（東本願寺）宗法公開: 大谷大学博物館学課程開設10周年記念. Kyoto: Ōtani Daigaku, 1996.

Ōtani Daigaku Shinshū Sōgō Kenkyūjo 大谷大学真宗総合研究所, ed. *Rennyo no sekai* 蓮如の世界. Kyoto: Bun'eidō, 1998.

——, ed. *Rennyo: hito to oshie: "Rennyo Shōnin Goichidaiki kikigaki" ni manabu* 蓮如: 人と教え: 『蓮如上人御一代 記聞書』に学ぶ. Kyoto: Higashi Honganji Shuppanbu, 2000.

Ōtani Eijun 大谷瑩潤. *Rennyo Shōnin* 蓮如上人. Kyoto: Ōtani Shuppansha, 1949.

Ōtani Kōichi 大谷晃一. *Oinaru saka: sei to zoku no kyojin Rennyo* 大いなる坂: 聖と俗の巨人蓮如. Tokyo: Kawade Shobo Shinsha, 1990.

——. *Rennyo: Honganji ōkoku wo kizuita kyojin* 蓮如: 本願寺王国を 築いた巨人. Tokyo: Gakuyō Shokyoku, 1998.

Pittman, Don, Ruben Habito, and Terry Muck, eds. *Ministry and Theology in Global Perspective: Contemporary Challenges for the Church*. Grand Rapids: Eerdmans, 1996.

Purejidentosha プレジデント社, ed. *Shinran to Rennyo: nayameru gendaijin no "dōgōsha."* 親鸞と蓮如−悩める現代人の「同行者」. Purejidento プレジデント, no. 12. Tokyo: Purejidentosha, 1989.

——, ed. *Tokushū: Rennyo: nenbutsu no kokoro* 特集: 蓮如−念仏のこころ. Purejidento, no. 11. Tokyo: Purejidentosha, 1997.

Rappaport, Roy. *Ritual and Religion in the Making of Humanity*. Cambridge, U.K.: Cambridge University Press, 1999.

Reiō (of Kaigoin 開悟院) 靈 (日+往). *Ofumi kihō–ittai butsubon–ittai dōiben fu gangyō gusokuben* 御文機法一体仏凡一体同異弁附願行具足弁. *Shinshū taikei*, vol. 35.

——. *Gaikemon ryakuben* 改悔文略弁. *Zoku Shinshū taikei*, vol. 9.

Rennyo Kenkyūkai 蓮如研究会, ed. *Shin Rennyo e no gokai* 新蓮如への誤解. Kyoto: Nagata Bunshōdō, 1997.

Rennyo Shōnin Kenkyūkai 蓮如上人研究会. *Rennyo Shōnin kenkyūkai kaishi (vol. 1–8)* 蓮如上人研究会会誌1–8. Kanazawa: Rennyo Shōnin Kenkyūkai, 1989–1994.

——, ed. *Rennyo Shōnin kenkyū* 蓮如上人研究. Kyoto: Shibunkaku Shuppan, 1998.

Rennyo Shōnin Eden Chōsa Kenkyūhan 蓮如上人繪傳調査研究班, ed. *Rennyo Shōnin eden no kenkyū* 蓮如上人繪傳の研究. Kyoto: Higashi Honganji Shuppanbu, 1994.

Rogers, Minor L., and Ann T. Rogers. *Rennyo: the Second Founder of Shin Buddhism*. Berkeley, Cal.: Asian Humanities Press, 1991.

Ryōshō (Myōonin 妙音院) 了祥. *Gaikemon kōsetsu* 改悔文講説. *Zoku Shinshū taikei*, vol. 9.

——. *Tannishō monki* 歎異抄聞記. *Zoku Shinshū taikei*, vol. 21; also printed as a separate volume ed. by Inaba Shūken, Kyoto: Hōzōkan, 1972.

Ryūkoku Daigaku 龍谷大学, ed. *Rennyo Shōnin kenkyū* 蓮如上人研究. Kyoto: Chūshu Daishi Yonhyakugojūkai Onkihōyō Jimusho, 1948.

Ryūkoku Daigaku Ōmiya Toshokan, ed. *Rennyo Shōnin ten: shiryō ga kataru shōninzō* 蓮如上人展：史料が語る上人像. English title: *Exhibition Rennyo Shonin: An Image of Rennyo from Historical Materials*. Kyoto: Ryūkoku Daigaku Ōmiya Toshokan, 1998.

Sakuma Tadashi 佐久間正, trans. and ed. *Abira Giron, Nihon Ōkokuki,* アビラ • ヒロン日本王国記, and Okada Akio 岡田章雄 trans. and ed. *Ruis Furoisu, Nichiō bunka hikaku* ルイス • フロイス日欧文化比較. Both translations in Daikōkai jidai sōsho, vol. 11. Tokyo: Iwanami Shoten, 1965.

Sano Manabu 佐野学. *Shinran to Rennyo* 親鸞と蓮如. Kyoto: Chōjiya Shoten, 1949.

Sasaki Hideaki 佐々木英彰. *Hōnen kara Rennyo made: shinshūshi no tsūnen wo minaosu* 法然から蓮如まで：真宗史の通念を見なおす. Tokyo: Shinsensha, 2000.

Sasaki Yoshio 佐々木芳雄. *Rennyo Shōnin–den no kenkyū* 蓮如上人伝の研究. Kyoto: Chūgai Shuppan, 1926.

Senmyō (of Enjōin 圓乘院) 宣明 (1749–1821). *Gojō ofumi taikō* 五帖御文大綱. *Shinshū taikei*, vol. 32.

——. *Ofumi taikō* 御文大綱. *Shinshū taikei*, vol. 32.

——. *Gaikemon ki* 改悔文記, in 2 fascicles. *Zoku Shinshū taikei*, vol. 9.

——. *Gobunshō manijukai* 御文摩尼珠海, in 2 fascicles. *Shinshū zensho*, vol. 49.

——. *Ofumi yōgi* 御文要義. *Shinshū zensho*, vol. 49.

Sharf, Robert, and Elizabeth Sharf. *Living Images: Japanese Buddhist Icons in Context*. Stanford, Cal.: Stanford University Press, 2001.

Shaw, Glenn W. *The Priest and His Disciples*. Tokyo: Hokuseido Press, 1922; rev. ed. 1926.

Shigematsu Akihisa 重松明久. *Chusei Shinshū shisō no kenkyū* 中世真宗思想の研究. Tokyo: Yoshikawa Kōbunkan, 1973.

——. *Honganji hyakunen sensō* 本願寺百年戦争. Kyoto: Hōzōkan, 1986.

——, ed. *Shinran, Shinshū shisōshi kenkyū* 親鸞 • 真宗思想史研究. Kyoto: Hozokan, 1990.

Shinkō no Zōkeiteki Hyōgen Kenkyū Iinkai 信仰の造形的表現研究委員会, ed. *Rennyo Shōnin ezō, Rennyo Shōnin eden, Shinshū shoha rekidai ezō, Kaiki mokuzō* 蓮如上人絵像；蓮如上人絵伝；真宗諸派歴代絵像；開基木像. *Shinshū jūhō shuei* 真宗重宝聚英, vol. 9. Kyoto: Dōbōsha, 1988.

Shinshū Ōtaniha Kyōgaku Kenkyūjo 真宗大谷派教学研究所, ed. *Rennyo Shōnin gyōjitsu* 蓮如上人行実. Kyoto: Shinshū Otaniha Shūmusho Shuppanbu, 1948, 1994.

——, ed. *Rennyo Shōnin no shōgai to oshie* 蓮如上人の生涯と教え. Kyoto: Shinshū Otaniha Shūmusho Shuppanbu, 1994.

——, ed. *Rennyo Shōnin to gendai* 蓮如上人と現代. Kyoto: Shinshū Otaniha Shūmusho Shuppanbu, 1998.

Shinshū Ōtaniha Nanba Betsuin, Asahi Shinbun Ōsaka Honsha Kikakubu 真宗大谷派難波別院 • 朝日新聞大阪本社企画部, ed. *Rennyo to Ōsaka: Ōsaka no machi to Rennyo Shōnin ten* 蓮如と大阪：大阪の町と蓮如上人展. Ōsaka: Asahi Shinbunsha, 1986.

Shinshū Ōtaniha Shūgakuin 真宗大谷派宗学院, ed. *Shūgaku kenkyū tokushūgō: Rennyo Shōnin kenkyū* 宗学研究特集号—蓮如上人研究. Kyoto: Shinshū Ōtaniha Shūgakuin, 1932.

Soga Ryōjin 曽我量深. *Tannisho chōki* 歎異抄聴記. Kyoto: Chōjiya, 1947; rev. 4th ed. by Kyoto: Higashi Honganji Shuppanbu, 1970.

——. *Kan'ō no dōri: Rennyo kyōgaku no chūshin mondai* 感應の道理：蓮如教学の中心問題. Kyoto: Chōjiya, 1952.

——. *Shūkyō no shikatsu mondai* 宗教の死活問題. Tokyo: Yayoi Shobo, 1973.

——. *Soga Ryōjin kōgishū* 曽我量深講義集. 15 vols. Tokyo: Yayoi Shobō, 1977–1990.

Soga Ryōjin and Soga Ryōjin Senshū Kankōkai 曽我量深選集刊行会, eds. *Soga Ryōjin senshū* 曽我量深選集. 12 vols. Tokyo: Yayoi Shobō, 1970–1972.

Sōgō Joseishi Kenkyūkai 総合女性史研究会, ed. *Nihon josei no rekishi: onna no hataraki chūsei* 日本女性の歴史：女のはたらき中世. Tokyo: Kadokawa Shoten, 1993.

Sōyō (of Myōkyōin 明教院) 僧鎔 (1723–1783). *Kaigemon ryakuben* 改悔文略弁. *Shinshū zensho*, vol. 62.

Sugi Shirō 杉紫朗. *Gobunshō kōwa* 御文章講話. Kyoto: Kōkyō Shoin 1933; repr. Kyoto: Nagata Bunshōdō, 1979.

Sugiura Minpei 杉浦明平. *Sengoku ranse no bungaku* 戦国乱世の文学.Tokyo: Iwanami Shoten (Iwanami Shinsho 557), 1965.

Sumida Chiken 住田智見. *Igishi no kenkyū* 異義史之研究. Kyoto: Chōjiya, 1960.

——, ed. *Rennyo Shōnin zensho* 蓮如上人全書. Kyoto: Hōzōkan, 1907.

Tabata Yasuko 田端泰子. *Nihon chūsei joseishi ron* 日本中世女性史論. Tokyo: Hanawa Shobo, 1994.

Tagami Taishu 田上太秀. *Bukkyo to seisabutsu* 仏教と性差別. Tōsho sensho 東書選書, No. 128. Tokyo: Tokyo Shoseki, 1992.

Taigan (of Jikinyūin) (直入院) 泰巌 (1711–1763). *Ryōgemon yōkai* 領解文要解. *Shinshū sōsho*, vol. 10.

Takamaki Minoru 高牧実, *Miyaza to sonraku no shiteki kenkyū* 宮座と村落の史的研究. Tokyo: Yoshikawa Kōbunkan, 1986.

Takamatsu Shin'ei 高松信英. *Gendaigo–yaku: Rennyo Shōnin goichidaiki kikigaki: nyorai no manako/watashi no me* 現代語訳：蓮如上人御一代記聞書、如来の眼 • 私の眼. Kyoto: Hōzōkan, 1990.

——. *Ofumi sama: Shinshū no katei gakushū*. 御文さま：真宗の家庭学習. Kyoto: Higashi Honganji Shuppanbu, 1996.

Takamichi Shōshin 高道正信. *Rennyo* 蓮如. Fukui: Shinagawa Shoten, 1970.

Take Kōichirō 岳宏一郎. *Rennyo natsu no arashi* 蓮如夏の嵐, 2 vols. (上下). Tokyo: Mainichi Shinbunsha, 1999.

Tanaka, Kenneth. *The Dawn of Chinese Pure Land Buddhism: Ching–ying Hui–yüan's Commentary on the Visualization Sutra.* Albany, N.Y.: SUNY Press, 1990.

Tanishita Ichimu 谷下一夢. *Shinshūshi no shokenkyū* 真宗史の諸研究. Kyoto: Heirakuji Shoten, 1941.

Taya Raishun 多屋頼俊, Ōcho Enichi 横超慧日, and Funahashi Issai 船橋一哉, eds. *Shinpan Bukkyōgaku jiten:* 新版仏教学辞典. Kyoto: Hōzōkan, 1995.

Terada Yakichi 寺田弥吉. *Rennyo seigo dokuhon* 蓮如聖語読本. Tokyo: Daiichi Shobō, 1937.

Terakawa Shunshō 寺川俊昭. *Tannishō no shisōteki kaimei* 歎異抄の思想的開明. Kyoto: Hōzōkan, 1978.

——. *Shinran no shin no dainamikkusu: ōkan nishu ekō no butsudō* 親鸞の信のダイナミックス：往還二種回向の仏道. Shikaidō, Chiba-ken: Sōkōsha, 1993.

——. *Rennyo Shōnin: gendai-teki igi* 蓮如上人：現代的意義. Kuwana, Mie-ken: Ōtaniha Mie Kyōmusho, 1995.

Terakura Noboru 寺倉襄. *Shinshū resso no kyōgaku* 真宗列祖の教学. Nagoya: Bunkōdō Shoten, 1973.

Thelle, Notto R. *Buddhism and Christianity in Japan: From Conflict to Dialogue, 1854–1899.* Honolulu: University of Hawaii Press, 1987.

Tōjō Gimon 東條義門. *Matsudai muchi ofumi wagosetsu* 末代無智御文和語説. *Shinshū zensho*, vol. 57.

Tokunaga Daishin 徳永大信. *Rennyo Shōnin no sōgōteki kenkyū* 蓮如上人の総合的研究. Kyoto: Nagata Bunshōdō, 1997.

Tokuryū (of Kōjuin 香樹院) 徳龍 (1772–1858). *Shōshinge taii kōgi* 正信偈大意. 講義. *Shinshū taikei*, vol. 29.

Tokushi Yūshō 禿氏祐祥, ed. *Kōchū Rennyo Shōnin ofumi zenshū* 校註蓮如上人御文全集. Tokyo: Bunkenshoin, 1922.

——, ed. *Rennyo Shōnin hōgoshū fu kaisetsu* 蓮如上人法語集附解説. Kyoto: Ryūkoku Daigaku Shuppanbu, 1924.

Tokyo Daigaku Shiryo Hensansho 東京大学史料編纂所, ed. *Dai Nihon shiryō* 12–9 大日本史料十二編之九. Tokyo: Tokyo University, 1901–1915.

Toyoshima Gakuyū 豊島学由. *Rennyo no shōgai* 蓮如の生涯. Tokyo: Kokusho Kankōkai, 1996.

Tsuji Zennosuke 辻善之助. *Nihon Bukkyōshi* 日本仏教史, 10 vols. Tokyo: Iwanami Shoten, 1944–1955.

Tsujikawa Tatsuo 辻川達雄. *"Yashi" Yoshizaki no Rennyo: Sono shisō to Jidai haikei* "野史"吉崎の蓮如: その思想と時代背景. Fukui: Rakunensha 落鮎舎, 1983.

——. *Rennyo: Yoshizaki fukyō* 蓮如—吉崎布教. Tokyo: Seikōdō Shinkōsha, 1984.

——. *Oda Nobunaga to Echizen ikkō ikki* 織田信長と越前一向一揆. Tokyo: Seikōdō Shinkōsha, 1989.

——. *Rennyo jitsuden 1: "Ōmihen"* 蓮如実伝第一部「近江篇」. Kyoto: Honganji Ijizaidan, 1995.

——. *Rennyo jitsuden 2: "Hokurikuhen I"* 蓮如実伝第二部 「北陸篇上」. Kyoto: Honganji Ijizaidan, 1996.

——. *Rennyo to shichinin no musuko* 蓮如と七人の息子. Tokyo: Seikōdō Shinkōsha, 1996.

Tsukamoto Zenryū 塚本善隆. *Shina bukkyōshi kenkyū: hokugi hen*. Tokyo: Kōbundō, 1942; repr. 1969.

Umehara Shinryū 梅原真隆. *Yoshizaki no Rennyo Shōnin* 吉崎の蓮如上人. Yoshizaki (Fukui): Yoshizaki Betsuin, 1926.

——. *Rennyo Shōnin kikigaki shinshaku* 蓮如上人聞書新釈. *Umehara Shinryū Senshū* 梅原真隆選集 vols. 32–33. Namerikawa (Toyama): Senchōji Bunsho Dendōbu, 1950.

——, ed. *Rennyo Shōnin goichidaiki kikigaki* 蓮如上人御一代記聞書. Kadokawa Bunko, no. 1842. Tokyo: Kadogawa Shoten, 1959.

Uno Enkū 宇野圓空, ed. *Rennyo Shonin* 蓮如上人. *Shinshū seiten kōsan zenshū* 真宗聖典講讃全集, vol. 8. Tokyo: Kokusho Kankōkai, 1976; repr. 1987.

Uno Gyōshin 宇野行信. *Seiten seminā: gobunshō* 聖典セミナ: 御文章. Kyoto: Honganji Shuppan, 1994.

Uryūzu Ryūshin 瓜生津隆真. *Gendaigoyaku Rennyo Shōnin goichidaiki kikigaki* 現代語訳蓮如上人御一代記聞書. Tokyo: Daizō Shūppan, 1998.

Valignano, Alejandro. *Sumario de las cosas de Japón, Adiciones del sumario de Japón* (1583), ed. Alvarez–Taladriz, José Luis. *Monumenta Nipponica Monographs*, No. 9. Tokyo: Sophia University, 1954.

Varley, H. Paul. *The Ōnin War.* New York: Columbia University Press, 1977.

Wada Sōkyū 和田蒼穹. *Yome odoshi nikutsuki no men ryaku engi: Rennyo Shōnin go–kyūseki* 嫁威肉附之面略縁起: 蓮如上人御舊跡. Sakai: Gankyōji 願慶寺, 1943.

Wakita Haruko 脇田晴子. *Nihon chūsei joseishi no kenkyū: seibetsu yakuwari buntan to bosei, kasei, seiai* 日本中世女性史の研究: 性別役割分担と母性 ● 家政 ● 性愛. Tokyo: Tokyo Daigaku Shuppankai, 1992.

Washio Junkei 鷲尾順敬, ed. *Kokubun tōhō bukkyō sōsho* 國文東方佛教叢書. Tokyo: Tōhō Shoin, 1925–1933.

Yamaori Tetsuo 山折哲雄. *Ningen Rennyo* 人間蓮如. Tokyo: Shunjusha, 1970; 2nd ed. Shunjusha, 1993; rev. and expanded ed. (増補版) Tokyo: JICC Shuppankyoku, 1993.

——. *Rennyo to Nobunaga* 蓮如と信長. Tokyo: PHP Kenkyūsho, 1997, 2002.

Yamaori Tetsuo and Ōmura Eishō 大村英昭, eds. *Rennyo: tenkanki no shūkyōsha* 蓮如—転換期の宗教者. Tokyo: Shōgakkan, 1997.

Yamamoto Kosho. *The Words of St. Rennyo.* Tokyo: Karinbunko, 1968.

Yanagida Chishō 柳田智照. *Rennyo Shōnin Goichidaiki Kikigaki kōwa* 蓮如上人 御一代聞書講話, 4 vols. Kyoto: Hyakkaen, 1984–1996.

Yokomichi Mario 横道万里雄 et al. eds, *Yōkyokushū* 謡曲集. *Nihon koten bungaku taikei,* vols. 40–41. Tokyo: Iwanami Shoten, 1960.

Yomiuri Shinbunsha 読売新聞社, ed. *Nenbutsu no kokoro: Rennyo to Honganji kyōdan* 念仏のこころ：蓮如と本願寺教団. Tokyo: Yomiuri Shinbunsha, 1991.

Yoshimura Shūki 吉村修基, ed. *Bukkyō kyōdan no kenkyū* 仏教教団の研究. Kyoto: Hyakka-en, 1968.

Secondary Sources: Articles

JAPANESE JOURNAL TITLES

Bukkyō daigaku sōgō kenkyūsho kiyō 佛教大学総合研究所紀要
Bukkyō shigaku kenkyū 仏教史学研究
Bukkyōshi kenkyū 仏教史研究
Chūō bukkyōgakuin kiyō 中央仏教学院紀要
Dōhō 同朋
Dōhō bukkyō 同朋仏教
Dōhō gakuen bukkyō bunka kenkyūsho kiyō 同朋学園仏教文化研究所紀要
Gekkan hyakka 月刊百科
Gyōshin gakuhō 行信学報
Indogaku bukkyōgaku kenkyū 印度学仏教学研究
Indo tetsugaku bukkyōgaku 印度哲学仏教学
Kanazawa daigaku kyōikugakubu kiyō 金沢大学教育学部紀要
Kenkyū kiyō (Kyōto Joshi Daigaku Shūkyō and Bunka Kenkyūsho) 研究紀要
Kokuritsu rekishi minzoku hakubutsukan kenkyū hōkoku 国立歴史民俗博物館研究報告
Kyōgaku kenkyūsho kiyō 教学研究所紀要
Kyōka kenkyū (Jōdoshū Sōgō Kenkyūsho) 教化研究
Kyōka kenkyū (Shinshū Ōtaniha Kyōgaku Kenkyūsho) 教化研究
Kyōto–shi rekishi shiryōkan kiyō 京都市歴史資料館紀要
Kyūshū Ōtani kenkyū kiyō 九州大谷研究紀要
Kyushū Ryūkoku tanki daigaku kiyō 九州龍谷短期大学紀要
Musashino joshi daigaku bukkyō bunka kenkyūsho kiyō 武蔵野女子大学仏教文化研究所
Musashino joshi daigaku kiyō 武蔵野大学紀要
Nenpō chūsei–shi kenkyū 年報中世史研究
Nihon bukkyō gakkai nenpō 日本仏教学会年報
Otani daigaku daigakuin kenkyū kiyō 大谷大学大学院研究紀要
Ōtani gakuhō 大谷学報
Rekishi chiri 歴史地理
Rekishigaku kenkyū 歴史学研究
Ryūkoku daigaku bukkyō bunka kenkyūsho kiyō 龍谷大学仏教文化研究所紀要
Ryūkoku daigaku ronshū 龍谷大学論集
Ryūkoku kyōgaku 龍谷教学
Ryūkoku shidan 龍谷史壇
Shindō 身同

Shinran kyōgaku 親鸞教学
Shinshū bunka 真宗文化
Shinshūgaku 真宗学
Shinshū kenkyū 真宗研究
Shisō 史窓
Shūgakuin ronshū 宗学院論集
Shūkyō kenkyū 宗教研究
Tōyō daigaku bungakubu kiyo shigakka 東洋大学文学部紀要史学科
Tōyōgaku ronsō 東洋学論叢

ARTICLES

Adachi Yukiko 足立幸子. "Shinshū no okite ni tsuite 真宗の掟について." *Indogaku bukkyōgaku kenkyū* 42 (1994), 734–736.

Aigun Nobuya 合群信哉. "Rennyo ni okeru kyōgakuteki kansei: Genshō shōjōju shisō no rikai wo megutte 蓮如における教学的陥穽: 現生正定聚思想の理解をめぐって." *Indogaku bukkyōgaku kenkyū* 39 (1990), 199–202.

Akamatsu Tesshin 赤松徹真. "Rennyo kenkyū (I) 蓮如研究 (I)." *Ryūkoku daigaku bukkyō bunka kenkyūsho kiyō* 30 (1991), 191–207.

——. "Rennyo kenkyū (II) 蓮如研究 (II)." *Ryūkoku daigaku bukkyō bunka kenkyūsho kiyō* 31 (1992), 168–178.

——. "Rennyo no shinshūshi–teki kenkyū (1) 蓮如の真宗史的研究 (I)." *Ryūkoku daigaku bukkyō bunka kenkyūsho kiyō* 34 (1995), 116–127.

Akatsu Tsuneyuki 吾勝常行. "Rennyo ni miru muga ni tsuite: 'Ningen chūshin apurōchi' wo shiten toshite 蓮如にみる無我について: 「人間中心アプローチ」を視点として." *Indogaku bukkyōgaku kenkyū* 44 (1995), 189–191.

——. "Rennyo ni okeru komyunikēshon no imi 蓮如におけるコミュニケーションの意味." *Shūkyō kenkyū* 71 (1998), 306–307.

——. "Rennyo ni okeru seken to buppō: Sono setten toshite no 'mi' wo chūshin ni 蓮如における世間と仏法: その接点としての「身」を中心に." *Indogaku bukkyōgaku kenkyū* 46 (1998), 217–220.

Akutagawa Shōju 芥川昭寿. "Rennyo Shōnin no chojutsu ni mirareru joshi no igi: 'ha' to 'ga' wo megutte 蓮如上人の著述に見られる助詞の意義:「は」と「が」をめぐって." *Ryūkoku kyōgaku* 31 (1996), 84–97.

Amagishi Jōen 天岸浄円. "Rennyo Shōnin kankei bunken mokuroku 蓮如上人関係文献目録." In *Rennyo Shōnin no kyōgaku to rekishi* 蓮如上人の教学と歴史, ed. Kimura Takeo, 366–399. Osaka: Tōhō Shuppan, 1984.

Aoki Kaoru 青木馨. *Ofumi–bon chōsa yori mita kinsei honganji kyōdan no tokushitsu* 御文本調査より見た近世本願寺教団の特質. *Shinshū kyōgaku kenkyū* 14 (1990), 87–97.

——. "Honganji Rennyo, Jitsunyo hitsu myōgō hikakuron 本願寺蓮如 • 実如筆名号比較論." *Bukkyō shigaku kenkyū* 37 (1994), 69–86.

——. "Honzon, eizō ron 本尊 • 影像論." In *Kōza Rennyo* 2 講座蓮如第二巻, ed. Jōdoshinshū Kyōgaku Kenkyūsho, 13–52. Tokyo: Heibonsha, 1997.

——. "Honganji monshusei ni kansuru ichi kōsatsu 本願寺門主制に関する一考察." *Shinshū kenkyū* 43 (1999), 88–105.

Aoki Tadao 青木忠夫. "Sengokuki Honganji hōonkō no 'gaike' ni kansuru ichi kōsatsu 戦国期本願寺報恩講の「改悔」に関する一考察." *Bukkyō shigaku kenkyū* 37 (1994), 80–118.

Aoyama Hōjō 青山法城. "Rennyo Shōnin kō: Ofumi to gyōjitsu 蓮如上人考: 御文と行実." *Shinshūgaku* 90 (1994), 122–124.

Asai Narumi 浅井成海. "Rennyo kyōgaku ni okeru 'tasuke–tamae to tanomu' no shisō haikei 蓮如教学における「たすけたまへとたのむ」の思想背景." In *Rennyo taikei* 2 蓮如大系第二巻, ed. Kakehashi Jitsuen, 212–232. Kyoto: Hōzōkan, 1996.

Asakura Masanori 朝倉昌紀. "Rennyo Shōnin ni okeru jōdo to genjitsu sekai no imi 蓮如上人における浄土と現実世界の意味." *Ryūkoku kyōgaku* 28 (1993), 24–32.

——. "Rennyo Shōnin no jingikan ni tsuite 蓮如上人の神祇観 について." *Ryūkoku kyōgaku* 30 (1995), 7–16.

——. "Rennyo to minzoku shinkō: Bukki ishiki wo chūshi ni 蓮如と民俗信仰：物忌意識を中心に." *Indogaku bukkyōgaku kenkyū* 44 (1995), 184–188.

——. "Shinshū ni okeru shukuzenkan no tenkai: Rennyo Shōnin no shukuzen no mondai wo chūshin ni 真宗における宿善観の展開：蓮如上人の宿善の問題を中心に." *Shūgakuin ronshū* 68 (1996), 1–18.

——. "Shinshū ni okeru soshi shinkō no tenkai 真宗における祖師信仰の展開." *Shinshū kenkyū* 40 (1996), 14–27.

——. "Rennyo no nyonin ojō shisō ni tsuite 蓮如の女人往生思想について." *Indogaku bukkyōgaku kenkyū* 45 (1997), 88–92.

Asano Kyōshin 浅野教信, Yata Ryōshō 矢田了章, Oka Ryōji 岡亮二, Fukagawa Rinyū 深川倫雄, and Hideno Daien 秀野大衍. "Rennyo Shōnin wo megutte [symposium] 蓮如上人をめぐって(シンポジウム)." *Ryūkoku kyōgaku* 28 (1993), 95–129.

Asao Naohiro 朝尾直弘. "Jūroku seiki kōhan no Nihon 十六世紀後半の日本." In *Iwanami kōza Nihon tsūshi* 岩波講座日本通史 vol. 11, ed. Asao Naohiro et al. Tokyo: Iwanami shoten, 1993, 1–68.

Blum, Mark. "Rennyo kyōgaku ni okeru ichinengi ni tsuite 蓮如教学における一念義について." *Indogaku bukkyōgaku kenkyū* 46 (1997), 51–55.

Chiba Jōryū 千葉乗隆. "Rennyo no ikonokurasumu 蓮如のイコノクラスム." In *Nihon no shakai to bukkyō: Chiba Jōryū Hakase koki kinen* 日本の社会と仏教：千葉乗隆博士古希記念, ed. Nihon Bukkyōshi no Kenkyūkai, 1–54. Kyoto: Nagata Bunshodō, 1990.

——. "Rennyo Shōnin wo megutte [lecture] 蓮如上人をめぐって (講演)." *Ryūkoku kyōgaku* 26 (1991), 99–104.

——. "Shinshu kyōdan ni okeru raihai taishō no suii 真宗教団における礼拝対象の推移." *Ryūkoku shidan* 98 (1991), 1–23.

——. "Rennyo Shōnin to kebōzu 蓮如上人と毛坊主." *Shinshū bunka* 8 (1999), 27–47.

Chiba Takafumi 千葉考史. "*Rennyo Shōnin goichidaiki kikigaki* ni tsuite no kenkyū 『蓮如上人御一代記聞書』についての研究." *Ryūkoku kyōgaku* 34 (1999), 40–50.

Chitani Kimikazu 智谷公和. "Rennyo Shōnin no gō ni tsuite (josetsu) 蓮如上人の業について (序説)." *Ryūkoku kyōgaku* 32 (1997), 99–111.

——. "Rennyo Shōnin no bonnō ni tsuite: akugō bonnō wo chūshin ni 蓮如上人の煩悩について：悪業煩悩を中心に." *Ryūkoku kyōgaku* 34 (1999), 75–85.

Daiki Naohiko 大喜直彦. "Butsuzō no shōshitsu 仏像の焼失." *Rekishigaku kenkyū* 675 (1995), 1–17.

——. "Minaosu, Rennyo kenkyū no shiten (research notes) 見直す ● 蓮如研究の視点 (研究ノート)." *Gyōshin gakuhō* 11 (1998), 128–142.

Davis, David. "*Ikki* in Late Medieval Japan." In *Medieval Japan: Essays in Institutional History*, ed. John W. Hall and Jeffrey P. Mass, 221–247. New Haven, Conn.: Yale University Press, 1974.

Dobbins, James. "From Inspiration to Institution: The Rise of Sectarian Identity in Jōdo Shinshū." *Monumenta Nipponica* 41 (1986), 331–343.

——. "Portraits of Shinran in Medieval Pure Land Buddhism." In *Living Images: Japanese Buddhist Icons in Context*, ed. Robert Sharf and Elizabeth Sharf, 19–48. Stanford, Cal.: Stanford University Press, 2001.

Dōwa Suishinhonbu 同和推進本部. "Rennyo Shōnin gohyakkai goenki ni mukete dōwa suishin honbu toshite donoyōna imi to kadai wo miidashite ikunoka: 'Kihonteki kadai' no seiri 蓮如上人五百回御遠忌に向けて、同和推進本部としてどのような意味と課題を見いだしていくのか:「基本的課題」の整理." *Shindō* 15 (1996), 2–11.

Eidmann, Phillip K. "Nyoshin and the *Kudensho*." *Pacific World: Journal of the Institute of Buddhist Studies* 1 (1982), 15–17.

Endō Hajime 遠藤一. "Ōmi no Rennyo: Sengokuki Honganji kyōdan keiseishiron, josetsu 近江の蓮如: 戦国期本願寺教団形成史論 • 序説." *Ryūkoku shidan* 99, 100 (1992), 361–380.

Fernandez, James W. "The Mission of Metaphor in Expressive Culture." *Current Anthropology* 15 (1974), 119–145.

Fugen Kōju 普賢晃寿. "Anjinketsujōshō to Rennyo kyōgaku 安心決定鈔と蓮如教学." *Shinshūgaku* 62 (1980), 1–29.

——. "Chūsei shinshū ni okeru ōbō to buppō 中世真宗における王法と仏法." *Kyōgaku kenkyūsho kiyō* 1 (1991), 59–97.

——. "Rennyo Shōnin no myōgōron to sono seiritsu haikei [lecture] 蓮如上人の名号論とその成立背景(講演)." *Ryūkoku kyōgaku* 30 (1995), 101–123.

Fugen Yasuyuki 普賢保之. "Rennyo to Shinne 蓮如と真慧." *Indogaku bukkyōgaku kenkyū* 43 (1994), 112–116.

——. "Rennyo Shōnin to Shinne Shōnin 蓮如上人と真慧上人." *Ryūkoku kyōgaku* 30 (1995), 67–77.

——. "Rennyo ni okeru metsuzai 蓮如における滅罪." *Indogaku bukkyōgaku kenkyū* 46 (1997), 34–38.

——. "Rennyo ni okeru 'nyorai to hitoshi' no igi to sono haikei 蓮如における 「如来とひとし」の意義とその背景." *Chūō bukkyōgakuin kiyō* 11 (1997), 17–34.

Fuji Yoshinari 藤能成. "Rennyo ni okeru 'yobikake no kyōgaku' 蓮如における 「呼びかけの教学」." *Shinshū kenkyū* 43 (1999), 120–135.

Fujii Jōgyō 藤井浄行. "Rennyo Shōnin gojigon honmatsu no kenkyū 『蓮如上人御持言本末』の研究." *Shinshū kenkyū* 40 (1996), 94–127.

Fujimoto Masaki 藤元正樹. "Rennyo Shōnin no kyōgaku 蓮如上人の教学." *Kyōka kenkyū* 103 (Shinshū Ōtaniha Kyōgaku Kenkyūsho, 1990), 6–28.

Fujisawa Keiju 藤澤桂珠. "Renshi *Hōshō* ni okeru 'gojūgisō' no jinshi. 蓮師『宝章』に於ける「五重義相」の深旨." *Ryūkoku kyōgaku* 26 (1991), 56–67.

Fujisawa Shinshō 藤澤信照. "'Goshō tasuke tamae' to ganshōshin 「後生たすけ たまへ」と願生心." *Ryūkoku kyōgaku* 29 (1994), 48–57.

Fujitake Myōshin 藤嶽明信. "Bonbu no butsu ni naru koto wa fushigi naru koto nari 凡夫の仏になる事は不思議なる事也." *Shinran kyōgaku* 72 (1998), 16–32.

Fujiwara Masanobu 藤原正信, "Kindai Shinshū to Fukuzawa Yukichi 近代真宗と福沢諭吉." In *Kōkakai shūkyō kenkyū ronshū: Shinran to ningen* vol. 2 光華会宗教研究論集: 親鸞と人間 第 2 巻, ed. Kōkakai, 107–129. Kyoto: Nagata Bunshōdō, 1983.

Fukagawa Nobuhiro 深川宣暢, Ogasawara Masahito 小笠原正仁, Okamura Yoshiji 岡村喜史, Asada Masahiro 浅田正博, Takada Shinryō 高田信良. "Buppō to ōbō [symposium] 仏法と王法 (シンポジウム)." *Ryūkoku kyōgaku* 32 (1997), 159–199.

Fukuhara Rengetsu 福原蓮月. "*Hōshō* no kihōittaisetsu no shin'i 宝章の機法一体説の真意." *Ryūkoku kyōgaku* 26 (1991), 68–78.

Fukuma Kōchō 福間光超. "*Gobunshō* shoshabon no chōsa, kenkyū 「御文章」書写本の調査 • 研究." *Ryūkoku daigaku bukkyō bunka kenkyūsho kiyō* 31 (1992), 135–168.

——. "Rennyo Shōnin to sono kyōdan [lecture] 蓮如上人とその教団 (講演). *Ryūkoku kyōgaku* 33 (1998), 102–144.

Fukunaga Seiya 福永静哉. "'Futsuto' kō 「ふつと」考." *Kyōgaku kenkyūsho kiyō* 1 (1991), 133–143.

Gamaike Seishi 蒲池勢至. "Rennyo eden ni miru sei to zoku: 'Rennyo' no minzokuka ni tsuite 蓮如絵伝にみる聖と俗: 「蓮如」の民俗化について." *Nihon bukkyō gakkai nenpō* 59 (1994), 197–207.

——. "Rennyo Shōnin eden no keifu" 蓮如上人絵伝の系譜, in *Rennyo Shōnin eden no kenkyū* 蓮如上人絵伝の研究, ed. Rennyo Shōnin Eden Chōsa Kenkyūhan, 122–152. Kyoto: Higashi Honganji, 1994.

Hamada Kazuo 浜田一男. "Rennyo Shōnin no *Tannishō* okugaki no imi suru mono 蓮如上人の歎異抄奥書の意味するもの." *Ryūkoku kyōgaku* 28 (1993), 15–23.

Hashimoto Hōkei 橋本芳契. "Yuimakyō to Rennyo kyōgaku: Ekōdō no shingi 維摩経と蓮如教学: 回向道の真義." *Indogaku bukkyōgaku kenkyū* 43 (1995), 49–57.

Hayashi Hiroki 林弘幹. "Rennyo to kō: 'yoriai dangō' no shakaigaku–teki kōsatsu 蓮如と講:「寄合談合」の社会学的考察." *Kyōka kenkyū* 103 (Shinshū Otaniha, 1990), 115–139.

Hayashi Nobuyasu. 林信康. "Rennyo no rinri shisō: ōbō to buppō wo chūshi to shite 蓮如の倫理思想: 王法と仏法を中心として." *Kenkyū kiyō* 8 (1995), 171–186.

Hayashi Tomoyasu 林智康. "Rennyo Shōnin to *Gobunshō* 蓮如上人と『御文章』." *Shinshūgaku* 86 (1992), 1–31.

——. "Rennyo Shōnin to igi 蓮如上人と異義." *Ryūkoku kyōgaku* 28 (1993), 60–78.

——. "*Rennyo Shōnin goichidaiki kikigaki* ni tsuite 『蓮如上人 御一代記聞書』について." *Shinshūgaku* 91,92 (1995), 253–277.

——. "Rennyo Shōnin ni manabu: *Tannishō* to *Gobunshō* 蓮如上人に学ぶ: 『歎異抄』と『御文章』." *Kyōgaku kenkyūsho kiyō* 4 (1995), 59–84.

——. "Rennyo Shōnin to jōdo iryū 蓮如上人と浄土異流." *Shinshū kenkyū* 39 (1995), 162–179.

——. "Rennyo Shōnin to goeika 蓮如上人と御詠歌." *Shinshūgaku* 93 (1996), 31–53.

Hayashi Tomoyasu, Ikeda Yūtai 池田勇諦, Asai Narumi 浅井成海, Katō Gitai 加藤義諦, and Mitsui Shūjō 満井秀城. "Rennyo Shōnin to jōdo iryū [symposium] 蓮如上人と浄土異流(シンポジウム)." *Ryūkoku kyōgaku* 30 (1995), 124–151.

Hayashima Yūki 早島有毅. "Jūgo seiki kōhan ni okeru bukkyō 'kyōdan' keisei ronri no ichirei: Honganji Rennyo ni yoru 'kyōdan' keisei no mondai jōkyō 十五世紀後半における仏教「教団」形成論理の一例: 本願寺蓮如による「教団」形成の問題情況." *Bukkyō shigaku kenkyū* 20 (1973), 1–31.

——. "Honganji Rennyo no myōgō honzon to sengoku shakai: jūji myōgō wo sozai to shite 本願寺蓮如の名号本尊と戦国社会: 十字名号を素材として." *Kyōto–shi rekishi shiryōkan kiyō* 10 (1992), 211–250.

——. "Chūsei shakai ni okeru Shinran monryū no sonzai keitai 中世社会における親鸞門流の存在形態." In *Rennyo to Honganji kyōdan* 2 蓮如と本願寺教団 (下), vol. 4 in the series *Rennyo taikei* 蓮如大系, ed. Kinryū Shizuka et al., 54–84. Kyoto: Hōzōkan, 1996.

——. "Honganji Rennyo no 'kyōdan' to sengoku shakai: ofumi wo sozai to shite 本願寺蓮如の「教団」と戦国社会: 御文を素材として." In *Kōza Rennyo* 1 講座蓮如第一巻, ed. Jōdoshinshū Kyōgaku Kenkyūsho and Honganji Shiryō Kenkyūsho, 205–250. Tokyo: Heibonsha, 1996.

——. "Chūsei bukkyō ni okeru honzon gainen no juyō keitai 中世仏教における本尊概念の受容形態." In *Nihon bukkyō no keisei to tenkai* 日本仏教の形成と展開, ed. Itō Yuishin, 330–342. Kyoto: Hōzōkan, 2002.

Hideno Daien 秀野大衍. "Ōsaka ni okeru kō no goshōsoku ni arawareta Rennyo Shōnin no kyōgaku 大阪における講の御消息に顕れた蓮如上人の教学." In *Rennyo Shōnin no kyōgaku to rekishi* 蓮如上人の教学と歴史, ed. Kimura Takeo, 61–78. Ōsaka: Tōhō Shuppansha, 1984.

Hiramatsu Reizō 平松令三. "Takada Senjuji Shinne to Honganji Rennyo 高田専修寺真慧と本願寺蓮如." In *Chūsei bukkyō to Shinshū* 中世仏教と真宗, ed. Kitanishi Hiromu Sensei Kanreki Kinenkai, 99–110. Tokyo: Yoshikawa Kōbunkan, 1985.

——. "Zenran gizetsujō no shingi ni tsuite 善鸞義絶状の真偽について," *Ryūkoku daigaku ronshū* 432 (1988), 19–30.

——. "Rennyo Shōnin no shosha shōgyo to Honganji dentō shōgyō [lecture] 蓮如上人の書写聖教と本願寺伝統聖教(講演)." *Ryūkoku kyōgaku* 32 (1997), 123–158.

Hirose Shizuka 廣瀬惺. "'Mida wo tanome' kō 「弥陀をたのめ」考." In *Ronshū Rennyo: sono shisō to bunka* 論集蓮如：その思想と文化, ed. Dōhō Daigaku Bukkyōgakkai, 129–150. Nagoya: Dōhō Daigaku Bukkyō Gakkai & Bunkōdō Shoten, 1998.

——. "*Ofumi* ni okeru 'goshōsanshō' kō 『御文』における「五障三従」考." *Dōhō bukkyō* 35 (1999), 25–41.

Hishiki Masaharu 菱木正晴. "Nyoshin wo on'o suru shisō 女身を厭惡する思想." In *Ronshū Rennyo: sono shisō to bunka* 論集蓮如：その思想と文化, ed. Dōhō Daigaku Bukkyōgakkai, 417–469. Nagoya: Dōhō Daigaku Bukkyō Gakkai & Bunkōdō Shoten, 1998.

Honda Yoshinari 本多至成. "Rennyo Shōnin to zensha no kōshō 蓮如上人と禅者の交渉." *Ryūkoku kyōgaku* 32 (1997), 112–122.

Hosokawa Gyōshin 細川行信. "Shinshū chūkō no shigan: tokuni Rennyo no Honganji saikō ni tsuite ." *Ōtani gakuhō* 48 (1969), 1–11.

——. "Rennyo Shōnin to Ōmi: toku ni katada monto to higashi Ōmi shu ni tsuite 蓮如上人と近江：特に堅田門徒と東近江衆について." In *Rennyo Shōnin kenkyū* 蓮如上人研究, ed. Rennyo Shōnin Kenkyūkai, 139–156. Kyoto: Shibunkaku Shuppan, 1998.

Ichiraku Makoto 一楽真. "Rennyo ni okeru ōbō 蓮如における王法." *Nihon bukkyō gakkai nenpō* 63 (1998), 163–177.

——. "Rennyo ni okeru shukuzen 蓮如における宿善." *Shinran kyōgaku* 71 (1998), 21–33.

Ichiraku Tenji 一楽典次. "Kie to gaike 帰依と改悔." *Kyōka kenkyū* 103 (Shinshū Ōtaniha, 1990), 29–53.

——. "Rennyo Shōnin to tanni no seishin 蓮如上人と歎異の精神." *Kyōka kenkyū* 110 (Shinshū Ōtaniha, 1993), 13–30.

Ienaga Saburō. "Japan's Modernization and Buddhism." *Contemporary Religions in Japan* 6 (1965), 1–41.

Igarashi Daisaku 五十嵐大策. "Shinran kyōgaku to Rennyo kyōgaku no hikaku kenkyū: Honkankan wo chūshin toshite. 親鸞教学と蓮如教学の比較研究：本願観を中心として." *Ryūkoku kyōgaku* 30 (1995), 44–57.

Igawa Yoshiharu 井川芳治. "Rennyo kafu no Shinran–Rennyo nison renzazō 蓮如下付の親鸞 • 蓮如二尊連座像." *Rennyo taikei* 3: *Rennyo to Honganji kyōdan jō* 蓮如大系 3：蓮如と本願寺教団上. Kyoto: Hōzōkan, 1996, 334–342.

Igawa Yoshiharu. "Rennyo uragaki no hōben hosshin sonzō kō: Taruichō Shinshū jiin no shinshutsu shiryō wo fumaete 蓮如裏書の方便法身尊像考：垂井町真宗寺院の新出史料を踏まえて." *Dōhō bukkyō* 32 (1997), 225–253.

Ikeda Makoto. 池田真. "Rennyo ni okeru shōshin no igi: *Shōshinge taii* wo chūshin toshite 蓮如における正信の意義：『正信偈大意』を中心として." *Shinran kyōgaku* 72 (1998), 33–51.

——. "Rennyo Shōnin ni okeru 'Shinshū saikō' no igi: 'Shōshinge' no chūshaku wo megutte 蓮如上人における「真宗再興」の意義：「正信偈」の註釈をめぐって." *Shinshū kenkyū* 43 (1999), 1–15.

Ikeda Yūtai 池田勇諦. "Rennyo Shōnin no nyonin jōbutsu setsu no kadai [lecture] 蓮如上人の女人成仏説の課題 (講演)." *Shinran kyōgaku* 60 (1992), 80–91.

——. "Sabetsu to tsumi: Rennyo Shōnin to gendai [lecture] 差別と罪：蓮如上人と現代 (講演)." *Shindō* 18 (1998), 4–22.

——. "Ofumi no kyōkei 御文の教系." In *Ronshū Rennyō: sono shisō to bunka* 論集蓮如：その思想と文化, ed. Dōhō Daigaku Bukkyōgakkai, 57–74. Nagoya: Dōhō Daigaku Bukkyō Gakkai & Bunkōdō Shoten, 1998.

——. "Kyōgyōshinshō to Ofumi 教行信証と御文." *Dōhō bukkyō* 35 (1999), 11–23.

Imada Minsei. 今田愍生. "Rennyo Shōnin no *Ryōgemon* ni tsuite 蓮如上人の領解文について." *Ryūkoku kyōgaku* 26 (1991), 33–43.

——. "Rennyo Shōnin *Gobunshō* shi no shi no sanshu eika ni tsuite 蓮如上人御文章四の四の三首詠歌について." *Ryūkoku kyōgaku* 28 (1993), 7–14.

Imada Norio 今田法雄. "Renshi ni okeru Yamashina zōei to sono haikei. 蓮師に於ける山科造営とその背景." *Shinshū kenkyū* 36 (1992), 143–157.

Inada Jōshin 稲田静真. "Rennyo Shōnin no 'gojū no gi' ni tsuite 蓮如上人の「五重の義」について." *Ryūkoku kyōgaku* 27 (1992), 30–40.

——. "Rennyo Shōnin ni okeru shinyaku no haikei: 'yoshonyoraitō,' 'bendōmiroku' tō ni tsuite 蓮如上人における信益の背景：「与諸如来等」、「便同弥勒」等について." *Shūgakuin ronshū* 66 (1993), 1–16.

Inaki Sen'e 稲城選恵. "Renshi kyōgaku no chūshin mondai ni tsuite [lecture] 蓮師教学の中心問題について (講演)." *Ryūkoku kyōgaku* 26 (1991), 105–132.

——. "*Gobunshō* no ronri: ware to nanji no nisha no tachiba 『御文章』の論理：我と汝の二者の立場." *Chūō bukkyōgakuin kiyō* 8–9 (1992), 1–19.

——. "Rennyo kyōgaku no honryū [lecture] 蓮如教学の本流 (講演)." *Ryūkoku kyōgaku* 34 (1999), 98–113.

Ishiguro Daishun 石黒大俊. "Rennyo Shōnin no o'uta ni tsuite 蓮如上人のお歌 について." *Ryūkoku kyōgaku* 26 (1991), 19–32.

Itō Akemi 伊藤曙覧. "Minzoku kara mita Rennyo Shōnin 民俗から見た蓮如上人." In *Rennyo Shōnin kenkyū* 蓮如上人研究, ed. Rennyo Shōnin Kenkyūkai, 317–338. Kyoto: Shibunkaku Shuppan, 1998.

Itō Shinichi 伊藤進一 et al., eds. "Sagara shi hōdo 相良氏法度." In *Buke kahō* 武家家法, *Chūsei hōsei shiryō shū*, vols. 3–5 中世法制史料集第3–5巻, ed. Itō Shinichi, et al., 35–113. Tokyo: Iwanami Shoten, 1965.

Iwasaki Chinei 岩崎智寧. "Shinshū ni okeru nyonin–ōjō ron to sei–sabetsu: tokuni Shinran wo chūshin to shite 蓮如における女人往生について." *Shūgakuin ronshū* 68 (1996), 19–41.

Izumoji Osamu 出雲路修. "Gojō ofumi no seiritsu wo megutte 五帖御文の成立をめぐって." *Kyōka kenkyū* 103 (Shinshū Ōtaniha, 1990), 72–83.

——. "'Ofumi kenkyūkai' shōroku: Ichijōme dai nanatsū wo chūshin ni 「御文研究会」抄録：一帖目第七通を中心に." *Kyōka kenkyū* 110 (Shinshū Ōtaniha, 1993), 44–58.

——. "Rennyo ni okeru otoko to onna 蓮如における男と女." *Kyōka kenkyū* 110 (Shinshū Ōtaniha, 1993), 31–43.

——. "Rennyo Shōnin no bunshō hyōgen [lecture] 蓮如上人の文章表現 (講演)." *Ryūkoku kyōgaku* 28 (1993), 79–94.

——. "Hakkotsu wo megutte 白骨をめぐって." *Ryūkoku daigaku ronshū* 450 (1997), 98–112.

Jinnai Masanobu 神内正信. "'Sorewa monpō to wa betsu' to iu koto no imi: Rennyo Shōnin to gendai [lecture] 「それは聞法とは別」ということの意味：蓮如上人と現代{講演}." *Shindō* 18 (1998), 26–38.

Kadono Yōmyō 葛野洋明. "Rennyo Shōnin no dendō: Amerika kaikyō no genjō wo tōshite 蓮如上人の伝道: アメリカ開教の現状を通して." *Ryūkoku kyōgaku* 29 (1994), 21–33.

———. "Rennyo Shōnin no shōkaron 蓮如上人の証果論." *Ryūkoku kyōgaku* 32 (1997), 7–19.

Kaginushi Ryōkei 鍵主良敬. "Rennyo ni okeru nichijōsei to muga: Daijō no shigoku kara mite 蓮如における日常性と無我: 大乗の至極から見て." *Nihon bukkyō gakkai nenpō* 63 (1998), 149–161.

Kagotani Machiko 籠谷眞智子. "Rennyo to 'yome odoshi' no ohanashi." *Shinshū kenkyū* 26 (1982), 128–136.

———. "Rennyo to 'yome odoshi' no kyōkun 蓮如と「嫁おどし」の教訓." *Kenkyū kiyō* 5 (1992), 23–50.

———. "Rennyo yonhyakukai enki hōyō no keii to ningyō jōruri 蓮如四百回遠忌法要の経緯と人形浄瑠璃." *Kenkyū kiyō* 6 (1993), 1–16.

———. "Rennyo to Nōgaku" in *Rennyo taikei* vol. 1, ed. Ueba Akio 上場顕雄, 288–316. Kyoto: Hōzōkan, 1996.

———. "Shinshū bunkashi no kenkyū 真宗文化史の研究." *Shisō*, 1954.

Kaihō Ryū 海法龍. "Monogatari no yukue: Rennyo Shōnin to gendai [lecture] 物語の行方: 蓮如上人と現代 (講演)." *Shindō* 17 (1998), 98–108.

Kakehashi Jitsuen 梯実円. "*Anjin ketsujōshō* to Rennyo Shōnin: kihō–ittai ron wo megutte 『安心決定鈔』と蓮如上人: 機法一体論をめぐって." In *Rennyo Shōnin no kyōgaku to rekishi* 蓮如上人の教学と歴史, ed. Kimura Takeo, 93–114. Ōsaka: Tōhō Shuppansha, 1984.

———. "'Tasuke tamae to tanomu' ni tsuite [lecture] 「タスケタマヘトタノム」について (講演)." *Ryūkoku kyōgaku* 31 (1996), 111–128.

———. "Seme no Rennyo to mamori no Rennyo 攻めの蓮如と守りの蓮如." In *Rennyo: tenkanki no shūkyōsha* 蓮如: 転換期の宗教者, ed. Yamaori Tetsuo and Ōmura Eishō, 258–266. Tokyo: Shōgakkan, 1997.

Kanda Chisato 神田千里. "Ikkō-shū to Kirishitan 一向宗とキリシタン." *Tōyō daigaku bungakubu kiyo* 50: *Shūshi gakka hen* 22 (1997), 1–30.

Kaneko Daiei 金子大榮. "Rennyo the Restorer (1)." *The Eastern Buddhist* 31:1 (1998), 1–11.

———. "Rennyo the Restorer (2)." *The Eastern Buddhist* 31:2 (1998), 209–218.

Kanno Takakazu 菅野隆一. "Rennyo to Zonkaku: *Gobunshō* ni okeru Zonkaku senjutsu no iyō ni tsuite 蓮如と存覚: 『御文章』における存覚撰述の依用について." *Kyōgaku kenkyūsho kiyō* 4 (1995), 109–131.

Kashiwagura Akihiro 柏倉昭裕. "Okite no ofumi 掟の御文." *Shūkyō kenkyū* 319 (1999), 386–387.

Katada Osamu 堅田修. "Rennyo Shōnin no eika 蓮如上人の詠歌." In *Ronshū Rennyō: sono shisō to bunka* 論集蓮如: その思想と文化, ed. Dōhō Daigaku Bukkyōgakkai, 151–168. Nagoya: Dōhō Daigaku Bukkyō Gakkai & Bunkōdō Shoten, 1998.

Kataoka Osamu 片岡了. "*Ofumi* no buntai 『御文』の文体." *Ōtani gakuhō* 72 (1993), 1–13.

Katō Chiken 加藤智見. "Rennyo Shōnin ni okeru kyōdankan no genten (lecture) 蓮如上人における教団観の原点 (講演)." *Ryūkoku kyōgaku* 30 (1995), 87–100.

———. "Rennyo to Lutā 蓮如とルター." *Indogaku bukkyōgaku kenkyū* 46 (1997), 46–50.

———. "*Ofumi* to kyōka to shūkyōsei 「御文」と教化と宗教性." In *Ronshū Rennyō: sono shisō to bunka* 論集蓮如: その思想と文化, ed. Dōhō Daigaku Bukkyōgakkai, 89–110. Nagoya: Dōhō Daigaku Bukkyō Gakkai & Bunkōdō Shoten, 1998.

Kawamura, Leslie. "The Myōkōnin: Japan's Representation of the Bodhisattva." In *Myōkōnin kenkyū* 妙好人伝研究, ed. Asaeda Zenshō, 40–55. Kyoto: Nagata Bunshōdō, 1987.

Keta Masako 気多雅子. "Katō Chiken *Rennyo to Rutå: shinkō no shūkyōgaku–teki kōsatsu* (review, introduction) 加藤智見『蓮如とルター: 信仰の宗教学的考察』 (書評 • 紹介)." *Shūkyō kenkyū* 64 (1990), 68–71.

——. "Rennyo ni okeru shūkō to seiji no kankei 蓮如における宗教と政治の関係." *Kanazawa daigaku kyōikugakubu kiyō* 41 (1991), 252–264.

Kigoshi Yasushi 木越康. "Rennyo to Shinshū kyōdan: 'Kirishitan monjo' ni yorinagara 蓮如と真宗教団: 「キリシタン文書」によりながら." *Shinran kyōgaku* 73 (1999), 31–49.

Kikuchi Takeshi 菊池武. "Rennyo jidai no ihōgi ni tsuite: Shinshū to shomin shinkō 蓮如時代の異法議について: 真宗と庶民信仰." In *Homyō Shōnin roppyaku–gojūkai go'onki kinen ronbun–shū* 法明上人六百五十回御遠忌記念論文集, ed. Yūzū Nenbutsu Shūkyōgaku Kenkyūsho, 403–411. Osaka: Dainenbutsuji, 1998.

Kikufuji Myōdō 菊藤明道. "Shinran, Kakunyo, Rennyo no rinrikan 親鸞 • 覚如 • 蓮如の倫理観." *Indogaku bukkyōgaku kenkyū* 44 (1995), 167–173.

King, Winston. "An Interpretation of the *Anjin Ketsujōshō*." *Japanese Journal of Religious Studies* 13 (1986), 277–298.

Kinryū Shizuka 金龍静. "Sengokuki Honganji kyōdan no uragaki–kō 戦国期本願寺教団の裏書考." *Nenpō chūsei–shi kenkyū* 13 (1988), 1–20.

——. "Rennyo kyōdan no mibun–teki, soshiki–teki kōzō 蓮如教団の身分的 • 組織的構造." In *Nihon no zenkindai to Hokuriku shakai* 日本の前近代と北陸社会, ed. Kusunose Masaru, 261–277. Kyoto: Shibunkaku, 1989.

——. "Sengokuki Honganji kyōdan no hōbutsu kō 戦国期本願寺教団の法物考." In *Shinshūshi ronsō* 真宗史論叢, ed. Fukuma Kōchō Sensei Kanreki Kinenkai. 327–350. Kyoto: Nagata Bunshōdō 1993.

——. "Ikkō-shū no shūha no seiritsu 一向宗の宗派の成立." In *Kōza Rennyo* 4 講座連如 第四巻, ed. Jōdo Shinshū Kyōgaku Kenkyūsho, 295–318. Tokyo: Heibonsha, 1997.

Kitajima Takaaki 北島隆晃. "Rennyo Shōnin ni okeru jōdo 蓮如上人における浄土." *Ryūkoku kyōgaku* 32 (1997), 20–32.

Kitanishi Hiromu 北西弘. "Hōnen shōnin to Rennyo Shōnin 法然上人と蓮如上人." *Kyōka kenkyū* 6 (Jōdoshū Sōgō Kenkyūsho, 1994), 2–24.

——. "Shinshūshi–jō no Hōnen Shōnin 真宗史上の法然聖人." *Bukkyō daigaku sōgō kenkyūsho kiyō* 2 (1995), 38–58.

——. "Kitanishi sensei ga kataru Hōnen, Shinran, Rennyo [dialogue] 北西弘先生が語る法然、親鸞、蓮如 (対談)." *Bukkyō daigaku sōgō kenkyūsho kiyō* 3 (1996), 42–63.

——. "Rennyo Shōnin to sono kazoku (lecture) 蓮如上人とその家族 (講演)." *Gyōshin gakuhō* 11 (1998), 191–207.

Kō Shimei 高史明. "*Tannishō* soshite Rennyo Shōnin no konnichiteki igi (lecture) 『歎異抄』そして蓮如上人の今日的意義(講演)." *Shinran kyōgaku* 71 (1998), 69–101.

Kōbai Eiken 紅楳英顕. "Shinran to Rennyo no nenbutsu shisō 親鸞と蓮如の念仏思想." *Shinshū kenkyū* 38 (1994), 125–138.

——. "Shinran to Rennyo: Genshō shōjōju ni tsuite 親鸞と蓮如: 現生正定聚について." *Indogaku bukkyōgaku kenkyū* 46 (1998), 221–227.

Kobayashi Hakumon 小林博聞. "*Ofumi* 'namuamidabutsu no sugata' kō (1) 『御文』「南無阿弥陀仏のすがた」考 (一)." *Kyūshū Ōtani kenkyū kiyō* 22 (1995), 15–24.

——. *Ofumi* 'namuamidabutsu no sugata' kō (2). 『御文』「南無 阿弥陀仏のすがた」考 (二)." *Kyūshū Ōtani kenkyū kiyō* 23 (1997), 1–16.

Koike Toshiaki 小池俊章. "Rennyo Shōnin ni okeru genjitsu sekai no igi 蓮如上人における現実世界の意義." *Ryūkoku kyōgaku* 27 (1992), 18–29.

——. "Tariki ekō no kenkyū: Rennyo Shōnin *Gobunshō* e no tenkai wo kangamite. 他力回向の研究: 蓮如上人『御文章』への展開を鑑みて." *Shūgakuin ronshū* 67 (1995), 104–117.

Kojima Michihiro 小島道裕. "Heichi jōkan ato to jiin, sonraku: Ōmi no jirei kara 平地城館と寺院・村落: 近江の事例から." In *Chūsei jōkaku kenkyū ronshū* 中世城郭研究論集, ed. Murata Shūzō, 397–430. Tokyo: Shinjinbutsu Ōraisha, 1990.

Kōshiro Yūmō 幸城勇猛. "Jōnai *Gobunshō* ni okeru shinjin no seiritsu konkyo 帖内御文章に於ける信心の成立根拠." *Ryūkoku kyōgaku* 26 (1991), 79–89.

——. "Rennyo kyōgaku ni okeru shinjin no tokushoku 蓮如教学における信心の特色." *Ryūkoku kyōgaku* 28 (1993), 50–59.

Kubori Shōbin 久堀勝敏. "Rennyo kyōgaku ni okeru shukuzen, mushukuzen ni tsuite: sono jo 蓮如教学における宿善、無宿善について: その序." *Ryūkoku kyōgaku* 26 (1991), 44–55.

——. "Renshi kyōgaku to rokujishaku: Shūso tono kakawari 蓮師教学と六字釈: 宗祖とのかかわり." *Ryūkoku kyōgaku* 29 (1994), 135–146.

——. "Rennyo Shōnin to goanjin 蓮如上人と御安心." *Ryūkoku kyōgaku* 34 (1999), 86–97.

Kusano Kenshi 草野顕之. "Rennyo kyōdan no naijitsu ni tsuite: Rennyo Shōnin to gendai (lecture) 蓮如教団の内実について: 蓮如上人と現代 (講演)." *Shindō* 17 (1998), 5–65.

Kusunoki Shōei 楠昭英. "Rennyo ni totte no 'eshin' 蓮如にとっての「廻心」." *Kyushū Ryūkoku tanki daigaku kiyō* 44 (1998), 1–36.

Maeda Egaku 前田恵学. "Kyōdan kakuritsu no kiso: Rennyo Shōnin no ichi–zuke 教団確立の基礎: 蓮如上人の位置づけ." In *Rennyo Shōnin kenkyū* 蓮如上人研究, ed. Rennyo Shōnin Kenkyūkai, 409–420. Kyoto: Shibunkaku Shuppan, 1998.

Mano Toshikazu 真野俊和. "Shinshū ni okeru sōsō girei no keishiki: Rennyo no baai 真宗における葬送儀礼の形式: 蓮如の場合." *Kokuritsu rekishi minzoku hakubutsukan kenkyū hōkoku* 49 (1992), 177–194.

Masaki Haruhiko 正木晴彦. "Zendō to Rennyo ni kansuru ichi danmen 善導と蓮如に関する一断面." *Indogaku bukkyōgaku kenkyū* 46 (1998), 17–23.

Matsuoka Masanori 松岡雅則. "Kiyozawa Manshi ni okeru Rennyokan 清沢満之における蓮如観." *Indogaku bukkyō gaku kenkyū* 46 (1997), 56–58.

Mikogami Eryū, "Shinshū kyōdan no honzon 真宗教団の本尊." In *Bukkyō kyōdan no kenkyū* 仏教教団の研究, ed. Yoshimura Shūki, 448–464. Kyoto: Hyakka–en, 1968.

Minamoto Ryōen 源了圓. "Bannen no Rennyo Shōnin no shisō, shinkō to myōkōnin no keisei (lecture) 晩年の蓮如上人の思想・信仰と妙好人の形成 (講演)." *Gyōshin gakuhō* 11 (1998), 188–236.

——. "Myōkōnin Asahara Saichi to Rennyo: hitsotsu no shiron 妙好人浅原才市と蓮如: 一つの試論," In *Rennyo Shōnin kenkyū I* 蓮如上人研究 I, ed. Jōdo Shinshū Kyōgaku Kenkyūjō, 217–300. Kyoto: Nagata Bunshōdō, 1998.

——. "Rennyo zenki ni okeru myōkōnin no keisei: Kanegamori no Dōsai wo megutte 蓮如前期における妙好人の形成: 金森の道西をめぐって." *Kyōgaku kenkyūsho kiyō* 7 (1998), 35–55.

——. "Rennyo Shōnin, Umeda Kenkyō, Asahara Saichi (lecture) 蓮如上人・梅田謙敬・浅原才一 (講演)." *Shinshū kenkyū* 43 (1999), 157–194.

Minowa Shūhō 箕輪秀邦. "*Ofumi ni manabu* 『御文』に学ぶ." *Dōhō* 1995, 34–41.

Mitsui Shūjō 満井秀城. "Renshi kyōgaku no rekishiteki igi ni tsuite 連師教学の歴史的意義について." *Shūgakuin Ronshū* 60 (1988), 26–50.

——. "Rennyo Shōnin 'ōbōihon' no rekishiteki haikei ni tsuite 蓮如上人'王法為本'の歴史的背景について." *Ryūkoku kyōgaku* 25 (1990), 21–32.

——. "Rennyo kyōgaku to jōdo kaigaku 蓮如教学と浄土戒学." *Shūgakuin ronshū* 66 (1993), 67–86.

——. "Rennyo kyōgaku kenkyū ni okeru shisōshi no hōhō ni tsuite 蓮如教学研究における思想史の方法について." *Ryūkoku kyōgaku* 29 (1994), 75–86.

Miura Shūkō 三浦周行. "Honen to Rennyo." In *Shinpen Rekishi to Jinbutsu* 新編歴史と人物, orig. by Miura Shūkō, rev. ed. Hayashiya Tatsusaburō and Asao Naohiro, 202–215. Tokyo: Iwanami Shoten (*Iwanami bunko* 33–166–2), 1990.

Miyata Noboru 宮田登. "Josei to minkan shinkō 女性と民間信仰." In *Nihon josei shi* 3: *Kinsei* 日本女性史3: 近世, ed. Joseishi Sōgō Kenkyūkai, 227–254. Tokyo: Tokyo Daigaku Shuppankai, 1982.

Miyoshi Etsuko 見義悦子. "Joseikan wo ronzuru toki: Rennyo Shōnin to gendai [lecture] 女性観を論ずる時: 蓮如上人と現代(講演)." *Shindō* 16 (1997), 35–41.

Mōri Katsunori 毛利勝典. "Shokugyō shūkyōka toshite no Rennyozō 職業宗教家としての蓮如像." *Indogaku bukkyōgaku kenkyū* 47 (1999), 179–181.

——. "Shokugyōteki shūkyōka toshite no Rennyozō: Shinshū shinjin no jittaika to sono mondaiten. 職業的宗教家としての蓮如像: 真宗信心の実体化とその問題点." *Shinshū kenkyūkai kiyō* 31 (1999), 1–20.

Mori Ryūkichi 森龍吉. "*Rennyo to Karuvan: keizai rinri o meguru Shinshū to Purotesutantizumu Tono hikakuron ni kanrenshite* 蓮如とカルヴァン: 経済倫理をめぐる真宗とプロテスタンティズムとの比較論に関連して." *Nihon bukkyo gakkai nenpō* 37 (1972), reprinted in *Rennyo Taikei* 2 (Hozokan, 1996, Nov.), 426–538.

Mori Shōji 森章司. "Shokan ni miru Shinran to Jishinbō Zenran 書簡に見る親鸞と慈信房善鸞." *Tōyōgaku ronsō* 28 (2003), 27–83.

Morita Giken 森田義見. "Joshōron no kenkyū: Rennyo Shōnin ni tsuite. 助正論の研究: 蓮如上人について." *Ryūkoku kyōgaku* 28 (1993), 33–44.

——. "Rennyo Shōnin no fukyō jissenron 蓮如上人の布教実践論." *Ryūkoku kyōgaku* 30 (1995), 29–43.

——. "Rennyo to Ikkyū 蓮如と一休." *Shinshū kenkyūkai kiyō* 28 (1996), 1–20.

——. "Rennyo Shōnin no honzonron: shoki ninpō ni yosete 蓮如上人の本尊論: 所帰人法によせて. *Ryūkoku kyōgaku* 32 (1997), 58–69.

——. "Rennyo Shōnin no shukuzenron 蓮如上人の宿善論." *Ryūkoku kyōgaku* 34 (1999), 51–62.

Morita Shin'en 森田眞円, Nishiyama Kunihiko 西山邦彦, Nishikawa Kōji 西川幸治, Kinryū Shizuka, Sei Shōsei 成照星, and Mitsui Shūjō. "Rennyo Shōnin wo megutte: Rennyo Shōnin no mezasareta mono [symposium] 蓮如上人をめぐって: 蓮如上人のめざされたもの (シンポジウム)." *Ryūkoku kyōgaku* 34 (1999), 130–169.

Murakami Munehiro 村上宗博. "Rennyo no gyōshinron 蓮如の行信論." *Indogaku bukkyōgaku kenkyū* 42 (1983), 124–126.

——. "Kakunyo kyōgaku to Ryōchū kyōgaku: rinjū raigō wo megutte 覚如教学と良忠教学: 臨終來迎をめぐって." *Ōtani daigaku daigakuin kenkyū kiyō* 6 (1989), 49–68.

——. "Kakunyo no gyōshinron: rinju raigō wo megutte 覚如の行信論: 臨終來迎をめぐって." *Shinshū kyōgaku kenkyū* 16 (1992), 46–55.

——. "Rennyo *Matsudai muchi no ofumi* ni kiku 蓮如『末代無智の御文』に聴く." *Shinshū bunka* 6 (1997), 48–88.

Nabata Takashi 名畑崇. "Muromachi no Rekishikan: *Hekizan nichiroku* wo megutte. 室町の歴史観: 『碧山日録』をめぐって." *Ōtani gakuhō* 75 (1996), 66–67.

——. "The Legacy of Rennyo Shonin: *Rennyo Shonin Itokuki*." *The Eastern Buddhist* 31–2 (1998), 245–262.

——. "Rennyo no oshie: Muromachi no sei to shi 蓮如のおしえ—室町の生と死." *Ōtani gakuhō* 78 (1999), 31–41.

Nabeshima Naoki 鍋島直樹. "Rennyo ni okeru mujōkan no tokushitsu (I) 蓮如における無常観の特質(I)." *Ryūkoku daigaku ronshū* 449 (1996), 1–43.

Nadamoto Aiji 灘本愛慈. "Shinran Shōnin to Rennyo Shōnin." In *Rennyo shōnin no kyōgaku to rekishi* 蓮如上人の教学と歴史, ed. Kimura Takeo, 55–58. Tokyo: Tōhō Shuppan, 1984.

Naitō Chikō 内藤知康, Sōma Kazui 相馬一意, Terazono Yoshiki 寺園善基, Kōbai Eiken, and Tōkō Kan'ei 東光寛英. "Jōdo to tengoku: Rennyo Shōnin wo megutte [symposium]. 浄土と天国: 蓮如上人をめぐって (シンポジウム)." *Ryūkoku kyōgaku* 31 (1996), 145–184.

Nakagaki Masayoshi 中垣昌美. "Rennyo Shōnin to nenbutsu komyuniti 蓮如上人と念仏コミュニティ." In *Rennyo Shōnin no kyōgaku to rekishi* 蓮如上人の教学と歴史, ed. Kimura Takeo, 319–337. Osaka: Tōhō Shuppansha, 1984.

Nakamura Eiryū 中村英龍. "Rennyo Shōnin to gensō ekōron no kanrensei ni tsuite 蓮如上人と還相回向論の関連性について." *Ryūkoku kyōgaku* 32 (1997), 48–57.

——. "Rennyo Shōnin ni okeru shin ryōge no tokushitsu 蓮如上人における信領解の特質." *Ryūkoku kyōgaku* 34 (1999), 30–39.

Nakamura Ikuo 中村生雄. "Honji suijaku to Shinshū shinkō 本地垂迹と真宗信仰." In *Rennyo: tenkanki no shūkyōsha* 蓮如: 転換期の宗教者, ed. Yamaori Tetsuo and Ōmura Eishō, 227–238. Tokyo: Shōgakkan, 1997.

——. "Rennyo no josei–kan, kazoku–kan 蓮如の女性観・家族観." In *Rennyo: tenkanki no shūkyōsha* 蓮如: 転換期の宗教者, 93–120. Tokyo: Shōgakkan, 1997.

Nanbu Matsumi 南部松見. "Rennyo Shōnin ni okeru ōbō, buppō: Kinsei, kindai 'shinzoku nitai' ron e no eikyō 蓮如上人における王法・仏法: 近世・近代「真俗二諦」論への影響." *Ryūkoku kyōgaku* 33 (1998), 9–23.

Naomi Genyō 直海玄洋. "Sukui: *Gobunshō* ni manabu [lecture] すくい―御文章に学ぶ (公開講座)." *Chūō bukkyōgakuin kiyō* 10 (1993), 40–77.

Neusner, Jacob. "Shalom: Complementarity." In *Ministry and Theology in Global Perspective: Contemporary Challenges for the Church*, ed. Don Pittman et al., 465–471. Grand Rapids, Mich.: Eerdmans, 1996.

Ninzeki Takashi 忍関崇. "Hokuriku ni okeru Rennyo kyōdan no tenkai ni tsuite: Hakusan Kaga Baba wo chūshin toshite 北陸における蓮如教団の展開について: 白山加賀馬場を中心として." *Bukkyōshi kenkyū* 28 (1991), 16–48.

Nishiguchi Junko 西口順子. "Ekeizu ni miru 'ie' no saishi 絵系図に見る「家」の祭祀." *Gekkan hyakka* 288 (1986), 18–29.

Nishikawa Kōji 西川幸治. "Rennyo no machi zukuri 蓮如の町づくり." *Ōtani gakuhō* 78 (1999), 42–63.

Nishikawa Masato 西河雅人. "Renshi kyōgaku ni miru jōgyōdaihi no genjitsuteki igi 蓮師教学に見る常行大悲の現実的意義." *Ryūkoku kyōgaku* 25 (1990), 9–20.

Nose Eisui 野世英水. "Rennyo *Ofumi* ni mirareru jingikan ni tsuite 蓮如『御文』に見られる神祇観について." *Indogaku bukkyōgaku kenkyū* 43 (1993), 179–182.

——. "Rennyo ni okeru shin to jingi 蓮如における信と神祇." *Shinshūgaku* 90 (1994), 78–102.

Obata Bunshō 尾畑文正. "Dōhō towa ikanaru sonzai ka: Rennyo Shōnin to gendai [lecture] 同朋とはいかなる存在か―蓮如上人と現代 (講演)." *Shindō* 16 (1997), 5–20.

——. "Rennyo Shōnin no kenryoku–kan: *Hakkotsu no ofumi* wo tōshite 蓮如上人の権力観: 「白骨の御文」を通して." In *Ronshū Rennyo: sono shisō to bunka* 論集蓮如: その思想と文化, ed. Dōhō Daigaku Bukkyōgakkai, 470–448. Nagoya: Dōhō Daigaku Bukkyō Gakkai & Bunkōdō Shoten, 1998.

Ōhashi Shunnō 大橋俊雄. "Rennyo Shōnin to jishū [lecture] 蓮如上人と時衆 (講演)." *Shūgakuin ronshū* 65 (1993), 75–96.

Okamura Ken'ei 岡村謙英. "Shūso kara Renshi ni miru 'byōdōhō' no yukue 宗祖から蓮師に見る「平等法」のゆくえ." *Ryūkoku kyōgaku* 29 (1994), 105–117.

——. "Renshi no shōmyō hōongi 蓮師の称名報恩義." *Gyōshin gakuhō* 10 (1997), 198–216.

——. "Buppōsha keshiki mienu furumai. 仏法者気色みえぬ振舞." *Ryūkoku kyōgaku* 33 (1998), 74–85.

Ono Renmyō 小野蓮明. "Rennyo ni okeru shinshū no kenyō 蓮如における真宗の顕揚." *Indogaku bukkyōgaku kenkyū* 46 (1998), 228–236.

Ōtani Kōshin, "Opening Address." In *Amerika no shūkyō wo tazunete: Hābādo daigaku sinpojiumu to Beikoku tōbu kenshū ryokō* アメリカの宗教を訪ねて：ハーバード大学シンポジウムと米国東部研修旅行; *Shin Buddhism Meets American Religions*, ed. Hābādo Daigaku Shinpojiumu to Beikoku tōbu Kenshū ryokōkan, 242–236. Kyoto: Nishi Honganji–nai Jibu, 1986.

Rogers, Minor L. "Rennyo and Jōdo Shinshū Piety: The Yoshizaki Years." *Monumenta Nipponica* 36 (1981), 21–35.

——. "The Shin Faith of Rennyo." *The Eastern Buddhist* n.s. 15 (1982), 56–73.

——. "A View of Rennyo's Early and Middle Years." In *Jōdokyō no kenkyū: Ishida Mitsuyuki hakase koki kinen ronbun* 浄土教の研究：石田充之博士古稀記念論文, ed. Ishida Mitsuyuki Hakase Koki Kinen Ronbunshū Kankōkai, 101–124. Kyoto: Nagata Bunshōdō, 1982.

Sapir, Edward. "Symbolism." In *Encyclopedia of the Social Sciences*, ed. Edwin Seligman and Alvin Johnson, 492–495. New York: Macmillan, 1934.

Seo Kenshō 瀬尾顕証. "Gyōgi no kakuritsu to sono ii: wasan, ofumi wo chūshin to shite 行儀の確立とその推移." In *Ronshū Rennyō: sono shisō to bunka* 論集蓮如：その思想と文化, ed. Dōhō Daigaku Bukkyōgakkai, 355–374. Nagoya: Dōhō Daigaku Bukkyō Gakkai & Bunkōdō Shoten, 1998.

Shibata Hideaki 柴田秀昭. "Rennyo Shōnin no kyōka ni manabu 蓮如上人の教化に学ぶ." *Kyōka kenkyū* 103 (Shinshū Ōtaniha 1990), 54–71.

Shibata Tōru 柴田泰. "Kakehashi Jitsuen, Nabata Takashi, Minegishi Sumio kanshū *Rennyo taikei* zen–gokan 梯實圓・名畑崇・峰岸純夫監修『蓮如大系』全五巻." Review of *Rennyo taikei*, all 5 volumes. *Indo tetsugaku bukkyōgaku* 13 (1998), 371–372.

Shigaraki Takamaro. "The Problem of the True and the False in Contemporary Shin Buddhist Studies: True Shin Buddhism and False Shin Buddhism." *Pacific World* 3 (2001), 27–52.

Shigematsu Akihisa 重松昭久. "Fukuzawa Yukichi to Bukkyō." In *Shinran—Shinshū shisōshi kenkyū*, ed. Shigematsu Akihisa, 377–434. Kyoto: Hozokan, 1990.

Solomon, Ira Michael. "Rennyo and the Rise of Honganji in Muromachi Japan." Ph.D. diss., Columbia University, New York, 1972.

——. "Kinship and the Transmission of Religious Charisma: The Case of Honganji." *The Journal of Asian Studies* 33 (1974), 403–413.

——. "The Dilemma of Religious Power: Honganji and Hosokawa Masamoto." *Monumenta Nipponica* 33 (1978), 51–65.

Sugihira Shizutoshi. "Rennyo Shōnin: The Great Teacher of Shin Buddhism." *The Eastern Buddhist* 8 (1949), 5–35.

Sumikura Hironobu 隅倉浩信. "'Tasuke tamae to tanomu' kō 「たすけたまへとたのむ」考." *Ryūkoku kyōgaku* 33 (1998), 38–51.

——. "'Tasuke tamae to tanomu' kō: Rennyo Shōnin no shinjin wo meguru shomondai. 「たすけたまへとたのむ」考：蓮如上人の信心を巡る諸問題." *Indogaku bukkyōgaku kenkyū* 46 (1998), 214–216.

Tagami Taishu 田上太秀. "Furoku: seisabetsu o jochōshita *Ketsubonkyō* 付録：性差別を助長した血盆経, appendix to his *Bukkyō to seisabutsu* 仏教と性差別. *Tōsho sensho* 東書選書, no. 128, 197–209. Tokyo: Tokyo Shoseki, 1992.

Taguchi Yukie 田口雪江. "*Gobunshō* nyonin jōbutsu『御文章』女人成仏." *Ryūkoku kyōgaku* 29 (1994), 34–47.

Takahashi Kotohisa 高橋事久. "*Tannishō* to *Gobunshō* 歎異抄と御文章." *Indogaku bukkyōgaku kenkyū* 43 (1994), 107–111.

——. "Rennyo no ōbō to buppō 蓮如の王法と仏法." In *Nihon no shakai to shinshū* 日本の社会と真宗, ed. Chiba Jōryū, 35–46. Kyoto: Shibunkaku Shuppan, 1999.

Takeda Kenju 武田賢寿. "Kakunyo Shōnin no Honganji kaisō to Rennyo Shōnin no Honganji saikō ni tsuite no ichikōsatsu 覚如上人の本願寺開創と蓮如上人の本願寺再興についての一考察." *Dōhō gakuen bukkyō bunka kenkyūsho kiyō* 14 (1992), 1–11.

Takeda Susumu 武田晋. "Rennyo Shōnin no ōjō shisō 蓮如上人の往生思想." *Shūkyō kenkyū* 67 (1994), 268–270.

Takemura Shōhō. "Rennyo Shōnin no dendō 蓮如上人の伝道." *Ryūkoku kyōgaku* 34 (1999), 114–129.

Takemura Takahiko 武邑尚彦. "Rennyo Shōnin ni manabu: Dendō to kyōgaku [lecture] 蓮如上人に学ぶ: 伝道と教学 (講演)." *Ryūkoku kyōgaku* 31 (1996), 129–144.

Takenaka Chishū 竹中智秀. "Rennyo Shōnin to gendai [lecture] 蓮如上人と現代 (講演)." *Shindō* 17 (1998), 66–97.

Tamamitsu Jūnshō 玉光順正. "Mieru kyōdan ni mukete: Rennyo Shōnin to gendai [lecture] 見える教団に向けて—蓮如上人と現代 (講演)." *Shindō* 18 (1998), 42–59.

Tanabe Shōei 田辺正英. "Rennyo ni okeru mujō ni tsuite 蓮如における無常について." *Shūkyō kenkyū* 65 (1991), 234–235.

Tani Shinri 谷眞理. "Rennyo Shōnin to gendai: Ningen no ichidaiji [lecture] 蓮如上人と現代: 人間の一大事 (講演)." *Shindō* 16 (1997), 21–34.

Tanishita Kazumu 谷下一夢. "Rennyo Shōnin no Yoshizaki senkyo ni tsuite 蓮如上人の吉崎占拠に就いて." *Rekishi chiri* 62 (1933), 313–328.

——. "Rennyo Shōnin jidai no honganji ni kansuru shūgai shiryō 蓮如上人時代の本願寺に関する宗外史料." In *Rennyo Shōnin kenkyū* 蓮如上人研究, ed. Ryūkoku Daigaku, 286–308. Kyoto: Chūshu Daishi Yonhyakugojū–kai Enkihōyo Jimusho, 1948.

Tashiro Shunkō 田代俊孝. "Rennyo ni okeru shi no jyuyō to chōetsu 蓮如における死の受容と超越." *Indogaku bukkyōgaku kenkyū* 46 (1997), 39–45.

Terakawa Shunshō 寺川俊昭. "Shinran to Rennyo: ōjō rikai wo megutte 親鸞と蓮如: 往生理解をめぐって." *Indogaku bukkyōgaku kenkyū* 46 (1997), 1–11.

Tezuka Yuichō 手塚唯聴. "Rennyo Shōnin no o–myōgō to Jitsunyo Shōnin no o–myōgō 蓮如上人の御名号と実如上人の御名号." In *Rennyo Shōnin no kyōgaku to rekishi* 蓮如上人の教学と歴史, ed. Kimura Takeo, 183–192. Osaka: Tōhō Shuppansha, 1984.

Tokunaga Daishin. 徳永大信. "*Gobunshō* ni miru shingeron 『御文章』にみる真仮論." *Indogaku bukkyōgaku kenkyū* 43 (1993), 183–187.

——. "*Gobunshō* ni miru kyōhanron 『御文章』にみる教判論.' *Indogaku bukkyōgaku kenkyū* 43 (1994), 58–61.

——. "*Gobunshō* ni miru kyūsairon 『御文章』にみる救済論." *Shūkyō kenkyū* 68 (1995), 339–340.

——. "*Gobunshō* ni miru shomondai: tokuni shinkeron, kyōhanron, kyūsairon ni tsuite 『御文章』にみる諸問題: 特に、真仮論、教判論、救済論について." *Kyushū Ryūkoku tanki daigaku kiyō* 41 (1995), 1–24.

——. "Gojōme *Gobunsho* ni miru bunshō hyōgen: tokuni sono sōjō to hakki ni tsuite 五帖目『御文章』にみる文章表現: 特にその相承と発揮について." *Ryūkoku kyōgaku* 31 (1996), 98–110.

——. "*Kyōgyōshinshō* shinmonrui to *Gobunshō*『教行信証』信文類と『御文章』." *Kyushū Ryūkoku tanki daigaku kiyō* 42 (1996), 1–10.

——. "*Kyōgyōshinshō* shinmonrui to *Gobunshō* 『教行信証』 信文類と 『御文章』. *Shūkyō kenkyū* 69 (1996), 186–187.

——. "*Kyōgyōshinshō* to *Gobunshō* to no ichi shiten: Tokuni sono bunshō hyōgen ni tsuite 『教行信証』と『御文章』との一視点: 特にその 文章表現について." *Shinshū kenkyū* 40 (1996), 170–182.

Tokunaga Michio 德永道雄. "*Anjinketsujōshō* to hongaku shisō: *Gobunshō* no hyōgen wo megutte. 『安心決定鈔』と本覚思想: 『御文章』の表現をめぐって." *Ryūkoku kyōgaku* 29 (1994), 147–159.

——. "Rennyo no kihō–ittai kan ni tsuite 蓮如の機法一体観について." *Shinshū kenkyū* 44 (2000), 91–107.

Toyoshima Gakuyū 豊島学由. "*Tannishō* kinsho–setsu hihan 「歎異抄」禁書説批判." In *Rennyo Shōnin no kyōgaku to rekishi* 蓮如上人の教学と歴史, ed. Kimura Takeo, 133–148. Osaka: Tōhō Shuppansha, 1984.

Toyoshima Gakuyū, Yamada Yukio 山田行雄, Uno Gyōshin 宇野行信, and Hata Seibun 波多正文. "Rennyo Shōnin wo megutte [symposium] 蓮如上人をめぐって (シンポジウム)." *Ryūkoku kyōgaku* 27 (1992), 93–125.

Troup, James. "The Gobunsho, or Ofumi of Rennyo Shōnin." *Transactions of the Asiatic Society of Japan* 17 (1889), 101–143.

Tsunemitsu Kōsei 常光香誓. "Rennyo Shōnin ni okeru tenjō no igi: Butsubon ittairon wo chūshin toshite 蓮如上人における転成の意義: 仏凡一体論を中心として." *Ryūkoku kyōgaku* 32 (1997), 33–47.

Uji Shin 宇治伸. "'Kō' no kinō to sonraku shakai kōzō: hokuriku chihō wo chūshin to shite 「講」の機能と村落社会構造: 北陸地方を中心として." In *Rennyo Shōnin kenkyū* 蓮如上人研究, ed. Rennyo Shōnin Kenkyūkai, 339–362. Kyoto: Shibunkaku Shuppan, 1998.

Ujitani Yūken 宇治谷祐顕. "Rennyo Shōnin ni okeru mon (myō) gi no bekken 蓮如上人における聞(名)義の瞥見." In *Ronshū Rennyō: sono shisō to bunka* 論集蓮如: その思想と文化, ed. Dōhō Daigaku Bukkyō Gakkai. Nagoya: Dōhō Daigaku Bukkyō Gakkai & Bunkōdō Shoten, 1998.

Uryū Tōshō 瓜生等勝. "Rekidai shūshu ni yoru *Gobunshō* no kankō: Kaihanzen oyobi Shōnyo ryō shūshu ni yoru kaihan, kankō 歴代宗主による『御文章』の刊行: 開版前及び 証如両宗主による開版 • 刊行." *Ryūkoku kyōgaku* 25 (1990), 33–46.

Uryūzu Ryūyū 瓜生津隆雄. "Rennyo no kefū ni tsuite (lecture) 蓮師の化風について (講演)." *Ryūkoku kyōgaku* 27 (1992), 83–93.

Ushiyama Yoshiyuki 牛山佳幸. "Ranse ni okeru Shinano Zenkōji to Zenkōji shinkō 乱世における信濃善光寺と善光寺信仰." In *Rennyo Shōnin kenkyū* 蓮如上人研究, ed. Rennyo Shōnin Kenkyūkai, 113–138. Kyoto: Shibunkaku Shuppan, 1998.

Wake Ryōsei 和氣良晴. "Rennyo kyōgaku to *Sanbu kana shō* 蓮如教学と『三部仮名鈔』." *Ryūkoku kyōgaku* 33 (1998), 24–37.

Weinstein, Stanley. "Rennyo and the Shinshū Revival." In *Japan in the Muromachi Age*, ed. John W. Hall and Toyoda Takeshi, 331–358. Berkeley: University of California Press, 1977.

Yamada Masanori 山田雅教. "Chūsei kōki ni okeru Takada monto to Honganji monto: Shinne to Rennyo no jidai 中世後期における高田門徒と本願寺門徒: 真慧と蓮如の時代." *Kyōgaku kenkyūsho kiyō* 4 (1995), 133–155.

——. "Girei kūkan toshite no Yamashina Honganji 儀礼空間としての山科本願寺." *Kyōgaku kenkyūsho kiyō* 7 (1998), 243–279.

Yamada Yukio 山田行雄, Kitanishi Hiromu, Inaki Sen'e, Fukuma Kōchō, Asai Narumi. "Rennyo Shōnin wo megutte [symposium] 蓮如上人をめぐって (シンポ ジウム)." *Ryūkoku kyōgaku* 26 (1991), 136–171.

Yamada Yukio, Aomo Jōhō 青雲乗芳, Kitabatake Rishin 北畠利親, Shimada Hōsen 嶋田法宣, Fujisawa Shōtoku 藤沢正徳, and Mori Shōyu 森昭雄. "Rennyo Shōnin wo megutte: Dendō kyōke no hōhō [symposium] 蓮如上人をめぐって：伝道教化の方法 (シンポジウム)." *Ryūkoku kyōgaku* 29 (1994), 184–217.

Yamamoto Osamu 山本攝. "Rennyo Shōnin no rokujishaku 蓮如上人の六字釈." *Gyōshin gakuhō* 8 (1995), 157–185.

——. "Rennyo Shōnin no shukuzenron 蓮如上人の宿善論." *Gyōshin gakuhō* 9 (1996), 155–176.

——. "*Rennyo Shōnin goichidaiki kikigaki* kaishaku no shomondai: 'Utagai' to 'nageki' 「蓮如上人御一代記聞書」解釈の諸問題：「疑い」と「なげき」." *Gyōshin gakuhō* 11 (1998), 71–87.

Yamazaki Ryūmyō 山崎龍明. "Shinran to Rennyo no shūkyō jōkyō ni tsuite: jingi–kan wo chūshin to shite 親鸞と蓮如の宗教状況について：神祇観 を中心として." In *Zoku Kokka to bukkyō: kodai, chūsei hen (Nihon bukkyōshi kenkyū 3)* 国家と仏教：古代・中世編 (日本仏教史研究 3), ed. Futaba Kenkō, 271–313. Kyoto: Nagata Bunshōdō, 1981.

——. "Rennyo ni okeru shinkō kōzō ni tsuite (3) 蓮如における信仰構造について (3)." *Musashino joshi daigaku kiyō* 18 (1983).

——. "Rennyo ronkō 蓮如論考." *Musashino joshi daigaku bukkyō bunka kenkyūsho kiyō* 14 (1996), 1–42.

Yasui Kōdo 安井廣度. "Ōtaniha gakujishi 大谷派學地史." In *Zoku Shinshū taikei* vol. 20, ed. Yasui Kōdo. Tokyo: Shinshū Tenseki Kankōkai, 1936.

Yokoyama, W. S., trans., and Nabata Takashi 名畑崇. Introduction. "The Legacy of Rennyo Shōnin: *Rennyo Shōnin Itokuki*." *The Eastern Buddhist* 31:2 (1998), 245–262.

Yonemura Ryuji 米村竜治. "Minzoku shakai ni ikiru 'Rennyo–san' 民俗社会に生きる「蓮如さん」." In *Rennyo: tenkanki no shūkyōsha* 蓮如：転換期の宗教者, ed. Yamaori Tetsuo and Ōmura Eishō, 239–249. Tokyo: Shōgakkan, 1997.

Yoshida Muneo 吉田宗男. "Rennyo no mujōkan: *Hakkotsu no ofumi* wo chūshin toshite 蓮如の無常観：『白骨の御文』を中心として." *Shūkyō kenkyū* 67 (1994), 267–268.

——. "Rennyo no shinkō 蓮如の信仰." *Shinran kyōgaku* 67 (1996), 53–64.

——. "Rennyo no shishōkan 蓮如の死生観." *Shūkyō kenkyū* 69 (1996), 206–207.

——. "Shi to mujō no setten: Rennyo no *Ofumi* wo chūshin ni 死と無常の接点—蓮如の『御文』を中心に." *Shūkyō kenkyū* 70 (1997), 244–245.

Yoshida Terumasa 吉田晃政. "'Tasuke tamae' ni tsuite no ichikōsatsu: *Taketori monogatari* inmon no gimon to tomoni 「タスケタマヘ」についての一考察：『竹取物語』引文の疑問と共に." *Ryūkoku kyōgaku* 34 (1999), 9–18.

Yoshii Katsunobu 吉井克信. "Ōsaka Honganji 'Ishiyama' hyōgen no sōshutsu ni tsuite 大坂本願寺「石山」表現の創出について." *Ōtani gakuhō* 73 (1993), 53–54.

Yotsutsuji Akira 四衢亮. "Hiraza to iu chihei: Rennyo Shōnin to gendai [lecture] 平座という地平：蓮如上人と現代 (講演)." *Shindō* 16 (1997), 42–47.

Yūki Yoshifumi 由木義文. "Rennyo Shōnin e no toikake 蓮如上人への問いかけ." *Indogaku bukkyōgaku kenkyū* 46 (1997), 30–33.

Index

The first text below includes the earliest known use of the term *monachos* for monk.[4] In the document, a civil petition dated in 324 C.E., the petitioner reports his rescue in a village dispute over a cow by "the deacon Antoninus and the monk Isaac." The presence of the monk Isaac in this village dispute raises serious questions about the association of the term *monachos* or "monk" solely with those persons who withdrew (*anachorēsis*) to the desert. Isaac is not a desert hermit separated from the world. He plays an active role in village affairs and functions in harmony with the church authorities represented by the deacon. Judge, who wrote the definitive article on this text, argued that Isaac represents a movement "different from and prior to the creation of either eremitism (in its Antonian form) or coenobitism."[5] The members of this "earlier" movement broke with their traditional domestic ties. They withdrew from family and led a celibate existence, but their "ethical" withdrawal was not translated into a physical withdrawal from society and church. Rather, they set up houses of their own within the towns and bound their "life of personal renunciation" with services to the church. Judge labels this development the "apotactic" movement. In the later literary sources, where the emphasis is on physical withdrawal to the desert or monastery, the apotactic monks are forgotten or disparaged as heretical.[6]

The translations of the seven letters to Paphnutius are based on the Greek edition published in 1924 by H. Idris Bell.[7] The letters, which date to the middle of the fourth century, offer direct passage into the Egyptian social world of that period. The monk Paphnutius is held in great reverence and awe by the writers of these letters. As an ascetic, he is the recognized recipient of revelation (P. London 1926), and his "noble way of life" calls for imitation (P. London 1927). He is a patron whose prayers offer salvation from every difficulty.[8] He functions as an intercessor to

---

Christianity (Tokyo: Yamamoto Shoten [Japanese] and Detroit: Wayne State University [English], forthcoming).

4. Columbia Papyrus 187 = P. Coll. Youtie 77. Greek text in *Collectanea Papyrologica: Texts Published in Honor of H. C. Youtie* (ed. Ann Ellis Hanson; Papyrologische Texte und Abhandlungen 19; Bonn: Rudolf Habelt, 1976). The basic and brilliant study of this text is by E. A. Judge, "The Earliest Use of Monachos for 'Monk' (P. Coll. Youtie 77) and the Origins of Monasticism," JAC 20 (1977) 72–89.

5. Judge, "The Earliest Use of Monachos," 85.

6. Ibid., 78–85; Goehring, "The Origins of Monasticism."

7. H. Idris Bell, *Jews and Christians in Egypt: The Jewish Troubles in Alexandria and the Athanasian Controversy* (1924; reprint, Westport, Conn.: Greenwood, 1972) 100–120.

8. Peter Brown, "The Rise and Function of the Holy Man in Late Antiquity," *JRS* 61 (1971) 80–101; reprinted in idem, *Society and the Holy in Late Antiquity* (Berkeley: University of California Press, 1982) 103–52.

rescue his clientele from "every temptation and from every plot of men" (P. London 1923). Both men and women write to him for healing (P. London 1926, 1928, and 1929), which they expect through his prayers or through oil that he sends to them (P. London 1928). The letters reveal a world in which the power and authority of the ascetics as holy men rivals that of the church.[9] Their direct documentary evidence of this popular appeal to the authority of the early ascetics corroborates the more literary evidence of the *Apophthegmata Patrum*.

The correspondence of Didyme and the sisters is translated from the Greek text published by Naldini.[10] The two letters date from the early fourth century and imply the existence of a community of Christian women actively involved in commercial transactions. The precise nature of this community remains unclear, and suggesting that it represents an early monastic community certainly goes beyond the evidence. The existence of this female community nonetheless raises questions about the role of the houses of virgins mentioned in various sources and their relationship to the burgeoning monastic movement.[11] The economic involvement of the present community does not necessarily preclude an ascetic self-understanding.[12]

The documentary papyri translated here offer only a select indication of the importance of this material. New sources continue to appear, and the evidence is becoming increasingly central to the study of early Christian monasticism.

TRANSLATION[13]

I. THE FIRST USE OF
THE TERM *MONACHOS* FOR MONK

Columbia Papyrus 171 = P. Coll. Youtie II 77

To Dioscorus Caeso, Commander of the Fifth Region, from Isidoros, son of Ptolemaeus, from the village of Karanis in your region:

9. Philip Rousseau, *Ascetics, Authority, and the Church in the Age of Jerome and Cassian* (Oxford: Oxford University Press, 1978).

10. M. Naldini, *Il Cristianesimo in Egitto: Lettere private nei papiri dei secoli II–IV* (Florence: Le Monnier, 1968) Nos. 36 and 37.

11. *Vit. Ant.* 3; Judge, "The Earliest Use of Monachos," 85; Goehring, "The Origins of Monasticism"; Susanna K. Elm, "The Organization and Institutions of Female Asceticism in Fourth Century Cappadocia and Egypt" (Ph.D. dissertation, Oxford University, 1986).

12. James E. Goehring, "The Social and Economic World of Early Egyptian Monasticism," in Jack Sanders, James E. Goehring, and Charles Hedrick, *Gnosticism and the Early Christian World: Volume Two of Essays on Antiquity and Christianity in Honor of James M. Robinson* (Sonoma, Calif.: Polebridge, 1990).

13. The translations are meant to be readable and are less concerned to present the

The young animals of Pamounis and Harpalus destroyed the planting that I have and, moreover, their cow grazed in the same place. As a result, farming has become useless for me. Then, when I captured their cow and was taking it to the village, they attacked me in the fields with a large club, threw me on the ground and beat me down with blows, as the marks on my body show, and then they took the cow. If I had not happened upon help from the deacon Antoninus and the monk Isaac, they would have killed me in the end. Therefore, I send on these charges to you, deeming it worthwhile that they be brought before you to save my case in prefectural court both about the planting and about the assault.

The Consuls-to-be for the fourth time, Payni 12.

II. LETTERS TO PAPHNUTIUS

1. London Papyrus 1923

Ammonius gives greeting in the Lord to Paphnutius, who is a pious, blessed friend of God:

I know always that I am saved because of your prayers from every temptation and from every plot of men. And now I beg that you remember me in your holy prayers. Our brother Didymus came to me and I went to him just as you had instructed about the matter. I pray that you be healthy for many years, sweetest father. May the God of peace keep you for the longest time.

2. London Papyrus 1924

Ausonius to the beloved father Apa Paphnutius:

Remembering the commands of your Piety, I sent for Horus of Philonikou and I advised him. I asked Gallus to advise me in all matters so that I might as far as possible display zeal on my part. I greatly entreat that you give direction in this and in all matters. Remember me in your prayers. May God keep you healthy and full of prayer for us, beloved father.

---

state of the texts than to give an idea of how the letters might have sounded in the ears of the original authors. Yet the original Greek is often awkward, ambiguous, and stilted and, therefore, so is the English.

3. London Papyrus 1925

Pianos gives greeting in the Lord God to the excellent Apa Paphnutius who is most desirous of knowledge:

Since a man was going to your Holiness, I took the opportunity and decided it was necessary to greet your Piety with a letter, praying to Christ that I might be deemed worthy to embrace you with my very eyes. It is yet possible to greet you in the spirit but each day. . . . I beseech your Holiness that you deem it worthy to pray on behalf of my sins so that God may save me from my [sins] and from the troubles that beset me. Give greeting to the brothers from me and give them greeting from me on behalf of the slave of Athanasius. For he happens to be one of those who love your Piety. I salute my lord Athanasius and Eusebius and Hareous and all the brothers who are with your Holiness. And his brother Dorotheus also salutes you.

I pray that you be preserved in the Lord for much time.

4. London Papyrus 1926

Valeria gives greeting in Christ to the most honored upholder of Christ, Apa Paphnutius, who has been adorned with every excellence:

I ask and beg you, most honored father, that you request [help] for me from Christ and that I receive healing. Thus I believe that I receive healing on account of your prayers, for the revelations of the ascetics and the worshipers are clear. For I am beset by a great sickness, a terrible difficulty in breathing. Thus I have believed and do believe that if you pray on my behalf, I receive healing. I pray to God, I also pray to you. Remember me in your hallowed supplication. If I have not come in the body to your feet, I have come to your feet in the spirit. I mention my daughters, Bassiana and Theoclia. Remember them also in your hallowed supplication. My husband also sends many greetings. Pray for him also. My whole household greets you. I pray that you be preserved, most honored father.

5. London Papyrus 1927

To the most honored brother and lover of God:

Dorotheus the Oxyrhynchite, the worthless slave, greets you in the spirit and in the love of Christ. Before all, I beg the God and the father of the savior Jesus Christ that he consider me worthy of finding grace before him and that you receive this letter from me. For in this I am going to be glad when the good slave receives me because of the letter and raises up prayers on my behalf to the master with enthusiasm and with a pure mind. For I believe that. . . .

. . . but because of your most holy and well-reputed way of life, and because you renounce the pretensions of the world and hate the arrogance of the vainglorious. We then rejoice even more in the report that you make manifest the most noble struggle. We rejoice that we imitate you in the same noble way of life because, as is presently fitting, God rejoiced to find for you a healthful renunciation corresponding to the times. "Redeeming the times," proclaims the thrice-blessed apostle, "because the days are evil."

I trust to see your countenance, if the Lord permits, as we are on the road. But I fear to come lest you [rebuke?] us and we are ashamed. Certainly we believe that if it is your will that we visit you, you will announce first through the one who is bearing the letter. Give him the message whether you want us to come up or not. . . . not with the result that we fulfill our love toward you and the brothers with you, you who are most honored in the spirit.

6. London Papyrus 1928

Heracleides to Apa Paphnutius, the father who is loved by God:

You always have the chance to pray on my behalf and I need help from you who are stronger on account of prayer. Both because of my name and because of the sickness that has seized and oppressed me, I now beg you to do this additional thing: send me the oil. . . . For I do not believe that I will be helped otherwise. May you hold up Christ as long as you have health. [second hand] I pray in the Lord Christ that you be preserved for much time, praying assiduously on my behalf, most God-revering father. The prophet also shouted, "In affliction I called out and he heard me." Now truly it is an affliction in which I live, where help can be received neither from a brother nor from any other, except for the hope through our Lord Christ expected on account of your prayers.

7. London Papyrus 1929

Athanasius gives greeting in the Lord God to the most honored and beloved father Paphnutius:

May God the omnipotent and his Anointed One allow that your piety remain for much time and remember us in your supplications. If your Holiness accomplishes this, we will be in good health everywhere. I beg you, therefore, more diligently: remember us. For the prayers you give are received on high because of your holy love and if you ask with your holy supplication, our affair will be well. I rejoice justly, believing that you make mention of us everywhere. For I know that you love us. I am concerned especially for Didyme and my mother, for Didyme and my mother are ill. The struggle then is greatest in me who am suffering and most weak. But I believe in the Savior of all. While living through these sicknesses, we rejoice that you thought to send our fine son Horion to us. Theodosius, . . . Antiochus, Didyme, my mother and all our household, we honor and salute you, most honored and beloved father. May divine Providence preserve and keep you for the longest time, always remembering us, you who are beloved and most honored.

III. CORRESPONDENCE OF DIDYME
AND THE SISTERS

1. Berlin Papyrus Inv. 13897

Didyme and the sisters give greeting in the Lord to my beloved sister Sophias:

To begin with, we believed it necessary to greet you. We received the travel supplies from brother Pipera and. . . . Greet her and [ask] that she visit us. . . .

The totals: we received for her from others seven double containers of wine and a leather sack of unripened grapes. If we find a way, we will send you by someone the sack and the containers as we can. We did not receive the other things. Make an effort that we may send you what you want through people who are known. I want you to know about Lucilius's cloth, which you sent, that I spent his money and immediately sent you two sandals bought from the linen weavers for four talents. You have not written back about these things. Also sent through Nautesiphares, son of Plousius, for Pansophius's wife were a large ostrich egg and a small basket, both in Phoenician wrappings. You also have not written back about these.

Give greeting to the sweetest Didyme and the most beloved Favorinus. Sweetest Didyme's implements were found in Severus's wool bag. Lady Valeriana, the other lady Valeriana, and those with Pilosophius,

Lucilas and Pansophus, greet you. Greet good Biceutia and ask if she has received a filet and two cakes from Aionius. Greet everyone, including Italia and Theodora, that they be preserved in the Lord. May the Lord keep them for us.

2. Oxyrhynchus Papyrus 1774

Didyme and the sisters give greeting in the Lord to Lady Sister Atien-ateia:

To begin with, it was necessary to give you greeting, praying that you be in good health. Write to us, my lady, about your health and about what orders you need, as you have the credit. Tell us if you have received your orders. We have 1,300 denarii, I think, remaining of the money for your orders. The cakes we have received for you will be paid for from that amount.

Greet blessed lady sister Asous and her mother and . . . and all. . . .

SUGGESTED READINGS

Barison, P. "Richerche sui monasteri dell'Egitto bizantino ed arabo secondo i documento dei papiri greci." *Aegyptus* 18 (1938) 29–148.

Emmett, Alanna. "Female Ascetics in the Greek Papyri." *XVI Internationaler Byzantinistencongress Wien, 4–9. October 1981.* Hrsg. von W. Hörander, C. Cupane und E. Kiolinger. Jahrbuch der österreichischen Byzantinistik 32,2. Wien: Der osterreichischen Akademie der Wissenschotlen, 1982.

Goehring, James E. "The Origins of Monasticism." In *Eusebius, Judaism and Christianity.* (Japanese) Tokyo: Yamamoto Shoten; (English) Detroit: Wayne State University, forthcoming.

————. "The Social and Economic World of Early Egyptian Monasticism." In *Gnosticism and the Early Christian World: Volume Two of Essays on Antiquity and Christianity in Honor of James M. Robinson.* Edited by Jack T. Sanders, James E. Goehring, and Charles W. Hedrick. Sonoma, Calif.: Polebridge, 1990.

Judge, E. A. "The Earliest Use of Monachos for 'Monk' (P. Coll. Youtie 77) and the Origins of Monasticism." *JAC* 20 (1977) 72–89.

————. "Fourth Century Monasticism in the Papyri." In *Proceedings of the XVI International Congress of Papyrology,* 612–20. Chico, Calif.: Scholars Press, 1981.

Chronological Tables

AFRICA

20 B.C.E.	Philo born (d. 50 C.E.).
185 C.E.	Origen born.
ca. 200	*Allogenes* written.
218–220	Origen writes *De principiis*.
ca. 251	Anthony born.
ca. 253	Origen dies.
253–257	Paul of Thebes (the Hermit) departs for desert.
285	Anthony withdraws to Pispir.
ca. 292	Pachomius born.
ca. 293	Macarius the Alexandrian born.
296	Athanasius born.
ca. 300	Macarius the Egyptian born.
304	Anthony emerges, joined by monks.
	Apollo born.
	Hilarion in Egypt, visits Anthony.
308	Hilarion departs for Gaza.
ca. 311	Anthony in Alexandria to encourage martyrs.
	Peter of Alexandria martyred.
	Amoun enters ascetic life.
313	Anthony withdraws to the Interior Mountain by the Red Sea.
	Pachomius baptized.
	Didymus the Blind born.
319	Athanasius ordained deacon by Alexander of Alexandria.

ca. 320	Pachomius founds community at Tabennisi.
	Ethiopian Moses born (d. 407).
324	Constantine sole emperor.
326	Ammonius founds monastic community at Nitria.
328	Theodore enters Pachomian community.
335	Athanasius's first exile (to 337).
338	Anthony visits Alexandria and Nitria.
	Foundation of Kellia.
339	Athanasius's second exile (to 346).
	Serapion bishop of Thmuis.
340	Athanasius, Ammonius the Tall, and Isidore in Rome.
	Monastic ideas spread in the West.
	Macarius the Egyptian ordained priest.
	Pachomian foundations around Panopolis.
	Paul of Thebes (the Hermit) dies.
	Pambo, Sisoes, John the Dwarf, Paphnutius, Pior, Carion, and his son Zacharias flourish.
345	Synod at Latopolis.
346	Pachomius dies.
	Athanasius returns.
ca. 350	John of Lycopolis enclosed.
351	Horsiesius calls Theodore to lead Tabennisian community.
355	Macarius the Alexandrian becomes a monk.
356	Anthony dies.
	Athanasius begins third exile in Egyptian desert.
357	Athanasius writes *Vita Antonii*.
ca. 357	Basil of Caesarea tours Egypt.
360	Duke Artemis searches Faou for Athanasius.
	Isidore of Pelusium born.
	Lucifer of Cagliari exiled in Thebaid.
362	Athanasius ends third exile.
	Athanasius begins fourth exile.
	Lucifer of Cagliari leaves Thebaid for Antioch.
	Synod of Alexandria (*Tomus ad Antiochenos*).
363	Athanasius in Thebaid, returns to Alexandria.
368	Theodore dies.
	Horsiesius resumes leadership of community.

373	Athanasius dies.
	Melania in Egypt (to 375).
	Rufinus in Egypt, Nitria, and Pispir.
375	Monks of Nitrian desert riot in Alexandria against Arian bishop Lucian.
375–380	Cyril of Alexandria born.
380	Timothy bishop of Alexandria.
382–383	Evagrius in Nitria.
383	Shenoute abbot of White Monastery of Atripe (to 466).
385	Jerome and Paula come to Egypt and visit Nitria.
	Apollo founds cenobium at Bawit.
	Evagrius at Kellia.
	Cassian and Germanus arrive in Egypt.
	Theophilus bishop of Alexandria.
387	Horsiesius dies.
388	Palladius comes to Egypt, visits Alexandria, Nitria, and Kellia.
	Vita Antonii in Latin.
ca. 390	Macarius the Egyptian dies.
391–392	Destruction of pagan temples, Serapeum.
	Temple at Canopus becomes Tabbenisian monastery.
	Floruit John of Lycopolis.
393	Dioscorus bishop of Hermopolis Parva (Damanhur).
	Macarius the Alexandrian dies.
394	Arsenius goes to Scetis.
	John of Lycopolis visited by Palladius.
	The Journey narrated in *Historia Monachorum in Aegypto*.
395	John of Lycopolis dies.
398	Didymus the Blind dies.
399	Evagrius dies.
	Theophilus's Paschal Letter against Anthropomorphism.
	Theophilus turns against Origen.
400–401	Alexandrian Synod condemns Origenism.
	Pilgrimage of Postumian.
403	Exiled monks return to their monasteries.

404	Jerome translates the *Pachomian Rule*.
ca. 405	Palladius in Rome to plead the cause of Chrysostom.
	(Greek) writing of the *Historia Monachorum in Aegypto*.
405–410	Rufinus translates the *Historia Monachorum in Aegypto* into Latin.
406	Palladius begins exile in Syene.
407–408	First devastation of Scetis by barbarian tribe of Maziben; Moses and his companions killed.
	Poemen, Joseph, Theodore, Agathon, and others leave Scetis.
	Palladius at Antinoe.
412	Cyril bishop of Alexandria.
	Palladius leaves Egypt.
	Palladius bishop of Aspuna at Galatia.
415	Murder of Hypatia.
	Cyril expels Jews from Alexandria.
419–420	Palladius writes the *Lausiac History*.
420	Cyril's Paschal Encyclical condemns christological dualism.
420–430	Cassian writes the *Institutes* and *Conferences* at Marseille.
424	Cyril's Paschal Encyclical condemns Arianism.
429	Cyril of Alexandria sends his encyclical *Ad Monachos Aegyptii, Ad Nestorium I*.
430	Cyril of Alexandria: *Ad Nestorium II, III*.
431	Cyril returns in triumph to Alexandria.
	Nonnus of Panopolis dies.
433	Communion restored with Orientals.
ca. 434	Second devastation of Scetis.
	Arsenius in Troe.
435	Isidore of Pelusium dies.
	Nestorius in exile in Oasis of Upper Egypt.
449	Arsenius dies.
451	Dioscurus deposed by Council of Chalcedon.
	Proterious bishop of Alexandria (to 457).
453	Peter the Iberian arrives from Palestine.
516	Dioscorus II bishop of Alexandria.
517	Timothy bishop of Alexandria.
518	Severus of Antioch arrives in Egypt.

ca. 530	Julian of Halicarnassus.
	Alphabetical Collection completed (Bousset).
535	Theodorus bishop of Alexandria.
537	Paul of Tabennisi bishop of Alexandria.
538	Severus of Antioch dies in Egypt.
542–543	Plague.
551	Apollinarius bishop of Alexandria.
ca. 565	John Philoponus dies in Alexandria.
570	John bishop of Alexandria.
574–584	Moschus in Egypt.
ca. 576	Death of Anastasis in Scetis.
ca. 577	Third devastation of Scetis.
	Theodore bishop of Alexandria.
578	Moschus in Oasis.
	Peter III bishop of Alexandria.
581	Eulogius bishop of Alexandria.
ca. 608	Moschus and Sophronius in Egypt.
610	John the Almsgiver bishop of Alexandria.
617	Persians take Alexandria.
	Moschus and Sophronius flee to Samos and then to Rome, where Moschus dies.
619	John the Almsgiver dies.
625	George bishop of Alexandria.
632–633	Sophronius, Maximus in Alexandria.
642	Alexandria falls to Arabs.
650	Thallasius the Libyan dies.

MOUNT SINAI

380 C.E.	Silvanus, twelve disciples settle temporarily at Sinai.
ca. 383	Egeria visits Sinai.
556–557	Justinian builds fortress on Sinai.
	Doulas hegoumenos.
565–566	Transfiguration apse-mosaic installed.
	Longinus hegoumenos, Theodore his second.
ca. 576	Justin II brings Gregory of Fara from Palestine to be hegoumenos of Sinai after death of Longinus.
579	Gregory patriarch of Antioch.
	John Climacus born.
ca. 584	Moschus at laura of Aeliotes on Sinai.

ca. 595	John Climacus comes to Sinai (to 649).
ca. 649	Death of John Climacus.
ca. 700	Anastasius of Sinai dies.

PALESTINE

ca. 300 c.e.	Chariton from Iconium settles at Fara.
	Hilarion born at Thavatha.
305	Hilarion visits Anthony in Egypt.
308	Hilarion returns from Egypt to Gaza.
324	Constantine sole emperor.
ca. 330	Monasteries (e.g., Epiphanius at Besanduk) begin to arise.
356	Hilarion leaves Palestine.
ca. 357	Basil tours Holy Land.
ca. 370	Innocent on Mount of Olives, outside Jerusalem.
ca. 375	Egyptian exiles at Diocaesarea, Melania present.
ca. 376	Melania on Mount of Olives.
ca. 377	Porphyry by Jordan.
ca. 380	Rufinus joins Melania on Mount of Olives.
382	Evagrius on Mount of Olives.
385	Jerome and Synodia in Bethlehem.
392	Porphyry Cross-warden.
397	Rufinus returns to the West.
399	Palladius briefly in Palestine.
400	Melania returns to the West.
	Tall Brothers come to Scythopolis.
404	Paula dies.
	Jerome translates *Pachomian Rule*.
	Rufinus translates *Historia monachorum*.
405	Euthymius comes to Jerusalem, settles at Fara.
410	Melania returns and dies in Jerusalem.
411	Euthymius and Theoktistos settle in the Wadi Mukellik.
	Hesychius of Jerusalem flourished.
415	Synod of Diospolis.
417	Eustochium and Bishop John die.
	Melania the Younger comes to Jerusalem.
ca. 422	Conversion of Peter Aspebet.
	Euthymius leaves Theoktistos in Wadi Mukellik.

422	Juvenal bishop of Jerusalem.
ca. 425	Euthymius settles at Khan el-Ahmar.
428	Juvenal, Hesychius at consecration of church at Euthymius's laura.
	Peter the Iberian comes to Jerusalem.
	Bessarion dies.
439	Melania the Younger dies.
443	Eudocia retires to Jerusalem.
444	Peter the Iberian retires to Maiuma.
ca. 450	Hesychius of Jerusalem dies.
458	Romanus returns from exile and goes to Eleutheropolis.
473	Euthymius dies.
474	Sabas in the desert.
475	Gerasimus dies.
478	Sabas at "St. Sabas."
479	Theodosius founds cenobium.
	John Rufus joins Peter the Iberian.
482	Cenobium of St. Euthymius consecrated.
483	Sabas founds Lavra (at Mar Saba).
486	Sallust bishop of Jerusalem.
	Marcion archimandrite.
489	Isaiah and Peter die.
490	Sabbas ordained priest.
	"God-built" church consecrated.
	Severus becomes a monk at Maiuma.
491	John of Colonia flees to Mar Saba.
492	Foundation of Castellium.
	Marcion dies.
	Theodosius and Sabas archimandrites.
494	Elias bishop of Jerusalem.
ca. 500	Palestinian Talmud.
501	Theotokos church at Mar Saba consecrated.
507	Foundation at new laura.
512	Sabas returns.
	Mamas of Eleutheropolis accepts Chalcedon.
513	Elias refuses Severus's synodicals.
516	Elias exiled to Aila.
	John bishop of Jerusalem.
518	Synod of Jerusalem proclaims four councils.

	Sabas carries news around Palestine.
	Aenas of Gaza dies.
524	Peter bishop of Jerusalem.
525	Kyriakos leaves Souka for desert of Natoupha.
529	Theodosius dies.
	Samaritan revolt.
530	Kyriakos in desert of Rouba.
531–532	Sabas visits Caesarea and Scythopolis.
532	Sabas dies.
535	Kyriakos at Sousakim.
537	Gelasius hegoumenos of Mar Saba.
537–553	Theodore of Raithu writes *Praeparatio* (De Incarnatione).
ca. 538	Procopius of Gaza dies.
542–543	Plague.
542	Kyriakos goes to cave of St. Chariton.
543	Sophronius (successor of Theodosius) dies.
	Consecration of new church.
	Cyril of Scythopolis comes to Jerusalem.
ca. 543	Seridius, John, and Barsanuphius die.
544	Cyril enters cenobium of St. Euthymius.
546	Gelasius dies returning from Constantinople.
547	George (Origenist) hegoumenos at Mar Saba, then deposed.
	Cassian installed.
555	Origenists removed from new laura.
	Kyriakos back at cave of St. Chariton.
556–557	Cyril writes *Lives*.
	Kyriakos dies.
564–574	Moschus at Fara.
583	Macarius dies.
	John III bishop of Jerusalem.
594	Amos bishop of Jerusalem.
	Moschus and Sophronius in Palestine.
614	Persians capture Jerusalem.
	Zacharius taken captive.
629	Battle of Muta.
631	Heraclius restores the cross to Jerusalem.
	Modestus bishop of Jerusalem, then dies.
634	Sophronius bishop of Jerusalem.

636	Battle of Yarmuk.
638	Sophronius surrenders Jerusalem to Omar.
	Sophronius dies.
ca. 675	John of Damascus born.
ca. 718	John of Damascus enters monastery of St. Sabas.
743	Cosmas bishop of Maiuma.

SYRIA

ca. 200 C.E.	*Acts of Thomas* written.
226	Ascendency of Sassanid dynasty.
256	Persians capture Antioch.
300	Eusebius of Emeas born.
ca. 300	Anonymous homily "On Virginity" written.
324	Constantine sole emperor.
	Eustathius bishop of Antioch.
326	Arian synod deposes Eustathius.
330	Eustathius exiled.
337–345	Aphrahat writes *Demonstrations*.
339	Libanius assumes chair of rhetoric.
	Christians persecuted in Persia under Shapur II.
354	John Chrysostom born at Antioch.
363	Ephraim leaves Nisibis for Edessa.
373	Ephraim in Antioch.
379	Synod at Antioch, Diodore, Meletius, 150 bishops condemn Apollinarianism.
381	Flavian of Antioch ordains Chrysostom to the diaconate.
383	Theodore of Mopsuestia ordained priest.
386	Simeon the Stylite born (d. 459).
	Chrysostom a priest (in Antioch to 397).
387	Monks riot in Antioch.
	Imperial statues destroyed.
392	Theodore bishop of Mopsuestia.
393	Theodoret born in Antioch.
	Diodore of Tarsus dies.
397	Chrysostom departs for Constantinople.
400	Rabbula becomes a Christian.
410	Council of Persian Church accepts creed of Nicaea.

412	Rabbula bishop of Edessa (to 435).
417	Theodotus bishop of Antioch.
420	Yazdegrad begins to oppress Persian Church. Qiyore the mepashqana initiates translations of Mopsuestia's scriptural commentaries into Syriac.
423	Theodoret bishop of Cyrus.
428	Theodore of Mopsuestia dies.
429	John I bishop of Antioch.
431	Nestorius confined to monastery in Antioch (to 435). Theodoret publishes *Refutation of Twelve Anathemas*.
433	Formulary of Union.
435	Ibas bishop of Edessa (to 457).
436	Rabbula dies.
442	Domnus bishop of Antioch.
444	Theodoret writes *Historia Religiosa*. Council of Antioch deposes Athanasius of Perre.
ca. 447	Theodoret writes *Eranistes*.
449–450	Theodoret writes *Ecclesiastical History*.
449	Jacob of Serug born (d. 521).
450	Maximus I bishop of Antioch.
ca. 457	Theodoret dies.
459	Symeon Stylites dies. Martyrios bishop of Antioch.
465	Severus of Antioch born (d. 538).
485	Philoxenus bishop of Mabbug. Begins writing *Discourses*. Peter the Fuller bishop of Antioch.
489	School of Edessa closed by Zeno, refounded at Nisibis.
490	Jacob Baradeus born.
499	Philoxenus in Constantinople.
502–505, 507	Persian War.
508	Philoxenus translates Bible. Severus in Constantinople with five hundred monks.
509	Synod of Antioch.
512	Flavian deposed.

	Severus bishop of Antioch.
	John Rufus writes *Plerophoriae*.
518	Justin emperor.
	Severus flees to Egypt.
519	Philoxenus exiled to Philippopolis in Thrace by Justin I.
	Writes letters to monks of Senun and Teleda.
	Paul II bishop of Antioch.
521	Euphrasios bishop of Antioch.
521	Philoxenus killed in Gangra of Paphlagonia.
526	Earthquake at Antioch.
528	Antioch destroyed by earthquake.
540	Persian wars, Syrian cities destroyed.
542	Jacob Baradeus bishop.
	Council of Antioch condemns Origenism.
545	Domnus (Domninos) bishop of Antioch.
547	Jacob consecrates Sergius bishop of Antioch.
551	Earthquake in Antioch.
553	Council of Constantinople condemns Theodoret's work.
559	Anastasios I bishop of Antioch.

CONSTANTINOPLE, ASIA MINOR, AND BABYLON

213 C.E.	Gregory Thaumaturgus born in Pontus.
233–238	Gregory Thaumaturgus in Palestine with Origen.
	Gregory meets Firmilian (later) bishop of Caesarea.
ca. 240	Gregory Thaumaturgus bishop of Neocaesarea.
260	Birth of Macrina the Elder.
265	Gregory Thaumaturgus at Council of Antioch.
ca. 273	Gregory Thaumaturgus dies.
ca. 306	Birth of Basil the Elder and Emmelia.
312	Constantine's profession of faith.
324	Constantine sole emperor.
325	Council of Nicaea.
	Gregory of Nazianzus the Elder converted from Hypistarianism by his wife, Nonna.
328	Birth of Macrina, sister of Basil.
329	Birth of Basil.

330	Foundation of the city of Constantinople.
	Gregory Nazianzus born.
337	Constantine dies.
	Constantius emperor in East.
340	Monastic groups surround Eustathius.
ca. 341	Council of Gangra rebukes Eustathius.
	Birth of Amphilocius of Iconium.
344	Birth of Peter (of Sebastia), brother of Basil.
	Death of the Elder Basil.
ca. 350	Marathonius embraces monastic life under Eustathius.
ca. 357	Basil baptized, departs for Egypt and Holy Land.
	Relics of Andrew and Luke brought to Constantinople.
	Death of Naucratius, brother of Basil.
	Gregory of Nazianzus baptized.
359	Basil ordained a deacon.
360	Basil at homoiousian council in Constantinople.
	Basil withdraws to Pontus.
	Gregory Nazianzus visits Basil; they compile *Philokalia*, two *Monastic Rules*.
363	Julian dies.
	Jovanian emperor.
	Basil begins *Contra Eunomium*.
364	Valens emperor.
365	Persecution by Emperor Valens.
	Basil withdraws to Pontus.
366	Valens baptized Arian.
368	Death of Emmelia, Basil's mother.
	Famine in Cappadocia.
	Philostorgius born at Borissus in Cappadocia Secunda.
370	Death of Eusebius of Caesarea, Basil bishop of Caesarea.
	Gregory of Nyssa writes *De Virginitate*.
	Amphilocius of Iconium withdraws from public life.
ca. 371	Valens divides Cappadocia.
	Gregory bishop of Nyssa.
	Gregory Nazianzus bishop of Sasima.

ca. 375	Basil writes *De Spiritu Sancto*.
ca. 382	Isaac founds "first" monastery in Constantinople.
390	Gregory Nazianzus dies.
	Amphilocius of Iconium, Synod of Side condemn Messalianism.
394	Gregory of Nyssa dies.
395	Theodosius dies.
	Arcadius emperor.
	Refunianai abandoned.
398	John Chrysostom consecrated bishop of Constantinople by Theophilus of Alexandria.
399	Eutropius seeks asylum, banished to Cyprus.
401	Tall Brothers in Constantinople.
403	Theophilus of Alexandria in Constantinople.
	Synod of the Oak deposes Chrysostom.
404	John Chrysostom exiled.
407	John Chrysostom dies in exile.
408	Theodosius emperor.
ca. 425	Alexander the monk arrives in Constantinople, founds monastery of *Akoimetai* ("sleepless monks").
ca. 430	Nilus of Ancyra dies.
	Mark the Hermit dies.
431	Maximianos bishop of Constantinople (to 434).
	Council of Ephesus recognizes Abbot Dalmatius (Isaac's successor) as archimandrite of all monks in the capital.
	Council condemns 18 propositions from (Simeon's) *Asceticon*.
434	Proclus bishop of Constantinople (to 446).
434–439	Philip Sidetes publishes *Christian History*.
435	Theodosius orders all Nestorius's writings burned.
	Armenian priests Leontius and Abel arrive in Constantinople.
439–450	Sozomen publishes *Church History*.
440	Basil bishop of Seleucia.
	Socrates publishes *Church History*.
446	Flavian bishop of Constantinople (to 449).
449	Kyriakos born in Corinth.

450	Monkis around Rhebus River.
	Monastery and convent on Mount Auxentius.
ca. 450	Diadochus of Photice in Epirus.
451	Council of Chalcedon (canon 4 subjects all monasteries to diocesan bishop).
	Tome of Leo.
459	Symeon Stylites dies.
460	Daniel mounts pillar near Constantinople.
493	Daniel Stylites dies.
508–511	Severus in Constantinople.
511–512	Sabas in Constantinople.
518	Justin I emperor.
	Chalcedon accepted.
	John II bishop of Constantinople (to 520).
520	Ephiphanius bishop of Constantinople (to 535).
527	Justinian emperor.
529	Edict against pagans.
531	Sabas in Constantinople.
586	John of Ephesus dies (*Lives of the Eastern Saints*).
ca. 600	Babylonian Talmud.
ca. 613	Maximus enters monastery at Chrysopolis (banished 655, d. 662).

WESTERN EUROPE

Ireland, Britain

354 C.E.	Pelagius born in Britain.
418	Germanus bishop.
432	Patrick begins Irish mission.
439	Secundius, Auxillus, Isernuis come to Patrick's aid.
461	Patrick dies.
475	Birth of Brigit.
ca. 500	Anglo-Saxon occupation.
ca. 550	Vinnian and Gildas flourished.
563	Iona founded by Columcille (d. 597).
ca. 591	Columbanus in Gaul.
612	Columbanus leaves Gaul.
615	Columbanus dies (*Regula monachorum*).
626	Maedoc, abbot of Ferns, dies.

630–650	Isidore writes *Etymologiae*.
	Anonymous *De Duodecim abusivis saeculi*.
632	Cumman's Paschal Letter to Segene of Iona and Beccan the Hermit.
	Roman Easter adopted.
634	Aidan arrives in Britain.
660	Donatus of Besancon dies.
664	Synod of Whitby.
664–667	Plague decimates monastic population.
672	Bede born (d. 735).
679	Adamnan abbot of Iona.
683	Plague.
ca. 688	Adamnan writes *Life of Columcille*.
697	Synod of Birr.
	"Law" of Adamnan.
699–705	*Life of Cuthbert* written.
704	Adamnan dies.
717	Dunnchad of Iona dies.

Continental Europe

ca. 100	Musonius Rufus dies (Italy).
ca. 150	Lucius, student of Musonius Rufus, publishes his teacher's discourses
324	Constantine sole emperor.
337	Ambrose of Milan born.
ca. 346	Rufinus and Jerome born.
348	Prudentius born.
354	Augustine born.
	Pelagius born in Britain.
357–360	Martin of Tours withdraws to Gallinara.
359	Hilary at Council of Seleucia.
360–367	Jerome student in Rome.
	Sulpicius Severus born in Aquitaneia.
ca. 363	Temple of Apollo on the Palatine at Rome burnt.
	Eusebius of Vercelli establishes monastic communities.
366–384	Pope Damascus I promotes women's asceticism.
	Ambrosiaster writes "On Sin of Adam and Eve."
367	Hilary dies.
370	Rufinus monk in Aquileai.

	Valentinian I exempts consecrated virgins from taxation.
ca. 372	Martin founds Marmoutier.
374	Ambrose bishop of Milan.
ca. 375	Orosius born at Braga.
376	Gothic migration under Ulfila.
	Paulinus of Pella born.
378	Paulinus of Nola enters Senate.
ca. 380	Faustinus priest in Rome.
381	Ulfila dies.
384	The question of the Altar of Victory.
	Siricius pope (to 399).
ca. 386	Conversion of Augustine.
	Paulinus meets Martin of Tours.
	Paulinus travels to Spain, marries Therasia.
	Jerome leaves Italy for Palestine.
ca. 389	Paulinus baptized.
	Paulinus and Therasia leave Gaul.
	Sulpicius Severus baptized.
391	Augustine ordained priest in Hippo.
393	Paulinus begins to sell his property.
394	Paulinus ordained priest by Bishop Lampius in Barcelon on Christmas day.
395	Augustine bishop of Hippo.
	Augustine writes *De continentia*.
	Paulinus and Therasia visit Rome on way to Nola.
397	Ambrose of Milan dies.
	Sulpicius Severus writes *Life of Martin of Tours*.
ca. 400	Julian of Eclanum (Italy).
400	Paulinus visited by Melania the Elder and Nicetas.
	Salvian born.
400–405	Paulinus active in building.
401	Augustine writes *De opere monachorum*.
402	Augustine writes *De virginate*.
	Innocent I pope (to 417).
403	Paulinus visited by Nicetas.
405–410	Honoratus and Caprasius settle in Lerinum.

ca. 408	Melania the Younger founds communities in Sicily, Campania.
410	Alaric sacks Rome.
	Rufinus dies.
	Pelagius in Africa (with Melania?).
411	Augustine begins anti-Pelagian writings.
ca. 416	Bishop Proculus gives Cassian Church of Saint Victor outside Marseilles.
	Julian bishop of Eclanum.
417	Zosimus pope (to 418).
418	Boniface I pope (to 422).
422	Celestine I pope (to 432).
ca. 423	Sulpicius Severus dies.
425–426	Cassian writes *Institutes, Conferences*.
428	Honoratus bishop of Arles.
429	Honoratus dies.
	Salvian ordained priest.
430	Augustine dies.
	Peter Chrysologus archbishop of Ravenna.
	Deacon Posidonius, envoy of Cyril of Alexandria, in Rome.
431	Paulinus dies.
ca. 432	Arnobius the Younger in Rome.
	Pope Sixtus II (to 440) founds Monasterium in Catacumbas.
ca. 433	Faustus of Riez abbot of Lerins.
434	Vincent of Lerins writes *Commonitoria*.
437	Valerian bishop of Cimiez.
440	Sabinus and Salonius found Saint-Martin d'Ainy at Lyon.
	Leo I (to 461) founds monastery (later called) Saint John and Paul.
449	Hilary dies.
ca. 450	Vincent of Lerins dies.
	Peter Chrysologus dies.
455	Rome sacked by Vandals.
458	Faustus of Riez in Provence.
461	Pope Leo dies.
468	Pope Simplicius (to 483).

477–485	Faustus of Riez in exile.
480	Benedict born at Umbria.
	Boethius born.
483	Pope Felix III (to 492).
ca. 490	Faustus dies.
492	Pope Gelasius I (to 496).
496	Anastasius II pope (to 498).
498	Symmachus pope (to 514).
ca. 498	Julian Pomerius dies (*De vita contemplativa*).
500	Dionysius Exiguus in Rome (to 545).
502	Caesarius bishop of Arles (to 542). (*Regula ad monachos, Reg. ad virg.*).
ca. 511	Eugippius writes *Vita s. Severini*.
514	Hormisdas pope (to 523).
ca. 515	Martin (of Braga) bishop in Pannonia.
523–526	Benedict writes *Regula monasteriorum*.
	Pope John I (to 526).
526	Pope Felix V (to 530).
529	Second Synod of Orange.
530	Boniface II pope (to 532).
533	Eugippius dies as abbot of Castellum Lucullanum.
	John II pope (to 535).
535	Agapetus pope (to 536).
536	Silverius pope (to 537).
537	Vigilius pope (to 555).
ca. 540	Cassiodorus retires to Vivarium.
542	Caesarius of Arles dies.
542–549	Cyprian of Toulon writes *Life of Caesarius*.
ca. 547	Benedict dies.
555	Pelagius I pope (to 561).
ca. 560	Isidore born.
561	John III pope (to 574).
573	Gregory bishop of Tours.
574	Benedict I pope (to 579).
579	Pelagius II pope (to 590).
580	Martin of Braga dies.
ca. 583	Cassiodorus dies.
589	Eutropius, abbot of Servitanum, bishop of Valencia.

590	Gregory I pope (to 604).
593	Gregory of Tours dies.
ca. 600	Isidore bishop of Seville.
604	Sabinianus pope (to 607).
607	Boniface III pope (to 608).
608	Boniface IV pope (to 615).
615	Boniface V pope (to 625).
625	Honorius pope.
636	Isidore of Seville dies.
649	First Lateran Synod (Pope Agatho).

Selected Bibliography of Summary or Comprehensive Treatments

Aries, P., and A. Bejin, eds. *Western Sexuality: Practice and Precept in Past and Present Times*, translated by A. Forster. Oxford: Basil Blackwell & Mott, 1985.

————. *Classical Mediterranean Spirituality: Egyptian, Greek, Roman*. New York: Crossroad, 1986.

Asioli, Emidio d'. *Spiritualità precristiana*. Brescia: Marcelliana, 1952.

Baker, A. "Early Syrian Asceticism." *Downside Review* 88 (1970) 393–409.

Balfour, D. "Extended Notions of Martyrdom in the Byzantine Ascetical Tradition." *Sobornost* 5 (1981) 20–35.

Baltensweiler, H. *Die Ehe im Neuen Testament: Exegetische Untersuchungen über Ehe, Ehelosigkeit und Ehescheidung*. Abhandlungen zur Theologie des Alten und Neuen Testaments 52. Stuttgart: Zwingli Verlag, 1967.

Benz, E. *Die christliche Kabbala*. Zurich: Rhein-Verlag, 1968.

Bieler, L. *THEIOS ANER: Das Bild des göttlichen Menschen in Spätantike und Frühchristentum*. Vienna: Oskar Höfels, 1935–36.

Black, M. "The Tradition of Hasidean-Essene Asceticism: Its Origin and Influence." In *Aspects du Judeo-Christianisme*, edited by M. Simon et al., 19–32. Paris: Presses Universitaires de France, 1965.

Brock, S. P. "Early Syrian Asceticism." In *Syriac Perspectives on Late Antiquity*, edited by S. P. Brock, I/1–19. London: Variorum Reprints, 1984.

Brock, S. P., and S. A. Harvey, eds. *Holy Women of the Syrian Orient*. Berkeley and Los Angeles: University of California Press, 1987.

Brown, P. *The Body and Society: Men, Women, and Sexual Renunciation in Early Christianity*. New York: Columbia University Press, 1988.

————. "The Notion of Virginity in the Early Church." In *Christian Spirituality: Origins to the Twelfth Century*, edited by B. McGinn, J. Meyendorff, and J. Leclercq, 427–43. New York: Crossroad, 1985.

————. *The Philosopher and Society in Late Antiquity*. The Center for Hermeneutical Studies: Protocol of the Thirty-Fourth Colloquy, edited by E. C. Hobbs and W. Wuellner. Berkeley, Calif.: The Center for Hermeneutical Studies, 1978.

————. "The Rise and Function of the Holy Man in Late Antiquity." *JRS* 61 (1971) 80–101.

Buechler, A. *Types of Jewish-Palestinian Piety from 70 B.C.E. to 70 C.E.: The Ancient Pious Men*. London: Oxford University Press, 1922.

Burrus, V. *Chastity as Autonomy: Women in the Stories of the Apocryphal Acts*. Lewiston, N.Y.: Edwin Mellen Press, 1987.

Bynum, C. W. *Holy Feast and Holy Fast: The Religious Significance of Food to Medieval Women*. Berkeley and Los Angeles: University of California Press, 1987.

Campenhausen, H. F. von. *Die Asketische Heimatlosigkeit im altkirchlichen und frühmittelalterlichen Mönchtum*. Tübingen: J. C. B. Mohr (Paul Siebeck), 1930.

————. *Die Askese im Urchristentum*. Tübingen: J. C. B. Mohr (Paul Siebeck), 1949.

Cartlidge, D. "Competing Theologies in Early Christian Asceticism." Th.D. dissertation, Harvard Divinity School, 1969.

Clark, E. A. *Ascetic Piety and Women's Faith: Essays on Late Ancient Christianity*. Lewiston, N.Y.: Edwin Mellen Press, 1986.

Cohn, J. "Two Studies in Classical Jewish Mysticism." *Judaism* 11 (1962) 242–48.

Colliander, T. *The Way of the Ascetics*. New York: Harper & Brothers, 1960.

Davis, K. R. *Anabaptism and Asceticism: A Study in Intellectual Origins*. Scottdale, Pa.: Herald Press, 1974.

Deems, M. M. "Early Christian Asceticism." In *Early Christian Origins: Studies for H. R. Willoughby*, edited by A. Wikgren, 91–101. Chicago: Quadrangle, 1961.

Dodds, E. R. *Pagan and Christian in an Age of Anxiety*. New York: W. W. Norton, 1965.

Dover, K. J. *Greek Popular Morality in the Time of Plato and Aristotle*. Oxford: Basil Blackwell & Mott, 1974.

Elm, S. K. "The Organization and Institutions of Female Asceticism in Fourth-Century Cappadocia and Egypt." D.Phil. thesis, Oxford University, 1987.

Foucault, M. *The Use of Pleasure. The History of Sexuality*, 3 vols. New York: Pantheon Books, 1985.

Fraade, S. D. "Ascetical Aspects of Ancient Judaism." In *World Spirituality*, vol. 13. *Jewish Spirituality: From the Bible to the Middle Ages*, edited by A. Green, 253–88. New York: Crossroad, 1986.

Frank, K. Suso. *Askese und Mönchtum in der alten Kirche*. Darmstadt, W.Ger.: Wissenschaftliche Buchgesellschaft, 1975.

Gryson, R. *Les origines du celibat ecclesiastique*. Gembloux: J. Duculot, 1970.

Hardman, O. *The Ideals of Asceticism*. New York: Macmillan Co., 1924.

Harnack, A. von. *Das Mönchtum*. Giessen: Ricker, 1921.

Heussi, K. *Der Ursprung des Mönchtums*. Tübingen: J. C. B. Mohr (Paul Siebeck), 1936.

Hickey, A. E. *Women of the Roman Aristocracy as Christian Monastics*. Ann Arbor, Mich.: OMI Research Press, 1987.

Kafton, J. *Die Askese im Leben des evangelischen Christen*. Potsdam: Stiftungsverlag, 1904.

Lauman, I., ed. *The Universal Jewish Encyclopedia*. New York: Ktav, 1969. S.v. "Asceticism" by S. Cohen.

Leipoldt, J. *Griechische Philosophie und Frühchristliche Askese*. Berlin: Akademie-Verlag, 1961.

Lohse, B. *Askese und Mönchtum in der Antike und in der Alten Kirche.* Munich and Vienna: Oldenbourg, 1969.

McGinn, B., J. Meyendorff, and J. Leclercq, eds. *Christian Spirituality: Origins to the Twelfth Century.* New York: Crossroad, 1985.

Meredith, A. "Asceticism—Christian and Greek." *JTS* 27 (1976) 313–32.

Miles, M. R. *Fullness of Life: Historical Foundations for a New Asceticism.* Philadelphia: Westminster Press, 1981.

Nagel, P. *Die Motivierung der Askese in der Alten Kirche und der Ursprung des Mönchtums.* Berlin: Akademie-Verlag, 1966.

Nichol, D. M. "*Instabilitas Loci:* The Wanderlust of Late Byzantine Monks." In *Monks, Hermits and the Ascetic Tradition,* edited by W. J. Sheils, 193–202. Padstow, Great Britain: Basil Blackwell, 1985.

Niederwimmer, K. *Askese und Mysterium: Über Ehe, Ehescheidung und Eheverzicht in den Anfängen des christlichen Glaubens.* Göttingen, W.Ger.: Vandenhoeck & Ruprecht, 1975.

North, H. *Sóphrosyne: Self-Knowledge and Self-Restraint in Greek Literature.* Cornell Studies in Classical Philology, vol. 35. Ithaca, N.Y.: Cornell University Press, 1966.

Parente, P. P. *The Ascetical Life.* St. Louis: Herder, 1947.

Phipps, W. E. *Was Jesus Married? The Distortion of Sexuality in the Christian Tradition.* New York: Harper & Row, 1970.

———. *The Sexuality of Jesus: Theological and Literary Perspectives.* New York: Harper & Row, 1973.

Pourrat, P. *Christian Spirituality.* New York: J. H. Kennedy, 1922.

Reitzenstein, R. *Historia Monachorum und Historia Lausiaca.* Göttingen: Vandenhoeck & Ruprecht, 1916.

Rousseau, P. *Ascetics, Authority and the Church in the Age of Jerome and Cassian.* London: Oxford University Press, 1978.

———. *Pachomius: The Making of a Community in Fourth Century Egypt.* Berkeley and Los Angeles: University of California Press, 1985.

Ruether, R. R. "Mothers of the Church: Ascetic Women in the Late Patristic Age." In *Women of Spirit: Female Leadership in the Jewish and Christian Traditions,* edited by R. Ruether and E. McLaughlin, 71–98. New York: Simon & Schuster, 1979.

Ruppert, F. *Das pachomianische Mönchtum und die Anfänge klösterlichen Gehorsams.* Münsterschwarzacher Studien 20. Münsterschwarzach: Vier Türme, 1971.

Safran, A. *Die Kabbala.* Bern: A. Francke, 1966.

Sheils, W. J., ed. *Monks, Hermits, and the Ascetic Tradition.* Padstow: T. J. Press, 1985.

Steinmann, J. *St. John the Baptist and the Desert Tradition.* New York: Harper & Brothers, 1958.

Strathmann, H. *Die Askese in der Umbegung des werdenden Christentums.* Leipzig: A. Deichert, 1914.

Swain, J. W. *The Hellenic Origins of Christian Asceticism.* New York: J. W. Swain, 1916.

Thomas, J. *Le Mouvement baptiste en Palestine et Syria.* Gembloux: Duculot, 1935.

Troeltsch, E. "Askese." In *Askese und Mönchtum in der alten Kirche*, edited by K. S. Frank, 69–90. Darmstadt, W.Ger.: Wissenschaftliche Buchgesellschaft, 1975.

Urbach, E. E. "Ascesis and Suffering in Talmudic and Midrashic Sources [Hebrew text with English summary]." In *Yitzak F. Baer Jubilee Volume*, edited by S. W. Baron, 48–68. Jerusalem: Historical Society of Israel, 1960.

Veyne, P., ed. *A History of Private Life: From Pagan Rome to Byzantium*. Cambridge: Harvard University Press, 1987.

Vööbus, A. *Celibacy: A Requirement for Admission to Baptism in the Early Syrian Church*. Stockholm: Papers of the Estonian Theological Society in Exile, 1961.

———. *Early Monasticism in Mesopotamia and Syria*. Stockholm: Papers of the Estonian Theological Society, 1960.

———. *The Origin of Asceticism: Early Monasticism in Persia*. Louvain: CSCO, 1958.

Whitchurch, I. G. *The Philosophical Bases of Asceticism in the Platonic Writings and in the Pre-Platonic Tradition*. New York and London: Longmans, Green & Co., 1923.

Wicker, K. O. "The Ascetic Marriage in Antiquity." *Bulletin of the Institute for Antiquity and Christianity* 15 (1988) 10–13.

Zöckler, O. *Askese und Mönchtum: Zweite, Gänzlich Neu Bearbeitete und Stark Vermehrte Auflage der 'Kritischen Geschichte der Askese.'* Frankfurt: Heyder und Zimmer, 1897.

———. *Kritische Geschichte der Askese: Ein Beitrag zur Geschichte christlicher Sitte und Kultur*. Frankfurt: Heyder und Zimmer, 1863.

INDEXES

Index of
Ancient Sources

BIBLICAL BOOKS (WITH APOCRYPHA)

Genesis		35:5	62 n.94
1:1-5	255 n.90	39	47 n.8
1:21	105 n.27	41	47 n.8
1:22	102 nn.13, 15; 105 n.27	45:24	257 n.107
1:26	416 n.104	Exodus	
1:27	103 n.20	2:23-24	252 n.59
1:28	102 n.14, 111 n.56, 112 n.58	5:22-23	252 n.60
2:7	162 n.4	8:15 (19)	105 n.28
2:8	53 n.38	12:2	55 n.54
2:13	185 n.35	12:29-30	343 n.73
2:15	106 n.33	15:1	269 n.14
2:16	110 n.49	15:1-18	154 n.81
2:17	110 n.49	15:9 (LXX)	252 n.61
2:24	89 n.15, 103 n.20, 161 n.3	15:19-21	154 n.81
3:1	111 n.54, 361 n.10	17:6	411 n.62
3:5	109 n.47	17:9-12	404 n.35
3:14	111 n.54	20:12	104 n.22
3:14-15	111 n.53	20:16	257 n.108
3:16	34 n.22, 111 n.55, 165 n.11	23:1	258 n.109, 293 n.146
3:17-18	112 n.60	24:15	229 n.12
3:22	59 n.83	24:18	23 n.13
3:23	296 n.160	25:30	153 n.80
5:24	420 n.128	29:32-33	153 n.80
14:20	420 n.129	32:4	25 n.21
14:22-23	248 n.36	32:27-28	355 n.16
16-17	180 n.18	Leviticus	
18:10	113 n.62	8:31	153 n.80
18:27	288 n.123	19:2	413 n.76
19:24-25	110 n.52	19:18b	249 n.37
21:2	113 n.62	21:1-2	217 n.10
22:5-6	37 n.38	21:11	217 n.10
22:11-12	403 n.34	23:40	56 n.64
		24:5-9	153 n.80

EARLY PATRISTIC BOOKS

TARGUMIC LITERATURE

MISHNAH AND RELATED LITERATURE

OTHER RABBINIC WORKS

NAG HAMMADI TRACTATES

CLASSICAL AND LATER CHRISTIAN LITERATURE

Index of
Subjects and Names

Index of
Foreign Words

GREEK

513

LATIN

HEBREW

SYRIAC

DATE DUE